THE ALLEGED FANTASY PROJECT

VOLUME I
FOUNDATIONS

THE ALLEGED FANTASY PROJECT

[2011 - 2021]

VOLUME I
FOUNDATIONS

J. Bartholomew Walker
and
Emma B. Quadrakoff

Quadrakoff Publications Group, LLC
Wilmington, Delaware
USA

Copyright © 2021 Quadrakoff Publications Group, LLC All rights reserved.

Except as noted, All Scripture passages taken from The Holy Bible, King James Version.
All NASB scriptures taken from The New American Standard Bible® Copyright © 1960, 1962, 1963, 1968, 1971, 1972, 1973, 1975, 1977, 1995 by the Lockman Foundation, LaHabra, CA.

Special thanks to the Lockman Foundation for the finest Bible version available; as well as for their permission to use the same. All Scripture passages taken from The Holy Bible, King James Version, are as noted.

ISBN: 978-1-948219-30-3

All rights reserved. No part of this publication may be reproduced, stored in a retrieval system or transmitted, in any form, or by any means, electronic, mechanical, recorded, photocopied, or otherwise, without the prior written permission of both the copyright owner and the above publisher of this book, except by a reviewer who may quote brief passages in a review.

The scanning, uploading, and distribution of this book via the Internet or via any other means without the permission of the publisher is illegal and punishable by law. Please purchase only authorized electronic editions and do not participate in or encourage electronic piracy of copyrightable materials. Your support of the author's rights is appreciated.

Any and all characters appearing that are not in any of the versions of the Bible are fictional. Any resemblance to any living person is strictly coincidental.

Printed in the United States of America.

Dedicated to The Holy Ghost—without Whom this Project would not have been possible.

"He that answereth a matter before he heareth it, it is folly and shame unto him."
—Proverbs 18:13 (KJV)

CONTENTS

Foreword ———————————————————— xxi

Introduction ——————————————————— xxv

Chapter 1
The Setup ————————————————————— 1

Chapter 2
What is Truth ————————————————————— 9

Chapter 3
Recollection and Imagination ——————————————— 25

Chapter 4
Unseen Cause—Seen Effect ———————————————— 57

Chapter 5
The Battlefield ————————————————————— 73

Chapter 6
"Insertions" ——————————————————————— 109

Chapter 7
Variations on the Planaō Theme —————————————— 125

Chapter 8
A Balancing Act ———————————————— 147

Chapter 9
Attack—Counterattack ————————————— 159

Chapter 10
True Talent ——————————————————— 183

Chapter 11
Talantŏn vs. "A-talantŏn" ——————————— 221

Chapter 12
It Sort of Has to Be So ———————————— 231

Chapter 13
Tsâbâ' Extraordinaire ————————————— 263

Chapter 14
Exercitum ex Ossium
(The Army of Bones) —————————————— 287

Chapter 15
The Separate and The Distinct ——————— 311

Chapter 16
Resurrection and Recourse ————————— 333

Chapter 17
Sowing, Reaping,
and Interference ——————————————— 341

Chapter 18
Faith—What on Earth Is It? ————————— 361

Glossary ———————————————————— 405

Bibliography ──────────────────── 443

About the MeekRaker Series ──────────── 477

FOREWORD

The knowledge is a very interesting thing. There is the *doxa*, the *epistēmē*, and the *techné*.

The *doxa* is the probable or the common knowledge. The good example of this is what many believe the Bible says. Doxa may be true; it may not.

The *epistēmē* is the more certain truth. Often this conflicts with the doxa; but unless the epistēmē is true; it is by definition not the epistēmē. The seeking of the epistēmē is for the sake of the epistēmē itself. There need not be the practical reason outside of the knowledge itself. Why seek the epistēmē? Because it is there. I want you should think about this.

But the *techné* is another type of the knowledge. The techné is the epistēmē plus something else. The something else, is the practical use for the epistēmē. When the epistēmē is sought with an end in mind that requires the epistēmē; whether in addition to because it is there or the not; this knowledge is then the techné.

It is true that those who seek the techné may have the different motivation than those who seek the knowledge only for the knowledge itself. This may limit of the fields that those who seek the techné study.

But the certainty of the knowledge is the more critical with the techné, as the (technical) device based on the doxa may not work.

Analysis of the Bible is considered to be the seeking of the epistēmē, as many only see the minimal utility of this knowledge— but this is not the so.

In these following pages is the much epistēmē, but there is also the much techné.

For many of the centuries there has been the doxa, that there is no possible of the techné with the epistēmē in this Bible. But this itself is the doxa and not the epistēmē; and it is not the truth. I want you should think about this too.

I am very much pleased to have the small contribution to this effort.

Erich Z. Petrovsky

INTRODUCTION

The Tale of Two Fantasies

> "A fanatic is someone who can't change his mind
> and won't change the subject."
> *(attributed to Winston Churchill)*

    In today's world, something is considered as a "fantasy," only when it is understood to be *fictional*. Another way to say this; would be that it is understood by all, that there is no *actuality* that exists, existed, or in some cases could possibly ever exist; that could or would reasonably produce the associated *reality* of that which it is that is considered as the fantasy.
    Actuality and *reality* must be clearly defined. *Actuality* is that which (actually) exists; while *reality* is that which is believed to exist solely based upon *perception*.
    But generally this is all known in advance; and the purposes for "fantasy," generally do not include the assessment of an actuality—at least anywhere outside of the fantasy. There is much written about the various spaceships, weapons, drive mechanisms etc.,

contained in fantasies; and much is written in great detail. But although much of this is written in a fashion quite similar to things that do in fact exist; the reader, (and writer), both know that this fantasy is in fact not actually so.

This is much more than a mere suspension of skepticism; but an admission and agreement by all that the "primary premise" is being at times deliberately and knowingly suspended—at least for a while. This "primary premise" being that it is all *fantasy*. Once this temporary suspension is done; not only can the detail become immense, but it also can be an amazing amount of fun. One can develop realities and get involved worlds and circumstances as though they in fact exist; but whether suspended or not; it is known by all that this is not so. One main difference between this type of fantasy and a lie; is that no one is supposed to believe that it is true, but only *make believe* that this is so—and only temporarily.

It is true that much that was once written as fantasy ultimately becomes fact. Much of early science fiction is now essentially history. Going to the moon; computers; hand held communication devices and such do exist, (are *actualities*), today. But at the time these *fantasies* were written, all; (or at least most); knew they simply did not exist *at that time*. In this sense, fantasy writers are in fact the experts in phenomena which have no actuality *at that time*—at least in the material realm in which we all physically "live."

There also seems to be a distinction between *fantasy* and *fiction*. By today's understood definition; all fantasy is fiction; but not all fiction is fantasy. To be considered a fantasy, today, there must be some type of "supernatural" component; and not merely a new type of "secret agent" working to combat evil; or a rather talented, (and incessantly quite lucky), detective making the world a better place in which to live.

According to Chambers, the origin(s) of the word "fantasy" is/are:

> "fantasy *n.* About 1350 *fantasie* use of the imagination; later, apparition or phantom (probably before 1375; * borrowed from Old French *fantasie*, learned borrowing from Latin *phantasia*, from Greek *phantasía*

Introduction The Tale of Two Fantasies

appearance, image, perception, imagination, from *phantázesthai* picture to one self..."¹¹

This root of "fantasy:" *fantasie*, is reasonably consistent with the common understanding of what today constitutes a "fantasy."

However; again regarding the origin(s) of the word "fantasy" Chambers also states:

> "... from *phantós* visible, from *phaínesthai* appear (middle voice to *phaínein* to show, related to *pháos*, *phôs* light). The Greek is cognate with Sanskrit *bhāma-s* light, Old Irish *bān* white, Albanian (Tosk dialect) *bënj* I make (appear), Armenian *banam* I open, make visible, and Tocharian A *pam* clear, from Indio-European * *bhā-/bhə*-shine (Pok. 104). The meaning of whimsical or visionary notion, illusion, appeared in Middle English before 1400, followed by the general sense of imagination, especially extravagant or visionary imagination, in early modern English (1539)."¹²

And also according to Chambers, another word derived from *phaínesthai* is the word "phenomenon."

> "phenomenon n. 1625, fact or occurrence, manifestation... borrowed from Latin *phaenomenon*, from Greek *phainómenon* that which appears or is seen, noun use of neuter present participle *phaínesthai* appear; see FANTASY"¹³

It must be noted that when there are two similar sources for a word, such as the above Latin and Greek sources for *phenomenon*, this is generally referred to as *cognate* or *cognates*. Hereafter any claim of *cognates* will interchangeably be referred to as the "Red Flag Rule." This is because of the extreme likelihood that *neither* claimed source represents the actual original source; and the actual definition of "cognates" is consistent with this. Meaning: that another different source likely exists, from which; if discovered; additional information can be obtained.

As often can happen, the analysis of the meaning of words leads to knowledge about a phenomenon or phenomena which require some explanation. Words are essentially symbols of or for phenomenon or phenomena; and are relied upon to produce accurate *realities*.

Sometimes; as in the case of *flammable*, and *inflammable* essentially being synonymous; this can easily become a problem. This is likely due to erroneous usage at some point, as a thing cannot be both "A "and "-A"—any etymologists claims of *inflame* as the root notwithstanding. *Seeded* grapes; unlike *seedless* grapes; is also not so easy to logically decipher.

The later meaning of *fantasy*; according to the above referenced etymology, is reasonably consistent with the meaning of *fictional* today; but also includes: "visible," "appear," "to show," "light," "white," "I make (appear)," "I open, make visible," and "clear."

The same can be said of "fancy;" which is derived from fantasy.

Regarding the origin of "fancy," Chambers, states:

> "fancy n. 1462-65 *fantsy, fansey*, in *The Paston Letters*; formed by contraction of FANTASY. *Fancy* and *fantasy* gradually differentiated in form and sense with *fancy* taking on the meaning of inclination, liking, desire, often whimsical, which became obsolete in *fantasy* in the 1600's."[14] p368 ,

"Fancy" today can refer to "fictional," or "desire;" or a "very high level of quality;" such as "fancy cashews." This particular use of fancy as an adjective is not used to convey the meaning that the purported level of high quality is fictitious—but rather, to convey the exact opposite. Neither is *fancy* generally used to indicate that the cashews in question do not exist, except in one's "imagination."

The "suffix" of the word *Theophany*, (phan); which literally means an *appearance* of God when combined with "Theo;" comes from this same (*phantós*) root. The word is not Theo*phony*; meaning to *hear* from God. Ergo; Theophany is not Theophony.

Whether or not one believes that Theophany is an actuality; i.e.; that God ever appeared to anyone at any time; is irrelevant to the meaning of the term. Whether or not one believes that Theophany ever happened; Theophany nevertheless still means a *genuine* appearance of God, or an *actual* phenomenon; and thus represents the one definition of fantasy, ("from *phantós* visible, from *phaínesthai* appear"); and *never* the other definition: ("use of the imagination").

Stated another way, one is free to believe that any and all *claims* of the existence of Theophany as an actuality or phenomenon, is or are *fantasy*, here meaning the: "use of the imagination." However; one cannot redefine the very definition of "Theophany" *itself* to mean this: "use of the imagination," *fantasy* definition. Should one attempt to do this, one might just as well change the meaning of *Theophony*, from "hearing God," to "phony God."

In fact; if, and to the very same extent that one asserts that another who claims to have experienced Theophany; or one who claims Theophany is an actual phenomenon is engaging in: "use of the imagination" type of *fantasy* in their *claiming*; there then is the required admission that actual claimed Theophany itself, represents the *other* type of fantasy: "from *phantós* visible, from *phaínesthai* appear;" or the *first* fantasy assertion simply will not work.

An examination of "profane" is also revealing. This is generally *literally* considered to mean "before temple." The "pro" meaning "before;" and "fane" meaning "temple;" spelled here with an "f." This could refer to a literal standing in front of a temple, being refused admission for lack of qualifications. Or the meaning could also be *chronological*; in the sense of the time or a time *before* one "knew better."

However, profane is generally used to indicate disrespect for; or defiling; of religion or God. Any confirmation of a relationship between *fanum* and the root of *fantasy* et seq., could not be reliably confirmed.

This naturally segues into the English words: *fane, fey,* and *feign*: *Fane* is a noun meaning a temple or church.

Fey is an adjective describing supernatural type quality or qualities. The relationship between the noun *fane*, and the adjective *fey*; can easily be seen—any "modern" etymological disagreements notwithstanding.

Feign is a verb which fairly means to give false representation(s).

Arguably, a similar situation exists with the non-English word *fakir*, and The English word *faker*; and there are even disagreements over meanings within the word "fakir" itself. A *fakir*; (including its alternate spellings); was capable of miraculous powers; but much like Jesus and Co., relied upon gifts from others. Or, *fakir* can sometimes mean a beggar, without any supernatural powers. And of course the English word *faker*, is much like *feign*.

The same can be said; although to a lesser degree; with another offspring of *fantasy*, namely: "fantastic." Although sometimes used to mean "impossible;" to state that something is "fantastic," generally indicates that whatever that particular "something" represents; is so far beyond any expected deviations from the norm; as to be equivalent to it being impossible for it to exist in actuality—nevertheless it does in fact exist.

Thus here in this usage; there is the requirement that whatever is considered as *fantastic*; must in fact have actual existence—as difficult as this may be to believe. This usage essentially represents the difference between what one *thought* was possible; and a reasonable understanding of what *actually is*. This then also represents a reality/actuality mismatch; in that the reasonably perceived *actuality*, produces a new reality far in excess of the previous reality of possibility. There is then a temporary sense of *awe*, until the new reality becomes the reference or standard.

In a sense, this is a means of extending the normal three degrees of comparison that exist in the English language. When something is "fantastic" in this meaning, it is so far beyond what could be considered or even conceived of as "best," or even "possible" for that matter; it nevertheless remains in fact so.

Thus, here the requirements of "best" are altered in such a manner as to represent a standard initially described as "fantastic; thereby maintaining the three degrees of comparison, but increasing the requirements for the *superlative*. What was previously *fantastic*, ultimately supplants what was previously considered as *best*. But once again, in this usage it must be the truth.

So it seems that there are two mutually exclusive definitions of the word "fantasy;" if one includes the word itself, as well as its associated progeny. The question is why is this so?

According to Chambers, we know that *fantasy* requires: "use of the imagination;" and that it was: "*later*, apparition or phantom." (emphasis added)

But also according to Chambers, *fantasy* also is: "appearance, image, perception, imagination;" and to: "... picture to one self." There is also: "visible, "and: "to show," "light," "I make (appear)," "I open, make visible," and "clear."

It seems to be a fair conclusion, that originally "fantasy" required an actuality to support whatever it was that was considered the *fantasy*. *Prophesy* and *retrophesy* would fall into this category. The former is concerned with what not yet is; such as "end times" prophesy. The latter refers to what was; but is or was not known—such as the writings found in early Genesis. After all, Moses was not there; and neither was any other human present as a witness. At the time Genesis was written, it was concerned with events that had already happened; and had happened long before its writing.

But in both cases; what is or was written, is concerned with what existed, or will *exist*. In both cases, there either was, or will be a corresponding actuality in the *immaterial* realm. This *immaterial* actuality either had already manifested on the *material* realm, (retrophesy); or *will be* manifested on the *material* realm at some point in "time," (prophesy).

The difference between *history* and *retrophesy*, is the *source* of the information.

History is generally written by researching contemporaries, or researching others who have already done so. This is done by gathering that which is on the *material* realm; and is largely a matter of *recollection*.

But *retrophesy* is obtained by gathering that which is on the *immaterial* realm; and in certain strict senses, is largely a matter of *imagination*. This is done by "assisted recollection," via *rhēma*.

These facts are not a subset of the set of facts contained in the "recollective reservoir" of the individual engaging in the *retrophesy*. Thus this cannot be any type of normal recollection.

Barring the use of *retrophesy*, how could the events in early Genesis have become known to man? Science may be considered a possibility up to a certain point. Science can determine the *effect*, (Big Bang); but not the *cause*,—the *creation* of the heavens of the earth, or by *Whom*.

Science is also not particularly adept at explaining actual *creation*; which is bringing something material into existence from nothing material—even in the general sense. This is largely because the cause *is* not, and *was* not at the time of Genesis 1:1, contained in the *material* realm under scientific study.

Prophesy is similar. Scientific *prediction*, (speak before), is based upon factors in the *material*. To the extent that these factors are accurately determined; accurate predictions are possible, by the mere application of logic.

But the source of *prophesy* is the *immaterial*; and here again with the imagination involved. If one proffers a logical prediction solely based upon known facts as "*prophesy*;" then a "no kidding" would be an appropriate response.

Fantasy can, in a sense; be a relativistic term, depending upon the definition chosen. What is imagined and qualifies as fantasy in the *original* meaning; becomes commonplace at some point in time: "At first I thought it was nuts, but..."

The problem is when the reverse happens. This is when what is commonplace, becomes fantasy in the *alternate* meaning. Since in the minds of most, "miracles" either do not exist, or are extremely rare today; then the miracles in the Bible are "fantasy" in the more "modern" sense—meaning that there is and was no such actuality.

This work is concerned with much that is nowhere near the current "norms." Some parts are concerned with what was much closer to "norms" many years ago; when society had both a connection to, and an understanding of, God; which was of a much greater magnitude than exists today. And some of this work is concerned with the inescapable logical corollaries of the same. As is the case when it is determined that Genesis 1:2 is not merely a recapitulation of what happened in Genesis 1:1 but in greater detail; and is concerned with conditions and events chronologically *after* Genesis 1:1 was completed; these corollaries are enormous.

The same can be said about the *creation* of man, (hosts); and the *formation* of Adam. Once it is understood that the bringing into existence of a material entity from nothing; and the bringing into existence of a material entity from something; cannot possibly be the same event—*everything* changes. Many old doors are closed, and many new doors become "blown" wide open—with one's pride being the only significant obstacle to one's entrance.

Great efforts were undertaken to determine what actually *was*; and to prove the same.

Great efforts were also undertaken to insure that only *solipsism* could be a reasonable argument against the presented facts, and these inescapable corollaries. The *quantity* of available information; and the *reliability* of information is much like a "see-saw." The 66 books of the Bible are agreed to as authentic, so reliability in using them is not an issue. Other "books" may have provided additional information, but at the price of reliability; as there is no clear consensus as to their *authenticity*, and thus their reliability is suspect. Had they been used, this would have opened the door to rational arguments in addition to solipsism; and thus these were neither "consulted" nor cited.

The title *"Alleged Fantasy"* is a suitable title, because it incorporates two potential groups of "allegers;" and two definitions of "fantasy." Thus, those who agree that a sufficient level of proof has been met for the facts and the necessary corollaries; will allege the *original* meaning of fantasy. And those who do not agree that a sufficient level of proof has been met for the facts and the necessary corollaries; for whatever reason(s); will allege the more *modern* meaning.

Chapter 1

The Setup

*"What senses do we lack that we cannot see
or hear another world all around us?"*

Frank Herbert
(as Paul Atreides
in *"Dune"*)

This question; in a surfeit of various forms; has plagued mankind for perhaps *hundreds* of millennia—yes *hundreds* of millennia. [See "*MeekRaker Beginnings...*" Ch. 1-4] The *premise* of this quote is that there *is* another world all around us; but the problem is that it cannot be *sensed*; e.g.; because it cannot be seen or heard. This "other world" is just that; "another world."

The question posed, has to do with what senses do we lack that we cannot see or hear this other world. However, this is a bit presumptive, because there are at least three inherent *presumptions* or perhaps even *assumptions*, contained in the question:

Firstly; that this other world *itself*; as opposed to the *effects* of this "other world;" is *capable* of being "seen or heard" in the usual "sense."

Secondly; that because of this assumed capability, that it is then our lack of sufficient senses; e.g.; seeing and hearing capabilities that are the problem.

And *thirdly*; that this other world thus cannot be otherwise "sensed," beyond seeing and hearing.

One thing that most "versions" of the Bible seem to agree upon; perhaps singularly and uniquely; is the meaning of very *first* verse, the same being Genesis 1:1. Although even here, whether "heaven" should be in the singular or the plural remains an issue.

Genesis 1:1 (KJV) tells us:

> *"In the beginning God created the heaven and the earth."*[1.1]

After Genesis 1:1, the confusion begins both in Genesis "real time"—meaning the relative times *when* these; (the events from the beginning of Genesis 1:2 onward); were all actually happening "back then;" as well as understanding the actual chronology today. When analyzing what Genesis 1:2 necessarily must then literally mean, this then produces even more confusion and disagreement with what must then also logically follow.

But most all or agree that *"In the Beginning"* God did in fact do *something*; in that He: *"created the heaven(s) and the earth."*

This causes a rather significant, but also a very interesting problem. Wherever God was just "before" He created the *material* realm, (the heavens and the earth, or *time*, *matter*, and *space*); He could not have been in that same realm which was yet to be created, prior to its creation. Thus He was either in another *material* realm "somewhere;" or He was in *that* other, (the *immaterial*), realm; "when" and "from which" He created the *material* realm.

Since there is a clear distinction made between "heaven(s)" and "earth;" it seems likely that *"heaven(s),"* (as opposed to *heaven,*); is what it was that He created in the beginning—in addition to the earth.

Here "heaven(s)" refers to the *space* between matter in the *material* realm, or "this world." Thus "heavens" here in the *plural*, in this usage refers to the space between matter in the *material* realm, or "this world;" while "heaven;" as in where God "art in;" refers to the *immaterial* realm, or this same "another world all around us."

If this were not so, and God was in another *material* realm; then it must be asked how it was that *that* material realm was brought into existence, and by whom? Ultimately there had to have been an initial realm from which God created *the*, or *these* material realm(s); the same necessarily ultimately being *the*, or *an*, *immaterial* realm. This will be addressed in greater detail in a later chapter.

The actual Hebrew word translated as "heaven" in Genesis 1:1 is:

> "8064 shâmayim; dual of an unused sing. shâmeh; from an unused root mean. to *be lofty*; *the sky* (as *aloft* the dual perh. Alluding to the visible arch in which the clouds move, as well as to the higher ether where the celestial bodies revolve)."[1.2]

From a scientific perspective, most agree that there was a beginning of the physical or *material* universe—and here the material universe usually means *all* of the matter, and *all* of the space. Often referred to as the "Big Bang;" it is "settled science," that the universe had a beginning at some point in "time."

Most scientists also agree that every effect has a cause, and every cause has an effect. It must be determined if this *effect*; (the physical universe being brought into existence); was somehow a unique *causeless* effect; or alternatively, if there was in fact a *cause* for this *effect*.

Is there any such thing as a "causeless effect?" The answer is yes, but there is only one; and this is referred to as the *"primum movens,"* or prime mover.

In order for any "thing" to ever exist or have existed as an *effect*; there ultimately must be something in existence, (an effect) which had *no cause*. That *"primem movens"* is what is known as God—no matter what He may be called, or whatever else may or may not be attributed to Him.

By this definition, the existence of "God" is a logical requirement; and thus this is not logically debatable from the *"primem movens"* viewpoint. The logical *necessity* for the existence of "God," is again of course an entirely different matter than any purported *attributes, desires,* or *anything else* regarding "God."

If for some reason(s), one takes the position that somehow uniquely there was *no* cause for this particular effect; (the physical universe being brought into existence); then the *primum movens* necessarily becomes the universe. This of course conflicts with science, as science knows there was a cause—even if little else is reliably known about this cause, other than that there was one.

Stipulating that science and Genesis 1:1 are both correct, at least in terms of this particular *event*; i.e.; that there was in fact a cause for the "creation of the universe;" it is a rather difficult argument to make, that said *cause* of the physical universe being brought into existence, could somehow have nevertheless existed in this same physical universe *prior* to the creation of the realm in which it is here claimed to have (pre) existed.

Thus from a *scientific* viewpoint, another realm is *required* in order to explain the creation of the material realm; else things get even more complicated. Even if simultaneity is claimed; this may explain the *time*, but not the *place*. There is no other reasonable scientific conclusion; other than there must have been, (and is), an *immaterial* realm, in which existed the *cause* for this *effect* known as the creation of the *material universe*; i.e.; creation of the *heavens* and the *earth*.

The "five senses" are by design a means by which to sense the manifestations in this *material* world or realm; and not necessarily any other world or realm; including an, or the, *immaterial* world;

The Setup

from which the *material* world was necessarily brought into existence.

One would not reasonably expect to be able to sense any phenomenon using a device that was designed to sense another phenomenon—particularly when an entirely *different* type of phenomenon.

This is true even *within* the material realm. One would not expect to see music; (except users of LSD—or so it is said). One does not try to listen to moonlight. All of these five senses are designed to provide limited input from the *material* realm; but not necessarily from the *immaterial* realm. In order to obtain input from the *immaterial* realm, one generally must perceive outside of the five senses; or *extra-sensory*.

However; *extra sensory perception* is not currently a reliable means of obtaining information about this "other world;" at least not for most people most of the time. In fact it is considered such an unusual event for most, that it can reasonably said that with few exceptions, that it is not reliable for anyone at any time—if it is expected that extra sensory perception were to operate in the same manner and with the same degree of *reasonable* but not infallible reliability as the five senses. The inclusion of "reasonable," cannot be overemphasized here.

Although much is known about the *effects* of the immaterial realm on the material realm; relatively little is known about the immaterial realm itself. Science, much to its credit, has studied certain *effects* of the immaterial realm; i.e.; effects upon that which comprises the *material* realm; but science knows little or nothing about either the actual immaterial causes of these material effects; or the realm whence it, (the material realm), necessarily came.

As a result, although there is a plethora of scientific and other terminology to describe the material realm; there is a paucity of "words" to describe the immaterial realm. This is not necessarily because there is so much about the immaterial realm that is ineffable; but rather that the sufficient and precise terminology simply does not exist. And that terminology that does exist, is often *subjective* and *non-specific*, and thus easily subject to error.

A prime example of this, is contained in the Book of Revelation, or what was originally titled the: "Apocalypsa," or roughly: "Revealed Things." The phenomena witnessed by John from Chapter 4 onward, were contained in the immaterial realm, which he was permitted to "see."

This is why the words "as" or "like" appear with such frequency in the translations. These were not similes; but rather *similarities*. John attempted to utilize the words describing phenomena in the *material* realm, which most closely resembled what he "saw" in the *immaterial* realm—hence the use of "like" or "as."

But these are only accurate as far as the true *similarities* are concerned. These differences; which are unknown to the reader unless pointed out; can, will, and do lead to grossly erroneous attributions of characteristics.

Thus *terminology* is always crucial. Often, disputes exist not because parties are truly in disagreement; but rather because they merely *believe* they are in disagreement. And the major reason that they believe they are in disagreement; is because there is an unknown miscommunication. The parties may in fact be in complete agreement, but do not know they are in agreement; because they are using different terminology to describe the same phenomenon, and simply are unaware of this. Thus; they *believe* each is describing something different than the other; but in fact are describing the same phenomenon, by unknowingly using different terminology to describe the same thing.

There is an illogical variant to this. This occurs when the parties are not in disagreement because of incorrect *terminology*, but rather because they are arguing entirely different "things." Here one party believes that the discussion is actually about the matter under discussion, (third person discussion); and the terminology is reasonably clear in this regard. And although the other party *appears* to be discussing this same matter, one is actually attempting to prove that he or she cannot ever be wrong, (a *tacit* first person discussion).

One party is largely *factual*; and the other is party largely *emotional*. Thus one party believes that both are standing looking at the matter under discussion; when in fact one of the parties is actually looking in the mirror. Therefore, here the *clearer* the terminology becomes, the *more* disagreement enters into the discussion.

And when the situation arises that both parties are actually looking in the mirror, while merely pretending to be examining the matter purportedly under discussion; logic generally departs entirely from the interchange.

Some simply will not pay the required price for being "set free" by the truth, as per James Abraham Garfield, our 20th president who is credited with having said:

"The truth will set you free,
but first it will make you miserable."[1.3]

It is not necessarily a problem when using incorrect terminology, as long as the incorrect terminology does *not* represent something else.

For example: in Boston, a "grinder" is essentially the same thing as a "sub" or a "hero" elsewhere. As long as the knowledge of what a "grinder" is remains unknown to the buyer, he or she may have to explain what it is they want; but it is not likely that they would receive something they do not want—assuming of course that they are in a restaurant, and not a hardware store.

The same cannot be said for a "Sloppy Joe." This could be a ground beef and sauce on a hamburger bun; or it could also be an elaborate and expensive delicatessen sandwich, solely depending upon *where* it is ordered. However as a precaution, it must be noted that "understanding" the meaning of a word strictly by its *contextual* usage can be dangerous, as it only permits one to know what that particular speaker *believes* it means.

In addition, *precise* terminology is also important in order to make necessary distinctions; as the more *complex*, (as opposed to *complicated*), an idea becomes; then the more *specific* the terminology must become. This is not merely in order understand it; but more importantly, in order to *describe* it with sufficient specificity, as to be able to accurately and precisely communicate the same.

For example: Today, it seems that the word "spirit," (Latin *spiritus*, "breath" or "breath-like"); is used to describe essentially anything and everything contained in, or *believed* to be contained in this "other world." The describing of entirely separate, distinct, and thus entirely different phenomena with the same word, only leads to misunderstanding and confusion.

There is a point to be made with respect to *terminology* vs. *words*. Although modern etymologists may not necessarily take this far enough back; the root of *"terminology"* is *"term"* or *"terminus;"* the same root being used in other words such as termination, terminal, etc.

This root, (term), generally implies *finality* or the *end* of some thing or process; in this case "lŏgŏs" or words—with an alternative meaning of "terminology" being the: "study of ends."

Thus if *communication* is the true purpose; then unless the words used to convey the subject of the communication succeed in this endeavor; meaning the recipient has or should have a reasonably *complete* understanding; then they are just words, and not *terminology*. If unsuccessful, then additional words must be used until the process is complete. *Precise* terminology saves time, and minimizes the likelihood of misunderstanding.

There is "that one" about the meaning of "diagnosis." There are two ways to break down and define this word. The first is believed by most to be the correct one: *"dia-gno-sis."* The prefix "dia," generally is defined as meaning through or thorough; "gno;" generally means knowledge; and the suffix "osis," generally referring to an abnormal condition. Thus, a fair definition is "a thorough knowledge of an abnormal condition."

But if the word is broken down as *"di-agnosis,"* we now have by definition two people, "di;"; who have *no* knowledge whatsoever, "agnostic;" about an abnormal condition, "osis"—the doctor and the patient.

The mentioning of "this one" could not be avoided here.

Chapter 2

"What is Truth?"

*A*ctuality can be defined as what exists, and thus is completely objective—"The thing is what it is, and *aint* what it *aint*." *Reality* is what we believe exists, or normally represents what is merely *subjective* or *perceived* actuality.

> "*Reality* is what is *perceived* or *believed* to be so. This is in contradistinction to *actuality*, which is what, (actually), *is* so. That which is a mirage, but is not known to be a mirage; represents a *reality* of water, with an *actuality* of "not water;" e.g.; sand. This *reality* of water will be acted upon by traveling a great distance, only to then ultimately find that the previous reality and the actuality are quite different; producing a new *reality* for this very same actuality.
> The seemingly disproportional response by the "petty" person; is considered as such, because of the *different* realities produced by the *same* stimulus, (an *actuality*)."[2.1]

One cannot "actually" ever "come back to reality," simply because for any conscious mind, one's reality is impossible to ever leave. This is irrespective of any similarities or differences between any given *actuality*, (that which exists); and one's *reality*, (perception), of this same actuality.

The correct but rarely used phrase would be to "come back to *actuality*;" but then of course the question arises as to come back to actuality from *where*? From one's *reality* would be the only reasonable response, here indicating that said reality is believed to be inconsistent with the actuality involved.

As stated, the *reality* of a mirage in the desert is water; but the *actuality* is not—if it is a mirage. The *reality* of a movie is characters, locations and a plot; but the *actuality* is merely light and sound. However; this actuality is known, (hopefully), by the viewers; and the idea is to "make believe" for the purpose of entertainment. For about two hours, we'll all just "let on" that it is an actuality.

The *reality* of a fictional book is similar to a movie; but the *actuality* is ink and paper representing another's *imagination*. This distinction can often at times be a bit more difficult with much of that which is proffered as: "non-fiction."

Thus it is fair to conclude, that the entire spectrum or set consisting of one's reality, must necessarily be contained within, or perhaps better phrased; be a *subset* of, this larger set of actuality—at least in order for our *reality* or *perceived actuality* to have any significance or meaning. Like a smaller sphere contained within a larger sphere, our reality or realities must at all times remain within the confines of what actually exists; else according to the very same extent that a given *reality* does not—it is likewise nonsense.

A liar will endeavor to alter the reality of his or her victim, in order to deliberately cause them to include in their *reality*, some thing or things that are not contained in the larger set of *actuality*.

The actuality or fact is that you "did do it;" and that fact is contained in this larger sphere of actuality. Lying in order to convince someone that "you did not do it;" is thus not included in this larger set or sphere of actuality.

"What is Truth?"

Oh most certainly the act of lying is an actuality, and said lie is contained in the sphere of actuality; but if successful, the victim does not know of this. However, there is not any intersection, (sometimes called union), or containment of this new "reality sphere" that the liar created in the mind of the victim, within the sphere of *actuality*. Whatever it is you actually lied *about*, (I didn't do it); as opposed to the fact of the actual *telling* of the lie, has no "actual" existence.

If there is an actuality that in fact exists, then *all* of the *perceived* parts or subsets, (reality), of that actuality must be consistent with that same actuality. If not; then the actuality *believed* to exist, (reality), is either the result of a *different* actuality; or there is no such actuality at all.

Proverbs 17:4 (KJV) tells us:

> "A wicked doer giveth heed to false lips;
> and a liar giveth ear to a naughty tongue." [12.2]

Regarding the *second* statement: "*a liar giveth ear to a naughty tongue;*" the first thing one must ask is: "Does any of this make any degree of sense?" This is one of those times where something sounds good initially; and because of this, the statement can easily be glossed over; and therefore *if* there is a true meaning, it can easily be missed.

Precisely which or whose tongue is it that the liar is "*giveth ear to?*"

A reasonable answer being, that it is the liar's *own* tongue, as to facilitate the concocting and deployment of a lie that will succeed. But it does not state *his* naughty tongue, which the tongue of a liar clearly is. It must be noted that this statement includes the *indefinite* article "*a*," which precedes "*naughty tongue;*" implying that the tongue being paid attention to could be "any old tongue" at all, provided it is "*naughty.*"

The NAS Bible translates this as a "*destructive*" tongue.

Here is the same Proverbs 17:4, but here (NAS):

"*An evildoer listens to wicked lips;
A liar pays attention to a destructive tongue.*"[2.3]

The actual Hebrew word translated here as "liar" is:

"8267 sheqer; from 8266; an *untruth*; by impl. a *sham* (often adv.): - without a cause, deceit (-ful), false (-hood, - ly), feignedly, liar, + lie, lying, vain (thing), wrongfully."[2.4]

As can be clearly seen, *sheqer* does not actually literally best translate as "*liar*," or "one who lies;" but rather in fact, instead refers to the very "untruth," or "sham" *itself*.

In fact the translation of the word *sheqer* as "*liar*," (the list of words appearing after the ": -"); represents the unique specific erroneous *translation* of *sheqer* as "*liar*" in the above Proverbs 17:4 KJV; as *sheqer* is not translated as "liar" anywhere else in the entire Old Testament KJV.[2.5]

Thus it actually should read that it is the lie or untruth *itself* that is paying attention to a "*naughty*" or "*destructive*" tongue. Repeat: according to Proverbs, it is the actual *lie itself*, (*sheqer*); and not a *liar* that is paying the attention to a "*naughty*" or "*destructive*" tongue. And yes; it would most certainly be fair, as well as quite appropriate at this juncture to again ask: "Does any of this make any degree of sense?"

John 8:44 (NAS) tells us:

"*You are of your father the devil,
and you want to do the desires of your father.
He was a murderer from the beginning,
and does not stand in the truth
because there is no truth in him.*

"What is Truth?"

> *Whenever he speaks a lie,*
> *he speaks from his own nature,*
> *for he is a liar and the father of lies"*[2.6]

Here Jesus appears to be speaking to the Pharisees; and these passages reveal much about the relationship between the *enemy*, and the *origins* of lies.

We are told that the devil is a *"liar,"* and the *"father of lies."* What this reasonably means, is that there was no such thing as an untruth or a lie—until there was an enemy. (This is very important in understanding Genesis 1:2, as well as Adam's situation much later.)

Furthermore, the enemy *"speaks from his own nature"* in the speaking of *"a lie."* But what does all of this mean, and how does it relate to the aforementioned second statement in Proverbs 17:4: *"A liar pays attention to a destructive tongue?"*

Genesis 1:1 tells us, that anything that exists in the *material* realm; has or had to *first* exist in the *immaterial* realm, in some "form," way, or manner. And casting all tautological risks aside; it must be stated that of course anything that exists in the *immaterial* realm, must exist in the *immaterial* realm.

Again here the distinction must be made between the existence or actuality of the *telling* of the lie, and the *contents* of the lie. The fact is that when the devil *tells* any given lie, this lie "telling" first exists or has "actuality" in the *immaterial* realm; as well as later in the *material* realm; and thus is contained within the sphere of actuality.

The fact is that he *did* tell the lie. However, regarding the *contents* of the lie, this is another matter. It is simply not possible that mutually exclusive facts can exist simultaneously—by *definition*. Either one "did do it" or one "did not do it;" if the subject matter concerns the same act at the same time. Thus, whatever *the truth* is, it exists or has actuality in the immaterial realm; and ultimately did, does, or will have existence or actuality in the material realm at the appropriate time of manifestation.

But the same, (actuality), cannot be said for the *content* or *contents* of the lie. The *contents* of the lie have no *actuality* whatsoever. It only has *reality*; and only for those who believe it at that. The perpetrator of the lie knows full well it is not an *actuality*, as well as does anyone else who sees through the ruse; i.e.; finds a part or a *subset* of the *actuality* that is inconsistent with the *purported actuality*.

So whence came the *content* of this or any lie? Jesus tells us that it comes from the enemy's "*own nature.*" The truth is not "*in him,*" and thus whatever he lies about comes not from *actuality*, whether material or immaterial, but rather from his "*nature.*"

According to Jesus, the enemy's ramblings come from "*his own nature,*" which is an actuality; but the *content* of said ramblings has no actuality, because whence could come the truth, or actuality, when it is not "in him?"

Distinctions must be made here regarding Jesus' descriptions of the enemy:

Firstly, the enemy "*does not stand in the truth,*" because "*there is no truth in him.*" This does not necessarily mean that the enemy never tells "*a truth,*" (as opposed to *the* truth); but rather that he cannot or does not *stand* in the truth.

The reason given for him not standing in the truth; is because the truth is not in him. Thus a relationship is established between being able to stand in the truth and having the truth in one; in the sense that in order to be able to stand in the truth, one must first have the truth in him. The King James translates this same Greek word as "*abode.*"[2.7]

Strong's initially places an asterisk by this word: "The asterisk indicates a different rendering (from that of the A.V. (Authorized Version)) adopted in that place by both the British (changed to stood) and American Revisers (changed to standeth)."[2.8]

This original Greek word translated as "abode," or "stand," or "standeth" is:

> "2476 histēmi; a prol. form of a prim. staō, (of the same mean., and used for it in certain tenses); to *stand* (trans. or intrans.), used in various applications (lit. or fig.): -

abide, appoint, bring, continue, covenant, establish, hold up, lay, present, set (up), stanch, stand (by, forth, still, up)."[2.9]

If we use the King James translation as *abode* or *abide*, then it would be fair to say that "one cannot *live* in the truth, unless the truth is in him." Using the literal definition for *histēmi*, *stand* seems the more accurate translation: "one cannot *stand* in the truth, unless the truth is in him."

Secondly; Jesus stated that *"Whenever he speaks a lie,"* implying that there are times when the enemy is not speaking a lie. This could simply mean times when the enemy is not speaking. There are many possibilities for "X," with regard to that old quasi-joke that targets many—most notably: politicians, attorneys, and alcoholics.

Q: "How can you tell when an X is lying?"
A: "When his/her lips are moving."

Or; this *"whenever"* in John 8:44; could refer to times when the enemy is speaking, but it is *not* a lie.

If the enemy is speaking, but not speaking a lie; then unless there exists a gray area where something spoken is neither a truth nor a lie; *and* the enemy exclusively speaks in said "gray area" when he is not lying; then at some point, the enemy necessarily speaks "a truth." "A truth" is again being distinguished here from "the truth."

Telling truth but not all of it, is a common technique for lying. "I got in trouble for something I did not do." being a prime example. What one did not do, was to show up for work on time, pay their taxes, perform the task their employer told them to do, etc. Technically, the statement is true. Meaning; that in the larger set of "the truth;" the "a truth" proffered, does in fact exist; or rather *is* contained therein. And with respect to the enemy, we know he does this, from his encounter with "that woman" who was given to Adam.

Since we know that "the truth" is not in him, and that each and every "a truth" must be a subset of "the truth," even if used with or for deceptive *intent*; then it is likely that if "the truth" is not in him, then any subset of the truth; i.e.; "a truth;" cannot be in him either.

It is not the "a truth" vs. "the truth" in terms of an *actuality* that is the issue. It is the *utilization* or *intent* of deceptively proffering "a truth," as "the truth;" which removes the "a truth," from a subset of "the truth;" in that specific instance.

This is done to cause a specific *reality* different from that which the *actuality* would reasonably justify. Proffering "I got in trouble for something I did not do," here can reasonably cause a *reality* that one was punished for some act of *commission* for which they are *innocent*. But "the truth," is that one was punished for an act of *omission*; i.e.; for *failing* to perform a *required* act of *commission*.

And it must be remembered that Jesus also said *"there is no truth in him."* This statement represents an unqualified and complete negation of the possibility of *any* truth being in him—*unless said "a truth" is utilized for deception*.

So then it would be fair to ask: When the enemy speaks any truth, since none of it is *within* him, whence does he obtain said truth? The only possibility left for the enemy who has *"no truth in him,"* and thus has no truth within, is to obtain any truth is from *without*.

Meaning that he observes, and repeats what he observes in furtherance of some form of deceit. This can easily be confused with the enemy *knowing* something from his *nature*, but careful examination will ultimately reveal that the source was *observation*; and is or was in no way any form of "supernatural" knowledge.

But back to Proverbs; and the "lie," and not "a liar," that is paying attention to a *"destructive"* or *"naughty"* tongue. There are two reasonable explanations for this, with one being *literal*; and one which is perhaps best described as *figurative* in nature; but each likely being true.

With regard to the *first* or the "literal" explanation, we are told the following by Peter, via either Mark or Silvanus, in 1 Peter 5:8 (NAS):

"Be of sober spirit, be on the alert.

"What is Truth?"

> *Your adversary, the devil,
> prowls around like a roaring lion,
> seeking someone to devour."*[2.10]

"There is clearly a consideration of space (prowling around) as well as time (seeking). It is true that part of Peter's statement may be read as a simile, but that would relate to the similarities of a roaring lion, and not necessarily the devil's actions. Or, and more likely; Peter is attempting to describe a phenomenon for which no correct word exists; thus providing a description using the word "like" to indicate the closest possible similarity is intended.

"If it is assumed that devour means consumption of whatever is the object of the "seeking;" then one might fairly ask why any animal would warn it's prey with roaring; prior to killing it for food? This would seem to substantially decrease the likelihood of success; or at a minimum, cause more effort to be required. If devour just means to destroy; to kill when it is not to be used for food; then likewise why would it make any sense to warn the prey?

"But what if Peter really meant that the prowling and roaring constitutes the first effort in his seeking; is in a sense similar to radar? In the use of radar, a signal is first sent or transmitted; and then the returned signal is examined in order to gain information—"stealth" aircraft being specifically designed to minimize this returned signal.

"In a likewise manner, the enemy "roars;" here actually meaning those "thoughts ideas and suggestions" humans get into their heads; often knowing not whence they came. He then watches one's reaction in order to determine their specific potential level of "devour-ability." His goal being to "get our attention" as he did with "the woman," so that he can

17

get a foothold with which to continue the process. Thus, he does not like it when it is the case where little or no signal is returned; meaning that he has been largely or completely ignored."[2.11]

When Jesus stated that the enemy was the father of lies, did he mean *some* lies or *all* lies? Jesus seems to have presented this as an absolute; as He did not state this in the particular, but rather in the general.

There is truth and there is untruth. Not all untruths are lies, but all lies are untruths. A child generally does not provide an answer on an arithmetic examination which indicates that $2 + 2 = 5$, in order to convince the teacher that this is in fact so, while knowing that it is not. [He/she may try a variation of this later with respect to the grade; but that is another matter]. There is an *untruth* here, but likely the child genuinely believed this untruth was truth. A *lie* is *knowingly* stating untruth; either *literally* or *contextually*; in order to *deceive* the recipient with respect to what is the truth.

As in the earlier examples, a lie can consist solely of truth, but not all of it; as the child did in fact get in trouble for something he in fact did not do—clean his room. It seems it is the *process* of lying, or deceit to which Jesus was referring. It is this *process*, and the *result* which was fathered by the enemy. It is a process deliberately designed to alter another's *reality*, or perception of actuality; so as to be *inconsistent* with the *actuality*. Adam and the woman had "no *knowledge* of evil." They knew not what a lie was, until the "hisser," (usually translated as *serpent*), arrived. It must be remembered that the "tree" was not the tree of good and evil, but rather the tree of the *knowledge* of good and evil.

This "hisser" requires a bit of explanation.

The actual Hebrew word for the "serpent" that "showed up" in "Eden" is:

"5175 nâchâsh; from 5172; a *snake* (from its *hiss*); - serpent."[2.12]

"What is Truth?"

"5172 nâchash a prim. root; prop. to *hiss*, i.e. *whisper* a (magic) spell; gen. to *prognosticate*: - x certainly, divine, enchanter, (use) x enchantment, learn by experience, x indeed, diligently observe."[2.13]

As can easily be seen, the usual translation of 5175 *nâchâsh*, as "serpent," is a bit misleading. *Nâchâsh* is *functional* and not *structural*. The assumption that this hisser was structurally a snake, would be akin to the assumption that something is a duck; when only one of the three commonplace "duck criteria," (looks, walks, quacks), have been met.

And there is also that matter of this "serpent's" belly. Genesis 3:14 (KJV) tells us:

"And the Lord God said unto the serpent,
Because thou hast done this,
thou art cursed above all cattle,
and above every beast of the field;
upon thy belly shalt thou go,
and dust shalt thou eat all the days of thy life:"[2.14]

Clearly, Genesis 3:14 represents a change in the status of this *nâchâsh*, or "hisser." Snakes generally have no need for shoes, because they are already "upon their belly." Here being *"upon thy belly"* represents a new and different condition for this particular "hisser." Ergo; either this "hisser" was a snake that for some reason(s) was not already *"upon thy belly;"* or it was not a snake.

It is very important to note two of the translations of the *root* of the "serpent" 5175 nâchâsh; the same being 5172 *nâchash*: "Learn by experience, x indeed;" and "diligently observe."

Much as any noxious, or otherwise unpleasant odor that is detected necessarily comes from the *source* of the odor; the same can be said of a lie. When an odor is detected; one is breathing in molecules from the source of the odor, in a concentration sufficient to be detected. And after a prolonged period of exposure, the olfactory system may *inhibit* the sensation of the odor: "I don't smell it anymore."

A lie is similar. Since the enemy is the father of the lie; then whenever we encounter a lie or engage in this process, we are dealing with the offspring of the enemy—whether *directly*, or *indirectly*; i.e.; via a surrogate.

And just as with an odor, we can become quite used to it. And also like an odor, we can lose the ability to distinguish what represents the truth and what is a lie; i.e.; "what stinks and what doesn't." We can then easily develop *habits*, which then lead us to determine truth not by actuality, but rather by what seems to benefit most us at that time.

When the enemy is "roaring;" (or perhaps better phrased as "hissing"); i.e.; *thoughts, ideas,* and *suggestions*, (as was done with the "woman"); he is disseminating lies—albeit that the lies may contain some incomplete level of truth. A lie is a bit like humor; in that generally neither will be successful unless containing some level of "truth;" whether actual, (actuality); or perceived, (reality).

As in the radar analogy, the enemy will observe which *lies* find a suitable environment, (host); and which do not. What he is seeking is a means of bearing fruit.

"Thoughts ideas and suggestions;" (hereafter interchangeably referred to as: "TIS"); is a *process*. The first, (*thoughts*), is the preliminary or *scouting* part of the mission. He first sows this *thought* in order to see who will "pay attention" to it. If so; meaning the lie was "successful;" he will then begin the *idea* process, laying the foundation for the final phase of *suggestion*: "Why don't you do this?"—with this entire *process* based upon some lie, or series of lies.

Needless to say, the enemy is looking for *destruction*—looking for *any* means of opposing God's desires, one of which is *increase* for his children. This is why a lie pays attention to a destructive tongue. It is being directed by its father, (the enemy); either directly or through a surrogate. Should the lie not sufficiently catch the attention of a host, he will then change the lie; find another "*destructive tongue*" in order to indirectly get the lie *to* the victim; or give up and return at a more "opportune" time.

"What is Truth?"

And with regard to the *second*, or the *"figurative"* explanation of "a lie," and not "*a liar*" paying attention to a "*destructive*" or "*naughty*" tongue; this relates to F = MA, along with equal and opposite reactions; or what is commonly referred to as *karma*.

Any lie represents a *totality*, and not just what it may appear to be on the surface. One cannot lie, and obtain only the *desired* result(s). Any and all "undesired" results may be referred to as "unintended consequences;" but this belief is merely a *reality*—either based upon, or due to, ignorance; and is not in any way actuality based.

Thus as is the case with any action; there is an equal and opposite reaction which will ultimately return to the source of the action. Thus in a sense; the lie "pays attention" to the *source* of the lie as the target for the return of this karma or compensation.

The previously addressed *second* part of the cited Proverbs 17:4 passage: "*A liar* (actually lie) *pays attention to a destructive tongue;*" goes hand in hand with the *first* part of the same.

Again, the *first* part of the above Proverbs 17:4 tells us:

"An evildoer listens to wicked lips;"

Precisely what is an *evildoer*? An implied distinction is present here. Namely; to distinguish *evil* from *wicked*. As will be seen numerous times, *evil* is acting against God's will. Any particular act may or may not in and of itself appear or seem *wicked*; as in the common definition or understanding of the term *wicked*. However, if any action or inaction is inconsistent with the will of God; it is by definition: *evil*.

The enemy will oppose God no matter what. Therefore, the enemy will likewise oppose anyone who is attempting to act according to the will of God. It makes little difference to him if it appears to be wicked or not. As long as whatever "it" is, represents any action or inaction in *furtherance* of the will of God; the enemy will oppose the same. Thus, the enemy literally is pure evil; not by ignorance of lack of sufficient quality information; but by choice.

The actual word translated as "evildoer" here is:

"7489 râ'a': a prim. root; prop. to *spoil* (lit. by *breaking to pieces*); fig. to *make* (or *be*) *good for nothing*, i.e. *bad* (phys., soc. or mor.):—afflict, associate selves [*by mistake for* 7462], break (down, in pieces), + displease, (be, bring, do) evil (doer, entreat man), show self friendly [*by mistake for* 7462}, do harm, (do) hurt, (behave self, deal ill, x indeed, do mischief, punish, still, vex, (do) wicked (doer,-ly), be (deal, do) worse."[2.15])

"7462 râ'âh; a prim root; to tend a flock, i.e. pasture it; intrans. To graze (lit or fig.); gen. to rule; by extens. to associate with (as a friend):—x break, companion, keep company with, devour, eat up, evil entreat, feed, use a friend, make friendship with, herdman, keep [sheep] (-er), pastor, + shearing house, shepherd, wander, waste."[2.16]

The difficulties of accurate translations of the original Bible terminology, are evident with the noted "mix-ups" of 7489 and 7462.

Here the "positive" meanings for the translations of 7489 râ'a', "associate selves, show self friendly"; are *incorrect* as noted by the inclusion of "[*by mistake for* 7462]." Thus in these instances when râ'a' appeared; which *should* have been translated as such with *negative* meanings; râ'a' was instead likely assumed to be 7462 râ'âh; and was translated with *positive* meanings.

It also appears from the definitions that the reverse happened; although this is not noted. Here with the *translations* of "*devour, eat up, evil entreat,*" as well as "*wander, waste*" as *negative* translations of 7462 râ'âh, it seems likely that 7489 râ'a', and not 7462 7râ'âh, was the actual original word.

It is interesting to ponder how such mistranslations may be responsible for the minor differences between religious sects. ["That one," about the fact that various religious sects do not recognize each other's "*church;*" but the Baptists do not recognize *each other* in the liquor store; will not be repeated here.]

Tracing the roots of the word "wicked" is a bit of difficult undertaking. It appears that the roots are the same as Wicca or witchcraft.

According to Chambers, the origin of "witch" is:

> "...wiche, in Genesis and Exodus; developed from Old English wicce female magician, sorceress,..."[2.17]

Exodus 22:18 (KJV) tells us:

> "*Thou shalt not suffer a witch to live.*"[2.18]

In Exodus 22:18 the Hebrew word translated as "witch," is actually:

> "3784 kâshaph; a prim. root; prop. to *whisper* a spell, i.e. to *inchant* or practise magic: —sorcerer, (use) witch (-craft)."[2.19]

This "whispering" may be another way of describing "hissing;" with the same being the actual meaning of the word generally translated as *serpent* or *snake*, with regard to Adam & Co, as previously stated. This aforementioned 5175 nâchâsh; "a *snake* (from its *hiss*); - serpent;" again is derived from 5172 nâchash; here also meaning: "to *hiss, i.e. whisper* a (magic) spell;" to describe or "name" the enemy at the time he attacked Eve. And the alternate *translations* of 5172 nâchash as: "learn by experience, x indeed, diligently observe;" should also not be overlooked.

The key here in the definition of *kâshaph*, is also the *whispering* of a *spell*. An *evildoer* (râ'a'); or *spoiler*, ("to spoil"); meaning one who purposely acts contrary to the will of God; will listen to this whispering, whether it be a spell or anything else. This "listening" is to be distinguished from one who *hears* the whispering, but dismisses it for what it is. This "listening" is the "return" the enemy is seeking, as success of the first step of the aforementioned TIS process.

This TIS *process*, or "thoughts ideas and suggestions" process (attacks); will be examined in much greater detail shortly.

Chapter 3

Recollection and Imagination

> *"A mentally insane person will have a reality which includes a sphere of reality with incomplete intersection/union or containment of this reality within the larger sphere of actuality."*
> —Emma B. Quadrakoff

Insane simply means not sane. The root of this word being the Latin *"sanus;"* relating to the state of *general* health; e.g.; healthy. The use of this root is seen in *"sanitarium"* or *"sanitorium"* and *"sanitize."*

The differences in the usages or meanings of these derivatives of *sanus* become a bit blurred. In the case of sanitarium or sanitorium, there is often a *subjective* decision made as to what *level* of health exists. This is a determination which is not a *binary*; but rather is merely an opinion based upon some type of scale or perhaps stated more accurately: "How unhealthy is the patient?"

Are they unhealthy enough to warrant being placed in a sanitarium?

Likewise *sanitizing*, as opposed to *sterilization*; merely reduces the number of microorganisms present to a previously determined, (by consensus), "acceptable" level. Thus this is also not actually a binary, as it is not the presence of *any* pathogens, as in sterilization; but rather the *number* of pathogens present that is the issue.

With regard to *mental* sanity or health, the greater the intersection or containment of any particular reality sphere is within the larger sphere of actuality, the greater the level of *mental* sanity. The less the intersection or containment of any given reality sphere is within the larger sphere of actuality, the greater the level of mental insanity. And if there is no intersection, then there is no mental sanity. But the key reference here must be the *actuality*, and not merely the *reality* of another.

In today's world, there seems to be an increase in the morbidity and prevalence of the mental process known as *confabulation*. Confabulation represents a kind of *hybrid* entity; consisting of some degree of mental insanity, and quasi-lying.

Here there is a blending of the *recollection* and *imagination* faculties; also resulting in a *reality* not completely contained within the sphere of *actuality*. Sometimes this is due to actual underlying *physical* disease or trauma; but more often it is *psychological* in origin. This is a type of *sophistry*; as whatever is confabulated has to "sound good;" but necessarily contains at least one fatal flaw.

For example: A tells B, that A began to distance themselves from B, because of B's incessant and picayune criticisms about some pro-bono construction work that A did for B at B's home.

As the "story" goes, this "distancing" was because A simply did not appreciate the fact that B constantly criticized the work done by A; work done strictly as a favor to B; so A simply got tired of it all, and thus walked away entirely from the relationship. This would not be an unreasonable position, in that who would appreciate this incessant criticism by B, for things done by A simply to help B out of the kindness of A's heart?

When A is then questioned by B, as to specifically what work it is to which A is referring, A cannot provide so much as even *one* example of any work that was ever done. *B* then asks *A* to name even one time that *A* was ever in *B*'s house, and could have possibly ever done any work whatsoever. *A* cannot name even one time that *A* was ever in *B*'s house and could possibly have done any type of work. *A*'s final response to *B* is that *A* "guesses" that he (*A*) does not have a very good memory.

As crazy as this all sounds, it is nevertheless a true story.

But the (true) *actuality*, was that it was because of *A*'s outrageous behavior, that in fact it was *B* that simply could no longer stand to be anywhere near *A*.

It was *B* who actually distanced himself from *A*, and in fact at the very same time, *A*'s wife was actually angry with *B* because of this distancing by *B*. Yet because of *A*'s pride, this was intolerable to *A*; so *A* then petitioned his *imagination*; knowingly or not; in order to come up with a scenario that made some degree of sense; and also protected *A*'s pride; and *A* actually convinced himself that this was a true *recollection*.

Thus at the very same *A*'s wife is angry at *B* for *B* distancing *him*self from *A*, which was the story *A* had previously told her; *A* now is now telling *B* that it was actually *he*, (*A*) who did the "distancing," and precisely why.

The difference between confabulation and lying; is that in the confabulator's mind, there is genuine belief that this new *reality* is an accurate recollection of an *actuality*—at least at the time they are "telling it." They genuinely do not know that this phenomenon has no basis in actuality, and exists only in their mind. They do not even know they are not telling the truth. (It doesn't stink anymore.)

Confabulation often represents an attempt of the reconciliation of *actuality* with *emotions*, via the creation of an altered *reality*; and then the subsequent representation of this *reality* as an *actuality*—and all while genuinely believing this represents truth.

Because one emotionally desires an actuality that is quite different than what the actuality in fact is; in confabulation, these emotions will then cause the *imaginative* faculties to devise a reality representing an actuality which is consistent with these emotional needs—irrespective of any inconsistencies with the (actual) actuality.

The "trick" here, is to successfully supplant the normal *recollective* faculties, (memory); with the result or product of these *imaginative* faculties. The result is an altered "recollection;" and a genuine belief that this new reality represents an accurate recollection of some past actuality. The "spiritual" mechanism(s) for this, will be discussed in greater detail in subsequent chapters.

This, (confabulation), again is to be distinguished from lying; as the liar knows full well that the lie represents some *imaginative* product, rather than a *recollection*.

Here with the *liar*, the "trick" is for the liar to knowingly successfully convince, (split infinitive(s) noted), the *victim* of the lie that this *imaginative* product, represents an accurate *recollection* of actuality.

But "success" in confabulation, is determined by the belief of the *confabulator*, at least temporarily; while as stated, "success in lying is determined by the belief of the *victim*," again for as long as it lasts.

From a *functional* standpoint, we do not "live," (abide), in actuality, but rather must almost always "live" in reality. Although it is true that "a thing that is, is; and cannot not be;" nevertheless, our judgments and decisions are based upon what we think or *believe* a "thing" is; (reality); rather than what it in actuality is. Because of this, emotions should always be reconciled with actuality, permitting a reality consistent with actuality; and never, (as with confabulation), attempt the reverse.

Thus a fair conclusion being; that in order for one's *reality* to in fact represent an objective existence of a "thing," it must remain at all times within the confines of that *actuality*.

How is *actuality* determined? This of course is a critical action, as it affects everything we do; and every decision we make. Generally; *actuality* is attempted to be determined by what one knows or thinks they know about the *objective* existence of phenomena.

One method is to determine actuality by direct sensory input; which of course is based upon input from our five senses.

Recollection and Imagination

Whatever one sees, hears, touches, tastes, or smells; has actuality.

This use of the five senses as a completely reliable means of determining actualities, of course presents at least two serious problems:

Firstly; the *five senses* are subject to error. A *mirage* or *hologram* can be very convincing, yet they are just that. The mirage and the hologram both have actual existence, but what they represent to the viewer is neither that of a mirage nor a hologram; but rather strictly what they *appear* to represent to the viewer.

It looks just like a body of water somewhere in the distance, but it is not. It looks like a large nut and bolt, but in fact is only an image from a thin piece of some other, (non-nut or non-bolt), material. In the absence of the knowledge of their *actualities*, the reality and actuality are assumed to be the same. In fact, it is not likely that any thought of these being any different than they appear would even be entertained; unless there existed some reason for questioning the *reality*, or *perceived* actuality.

Secondly; these five senses, even if completely accurate; are generally grossly insufficient to perceive even a small percentage of what actually exists. The audible spectrum is very limited; the sight spectrum is even more so. There are audio frequencies far beyond our ability to sense, and the visual spectrum is likely not even an octave. Thus there are phenomena which clearly have "actual existence;" yet we are completely oblivious to their existence. Much wildlife can hear octaves above what humans can hear.

Another unreliable means would be by *indirect* sensory input. One knows there must be voices in the room, because they are coming out of the radio; and since the battery-powered radio is not connected to anything outside the room, there *must* be someone "in there." Granted, these voices are superimposed on a radio frequency that cannot be detected by humans, but nevertheless they must be somewhere in the room in order for the radio to convert them into audible, (as opposed to inaudible), sound. So then precisely what actuality is in the room? Is it the voices picked up by the human senses, or the radio frequency?

Another unreliable means is based upon "knowledge," whether this is personally observed or not. We all know atoms exist, but how many of us have actually seen one? And once told what an atom should look like, and then shown what we are told is an atom; all we would know would be that the observation matched the knowledge—while not in any way being certain that the original knowledge was in any way an accurate description of an actuality.

Thus we have a distinction between reality as a result of personally "verified" actuality; and reality as a result of *believed* actuality; irrespective of what correlation may exist between said believed realities and the actuality. "I *know* from experience that it will hurt if I hit my thumb with a hammer;" as opposed to being *told* that it will hurt if one hits his or her thumb with a hammer.

For each and every *cause* in the universe, there is an *effect*; and for each and every *effect*, there is a *cause*; and this is inescapable. The only exception to this of course, is again the logical requirement for a *primum movens*, or "prime mover;" which is generally referred to as God. This is the only effect with no cause.

Actuality will generally become our reality, because of an actuality's *perceived* effects on us; but only to the extent it is perceived by us. But a thing is what it actually is, and not necessarily limited to what its *effects* upon us, *represent* to us. Neither does any particular *actuality* in any way necessarily resemble what our *reality* suggests to us that the actuality in fact is.

It must also be understood, that again, actualities necessarily are almost always much greater and more complex than that which is comprehended; or arguably can ever be comprehended—at least from one's viewpoint or perspective from the *material* realm. Generally, only a tiny portion of any given actuality is ever "actually" perceived.

The "figurative" meaning of a lie paying "*attention to a destructive" tongue*," is a good example of this. The actuality of a "lie," consists of everything that comprises the lie; and not merely what one *thinks* or *believes*, (the *reality* of the lie), comprises the lie. Whatever *benefit* one believes is derived from lying, is only one part of the actuality of the lie. The *damage* that this lie causes, as well as the *karmic* debt incurred by the telling of a lie, is also part of the total package that is called a lie—even if one is completely unaware of this fact.

Thus, it is almost without exception that even accurate realities, represent only a portion of the associated actuality or actualities, that precipitate(s) these associated reality or realities. This presents substantial problems; as again, we live, think and act in realities, and not actualities; and yet we are ultimately faced with the "actuality" of actualities.

Can one determine if a radio antenna or cell tower is in use or disconnected, merely by visual inspection? Can one visually determine if an electrical wire is "hot?" Can one see the total actuality of electric current flowing through said wire, including the electromagnetic field around the wire, as well as the air and material temperature changes surrounding this wire?

This gets even more complex and fallible when the *immaterial* realm is considered. Distinctions must be made here between non-detectable *material* phenomena, as opposed to *immaterial* phenomena. The actualities in the previous paragraph, all refer to the former, as they all have *material* existence.

Actuality breaks down into four categories of phenomena:

1. Detectable material phenomena
2. Non-detectable material phenomena
3. Detectable immaterial phenomena
4. Non-detectable immaterial phenomena

A distinction must also be made between detecting the actual phenomenon/phenomena *itself*, and merely detecting the *result*(s) of said phenomenon/phenomena; as well as there being a need to be capable of accurately determining precisely which is which. All; (including *solipsists*, if sufficiently intoxicated); believe that those results described in Genesis 1:1, (creation of the heavens and the earth), exist; even if there is much disagreement as to the phenomenon responsible for the same.

The first two; (detectable material phenomena and non-detectable material phenomena); are relatively easy.

The aforementioned common electric current is usually deliberately made by man, and has an actuality or actualities, many or most of which, (but not necessarily all), can be detected. These detections have increased over time, and continue to increase.

Visual inspection does little, but equipment designed to detect these phenomena exist; and these detection devices are *material* in nature. The more sophisticated the equipment, the greater the likelihood of detection of these various actualities. Thus there is, and has been an increase of *material* phenomena placed in the detectable category and a decrease in the non-detectable category.

Electricity is the *movement* of electrons, (matter). The *fields* created, are essentially material as they can result in generation of electrical current. Any temperature changes, (result), essentially represent merely faster moving or faster vibrating previously existing matter. If the light goes on when the switch is closed, we also can see the *result*.

But the *immaterial* realm is quite different. The *material results* of phenomena in the immaterial realm; such as the *effect* of *creation*, and subsequent *existence* of universe; can often easily be determined. However, detecting these causative *immaterial* actualities themselves, whether direct or indirect, is another and entirely different issue. (The use of: "entirely different matter," is purposely avoided here for obvious reasons.)

This is all further complicated by the fact that the immaterial realm has neither time, nor distance, nor space. Thus it is more than arguable that actual immaterial phenomena all exist at once, and essentially all in the same "place."

Since there is no *time* in the immaterial, it does not seem that there is any determination of the *sequence* of the creation or existence of immaterial phenomena possible from that realm. Again, this refers to the *actuality* of the very *immaterial* phenomena itself; and not merely any *material* result or influence upon the *material*.

And likewise with no *space*, it seems there cannot be any particular *place* of congregation or concentration of the actuality of immaterial phenomena. These are additional problems that John experienced as accounted in Revelation—again at least from Chapter 4 onward.

Thus to the extent that we "hosts" are influenced by *immaterial* phenomena, it is more than logical; in fact it is a *requirement*; to conclude that said influences are the result of the portions of said immaterial phenomena causing said influences. This may seem to be a "no brainer," but this often remains unrecognized, or perhaps better stated: *unrealized*.

However, no further determination of the true magnitude or nature of these *immaterial* actualities, can *easily* be made outside of the influential portions, (effects), of the same.

Nevertheless the fact remains, that except for the aforementioned *primum movens*; for every *effect*, there is and must always be a *cause*. If and when it can be correctly determined that no cause in the *material* realm could have possibly *caused* said given *effect* in the *material* realm; then the *causative* factor of said *material* effect cannot reside in the *material* realm. This is precisely why the event described in Genesis 1:1, AKA: "The Big Bang," *requires* the existence of an *immaterial* realm; as at that "time," no such *material* realm even existed in which to contain this *cause*.

This is stated with the caveat that the reliability or veracity of this "immaterially caused" conclusion, is in direct proportion to the level of confidence or certainty with which the determination of non-existence of the causative factor residing in the material realm was concluded.

In other words; to the extent that it is "certain" that there is no material cause possible for a material effect; then to that same extent the cause *must* reside in the immaterial—as long as the perceived *effect* is in fact an *actuality*. So with respect to the event described in Genesis 1:1, AKA: "The Big Bang;" since there was not yet a material realm where the cause for the creation of the material realm could have existed; the evidence for an *immaterial* cause is both dispositive and conclusive.

And of course the realms are a *binary*, as the very terminology itself is based upon whether or not there exists "matter" in that realm. Whichever realm it is that is under discussion, must either be *material* or *immaterial*; there being no possibility of an actual third. The only possible exception to this would be the *nether* or *neither* realm, and the *kŏlpŏs*; AKA: Abraham's Bosom, Limbus

Patrum, or "air conditioned section of hell;" contained *within* this nether or neither realm. But this nether or neither realm, or any "subdivisions" of the same, is not actually *another* realm, but rather a *neither* realm. [See *"Ostium Ab Inferno—The Opening From Hell."*]

Thus, if a thing exists, (here as a causation factor); and this "thing" does not exist in the *material* realm; then there remains no other realm in which it can exist, other than the *immaterial* realm. It must be remembered that that which resides in the neither or nether realm, was once contained in the *immaterial* realm, but was banished from the same.

In addition, when it becomes a *certainty*, that in order for any material *cause* to be responsible for a given material *effect*, requires the *violation* of natural law; then it is simply not possible for the *causative* factor itself, as opposed to the material *result* or the *effect*, to reside or exist anywhere within the material realm.

When the effect under consideration pleases us immensely; and it is certain that no material cause could possibly exist that would produce said effect; this is generally referred to as a *miracle*.

It must be asked precisely what *material* causative factor could have there been for the introduction of manna from the sky as foodstuff for forty years; and, (at least arguably), never to be seen again? The recipients of this manna had obviously never encountered it before; which is precisely why they named it "manna." Manna literally means: "What is it."[3.1]

A word must be said about *Supernatural* vs. *Paranormal* vs. *Immaterial*. Although often considered synonymous; they are *similar*, but not necessarily *synonymous*. Sometimes they can successfully be used interchangeably; and sometimes they cannot.

Supernatural, is the mere addition of the prefix *"super"* to the word *"natural."* The root of natural is *nat*, or *natal*; which generally refers to birth. This is also seen in words such as nativity, natal horoscope, (a look at, or looking at (scope), the hour of birth), naturalized citizen, etc. And *"super"* generally means "above." Thus *supernatural* refers to that which is *above* that which was "born." Both science and the Scriptures agree that the universe was "born." Supernatural refers to that which is and was *above* the universe—the same being the *source* of the *cause*, for the *result* or *effect*, that was the creation (birth) of the universe.

Here again the distinction between "heaven," and "the heavens," is appropriate. "Heaven" here is referring to that which existed *before* the "heaven(s) and the earth" were "born" by creation. There was an *immaterial* realm, (heaven); *before* there was a natural realm, (the heavens and the earth); but this term *supernatural* could have no meaning unless and until there was a *natural* realm. And of course this is only from the "current" perspective of the natural realm; as the concepts of "before" and "after" in the supernatural realm, are both ineffable, and difficult to even imagine.

Paranormal is a bit trickier. Here we have the prefix, "para;" which generally means "next to" or "beside."

> "3844 para; a prim. prep.; prop. *near*, i.e. (with gen.) *from beside* (lit. or fig.), (with dat.) *at* (or *in*) the *vicinity* of (obj. or subj.), (with acc.) to the *proximity* with (local [espec. *beyond* or *opposed* to] or causal [*on account* of])..."[3.2]

But it must be asked, precisely what is "that thing" described as *paranormal*, that is *next to* or *beside* this "something?" It must also be asked, what is "the thing" that the something described as *paranormal*, is actually beside or next to?

The *root* of paranormal, "normal," is:

> "...norma carpenter's square, rule, NORM... Normalcy 1857, mathematical condition of being at right angles..."[3.3]

In studying a block of mass on an inclined plane, the *norm* is that amount of weight or force on the *inclined* surface itself. On a flat or horizontal surface; meaning that the weight is at a "right angle" to the plane, the norm is equal to the object's weight. As the inclined surface approaches vertical, this *norm* decreases, and will becomes zero when the plane is vertical. But the *weight* of the object itself remains essentially constant. The magnitude of this "norm," is dependent upon this angle.

Paranormal, as per the above definition of its root *normal*, would fairly then refer to phenomenon or a phenomena; which is *next to*, or *beside*, something that involves a *right angle*.

Paranormal is rarely used to describe a person "next to" a block on an inclined plane. Rather, paranormal meaning being "next to" a right angle or norm, likely refers to the intersection of that which is of the *immaterial*, and that which is *material*; and particularly, although not always necessarily; referring to that which is *physically alive*.

Human beings; although designed to be "vertical" creatures while in the *awake* state; are in fact also designed to exist on a *horizontal* surface. [This is stated with the understanding of the existence of differences between Euclidian and non-Euclidian geometry; and the fact that the earth is actually an oblate spheroid.]

Throughout time, the *material* realm is generally represented as the *horizontal*; with the *immaterial* generally represented by the *vertical*.

When humans are physically alive; they have that "vertical" breath of life or "soul;" as well as other things intersecting this horizontal material existence from the "above." This is that "normal" condition of physical life; and at lease allegorically, resembling a cross.

Thus *paranormal* describes something that is *para* or: "*near*, i.e. (with gen.) *from beside* (lit. or fig.), (with dat.) *at* (or *in*) the *vicinity* of (obj. or subj.), (with acc.) to the *proximity* with (local [espec. *beyond* or *opposed* to];" this *norm* or right angle intersection of body and soul. Without this right angle body soul intersection, (physical life); there can be no *paranormal*. There can be "paraphysical," or next to the *physical* or *material*; but there cannot be true *paranormal*.

Sometimes interlaced triangles are used to represent the condition of the immaterial and material intersection. The triangle with the apex pointed down represents the *immaterial*. The triangle with the apex pointed up, with the base on the bottom and horizontal, represents the *material*. The "Star of David," is derived from these interlaced triangles.

When this *intersection* of the immaterial with material ceases, the human no longer is physically alive; and generally is no longer capable of being a *vertical* entity; with what remains, (the remains), usually "remaining" on the horizontal.

This "vertical" portion continues to exist, but no longer intersects the horizontal. This vertical portion *ideally* remains in the immaterial realm from which it likely never actually exited, but rather only ever *intersected* the material. Numerous theories such as those regarding heaven, hell, purgatory, limbo, (now considered extinct); all have one very important thing in common: Each require the continued existence of this *vertical* portion or soul.

The *horizontal* portion remains in the material; but no longer is capable of maintaining this intersection. Thus the previously alive matter is no longer capable of *homeostasis*, and the decay process begins.

This concept of this intersection as a "right angle" or norm, commonly appears in "normal" vernacular: "I wasn't brought up that way." "I wasn't raised that way." "Where were you brought up?" These express the process of the *vertical* component maintaining this "right," or ninety degree angle with the *horizontal*.

This can also be seen in expressions such as: "He is on the level;" "He is a level headed guy;" or seen in the concept of "square deal," or "cutting corners." When it is suspected that this ninety degree relationship with the "vertical," (lack of rectitude), of soul or mind is not being maintained with the "horizontal" or material; it is often asked: "What's his angle?"

If true, the literal answer would be: "not ninety degrees," or not "on the square," or not a right angle—and is alluded to by the very asking of the question.

Upright behavior is behavior on the horizontal or material realm, that is consistent with this vertical portion. A "square deal" is a fair and honest transaction. When things are not "square" or "on the level," imbalances are caused, and will ultimately require resolution.

And what about specific "behavioral norms?"

In a free society, certain behaviors are desired; and certain behaviors are not. Of those that are not desired, there are tolerances established with respect to how much deviation from these desired behaviors will be permitted without intervention. If behaviors are placed on a "bell curve," two vertical lines, one on either side of the "peak" can be used to mark this boundary. Whatever behaviors are contained within these lines can be considered as behavioral *norms* at that time; and this represents that society's behavioral "tolerances" at that time.

The farther any given behavior outside of these lines deviates from this "peak," the more severe the penalty for said behavior. The illegal parking of an automobile may lie just outside of these boundaries, but murder would be much farther away.

A similar system could be established, if it could be objectively and precisely determined how far a given behavior deviates from the right angle formed by the intersection of this *immaterial* part of man with the *material* part.

Abnormal is the addition of the Latin prefix *ab*, added to this "normal." *Ab* generally means *away from*; so in this usage abnormal simply means away from the norm or normal, or this ninety degree or right angle. Behavioral *norms* change over time, but the standards of the actual norm or intersection of the immaterial with the material does not. But how can this be so?

The answer lies in realities which are *inconsistent* with *actualities*—most notably with the misunderstanding of God's Word. Sometimes this is innocent—but often times it is not. As will be seen, *free will* and *balance* are two of the most important concepts in understanding this vertical portion. Free will—as long as one's exercise of his or her free will does not interfere with another's free will; and with balance meaning reaping what one sows. [See the Monograph: *"Inevitable Balance."*]

As stated, the *material effects* of the *immaterial*; are generally the only way that the *immaterial* realm is detected *materially*.

When a fetus breathes his or her *first* breath, it becomes a living soul or being; and the Scriptures confirm this with the process described in formation of Adam in Genesis 2:7.

When the *last* breath is breathed, the immaterial portion exits the physical body. The former being the causation of this intersection or right angle; and in the latter, this intersection or right angle ceases to exist.

So then again, a fair definition of the *paranormal*, would be that which exists *next to* or *beside* this *norm*, or right angle; or immaterial/material intersection. These entities that exist next to or beside this norm; or immaterial/material intersection; must be either material or immaterial.

If they are *material*; then the study of the same is what comprises the various physical sciences, and although technically correct, this is not generally referred to as *paranormal*.

It is generally understood that only when these phenomena are *immaterial*, that the term *paranormal* is used to describe them; with *parascience* meaning "to know" about these "paranormal" phenomena. And just as in "material" science, there are subcategories of *parascience*: Angelology, Demonology, Theology, etc.

Those parascientists, or paranormal investigators; who make a serious study of the paranormal, whether termed scientists or investigators; utilize various *material* devices in order to attempt to detect and or communicate with these *immaterial* paranormal entities.

Whether it is a "spirit box," thermographic equipment, or cameras designed to record from ultraviolet through infrared; these are nevertheless designed to detect changes in the *material* environment as a result of this *immaterial* paranormal, (from the immaterial realm), activity. As previously stated, it is very difficult to detect any phenomenon, (here immaterial), which is dissimilar to that phenomenon for which the detection device, (material), was designed.

As a contrast, the word "parallel" comes from:

> "parà allélois beside one another, side by side (parà beside and allélois each other...)"[3,4]

Here there is an implication of similar phenomena—such as in parallel lines. When two things are truly parallel, there can be no intersection, including a "right angle" or *norm*—at least according to Euclidian geometry. But even in non-Euclidian geometry, although these "lines," ultimately may actually be circles, and thus may ultimately "intersect" with themselves; any intersection with each other seems unlikely.

If it is so stipulated that this immaterial realm has neither time nor space; then why is it that so many paranormal investigators often travel great distances in order to get to an environment where these paranormal activities are believed to be present?

This is in actuality a twofold question: The detection of the paranormal *activity*; and the detection of the paranormal *entity*; are entirely different things. In this sense, the paranormal *entity* is the *cause*; and the paranormal *activity* is the *effect*.

With regard to the *activity*, this may in fact sometimes be location dependent. Without delving into the subjects of portals, vortices and such, information about which is generally less than "scientific;" there may be specific physical locations that provide some type of means for this activity to manifest, for varieties of reasons. And it must also be noted that this *activity*, is generally only that which results in changes detected in the *material* realm—at least with regard to the aforementioned detection devices.

This is an important distinction. A "light orb," assuming these are actualities; is neither the immaterial *entity*, nor the immaterial *activity*. Said "orb" merely represents only the *material* effect of the immaterial entity, or the immaterial entity's immaterial activity. A "shadow figure," again assuming these are actualities, likewise represents only the effect on the *material*, that is caused by either the immaterial *entity*, or the immaterial entity's immaterial *activity*.

With respect to the paranormal *entity itself*; given that there is neither time nor space; the real question would not be how is it that one gets *to* these paranormal entities; but rather how could one's *immaterial* portion; i.e.; "soul;" ever get *away* from them.

One exception to this; would be any entity that is misplaced. Meaning; any entity originally designed to exist in one realm, (here the *immaterial* realm); but was for whatever reason(s) banished from this *immaterial* realm to either to the *material* realm, or to an "X" realm; i.e.; the *neither* or *nether* realm; AKA "hell."

"Revelation 12:7-9 (KJV) tells us:

> "*And there was war in heaven:
> Michael and his angels fought
> against the dragon; and the dragon
> fought and his angels,*
>
> *And prevailed not; neither was
> their place found any more in heaven.*
>
> *And the great dragon was cast out,
> that old serpent, called the Devil, and Satan,
> which deceiveth the whole world:
> he was cast out into the earth, and
> his angels were cast out with him.*"[O1]

"Here we have a description of what happened; (most likely at some point in time between Genesis 1:1 and Genesis 1:2); when sin attempted to contaminate the immaterial realm or heaven. Although very little is known regarding the circumstances surrounding this battle, what is clear is that there was then no place "any more" for the enemy or "his angels" in the *immaterial* realm or "heaven," and they were "cast out."

"The actual Greek word translated as "angels" is:

> 32 "aggĕlŏs; from aggĕllō; (prob. der. from 71; comp. 34) (to *bring tidings*); a *messenger*; esp. an "*angel*"; by impl. a *pastor*:- angel, messenger."[O2]

"The word aggĕlŏs is the only word used for "angels" in the entire New Testament except in Luke 20:36 which is:

"2465 isaggĕlŏs; from 2470 and 32; *like an angel*, i.e. *angelic*: - equal unto the angels."[O3]

"Just for reference, Luke 20:36 (KJV) tells us:

"Neither can they die any more: for they are equal unto the angels; and are the children of God, being the children of the resurrection."[O4]

"The definition of the aggĕlŏs requires three things. First; one who sends a message or tidings. Second; the message or tidings itself or themselves. And third; a recipient for the message or tidings. The significance of this will be addressed later.
"It must be noted that the actual Greek word translated as "deceiveth" is:

"4105 planaō; from 4106; to (prop. *cause to*) *roam* (from safety, truth, or virtue): - go astray, deceive, err, seduce, wander, be out of the way."[O5]

"Thus here there are actually two matters to consider. The *objective of* these particular aggĕlŏs, is or was planaō; or "to (prop. *cause to*) *roam* (from safety, truth, or virtue): - go astray, deceive, err, seduce, wander, be out of the way." The "these," in this context, is important because not all angels or aggĕlŏs seek planaō. It was only *these particular* angels or aggĕlŏs; those "cast out" with him; who sought and seek planaō.

Those who were not "cast out;" i.e.; are not with the enemy, are likewise aggĕlŏs; but they do not seek planaō.

"As an aside, it is considered "common knowledge" or *doxa* that the enemy took *one third* of the angels with him; however there seems to be little Biblical evidence for this.

"Revelation 12:4 is usually cited as the source for this "took one third" belief:

"Revelation 12:4 (KJV) tells us:

*"And his tail drew the third part
of the stars of heaven,
and did cast them to the earth:
and the dragon stood before the woman
which was ready to be delivered,
for to devour her child as soon as it was born."*[06]

"There are several problems with citing this verse as evidence for the "one third" theory: Revelation 12:9 tells us the enemy: *"was cast out into the earth, and his angels were cast out with him."* Thus it was not the enemy who did any casting out of these *aggĕlŏs*; whether by utilizing his tail, or by any other means—they were "thrown out" together.

"Neither Satan nor these aggĕlŏs were active parties in this expulsion event; i.e.; they were the "baseballs" and not the "batter." And given the context, the timing is way off, unless one believes that *"the woman which was ready to be delivered, for to devour her child as soon as it was born;"* had already occurred long long ago. And also given the context, it seems that this "tail action" relates to an entirely different event, and an event in the far future.

"There are both similarities and differences with respect to the enemy and a contaminated soul:

"The enemy was *cast out* of the immaterial realm; (*heaven* but not the *heavens*); because of the contamination of sin committed while in that realm.

"The actual word here in this passage of Revelation translated as "into" is:

> "*1519* ĕis *to* or *into* (indicating the point reached or entered) of place, time, or (fig) purpose (result etc.)"[O7]

"So at this point it is unclear whether "to the earth" or "into the earth" represents the correct translation.

"Man is refused *reentry*, because of sin committed while in the condition of physical life.

"Although the actual genesis of the enemy is not known, it seems clear that the enemy is an immaterial entity, and was designed to exist, and did in fact exist, in the immaterial realm; and thus was not designed to exist in the material realm. We are told that he was cast out of the immaterial realm, either *to* the earth or *into* the earth. But as a *material* entity on the *material* realm, the enemy is not generally recognizable as such.

"At the risk of a "double tautology," it must again be stated that the immaterial part of man is immaterial in nature, and the material part of man is material. The true part or essence of man (the part that is created equal), is the immaterial part; with the material part representing a vessel for earthly (material) existence. The immaterial part is immortal, but the physical part, under normal circumstances, is not—at least by the "normal" rules of the material realm.

"For clarity, distinctions must be made. It is beyond any rational dispute, that there is an immaterial realm with "current lawful occupants." God and angels (*non-planaō* seeking angels) come to mind first. To the extent that there are other *immaterial* entities that exist, these either "lawfully reside" in the immaterial realm as per design, or they do not. To be clear, this: "do not" does not mean *unlawful* residence in the immaterial realm, as we are told what happens when this is attempted. This refers to immaterial entities that may in fact exist, but do not exist or "reside" in the immaterial realm. There may be a plethora of other entities legitimately residing in the immaterial realm, or there may not be. However the enemy and "his angels" although they continue to exist, we are told they no longer reside in the immaterial realm as they by design should—and by design they do not possess an earthly vessel, and thus cannot have any type of "normal material" existence.

"The material and immaterial realms are a binary; in that there is either matter or there is not. Any entity who either cannot re-enter the immaterial realm (contaminated soul); or one who was "cast out" of the immaterial realm, cannot exist in or on that realm. And if *neither* has the physical vessel to exist in the material realm; e.g.; an entity originally designed for immaterial existence, or a soul departed from said physical vessel (no longer has an "earth suit"); then neither can either of the same truly exist in the material realm.

"The "nether world" is generally considered to be that which is down or beneath the surface of the earth; arguably the "bad section" of the *immaterial* realm; with perhaps the surface of the earth being the "tracks" which this nether world is on the "bad side" of. This would be consistent with the "cast out *into* the earth" translation of the aforementioned *ĕis*.

"Merriam Webster defines "nether" as:

> "1: situated down or below: lower; 2: situated or believed to be situated beneath the earth's surface."[08]

"But although this "nether world" may not be material, "neither" is it necessarily any part of the immaterial realm.

"It could in fact be; any "etymological sources" to the contrary not withstanding; that this "nether" merely represents a misspelling of "neither."

"If so, this would represent both a kind of third realm; and *not* a third realm simultaneously. Meaning; that the "*neither world;*" as opposed to the common usage of "*nether* world;" actually means *neither* realm or "world;" or "stuck" between the two realms. This would be an "X realm;" and is not *either* realm; but rather *neither* realm, or *no realm*.

"This may have been the actual source of the now abandoned concept of "Limbo." The Catholic doctrine of Limbo was concerned with that place where those who were not "Baptized;" usually infants; supposedly went upon physical death. The belief is or was; that *all* (except Jesus) are born with "original sin," which is removed only with Baptism. Since the belief is that no one can go to heaven unless cleansed of this and all other sins; there then had to be a place for infants who are all born with original sin; but yet could not have sinned of their own free will. No attempt is being made here to attest to the truth or falsity of any particular religious beliefs, including this one; but merely to present them.

"Thus this concept of "Limbo" represented a destination between heaven and hell. According to this doctrine, the infant *could* not go to heaven because of the original sin; yet *should* not go to hell because infants do not know right from wrong, and thus cannot sin of their own free will. Hence there had to be a benign place that was in the immaterial realm, but technically not part of "heaven."

"However; it is possible that originally this concept of "Limbo" referred to not a section of the *immaterial* realm outside of heaven, but rather to be caught *in between* the material and immaterial realms—this *neither* world, AKA: the "X" or the "no realm."

"The word "limbo" can refer to either a dance which was popular in the 1950's and/or the 1960's; or it refers to something else. That something else can be seen from the root of the word.

"Limbo is derived from:

"Latin (in) *limbō* (on) the edge, ablative case of *limbus* edge, border..."[O9]

"Limbo originally likely meant this border or edge between the two realms; rather than a separate place within a realm; here a separate "place" as or like the immaterial realm; in terms of including no space, time, or matter; but not actually within either realm. This can also be seen with the common usage of "stuck in limbo;" which means stuck between two things, and unable to move forward or backward.

"The common concept (doxa) of "hell" requires a bit of analysis. It is generally considered as a possible destination for the immaterial portion of life forms—those with the "breath of life." However the origin of the word "hell" seems a bit sketchy.

"According to Etymonline.com, "hell" is from:

"Old English hel, helle, "nether world, abode of the dead, infernal regions, place of torment for the wicked after death," from Proto-Germanic *haljō "the underworld" (source also of Old Frisian helle, Old Saxon hellia, Dutch hel, Old Norse hel, German Hölle, Gothic halja "hell").

> "Literally "concealed place" (compare Old Norse hellir "cave, cavern"), from PIE root *kel-(1) "to cover, conceal, save." The English word may be in part from Old Norse mythological Hel (from Proto-Germanic *halija "one who covers up or hides something"), in Norse mythology the name of Loki's daughter who rules over the evil dead in Niflheim, the lowest of all worlds (nifl "mist"). A pagan concept and word fitted to a Christian idiom.
>
> "In Middle English, also of the Limbus Patrum, place where the Patriarchs, Prophets, etc. awaited the Atonement."[O10"3.5] [Excerpt from *"OSTIUM AB INFERNO"* Copyright © 2019 Quadrakoff Publications Group, LLC All rights reserved. Reprinted by permission]

Thus distinctions must be made with respect to all *immaterial* entities, regarding precisely "where" said entities are "currently located." It is unclear how the physical limitations of the material realm affect these entities; but they likely are all affected to some extent by these limitations. However; these limitations may be much different depending upon the *nature* of the immaterial entity, as well as the immaterial entity's "location."

Some "common" *paranormal* entities; such as demons, and Satan himself; (or perhaps better termed Satan itself); likely fall into this, "nether or neither world," category.

As Revelation tells us, these were *aggĕlŏs*, or messengers; who were banished from the immaterial realm, because they were engaging in *planaō*, or; "to (prop. *cause to*) *roam* (from safety, truth, or virtue.") This is described in Revelation as: "*called the Devil, and Satan, which deceiveth the whole world.*"

These are entities which were designed for existence in one realm, (immaterial); but now must exist "elsewhere." Other immaterial entities such as God Himself, true, (*non-planaō*), angels, and most "ghosts;" likely can, but do not have to, (shall); leave the immaterial realm. (Here "ghost" is utilized to mean a disembodied soul.)

The word "haunt" is a *verb*, and is likely derived from:

> "v. go often to, visit frequently. Probably about 1200 *hanten* practice habitually; later *haunten* (before 1250), and in the sense of visit frequently (probably before 1300); borrowed from Old French *hanter* to frequent, resort to, be familiar with (originally, of a spirit coming back to the house he had lived in)."[3.6]

It is thus clear that the verb *haunt*, requires a *destination* of some sort, along with *repetition*. This destination refers to either a person place or thing, and does *not* refer to the active *entity* itself; i.e.; the *haunter*. It is that *visitation* to a *destination*; usually in the *material* realm; and clearly not that entity that *haunts*, the actions to which this term *haunt*, as a *verb*, refers.

The word "poltergeist" is a *noun*, and is defined as:

> "n. noisy spirit or ghost. 1848, borrowing of German *Poltergeist* (*poltern* make noise, rattle, rumble + *geist* GHOST)."[3.7]

Assuming that a parascientist is seeking a *ghost*; it seems that a *poltergeist* is what would be considered "low hanging fruit." And that the purpose of the detection instrumentation, essentially is to simply lower the threshold for categorization as a poltergeist. This instrumentation allows what would otherwise be a somewhat quiet ghost, to be detected as though a poltergeist. It is this "noise" as evidence, which the parascientist seeks.

However; it cannot be overemphasized that not all paranormal entities are *ghosts*. Simply because one is seeking a ghost, or believes that it is a ghost that is being detected; this in no way necessarily means that the detected paranormal entity is in fact a ghost. Malevolent paranormal entities, are both cunning and wise;

as well as quite experienced. The previous alternate *translations* of nâchash as: "learn by experience, x indeed, diligently observe;" are quite pertinent here.

But actual "ghosts" are of, and from God, and are designed to reside in a material vessel. In fact; until perhaps the 1960's, God Himself had "The Holy Ghost" nomenclature utilized to describe one part of the Trinity. There is no reason to *always* necessarily believe that ghosts are to be considered as in any way harmful—if it is in fact a ghost. These are by design part of what it is that God breathes "into the nostrils" at the time of birth, resulting in a physically living being.

However; there are other entities in the *immaterial* realm, or in the "X" realm, in addition to ghosts; and some are of God, (true angels, in the immaterial); and some are not, (those in the "X" realm).

So when a *paranormal* investigation takes place and is "successful;" it is important to determine precisely what entity it is that is being detected, and/or is communicating. Malevolent entities are deceitful, clever; and as stated, have had a long time in which to practice. *Assuming* that the investigator can somehow *limit* what is being contacted to only that which is desired; can be both imprudent, and downright foolish.

Likewise; grouping all paranormal entities into one category such as "a spirit," is also extremely unwise. Each of these types of entities is likely different; has different capabilities; and has different desires.

It seems that it would be fair to state that if the *effects* of these paranormal entities on the *material* realm are that which is desired; then the detection *method* would likely have to be *material* in nature. Likewise, if the detection of *immaterial entity itself*; or its actions from *within* the *immaterial* realm; unrelated to or independent from any effect on the material realm is that which is desired; then any such detection device would likely have to be *immaterial* in nature.

One might fairly ask: "How is it possible to create a detection device that is immaterial in nature?" There is one answer and one comment: The *answer* is that this is not currently known. The *comment* is that one already exists, and thus although the creation of immaterial instruments would be desirable for highly *objective* detection or reception; these are not necessarily necessary for *any* detection or reception.

The vertical portion of the intersection or right angle of the human being; (e.g.; mind or soul); by design, *is* a paranormal detection device. Simply because this device is only partially acknowledged and underdeveloped, does not mean that it does not exist.

Neither can it be said that simply by not *attributing* any given perception to direct *immaterial* perception, does not mean it is not happening. False premises lead to false conclusions. And all along it was believed to just be a "hunch." The very next chapter is concerned with direct and indirect reception of *malevolent* immaterial phenomena.

As an aside; the word *parapsychology* generally refers to things such as psychic abilities, clairvoyance and the like. This concept of a "mind or soul" which is "next to or beside" a "mind or soul," in this usage, seems to represent an underestimation of the true capabilities of the human mind as per design.

Reliable reference sources regarding the specifics of these various immaterial entities; whether malevolent or benign; cannot be found. Sprites, undines, incubuses, succubuses, may or may not exist. What most can agree upon; is that there are malevolent entities although not actually in, but *near* this immaterial realm. Whether there are numerous types or only one type, unfortunately cannot be under discussion here; as most available information seems at this time at best unreliable. This is largely because *aggĕlŏs* refers to *function*, and not *structure*.

Irrespective of their origins, *malevolent* immaterial entities, by definition, are not at this time in any way of God. Whether they once were, or were not; or could, or could not be of God, is a matter of opinion. But by definition, they *currently* are not of God. [This stated here, because a fair argument exists that the *story*, (not parable), of "Legion;" may represent "saved" demons—and that this is, or was, the very purpose for the inclusion of the *story*.]

"Limbo" originally likely meant this "border," or "edge" *between* the two *realms*; rather than a separate place *within* some realm. This can also be seen with the common usage of "stuck in limbo;" which means stuck between two things, and unable to move forward or backward.

The mention of "Limbus Patrum" in the above definition of hell—literally the "Limbo of the Father;" supports this concept of a edge or border; but here the Limbus Patrum is contained *within* the border of this "X" realm; and not contained in either, (material or immaterial), realm.

According to this belief; as good as Abraham, Isaac, Jacob, and Moses may have been, each and all sinned. Therefore, none were eligible to be connected to, or in the presence of, God at the time of their physical deaths. The belief is that they remained in this Limbus Patrum awaiting salvation.

This previously referenced separate place contained *within* the "X" realm; which is often erroneously referred to as "limbo," is the Greek:

> "2859 kŏlpŏs; appar. a prim. word; the *bosom*; by anal. a *bay*: - bosom, creek."[3,8]

This *kŏlpŏs*, or *Limbus Patrum*, or *Abraham's Bosom*; is the "area" for those who physically died before the availability of salvation.

As appears in the definition, it seems that the original meaning of hell had much more to do with a "concealed place" or "to cover, conceal;" rather than a fiery place where some souls go for eternal punishment. It must be asked as to precisely from what it is that this "place" known as hell provides concealment?

There are two types of "death," or "disconnection:"

There is *physical* death: where the soul et al. is no longer "contained" in the body.

There is also so called *spiritual* death: where after physical death, this soul cannot be (re)connected to or in the presence of God because of sin.

Cemeteries, mausoleums and the like; are generally not considered as in any way synonymous with hell. Thus, the above definition of hell as "abode of the dead" cannot in any way refer to the abode of the *material* portion of man. Ergo, it is only the *immaterial* portion of man which can abide in hell.

But the immaterial portion of man is immortal; else how could there be eternal punishment in hell; or eternal happiness in heaven? It can and should be fairly asked, how it could be that this *immaterial* portion of man itself could actually die?

The answer is that it does not. This "death" is *spiritual* death, and refers to the *immaterial* portion not being connected to or in the presence of *God* after *physical* death.

There are entities which are designed to be in the immaterial realm, and *are* in the immaterial realm.

There are also entities that were designed to be in the immaterial realm, and at one point in time were; but no longer are. These are contained in this "X" realm or hell, in one, (the bad), side of this *kŏlpŏs*.

This is important with respect to physically alive man. This is because with the condition of physical life, and the presence of the aforementioned "norm," or right angle intersection of the "vertical" immaterial portion of man; with the "horizontal" material portion of man; these "concealed" entities are technically *paranormal*—next to this particular "norm."

Man is designed to be in both realms when physically alive. This is also important, because that *immaterial* portion of man by which man is physically alive, *could* technically become *paranormal*, once it leaves the physical body. It can be returned to, and remain in, the immaterial realm; or it could be "stuck" between the two realms.

Whenever an entity designed for one realm is *not* in the realm for which it is designed, there is necessarily an imbalance present. There is also an argument to be made with respect to chronology. Meaning; that there may be a choice as to whether a disembodied soul; i.e.; ghost; remains in this no realm, or moves on to the immaterial realm.

If for whatever reason(s), an "eligible" disembodied soul chooses to not "go toward the light," this decision is respected. However; as is *always* the case, there is a *balance* to this decision. The same being that the decision to not re-enter the immaterial realm, does not necessarily mean a return to the "normal" or right angle state; [see: "*REINCARNATION—A REASONABLE INQUIRY*"]; and thus they could remain in this "neither realm" state.

Neither is this decision necessarily a permanent decision. This is likely why some who are experts in certain paranormal areas, refer to assisting these entities in: "moving on." If there were no means by which this decision could be changed, this "moving on" option" simply could not exist.

This is also the likely state of those who are unsaved; except it is not necessarily voluntary. The *immaterial* portion or soul cannot be in the presence of, (contaminate), God because of sin. The use of the nomenclature "Limbus Patrum," exhibits a bit of hubris; in that this particular name, ("*Limbus Patrum*"), only seems to apply to those men of great earthly works. But the correct Biblical word, the aforementioned *kŏlpŏs*; describes this (good) section of the "X area," and thus the *concept* of this "area" nevertheless remains correct.

All who have sinned and remain "unjustified," simply cannot be in the presence of God. Whether it is a matter of willful sin of the "Patrum;" or the willful sin of someone of no *earthly* notoriety whatsoever; the rules are the same for all. If "original sin" exists; which is a highly dubious proposition; then the rules would also apply to involuntary original sin.

However God does have other options:

In the case of those who *voluntarily* decide to not re-enter the immaterial realm, He has provided those aforementioned who can assist them in the process.

In the case of those who *cannot* voluntarily enter His presence, it is at least arguable that He may provide other options. He is after all the God of second chances.

This "X," area," or original meaning of Limbo, or "hell," or "neither world;" can be a crowded "place." It must be remembered that it was *aggĕlŏs*, or *messengers*; engaging in *planaō*, or "(prop. cause to) roam (from safety, truth, or virtue);" i.e.; "*which deceiveth the whole world*"), who were originally "sent there."

As previously stated, *aggĕlŏs* is a *functional* definition; and not a *structural* one. What we do know is that these were *immaterial* entities; who by design, were supposed to be messengers. It is not known what their precise *structure*; whatever that may mean in the immaterial realm; was or is. Neither is it known what *variety* of these "structures," may be "present" in either the *immaterial* realm; or "present" in this "neither realm."

What is also known is that those sent there, had been engaging in *planaō*, or in English: *"deceiveth the whole world."*

It is true that some of these entities may have been sent to the "abyss," as "Legion" originally feared.

It is possible that some may have repented, and returned to active status; (*aggĕlŏs* minus the *planaō*); as possible one "read" of the story of Legion would suggest.

It is true that the power of these entities, and thus the "power difference" or Δ, changed dramatically at Calvary.

But there is no reason to believe that the *objectives*, or the *amount* of activity has been reduced in any meaningful way— except perhaps for those, who unlike Legion, may have been sent to the "abyss."

Alleged Fantasy Foundations Volume I

Chapter 4

Unseen Cause—Seen Effect

Granted this is not news, but: "Anything that can go wrong will go wrong," is often identified as: "Murphy's Law." But what does this actually mean? The two key words in this "law" are: "*can*" and "*will.*" Rephrased it would read: "It is a certainty that anything that is *capable* of going wrong, or has the *ability* to go wrong; *shall* or *will*, (not *may*, or *might*), go wrong."

Or alternately: "If it is *possible* for something to go wrong, then it *will* go wrong."

Thus, this represents a situation expressed as a "law;" where in fact any undesired event with the *probability* of greater than zero, (P>0), of occurring; necessarily results in the probability of 100%, (P=1 or certainty); that this same event will in fact occur.

To the extent that this "law" has validity; something which most would agree that at least *empirically*, it in fact does; even if not as an actual "law;" then in a general sense, this is so for one of two possible reasons: It is simply the result of "random" chance, based upon *material* or *natural* law; or it is not.

Perhaps this "law," is merely a result of complexity and probability. Meaning for instance, that a process with ten distinct steps; all of which must succeed in order for the entire process to be considered a "success;" will ultimately fail, because success requires *all* ten steps must succeed for success; and only *one* of the ten has to fail for the process to be considered as a failure.

For example: In order to "win," one must toss a coin with ten "tails" in a row. Each toss has the approximate probability of 0.5, (50%), that "tails" will be the result; but to succeed, you must get "tails" in all ten tosses. Thus the likelihood or probability this particular "success" is very low, as landing on "heads" *can* happen, and likely *will* happen, in at least one out of ten tosses. Ergo, whatever *can* go wrong, (here "heads"); likely *will* go wrong. However, whomever it was that bet against you experienced no such thing; if their success is defined as your failure. Thus, here an *even*, and long term *likely* statistical distribution of 5 "heads" and 5 "tails" constitutes "going wrong."

This phenomena described, (although not explained), by Murphy's Law; does not usually refer to "games of chance" type events. If it were a certainty, as Murphy's Law seems to indicate, that whatever *can* go wrong, (losing), in games of chance, *will* most certainly go wrong; then no sane person would ever engage in any games of chance.

This of course is entirely different than in the long term, the odds always being with the house—as they necessarily must be. It is not long term, but short-term gains for which gamblers seem to gamble, as they know that no business can exist with less than 50% or ($P=.5$) odds in their favor; and yet still somehow manage to pay for the overhead required to provide these services.

Honest games of chance rely on what appear to be *random* events. Random in this sense meaning: that the outcome of any particular event is unpredictable prior to the occurrence of the event; generally because of the incalculable number of variables. It is true that overall long-term results are somewhat predictable, and the greater number of events used as a statistical universe, the more accurate the long-term prediction. But this predictive ability does little to predict the outcome of a single event, or a small number of events.

So then, how can it possibly be that there could be any truth in Murphy's Law, that, (paraphrased): "Any undesired event with the probability of occurrence of a value which is only *greater* than zero, (P>0); will necessarily result in the probability of 100%, (P=1 or certainty), that this same event will in fact occur?"

This makes no sense with respect to random events; and in fact is more than *oxymoronic*, but is in fact *contradictory* in nature. To state that if P is *less* than one, (P<1); or better stated, as long as P is greater than zero, (P>0), however small the probability is; then it will necessarily be the case that P=1 with respect to normal random events, would be absurd. Nevertheless; even if some degree of hyperbole is factored into "Murphy's law," the probability of anything will go wrong is still a very good bet.

There are corollaries to Murphy's law regarding which way a piece of bread will land on the floor with respect to the buttered side; as well as the relationship of how long a "job" will take with respect to the time allocated for it. (Actually, the *time* "corollary," seems to more likely be "Parkinson's law," circa 1955.[4.1])

Nevertheless, it is generally attributed to Murphy. There is *not* however, any known corollary to Murphy's Law, or any other law attributed to anyone else which states: "Anything that can go *right*; will go *right*."

Thus, to the extent that Murphy's Law is valid, it is to this very same extent that these "predictable" outcomes of "going wrongness;" are not, and cannot, merely be the result of random chance.

The origin of the term "Murphy's Law," is a matter of substantial contention. What does not seem to be a matter of contention however, is that the name Murphy generally refers to, or is derived from, "sea warrior." Perhaps this is a mere "coincidence;" and then again perhaps not.

Genesis 2:1 (KJV) tells us:

"Thus the heavens and the earth were finished,

*and all the host of them."*⁴·²

    Here, the extremely important answer to the age-old question of "Why are we here?;" is both hidden and quite obvious in this passage. All one need to do to discover this answer, is simply to look up one word.
    This is clearly delineated by God's use of the term translated here as: "host," or "hosts" in other "versions."
    The actual original Hebrew word translated as "host" or "hosts" here is:

> "6635 tsâbâ' or tsᵉba'ah from 6633; a *mass* of persons (or fig. things), espec. reg. organized for war (an *army*); by impl. a *campaign,* lit. or fig. (spec. *hardship, worship):* - appointed time, (+) army, (+) battle, company, host, service, soldiers, waiting upon, war (-fare). 6633 tsâbâ' a prim. root; to *mass* (an army or servants): - assemble, fight, perform, muster, wait upon, war."⁴·³

    This "tsâbâ' or tsᵉba'ah...; a *mass* of persons (or fig. things), espec. reg. organized for war (an *army*);" provides irrefutable evidence of the purpose for mans creation and existence on the earth—at least according to God.
    Prior to this, and long before the *formation* of Adam in Genesis 2:7; God had told *created* man of this very purpose. Here in Genesis 1:28, these *created* hosts were told by God precisely what it was that they were to do:
    Genesis 1:28 (KJV) tells us:

> *"And God blessed them, and God said unto them,*
> *Be fruitful, and multiply, and replenish the earth,*
> *and subdue it:*
>
> *and have dominion over the fish of the sea,*

Unseen Cause—Seen Effect

*and over the fowl of the air, and over
every living thing that moveth upon the earth."*[4.4]

The original Hebrew word translated as "subdue," here with regard to the earth is:

> "3533 kâbash; a prim. root; to *tread* down; hence neg. to *disregard*; pos. to *conquer, subjugate, violate*: - bring into bondage, force, keep under, subdue, bring into subjection."[4.5]

It is from this Hebrew word *kâbash*, that the English word *kibosh*, as in: "Put the kibosh on it," is derived.

One is free to *not* believe that the Bible represents the Word of God. But if one *believes* that the Bible does in fact reasonably represent the Word of God; one is then *not* free to provide any other explanation of the purpose of man, which would be *inconsistent* with that which God Himself literally stated regarding the same.

This answer of course obviously being, that we are here to fight a war.

The *English* words *hostile* and *hostage*, are derived from this root of the *English* translation of tsâbâ' as: "host" or "hosts."

Thus, it appears that the relationship between events as described by Murphy's Law; which makes little sense based upon random events, and is or are arguably statistically impossible; will reliably occur when one or more of those individuals that God designated as "mass of persons organized for war," are endeavoring to obtain certain types of specific positive results.

When said desired result is "upright," or consistent with a "right angle;" then anything that has the capability of going wrong, will go wrong; and the name of this "Law" is likely derived from "sea warrior."

There would be no reason for God to establish a mass of persons to conduct war *by design*, if there was or were no enemy or enemies. Thus this "going wrong," is not always *random*; but rather is often contributed to, or as a direct result of, the reaction(s) of the enemy that opposes man in this war.

Why was a name that arguably means "sea warrior" used to describe this law, instead of merely warrior? Perhaps this is merely coincidental; or perhaps this goes back to the "without form and void" period, when the earth was covered with "water."

Approaching this from a bit of a different angle, it has often been said that: "If you factor the devil in, then you factor the devil out."

Perhaps a better way of stating this would be: "To the extent that one factors an enemy in, to that same extent that enemy is factored out." This is simply a way of minimizing or eliminating the "anything that can go wrong" part, in order to minimize or preclude the anything that "will go wrong" part. This is because; to the extent that the enemy cannot be a factor in the *process*; he has necessarily been factored out of the *outcome*.

This is also not a revelation, but the devil is not God. After Calvary, the enemy has very few actual capabilities of substance—except if and when granted special dispensations by God. His main areas of activity are now largely *indirect* in nature; and thus he generally relies upon the mental *perversion* of the "hosts," in order to engage in "direct" action on his behalf.

Said attempted host *perversions*, will be *direct* "personalized" *thoughts*, *ideas*, and *suggestions*, to the *subject* host; or *indirect* when done through a *surrogate* host, or *surrogate* hosts.

Direct physical or *supernatural* capabilities, and *direct* "TIS" attacks are entirely different; e.g.; *directly* murdering a host; as opposed to "suggesting" *directly* to a host, to murder another host. In fact this very suggestion, likewise suggests that the enemy *cannot* do it himself; as opposed to *will not* do it himself.

Ephesians 6:12-17 (NAS) tells us:

> *"For our struggle is not against flesh and blood,*
> *but against the rulers, against the powers,*
> *against the world forces of this darkness,*
> *against the spiritual forces of wickedness*
> *in the heavenly places.*

Unseen Cause—Seen Effect

*Therefore, take up the full armor of God,
so that you will be able to resist in the evil day,
and having done everything, to stand firm.
Stand firm therefore,*

*HAVING GIRDED YOUR LOINS WITH TRUTH,
and HAVING PUT ON THE BREASTPLATE
OF RIGHTEOUSNESS,
and having shod YOUR FEET WITH THE
PREPARATION OF THE GOSPEL OF PEACE;*

*in addition to all, taking up the shield of faith
with which you will be able to extinguish
all the flaming arrows of the evil one.
And take THE HELMET OF SALVATION,
and the sword of the Spirit,
which is the word of God."*[4.6]

"Many would say: "This is all very nice. In a perfect world this might actually have some value, but I live in the real world. There are real flesh and blood enemies who must be defeated, if one is going to survive. None of this will help with the mortgage, the bill collectors, the problems at work, etc."

"Although this type of response may be perfectly understandable, it clearly indicates a lack of knowledge regarding the *actual* war in which we "hosts" are engaged. All of these stated problems are quite actual; however, they represent neither a battle nor the war. These are either the results of battles already lost, or interventions in our lives by person or persons who have lost their own personal battle(s) with the enemy. The former is of our own making; the latter is the most common means by which the enemy attacks us via surrogates."[4.7]

The actual Greek word translated as "arrows" is:

"956 bĕlŏs; from 906; a *missile*, i.e. *spear* or *arrow*: - dart."⁴·⁸

"906 ballō; a prim. verb; to *throw* (in various applications, more or less violent or intense): - arise, cast (out), x dung, lay, lie, pour, put (up), send, strike, throw (down), thrust."⁴·⁹

The actual Greek word translated as "fiery" is:

"4448 purŏō; from 4442; to *kindle* i.e. (pass.) to *be ignited*, *glow* (lit.), *be refined* (by impl.), or (fig.) to *be inflamed* (with anger, grief, lust): - burn, fiery, be on fire, try."⁴·¹⁰

The above Ephesians 6:12-17, is a bit more revealing if the *chronology* of the recommendations is changed a bit:

"For our struggle is not against flesh and blood, but against the rulers, against the powers, against the world forces of this darkness, against the spiritual *forces* of wickedness in the heavenly *places*."

"Therefore, take up "the sword of the Spirit, which is the word of God;" but before you do this, properly prepare yourself for battle by firmly and resolutely deciding to:

"Take up the full armor of God, so that you will be able to resist in the evil day, and having done everything, to stand firm.

"Stand firm therefore, HAVING GIRDED YOUR LOINS WITH TRUTH, and HAVING PUT ON THE BREASTPLATE OF RIGHTEOUSNESS, and having shod YOUR FEET WITH THE PREPARATION OF THE GOSPEL OF PEACE; in addition to all, taking up the shield of faith with which you will be able to extinguish all the flaming arrows of the evil *one*. And take THE HELMET OF SALVATION."

Unseen Cause—Seen Effect

This is introduced here, but will be examined in greater detail in a later chapter.

The devil must at all times "respect" our free will. He cannot act against our free will without "license"—else he would do so. Why would he bother utilizing thoughts, ideas, and suggestions, (his main armaments of today); in order to convince us to do things that we are otherwise not doing, (or to not do things we *are* doing); if he could merely force his will upon us? He wouldn't. He would just make us do it. He does not operate this way because he simply and solely cannot.

Despite this, many hosts get into serious trouble, because often times their *true* will is either wrong or unclear to them; and the enemy will facilitate this process—most particularly exploiting this Δ, or difference between what our true will is; and what we *believe* our true will is at any given time.

For example: People will often get into financial difficulties because they will confuse what they *need*, with what they *want*. If it becomes one's will to run up the credit card with things one cannot afford because of this confusion; then the enemy will help them do it, and also help them with the justifications.

Or, perhaps one will have a much higher opinion of their value, simply because of the nature of the work they perform. They believe that they are entitled to certain vacations and other expenditures; with all obviously being luxury expenditures— something with which their salary level clearly disagrees.

Nevertheless; it becomes their will to spend according to their inflated assessment of their value, and there is plenty of help from the enemy. Or, they genuinely believe that they need a large home; when what they really want is to impress people. The enemy will assist in finding that home; but when the mortgage becomes in arrears, any suggestions made by him as to what to do about it will likely make matters worse.

Why is any or all of this important to know? The answer to this requires a bit of an explanation:

At the "time" of "In the Beginning," as per Genesis 1:1; which of course occurred *before* Genesis 1:2; things were substantially different than they are today. The reason that the Bible begins with: "In the Beginning," is to differentiate all of what follows as occurring at different and much later times. It was "In the Beginning" that the Heavens and the earth were created, with this "Beginning" *ending* at the end of Verse 1.

Any "title" describing the Book of Genesis that overwhelmingly emphasizes the word "creation;" e.g.: "The Book of Creation," is extremely misleading. This is because even a cursory read will reveal that the majority of Book of Genesis; and even the majority of the first chapter; has do with some, but very little, actual *creation*.

The first action the Bible tells us "God did;" was to create the heavens and the earth.

Genesis 1:1 (KJV) tells us:

"In the beginning God created the heaven and the earth."[4.11]

As can easily be seen, the first action the Bible tells us what "God did;" was to create the heaven(s) and the earth; is not literally true.

With regard to creating the material realm, His *first* action was actually to make the *decision* to create the heavens and the earth. His *second* action was to put this decision into action, with the result being the creation of the heavens and the earth. And the characterization of "first" and "second," likely only applies with respect to the *material* realm—unless one assumes that God had never done anything else prior to the creation of the material realm.

What occurred in Genesis 1:1 *chronologically*, did not happen anywhere near the time of Genesis 1:2; but rather a long and unspecified time before Genesis 1:2.

Genesis 1:2 (KJV) tells us:

"And the earth was without form, and void; and darkness was upon the face of the deep.

And the Spirit of God moved upon the face of the waters."[4.12]

Genesis 1:1 represents a *completed* process, that actually begins with God's decision to create the material realm; and ends with the appearance of the word "earth" in Genesis 1:1; with Genesis 1:2 onward, again occurring an unspecified, but long period of time *after* this, (Beginning), process was completed. The "end" of this "Beginning," was the creation of the heaven(s) and the earth.

Thus Genesis 1:2 onward is *not* a description or recapitulation of any of the *process* described in Genesis 1:1; as Genesis 1:1 tells us that this process was completed. In fact, the Interlinear Bible translates Genesis 1:2 as: "*she* (the earth) *became*" without form and void.[4.13]

The Bible does not begin with "Once Upon a Time"—despite the secular world believing that it probably should. "Once Upon a Time" generally describes the time before which whatever follows—happened. The Bible is not a fairy tale occurring in some unspecified time or place. It tells us what God did in the beginning; with the events in Genesis 1:2 onward occurring at times other than, (and then necessarily *after*), this "Beginning" ended.

There can only be one *beginning* of any particular phenomenon—any common usage of "first introduced" notwithstanding. When were the heavens and the earth created? They were created in the "Beginning."

What was this the actual beginning of? It was the beginning of time, space, and matter; and this "Beginning" ended with the creation of time, space, and matter, including the earth.

Genesis 1:2 presupposes, and in fact *requires* the prior existence of the *completed* earth, in order for those conditions and events described to exist and occur, respectively.

What about the so called "Big Bang" theory? Is it not a fact, that at some point in time, all of the matter in the universe was located in one particular place; and then this matter "exploded," and was scattered across the universe? And is it in fact not so that most or all of it is still moving? After all, it was a *very* big bang, and the "universe" is rather large; and according to some, arguably still expanding.

Perhaps this is so, but the mechanism of the *scattering* of all known matter across the universe, does nothing to explain its *source*.

Neither does this "Big Bang" theory in any way preclude intelligent design—substantial ongoing secular attempts at said preclusion notwithstanding. This theory does nothing to explain the *source* or *cause* of this manifestation of matter; but rather is often, if not exclusively, proffered as an attempt to *preclude* intelligent design—as though somehow an explanation of the mechanism of the *distribution* of matter across the universe explains its *source*. The fact is; that the *motion* of an object or a mass when a force or forces are imparted upon it, has nothing whatsoever to do with the *origins* or *source* of said object or mass; i.e.; *matter*.

"I want you to push that thing over there."
"What thing over there?"
"You know that thing over there."
"No I don't know that thing over there, as there isn't anything over there."
"Oh. Sorry, I forgot. I didn't put it there yet.

Silly? Of course, but this illustrates a point. One cannot impart a force on "a thing," until after it exists. Thus, to explain the *motion* of all of the matter in the universe as a substitute for its *source* or *origin* is nonsensical; and generally the more one makes this attempt, the sillier it becomes. First the matter would have to exist, and then it could go *boom*; no matter how short the time interval involved.

The most reasonable explanation for this "Big Bang," is that it represents what a hypothetical observer would have witnessed at the time of Genesis 1:1. When God created the heavens and the earth, this "Big Bang" was part of the method employed to obtain the, (His), desired result. Science tells us part of what happened; i.e.; the distribution *process*, and the result; but science tells us nothing about Who it was that made it happen. The Bible tells us *Who* it was that made it happen; but describes only the result; telling us nothing about the details of the actual *process*.

How did God create the heavens and the earth? As stated, the Bible doesn't tell us. But if he created, (*bârâ'*), the heavens and the earth in the same way and manner that He created other things that He created; (at least those creations described in the Bible); then He likely "spoke" it into existence, in some way or manner. This is stated with the understanding that "spoke" can have meanings beyond the common understandings.

We are not actually told that that "God said, let us make the heavens and the earth;" but this represents the most reasonable explanation. It could not read: "Then God said....," because there then would have had to have been a *now* prior to the *then*; which represents a rather difficult undertaking prior to the existence of time.

> "Most believe that early Genesis is fraught with "creating." However an unbiased analysis of the actual events based upon actual terminology, strongly suggests otherwise.
>
> "Words mean things, and perfect synonyms are difficult, especially in translations. Actually, it is not certain that there are any perfect synonyms within the same language. "In the Beginning," it was the heavens and the earth that was created. In fact, the terms "created" or "creature," do not appear again in Genesis 1, until verses 21 and 20 respectively."[S1]

"This would also be consistent with the concept of beliefs regarding an Atlantis or Lemuria—at least in terms of *some* life forms being present at that time; (between Genesis 1:1 and 1:2; or between the words "*earth*" and "*without form and void*").

Those who scoff at this idea, generally claim ignorance of plate tectonics on the part of the proponents, as the reason for this belief.

However; although "evidence" regarding the timeframe is sketchy at best; *if* some type of continent such as Atlantis existed, it existed at a time between one million and one hundred million years ago— chronologically likely long before the *created* hosts and the kibosh (English) directive; and even longer before the *formation* of A & E. The "plates" can move substantially in one hundred million years. If something similar to Atlantis existed, it is generally believed to ultimately have become covered in water. If this sounds familiar to those who understand early Genesis, there are very good reasons for this familiarity.

So to those who might still maintain that the *creation* of the earth was a process extending far beyond the end of Genesis 1:1, the question becomes this: Why would God create an earth that required replenishment, and subduing, (putting the *kibosh* on), and dominating, and then refer to created man as hosts; which is a fighting force; rather than creating an earth perfectly suitable for man? The simple answer is that He *wouldn't*; and He *didn't*.

Most agree that the Bible is primarily a book about redemption. But few understand what this actually means; i.e.; the actual *extent* of this redemption. It is generally, (erroneously), understood; that it is solely the redemption of man with which the Bible is concerned. However; the Bible is not merely concerned with the redemption of man, but also the redemption of the very earth itself—perhaps even the entire material ream.

> "This can easily be seen in the latter half of Genesis 1:2 and onward, where God begins to take redemptive action. Then the created hosts are advised to take redemptive action. Then likely through the formation of Adam, the seeds are sown for the Son to engage in the (immaterial) redemptive process; along with, and with assistance of the hosts."[4.14]

At some point after the earth was completed, something very bad happened. The result was that the earth was without form and void; covered in "water," and all was dark. Is or was this actually the story of Atlantis, which is sometimes called Lemuria? Who knows? Perhaps this is so. If all of the earth's land mass was one at that time, unlike the separated "jigsaw puzzle" appearance the continents have today, it is possible. Nevertheless, God had to intervene and push back the darkness. But he did not *completely* obliterate the darkness, but rather ultimately caused an *"evening."*[4.15]

It is likely at this point in time, (between Genesis 1:1 and Genesis 1:2), when all of that *"deceiveth the whole world,"* business previously described in Revelation 12:7-9 actually took place. It is the erroneous belief that Revelation is concerned only with the future that obscures this knowledge. The truth is that John actually witnessed past, present, and future events all "at once;" as he was permitted to see into a realm with no time.

Thus we are currently in a "transitional and partial" state between what conditions were during and after Genesis 1:2; and what conditions will ultimately become at the end. These latter and later conditions being the same as they were for an unspecified time *after* Genesis 1:1, before that which is described in Genesis 1:2.

In the interim: we are, and continue to be at war. Whether man realizes this or not, will affect the success of many *battles*, but will not affect the *existence* of this state of war.

Chapter 5

The Battlefield

Soul is often described as: "will intellect and emotions." But as will be seen, although soul actually represents much more than this; it is nevertheless these three areas that represent the battlefield on which this war is most directly waged; most particularly in the *judgment* portion of the intellect.

God gave us *free will*, and will not manipulate us. He will give us the answer sheet, but we must provide the answers ourselves. He will give us all the wisdom necessary to make a good decision; but *we* must ultimately decide. Of what possible use would it be for God to empower man, and charge man with a task; and then do it all Himself? This is of course an entirely different matter than *why* it is that God created man; and then sought recourse from His created hosts.

The enemy of course, will do anything and everything he is capable of, in order to manipulate our will in furtherance of his desires—including incessantly trying to convince us that "revelation" is in fact "manipulation."

The following is a graphic representation of the forces involved:

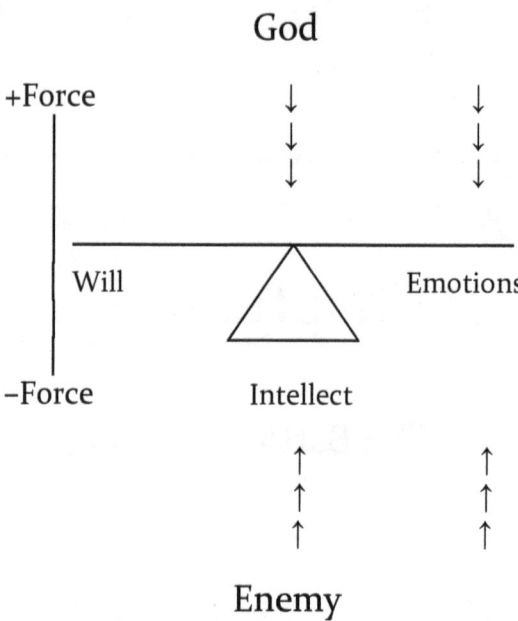

These are the three interrelated portions of the human soul, (will, intellect, and emotions); which represent the battlefield where "the hosts," or perhaps better phrased: "we hosts," are constantly engaged in battle. God and the enemy are each extremely interested in the actions or resultant forces we humans decide upon, or choose to create.

These "forces" created by humans, (and other life forms with the breath of life); are the very same types of forces collectively, (F_A x F_R), with the product referred to as F_T. Here F_A represents the *action* undertaken; F_R ,represents the *reason* for the action undertaken; and F_T represents the actual force. This is in accordance with Newton's F = MA; but here there is an *immaterial* component, (F_R), included in the calculation. [A detailed explanation of this appears in "*MeekRaker Beginnings... Second Intermission*"]

That which is normally considered as *emotions*, often represent the *driving* the "forces" behind our actions. Joy, happiness, contentment, love, peace; these are some of the emotional states/stimuli sent by God from above. He likely does not have to "throw" them. He probably just opens the "windows of heaven" and they simple pour down—like manna. These "push downward" on the emotional portion of our souls, stimulating or triggering similar emotions within us.

What God is looking for; is as a result of these emotions pushing downward on the emotional side of the soul, (or the right side of this "seesaw"); that our "will" will result in positive, (upright), forces being created. These types of desired resultant forces are represented by the "will" on the left side of this "seesaw" or line moving in the *upward* or *positive* direction.

What hangs in the balance is our intellect. Our intellect is also subject to "forces" from both above and below. Here in the *intellect*; rather than God providing *emotional* stimuli; He is providing us, often simultaneously, with truth, revelation, and guidance, (that which *is*).

Although the enemy is also capable of "emotional manipulation" to some significant extent; the main weapon of the enemy, is the provision of lies, (that which *is not*), in the form of the aforementioned *thoughts*, *ideas* and *suggestions*. These lies are provided not only to cause us to factor in false information; but also in an attempt to increase the emotional driving forces he, (lower case), is exerting upon us. He, (the enemy), lies to us about many things; often including how much more important or greater we are than someone else.

We then use our intellect to make the decision as to what to believe or not believe; and make a decision to act or not act. A quality decision not only requires good *judgment*, but also requires quality *information*.

> "Practically everyone knows that there are Ten Commandments; written in stone; which we all have been commanded by God to obey. After all, they are called *commandments* and not suggestions. Thus it

would seem clear that God has commanded us to obey them.

"There are two problems with what here is universally considered to be *epistémē*, or certain knowledge; but what is in fact actually *doxa*, (less than certain), knowledge:

"The first; is that in fact there are not and have never been Ten Commandments—at least contained in Exodus 20; but rather there actually are, and have always been only nine. For example: In one attempt to get to ten, it seems that at some point some person or persons, for some reason or reasons; chose to "bust out" the coveting of a wife from the rest of the coveting, thus providing an additional "Commandment."

"This likely happened prior to the "modern" era, as it is "wife," and not "spouse" or "partner," that appears in the translations. Others break up the first Commandment into two; with the "no other Gods" and "graven images" parts receiving their very own separate Commandment status and number. Except for perhaps some numerological or Kaballistic concerns, this appears to be a relatively minor point and not particularly germane to the subject at hand—at least at this time.

"The second problem; is the purported *requirement to obey* these commandments, which of course is another matter. This is not to say that God does not want us to obey these Commandments; that He would not prefer that we obey these Commandments; or that there are not serious repercussions each and every time these commandments are not obeyed. Rather, the issue is whether or not He actually told or "commanded" us to obey them.

"There is a difference between stating what the laws are; and asking or requiring one to obey them. The former is *informative* in nature; with the latter being at least arguably *manipulative* in nature.

The Battlefield

"The Commandments appear for the first time in Exodus 20.

"In Exodus 20:6 (KJV) we are told:

> *"And shewing mercy unto thousands of them that love me, and keep my commandments."*[SH1]

"One might reasonably first ask what need there would be for mercy to be shown, (shewn), to those who both love God and also keep, (i.e.; obey), (His) commandments? *Mercy* generally refers to not getting what one deserves, and is usually in the *negative*; as opposed to *grace*, which is getting what one does not deserve, and is usually in the *positive*. So then it must be asked that if "keep" means *obey*; then why would there be any need for any type of mercy to be shown to those "thousands" who are obeying said Commandments? The answer of course: is that by definition there would be no need whatsoever for any such mercy.

The actual Hebrew word translated here as "mercy" is:

"2617 checed; from 2616; *kindness*;..."[SH2]

"2616 châcad; a prim. root; prop. perh. to *bow* (the neck only [comp. 2603] courtesy to an equal), i.e. to *be kind*;..."[SH3]

"2603 chânan; a prim. root [comp. 2583]; prop. to *bend* or stoop in kindness to an inferior; to *favor bestow*..."[SH4]

"A distinction is made here with regard to the roots of the Hebrew word originally contained in Exodus 20:6 which is translated as "mercy," (*checed* from *châcad*). It seems that the actual definition of *checed*, is concerned with showing or providing kindness or courtesy to an *equal*; versus the similar word *chânan*, which is concerned with providing kindness to an *inferior*.

"Thus it remains unclear as to why the translators chose "mercy" as the English translation of *checed*; as this seems antithetical to its actual meaning. More precisely; generally in order to show "mercy," one must necessarily be in a position of superiority with regard to the potential recipient of any "mercy"—at least with respect to that particular situation. Here with the use of *checed* a position of equality is required.

"In Exodus 20:6 it is God who is or was communicating, so it seems likely He would have known which Hebrew word to choose to convey His precise meaning. And He chose the word *checed*, and not *chânan*. Thus what is clear, in at least in this regard; is that from this standpoint; (with regard to showing kindness in *this* context); He (God) considers or considered us to be equals—else He would have used *chânan*—which He did not.

"This may be disturbing to those who attempt to reconcile that which is originally and by design brought into existence in the "image and likeness of God, (H. Sapiens);" with their view of the actual, (real time), current state of the same. This is the inevitable result of conflating the original pure and perfect product, with the current polluted result.

"But it seems there is an additional requirement in order to obtain said kindness from the standpoint of being shown kindness as an equal and not as an inferior; as it must be remembered we were told: *"And shewing mercy unto thousands of them that love me, and keep my commandments."*

"This can be rephrased as a reversed "if then" declaration: "

> "I, (God), will show you kindness from the standpoint of an equal, if you both love me, *and* also keep my commandments."

"The actual Hebrew word translated as "love" is:

> "157 'âhab or 'âhêb; a prim. root: to *have affection* for (sexually or otherwise): - (be-) love (-ed, -ly, -r), like, friend."[SH5]

"Thus the translation as "love," seems reasonably straightforward.

"The answer to this "obedience" matter, lies in the actual word which is translated here as "keep."

"The actual Hebrew word translated here in Exodus 20:6 as "keep" is:

> "8104: shâmar; A prim. root; prop. to *hedge* about (as with thorns), i.e. *guard*; gen. to *protect, attend to,* etc.: - beware, be circumspect, take heed (to self), keep (-er, self), mark, look narrowly, observe, preserve, regard, reserve, save (self), sure, (that lay) wait (for), watch (-man)."[SH6]

"As can easily be seen, the Hebrew word *shâmar*, does not in any way mean *obey*; but rather to *protect* as though surrounded by a "hedge" of "thorns."

"In fact, as can bee seen; according to Strong, *shâmar* is not translated as "obey" anywhere in the entire Bible. (See the above provided list of words after the ": -," as these represent all of the Biblical translations of *shâmar*.)

"Perhaps God made an error, in that He actually meant to use a word that meant "obey," but was just preoccupied with the ongoing follies of His Chosen Ones at the time.

"Or perhaps in fact He actually did use a word that meant "obey," and somehow an error just cropped up in the translation.

"Or perhaps Moses actually spoke Hebrew with a serious "Brooklynese" accent, and thus just misunderstood God.

"The first of course is impossible. The second is possible; but the problem with this, as well as the latter "perhaps;" is the pesky matter of the "written in stone" part for the content. If God was that serious about not being misunderstood about the rules, He would likely be just as clear about what to do with them.

"Much later, Jesus addressed this same issue of love and "obeying" the Commandments.

"In John 14:15 (KJV) Jesus tells us:

"*If ye love me, keep my commandments.*"[SH7]

"So it seems clear that Jesus is merely saying: "If you love me, then show it by obeying My commandments."
"Or is He?
"Here the actual Greek word translated as "keep" is:

"5083 tērĕō; from tĕrŏs (a *watch*; perh. akin to 2334); to *guard* (from *loss* or *injury*, prop. by keeping *the eye* upon..."[SH8]

"Thus the Greek word *tērĕō*, is very synonymic to the aforementioned Hebrew word *shâmar*. And neither *shâmar* nor *tērĕō* is even remotely concerned with obeying the Commandments, or showing *obedience* to anything else.

"It is clear that Jesus was not asking for, or even addressing *obedience* either.

"In Exodus 20:6, when the Father addressed the matter, He said to shâmar His Commandments—meaning that we should *protect* His Commandments as though to surround them with a hedge of thorns.

"Then when Jesus addressed this same matter in John 14:15, the best Greek word for whatever Aramaic word it was that Jesus actually spoke, was the Greek word *tērĕō*—meaning to watch or guard from loss or injury by "keeping the eye upon," His (My) Commandments. In neither case was any type of actual *obedience* to the Commandments sought.

"So when God referenced keeping his commandments: *"And shewing mercy unto thousands of them that love me, and keep my commandments*; what is under discussion with regard to His Commandments, is to *protect* (them) as though surrounded by a hedge of thorns. And much later Jesus essentially stated the very same thing."[5.1] [Excerpt from: *"Wisdom Essentials"* Reprinted by permission]

Thus these "Commandments," as well as much more information contained in the Bible and elsewhere; can provide that which is needed to make quality decisions. But it is up to man to decide what it is he will and will not be doing in furtherance of that with which man was charged in Genesis 1:28: *"And God blessed them, and God said unto them, Be fruitful, and multiply, and replenish the earth, and subdue it* (put the kibosh on it)*: and have dominion over the fish of the sea, and over the fowl of the air, and over every living thing that moveth upon the earth."*

For clarity, a distinction should again be made between *feelings* vs. *emotions*. Generally they are considered as synonymous. For the purposes of this discussion, they are in no way the same thing; with emotions being as previously described above.

Feelings however, are to be considered as *sensory* input, similar to the types of data provided by the normal five senses. Feelings can, and often will result in an emotional response or change; nevertheless, there is a time delay, no matter how infinitesimal, between the reception of a *feeling* and any change in one's *emotional* state. Emotions as a specific driving force will be addressed in greater detail shortly.

Thus when one's "feelings are hurt," this would literally describe some *sensory overload* to the point of pain; rather than negative *emotions* produced *because* of, or as the *result* of, some type of *information* obtained from sensory input—at least for the purposes of these discussions.

"It just doesn't feel right," is a phrase we have all said or heard; as opposed to: "Will you give me two tens for a five?"

With respect to the *latter*, "it just doesn't feel right" would never be proffered as the rationale for refusing this exchange. The issue is not that it doesn't feel right, but rather that we *know* it is not right. This conclusion is strictly based upon our *knowledge* that at least in this universe, ten plus ten does not equal five.

With respect to the *former*, said *feelings* are the imparting of information to us beyond the normal five physical senses; or perhaps better termed: "extrasensory" information, which is designed and provided for us to "perceive" at that time. Sometimes, this can be God communicating "real time" with His hosts as situations emerge. ("Emerge" being the root for emergency.) Sometimes, it is simply a matter of the recollection of information previously stored in the area or repository referred to as "memory," or sometimes stored in or as the "conscience."

Psalms 37:4 (KJV) tells us:

> "Delight thyself also in the LORD;
> and He shall give thee the
> desires of thine heart."[5.2]

This can be read two ways: This could refer to God *giving* us the actual desires of our heart; or it could refer to God *fulfilling* the desires of our heart.

The actual Hebrew word translated as "give" is:

> "5414 nâthan; a prim. root; to *give,* used with greatest latitude of application (*put, make,* etc.)"[5.3]

Likely, Psalms 37:4 refers to both *desire* and *fulfillment*. God will *place* desires in our hearts; desires which are consistent with and in furtherance of His divine purpose for us. Then, to the extent that we permit Him, He will also be involved in the *fulfillment* of these desires. [The subject of the *talantŏn*, will be addressed in a later chapter.]

In Matthew 7:13-14 (KJV), Jesus is speaking and He tells us:

> *"Enter ye in at the strait gate:*
> *for wide is the gate, and broad is the way,*
> *that leadeth to destruction,*
> *and many there be which go in thereat:*
>
> *Because strait is the gate,*
> *and narrow is the way,*
> *which leadeth unto life,*
> *and few there be that find it."*[5.4]

This *above* passage is usually considered to be related to *salvation*, as the case with Luke 13:24 below; but there is a difference. This is because in the following from Luke below; it is quite clear that here in Luke *below*; unlike in Matthew *above*; that here in *Luke*, Jesus is in fact speaking about *salvation*.

Luke 13:23-25 (KJV) tells us:

> *"Then said one unto him, Lord,*
> *are there few that be saved?*

> *And he said unto them,*
> *Strive to enter in at the strait gate:*
> *for many, I say unto you,*
> *will seek to enter in,*
> *and shall not be able.*
>
> *When once the master of the*
> *house is risen up,*
> *and hath shut to the door,*
> *and ye begin to stand without,*
> *and to knock at the door, saying,*
> *Lord, Lord, open unto us;*
> *and he shall answer and say unto you,*
> *I know you not whence ye are:*"[5.5]

Since both Luke and Matthew mention either a *gate* or a *door*, and to *enter*; and references are made to how *strait* or *narrow* these *gate(s)* or *door(s)* may be; it is easy to see how these can be conflated into one *set* of knowledge; i.e.; *recapitulations* of the very same message from Jesus.

But if it is so stipulated that it is at least *possible*, that these two sets of passages may *not* refer to the same subject, (salvation); then prudence requires an examination of the similarities and differences, in order to reasonably determine what additional information may be hidden, (*occultus notitia*), therein.

In Matthew, there appear the translations of: *gate, gate, way, gate,* and *way*; and in this very order.

In Luke, there appear the translations of: *gate, door,* and *door*; and in this very order.

The original Greek word in *Matthew* that is translated three times as "*gate*;" and the original word in *Luke* that is translated once as "*gate*," is:

> "4439 pulē, appar. a prim. word; a *gate*, i.e. the leaf or wing of a folding *entrance* (lit. or fig.): - gate."[5.6]

The Battlefield

With regard to the translation twice as "way" in *Matthew*, the original Greek word is:

"3598 hŏdŏs; appar. a prim. word; a *road*; by impl. a *progress* (the route, act or distance); fig. a *mode* or *means*: - journey, (high-) way."[5.7]

With regard to the translation twice as "door" in *Luke*, the original Greek word is:

"2374 thura; appar. a prim. word [comp. "door"]; a *portal* or entrance (the opening or the closure, lit. or fig.) – door, gate."[5.8]

The original Greek word translated as "enter" both in passages is:

"1525 ĕisĕrchŏmal; from 1519 and 2064; to *enter* (lit or fig.); - x arise, come (in, into), enter in (-to), go in (through)."[5.9]

However, the original Greek word in Luke for "strive" is:

"75 agōnizŏmai; from 73; to *struggle*, lit. (to *compete* for a prize), fig. (to *contend* with an adversary), or gen. (to *endeavor* to accomplish something): - fight, labor fervently, strive."[5.10]

It must be noted that the common understanding of the meaning of the word *agony* or *agonize*, is generally considered to be *pain*. But although here the original *agōnizŏmai* makes reference to *struggle*, there is no reference to *pain*.

Also, as will be addressed in detail in a later chapter; in the *New Testament*, the actual Greek word often translated as "sin" is:

"264 hamartanō; perh. from *1* (as a neg. particle) and the base of *3313*; prop. to *miss* the mark (and *so not share* in the prize), i.e. (fig.) to *err*, esp. (mor.) to *sin*."[5.11]

Clearly *agōnizŏmai* requires some type of *adversary* or *counterpoise* with which to "struggle;" and thus the existence of some type of *adversary* or *enemy* is presupposed. In fact, the above definition of *agōnizŏmai* includes: "(to *compete* for a prize), fig. (to *contend* with an adversary)."

And *hamartanō* is when the "mark" is missed, and one does not "share in the prize;" and this is translated as *sin*. Clearly here there is also some type of *adversary* or *enemy* presupposed, with regard to not "hitting" this "mark."

Thus there is some commonality with *agōnizŏmai* and *hamartanō*; with *agōnizŏmai* or the "struggle" being the "event;" and *hamartanō*, (translated as "*sin*"), being the "result" when this "struggle" is lost. And as the result of this loss, one then does not share in the "prize," that is referenced in both definitions.

Here in Luke, it seems Jesus is clearly referring to salvation, as that was the subject of the inquiry to him: "*are there just a few who are being saved?*"

The original Greek word translated as "saved" in Luke 13:23 is:

> "4982 sōzō; from a prim. sōs (contr. for obsol. saŏs "*safe*"); to *save*, i.e. *deliver* or *protect* (lit. or fig.): - heal, preserve, save (self), do well, be (make) whole."[5.12]

But it must be asked if there is *agōnizŏmai* or a "struggle," required in order to *obtain* salvation; and it must also be asked if salvation reasonably represents a "prize," for prevailing in this struggle—assuming a struggle is required to begin with.

If so, then clearly this represents salvation as the direct result of *works*—a doctrine clearly known to be literally Biblically *false*, except perhaps by the *pseudo-statists*. [See: "*Statists Saving One*," Chapter 10: "*The Pseudo Statists*"]

Biblically speaking; "OSAS," (Once Saved Always Saved), is proven beyond a reasonable doubt. Thus this *struggle* does not refer to the actual *obtaining* of salvation.

The *context* of Jesus' answer to the question, is critical in understanding the meaning of these passages. The *question* had to do with *how many* are being saved: "*are there few that be saved?*"

The Battlefield

Thus it seems reasonable that Jesus' *answer* would, at least in some way or manner, be concerned with this very same matter.

The actual Greek word translated as "strait" here in Luke 13:24: "*Strive to enter in at the strait gate,*" is:

> "4728 stěnŏs; prob, from the base of *2476*; *narrow* (from obstacles *standing* close about): - strait."[5.13]

Here there is a sense of "narrow" or a "strait," as it relates to the presence of *obstacles*. The common definition of *strait* is consistent with this, (see *stenosis*). But if "strait" is *spoken* instead of *read*, many would hear the word "straight," as in non-crooked, or the shortest distance between two points.

The *struggle*, has to do with whether few or many will obtain salvation by entering the "*strait*" door, or via Jesus himself; as He is the only "door" to salvation. In fact, today there are many more obstacles causing a narrowing or an even "straiter strait." Much of this additional narrowing, is the direct result of governmental actions—most particularly the courts.

However, by placing "price tags" on salvation, (proffering non-OSAS); many *religions* are also quite guilty of "obstacle placement." The aforementioned Chapter 10, "*The Pseudo-Statists,*" in "*Statists Saving One;*" provides much illumination about the reasons for this. [It must be noted here, that the use of *hamartanō* and *agōnizŏmai* can be a much more broad usage than just relating to *salvation*. It is just that here in Luke, the subject under discussion is *sōzō*, or *salvation*.]

Jesus then goes on to describe that this choice is "time sensitive," and what conditions will be like when it is "too late."

As previously referenced, many nevertheless erroneously believe that this word "*strait*" is "straight," again indicating the shortest distance between two points; said two points being the location of the host, and the location of the door or gate. However, this is rarely if ever the case. This is because of the *stěnŏs*, as the result of *obstacles*, which must either be traveled around or destroyed—if one is to get to that gate.

It is interesting to analyze Luke 13:23-25, and also to place it in terms of contextual chronology:

Firstly, Jesus is being asked if there *presently* are just a few who are saved: "*are there few that be saved;*" but Jesus does not in any way *directly* answer that question. He is being asked if there are, (present tense); just a few "*be saved;*" but He makes no comment whatsoever about those who are currently saved; neither numerically nor in any other manner.

Instead, He first comments about the "*strait gate,*" or *stĕnŏs pulē*; and striving or *agōnizŏmai*, to "*enter*" or *ĕisĕrchŏmal*; and this is all translated as in the *present* tense.

Jesus then speaks about those in the future, as he comments about those who "*will* (future tense) *seek to enter and not be able.*"

As of this writing, (today), everyone is "*able*" to be saved. It is not a matter of *ability*, but rather of *will*. At the present, all who *seek* salvation, are *able* to receive salvation; and must only be *willing* to receive the same. But in actuality, in these passages in Luke, Jesus is speaking about a time when there will be those who will seek salvation, (are *willing*), but will not be *able*.

Jesus advises us about the "time sensitivity" by stating: "*When once the master of the house is risen up, and hath shut to the door.*" "When" will this" "*door*" be "*shut?*" In an unspecified time in the *future*; after the event of: "*When once the master*" rises up has happened.

At this *future* time after the "door" has been "shut," many will *then* want to be admitted; but this master who shut the door will state: "*I know you not whence ye are.*"

As of today, the "*master of the house*" has not yet shut the door; indicating that at the time Jesus made these statements, the door was yet, (actually would be), open—albeit with substantial *stĕnŏs* to get to this door, because of obstacles.

These passages clearly are about *salvation*; and why one should not procrastinate, as no one knows when the door will actually be shut. (Heck; any religious doctrines notwithstanding, salvation is *completely* free—quasi-tautology noted.)

One might say that this "shutting" refers to "end times;" and there likely will be a seven year window in which to make up one's mind before the door is shut. Of course then by this same thinking, one would then have missed the rapture, (assuming of course that there will be a rapture), that surely no one knows the timing of, (except the Father); and would then have to make this decision during the tribulation and associated judgments.

Thus this "shut door," likely refers to the very end, when God simply runs out of either *grace* or *mercy*—depending upon one's perspective. Man's free will is at all times respected, but there comes, (*will* come), a point in time; where there is, (*will* be), simply no more *time* to decide.

But back to Matthew. Again it must be asked if these passages in Matthew 7:13-14 are also concerned with salvation, or if not; specifically what subject is it with which these words are concerned?

Here again is Matthew 7:13-14 (KJV), where Jesus is speaking; and He tells us:

"Enter ye in at the strait gate:
for wide is the gate, and broad is the way,
that leadeth to destruction,
and many there be which go in thereat:

Because strait is the gate,
and narrow is the way,
which leadeth unto life,
and few there be that find it."

At this juncture, in order to provide proper *context* for Matthew 7:13-14 above, it would be appropriate, arguably *necessary*, to consider the verses being those which *directly precede* the above Matthew: 7:13-14, namely Matthew 7:7-12.

It then becomes obvious that the topic Jesus is speaking about here in these *preceding* verses, Matthew 7:7-12, is *not* salvation, or even related in any way to salvation; but rather aspects of our *behavior*.

Matthew 7:7-12 (KJV) tells us:

> *"Ask, and it shall be given you;*
> *seek, and ye shall find; knock,*
> *and it shall be opened unto you:*
>
> *For every one that asketh receiveth;*
> *and he that seeketh findeth;*
> *and to him that knocketh it shall be opened.*
>
> *Or what man is there of you,*
> *whom if his son ask bread,*
> *will he give him a stone?*
>
> *Or if he ask a fish,*
> *will he give him a serpent?*
>
> *If ye then, being evil,*
> *know how to give good gifts unto your children,*
> *how much more shall your Father*
> *which is in heaven give good*
> *things to them that ask him?*
>
> *Therefore all things whatsoever*
> *ye would that men should do to you,*
> *do ye even so to them:*
> *for this is the law and the prophets."*[5:14]

Firstly, it must be determined precisely what the meaning of the two "its" are in verse 7: *"Ask, and it shall be given you,"* and: *"knock, and it shall be opened unto you;"* as well as the meaning of the singular "it" in verse 8: *"to him that knocketh it shall be opened;"*—respectively.

The *second* "it" in verse 7, (*"knock, and it shall be opened unto you"*); sounds suspiciously like the *salvation* door in Luke, which will be closed at some point in time.

The Battlefield

But the *first* "it" in verse 7, (*Ask, and it shall be given you*); reads a bit differently. Here the "it" is something that will be given, and given in accord with whatever it was that was "asked for."

Thus it seems that in order for this particular, (the *first*), "*it*" to be limited to something related to a *door*; it seems one would to have had to have *asked* for a door—assuming the "*knock*," "*knocketh*," and "*opened*;" refer to actions taken upon a door.

The "*it*" in verse 8, ("*and to him that knocketh it shall be opened*"); is provided as part of an *explanation* of some type of principle, as we are told: "*For* (because) *every one that asketh receiveth; and he that seeketh findeth;*" appearing just before: "*and to him that knocketh it shall be opened.*"

There are then some examples cited, and we are then provided with the conclusion beginning with a "*therefore;*" or what an attorney might phrase as: "For all of the foregoing reasons: "*Therefore*; ("For all of the foregoing reasons"); *all things whatsoever ye would that men should do to you, do ye even so to them.*"

This is Jesus explaining what is contemporarily referred to as the law of *karma*, or law *compensation*—no matter how angry some "Christian folk" may become by associating *Jesus'* teachings, with a word of *Buddhist* origin.

In the material realm we have Newton's Laws of Motion, most particularly: equal and opposite reactions, and the previously referenced: F = MA. And as we were just told, there are similar laws regarding the nexus between the two realms. [See "*Wisdom Essentials – Inevitable Balance*"]

Jesus concluded these passages with: "*for this is the law and the prophets.*"

The actual Greek word translated as "law" is:

> "3551 nŏmŏs; from a prim. nĕmō (to *parcel* out, espec. *food* or *grazing* to animals); *law* (through the idea of prescriptive *usage*), gen. (*regulation*), spec. (of Moses [include. the volume]; also of the Gospel), or fig. (a *principle*): - law."[5.15]

The actual Greek word translated as "prophets" is:

> "4396 prŏphētēs; from a comp. of 4253 and 5346; a *foreteller* (*"prophet"*); by anal. an *inspired speaker*; by extens. a *poet*: - prophet."[5.16]

After this discussion of *karma*, which obviously has nothing to do with obtaining *salvation*; Jesus then immediately begins those previously cited familiar passages in Matthew 7:13-14 (KJV):

> *"Enter ye in at the strait gate:*
> *for wide is the gate, and broad is the way,*
> *that leadeth to destruction,*
> *and many there be which go in thereat:*
>
> *Because strait is the gate,*
> *and narrow is the way,*
> *which leadeth unto life,*
> *and few there be that find it."*

The actual Greek word translated as "strait" in *"strait gate"* here in Matthew 7:13 is also *stěnŏs*.[5.17]

The actual Greek word translated as "gate," is as was seen previously in Luke:

> 4439 pulē; appar. a prim. word; a *gate*, i.e. the leaf or wing of a folding *entrance* (lit. or fig.): - gate."[5.18]

The actual Greek word translated as "wide," is:

> "4116 platus; from *4111*; spread out *"flat"* (*"plot"*), i.e. *broad*: - wide."[5.19]

The actual Greek word translated as "broad," is:

The Battlefield

"2149 ĕuruchōrŏs; from ĕurus (*wide*) and 5561; *spacious*: - broad."[5.20]

The actual Greek word translated as "strait," (strait gate) in Matthew 17:14 is again *stĕnŏs*.[5.21]

However; the actual Greek word translated as "*narrow*," ("*narrow way*"), here in Matthew 7:14 is not *stĕnŏs*, but rather:

"2346 thlibō; akin to the base of 5147; to crowd (lit. or fig.): - afflict, narrow, throng, suffer tribulation, trouble."[5.22]

"5147 tribŏs; from tribō (to "rub"; akin to tĕirō, truō, and the base of 5131, 5134); a rut or worn track: - path"[5.23]

The actual Greek word translated as "destruction" is:

"684 apōlĕia; from a presumed der. of 622; *ruin* or *loss* (phys., spiritual or eternal): - damnable (- nation), destruction, die, perdition, x perish, pernicious ways, waste."[5.24]

"622 apŏllumi; from 575 and the base of 3639 to *destroy* fully (reflex. to *perish*, or *lose*), lit. or fig.: - destroy, die, lose, mar, perish."[5.25]

And according to Strong, the *only* time the word *apōlĕia* is ever translated as *destruction* in the entire four gospels, (MMLJ), is in this (Matthew 7:13 KJV), passage.[5.26]

In another unrelated chapter of Matthew, (Matthew 26:8 KJV); when the woman pours the expensive ointment or perfume on Jesus' head, the disciples asked: "'*To what purpose is this waste?*'"[5.27] The actual word translated in this passage as "waste," is also *apōlĕia*.[5.28]

Likewise in Mark, (Mark 14:4, KJV); when recounting the same story, the word *apōlĕia* is also translated as "waste" in: "'Why was this waste of the ointment made?'"[5.29]

Thus, it seems that "ruin, loss or waste" represents a better definition or translation of the original Greek word *apōlĕia*, than would be *destruction* or *death*.

However, one problem with this position; is that there is at least an implied comparison between the translation of *apōlĕia* as destruction or death; because at least at this juncture, it seems that Jesus indicated that those who find this gate will find life, instead of destruction or death. So because of this, it might also seem fair to consider that the appropriate translation of *apōlĕia* would be as destruction or death; based upon this implied comparison of *apōlĕia* with life; with life being the *opposite* of destruction or death.

But then again, it must be asked that if *destruction* or *death* instead of *waste*, was the correct meaning for what Jesus spoke in Aramaic; then why was it that the above *"apŏllumi*: "... to *destroy* fully (reflex. to *perish*, or *lose*), lit. or fig.: - destroy, die, lose, mar, perish," *not* chosen as the most synonymic Greek word? Instead it was *apōlĕia*; albeit derived from *apŏllumi*; which was chosen as most synonymic.

Thus a fair translation of Matthew 17:13, based upon the original Greek would be:

"Enter (ĕisĕrchŏmal) *ye in at the narrow*
from obstacles standing close about (stĕnŏs) *gate;*
for spread out flat, (platus), *is the gate;*
and (wide) *and spacious,* (ĕuruchōrŏs), *is the road,*
(hŏdŏs), *that leadeth to waste ruin or loss,* (apōlĕia);
and many there be which go in thereat"

There is no mention of *salvation*, either here in Matthew 17:13, or in the verses preceding it. So if it can be stipulated that Jesus was *not* speaking about *salvation* here Matthew 17:13, it must be asked precisely what it was of which He was in fact speaking?

There is the one gate or door that is *narrow* because of obstacles. At this juncture, it is unclear as to precisely what it is that is on the other side of this gate or door.

And there is another gate or door; that is a "spread out flat" gate; as well as a "wide and spacious" road leading to this "other gate, or door."

But we are told precisely what is that is on the other side of this "spread out flat," gate or door:" *apōlĕia*, or *"waste ruin or loss."*

And we are also told, that with respect to this "spread out flat," or *apōlĕia*, gate or door: "*many there be which go in thereat.*"

At this juncture; it can reasonably be inferred that if: "*many there be which go in thereat*;" with respect to this "spread out flat," gate or door; then likely "few" "*there be which go in thereat,*" with regard to the narrow door.

And the *conclusion* is contained in the very next verse, here again is Matthew 7:14 (KJV):

> *"Because strait is the gate,*
> *and narrow is the way,*
> *which leadeth unto life,*
> *and few there be that find it."*

Here in verse 14, we are told precisely *why* that which is contained in verse 13 is true, as verse 14 begins with the word: "*because.*"

As previously cited, here the original Greek word for "strait" in describing this "*gate*" is again *stĕnŏs*; and the original Greek word translated as "gate" is again *pulē* But the original Greek word for "narrow" here in describing the "*way*" is not *stĕnŏs*, but rather *thlibō*.

And we are now also told what is on the other side of this particular, (verse 14) gate, as *this* gate: "*leadeth unto life, and few there be that find it.*"

Life means *connection*; and death means *disconnection*. There is *physical life* when the soul is connected to the physical body; and *physical death* when disconnected. There is *spiritual life* when the soul is connected to its original source, (God); and *spiritual death* when disconnected.

But it seems that *all* to whom these words were spoken, were already *physically* alive. So a fair question for Jesus' audience, would be: "Why should I mess with that *stěnŏs*, and all of those obstacles close by; when I am already 'alive?'" Or perhaps: "But I am already on the other side of this gate."

An alternative explanation would be that this *"life,"* actually means: "spiritual life;" and so then it actually is *salvation*; just like in Luke; that Jesus was speaking of in these passages. But if this is stipulated as so, then Jesus would have simply "jumped into" this discussion completely out of context.

Thus we are faced with the choice of believing that Jesus was telling physically alive persons to enter this gate in order to attain physical life. Or; that Jesus was referring to "spiritual life," just as in Luke; with *no additional knowledge* available to us in these passages. Or that Jesus was referring to "X."

The actual Greek word translated here as "life" is:

> "2222 zōē; from *2198*; *life* (lit. or fig.): - life (-time). Comp. 5590."[5.30]

> "2198 zaō; a prim. verb; to *live* (lit. or fig.): - life (-time), (a-) live (-ly), quick."[5.31]

> "5590 psuchē; from *5594*; *breath*, i.e. (by impl.) *spirit*, abstr. or concr. (the *animal* sentient principle only; thus distinguished on the one hand from *4151*, which is the rational and immortal *soul*; and on the other from *2222* which is mere *vitality*, even of plants: these terms thus exactly correspond respectively to the Heb. 5315, 7307 and 2416): - heart (+- ily), life, mind, soul, + us, + you."[5.32]

> "4151 pněuma; from *4154*; a *current* of air, i.e. *breath* (*blast*) or a *breeze*; by anal. or fig. a *spirit*, i.e. (human) the rational *soul*, (by impl.) *vital principle*, mental

disposition, etc., or (superhuman) an *angel*, *doemon*, or (divine) *God*, Christ's *spirit*, the Holy *Spirit*: - ghost, life, spirit(ual, ually), mind. Comp. 5590."[5.33]

Here in the definition of *psuchē*, as per Strong's suggested comparison of *zōē* with 5590 *psuchē*, distinctions are easily seen. Here it is "mere *vitality*, even of plants," which represents the definition of *zōē*, as appears in the definition of *psuchē*.

Neither the immaterial part of man as *psuchē*: "the *animal* sentient principle only;" nor the immaterial part of man as *pněuma*: "the rational and immortal *soul*;" is not only *not* included in the definition of *zōē*, but each are specifically *excluded* from being in the definition of *zōē*—at least according to Strong.

Since it is only *pněuma*, and some may even argue *psuchē*, that is or are in need of *salvation*; and since it appears that each is *precluded* from being included in the definition of *zōē*; it could not have been *salvation*, (the *means* for attaining *spiritual* life), about which Jesus was speaking at that time, as per what is contained here in Matthew.

And since all that could hear Jesus at that time were already physically alive, it could not have been *physical* life about which, ("*leadeth to*") Jesus was speaking at that time.

By Hobson's choice, it must then have been "X"—whatever this "X" may in fact represent.

Precisely what is life *in-toto*, or "lifetime" (*zōē*)?"

A cynic may define "lifetime," as: "That period of time between when a human being exits one type of container; and is ultimately placed in another type of container." And another definition; would be that period of time from the *first* breath to the *last*.

But how does God define lifetime; and why did Jesus speak an Aramaic word best represented *not* by *psuchē* or *pněuma*, but rather by *zōē*?

This will be revisited many times throughout this work. *Actuality* is what exists; i.e.; that which *is*. *Reality* is that which is *believed* to exist; and "normally," said belief is based upon the accurate *perception* of subsets of an actuality. No actuality can ever be perceived 100% by any physically alive human being.

Man's perception of, and subsequent reality of, "lifetime;" is "man centered." Man understands he exists, and views the entire universe from this perspective. Man is "in the middle" of the *material* realm, and thus perceives his "lifetime" from this *material* perspective.

And because of the *time* component in the material realm, there is a chronological "event based" perception of "lifetime." In fact, with regard to what man *perceives*, and the subsequent *realities* created as a result of perception; the *solipsists* have a valid point if "truly known" is the "test."

But it must be remembered why God first *created* man. Some of this evidence has already been presented.

We know that God called created man "host" or "the hosts," (depending upon "the version"), because He said so; as again, in Genesis 2:1 (KJV), we are told: *"Thus the heavens and the earth were finished, and all the host of them."*

And again we know the actual Hebrew word translated as "host" or "hosts" is: "6635 tsâbâ' or ts^{e}ba'ah from 6633; a *mass* of persons (or fig. things), espec. reg. organized for war (an *army*); by impl. a *campaign*, lit. or fig. (spec. *hardship, worship*): - appointed time, (+) army, (+) battle, company, host, service, soldiers, waiting upon, war (-fare). 6633 tsâbâ' a prim. root; to *mass* (an army or servants): - assemble, fight, perform, muster, wait upon, war."

And we know what it is that God instructed man to do, as again Genesis 1:28 (KJV) tells us: *"And God blessed them, and God said unto them, Be fruitful, and multiply, and replenish the earth, and subdue it: and have dominion over the fish of the sea, and over the fowl of the air, and over every living thing that moveth upon the earth."*

And we also know what this *"subdue"* means: "3533 kâbash; a prim. root; to *tread* down; hence neg. to *disregard*; pos. to *conquer, subjugate, violate*: - bring into bondage, force, keep under, subdue, bring into subjection."

And we know it is from this Hebrew word *kâbash*, that the English word *kibosh*, as in: "Put the kibosh on it!" is derived.

Thus God first *created*, (and much later *formed*) man; with a specific *function* or *functions* in mind. For reasons beyond the

The Battlefield

scope of this work; (See the Monograph: "*Its Not Just a Theory*"); man has a limited amount of time to be physically alive on the earth. It seems reasonable, that God would prefer as much "progress" as possible in that limited amount of time.

It seem inarguable that God views "lifetime" from a much different perspective than does any physically alive man. God resides in the *immaterial*, ("art in heaven"), realm; and not within the *material* realm. In the absence of a time component in the immaterial realm, (however inconceivable this may be to man); surely God is much more capable of viewing man's "lifetime" *in-toto*, than is man.

Thus from Gods viewpoint, "lifetime" likely represents an opportunity for each human being to engage in the activities for which man in the *general* sense was created. It must be remembered what it is that is on the other side of the *wide* gate; with the same being *apōlĕia*; *or waste ruin or loss*. Waste, ruin, or loss of what? From God's perspective; man's *zōē* or "lifetime;" *as a host* of course.

And it gets a bit more complicated when the "obstacles" or *thlibō* on the narrow *way*, (as opposed to the narrow or *stĕnŏs gate* or *door*), are considered. Precisely *what* is or are these *thlibō*, *why* are they there, and *who* placed them there?

To understand the answers to these questions, "kind of flipping it around," might shed some light.

If someone decides to climb a mountain, this can be a very difficult and dangerous undertaking. The *purpose* of this endeavor generally, is of course to get to the top. In this sense, the *summit* represents the "strait" or *stĕnŏs gate* or *door*, just as the *destination* is described in Matthew. And that which the climber must negotiate and overcome to get there, represent the "obstacles" which make the *path* to the summit *narrow*.

These *physical* "obstacles" *on the path* to the summit, care not one whit about the mountain climber. Many of these were present for perhaps billions of years before the creation of man. And anyone who contemplates climbing this or any other mountain, generally can obtain precise information about each and every obstacle; as well as the experiences of others who made this same attempt. These obstacles are *objective*, and will not by themselves significantly change—no matter *who* it is that is attempting to overcome them.

But with regard to the obstacles *on the path* referenced in Matthew, the same cannot be said. If it is so stipulated that it is God's desire for a particular host to *get to* a particular door; these obstacles *on the path* are *specifically* designed, and *specifically* placed there; in order to try and stop that *specific* host, from getting to that, or perhaps better phrased, *their* specific door.

As previously stated, the actual Greek word translated as *narrow*, (in: "*narrow is the way*"), here in Matthew 7:14 is *not* stĕnŏs, but rather *thlibō*. What is the difference, and why does this matter? It must be remembered that it is the *way* or: "3598 hŏdŏs; appar. a prim. word; a *road*; by impl. a *progress* (the route, act or distance); fig. a *mode* or *means*: - journey, (high-) way;" and not a *door* that is described here as *thlibō* in Matthew.

Here again are the respective definitions:

> "4728 stĕnŏs; prob, from the base of *2476*; *narrow* (from obstacles *standing* close about): - strait."

> "2346 thlibō; akin to the base of *5147*; to crowd (lit. or fig.): - afflict, narrow, throng, suffer tribulation, trouble."

> "5147 tribŏs; from tribō (to "rub"; akin to tĕirō, truō, and the base of 5131, 5134); a rut or worn track: - path"

The reasons for the use of *thlibō* and not *stĕnŏs* to describe this *hŏdŏs*; or actually a "road," or by implication an "act;" become obvious here:

Stĕnŏs appears to be an *adjective*, and refers to the actual *result* of being "narrow," such as from literal physical obstacles.

But *thlibō* appears to be a *verb*, describing the *process* of *crowding*; i.e.; "to crowd." There is the sense of *pressure* from too much of something in one area, as per the "akin" of *tribŏs*, or: "to rub."

And the other translations of *thlibō* as: "afflict," "suffer tribulation," and "trouble;" strongly suggest that the *results* can also be much more *mental* or *emotional*; unlike *stĕnŏs*, describing *narrow*, as in a *physical* strait.

In the previous Luke 13:23-25 passages that relate to salvation, it is the *gate* or *pulē* that is *narrow* or *stĕnŏs*; because it is surrounded by the aforementioned obstacles—including obstacles deliberately placed there by some religions, even at that time. Here Jesus is speaking with respect to a question about *salvation*, or *sōzō*. When Jesus speaks of the *"many,"* who: *"will seek to enter in, and shall not be able,"* (future tense), it would be easy to assume that this is because of their inability to successfully struggle against the *stĕnŏs*.

But the more compelling argument is that this in fact is not so. This is because of that which immediately follows: *"When once the master of the house is risen up, and hath shut to the door, and ye begin to stand without, and to knock at the door, saying, Lord, Lord, open unto us; and he shall answer and say unto you, I know you not whence ye are:"*

Thus it is likely not the *stĕnŏs that* is responsible for those referenced who: *"will seek to enter in, and shall not be able;"* but rather because *at that time*, this door is, (will be), *"shut."*

In the case of *salvation*, that "door" in Luke; that is, the "door to salvation" door; is not really any type of "door" at present; because it is currently open 24/7. It is true that we are told that it is *stĕnŏs* because Jesus is the only "door" to salvation. The only real significance of this as a "door;" is because it can be, and at some point *will* be closed. Before that time, it is just as though there is only an opening or portal, but not an actual door.

But in Matthew 7:13-14 things are quite a bit different.

In both Luke and Matthew, we are told to enter or *ĕisĕrchŏmal*, the, narrow because of obstacles about it or *stĕnŏs*, gate or door.

In the passages in Luke, we are told about this gate or door being shut in the *future*, but we are not told about any other type of gate or door; or who or what may be on the other side of any such *second* door—whether wide, narrow, or otherwise. Since the question asked Jesus was about *salvation*; it seems likely that the audience already knew that which would be, should they *not* enter this recommended gate or door to *salvation*. And in Luke, we are not told anything about the nature of the *way*, to get *to* this gate or door of salvation.

However in Matthew, we are told of *two* gates or doors, as well as *two* paths.

One gate or door is wide, or *ĕuruchōrŏs*; and there are "*many that be*" who enter it. And we are told to where this particular gate or door leads. This gate or door, the *wide* one; leads to *apōlĕia*; or waste, ruin, or loss; with *destruction* as a translation of *apōlĕia*, appearing nowhere in the entire New Testament—except here.

But in fact we are not specifically told in this specific verse, either precisely or otherwise, *what it is* that will be: wasted, ruined, lost; or possibly destroyed: "*Enter ye in at the strait gate: for wide is the gate, and broad is the way, that leadeth to destruction, and many there be which go in thereat.*"

But since we are told in the very next verse where the *second* door "*leadeth*;" it is reasonable to conclude that it is that where this *second* door "*leadeth*," will be that which is wasted, ruined, lost; or possibly destroyed, if one chooses the "wide" door.

This *second* or other *door* or *gate*; is not at all *wide*, but rather is *narrow* or *stěnŏs*. And again unlike in *Luke*, here in *Matthew*, we are also told about the *way* or *road* to this, (narrow), gate or door. The "narrowness" of this very *road* or *way* itself, (or by implication even an "act,"), or *hŏdŏs*;" although *translated* as "*narrow*," it is actually the *verb*, *thlibō*, that is translated as "*narrow*" here; and is not the *adjective*, *stěnŏs*.

Unlike *stěnŏs*, which is the *result* of some past act; *thlibō* on the other hand, is a *verb* describing the *process* of crowding; i.e.; "to crowd;" along with the sense of pressure from too much of something in one area, as per the "akin" of *tribŏs*, or to "rub"—and thus this *thlibō*, appears to be happening "real time."

With regard to the ultimate *results* of *thlibō*, again these are sometimes translated as: as "afflict," "suffer tribulation," and "trouble;" and thus strongly suggest that the *results* of *thlibō*, can also be much more *mental* or *emotional*. In fact a fair argument exists, that the main purpose of *thlibō*, is to affect not so much

The Battlefield

what *can* be done by man, (what man is *able* to do); but rather to affect what *will* be done by man, (what man is *willing* to do).

Thus *stĕnŏs* would be more like *physical* "obstacles *standing* close about," as in a "strait," which interfere with what man is *able* to do. But *thlibō* would be more like *non-physical* "objects," which by *crowding*, interfere what man *will* to do.

A translation of *thlibō* as "afflict," (here as *afflicted*), appears in: 1 Timothy 5:10[5.34] (KJV):

> "Well reported of for good works;
> if she have brought up children,
> if she have lodged strangers,
> if she have washed the saints' feet,
> if she have relieved the afflicted,
> if she have diligently followed
> every good work."[5.35]

A translation of *thlibō* as "suffer tribulation," appears in: 1 Thessalonians 3:3-4[5.36] (KJV):

> "That no man should be
> moved by these afflictions:
> for yourselves know that
> we are appointed thereunto.
>
> For verily, when we were with you,
> we told you before that we should suffer tribulation;
> even as it came to pass, and ye know."[5.37]

Here we see an example of *thlibō*, purportedly translated as "suffer tribulation;" but this is not entirely true.

The word "*suffer*," is not actually included here as part of *thlibō*. Instead, the actual Greek word translated as "suffer" here in 1 Thessalonians 3:4 is:

"5302 hustĕrĕō; from 5306; to *be later*, i.e. (by impl.) to *be inferior*; gen. to *fall short* (*be deficient*): - come behind (short), be destitute, fail, lack, suffer need, (be in) want, be the worse."[5.38]

It must be noted that at first blush, the *definition* of the word *hustĕrĕō* sounds a bit like the previously cited word *hamartanō*; which is usually translated as: "sin:" "hamartanō perh. from *1* (as a neg. particle) and the base of *3313*; prop. to *miss* the mark (and *so not share* in the prize), i.e. (fig.) to *err*, esp. (mor.) to *sin*." Each involves "falling short" or being *deficient* or *erring*.

The actual word in verse 3 above translated as "*afflictions*" (not tribulation), is:

"2347 thlipsis; from *2346*; *pressure* (lit. or fig.): - afflicted (-tion), anguish, burdened, persecution, tribulation, trouble."[5.39]

So *thlibō* is translated as "afflict," (as *afflicted*), in: 1 Timothy 5:10, but is translated as "tribulation" in 1 Thessalonians 3:4; with yet another word, *thlipsis*, translated as "afflictions" in 1 Thessalonians 3:3, with *thlipsis* being "from *2346*" which of course is *thlibō*.

A translation of *thlibō* as "trouble," appears in 2 Thessalonians 1:6[5.40] (KJV):

"Seeing it is a righteous thing with God to recompense tribulation to them that trouble you;"[5.41]

Here in 2 Thessalonians 1:6, *thlibō* is the original Greek word translated as "*trouble*," but the original Greek word translated here as "tribulation" is again the above: "2347 thlipsis; from *2346*; *pressure* (lit. or fig.): - afflicted (-tion), anguish, burdened, persecution, tribulation, trouble."[5.42]

The Battlefield

What the commonality is between *thlibō* and its derivative *thlipsis*, is that of *crowding*, (thlibō); and *pressure*, (thlipsis). These can often be manifestations of the same phenomenon. When physical molecules are *pressurized*, say of an inert *gas*; the permitted volume could reasonably be described as "crowded." And likewise when something becomes *crowded*, generally there is increased *pressure*.

Who or what is it that is causing this *crowding*, and for what purpose(s)? Whomever or whatever this "causer" may be, the purpose is to make it as difficult as possible for man to get to this particular *zōē* gate or door.

Therefore that which is *desired* by this "causer," or "causers," of this crowding and pressure; is *apōlĕia*; *or* waste, ruin, or loss, of something; by making the alternative or wide path and door, the *apōlĕia* door, the more attractive alternative. And that very something, is necessarily that very same thing which we are told this particular gate or door would "*leadeth*" us to; the aforementioned *zōē*, or "lifetime."

How can this "crowding pressure" be removed? The easiest way would be to head towards the *apōlĕia* door. Once one does this, the pressure will diminish quite rapidly.

It must be restated here, that this *thlibō* primarily has to do with that which man will *choose* to do, (will do); and not so much what man is *capable* of doing, (can do).

If as God Himself stated, man's main purpose is that of being a *host*, or again in the original Hebrew: "6635 tsâbâ' or ts^{e}ba'ah from 6633; a *mass* of persons (or fig. things), espec. reg. organized for war (an *army*)...;" then it is clear that it is God's *adversary*, (God cannot be killed); and man's *enemy*, (man can be killed); that is responsible for this *thlibō*, in furtherance of *apōlĕia* of man's *zōē*, or "lifetime;" and Satan literally means "adversary." And this capability of *thlibō* to "afflict," "suffer tribulation," and "trouble;" is related to the previous diagram.

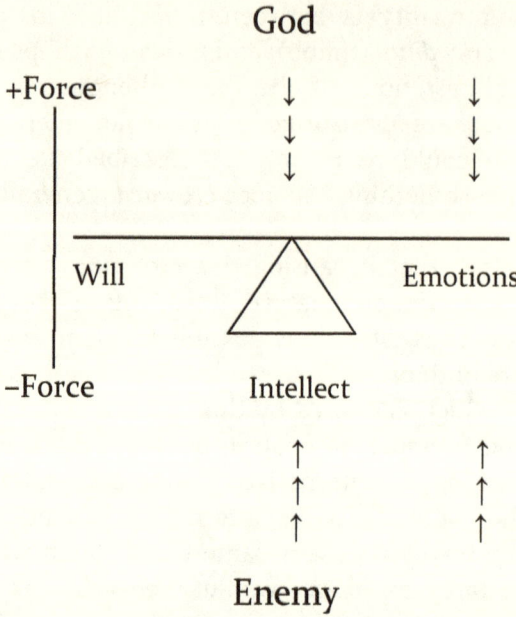

Thus to the extent that this narrow gate or door described in Matthew is *entered*; there is to this very same extent, *less apŏlĕia*. To the extent that there is *less apŏlĕia*, then to this same extent man's "lifetime" or *zōē* is: "unwasted," "unruined," and/or "unlost." And to the extent that man's lifetime or *zōē* is "unwasted," "unruined," and/or "unlost;" there is greater success in man's primary function as *tsâbâ'*. And the enemy has known all of this for quite some time.

How many have found this gate or door? Unlike *salvation*, which *many* find; and unlike the *wide* gate or door which *"many there be which go in thereat;"* Jesus tells us: *"few there be that find it."*

Why do few find it? Because *the way* to this particular "narrow" gate or door is *thlibō*; but the other gate or door is *"wide;"* and the *path* to this wide gate not *crowded*, but is *"broad."* It is simply much less difficult, which is why: *"many there be which go in thereat."*

The Battlefield

What is it that is actually on the other side of this, (the good), gate or door? The answer collectively is: wisdom, (knowledge plus understanding), "actionable intelligence," power, and most importantly; *unpredictability*.

That which is available upon entering this door is not the same for everyone. It is not simply God's *general* plan for man's zōē. It is God's plan for each *individual's* zōē. Each individual is different, and each is brought into existence for different *objectives*; but all are brought into existence for the same *goal*.

And that *goal*, is to bring to fruition that which is stated in Genesis 1:28: *"And God blessed them, and God said unto them, Be fruitful, and multiply, and replenish the earth, and subdue it: and have dominion over the fish of the sea, and over the fowl of the air, and over every living thing that moveth upon the earth."*

Most "believers" talk *to* God. Whether this is done and called prayer; or whether it is done in any other conscious manner, it is nevertheless talking *to* God. Sometimes it is even done unconsciously as in: "Oh my God." But if anyone states that God answered them back, eyebrows are usually raised.

And generally, people will speak to God and once finished, their minds are immediately filled with whatever it was that occupied their minds before. God either *cannot*, (because of man's free will), or *will* not penetrate the "static."

Capacious and lavish edifices are constructed for the purposes of prayer and worship; and sometimes with each occupied by many thousands when in use. Yet if the communication "street" should become "two way;" it is considered either insanity; or if actually believed, is considered a *miracle*.

The *"few"* know better. But to be one of the "few," one first has to *enter* this gate or door. And to get *to* this door, one must overcome the *thlibō*.

Alleged Fantasy Foundations Volume I

Chapter 6

"Insertions"

In the previous chapter, passages in Luke and Matthew were analyzed; most particularly Matthew 7:14: *"Because strait is the gate, and narrow is the way, which leadeth unto life, and few there be that find it."*

Here we are told about this *"strait"* or narrow *"gate"* or door, leading to *"life,"* which in the original Greek is *zōē*. *Zōē* is translated as "life" in the KJV; but as was shown, translates more accurately as "lifetime." "Lifetime" can reasonably be considered as that time when man is *physically* alive—from the first breath until the last breath. And since physically alive human beings were the recipients of this message, it can be inferred that at a minimum, *zōē* here refers to the *human*: "lifetime."

We are also told in the previous verse, (Matthew 7:13), that if humans instead choose the *"wide"* gate, whose path is *"broad;"* there will be *apōleia*, or "waste, ruin, or loss" of something unspecified therein.

It is not likely that this unspecified thing will be *fully* destroyed, as the original word is *apŏlĕia*, and not *apŏllumi*: "622 apŏllumi;

from 575 and the base of 3639 to *destroy* fully"—albeit we are told that *apŏlĕia* is *derived* from *apŏllumi*.

And by knowing where the other referenced or the "narrow" gate leads, (zōē); it can be reasonably inferred that it is man's *zōē* or "lifetime" that will be *apŏlĕia*, or subject to "waste ruin, or loss" if this other "wide gate" is chosen.

We are also told about the *way* or *path* to this "narrow" or "strait" door. Although translated as "narrow," ("*narrow is the way*"), again the original Greek word is not: "4728 stĕnŏs; prob, from the base of 2476; *narrow* (from obstacles *standing* close about);" but rather is in fact: "2346 thlibō; akin to the base of 5147; to crowd (lit. or fig.): - afflict, narrow, throng, suffer tribulation, trouble."

Thus this "narrow way," is in fact actually an *actively* "crowded way."

Is this a *physical* way or path, leading to a *physical* door? As previously indicated, the original Greek word for *way* or *path* is: "3598 hŏdŏs; appar. a prim. word; a *road*; by impl. a *progress* (the route, act or distance); fig. a *mode* or *means*: - journey, (high-) way."

If this were a *physical* way or path, leading to a *physical* door; then it seems Jesus forgot to tell anyone precisely where it was. And as can be seen in the definition of *hŏdŏs*: "by impl. a *progress* (the route, act or distance); fig. a *mode* or *means*;" and there are "allegorical" meanings likewise possible.

Jesus' words in these passages, seem to be somewhere between an *allegory* and a *parable*. Here Jesus was speaking about *choices* man must make; with respect to the very purposes for which man was designed, and brought into existence. His words presume that a physically alive person is already "standing" somewhere; and here is being advised by Jesus as to both the *choices*, and the *consequences* of man's chosen "movement."

Thus unlike the *stĕnŏs*, or *physical* and *fixed* obstacles in the mountain climber example in the previous chapter; this *thlibō* crowding is *non-physical*, and *fluid*; as evidenced by the *translations* of *thlibō* as: "afflict, narrow, throng, suffer tribulation, trouble."

"Insertions"

So then precisely where is this "crowd?" [It must be noted, and as will be seen, this crowd is not in any way the: "in-crowd."]

In Chapter 3, the intersection of the "vertical," or *immaterial* part of man; with the "horizontal" or *material* part of man, was described as a right angle;" or *norm*. Thus as previously stated; that which is next to, (or *para*), this right angle, (or *norm*); is by definition the *paranormal*.

It is difficult to imagine any type of crowding, or "to crowd" possible; without some crowding *factor*, (that which is engaging in the crowding), in some way or manner being "next to" that which is being crowded—here under "normal" circumstances, that which is the *immaterial* part of man.

If it is stipulated that the *material* realm is such that it contains *time, space,* and *matter*; and the *immaterial* realm is such that there are *no* actualities of *time, space,* or *matter*; then how could there *not* be some type of incessant crowding in the immaterial realm—at least from the *material* perspective, and the *material* understanding, of *material* "crowding?"

It is this very *act* of "crowding," which *results* in that or those phenomena that are then referred to as *paranormal*; as these entities are now "next to," (para), this *normal* soul body intersection.

The desire for "crowding" is the *cause*; and that which is doing the crowding, then being "next to" or "beside," (para), the "right angle" of the soul/body connection, (norm), or together *paranormal*; that is the *result*.

"But wait; are there not *angels* in and among this "paranormal crowd?"

The answer to this depends upon one's perspective. It must be remembered that there are actually two, (*either* the material or immaterial), realms; and one *nether* or *neither*, (neither the material nor immaterial), "realm." And it should also be remembered that this *neither* realm, has or had a "separate" area, (the "air conditioned" section), or *kŏlpŏs*; which is sometimes referred to as: "Abraham's Bosom." This *kŏlpŏs* is or was the "place," where souls who physically died before the availability of

111

salvation "reside," or "resided." [See: "*OSTIUM AB INFERNO—The Opening From Hell*"]

But "to crowd," has another meaning; which is in addition to the mere *presence* of that which is involved in this "crowding," or this "crowdogenic factor," as the *cause*. And that other meaning; is the *effect* on that which is being *crowded*.

A *crowded* area; is often an area where *movement* is difficult or impossible. Here it is the reference to specific movement *toward* this narrow gate or door, where zōē or "lifetime" can be "found;" (*"few there be that find it"*). Thus *thlibō* or "to crowd," can refer to either the *cause*, or the concentrated *presence* of those entities that are next to this soul/body intersection; or refer to the *effect* that this "crowding" may have upon that particular physically alive individual.

From this standpoint; meaning the *effect* on that which is trying to "move;" it would seem that if "that which is of God," were "present;" in the sense of "being in the crowd;" these would likely be *assisting* movement *toward* this "zōē door;" and not in any way impeding movement by "getting in the way."

Thus although some immaterial entities *not* in the neither realm *may*, and *may* cannot be overemphasized, be part of the "crowd" in the literal "physical" sense—whatever this may mean in the *immaterial* realm; they likely are not *participants* in the *effect* of "crowding" any physically alive human beings in terms of *movement*. In fact if anything, the reverse is likely true.

It is likely that that which is "contained" in this *neither* realm, is primarily that which is involved in this "crowding," to which Jesus was referring. And it is not likely that the "residents" of the "air conditioned" section of the neither realm, or the *kŏlpŏs*, or "Abrahams Bosom;" are in any way involved—assuming of course this *kŏlpŏs* still exists.

This is not to say that some disembodied souls are not also in this neither realm; either by refusing to re-enter the immaterial realm, or because re-entrance was not permitted. Neither does this mean that some "disembodied souls," cannot be, or are not also "willing" participants in this "crowding."

"Insertions"

It must be remembered that it was *aggĕlŏs*, (original Greek word translated as "angels"), or "messengers;" involved in the aforementioned *planaō*, or: "4105 planaō; from 4106; to (prop. cause to) roam (from safety, truth, or virtue): - go astray, deceive, err, seduce, wander, be out of the way;" who we are told in Revelation, were sent to this *neither* or *nether* realm, or world.

In fact; a fair read is that there was no need for this, or any other *neither* realm, until these *aggĕlŏs* engaged in *planaō*. Although we are told of this event in Revelation; formerly known as "The Apocalypsa, or "revealed things;" this event nevertheless likely occurred somewhere between Genesis 1:1, and Genesis 1:2. When John was permitted to "see" into the immaterial realm, again there was no time reference.

Aggĕlŏs is a *functional* and not a *structural* term. This means that the *commonality* for all *aggĕlŏs* lies in *function*, and not *structure*. There may be one type of structure, or a plethora of structures that are characterized as *aggĕlŏs*—irrespective of the lack of understanding of, or even a definition of what constitutes "structure" in the immaterial realm.

True *aggĕlŏs* have the commonality of being "messengers" or bringers of "tidings"—despite any possible differences in *structure*. These true *aggĕlŏs* remain on or in the immaterial realm, except perhaps under rare circumstances.

Those *aggĕlŏs* who were banished from the *immaterial* realm to this *nether* or *neither* world, were banished because they were engaging in *planaō*; translated in the KJV as: "*deceiveth*."

When man is "standing" there, and considering some type of movement; we are told that man should: "*Enter ye in at the strait gate,*" and we are told why: "*Because strait is the gate, and narrow is the way, which leadeth unto life, and few there be that find it.*"

But this *way* to the "lifetime door" is "crowded," and because of this crowding; there is an alternate *path* to another *door*, that has much less *resistance*. Thus with regard to this *other* door, the *apōlĕia* door; not only is the path "*broad*;" but the door itself is "*wide*." There is much *less* resistance to both "getting to," and "entering" this "wide" door, which is why: "*many there be which go*

113

in thereat." The problem here; is that *apōlĕia, or* "waste, ruin, or loss," are on the other side of that "wide" door.

We already know which door to "enter," as Jesus told us. Thus those entities is engaging in the *crowding* process, are trying to thwart man from entering the narrow door; and instead, provide a "clearer path" to the "wide," and "waste, ruin, or loss," door. If these entities were of God, the reverse would be true. If these were true *aggĕlŏs*, their "messages" and "tidings" would then be *consistent* with Jesus' "advice."

Thus with respect to getting to, and entering the correct door; these entities are literally *currently* providing yet more *planaō*: "from 4106; to (prop. cause to) roam (from safety, truth, or virtue): - go astray, deceive, err, seduce, wander, be out of the way."

They engaged in *planaō* while they were *there*—in the immaterial realm, for which they were expelled *from* the immaterial realm; and they continue engaging in *planaō from* this *neither* or *nether* realm, *to* which they had been banished.

The purpose of their *planaō here*—is to minimize the numbers that "get to" and thus are able to *enter* this narrow door; or stated another way, *minimize* the number represented by the *"few"* in: *"few there be that find it."*

These *planaō* entities *fear* man getting to this door, and for good reason(s), which will be addressed in detail later. And this is *fear* in the *literal* sense; as any host approaching this door represents approaching *danger* to their objectives and main goal. But in the very general *scientific* sense, what is the nature of this *process*?

> "In the physical science of electricity, one of the most fundamental laws is Ohm's Law; expressed as $E = IR$. Here E is Electromotive force or voltage; I is the current, flow of electrons or Intensity; and R is the Resistance to that flow.
>
> "This law describes the relationship of the simple circuit. In order for current to flow, there must be: a current or movement of electrons; a force driving that current; and a load through which to drive it.

"Insertions"

"As stated in this law, the larger the driving force (E), the greater the amount of electron flow (I), through a given resistance or load (R); and the greater this resistance (R), the lesser amount of electron flow (I) for a given force (E). [Step on a garden hose and less water flows, unless the pressure is increased.]

"Ohm's law is a *material* law; and like all material laws, there is a corresponding law in the *immaterial* from which it came. One example of this law in the immaterial; relates to the intentions and actions of the enemy to supplant that which is in, or is of the image and likeness of God; with that which is of him—that is; that which is not of God but is of the *enemy*.

"That which is of him, (the enemy), and not of Him; is analogous to the current. The enemy needs to get his current to flow into the hosts, (H. Sapiens). As in an electrical circuit, once the current gets into the hosts; then changes begin.

"The enemy does this in two very basic ways with respect to this same $E = IR$ law; with each method attempting to use forces, but with different tactical; (but the same strategic); intentions.

"Firstly; he does this by the utilization of forces against the hosts that are analogous to voltage. He "cranks up" this voltage in order to get current to flow from him to the hosts. Much "actionable intelligence" can be gained by carefully observing the nature of these "voltage increases." This is because unlike voltage, there is a *subjective* component. What would be low voltage to one host, can be the same as high voltage to another; and vice versa. (This can often be the reason for what seems to be pettiness.) These forces are custom designed to produce the maximum voltage, (and ultimately maximum current flow); *for that particular host*; and thus there is much intelligence that can be obtained by the design and timing of the attack—but it also must be remembered that the enemy is not always correct.

"However; just as in Ohm's law, in order for this to work; there must be the load, and that load of course is the host. But being made in the image and likeness of God; that load, (host), is not a particularly good *conductor* for the enemy's "current." This necessarily means that the host *is* a particularly good *resistor*. In order to maximize the current flow for a given voltage, the enemy will also attempt to lower the host's *resistance*. Here also much "actionable intelligence" can be gained by carefully observing the nature of these attempts at lowering resistance; as the enemy will attack those areas he or it perceives as weak. But again, it must be remembered that the enemy is not always correct.

"Job 1:10 (KJV) tells us:

> "Hast not thou made an hedge about him,
> and about his house,
> and about all that he hath on every side?
> thou hast blessed the work of his
> hands, and his substance is
> increased in the land."[T1]

"Here Satan is complaining to God that He has "*made an* (sic.) *hedge*" around Job. This "hedge" results in increased resistance. And according to Ohm's law, increased resistance means less current flow, for a given voltage. Satan is essentially complaining here that the resistance is way too high, and he cannot get significant current to flow into Job. But he admits here that God is the one who "made" this hedge.

"This "hedge" is actually:

"Insertions"

> "7753 sûwk a prim. root; to *entwine*, i.e. *shut in* (for formation, protection or restraint):- fence, (make an) hedge (up)."[T2]

"This may seem unrelated at first, but is in fact quite relevant:

"When God refers to "keeping" His commandments in Exodus 20, most believe that this "keep" or "keeping" means *obey*.

"Here in Exodus the actual Hebrew word is:

> "8104: shâmar; A prim. root; prop. to *hedge about* (as with thorns), i.e. *guard*; gen. to *protect, attend to,* etc.: - beware, be circumspect, take heed (to self), keep (-er, self), mark, look narrowly, observe, preserve, regard, reserve, save (self), sure, (that lay) wait (for), watch (-man)."[T3]

"Thus God is not talking about *obedience*; but *protecting* His commandments with an (allegorical) "hedge." To the extent that this "hedge" is built; this also increases the host's resistance, thus making the enemy's current flow to the host difficult. This is similar to the hedge around Job; but here this "hedge" or the act of *shâmar* must be *chosen* to be made by *man*.

"A fair argument can be made that in a sense, this "God made" "hedge" or *sûwk* in the case of Job, is or was primarily for the *material*; and the "man made" "hedge" or *shâmar* is for the *immaterial*. It could further be argued that this "God made" hedge varies with *action*; and the "man made" hedge varies with *thoughts*.

"As this "hedgeogenic" resistance increases, either less current will flow; or the enemy must somehow "crank up" the voltage. And there are limits; albeit sometimes changeable; to the "voltages" available to him.

"What about the hosts not merely maximizing the *resistance*, but also affecting the *voltage* applied by the enemy?[6.1] [Excerpt from: *"It's Not Just a Theory"* Reprinted by Permission]

This excerpt is primarily concerned with *physical* disease imposed upon human beings, by "duly licensed" *immaterial* interference to the *Vital Life Force, Chi*, or what chiropractors have been calling *"Innate Intelligence;"* for well over one hundred years. [Chiropractors remove *material* interference to this Vital Life Force. Traditional Chinese Medicine; such as acupuncture, moxibustion, etc.; modify, correct, or restore this VLF "locally," as does homeopathy. This will all be addressed in great detail later on.]

However; this *mechanism* is not limited to physical disease, but rather is also applicable to other "non-physical" attacks by these "crowders."

This *thlibō* or crowding, at least in the context of these passages in Matthew, represents a *cause*; and the *result* is much phenomena accumulating in the *paranormal*; or next to, (*para*) that "right angle," (*norm* or *normal*), junction of the immaterial soul with the material body. But unlike the *inanimate* obstacles one might encounter in the previous mountain climbing example; these are neither *physical*, nor are they the same for each individual.

As the previous diagram indicates, these "crowders" are seeking to alter the *will* of man from that which is of *God's* liking; to that which is of *their* liking. And this is done utilizing *planaō* or: "(prop. cause to) roam (from safety, truth, or virtue): - go astray, deceive, err, seduce, wander, be out of the way." Simply put: "They lie."

In fact; *if* the door Jesus advised us to enter is the *desired* destination, *then* crowding the "way" causes many to "roam;" and "many of the many," end up at the *undesired*, (wide), door.

It is the Δ or difference between *truth*, (that which is); and *falsehood*, (that which is not); that provides these "crowders" with power over man. Better stated, it is the Δ or difference between

"Insertions"

man's *reality* of "a thing;" "and the *actuality* of that very same "thing;" that provides power to the enemy.

In certain senses, this reality/actuality Δ; is similar to the Δ or difference of potentials with *voltage*. In each case, this Δ provides that which is necessary to cause changes that would not otherwise be possible without it. [Similarly; many insurance companies obtain much *wealth* and *power*, by deliberately causing a Δ or difference between what their "insureds" are told will be covered in their policy—coverage which they believe they have, (*reality*); and for which they pay premiums, (*actuality*); and that which the insurance company will *actually* end up "covering" after "many words."]

And how do these "crowders" get man to believe these *intellectual* falsehoods? One way is the *emotional* factor.

A *mirage* is benign in terms of *causation* for a reality/actuality Δ. *Benign* here in the sense that this is easily explained by physical factors alone. Of course a mirage can be *deadly* in terms of the effect it may have upon travelers. It is just that there is generally no active participant in the *causation* of this particular type of illusion.

But there are other types of "quasi-mirages," which are *not* in any way *benign* in terms of *causation*.

For example: Because of some type of emotional "hook," a homeowner is caused to believe that a repairman approaching their home is no repairman; but is in fact a *murderer*, who is "coming to get them." Perhaps the emotional "hook," is from past experiences, paranoia, a movie, or whatever. The important thing here; is that the homeowner has a *reality* of a murderer, when in fact the *actuality* is a repairman. That which "causes" this "thought" is "next to," or *paranormal*; and is engaging in *planaō*.

This reality/actuality Δ in the mind of the homeowner; is then capable of justifying their actions to be consistent with a "known" murderer approaching them; rather than a repairman. Of course there then will likely come some "suggestion" of some action in furtherance of "self-defense." Should the homeowner choose to "take out" this "murderer" in "self defense;" in all likelihood, this same homeowner will likewise but unknowingly "take out" themselves—at least in terms of any meaningful future ability to *kibosh*.

This of course being the main objective of the "crowder" all along; as the outright physical killing of a human being requires either that the "crowder" obtain a special *license*, one that was not even afforded to Satan himself with Job; or require some degree of *consent* of the victim. [Much about this second one will be addressed later.]

A mirage alone represents no danger whatsoever—*as long as it is known by all that it is a mirage.* Had the above homeowner understood this *planaō*, and instead of *acting* based upon this *planaō*, simply *stated*: "Nice try!" the outcome would be much different.

Here with a *known* mirage, whether quasi or true, there is no reality/actuality Δ; as all know precisely what it is. If any actions are undertaken with respect to this *known* desert mirage; then whatever the contemplated set of possibilities may be with respect to the *effects* of these same actions; it is well understood by all that the acquisition of water, is not, and cannot be, a subset of this set of contemplated effects.

But the *unknown* quasi-mirage, is different. This is like a desert mirage that is *not* known to be a mirage; but instead is believed to represent the actuality of water. And unlike a true mirage, this quasi-mirage is deliberately caused by that which crowds, (*thlibō*); and is "custom designed" by these "crowders" to change a specific host's behavior to their liking via *planaō*.

The police place a home in a wooded lot under observation. Since the front of the house faces the South; officers are placed at the cardinal points: North, South, East, and West. The officer observing from the South is asked: What color is the house?

He responds: "Kind of reddish." (It is actually brick.)

The officer observing from the North, (the rear of the house); is then asked the same question.

She responds: "Light green."

The other officers, (those observing from the East and West), are then asked this very same question, and each responds: "White."

Each officer is extrapolating their *perceptions* of the actuality, (reality); to include that which was *not actually perceived* by them. The truth is that each officer can only provide the information

"Insertions"

perceived by them—at least if accuracy is a concern. The correct answer would be: "The house is "X" color on *this* side."

What are the rules for determining the color of a house? The presence of red brick on the South side, mold on the North side, and white siding on the East and West sides; provide conflicting information as to the actual color of the house.

Is it the front of the house that determines the color of the house? If so then here the house is red. Or is it the color that covers the maximum square feet that determines the color of the house? If so, here the house is white.

Could it be the case that past experiences or "taste" affect these determinations? Meaning; that since the officer seeing the front absolutely loves brick houses; and since this particular house belongs to a suspected criminal; this officer instead contemplates only characterizing the house as "reddish," and not "brick." After all, this officer wants no commonality with a criminal.

The officer who views the rear of the house, in fact has a problem with mold on her own house, which she repeatedly has tried to remove. Could this in any way affect her decision to characterize the color as "light green" rather than "moldy?"

Could the officers seeing the sides of the house, somehow in any way be caused to make the aforementioned *extrapolation* as to color of the entire the house because of past experiences; or because of "taste?"

This may in fact all sound a bit silly, but is provided to illustrate a point. And that point is that *emotion* can often play a major role in what we "hosts" determine to be "facts." And again, *emotions* are to be distinguished from *feelings*.

Here these are all highly trained, and well experienced, law enforcement professionals. Thus allowing emotion to influence factual recounting is highly unlikely. This is because even any *possibility* of this, was likely "trained and experienced" out of them—at *least* in, but perhaps *only* in, their professional actions.

If this was "'trained and experienced'" out of them, then it likely was present to some degree prior to this. And the truth is that immunity from emotional interference likely can never be *completely* eradicated from anyone. And another truth; is that training and experience, likely does not affect each and every other area of their lives, each and every time.

Earlier it was stated:

> "It is this Δ or difference between *truth*, (that which is); and *falsehood*, (that which is not); that provides them with power over man. Better stated, it is the Δ or difference between man's *reality* of "a thing;" "and the *actuality* of that very same "thing;" that provides power to the enemy. In certain senses, this reality/actuality Δ; is similar to the Δ or difference of potentials with *voltage*. In each case, this Δ provides that which is necessary for the enemy to cause changes that would not otherwise be possible without it."

And unlike the true mirage, which is merely the result of inanimate and physical phenomena; the quasi-mirage is the desired result of the aforementioned *planaō* or: "(prop. cause to) roam (from safety, truth, or virtue): - go astray, deceive, err, seduce, wander, be out of the way." *Planaō* is the *means*; and if successful, and to the very same extent that *planaō* is successful; this Δ or *power* is the *result*.

If something, (a thing), *exists* (is an actuality); then this power to the enemy is roughly:

$$P_E \approx T_A/T_R$$

Where P_E represents the power available to the enemy, T_A represents the "actual truth" about an actuality, and T_R represents that "reality truth" or a host's *reality* about this same actuality.

As can be easily seen, if the *reality*, (T_R), of an actuality is zero, then this provides a very large amount of power to the enemy. If these were actual mathematical expressions, either "undefined;" or ∞ or infinite power would then be provided, as any number divided by zero, (except perhaps zero itself), is ∞, or infinity.

"Insertions"

This condition of zero reality, is precisely what the enemy desires with regard to man's knowledge of man's true purpose, and the power available to him.

But here if the reality of an existing actuality is the *same* as the actuality, ($T_A = T_R$) then the power to the enemy is only "one." However, as previously stated; no actuality can ever be 100% perceived, so *reality*, even if completely consistent with the actuality, is always less than the *actuality*.

And also as earlier stated, when one approaches the *zōē* or "lifetime" gate or door; one obtains: "wisdom, (knowledge plus understanding), "actionable intelligence," power, and most importantly; *unpredictability*." It is this *unpredicatibilty* that often act as a weapon, and can often times become "nuclear," against the enemy.

This is because the enemy likewise acts upon his or its *reality* of a given host; and this *reality* is never 100% either. This reality is largely based upon observation and past experiences. The enemy will act in a manner that can be predicted to attain the outcome he desires, based upon this reality. Thus, his or its reality can easily fail when a host becomes unpredictable; and the results can instead become a major disaster to or for him.

But if something, (a thing), *does not exist*, (is *not* an actuality); then "things are different," and thus T_A cannot be greater than zero, because there is no actuality to have any amount of *truth* about.

Here this power to the enemy is roughly:

$$P_E \approx T_R/T_A$$

Here it is the *reality* of the existence of a non-existent "thing" *alone*, which is the sole source of this power; and no matter what the numerical value of T_R, here again the quotient is the result of a dividend greater than zero, and a divisor of zero; again resulting again in a quotient of either "undefined;" or ∞ or infinite power—if this were an actual equation. [This is likely the reason for "demons" reputedly appearing as a: "nine foot tall goat;" or some such truck.]

But if there is no reality of the non-existent actuality, then again the power available to the enemy is o/o, and either "zero," or only "one." (Once again, some also believe that this is also "undefined.")

These are provided not as absolutes or actual mathematical expressions, but rather only to illustrate how *planaō* affects the capabilities of the enemy—which is precisely why he engages in *planaō*.

What the enemy desires, is to increase the reliability of: "The assumption of safety, by the conclusion of stupidity." Here there is commonality with many politicians, and for good reasons.

But here the "stupidity" is not the common understanding of low intelligence; but rather the more literal meaning of stunned or amazed, more akin to *stupor*; and due to either inadequate or no knowledge; or *falsehood*.

Chapter 7

Variations on the Planaō Theme

In addition to the provision of falsehood, (that which is not); what the enemy is also doing, is what appears in Ephesians 6:12-17, and was cited back in Chapter 4. He is pushing upward from below, or perhaps better phrased *throwing*, (ballō) these *arrows* (bĕlŏs), with all sorts of *"flaming"* (purŏō) emotions such as pride, anger, hatred, envy, jealousy etc.

His objective in attempting to push the right or emotion side of this "seesaw" or line upward; is to ultimately push the left side of this line or "seesaw" downward into the negative forces area.

All of these tailor made "messes," are designed to assist in the *crowding* and *pressure*, "to crowd," (thlibō), the "way;" in order to inhibit our movement towards that narrow *zōē* door; and are in furtherance of getting us to *choose* the other, (wide), door; as well as to do, or to not do many other things.

Here again is the "diagram:"

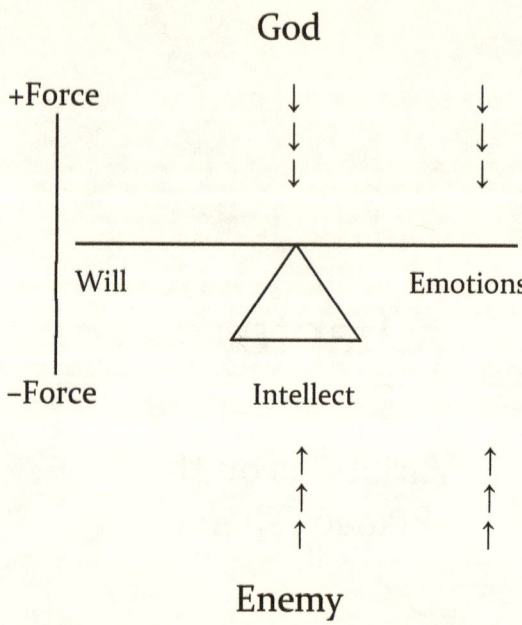

A distinction must be made here regarding the actions of the enemy. The *emotional* pressure exerted on the right side of the diagram, and the *intellectual* attacks are quite different. The *emotional* pressures may be considered as an attack, but this would be a bit of a mischaracterization. The purpose of the emotional attacks, in addition to just plain wickedness; is to set the stage for the actual attack. The emotional pressure itself, directly benefits the enemy very little; and may in fact ultimately be detrimental to his purposes—unless accompanied by the true attack.

There are only two *sources* of "information" available to the intellect. Irrespective of any *apparent* source, the ultimate source must either be God or the enemy; with each either acting *directly*; or acting *indirectly* through surrogates in the dissemination of this "information." There simply is no third ultimate source possible.

"A thing" either is, or is not, at any given "time." If it *is*; then it *cannot not be* at the very same time that *it is*. If it *is not*, then it *cannot be* at the same time that it *is not*. The above term

Variations on the Planaō Theme

"information," is used very broadly here; to include not just truth, but also falsehood from the enemy.

The purpose of *emotional* pressure is generally *motivational* in nature. This is true with either source. But there is a difference. The enemy is trying to *manipulate* the host to either do, or not do something. He wants to create a *negative* emotional imbalance, to be resolved by the exercise of our will. Should the emotional pressure not be followed by the enemy providing thoughts, ideas, and suggestions; then the only *new* information that the intellect could use from that point onward would be from God, and thus be truth.

For example: The enemy exerts emotional pressures which result in a bout of "depression." This bout of depression sets the stage for the actual attack. If this emotional imbalance is not ultimately followed by a suggestion such as: "Might as well kill yourself," (which is what in many ways he is ultimately after anyway); then this imbalance is temporarily left "open," so to speak.

If there then is no subsequent attack with thoughts ideas and suggestions—either directly or otherwise; then the only new information at the host's disposal would ultimately be from God, and thus be truth. This is not a particularly beneficial situation for the enemy. This is both because of the ultimate *action* the host may undertake; but also because of *karmic* matters.

It must also be noted that these "thoughts, ideas, and suggestions;" need not come *directly* from the enemy, or any "demonic" source. The enemy will also utilize *surrogates* in the dissemination of falsehood; in order to get the same introduced into the host's intellect, in order to affect the *judgment* process of the target of the attack.

These *surrogate* TIS attacks, (thoughts, ideas, and suggestions); actually come in two varieties or "flavors:" the *benign* and the *malignant*.

The *benign* surrogate TIS attack, is when the enemy convinces a surrogate; e.g.; friend, family member, or even a stranger; to engage in an attack, but the surrogate would have no way of reasonably knowing there is any type of attack or wrongness involved. It is legitimately an innocent, (*non-nocere*, or no harm), undertaking from the perspective of the surrogate.

As with *benign* tumors; which generally cause trouble by *pressure*; the "benign surrogate TIS attack," functions in a similar manner. The surrogate is not aware that they are doing anything which in and of itself is wrong, because they are not. There are no sinful, or immoral, or unethical, etc., behaviors involved. As is the case with the capsule surrounding most benign tumors, there are boundaries based upon character, which here the surrogate simply will not cross.

The *efficacy* of this type of attack, ("benign surrogate TIS attack"); is primarily dependent upon *situational* considerations, and most especially *timing*. The "benign surrogate TIS attack," is tailor made for the actual host under siege. They are primarily designed exert *pressure*, in order to have a negative effect on the judgment *process*.

Two true "anecdotellas" regarding *benign* TIS attacks:

> A couple is home all weekend and the telephone has not rung even once since Thursday. They are cleaning the basement and find a snake, lying on the cool concrete floor between two boxes. It appears to be dead. The husband does not want to take any chances, so he places a large clear plastic container upside down over the snake. The snake now wakes up and becomes quite active; trying to escape the enclosure. Within seconds, each of the many phones in the house begins ringing. People they have not heard from in a long time, including from different parts of the country, suddenly begin calling.

Were these callers doing anything wrong? Of course not. Rather, "something" just gave the callers the *thought* about someone or some thing; the *idea* to make a contact; and the *suggestion* to make the call *when* they did. They may have even stated out loud to themselves or someone else: "You know what? I am going to give them a call."

Variations on the Planaō Theme

The idea is to put pressure on the receiving host(s), in order to alter their judgment faculties to get them to do something careless or stupid—and quite ironically, here with a snake. But none of the callers were aware of the situation, and thus all of their actions were benign. However, it did not work, as the couple; being keenly aware of these tactics; simply thought it was hysterical.

Here is another:

> One is sitting in the car in a supermarket parking lot with a puppy, while the wife runs in for a few items. He parked far away from the store, so that he could play with the puppy without anyone seeing how silly he was behaving. There is not a car anywhere close by design. The wife comes out and gets into the car. All of a sudden there are cars everywhere. What was just an area of desolation; has now become a traffic jam. The best course of action is determined to be to just wait until the traffic clears before even attempting to leave.

Why is it that all of these cars suddenly appeared? Why is it that this desolate area suddenly became so attractive to so many motorists? Why is it that they all had the same idea and at the same time? It may occur to one to tell the wife that all of these people saw her, and then had to come in for a closer look; but what does he actually believe?

The truth is that it was either "random chance;" or there was a *causative* factor. And likely none of the motorists believed; neither should they have believed; that they were doing anything wrong, because they likely were not.

Malignant surrogate TIS attacks are quite a bit different. The *malignant* surrogate TIS attack, is when the enemy convinces a surrogate to engage in an attack; and the surrogate fully knows, or should reasonably know; that either there *is* some type of an *attack*, or that there is *wrongness* involved. [A lie seeking a destructive tongue perhaps?]

This *malignant* surrogate TIS attack is *not* an innocent undertaking. The surrogate may not realize that they are merely a "go-between;" but their intention is nevertheless to do some type of harm to the target.

As is the case with *malignant* tumors; which generally cause trouble by invasion or infiltration; the *malignant* surrogate TIS attack is similar. Here the surrogate is fully aware, or should be fully aware, that they are doing something which in and of itself is wrong; because they are. Here in the malignant TIS attack, there are sinful, immoral, unethical, etc.; behaviors that are involved.

And as is the case with most malignant tumors, there is essentially little or no "capsule" involved based upon any character issues; but rather the surrogate's behavior is generally only limited by things such as fear; fear of things such as legal repercussions or physical harm; and all too often, not even by these. The efficacy of this type of attack is primarily dependent upon *informational* matters.

This *malignant* surrogate TIS attack, is also tailor made for the actual host target under siege; but the surrogate may have little or no knowledge of their actual role in a much larger attack. Instead; they are merely substituting whatever may be their *emotionally* driven perceived need to attack the target, as their primary or even sole reason.

These *malignant* surrogate attacks; unlike the *benign*, which are designed to primarily affect the judgment *process* itself; *malignant* surrogate attacks are designed primarily to infiltrate or invade the *knowledge* base, in order to have a negative effect on the *information* utilized in the judgment process.

As with many actualities, the differences are as not cut and dried as they may seem to appear. There can be attacks within attacks within attacks. Precisely what type of attack on the surrogate, resulted in the malignant attack on the actual intended host? One must often "peel back the onion" to determine the actual causative factors, and this can be time consuming; and can also be a diversion from whatever the actual, (the *primary*), target was doing that "got the enemy's attention" in the first place.

It is also true, that many previous attacks of thoughts, ideas, and suggestions, may in fact *precede* a given manipulative *emotional* event. If so, this can represent a "set up," via the recollection of

Variations on the Planaō Theme

these previous attacks, that may be utilized by the intellect; instead of a *new* and *post-emotional* event provision of a (new) TIS attack. But this represents a much less effective battle technique. It is essentially waging the battle backwards, (TIS *first* and then the *emotional* attack); and thus is a much less reliable means of battle.

In the absence of the actual *post-emotional* TIS attack, relying on the target's recollection of previous "informational" attacks is unreliable; not only because of potential recollective inadequacies; but also because without subsequent "informational" intervention; the enemy has no substantial control over precisely what it is that will be recollected. And to make it even worse for him, all of this is happening while God is being extremely active in the dissemination of truth.

The enemy is involved with these attacks for many reasons; but the most serious motivation to the enemy, is *his* or *its* knowledge of how much *his* or *its* situation will deleteriously be affected should any currently physically alive hosts ever find that *zōē* gate, that *"few find."*

This "gate finding," represents a situation resulting in synergy. When this narrow gate is reached and entered, then our individual divine design; and our individually divinely intended purpose(s); become "in phase." And that can pack a level of power far beyond one's ability to think or imagine.

The enemy may have little knowledge of the specifics of any particular gate; but he "maintains" incredibly detailed records as to the course of events whenever these gates have been reached in the past; irrespective of the percentage of the time, (*"few there be that find it"*), that this has happened. He knows in a general sense, the severity of what is in store for *him*, if any host reaches that gate that is there for him or her; arguably a gate that already has his or her name inscribed upon it.

From chapter 4, here again is Ephesians 6:12-17 (NAS), which tell us:

> *"For our struggle is not against flesh and blood,*
> *but against the rulers, against the powers,*

*against the world forces of this darkness,
against the spiritual forces of wickedness
in the heavenly places.*

*Therefore, take up the full armor of God,
so that you will be able to resist in the evil day,
and having done everything, to stand firm.*

*Stand firm therefore,
HAVING GIRDED YOUR LOINS WITH TRUTH,
and HAVING PUT ON THE BREASTPLATE OF
RIGHTEOUSNESS,
and having shod YOUR FEET WITH THE
PREPARATION OF THE GOSPEL OF PEACE;*

*in addition to all, taking up the shield of faith
with which you will be able to extinguish
all the flaming arrows of the evil one.
And take THE HELMET OF SALVATION,
and the sword of the Spirit,
which is the word of God."*

Again, the actual Greek word translated as "arrows" is:

"956 bĕlŏs, from 906; a *missile*, i.e. *spear* or *arrow*: - dart."

"906 ballō a prim. verb; to *throw* (in various applications, more or less violent or intense): - arise, cast (out), x dung, lay, lie, pour, put (up), send, strike, throw (down), thrust."

Again the actual Greek word translated as "fiery" is:

"4448 purŏō, from 4442; to *kindle* i.e. (pass.) to *be ignited*, *glow* (lit.), *be refined* (by impl.), or (fig.) to *be inflamed* (with anger, grief, lust): - burn, fiery, be on fire, try."

And again, the above Ephesians 6:12-17, is a bit more revealing if the *chronology* of the recommendations is changed a bit:

> *"For our struggle is not against flesh and blood, but against the rulers, against the powers, against the world forces of this darkness, against the spiritual forces of wickedness in the heavenly places."*
>
> *"Therefore, take up..." "the sword of the Spirit, which is the word of God;"* but before you do this, properly prepare yourself for battle by firmly and resolutely deciding to:
>
> *"Take up the full armor of God, so that you will be able to resist in the evil day, and having done everything, to stand firm."*
>
> *"Stand firm therefore,* HAVING GIRDED YOUR LOINS WITH TRUTH, *and* HAVING PUT ON THE BREASTPLATE OF RIGHTEOUSNESS, *and having shod* YOUR FEET WITH THE PREPARATION OF THE GOSPEL OF PEACE; *in addition to all, taking up the shield of faith with which you will be able to extinguish all the flaming arrows of the evil one. And take* THE HELMET OF SALVATION."

The original Greek word translated as "heavenly" is:

> "2032 ĕpŏuraniŏs; from *1909* and *3772*; *above* the *sky*: - celestial, (in) heaven (-ly), high."[7.1]

With respect to *individual* battles, as Paul tells us in here in Ephesians 6:12-17, we are not at war with *"flesh and blood;"* but *"spiritual forces of wickedness."* And this is further confirmed, because Paul tells us where these non-"flesh and blood" entities are. They are not on earth per-se, but in *ĕpŏuraniŏs*, or "above the sky" places.

But it is known that these *"spiritual forces of wickedness,"* were ejected from the immaterial realm because these engaged in *planaō*. Thus the use of *ĕpŏuraniŏs* is likely used to mean not "flesh and blood;" or not physically alive, body and soul connected, entities, as per the "not against flesh and blood" comparison.

The King James version of Ephesians 6:12 tells us:

> *"For we wrestle not against flesh and blood,*
> *but against principalities, against powers,*
> *against the rulers of the darkness of this world,*
> *against spiritual wickedness in high places."*[7.2]

This first passage, (verse 12), begins with that which is translated as "*For*."

The actual Greek word translated as "for" in Ephesians 6:12 is:

> 1063 gar; a prim. particle; prop. assigning a *reason* (used in argument, explanation or intensification; often with other particles): - and, as, because (that)..."[7.3]

Thus this can be translated in more modern terms as: "because." A reasonable analysis would then necessarily have to refer back to what was stated *prior* to the appearance of this *gar*, in order to determine to precisely what it is that is being assigned this causation; (That which preceded the *gar* or "*for*," that which is so *because* or "*for*").

The verses that immediately precede Ephesians 6:12, are Ephesians 6:8-11, here (KJV):

> *"Knowing that whatsoever good thing any man doeth,*
> *the same shall he receive of the Lord,*
> *whether he be bond or free.*
>
> *And, ye masters, do the same things unto them,*
> *forbearing threatening:*
> *knowing that your Master also is in heaven;*

Variations on the Planaō Theme

> *neither is there respect of persons with him.*
>
> *Finally, my brethren, be strong in the Lord,
> and in the power of his might.*
>
> *Put on the whole armour of God,
> that ye may be able to stand
> against the wiles of the devil."*[7.4]

The first thing Paul does in these passages, is confirm the law of *karma*—at least with regard to the *"good thing;"* i.e.; that the previously discussed application of F = MA with regard to the *immaterial* is in fact valid: *"Knowing that whatsoever good thing any man doeth, the same shall he receive of the Lord."*

Paul then instructs the *"masters,"* (lower case), to behave in the same manner; essentially telling them that they are subject to the same rules, and that no matter what they may think of themselves, they have the same *"Master,"* (upper case). And furthermore, that this Master cares not one whit who they may think they are, or their status on the material realm.

Thus far, this is all about "man to man" behaviors on the material realm. This "section" concludes, (*"finally"*), with the audience being advised to: *"Finally, my brethren, be strong in the Lord, and in the power of his might."* This sentence *concludes* these previous instructions with regard to man's behavior toward man on the material realm.

The next sentence begins an entirely different matter: *"Put on the whole armour of God, that ye may be able to stand against the wiles of the devil."*

The actual Geek word translated as "wiles" is:

> "3180 měthŏděia; from a comp. of 3326 and 3593 [comp. "method"]; *traveling over, i.e. travesty (trickery):* - wile, lie in wait."[7.5]

The actual Geek word translated as "devil" is:

> "1228 diabŏlŏs; from *1225*; a *traducer*; spec. *Satan* [comp. 7854]: - false accuser, devil, slanderer."[7.6]

It is interesting to note that if the etymology of "traduce" is researched, there seems to be little or no distinction made between *traduce* and *transduce*. Perhaps *calumniate* would have been a better translation—perhaps not.

> "traduce (v.)1530s, "alter, change over, transport," from Latin traducere "change over, convert..."[7.7]

> "transducer (n.)1924, "device which converts energy from one form to another," from Latin transducere/ traducere..."[7.8]

A *transducer* is a device that converts one form of energy to another. A loudspeaker converts electrical energy into sound energy; while a microphone does the reverse. In fact, some intercom systems use a loudspeaker for both functions, although obviously not simultaneously.

Thus depending upon one's perspective, it could be said that a *traducer* is that which attempts to convert truth into falsehood, and convert falsehood into truth. Whether or not this *traducing* is successful or not depends upon man. It must be remembered that *defamation*; i.e.; libel or slander; must be *false* in order to be considered as either. Distribution of *truth* that harms the reputation of another, does not generally constitute defamation.

Again the section concerned with man's behavior toward *man* concluded with: "*Finally, my brethren, be strong in the Lord, and in the power of his might.*"

And the new topic in the very next section begins with: "*Put on the whole armour of God, that ye may be able to stand against the wiles of the devil.*"

Thus there is a strong implication that what we were told about man's behavior toward man is not applicable to the devil, the same being: "*Knowing that whatsoever good thing any man doeth, the same shall he receive of the Lord, whether he be bond or free.*"

Variations on the Planaō Theme

Man's role with regard to *other men* is clear, as we were told in Matthew 7:12, back in Chapter 5: *"Therefore;* ("For all of the foregoing reasons"); *all things whatsoever ye would that men should do to you, do ye even so to them: for this is the law and the prophets."*

Man's role with regard to some type of enemy is likewise clear, because again God himself refers to man as: "6635 tsâbâ' or ts^{e}ba'ah from 6633; a *mass* of persons (or fig. things), espec. reg. organized for war (an *army);* by impl. a *campaign,* lit. or fig. (spec. *hardship, worship):* - appointed time, (+) army, (+) battle, company, host, service, soldiers, waiting upon, war (-fare). 6633 tsâbâ' a prim. root; to *mass* (an army or servants): - assemble, fight, perform, muster, wait upon, war."

And man's role with regard to the earth is also clear, because again God Himself instructed man to: "3533 kâbash; a prim. root; to *tread* down; hence neg. to *disregard;* pos. to *conquer, subjugate, violate*: - bring into bondage, force, keep under, subdue, bring into subjection."

Thus what is a *"good thing"* with man's treatment of *man;* is as stated above in Matthew 7:12. This is what God desires; and He told us this is what He desires.

But the *"good thing"* with man's treatment of the *devil,* must be consistent with man's role as stated by God as *tsâbâ';* and must also be consistent with mans instructions by God to *kâbash;* the earth. This is what God desires; and He told us this is what He desires.

These are not only *not* the same; but are arguably *mutually exclusive.* Distinctions must again be made with respect to: *good* and *wicked;* and: *upright* and *evil.* There must be terminology to describe the *act itself;* as well as terminology to describe whether or not any given act is consistent or inconsistent with the *will of God*—as these are not always the same.

The Crucifixion was a horrible, (*wicked*), act; but it was consistent with the will of God, and so not *evil.* Had Jesus decided at Gethsemane to "not go through with it;" the *wicked* act would have been avoided; but this would have been *evil,* as it would have been *inconsistent* with Gods will.

The rules for behavior toward the enemy must be *consistent* with that which God instructed us to do; even if *inconsistent* with how God told us to treat our fellow man. This is not in any way any type of "double standard," as will be shown shortly.

Paul begins this next section which is about the *devil* with: "*Put on the whole armour of God, that ye may be able to stand against the wiles of the devil.*" And we are given the reason for this particular instruction in the very next verse: "*For* (because) *we wrestle not against flesh and blood,* (as was just discussed up to the end of the sentence beginning with *"finally,"*) *but* (now here we are discussing behavior) *against principalities, against powers, against the rulers of the darkness of this world, against spiritual wickedness in high places.*"

Here again is Ephesians 6:12-17 (NAS):

"*For our struggle is not against flesh and blood,
but against the rulers, against the powers,
against the world forces of this darkness,
against the spiritual forces of wickedness
in the heavenly places.*

*Therefore, take up the full armor of God,
so that you will be able to resist in the evil day,
and having done everything, to stand firm.*

*Stand firm therefore,
HAVING GIRDED YOUR LOINS WITH TRUTH,
and HAVING PUT ON THE BREASTPLATE
OF RIGHTEOUSNESS,
and having shod YOUR FEET WITH THE
PREPARATION OF THE GOSPEL OF PEACE;*

*in addition to all, taking up the shield of faith
with which you will be able to extinguish
all the flaming arrows of the evil one.
And take THE HELMET OF SALVATION,
and the sword of the Spirit,*

Variations on the Planaō Theme

which is the word of God."

What constitutes winning? To *"resist in the evil day, and having done everything, to stand firm?"* Most of what we have to use as described by Paul in this passage is *defensive* in nature. He essentially advises us put on armor: Truth, righteousness, the gospel (good news) of peace, the shield of faith, the helmet of salvation etc.; all of which is *defensive*.

There is a bit of a difference between standing firm and resistance, and extinguishing the arrows of the enemy. But both standing firm and resisting are essentially *defensive* measures. Standing firm is absorbing the forces of his blows. And extinguishing the arrows is destroying his weaponry, but this is essentially also *defensive*, like the Patriot missile defense system. But one cannot win a battle or a war by acting purely *defensive*, and simply waiting until the enemy becomes tired and leaves you alone.

Tucked in here at the very end of a long list of *defensive*, (increasing resistance), measures in all of the verses preceding verse 17, and beginning here in verse 17 after the second "and;" something rather interesting appears. In fact; therein lies a "bomb." And it is a rather interesting and quite powerful "bomb;"—the same representing the provision of a key instruction:

*"(take) the sword of the Spirit,
which is the word of God."*

This instruction is the only *offensive*, (voltage lowering), instruction given in these famous, (Ephesians 6:12-17), verses.

What does "(take) *the sword of the Spirit, which is the word of God"* actually mean?

The actual Greek word translated as "sword" is:

"3162 machaira; prob. fem. of a presumed der. of *3163*; a knife, i.e. dirk; fig. *war*, judicial *punishment*: - sword."[7.9]

139

As can be seen, the translation as *"sword"* is misleading. A *dirk* is not a sword. "Knife" or "dagger" would be a better translation. These are designed for "up close and personal" combat. This is important because this, (close up and tailor made); is precisely how the enemy attacks.

The "figurative" meaning should also be noted—that of "judicial punishment." There is an old saying: "Don't stick your head in the boxing ring if you don't want to get punched." It is the enemy who chooses to institute an attack. If the result is encountering a counterattack with a dirk, and he/it leaves a bit "bloodied;" then he or it deserved it. But again, this should never be combined with anything that is of the enemy such as anger, hatred, etc. It is *justice*, ("judicial punishment"); and not *vengeance*, that should be sought. If that which is of the enemy is *at any time* utilized, this can then easily be utilized by the enemy as a foothold.

The actual Greek word translated as "spirit" is:

"4151 pněuma; from 4154; a *current* of air, i.e. *breath* (*blast*) or a *breeze*; by anal. or fig. a *spirit*, i.e. (human) the rational *soul*, (by impl.) *vital principle*, mental *disposition* etc..."[7.10]

Thus; "the knife of the soul" is a better translation. And precisely what is this "knife of the soul?"

It is the *"word of God."* What is this "word," and why is it a *machaira* or "knife?"

The actual Greek "word" translated here in Ephesians as "word" is:

"4487 rhēma; from 4483; an *utterance* (individ., collect. or spec.); by impl. a *matter* or *topic* (espec. of narration, command or dispute); with a neg. *naught* whatever..."[7.11]

John 1:1 (KJV) tells us:

"*IN THE beginning was the Word,*

Variations on the Planaō Theme

*and the Word was with God,
and the Word was God."*[7.12]

However the actual Greek word translated three times here in John as "word," is not *rhēma*, but rather:

"3056 lŏgŏs; from 3004; something *said* (including the *thought*); by impl. a *topic* (subject of discourse), also *reasoning* (the mental faculty) or *motive*; by extens. a *computation*; spec. (with the art. In John) the Divine Expression (i.e. Christ)..."[7.13]

So it must be asked what the difference is between these two Greek words, each translated as *"word?"* The same being *rhēma* and *lŏgŏs*, and furthermore; why it was *rhēma* that was used in *Ephesians*; but it was *lŏgŏs* that was used in *John?*

Paul was giving us instructions for *future* behavior; and John was recollecting *past* events. Thus *rhēma*; meaning an *utterance*, refers to what God *is* or *will be* saying "real time." *Lŏgŏs* refers to what God has or had already "said."

Assuming Moses actually wrote early Genesis, what he recorded was the *rhēma* he was receiving "real time" from God; as he was not physically alive when those events in early Genesis transpired. In fact it seems no one was. (This process is what is referred to as *retrophesy* in "MeekRaker Beginnings...") Once it was recorded, however, and not being received "real time;" it then became *lŏgŏs*. The *means* of said recording; e.g.; oral memorization, long continuous scrolls, or today's Bible format; changes nothing with regard to this.

Thus this *rhēma* in *"word of God,"* refers primarily to what God *will be* uttering "real time;" and represents the "knife" portion of this "knife of the soul." But this is not to say that in the absence of the reception of any *rhēma*, that *lŏgŏs* cannot be utilized just as Jesus did when the enemy attacked Him in the desert, after He fasted. It must be remembered that the enemy "ran away" after this particular event.[7.14]

Paul's use of *rhēma*, and not *lŏgŏs*, indicates a *preference*, but does not necessarily represent an absolute. Again, Jesus seems to have done pretty well with the: "It is written. . ." It is not clear that any *Greek* word exists, that includes both *rhēma* and *lŏgŏs*.

Thus when attacking the enemy with the "knife of the soul," *rhēma* is preferred; but *lŏgŏs* is also an option. It must be noted that each contains that which is of God; and the *original* verbiage contains nothing which is of the enemy. ["*Original*" cannot be overstressed here, because as can be seen; translating both *rhēma* and *lŏgŏs* merely as "*word*," is at best inadequate.]

It should not be overlooked that the definition of *lŏgŏs* also includes: "something *said* (including the *thought*)..."; "*reasoning* (the mental faculty) or *motive*...;" and "the Divine *Expression* (i.e. *Christ*)..."

Thus contained in the definition of *lŏgŏs* are the various aspects; both *material* and *immaterial*; to what may seem to be mere speech or merely "saying something." This seems to confirm the immaterial component of *any* action—here speech. The *action*; the *thought*, the *reason*, and the *motive*; are all components of the actuality. And as there are equal and opposite reactions for the *material* part; the same will necessarily occur for the *immaterial* components.

It must also again be noted that according to Strong, the use of *lŏgŏs* can also refer to: "the Divine *Expression* (i.e. *Christ*)." Strong did not say *Jesus*; but rather: "i.e.," (Latin: *id est*), or "in other words:" "Christ." This "Divine Expression" (caps noted), thus does not likely refer to Jesus; who is *The* Christ (*the* Anointed One); but rather to *the* Christ or the Anointing itself; which of course refers to The *Holy Ghost* or Third part of the Trinity, and not to the *Son*, or Second part.

Thus this last part of the definition of *lŏgŏs*; the "Christ" or Holy Ghost part of *lŏgŏs*; seems to also describe a complete process such as: "Let there be light" and there was light. Again there are equal and opposite reactions as the result of the exercise of will.

Some of this "Word," (lŏgŏs), is contained in the Bible; most especially in The; (believed by many to be ten); Commandments. Some of this Word is in Science; some is in Mathematics; and some

Variations on the Planaō Theme

is found in Justice. In fact; wherever there is truth—therein is found the Word (lŏgŏs) of God.

Omniscience means that; among other things; there is nothing to learn. The enemy is not omniscient. [The temptation to state "in any way omniscient" is resisted here, as omniscience is a binary.] Ergo; the enemy can and does learn; and to do so "by observing" is common. When he encounters "judicial punishment" attacks via the "dirk or knife of the soul—which is 'the Word of God;'" he remembers to: "Be careful with that one. He's crazy. He 'knows what time it is,' and he fights back—and it hurts. I've still got the scars to prove it."

This will have a serious effect at the applied "voltage," forcing him to return at a more opportune time. It must be remembered that in order to *return*, he must first *depart*. . . shall we say *retreat*?

A sword in the material realm is an *offensive* weapon and can do some serious damage. If fact; to the extent that a sword can reach its target, there is almost no defense possible. The *defensive* trick is to consistently prevent contact from this weapon; or to *offensively* make certain the enemy *cannot* prevent contact from this *offensive* weapon; with the measure of success depending upon one's perspective.

The "the sword of the Spirit, which is God's Word," can be the *immaterial* equivalent of a sword in the material realm. It also can do serious damage; but serious damage in the immaterial realm, with corresponding results in the material. And that sword is based upon the Word of God.

All of these things currently under discussion represent *forces*. It is important to remember that these immaterial battles represent a battle, or battles of forces. The resultant actions both God and the enemy are attempting to achieve as illustrated on the left side of the "will intellect and emotions" diagram represent forces. All forces; whether material or immaterial; obey the very same rules—irrespective of mans *understanding* or even *knowledge* of the same.

When the enemy chooses to attack and does so, he has made a decision to impart a force or forces upon his victim. This force of his attack, or F_T, (as with tithing), is also calculated like many, if not all, immaterial forces, in that $F_T = F_A \times F_R$, meaning; that the enemy undertakes a specific action or F_A, with as specific reason or F_R, and the resultant force is F_T.

As in all forces, there are simultaneously created equal and opposite reactions; which when dealing with the *immaterial* realm, often initially are present as *potentials*; and these potentials are often referred to as *karma,* or if negative, "karmic debts."

> "...In an unrealistic "all other things being equal" sense, an immaterial *potential* energy or difference of potential *increase,* represents the *difference* between the existing level of "balance" *prior* to the introduction of the new stimulus; and the magnitude of the *total* imbalance, including that which was caused by said new stimulus.
>
> "With respect to the, (an), "insult" scenario; since no one is completely "balanced," *relative* degrees of imbalance must be utilized.
>
> "It is true that the level of any prior imbalance can disproportionately affect the increase in imbalance caused by a new stimulus; but that is "on the recipient." Meaning; that if it is true that "he's just crabby," or "she's just upset about something else;" disproportional increases in immaterial potential energy will exist, but not necessarily having been solely caused by that stimulus.
>
> "This Δ or change, (here increase), in *imbalance* from that level which existed prior to the new stimulus; represents the immaterial potential energy *increase* for that particular new stimulus. Thus the increase in "difference of potential," is this Δ for that particular new stimulus.
>
> $$IPE_T = IPE_O + IPE_S$$
>
> or
>
> $$IPE_S = IPE_T - IPE_O$$

"Here the total immaterial potential energy, (IPE_T); is equal to the *original* immaterial potential energy, (IPE_O); plus the additional imbalance created by the *new* stimulus, (IPE_S).

"Or; the increase in immaterial potential energy due to the stimulus, (IPE_S); is equal to the "post stimulus" total, (IPE_T), minus what was originally present prior to the new stimulus, (IPE_O).

"Just as there are virtually unlimited possibilities for this Δ, or increase in immaterial potential energy because of differences in the perceptions of people and situations; the same can be said for that which then becomes the *kinetic* energy (response).

"Thus the ultimate *balancing* of the increase in immaterial *potential* energy, is also subject to these same possibilities. What can and should be said however; is that the sane *objective* of any response should be *justice*, with the *goal* being *balance*..."[7.15]

"...One such "working model" from the *material* perspective, would be to establish one definition of *immaterial kinetic energy* as: "That which provides the means by which that which is in the *immaterial*, enters the *material*."

"*Bârâ*, or true creation, is one example of this, but there are others.

"Here "the thing" being "in motion," would not be with respect to *space* as is the case in the material realm; but rather would be "realm dependent."

"When that which is in the immaterial realm as a *potential*, enters the material; this is the *kinetics* or motion.

"Thus *immaterial kinetic*, is motion *between* the realms; i.e.; *immaterial* to *material*; rather than material kinetic motion *within* the *material* realm, as commonly understood..."[7.16] [Excerpts from: *"Inevitable Balance"* Reprinted by Permission]

Chapter 8

A Balancing Act

Romans 6:22-23 (KJV) tells us:

*"But now being made free from sin,
and become servants to God,
ye have your fruit unto holiness,
and the end everlasting life.
For the wages of sin is death;
but the gift of God is eternal life
through Jesus Christ our Lord."*[8.1]

With regard to the second verse, often; the word "penalty" is erroneously attributed to Paul, and not the word "wages;" thus making this "penalty of sin." Any such erroneous attribution, would of course change the meaning entirely.

The actual Greek word translated as "wages" is:

"3800 ŏpsōniŏn; neut. of a presumed der. of the same as 3795; *rations* for a soldier, i.e. (by extens.) his *stipend* or *pay*: - wages."[8.2]

"3795 ŏpsariŏn; neut. of a presumed der. of the base of 3702; a *relish* to other food (as if cooked *sauce*), i.e. (spec.) *fish* (presumably salted and dried as a condiment): - fish."[8.3]

Clearly there is an implication of the giving of what is *due* here, without regard to any type of penalty or reward; but rather *balance*. Wages or *ŏpsōniŏn* are paid as a matter of *entitlement*, and are required for that which has been performed. Wages usually represent something *positive* that benefits the worker, for his or her *previous* efforts that benefitted the person paying the wages.

However; in a sense, most criminal "penalties" also represent wages; but here in the *negative* sense. These criminal "wages" or *ŏpsōniŏn*, usually represent something *negative* that harms the "worker," for his or her *previous* act or acts of omission or commission, which resulted in *injury* to some party or parties. These are required in order to *balance* said act or acts of omission or commission, that resulted in injury to some party or parties.

Clearly when Paul uses that which is translated as *ŏpsōniŏn* with regard to *"sin,"* he is not referring to the former *positive ŏpsōniŏn*; but rather the latter *negative ŏpsōniŏn*, as contextually, said *ŏpsōniŏn* is "death."

It is also interesting that *ŏpsōniŏn*; according to Strong, refers to *soldiers*. This may be because again, according to the Father; (see Genesis 2:1 and elsewhere); all H. Sapiens are "hosts," (English), or "tsâbâ'," (Hebrew);" and thus were created and designed to engage in warfare; for redemption of something beyond themselves.

When the enemy chooses to attack us, this attack represents the creation of a force F_T; as well as the simultaneous creation of *potential* equal and opposite reactions, or *karma*. This represents *immaterial potential* energy. With respect to the forces being created and utilized by the enemy in an attack against us, these

A Balancing Act

karmic debts fall into two general categories: *intrinsic* and *extrinsic* battle karma.

Intrinsic battle karma, represents that which we "hosts" are permitted to do to, or extract from the enemy; in return for; and because of, and based upon, his *specific* attack upon us. It is *personal* and *event* specific.

Intrinsic battle karma is based more upon the "wickedness" of the act itself, more than it being *evil*; with *evil* again here meaning: *against the will of God*. The "wickedness" of the Crucifixion itself resulted in *intrinsic* battle karma—irrespective of this event being *consistent* with the will of God. And a fair read of the Scriptures indicates that the "payback," was immense.

Normally; if one person attacks another, the attacked person is generally permitted to attack in return; but that attack should be commensurate with the intensity or seriousness of the initial attack. If one is kicked in the shins, shooting in the head the person who did the kicking; is neither reasonable nor defensible. If this same attacker had presented and pointed a bazooka to the victim's head; then under these circumstances, killing the attacker in self-defense might be a justifiable response—perhaps even the only available response which includes the victim's survival.

But the enemy constantly and consistently seeks to destroy or "devour" us. Thus the *appearance* of his or its attacks can often be subterfuge. Given these facts, the value or quantity of the F_T of his attacks is always extremely high. This is because his *intentions* of *destruction*; e.g.; physical death, eternal separation, loss of our faith, etc. Ergo; the F_R, or the *reasons* for his actions are about as high they can get; even if the value of the F_A appears somewhat small. ("It was only a white lie." or: "That fruit over there will be good for you.")

It is clear from the meaning of the actual word erroneously translated here as "sword"—*machaira* and its roots; that that which is actually a *dirk* or *knife*, which is based upon the "Word of God;" is not what it may commonly be believed to be.

Most likely believe that this *machaira* represents something like reading Psalms to the devil, after he just attacked with everything he could muster.

Or perhaps something even more ridiculous such as: "Well, the Bible says I am supposed to suffer, so I guess it's alright." And it must be noted that it is *not* evident, that Jesus ever suggested that one do anything with a particular cheek when dealing *directly* with the enemy. That act of "mercy," is reserved for fellow, but *misguided*, hosts.

Would any person reasonably characterize any of these actions as fitting the literal definitions of *machaira*? It also must be remembered that *suffer* can also mean to permit or allow.

Here again is the actual Greek word translated as "sword."

> "3162 machaira; prob. fem. of a presumed der. of 3163; a *knife*, i.e. *dirk*; fig. *war*, judicial *punishment*: - sword."

As also stated here; again, another translation of *machaira* is "*judicial punishment.*" The "*judicial*" part of this definition fits with the concept of this *intrinsic* karmic debt. The "*punishment*" portion is another matter. This represents one possible purpose for the use of this *machaira* by hosts.

When Paul told us in Ephesians 6:12-17: "*For our struggle is not against flesh and blood, but against the rulers, against the powers, against the world forces of this darkness, against the spiritual forces of wickedness in the heavenly places;*" he was confirming *what* the battles actually are, and *where* the battles actually take place. Thus the true battle takes place in some part of the "*spiritual*" realm, or "*heavenly places*," in the aforementioned sense of non-material. There may or may not be components in the material realm, but the material realm is not the true battlefield. It is the F_R, or the *reason* component of any action that is the "nuke."

Extrinsic battle karma is the karmic debt the enemy incurs simply by attacking us.

Extrinsic battle karma is based more upon the "evilness" of the act, more than it being *wicked*; again with *evil* here meaning: *against the will of God*. The "evilness" of the enemy in Gethsemane when he attempted to get Jesus to *not* go through with Crucifixion itself resulted in *extrinsic* battle karma—as this event, (the Crucifixion), taking place was *consistent* with the will of God. And since the *intent* of the enemy was success, even though he failed; this *attempt* "counts" too.

Because the enemy chooses to "concoct" and enact an F_T with which to attack us, this very act alone; irrespective of *our* response; gives God license to do something about it. Because the enemy chose to treat God's children, (as soldiers or hosts), in this manner; and simply because of what we had to endure; this creates a karmic debt; a debt which God will collect in full; both to the detriment of the enemy, and to the benefit of His hosts.

Intrinsic and *extrinsic* battle karmas, can be considered as analogous to portions of our judicial system today:

Intrinsic battle karma is similar to our *civil* justice system. When the enemy attacks a specific child of God, this is similar to a citizen engaging in a specific "actionable" activity against another citizen, and causes him harm, (*nocere*). Here a private citizen will petition the courts for compensation due to the actual injuries caused him by another citizen. Again although a moving party is required here, it is the injured party and not the government that moves the civil case through the system. But unlike *criminal* penalties, it is the injured party who receives directly the just compensation due him or her.

Unlike a civil proceeding, in the case of *intrinsic* battle karma, again most of this process is unnecessary; as God knows the truth, and God decides the specific penalty; which again remains a karmic debt until it is paid. And also once again, since God has no need for the proceeds of this penalty, and since His desire is balance, the injured party is to be compensated by the enemy for the specific injuries he caused the individual or individuals.

Extrinsic battle karma is similar to our *criminal* justice system. When the enemy attacks a child of God, this is similar to a citizen engaging in *criminal* activity against another citizen. In our system of justice, the government takes upon the role of the injured party; and will ultimately extract penalties from the perpetrator, because of his or her actions or inactions against another citizen. If one injures an individual citizen or group of citizens; then one injures the entire society; and the government, acting on behalf of and with the consent of the governed, will extract a payment.

The purported purpose of any trial, is to arrive at the truth; and a group of citizens, (the jury), determine what is the truth, or are concerned with issues of *fact*. This same group will then decide if beyond a reasonable doubt, that this truth does or does not prove that the accused is guilty. If found guilty, then normally it is the judge; within previously agreed upon parameters; who will then decide what penalty is to be extracted from the guilty party, with said penalty representing, and continuing to represent a *debt* until it is paid.

One difference here is that in the *criminal* justice system; unlike *extrinsic* battle karma; this payment is extracted and or retained by the governing authority; and not generally distributed to the actual injured party. Penalties may include: monetary, incarceration; and/or removal of other previously existing rights previously enjoyed by the perpetrator.

However, *unlike* a criminal proceeding; in the case of *extrinsic* battle karma, most or all of this *trial* process is unnecessary; as God already knows the truth; and God decides the penalty; which again remains a karmic *debt* until it is paid. [One could fairly argue, that *a* penalty, (or *a reward*), is automatically chosen when the choice is made to commit the act. But "*a* penalty," and "*the* (actual) penalty," need not be the same.]

Since again God has no need for the proceeds of this penalty; and since his desire is balance; He will see to it that the suitable proceeds are *ultimately* distributed to the injured party; or to others He determines appropriate, to the benefit of the same. It is also a bit different as this process is a universal law, and thus *extrinsic* battle karma does not necessarily require a "moving party," (i.e.; a prosecutor), to agree to move the case forward, as is required in man's legal system.

There are potentially four interrelated karmic events being precipitated when the enemy attacks a child of God: Two forms or subcategories of *intrinsic* battle karma; and two forms or subcategories of *extrinsic* battle karma. Likely; the best way to describe these two subcategories would be as *compensatory* and *punitive*.

A Balancing Act

As an "earthly" example: While shopping in a convenience store, one is accosted by an individual brandishing a knife. Said individual demands the wallet of the shopper. Instead, the shopper breaks both of the arms of the perpetrator, and the *shopper* also sustains injuries in the process. There is no question as to the *facts* surrounding this event, as it is captured on video.

The shopper was entitled to protect himself, and thus the injuries sustained by the perpetrator were not only deserved; but were also necessary in order to stop the ongoing process. Thus the victim is and was entitled to inflict bodily harm upon the perpetrator, in order to protect himself from the actions of the same. This can be viewed as analogous to *punitive* intrinsic battle karma. It must be made clear, that the purpose of the actions of the victim must be for the purposes of self-defense, and not vengeance. If the actions of the victim far exceed those reasonably required in order to protect himself; then the victim may incur his or her own "negative" karma for that portion of his or her actions.

In addition, the victim would likely be entitled to compensation in civil court for the injuries he sustained while neutralizing the threats to his physical person. This can be viewed as analogous to *compensatory* intrinsic battle karma.

There are also similar "earthly" ramifications analogous to *extrinsic* battle karma; which is or are also the inescapable direct or indirect product or products of the perpetrator's actions.

Society will force the above perpetrator to pay this debt, via methods which will differ according to the mores of the specific culture. In the USA, there are prohibitions on what is considered "cruel and/or unusual punishment." But in other cultures, the perpetrator could easily face the precise level of physical harm, or even more; that the victim sustained or reasonably could have sustained, as well as other penalties. This is not to comment on the propriety or impropriety of any system of justice, but rather to show the similarities of man's judicial system, and *compensatory* extrinsic karmic debt.

Nevertheless, any incarceration, or the removal of previously enjoyed rights or privileges, is or are analogous to *punitive* extrinsic battle karma. Any fines levied against the perpetrator would be analogous to *compensatory* extrinsic battle karma. The proceeds of the same, are generally retained by the governmental authority on behalf of the entire society; as it is the society as a whole whom the government actually represents.

There is a key issue with respect to *compensatory intrinsic* battle karma. As in the case of a civil action, there must exist a moving party in order to extract payment for the *compensatory* portion of the *intrinsic* battle karma; and that moving party is the victim. But in order for the victim to obtain payment for this *compensatory intrinsic* battle karma, the victim must know of this *system*, and know that he or she is *entitled* to payment.

No entity is immune to the laws of physics, irrespective of the realm. When the enemy attacks, he begins the $F = MA$ process, and just as in tithing, the "Newtonian" rules apply. The karmic duality, (extrinsic and intrinsic), comes from the fact that we are both hosts and children of God; and thus when the enemy attempts to injure us, he is simultaneously attempting to injure God.

And just as also is the case in man's judicial system; failure in the injury attempt, does not negate the penalties for the attempt. In fact, some laws; such as those for mail fraud; often make no distinction between the penalties imposed for merely attempting, and those imposed for actually succeeding.

Thus each and every individual is entitled to specific compensation for acts committed, or attempted to be committed, against him by the enemy. The amount of said compensation is determined by God, but it is important that we understand the same rules of physics apply.

This may at first seem irrelevant, but it is not. God is omnipotent, but he also maintains balance. This is why there exists the mechanism of intercessory prayer. Simply because God wishes to do something and is perfectly capable of performance of the same; does not necessarily translate into God being able to perform this action and yet still maintain *balance*. Intercessory prayer is a means of providing a force or F_T, (amount of prayer multiplied by the reasons for the prayer), which, assuming the F_T is sufficient, then allow Him to maintain balance while granting the request; which is the MA.

A Balancing Act

When Satan went to God about Job, he essentially went there for *permission*. (see: *"MeekRaker Beginnings..., Chapter 9, Job's Predicament"*) Because of the negative forces that Job had created because of acting on his *fear*, there was a karmic debt incurred; for which Satan went to God for permission to "collect."

This is known, because when Satan went to God; he was complaining about the hedge God had around Job. Had the hedge already been sufficiently lowered automatically, then Satan would have just attacked Job; as it is likely that he did not enjoy going to God to ask for God's permission.

Thus as it reads, it seems that God was not going to lower this hedge around Job, unless and until He was requested to do so. This is neither the "common understanding," nor "common belief," (doxa), of what God said to Satan about Job. Most believe that God offered up Job to Satan, because the "modernized" translation, or perhaps better phrased; "modernized version" reads that way to many. However this is incorrect. God never offered Job to Satan; rather God essentially asked Satan: "Are you sure you want to do this?"

In order to keep balance, the same rule applies to *the*, or our, *compensatory* portion of intrinsic battle karma. We must know we are entitled to this compensation, and must request the same. Likely this was instituted to protect us in a sense, from the enemy being able to *automatically* collect because of the mistakes of the hosts. When hosts "mess up," we create these negative karmic forces, which then benefit the enemy to our detriment.

A word about here about "hedges:" When a child is born, there is a "hedge" around him as a matter of "entitlement" for protection. But as the child grows; this "hedge" remains at the same "height;" unless caused to grow by the young host or others. As the child becomes taller, unless this "hedge" likewise grows, there will be more exposure on unprotected areas.

For clarity, a quick recap seems reasonable:

The *extrinsic* karmas fall into both *punitive* and *compensatory* subcategories. These are determined and collected by God simply because the enemy attacked or attempted to attack a child of God. A good example of the collection of an extrinsic *punitive* battle karma, is or was what God did to Satan after the crucifixion. The majority of Satan's powers were taken from him because of his actions, which is probably best *euphemistically* described as being analogous to Satan's loss of some particular body part or parts—and this time it was not his "legs."

It is argued by some, that these powers, or at least a portion of them, may be returned to him temporarily during the "tribulation," for reasons not easily understood. However; even if so, he still lost the same from the crucifixion onward, until that time—assuming this particular position has merit.

The intrinsic battle karmas also fall into both *punitive* and *compensatory* subcategories. The *punitive* being damage that we are permitted to do to the enemy, and the *compensatory* being what we are entitled to; all because of the specific damage done or attempted to be done to us *specifically*; or because of what he has taken or tried to take from us *specifically*.

Back to *intercessory prayer*. From a *result* centered viewpoint, compensatory intrinsic battle karma can be a different form of exactly the same thing.

When we *sincerely* pray, we create an F_T, which at that time represents *potential* energy; creating an imbalance in the immaterial realm. This imbalance *must* be balanced. Thus, although we may or may not be granted our request, something *must* be done in order to restore balance. If the F_T is sufficient, and the object of our prayer is consistent with the will of God; then our request will be granted. This is why often many people will all pray for the same thing, as this can dramatically increase the magnitude of the F_T.

But even if the magnitude of the F_T is or was insufficient to warrant the specific request, or the request was not consistent with His will; nevertheless this imbalance must still be balanced. God must then do something which *is* consistent with His will; thereby transforming the potential energy into kinetic energy, and this is done according to $F = MA$.

We generally remain fixed upon our specific request, (M), being brought into the material realm, (A); and if after some unspecified period of time manifestation does not seem to have occurred, we

A Balancing Act

tend to believe that God did not and will not answer out prayer(s). The fact is that the F_T may have been insufficient; or the request may have been contrary to His will; or the request is in the *process* of being answered; or may have been answered, but not in any manner we were anticipating.

It is important to remember that there are essentially an infinite number of combinations of the magnitudes of M and A whose product will equal the F_T. This can range from a large mass with a slow acceleration, to a small mass with a large acceleration, or anywhere in between. Thus if it is a large request (M) and you want it faster (A fast acceleration); it would be wise to increase the magnitude of the F_T, with the easiest way being to get more people to pray.

Nevertheless, He *must* balance the F_T according to its magnitude and His will. Simply because we may be disappointed, and thus not *see* any relationship between our prayers and whatever he chooses; this does not mean that there was no restoration of balance, by the prayer being answered in some way or fashion.

But again, what does any of this have to do with intrinsic compensatory battle karma? The inescapable fact; is that when the enemy attacks a host, he creates a person specific imbalance in the *immaterial* realm, in addition to the other three imbalances. This imbalance is an F_T, just like the F_T created with intercessory prayer; but *negative* with respect to the enemy, which would be similar to a host stealing.

The magnitude of this force is of course equal to the product of: what *action* he undertook, and the *reasons* for which it was undertaken. Because he acted in a manner contrary to God's will, as well as contrary to his function by original design; this imbalance "licenses," if you will, God to do something in order to balance this imbalance, or negative F_T created by the enemy.

Thus, when the enemy attacks and creates this negative force with respect to God's or *His* will; the returned "opposite" reaction is negative with respect to the enemy or *his* will, which essentially by definition results in something that he will not like, and something from which his enemy (God and the hosts) will obtain equal benefit. This "equal benefit" will always be greater than the value of the original act alone, because of the multiplicative effect of the motive.

Chapter 9

Attack—Counterattack

When the intellect is cognizant of the word of God, and correctly utilizes this knowledge in the decision making process of the intellect; and then carries this decision through to fruition; a force is created. And this force can act as though it were a *material* offensive weapon thrust upon the enemy. This is the force represented by the line on the left side of the diagram.

This resultant force should always be "positive" in nature, but unfortunately it often is not. This is because often it is not the Word of God that is utilized; but rather the emotional or intellectual pressure or forces exerted by the *enemy*; forces that are often permitted by the host to interfere with the Word of God, and it is these that instead "guide" the decision making process. And unfortunately, there is often much assistance in this interference from many in the religious communities.

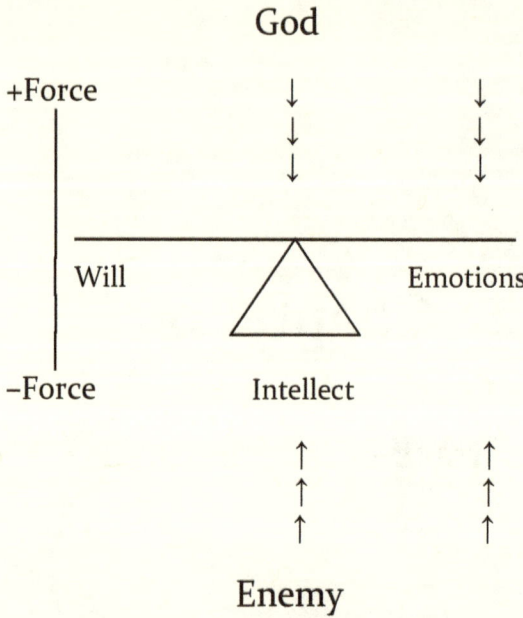

Either way, our action also represents an F_T, (where $F_T = F_A \times F_R$). And just like with any other force or action; there always occurs an equal and opposite reaction. It must be remembered here, that this "opposite" refers to the *direction*; with "opposite" meaning either from us or towards us, depending upon the direction of the original force.

With respect to *tithing*, the Bible is reasonably clear that we are all required to tithe ten percent of our increase; and a fair conclusion is that to do anything less is to "rob God," and thus ultimately "rob ourselves."

When it comes time to do this, (tithe), then here come the attacks of the enemy. What he is trying to accomplish with respect to tithing, is to manipulate one into choosing a course of action which results in either no tithe; a tithe less than the required amount; or a tithe with or for wicked or evil reasons.

Attack—Counterattack

This pressure will be emotional in nature, such as fear of the other bills one is required to pay. And the intellect will be attacked with untruths. This is all being done in an attempt to change the resultant force into the zero, or negative region of the diagram. He must get *us* to do it, because he simply does not have any way to accomplish this directly. Surely, he can create additional financial pressures, particularly through others; but he cannot choose that tithing action or force for us. He cannot "force the force," so to speak.

A fair analogy can be made here between the use of an old fashioned, (non-digital), thermostat with a heating system. These thermostats were relatively simple devices that required *no power* to function. They essentially consisted of a glass cylinder, with two wires inserted from one end of the cylinder; with these wires inside the cylinder not being connected to each other; and the other ends of these two wires were connected to the furnace, as an off and on switch. Inside the cylinder was also a small amount of (liquid) mercury. This cylinder was then mounted on a flat copper coil. As the temperature dropped, this copper band would contract and change the angle of the cylinder until the liquid mercury would roll down the inside of the cylinder to the two wires and complete the circuit. Once the circuit was completed, the furnace would come on.

The real power in this system is the furnace. The thermostat was a small simple and essentially *powerless* device; but nevertheless was able to cause or manipulate this powerful system into producing enough heat to heat an entire stadium, simply by the change of the angle of a small mercury switch.

The workings of the enemy are quite similar. When he or it is exerting forces on our emotions and intellect; these are essentially *powerless* forces with respect to our actions—unless we listen to them. When we do listen; as opposed to just hear; he is then able to change the angle of the line on diagram and manipulate our will; just like the thermostat connected to the furnace; into creating forces of his liking. But just like the old thermostat, he has no real power. It is the "hosts" who have the power. He knows this very well, but he hopes that the hosts never find this out.

His attacks are individually and tailor made. This is not because he can read our minds; and neither is this because he is omniscient; but rather, because he is an experienced and expert observer; and keeps amazing records on each of us. This individualized attack must be distinguished from his armaments. He is always spewing the same trash; he merely individualizes or personalizes the form that the trash takes on in order to maximize its efficacy.

So what we are instructed to do; is to put on all of the armor, resist the attack, extinguish the force of the arrows; and utilize the Word of God in the intellectual decision making process. This last action then creates a positive action or force, and to the enemy; this represents not the equivalent of a sword, but rather a *dirk* or a *knife*, because as previously stated, it is: "up close and personal."

2 Timothy 2:15 (KJV) tells us:

> *"Study to shew thyself approved unto God,*
> *a workman that needeth not to be ashamed,*
> *rightly dividing the word of truth."*[9.1]

The original Greek word translated as "rightly dividing" is:

> "3718 ŏrthŏtŏmĕō; from a comp. of 3717 and the base of 5114; to *make* a *straight cut*, i.e. (fig.) to *dissect* (*expound*) *correctly* (the divine message): - rightly divide."[9.2]

The reference to "straight cut" in *ŏrthŏtŏmĕō*, should not be overlooked with regard to the previous words: "normal," or "norm," and a "right angle;" when previously defining *paranormal*.

But there are actually two things going on with regard to "rightly dividing."

When the rocks *split* after the crucifixion, the actual word used there is the Greek word *schizo*.[9.3] This word means split, and is still used in today in terms such as schizophrenia.

Attack—Counterattack

Thus the *literal* definition of *ŏrthŏtŏmĕō* meaning to: "*make a straight cut*," would be similar to *schizo*; in that this is the act of merely separating. But is this the same as a *dividing* or *division*?

The *figurative* definition of *ŏrthŏtŏmĕō* is more than just the mere separating. Here in the *figurative* sense, there is also: "dissect (expound) correctly (the divine message)." Thus this implies a *purpose* to the "straight cut;" other than, and in addition to, the mere act of the separating.

If it can be stipulated that the word "division" is actually di-vision or *two visions*; or to "see two"—any etymological opinions to the contrary notwithstanding; then this actual *division* must occur *after* the splitting or making the "straight cut," as one cannot see the two resultant pieces until *after* they exist.

First the "straight cut" must be made; and then *two* are seen. The "straight cut" is the stimulus, or *cause*; and "seeing two" is the response, or *effect*.

> "In *deliberate* mancy, the active party is in search of something; e.g.; information; and deliberately undertakes some type of action (mancy), in furtherance of, and with the hope of, obtaining the same. This is usually *specific*, in the sense that something specific is desired. Many people will just randomly open a Bible to learn something about a particular problem currently in their lives. This is deliberate, and specific; i.e.; *deliberate specific mancy*. These are utilizing bibliomancy, but likely most do not realize this.
>
> "Other people will just randomly open a Bible to learn "something." This is deliberate, but not necessarily specific; i.e.; *deliberate non-specific mancy*. They are merely seeking "wisdom for the day." These are also utilizing bibliomancy, and also likely most do not realize this."[9.4]

Here the original Biblical text is that which is to be "divided." One of the "two seen" is just that; the original text. And the "other" that is seen, is that which is revealed to the "divider" who is endeavoring to *ŏrthŏtŏmĕō*, as per the instructions contained in 2 Timothy 2:15 above.

The Bible is the Word of God, and the Bible originally consisted entirely, (only), of the Word of God. But this is not necessarily a reversible statement, meaning: that the entire word of God is not necessarily contained in the Bible. The Bible is a book about redemption, and most "experts" agree with this. The problem is that most if not all do not understand what this actually means; but rather instead believe this refers exclusively to *man's* redemption.

This is being stated with the understanding that salvation was paid for; and thus in that sense is in fact *redemptive* in nature. But the redemption of the *earth* was necessary before man was even created, and then instructed by God to ""put the kibosh" on the earth in Genesis 1:28.

Thus the *primary* purpose of the Bible being redemptive in nature, however this is defined; it is necessarily and by design an *incomplete* version of the entire "Word of God;" as it is *redemption* that is the main concern.

This is an important concept, because the "Word of God" and "The Bible" are generally considered as synonymous. Whenever the: "Word of God" is seen, it is an automatic response to assume that this refers exclusively to the Bible; and many times this may in fact be an accurate assumption. However, to assume that if something is not contained in the Bible; then it cannot be the "Word of God;" is not only erroneous, but can also be quite dangerous.

It seems logical that God would also provide wisdom to His "other children;" here meaning people other than Hebrews/Jews, and subsequently to Christians—particularly if the reason for this "other wisdom," was for something "other than," redemption. This is likely why there exist some amazing parallels in other religions and cultures, (and even in some video games)—the fact that His word may have been adulterated by man over the centuries notwithstanding. And it is important to note that The Bible has also had its share of "modernizations."

Loosely speaking; today the term *"lŏgŏs"* generally refers to the *written* word of God; and is generally understood to mean the Bible.

Attack—Counterattack

The term *"rhēma"* today, or at least in this work; is meant to mean the *unwritten* or spoken "real time," word of God.

It is an undeniable fact that when one seeks wisdom via the *lŏgŏs*, that God will often provide wisdom via the *rhēma*. One may read a passage of the Bible that has been read many times, but God often will provide wisdom via *rhēma* to the reader at the same time or shortly thereafter.

This *wisdom* provided to the reader via *rhēma*, is wisdom that usually pertains to something that is going on, or something that *should* be going on in their lives; for which divine wisdom is necessary. "Wow! I must have read that passage 100 times and never saw that before." is not an uncommon response to this type of revelation.

As previously stated, the actual word in Ephesians 6:17; " *the sword of the Spirit, which is the word of God;*" which is translated as "word of God" is this: "4487 rhēma from 4483: an utterance (individ., collect. or spec.); by impl. a matter or topic (espec. of narration, command or dispute); ..."

The key here is emphasis upon the unwritten or *"utterance"* or *"narration"* means of obtaining the word of God. If one is "rightly dividing," or *ŏrthŏtŏmĕō* the *lŏgŏs*, (here first seeing only the one); one will then receive *rhēma*; and will now "see two;" the original *general lŏgŏs*, and now also the *specific* and *personal rhēma*.

Proverbs 2:6 (NAS) tells us:

> *"For the* LORD *gives wisdom;*
> *From His mouth come*
> *knowledge and understanding."*[9.5]

Note that the tense here is *present* tense. It does not state that the Lord *gave* wisdom. It does not state that knowledge and understanding *came* out of His mouth, as would necessarily be the case with His *lŏgŏs* or written word; e.g.; The Bible.

But this is not to say that writers such as Moses, did not also experience "real time" *rhēma* while writing the various portions of the scriptures. In fact since Moses was not present or even alive at the time of early Genesis, it likely was *rhēma* in furtherance of the *retrophesy* contained therein.

Neither does Proverbs 2:6 in any way refer to or in any way state, that there is anything wrong with obtaining knowledge and understanding from *lŏgŏs*, or what others wrote in the past.

Proverbs 2:6 essentially has nothing to do with the *lŏgŏs*, but is strictly concerned with the *rhēma*; or the uttered or narrated form of God's word. It is concerned with the provision of *wisdom*; which is often described as "knowledge plus understanding"; provided in "real time," as it *is* in the *present* tense.

And we are also told the source of this narrated or uttered wisdom. It is from the *mouth* of God. There is no suggestion in this particular passage, of any intermediaries, such as *prophets*. Again this is not to in any way to suggest that wisdom cannot or should not be obtained via the writings of the prophets, it is just that this passage is not concerned with that particular source of wisdom.

At this juncture, a distinction should be made between "head voices," and "room voices;" (authors' terminology).

"*Room voices*" are just that. They are voices one hears as though said voices are actually in the room, often including from a specific identifiable direction within the room. Generally today; although certainly not always; unattributable *room* voices are usually not the voice of God.

There are likely at least three reasons for this:

Firstly, God speaking in a "room voice" would likely result in some type of material manifestation beyond his voice. [What if God simply said: "Let there be...!"? Wait—He already did!]

Secondly, *rhēma* is generally provided in a *timeless* manner—meaning that this *rhēma* is provided instantaneously from the immaterial realm. Certainly it may take prolonged periods of time for us to absorb or to make sense out of this wisdom; but this is due to our limitations, and not the means of provision.

And thirdly, God does not generally use "room voices," simply because He does not have to.

Attack—Counterattack

But *"head voices"* are another matter. These may be similar to recollecting speech from the past; but here these cannot be attributed to anything in the past that can or could possibly be recollected. And sometimes, these can even take the form of a substantial rebuke.

Unfortunately, the enemy will also use this technique. This is very often utilized in his thoughts ideas and suggestions attacks. How does one tell the difference? Does what the voice is telling you sound like God? Not necessarily the *voice* itself, but rather the *content*. Would God give you that suggestion when He knows you are married? Do you honestly believe that you are entitled to any portion of that person's wealth because "he already has enough;" or "because he won't even miss it?"

The enemy will introduce this garbage from *without*; and then, even if, or perhaps *especially* if, you reject it; he will then try to make one think it came from *within*, and then try and make one feel guilty about it. This way, he or it can win no matter what happens—*as long* as *it is believed that the source was from within.*

"I cannot believe that that thought was in, or even entered my mind." The *first* part of this statement is literally correct, as "that thought" initially was never in the mind; but was *brought* into the mind. And thus the *source* of "that thought" resided nowhere "within." And the second part of this statement shows how "sneaky" these tailor made attacks can be.

There is no one in the room, no one even in earshot, and perhaps no one around for miles; and yet one must ask, perhaps even out loud: Who am I arguing with? Or perhaps: "Yeah, who does he thing he is?" Note the "yeah," as if in *agreement*.

If any of this sounds familiar, then you are familiar with the enemy's "head voices." The purpose of these, is to influence the intellect "triangle," by presenting falsehood as truthful information to then be utilized in the decision making process. These will also act to augment the emotional pressures the enemy is sending to us, (right side of the diagram), in order to get us to act in the manner in which he wishes; after all he cannot force us to do anything. It must be remembered, that it is believed that *functionally*, the enemy originally was an angel or messenger (*aggĕlŏs,*); and as "messengers" angels are supposed to work *for* us.

The enemy's attacks will generally be both *long term* and *progressive* in nature. First he gets the "conversation" going; perhaps with something seemingly innocent, (good fruit over there); but in a *progressive* manner, he will eventually get around to what it is he is actually after. By doing it this way, he hopes only the *interval* and not the *absolute* will draw any degree of attention from the host; or likely in his or its view: "the mark."

This is exemplified by stealing. After all, "It's only a dollar." So one goes from not stealing at all, to stealing one dollar; this being a one dollar interval. Stealing a dollar now becomes the norm, so when it now becomes two dollars, it is the same one dollar interval increase. In a relatively short time, one could easily find himself seriously planning to steal credit card information, without even knowing how they got to that point. [Political *progressives* utilize the very same tactic, as progressivism is not known as such because of any particular *ideology*, but rather as a *tactic* or a *strategy*.]

But when it is *God*, it is more like flash. Again, it may take a while to sort it all out; but the actual transference of the knowledge and wisdom is done very quickly. Perhaps He does this with speed, like the languages utilized in "speaking in tongues," in order to confound the enemy. But more likely since it is *immaterial* to *immaterial*, and consistent with man's *design*; there is no time necessary, present, or even possible.

There is also the matter of *listening*. As previously addressed, most people will clear their minds when they pray; and then at the conclusion of the prayer will allow their minds to become refilled with their problems; and then simply not understanding why God: "never answers them."

Two questions of course arise: Firstly, how would you know if He did answer, as no room has been left in the consciousness to hear His answer? And secondly, why should He compete for someone's consciousness—someone who just told Him how much they trusted Him?

There is also something to be said about returning or repeating God's word back to him.

Proverbs 22:21 (NAS) tells us:

> *"To make you know the certainty
> of the words of truth
> That you may correctly
> answer him who sent you?"*[9.6]

Although it is not generally thought about in quite this way; as previously alluded to, it can also be said that most if not all knowledge, (if it *is* knowledge and not merely "a truth" by consensus); also came and comes from God. This includes mathematics and science, (the word "science" usually defined as "to know"); as well as just about any and all other fields of actual knowledge.

The essence or force emanated by God, which brought into material manifestation His will to create *materiality*, is often referred to as "spirit." It is often stated that "God is a Spirit." The name of the Third Part of the Trinity was changed from Holy Ghost to Holy Spirit. "Spirit" is derived from Latin *spiritus*, roughly meaning "breath or breath-like"—here essentially meaning *immaterial*. Thus *anything* immaterial in nature; could be described as *spiritual*, at least in this sense.

Back in chapter one, it was stated: "It is not necessarily a problem when using incorrect terminology, as long as the incorrect terminology does *not* represent something else."

Thus one should be quite careful to be sure that not only that: "one knows what he is talking about;" but also that: "one knows what *it is*, that he is talking about."

The *first* refers to correctly ascribing attributes to "a thing" under discussion, when the "thing" under discussion is clearly known. The *second* refers not to knowledge regarding the *attributes* of "a thing;" but rather knowledge of what the "thing" itself under discussion in fact is. It is at best pointless to ascribe attributes to a thing, when the knowledge of what that thing in fact is, is incorrect.

John 4:24 (KJV) tells us:

> *"God is a Spirit: and they that worship him must worship him in spirit and in truth."*[9.7]

The original Greek word translated as "spirit" here both times is the previously referenced:

> 4151 pnĕuma, from 4154; a *current* of air, i.e. *breath* (*blast*) or a *breeze*; by anal. or fig. a *spirit*, i.e. (human) the rational *soul*, (by impl.) *vital principle*, mental *disposition*, etc., or (superhuman) an *angel*, *demon*, or (divine) *God*, Christ's *spirit*, the Holy *Spirit*: - ghost, life, spirit (-ual - ually), mind. Comp. 5590."[9.8]

The original Greek word translated as "truth" here is:

> "225 alēthĕia; from 227; *truth*: - true, x truly, truth verity."[9.9]

> "227 alēthēs; from *1* (as a neg. particle) and *2990*; *true* (as *not concealing*): - true, truly, truth."[9.10]

> "2990 lanthanō; a prol. form of a prim. verb, which is used only as an alt. in certain tenses; to *lie hid* (lit. or fig.); often used adv. *unwittingly*: - be hid, be ignorant of, unawares."[9.11]

Thus here "God is a *pnĕuma*, ("rational *soul*,"); and they that worship him must worship him in *pnĕuma*, ("rational *soul*,"); and in *alēthĕia* or truth;" with the understanding that here *"truth"* etymologically refers to not *hiding* anything. Thus "the truth," and not "a truth;" or perhaps better stated: "the whole truth," is what is required. Thus translating *pnĕuma* as *"spirit"* instead of "soul," opens up the door to much confusion about these instructions.

Luke 23:46 (KJV) tells us:

Attack—Counterattack

> *"And when Jesus had cried with a loud voice,*
> *he said, Father, into thy hands I commend my spirit:*
> *and having said thus, he gave up the ghost."*[9.12]

Here the actual Greek word translated as "spirit" is 4151 *pněuma*.[9.13]

And the actual Greek word translated as "ghost" is:

> "1606 ěkpněō; from 1537 and 4154; to *expire*; - give up the ghost."[9.14]

> "1537 ěk, or ěx; a prim. prep. denoting *origin* (the point *whence* motion or action proceeds)..."[9.15]

> "4154 pněō; a prim. word; to *breath* hard, i.e. *breeze*: - blow comp..."[9.16]

So what it was that Jesus "*commended*," (not *commanded*), into the Father's hands was his *pněuma*—but here is translated as "*spirit*," and is not translated as *ghost*.

But what He *then* actually "*gave up*," or *ěk*; was His *pněō*, (translated here as "*ghost*"); which is the root of *pněuma*, (translated earlier in this same sentence as "spirit"); with the *ěk* or *ěx*, as the "*gave up*" or "denoting *origin* (the point *whence* motion or action proceeds)" prefix added to *pněō*.

Again: "It is not necessarily a problem when using incorrect terminology, as long as the incorrect terminology does *not* represent something else."

And as was the case when the Bible tells us *strait*, and most believe the word is *straight*; here the Bible tells us *commend*, and most believe the word is *command*—but at least the *translation* is "*commend*" in this version.

Thus Jesus did not *command* his *pněuma*, as many believe; but rather *commend*(ed) his *pněuma*.

The original Greek word translated here as "commend" is:

"3908 paratithēmi; from 3844 and 5087; to place alongside, i.e. present (food, truth); by impl. to deposit (as a trust or for protection)..."[9.17]

The use of *paratithēmi* translated here as "*commend*," requires a *destination* of some sort, in this case: The Father's "*hands.*" [The appearance of *para* as the prefix for a word *in-toto* meaning: "to place alongside," should not be overlooked.]

The actual Greek word translated as "hands" is:

"5495 chĕir; perh. from the base of 5494 in the sense of its congener the base of 5490 (through the idea of *hollowness* for grasping); the *hand* (lit. or fig. [*power*]; espec. [by Heb.] a *means* or *instrument*]: - hand."[9.18]

What is easy to miss, is that this is or was a two-step process. This is known because we are told: "*having said thus.*"

First was the "*commend*" or *paratithēmi* of the *pnĕuma*, (with the root of *pnĕuma* being *pnĕō*, but *pnĕuma* nevertheless is translated here as "*spirit*"); and *then*, "*having said thus*;" and He then "*gave up*," (ĕk or ĕx), what is translated here as: "*the ghost*" (pnĕō). This is important because it proves volition and/or the ability of Jesus to willfully *paratithēmi*, and then *ĕkpnĕō* His *pnĕuma*.

Jesus did not *lose* his *pnĕuma* because of the physical damage done to His body. Rather He *willfully* placed, ("*gave up*"), his *pnĕuma* into the Father's hands. Usually death is when the physical body can no longer contain the *pnĕuma*, and it is released. But in the case of Jesus, He *willed* the process. Ergo; Jesus was neither killed, nor murdered.

This word, *pnĕuma*, appeared previously; particularly when determining the actual meaning of *zōē*, in terms of that "lifetime" which will be "wasted, ruined, or lost;" but not totally destroyed. And the following words also appeared in this previous analysis of *zōē*:

> "2222 zōē; from 2198; *life* (lit. or fig.): - life (-time). Comp. 5590."
>
> "2198 zaō; a prim. verb; to *live* (lit. or fig.): - life (-time), (a-) live (-ly), quick."
>
> "5590 psuchē; from 5594; *breath*, i.e. (by impl.) *spirit*, abstr. or concr. (the *animal* sentient principle only; thus distinguished on the one hand from 4151, which is the rational and immortal *soul*; and on the other from 2222 which is mere *vitality*, even of plants: these terms thus exactly correspond respectively to the Heb. 5315, 7307 and 2416): - heart (+- ily), life, mind, soul, + us, + you."

By the inclusion of: "thus distinguished on the one hand from *4151*, which is the rational and immortal *soul*" [4151 pněuma, from 4154; a *current* of air, i.e. *breath* (*blast*) or a *breeze*; by anal. or fig. a *spirit*, i.e. (human) the rational *soul*], in the above definition of *psuchē*; it can be seen that 4151 *pněuma*, is in fact this: "rational and immortal *soul*," and should be translated as such, and not as "spirit."

Thus again with regard to the previous John 4;24 which reads: "*God is a Spirit: and they that worship him must worship him in spirit and in truth*;" it should read: "God is a "rational and immortal *soul*:" and they that worship him must worship him in the "rational and immortal *soul*" and in complete, (nothing hidden),truth."

With regard to the *Old Testament*, according to Strong, there are in fact only three words in original *Old Testament* Hebrew translated as "spirit,"[9.19] with one caveat:

The *first* is the most common:

> "7307 rûwach; from 7306; *wind*; by resemblance *breath*, i.e. a sensible (or even violent) exhalation; fig. *life, anger, unsubstantiality*; by extens. a *region* of the sky; by resemblance *spirit*, but only of a rational being (includ. its expression and functions..."[9.20]

Here is seen the confirmation of "spirit" as immaterial-like or "unsubstantiality," or having "no substance."

The *root* of *rûwach* (7307) is:

> "7306 rûwach; a prim. root; prop. to *blow*, i.e. *breathe*; only (lit.) to *smell* or (by impl. *perceive* (fig. to *anticipate, enjoy*): - accept, smell, x touch, make of quick understanding."[9.21]

Despite *rûwach* as *7306* being the root of *rûwach* as *7307*; as can be seen, *rûwach* as *7306*, is not translated as "*spirit*" *anywhere in the entire Bible*, but rather translated, (the words appearing after the : -), only as: "accept, smell, x touch, make of quick understanding."

And it must be noted that there is yet another rûwach, which is the *Chaldean* form of rûwach.

> "7308 rûwach (Chald.); corresp. to 7307: - mind, spirit, wind."[9.22]

The first appearance of *rûwach* (as 7307) is in Genesis 1:2 (KJV):[9.23]

> *"And the earth was without form, and void;*
> *and darkness was upon the face of the deep.*
> *And the Spirit of God moved*
> *upon the face of the waters."*[9.24]

The only appearance of the Chaldean *rûwach* (as 7308) is in Daniel 4:8 (KJV):[9.25]

> *"But at the last Daniel came in before me,*
> *whose name was Belteshazzar,*
> *according to the name of my God,*
> *and in whom is the spirit of the holy gods:*

and before him I told the dream, saying..."[9.26]

The *second* Hebrew word translated as "spirit," appearing as "familiar spirit" is:

> "178 'ŏwb; from the same as 1 (appar. through the idea of *prattling* a father's name); prop. a *mumble*, i.e. a *water-skin* (from its hollow sound); hence a *necromancer* (ventriloquist, as from a jar: - bottle, familiar spirit."[9.27]

And the *third* Hebrew word *translated* as "spirit" is:

> "5397 nᵉshâmâh; fr. 5395; a *puff*, i.e. *wind*, angry or vital *breath*, divine *inspiration*, *intellect*, or (concr.) an *animal*: -blast, (that) breath (-eth), inspiration, soul, spirit."[9.28]

When it comes to any original *Greek* words translated as "soul" in the *New Testament*, there is only one,[9.29] and that is the previously discussed:

> "5590 psuchē; from 5594; *breath*, i.e. (by impl.) *spirit*, abstr. or concr. (the *animal* sentient principle only; thus distinguished on the one hand from *4151*, which is the rational and immortal *soul*; and on the other from *2222* which is mere *vitality*, even of plants: these terms thus exactly correspond respectively to the Heb. 5315, 7307 and 2416): - heart (+- ily), life, mind, soul, + us, + you."[9.30]

It is interesting, that contained in the very *definition* of the *only* Greek word translated as *soul*, (psuchē), in the entire New Testament; is the fact that this word, uniquely *translated* in the New Testament as *"soul,"* (psuchē), nevertheless in fact does *not* mean: "the rational and immortal *soul*"—as confirmed here in the very definition of *psuchē*.

Rather it is "the *animal* sentient principle only" to which *psuchē*, the only word in the New Testament translated as "soul," actually refers.

When it comes to original *Hebrew* words translated as "soul," and "souls" in the *Old Testament*; with only two exceptions,[9.31] the word is:

> "5315 nephesh; from 5314 prop. a *breathing* creature, i.e. *animal* or (abstr.) vitality; used very widely in lit., accommodated or fig. sense (bodily or mental)..."[9.32]

But even this may not be as simple as it may seem.
In Genesis 2:7 (KJV) we are told:

> *"And the Lord God formed man*
> *of the dust of the ground,*
> *and breathed into his nostrils the breath of life;*
> *and man became a living soul."*[9.33]

Here the actual Hebrew word translated as "soul," is the above *nephesh*.[9.34]

Here the actual Hebrew word translated here as "living" is:

> "2416 chay; from 2421 *alive*; hence *raw* (flesh); *fresh* (plant, water, year) *strong*; also (as noun, espec. in the fem. sing. and masc. plur.) *life* (or living thing), whether lit.or fig..."[9.35]

Thus we seem to have a *chay*, or "alive;" and a *nephesh*, or "breathing creature"—an "alive breathing creature."

It also seems that with *nephesh* literally defined as a "breathing creature," *nephesh* alone better represents the *physically alive* state of body and soul connection; rather than that immaterial portion alone, (soul); whether it is contained in the physically alive body or

Attack—Counterattack

not. This is despite the fact that the translations of "soul," and "souls" in the *Old Testament* is *nephesh*, with only two exceptions.

That "breath" that is "breathed into his nostrils" is:

> 5397 n^{e}shâmâh; fr. 5395; a *puff*, i.e. *wind*, angry or vital *breath*, divine *inspiration*, *intellect*, or (concr.) an *animal*: - blast, (that) breath (-eth), inspiration, soul, spirit."[9.36]

Here *n^{e}shâmâh*; previously being one of the three Hebrew words translated as "spirit;" is translated as *"breath;"* with the *"of life"* description or qualifier being the above *chay*.[9.37]

The *first* exception to the translation of "soul" being *nephesh* is in Job 30:15 (KJV):

> *"Terrors are turned upon me:*
> *they pursue my soul as the wind:*
> *and my welfare passeth away as a cloud."*[9.38]

The original Hebrew word translated here in Job 30:15 as "soul" is:

> "5082 n^{e}dîybâh; fem. of 5081; prop. nobility, i.e. reputation: - soul."[9.39]

As can be easily seen, the correct translation of n^{e}dîybâh should be "nobility" or "reputation;" and not "*soul.*"

The *second* exception for the translation as "soul" being *nephesh* is in Isaiah 57:16 (KJV):

> *"For I will not contend for ever,*
> *neither will I be always wroth:*
> *for the spirit should fail before me,*
> *and the souls which I have made."*[9.40]

The original Hebrew word translated here in Isaiah 57:16 as "soul" is the previous:

> "5397 nᵉshâmâh; fr. 5395; a *puff*, i.e. *wind*, angry or vital *breath*, divine *inspiration*, *intellect*, or (concr.) an *animal*: - blast, (that) breath (-eth), inspiration, soul, spirit."[9.41]

If *nᵉshâmâh* sounds familiar, this is because *nᵉshâmâh* was listed above as the *third* Hebrew word *translated* as "spirit;" and then seen in Genesis 2:7 with "Adam," there *translated* as "breath," (but not "breath of life" absent the *chay* qualifier); but here in Isaiah 57:16 *nᵉshâmâh* is *translated* as "soul."

1 Corinthians 14:33 (KJV) tells us:

> *"For God is not the author of*
> *confusion, but of peace,*
> *as in all churches of the saints."*[9.42]

The most common original Greek word translated as "resurrection" in the New Testament[9.43] is:

> "386 anastasis; from *450*; a *standing up* again, i.e. (lit.) a *resurrection* from death. . ."[9.44]

According to Strong, the word "reincarnation" does not appear in the King James Bible, as it is not listed anywhere in Strong's Concordance. As can be seen in the above definition of *anastasis*, it is: "(lit.) a *resurrection* from death," and not *reincarnation* that represents this "standing up again."

But in fact technically, *anastasis* could represent either. This is not necessarily a problem when it is contextually clear that the event must be a *resurrection*, as in the case with Lazarus. But when

Paul is speaking of what He believes as a "Pharisee," translating *anastasis* only as "resurrection," is at best misleading.

This misrepresentation then necessarily causes gross inconsistencies when analyzing the matter of John the Baptist and Elijah—no matter what one believes represents the truth with regard to *reincarnation*.

But since the Bible translators believe that they know or knew the mind of God so well; there could not possibly be any reason whatsoever to translate *anastasis* as anything other than *resurrection* at any time, or for any reason—even *hypothetically*, and solely for the purpose of argument.

In furtherance of understanding precisely what it is that is under discussion; prudence requires that some terms be defined, as used in this endeavor:

- "actuality" is "what a thing is or is not" irrespective of any reality of the same
- "alive" in the *general* sense, refers to a *connection*, or connected
- "body" or "soma" refers to that *material* or *physical* part of man; i.e.; the physical structure which is designed to contain the immaterial part of man
- "dead" in the *general* sense refers to a *disconnection*, or disconnected
- "death" is roughly synonymous with "dead," but refers to the *event* of disconnection, rather than that *general state* where there is no connection—"death" is when this disconnection occurs; and "dead" is the state after this occurrence
- "life" or "living" is reasonably synonymous with "alive," and thus also refers to that *general* state where there is some type of connection
- "physical death" refers to that state where the immaterial part of man (soul), is no longer connected to the material part of man (body)
- "physical life" is that condition where the immaterial part of man (soul) is connected to the material part (body)

- "reality" is that belief or "understanding" of "what a thing is or is not," and is based upon some level of *perception*
- "soul" refers to that *immaterial* part of man, often inadequately described as "will, intellect and emotions"
- "spiritual" can refer to a myriad of immaterial or "breath like" entities
- "spiritual death" refers to that state where the immaterial part of man (soul) is disconnected from its original source
- "spiritual life" refers to that state where the immaterial part of man (soul) is connected to its original source

As stated, when Paul speaks of the "Sword of the Spirit, the actual Greek word which is translated as "sword" is *machaira*; "a *knife*, i.e. *dirk*; fig. *war*, judicial *punishment*;" and that which is translated as "Spirit" is *pněuma*, better translated as "soul." Thus "knife or dirk of the soul" is the more correct translation.

These are important distinctions, because as also stated, a knife or dirk is for "close up and personal" weapon in furtherance of "judicial punishment," as included figuratively in the definition of *machaira*. And a "soul" is an individual entity, with likely no two being identical.

This means that this "knife," or "dirk;" is unique for each individual; i.e.; no two "dirks or knives" are identical, but rather each is custom designed for each individual.

Where can these weapons be found? They are on the other side of that narrow door that *"few find."* There is a unique door for each person; and is one that can only be opened by that person. And on the other side of that door lie these custom made weapons for "up close and personal" battle. This is why the *path* to this door is so crowded.

Battle usually has both defensive and offensive "sources and methods." Most "hosts" have some working knowledge of the *defensive* measures; measures such as the "armor," "resistance" etc.; but the idea of going on the *offensive* against the enemy is generally a foreign concept to most; unless it is based in anger or hatred—which of course tends to play into the enemy's strong suit.

Attack—Counterattack

Why? It is because of the negative nature of the F_T, when the F_R is based upon hatred or anger; and that is precisely what the enemy is after in the first place.

Most hosts spend their time quenching arrows, (or *trying* to quench arrows); and *resisting*—actually believing that this is the war, and it is *they* who are the main objective. Perhaps this is a bit narcissistic; but nevertheless this is so. If they could just win these personal battles, then God would be pleased with them.

However, since we are all made in the image and likeness of God; Who is perfect; this "success" then would merely represent a return to the "starting line." It simply doesn't seem to make very much sense for God to send us here as hosts in His "image and likeness;" and then for *success* to consist of merely becoming as unadulterated as possible before returning to him; and absent salvation, we cannot even return at all.

Others believe that despite being told the contrary by Paul, the war actually consists of battles against "flesh and blood." This meaning; that it is the fellow hosts who are the problem. Any of those "other" hosts who are wrong; either because they made a mistake, or they do not agree with their accuser; are "the enemy." "I am glad that I am not a sinner like that tax collector over there."

One finds himself commenting about the speck in their neighbor's eye, and is totally unaware of the railroad ties sticking out of theirs. There must be another word to describe this type of battle or struggle with other individuals; individuals who disagree with or are not as perfect as the accuser.

Each of these viewpoints is a prideful and self-centered diversion. This is not to say that one should not fight the personal battles within them, as they should. In fact, many Muslim scholars believe that this inner battle is precisely the original meaning of *jihad*. Neither should one refrain from helping others who are in need or in error; but neither is this the war that the hosts are supposed to be fighting.

The actual war is as Paul describes it: not against flesh and blood, but against powers and forces. This war is not against the *material*, but against the *immaterial*. Defensive measures are necessary and fine; but one cannot win this war, or any war, without going on the *offense*.

How does one win a war against that which is *immaterial*, by utilizing weapons that are available in the *material*? The answer is that one does not.

Immaterial offensive weaponry is required; and although many already have some immaterial offensive weapons, the problem is that generally these are *non-nuclear*.

John 14:12 (KJV) tells us:

> *Verily, verily, I say unto you,*
> *He that believeth on me,*
> *the works that I do shall he do also;*
> *and greater works than these shall he do;*
> *because I go unto my Father."*[9.45]

Chapter 10

True Talent

Some consider *electricity* and *magnetism* to be entirely *separate*, and entirely *distinct* entities. From this viewpoint, we have electricity and we have magnetism; and although they can be related, they are not the same thing.

Others believe that the "true actuality," is *electromagnetism*; of which electricity and magnetism are two manifestations or, subsets of one phenomenon.

"Radio waves" are in fact electromagnetic phenomena, with both electric and magnetic components. In fact, antennas exist that are purportedly capable of filtering out the *electrical* component of the wave, leaving only the *magnetic* portion; from which the contents of the signal can be derived. Why is this necessary? It is necessary because most of the interference caused by man is *electrical* in nature. This man made noise or "QRM," increases every year, and renders many frequencies noisy, and often unusable.

When electricity flows, there is a magnetic field created around the conductor. If another conductor enters this field, an electrical current will be produced in this second conductor, and this current will be opposite of the original current—lest the universe explode (again). But this will happen only when there is *movement*. The conductor simply *remaining* in a direct current produced field, will produce no additional electricity.

One can move the *conductor* in and out of the magnetic field as in the case of a generator; or utilize *alternating* current where the electricity and thus the magnetic field changes; but in either case, in order to obtain *manifestation*, there must be *movement*.

Likewise, man can be a conductor of that in the *immaterial* which he is designed to conduct; and is readily available for the express purpose of empowering him. And here it seems that this is likewise of little or no value, without *movement*.

In Matthew 25:14-30, we are told the famous parable of the *talents*. We know that this is a *parable* and not an actual *story*; because generally when Jesus told parables, no proper names were used. When it is a story, a recollection of actual events; usually proper names were used.

It must be noted that in Luke 19:12-27 there exists a similar parable. These two parables can easily be conflated, but there are very significant differences between them. Because of these differences, it seems unlikely that Matthew and Luke are merely have differing accounts of the same event; but rather that only one account is correct—that of course being the one that makes the most sense.

In order to maintain intellectual honesty, this parable is first presented here in its entirety.

Following is Matthew 25:14-30 (NAS):

> *"For it is just like a man about to go on a journey,*
> *who called his own slaves*
> *and entrusted his possessions to them.*
>
> *To one he gave five talents,*
> *to another, two, and to another,*
> *one, each according to his own ability;*
> *and he went on his journey.*

True Talent

*Immediately the one who had received the five
talents went and traded with them,
and gained five more talents.*

*In the same manner the one who had
received the two talents gained two more.*

*But he who received the one talent went away,
and dug a hole in the ground
and hid his master's money.*

*Now after a long time the master of those slaves
came and settled accounts with them.*

*The one who had received the five talents
came up and brought five more talents,
saying, 'Master, you entrusted five talents to me.
See, I have gained five more talents.'*

*His master said to him, 'Well done,
good and faithful slave.
You were faithful with a few things,
I will put you in charge of many things;
enter into the joy of your master.'*

*Also the one who had received the
two talents came up and said,
'Master, you entrusted two talents to me.
See, I have gained two more talents.'*

*His master said to him, 'Well done,
good and faithful slave.
You were faithful with a few things,
I will put you in charge of many things;
enter into the joy of your master.'*

*And the one also who had received the
one talent came up and said,
'Master, I knew you to be a hard man,*

> *reaping where you did not sow and*
> *gathering where you scattered no seed.*
>
> *'And I was afraid, and went away and*
> *hid your talent in the ground.*
> *See, you have what is yours.'*
>
> *But his master answered and said to him,*
> *'You wicked, lazy slave, you knew*
> *that I reap where I did not sow and*
> *gather where I scattered no seed.*
>
> *'Then you ought to have put my money*
> *in the bank, and on my arrival*
> *I would have received my money back*
> *with interest.*
>
> *Therefore take away the talent*
> *from him, and give it to the one*
> *who has the ten talents.'*
>
> *For to everyone who has,*
> *more shall be given,*
> *and he will have an abundance;*
> *but from the one who does not have,*
> *even what he does have shall be taken away.*
>
> *Throw out the worthless slave into the*
> *outer darkness; in that place there will*
> *be weeping and gnashing of teeth."*[10.1]

The way it reads, this slave master decides to go on a journey. So before he leaves, he calls his three slaves in for a meeting, and distributes all of his possessions to these three. It doesn't actually say *all*, but that is a fair read. He gives them these *talents* according to their *ability*. Likely the *head* slave got five, the *middle* slave two, and the *apprentice* slave one.

True Talent

He then gives no instructions whatsoever as to what should be done with these possessions. Neither does he indicate *if* or *when* he will be returning; nor is there any indication as to *if* or *when* what he "*gave*" the "slaves;" it does state "gave;" is to be returned to him.

He finally comes back. In his absence, two of the slaves traded the talents and resulting in 100% profit. One slave hid the talent by burying it in the ground.

So what does the slave master then do? He congratulates the two who risked his money by having "traded" them; and allows them both to keep not only all of the original money, but also lets them keep their profits as well. But to the one who hid the money; a rather conservative investment guaranteeing principal; he rebukes him, takes the money back and gives it to the one who now has ten, making it eleven for one servant, and zero for the other.

What principle are we to learn from this parable? "*For to everyone who has, more shall be given, and he will have an abundance; but from the one who does not have, even what he does have shall be taken away.*"

So then by this reasoning; in life, the appropriate *Christian* thing to do would then be to find the "least of these" and take away some of what they already have. Since this clearly would *contradict* many of Jesus' other teachings, this simply cannot be the point of this story.

In order to understand the wisdom contained in this parable, the logical very first question to be asked is precisely what was it that Jesus was actually speaking *about*? Part of this answer is contained in the very first sentence, wherein it states: "*For it is just like...*"

The question then becomes: "Precisely what is it in this particular parable that "it" represents, that is "*just like*" that which follows?"

"It" is a third person pronoun, referring to something else. "It" represents a rather large category of actualities. In fact, it seems that anything not being masculine or feminine in nature would qualify to be included in this "it" category.

To find the meaning of this particular "it," going all the way back to the beginning of the chapter where this story later appears; Matthew 25:1; provides some insight.

Matthew Chapter 25 begins with 25:1 (NAS), where Jesus is speaking and tells us:

> *"Then the kingdom of heaven
> will be comparable to..."*[10.2]

Thus it seems likely that Jesus is also speaking about this very same *"kingdom of heaven,"* in this parable which is also contained in Chapter 25, but in later verses 14-30—in some way or manner.

However, it must be noted that here in verse 1, Jesus is speaking about what *"will be;"* whereas later in verse 14, (where this "Talent Man" story begins), He is speaking about what currently *"is:" "For it is just like a man..."*

Jesus indicated in verse 1 what the Kingdom of Heaven *"will be;"* and will be *"then,"* or at some *future* time; as the verse begins with *"then."* Therefore this *"will be"* cannot be now, or at least was not yet at the time Jesus said this. This is an important distinction, because what the *"kingdom of heaven"* currently *"is"*, is something which affects our lives *now*; as opposed to what it *"will be,"* at whatever time the *"then"* represents; which *will not* affect us, at least not directly, until the *"then."*

Precisely what is this "kingdom of heaven?" Generally, there are two definitions of "heaven," depending on whether the singular or the plural is used; and whether or not preceded by the definite article: "the."

Heaven in the singular is generally understood to be where God resides, (art in); and the place where our immortal *pneuma*, or *soul*, begins its journey; and with salvation, the place to where it will ultimately return. It is never, (except by Petrovsky), referred to as "the heaven."

"The heavens" however, generally refers to the sky and outward. "Heavens" is generally referred to in the plural, and rarely *without* the "the." The appearance of the "s" in the phrase: "For heaven's sake," is possessive and not plural.

True Talent

It is interesting to again inquire as to precisely where God was when he created the heavens and the earth. Clearly he was not yet residing in a place that had yet to be created. Thus, as previously addressed, clearly there must be two different meanings for this word "heaven."

The actual Greek word in Matthew 25:1 which is translated as "heaven" is:

> "3772 ŏuranŏs; perh. from the same as 3735 (through the idea of *elevation*); the *sky*; by extens. *heaven* (as the abode of God); by impl. *happiness, power, eternity*; spec. the *Gospel, (Christianity)*: - air, heaven ([-ly]), sky."[10.3]

> "3735 ŏrŏs; prob. from an obsol. ŏrō (to *rise* or "*rear*"; perh. akin to *142*; comp. *3733*); a *mountain* (as *lifting* itself above the plain): - hill, mount (-ain)."[10.4]

In Luke 11:2; where the "Lord's prayer" appears; (≈Our Father who art in heaven. . .); "heaven" is also 3772 ŏuranŏs.[10.5]

If a fair analysis of this word "heaven" or ŏuranŏs is undertaken, it would initially seem that the meaning has much more to do with physical elevation, air, to rise or to rear, lifting, a hill, or a mountain, rather than the abode of God; which according to Strong's, is derived only by "extension" of ŏuranŏs.

However; from Jesus Himself using an Aramaic word which translates to the Greek word ŏuranŏs; both in Luke when providing the "Lord's Prayer," and here in Matthew, at the beginning of Chapter 25; it seems clear that He is speaking of "Heaven" where the Father is, and not "the heavens," where the celestial bodies "reside."

Furthermore; this parable in no way resembles any type of Astronomy lecture. One might try to argue that the "Master" represents the Sun, and the three servants the three innermost planets or some such; but this would likely be highly unsuccessful—unless some type of hallucinogens were also involved.

The actual word translated as "kingdom" is:

189

"932 basilĕia; from 935; prop. *royalty*, i.e. (abstr.) *rule*, or (concr.) a *realm* (lit. or fig.): - kingdom + reign."[10.6]

So it would seem reasonable to conclude that the *"it"* to which Jesus is referring with respect to the *parable*, is likewise the *"kingdom of heaven."* And this *"it"* likely refers not only to the "place" in which God resides; but rather, refers to the entire *immaterial* realm; and more importantly, the *rules* associated therein.

"In verse 1 of Matthew 25, Jesus referred to what the kingdom of heaven *"will be"* at the *"then."* Here in this parable, in verse 14 of Matthew 25, He is speaking of what heaven *"is,"* and *is now*.

The parable was spoken by Jesus in Aramaic, and written in Greek. There are only inexact synonyms for terminology among Aramaic, New Testament Greek and the Old Testament Hebrew equivalents; and that is only part of the problem.

Jesus told us: *"For it is just like a man about to go on a journey, who called his own slaves and entrusted his possessions to them. To one he gave five talents, to another, two, and to another, one, each according to his own ability; and he went on his journey."*

According to Strong, the word *slave* (singular) actually appears only once in the entire Bible; in Jeremiah 2:14, where a distinction is being made between a *slave* and a *servant*.[10.7]

And the word *slaves* (plural), only appears once in the entire Bible, and is in Revelation 18:13. And in Revelation, the actual word translated as "slaves" is the Greek *soma*, generally meaning body.[10.8]

The actual Greek word translated as "slaves" here in Matthew is:

"*1401* dŏulŏs; from *1210*; a slave (lit. or fig., invol or vol.; frequently therefore in a qualified sense of subjection or subserviency): - bond (-man), servant."[10.9]

This may seem a bit crazy; in that Strong's does not list *slave*, (singular), as appearing anywhere in the entire Bible, except in Jeremiah 2:14; and yet the very first two words in the *definition* of *dŏulŏs* are "a slave." It gets a bit worse, as Strong provides *nothing*

True Talent

for the actual word in Jeremiah that Strong claims is translated as *slave* (singular).[10.10]

Thus it is a fair conclusion, at least according to Strong, that there is no original word known in the entire Bible that corresponds to slave in the singular, except in Jeremiah 2:14; and only a word meaning *body* that is translates as slaves in the plural; the first two words in the definition of *dŏulŏs* notwithstanding.

In fact, Strongest Strong's classifies the word "slave" as "NIH" meaning "Not in Hebrew," citing Jeremiah as the example of an *added* word.[10.11]

Based upon the word *dŏulŏs* appearing elsewhere in the Bible, and always being translated as "bond (-man)," or "servant" every other time; it seems likely that *slave* would be an incorrect translation. (This of course relates to the New Testament Greek.)

Furthermore; according to Strong, *dŏulŏs* can be voluntary or involuntary, and thus could be either. Thus *dŏulŏs* appears to have to do with the overall *condition* of subservience or submission, rather than any specific type of *relationship* that produced this condition.

It is unclear precisely what it is that constitutes "voluntary slavery." Thus, *servant* seems to be the better definition for *dŏulŏs*—particularly in the context of the parable. In this parable, Jesus seems to be explaining a mechanism by which God's servants, (H. Sapiens), voluntarily; i.e.; free will choosing; to serve him.

The Old Testament mistranslated word "talent," has several definitions. It is sometimes a unit of weight which can range from 75 pounds for a *common* talent, to 150 pounds for a *royal* talent.[10.12]

In the entire *Old Testament*, the only Hebrew word *translated* as "talent" is:

> "3603 kikkâr; from 3769; a *circle*, i.e. (by impl.) a circumjacent *tract* or region, espec. the *Ghôr* or valley of the Jordan; also a (round) *loaf*; also a *talent* (or large [round] coin): - loaf, morsel, piece, plain, talent."[10.13]

The only other actual word translated as 'talent' in the Old Testament, is the *Chaldean*:

"3604 kikkêr (Chald.); corresp. to 3603; a *talent*; - talent."[10.14]

Thus the idea that "talent" is any type of Hebrew unit of measure; whether common or royal; is in no way supported factually. For whatever reason(s), translators elected to insert the word "talent" for *kikkâr* and *kikkêr* in the *Old Testament* translations.

But the actual *Greek* word appearing in Matthew 25 translated as "talent," is in fact:

"5007 talantŏn; neut. Of a presumed der. of the orig. form of tiaō (to *bear*; equiv. to *5342*); a *balance* (as *supporting* weights), i.e. (by impl.) a certain *weight* (and thence a *coin* or rather *sum* of money) or "*talent*": - talent."[10.15]

Here the concept of *talent* representing a *certain* weight is only by *implication*. This "implication" explanation, is likely the "tail wagging the dog;" as Strong did his work in the late 19th century, long after many of the Old Testament mistranslations by the "experts," had taken place.

The above stated "equivalent" word for talantŏn is:

"5342 phěrō; a prim. verb... to "*bear*" or *carry*"[10.16]

And of course, there is the *common*, the English word, definition of talent, (doxa); which refers to capabilities, generally considered to be innate; allowing someone to be able to, or have the capability to perform certain things in a manner which far exceeds the norm. *Talent* refers to this capability, *talented* refers to the individual who has the talent; and *gifted* is a term often used to describe the process whereby, or the reason why the talented individual received or has said talent. But as will be seen, "gifted;" is more than arguably a misnomer.

There is a distinct difference between the meanings of the Old Testament Hebrew *kikkâr* or *kikkêr*; irrespective of its incorrect translation as *talent*; and the New Testament Greek *talantŏn*. The

Hebrew *kikkâr* essentially means circle, the meaning related to money likely only from the shape of a coin. [*There exists a derogatory word for Jewish people which will not be repeated here. Many believe that the root of this word is kikkâr. The reason likely has to do with illiterate Jewish immigrants to the United States having to sign their name and refusing to sign with an "X," because of the similarities to the Christian cross; thus instead signing their name with a circle.*]

The Greek word *talantŏn* has nothing whatsoever to do with any shape; including the circle. Rather, it represents bearing, balance and perhaps; but only by *implication*; a specified and accurate weight. A twenty dollar US gold coin is just shy of one ounce troy pure gold. It is circular, but also represents a specific certain weight of gold. *Kikkâr* could be used to describe this as a coin, or its value as a coin, and some small fraction of the weight of the Hebrew "phantom" talent could *incorrectly* be used to describe its weight in gold. The confusion between the meanings of the terms may have arisen from this relationship.

However, the original Greek word used in the parable is *talantŏn*. Thus it would be prudent to assume that the *actual* definition of the *actual* word *actually* used, is what Jesus *actually* meant. Therefore, it would be fair to say that each of the servants was given a weight to bear, a weight or something as a balance to something else, and from the *immaterial* perspective a "certain" weight. The use of "certain weight" can be interpreted two ways. It can refer to the *amount* of the weight as certain, such as one ounce troy; or it can refer to the *existence* of some *balancing* weight as a *certainty*, irrespective of the amount.

Since the definitions of *talantŏn* primarily have to do with the act of bearing, carrying, balancing etc., irrespective of the *amount* of any weight, this appears to be the correct meaning; rather than a sum of money or weight of precious metals equivalent to some agreed upon value. The use of *talantŏn* as money, is never literal, but only by implication.

How much *talantŏn* was each given and why? They were each given different amounts based upon their abilities. It must be noted that they were not each given *talantŏn* according to their *accomplishments*, but rather according to their *abilities*—not according to what they had *done*, but rather according to what they were *capable* of doing.

The actual Greek word translated here as "ability" is:

> "*1411* dunamis; from *1410*; *force* (lit. or fig.); spec. miraculous *power* (usually by impl. a *miracle* itself): - ability, abundance, meaning, might (-ily, -y, -y deed), worker of) miracle (-s), power, strength, violence, mighty (wonderful) work."[10.17]

This word *dunamis*; must clearly be distinguished from the English word "dynamic;" which is derived from the Greek word *dynamikós*, which means "powerful;" *dýnamis*, which means "power;" and *dýnasthai*, which means "be able, have power."[10.18]

The abilities referenced in this parable were their *supernatural* or *miraculous* abilities, (dunamis); and not any type of *natural* abilities, (dynamikós). This is not to say that they did not have any *natural* abilities; but rather that their natural abilities are not referenced, and thus have nothing to do with the parable.

In physics, the derived word *dyne* represents a measurement or unit of *natural* force existing in the *material* realm; which when applied to a *mass*, results in *work* or the movement of the mass.

There seems to yet be no equivalent word derived from *dunamis*; which would represent a measurement or unit of *supernatural* force in the *immaterial* realm; which when applied, results in work or the possible movement of *immaterial* phenomenon; or more relevant to this parable, capable of ultimately making resultant changes in *material* phenomenon; but here from *dunamic* (supernatural) and not *dynamic* (natural) factors.

This being the case, the word *duna* is hereby coined, and is defined as the unit of measure of *immaterial* force, capable of making *material* changes *via* the *immaterial* realm. It must be pointed out that although the force acts from the *immaterial* realm, the ultimate purpose is to affect changes in the *material* realm; and thus this does not exclusively result in changes solely in the *immaterial* realm.

Although an exact accepted value, quantity or magnitude of a *duna* cannot actually be numerically calculated at this time, it can nevertheless be used to measure *relative* amounts of supernatural power.

If this seems idiotic, absurd or a useless endeavor; it must be remembered that in mathematics, "i" represents a quantity equaling the value of the square root of negative one. With respect to "i," this represents an *imaginary* number; as there is no known number when multiplied by itself will yield a negative product; hence the choice of that particular letter for this "variable." The square root of a negative number simply does not exist; or at least has no actuality in our material world. But with respect to *duna*, *immaterial* power does in fact exist—else no *material* universe could have been created.

Thus unlike in mathematics; where a term was selected to quantify a non-existent entity; here it is a bit different, in that it is the *quantification* of the something which *does* exist into a unit, albeit that only the *relative* value, and not the *actual* value is known.

Again, the key to this definition of *dunamis* is that it is *supernatural* or "miraculous," or a "miracle," or "wonderful," (full of wonder), force or power. This is not merely *natural* or *dynamikós* power or ability, but rather a *supernatural* or *miraculous* type of power.

Thus, each "servant" was given a *talantŏn* or weight to bear or balance or support; arguably of denoted measurable value, according to the amount of *dunamis* or supernatural power each had. There is a relationship between the terms. Because of the amount of *dunamis* or supernatural power given or possessed, there is a corresponding balancing weight or *responsibility* or *talantŏn*.

In order to avoid confusion, it would be prudent at this juncture to assign a term to describe and relatively quantify this amount of weight to bear or responsibility (*talantŏn*). This is necessary as said *talantŏn*, in this usage does not refer to *objective* physical weight as could be measured on a physical scale, but rather the *subjective* weight to the host.

This being the case, the word *tala* is hereby coined, and is defined as a unit of measure of immaterial, subjective, psychological, or emotional weight, capable of causing the host to exercise; and arguably is required to balance; his or her level of *dunamis*. The term *tala* must be used to avoid confusion with the *erroneous* translation as *talent* as a unit of *physical* weight, (pound, ounce, etc); or *talent* as some innate *skill* which is "completely free;" e.g.; "gifted."

One could hypothetically assign a value of one *duna* per *tala*. Thus the servant who received five *tala*, was given this "weight" of five *tala*, because he had five *duna* of *supernatural* power. Likewise; the same could be said for the two, and for the one "talent" servants.

The failure to realize this, would likely result in a classic example of the failure to perceive sufficient actuality; or perhaps better phrased; a failure to sufficiently perceive *the* actuality. Given that this may seem somewhat tautological or oxymoronic; this includes: to fail to perceive even in a somewhat limited sense; the; or an; actuality *in-toto*.

The presence of *dunamis* or supernatural power is often incorrectly perceived and is generally considered to be a stand alone entity—meaning that the *dunamis* alone represents the entire actuality. But in fact, it is *both* the *dunamis* or supernatural power; *and* the *talantŏn* or the balancing weight or responsibility; that comprises the true one actuality. They each individually represent only a part of the actuality. This is why using the term "gifted" would be inaccurate; as "gifted" recognizes only the *dunamis*; and not the associated and inextricably linked *talantŏn*.

Proverbs 30:1 (NAS) begins with the following:

> *"The words of Agur the son of Jakeh, the oracle."*[10.19]

The King James translation is: *"even the prophesy,"* in place of *"the oracle."*[10.20]

And Malachi 1:1 (NAS) begins with the following:

> *"The oracle of the word of the
> LORD to Israel through Malachi."*[10.21]

In each of these two NAS verses, the word *"oracle"* appears. A fair interpretation of an *"oracle;"* is one who is able to provide *revelation.* Whether providing *prophesy* or *retrophesy,* (true) oracles clearly exercise *dunamis;*—at least when acting in the capacity of an oracle.

However; the *King James* translation of this very same Malachi 1:1, provides *"burden"* as the translation, rather than *"oracle:"*

The KJV of Malachi 1:1 is:

> *"The burden of the word of
> the LORD to Israel by Malachi."*[10.22]

The actual word translated as "oracle" in NAS version of Proverbs 30:1 and Malachi 1:1; but "burden" in the KJV of Malachi 1:1 is:

> "4853 massâ'; from 5375; a *burden*; spec. *tribute*, or (abstr.) *porterage*; fig. an *utterance*,...." chiefly a *doom,* espec. *singing;* mental, *desire:* - burden, carry away, prophesy, x they set, song, tribute."[10.23]

> "5375 nâsâ' or nâcâh; a prim. root; to *lift* in a great variety of applications."[10.24]

"Porterage" generally refers to carrying a weight or burden; e.g.; a porter.

Thus there are several seemingly unrelated meanings to *massâ' et seq.* They can be translated as an *"utterance,"* likely prophetic or retrophesitic in nature; as well as a *"burden"* or *lifting*; as well as *"desire."*

As a result, it seems clear that *massâ'* represents the understanding or comprehension of a given actuality in Hebrew; for which the use of both *dunamis*, as well as *talantŏn*, and comprehending their relationship; is required for understanding or comprehending of the very same actuality in Greek:

(Hebrew) *massâ'* = (Greek) *dunamis* + (Greek) *talantŏn*

Dunamis may *appear* to exist alone; but cannot exist without the corresponding *talantŏn*. However; the mere *existence* of the *talantŏn*, does not necessarily mean it will be "carried."

Luke 12:48 (NAS) confirms this spiritual or immaterial rule of balance by telling us:

*"...From everyone who has been given much,
much will be required;
and to whom they entrusted much,
of him they will ask all the more."*[10.25]

Here in Luke, the aforementioned concept of the Hebrew word *massâ'*; or the requirement that among other things; the quantity of both *"dunamis + talantŏn"* necessarily be considered in order to ascertain the actuality, is confirmed.

And Jesus goes on with the parable: *"Immediately the one who had received the five talents went and traded with them, and gained five more talents. In the same manner the one who had received the two talents gained two more. But he who received the one talent went away, and dug a hole in the ground and hid his master's money."*

A cursory reading seems pretty simple. Two of the men took the money and traded with it, resulting in a profit of 100%—except for two minor problems. The same being: that it (*talantŏn*) was not money, but rather that burden which is necessarily associated with supernatural power; and it is not precisely known what is actually meant here by "traded."

The original Greek word translated as "traded" is:

> "*2038* ĕrgazŏmai; mid. from *2041*; to *toil* (as a task, occupation, etc.)..."[10.26]

> "*2041* ĕrgŏn; from a prim. (but obsol.) ĕrgō (to work); *toil* (as an effort or occupation); by impl. and act: - deed, doing, labour, work."[10.27]

Ĕrgazŏmai is the root of the terms *ergs*, *energy*, and *ergonomics*.

The term *"traded"* can be misleading, as it can refer to a situation where possession of items can be exchanged or swapped, without any corresponding increase in total wealth. "Trading" may result in increase in *subjective* wealth for the parties involved in the exchange, but there is no increase in *total* societal wealth. There is no actual "work" being done in the literal sense, so there is no increase in total *objective* wealth. Thus "worked" seems to be a much better translation of *ĕrgazŏmai*, than would be "traded."

Clearly the definition of *ĕrgazŏmai* requires actual "work," "toil," effort, etc., and thus can refer to "trades" such as the construction *trade*; which *can* increase total wealth, because the value or amount of wealth in the final product, exceeds the value or wealth of the components.

Precisely what type of work or *ĕrgazŏmai* was it in which these servants engaged? It appears from the definition of *dunamis*, that it likely was *miraculous* work; "spec.(ifically) miraculous power (usually by impl. a miracle itself)."

Here they worked their *dunamis*; or supernatural power, and not any *dynamikós*; or natural power.

Proverbs 14:23 (NAS) tells us:

> "*In all labor there is profit,*
> *But mere talk leads only to poverty.*"[10.28]

The parable continues:

"*Now after a long time the master of those slaves came and settled accounts with them.*

"*The one who had received the five talents came up and brought five more talents, saying, 'Master, you entrusted five talents to me. See, I have gained five more talents.' "His master said to him, 'Well done, good and faithful slave. You were faithful with a few things, I will put you in charge of many things; enter into the joy of your master.'*

"*Also the one who had received the two talents came up and said, 'Master, you entrusted two talents to me. See, I have gained two more talents.' "His master said to him, 'Well done, good and faithful slave. You were faithful with a few things, I will put you in charge of many things; enter into the joy of your master.*"

What seems to be happening here, is that these two servants went out and "worked" their *supernatural* or *miraculous* abilities, far beyond what was required by the magnitude of their responsibilities.

They began by being given a quantity of *tala* or weight to bear, according to the number of *duna* they each had possessed; as that is essentially what is stated. If the hypothetical relationship holds; one was given 5 *tala*, because he had 5 *duna*. The other was given 2 *tala*, because he had 2 *duna*. But they fulfilled their responsibilities so well, that they were ultimately given more *tala*. But the *actuality* includes both *tala* and *duna*. Meaning; that one cannot have one without the other.

And the "master's" response was consistent with this. They were put *"in charge of many things."*

The *"in charge of"* is actually:

> "2525 kathistēmi; from 2596 and 2476; to *place down* (permanently), i.e. (fig.) to *designate, constitute, convoy*:
> - appoint, be, conduct, make ordain, set."[10.29]

The word *"things"* does not appear in the original Greek. There exists no word which could be translated as *"things"* in this passage.

200

The word "*things*" appears to have been added at some point in time, for whatever purported reason(s).

This later addition of "*things*" results not in clarity, but confusion and obfuscation; by opening up tremendous and arguably unlimited possibilities as to what these "*things*" actually were. This is not quite as misleading as the previously shown tendency to call anything and everything immaterial "spirit;" but nevertheless results in substantial confusion. The "*few*" and the "*many*" appear to be correct; but no other word or words appear in this section regarding to what the "*few*" and "*many*" refer.

Thus, there is no explanation whatsoever provided as to the nature of the additional "*things*" they were put in charge of. Neither is there any detailed explanation of the original "*few*" with which they were "*faithful;*" except as stated in the beginning of the parable.

Thus the *few* and *many* were likely related to either these *supernatural* or miraculous powers, or *dunamis*; or they were related to the *talantŏn*; or to "bear or balance as supporting weights."

Since they had already received the additional *talantŏn* or units of *talas* as a result of their work or "ergs;" then by Hobson's choice, both the "few" and the "many" must refer to the units of *duna*.

It is the case that the few things with which they were faithful represented these miraculous powers; and it is also the case that no additional description is provided about the additional "*many*" over which they were given *kathistēmi*, but only that there is some relationship between what was done with the "*few*" as a causative factor resulting in the statement about the "*many*."

Had there been a difference between the types of "*things*" that the "*few*" represented, and the subsequent "*many*" "things;" then likely this would have been stated. Thus, unlike it being possible by the translators later addition of "*things;*" it is not the *character*, *characteristics*, or *nature* of the additional "*things*" over which they were given charge that is being stated; but rather solely concerning the *number* or *amount* of something.

This of course makes perfect sense, as the additional units of *tala*, or balancing weight taken on by them; had to be counterbalanced by obtaining additional units of *duna*.

The alternative explanation being; that the "*few*" and the "*many*" simply refer to the amount of *money* originally given to each of them; this arguably being like being given charge over "*few*" and many "dollars." Aside from the previously mentioned problems associated with this position, there are more:

Firstly, if the position is taken that the above is all gibberish, and talent is merely a unit of *normal* "weight;" then likely between 375 and 750 pounds of weight was originally given to the *five* talent man; as it does not state whether these "talents" were *common* or *royal*.

Thus, when he returned, he would have been carrying between 750 and 1,500 pounds of weight. Along with this, is the problem that unless it is known what *material* it was of which the five talent man was originally carrying between 375 and 750 pounds; there is no way to determine the *value*, if any, of either the original five, or subsequent five.

Second, is the use of the word "*few*." This term *few* is usually reserved for a quantity of more than two; as two is generally referred to as a *couple*; yet the very same thing was stated to the two talent man. Thus, it seems more than just speculation to suggest that he would have said the same thing to the one talent man, had he been "faithful" with that one talent.

Third, there is the "*faithful*" issue. There is no mention of what it was these servants were either instructed or expected to do with these talents. Yet upon their return, there actions are described as "*faithful*." This implies prior knowledge on the part of the servants with respect to this.

Fourthly, would or does the *amount* of money, rather than "money" itself qualify numerically for these statements about "*few*" and "*many*?" If so then the five talent man was given a *large* few, the two talent a *medium* few, and the one talent man arguably a *small* few. Or does it make more sense that the few and the many refer to either the numbers of *dunas* or to the number of sub-types of *dunamis* or supernatural/miraculous power?

True Talent

If this part of the parable were told in English today, it would begin as: "The rule of the immaterial realm is like a man who called his persons of subservience and entrusted his possessions to them. To one he gave five tala of balancing weight, to another two tala and another one tala. This was done to each according to said servant's supernatural power, or ability to do miraculous things."

This would be perfectly consistent with the previous will, intellect and emotions diagram; albeit that this *balancing* weight is not the only type of force exerted by God; and that there is more to *"talent"* than weight. In fact, given that it is the bearing or balancing that truly defines *tala*; it is at least arguable, that there is no *literal* relationship of *tala*, to *physical* weight whatsoever.

The following rules provide some keys to the understanding the interplay of natural and supernatural forces:

> I. "Nature will not permit the continued existence of an unbalanced actuality."
>
> II. "The universe will obey your will to the extent that it is not inconsistent with; nor contradictory to; the will of God."
>
> III. "When perceiving an *actuality*, one must exercise caution as to perceive as much of the actuality as possible, as this will determine one's *reality*; and it is our reality upon which we base our thoughts and actions. Likewise, caution must be exercised in order to not perceive as one actuality, that which is or are aspects of two separate actualities; or the reverse."
>
> [These are introduced here as they are relevant to this story, but will be discussed in greater detail later.]

And the parable is concluded in two distinct parts:

First part:

"And the one also who had received the one talent came up and said, 'Master, I knew you to be a hard man, reaping where you did not sow and gathering where you scattered no seed. 'And I was afraid, and went away and hid your talent in the ground. See, you have what is yours.'"

Here in the first part, the *servant* is making three distinct statements:

1. He is calling the master a hard, (not meek), *thief*; as what other word better describes one who *reaps* where he did not *sow*, and *gathering* where he had scattered no seed?
2. Secondly, he is stating that he was afraid of something, and because of this fear hid the talent in the ground.
3. Thirdly, the servant then seems to be trying to placate the master; by telling him that he now has something that belongs to the master; after just accusing him of whatever was his, (the master's); wasn't legitimately his, (the master's); in the first place.

Second part:

"But his master answered and said to him, 'you wicked, lazy slave, you knew that I reap where I did not sow and gather where I scattered no seed. Then you ought to have put my money in the bank, and on my arrival I would have received my money back with interest. Therefore take away the talent from him, and give it to the one who has the ten talents." For to everyone who has, more shall be given, and he will have an abundance; but from the one

who does not have, even what he does have shall be taken away."

There are cause-effect relationships *implied* in this portion. This is so because of the appearance of the words "then" and "therefore"

What is actually being said by the master is: "*if*" what you (servant) are saying is true, "*then*" you ought to have. . ." Or more contemporarily phrased: "You knew that I was a thief huh? Then you should have. . ."

The talent being referred to as *money* in the story only happens two times:

The first is in Matthew 25:18, (appearing once: "*hid his master's money*"); when this servant's actions were described as if by a "third party" narration.

And then again (appearing twice here: "*Then you ought to have put my money in the bank, and on my arrival I would have received my money back with interest.*") by the *master* in this passage.

The servant never refers to the talent as *money*; but rather maintains that it is *talent*.

And the master refers to the talent as money, only *after* the "*then*" or conditionally, and this is only pertinent *if* the servant's characterizations: "*you knew that I reap where I did not sow and gather where I scattered no seed;*" of the master were in fact true.

But when the master then speaks to someone else regarding the servant; and is no longer speaking with the condition of the "if" hypothetically having been met; he *then* refers to it as *talent*, ("*take away the talent from him*"); and not *money*.

It is as though the usage of the term "*money*" is strictly reserved for use by others only, and used only by what the speaker, (the "master"), believes would be suitable from the servant's perspective—even though that term is never once used by the servant.

The actual word translated here and also in Matthew 25:18 translated as "money" is:

"694 arguriŏn; neut. Of a presumed der. of 696; *silvery*, i.e. (by impl.) *cash*; spec. a *silverling* (i.e. *drachma* or *shekel*): - money, (piece of) silver (piece)."[10.30]

And with respect to *arguriŏn* being derived from 696, the same is:

"696 argurŏs; from argŏs (*shining*); *silver* (the metal, in the articles or coin): - silver."[10.31]

This sounds somewhat reasonable, in that *money* would be a fair translation of *arguriŏn* meaning "*silvery;*" if actually derived from *argurŏs*, meaning: "(*shining*); *silver* (the metal, in the articles or coin): - silver;" given what was purportedly in use back in "those days."

However; note the qualification by Strong, that the derivation of *arguriŏn* from 696 *argurŏs* is merely "*presumed.*"

There is also another problem developing here. This definition of *argurŏs* contains these two things: Firstly that 696 *argurŏs* is derived: "from *argŏs*;" and *then* the definition of *argurŏs* as "(*shining*); *silver* (the metal, in the articles or coin): - silver;" is provided. Again it is noted that it is the definition of *argurŏs* and not *argŏs* which is provided as: "*silver* (the metal, in the articles or coin): - silver.*"

When comparing *arguriŏn*, *argurŏs*, and *argŏs*; there seems to be either additional or missing letters, (ur), depending upon one's perspective; which seems to be a source of considerable confusion.

According to Strong, this word from which *argurŏs*, meaning: "(*shining*); *silver* (the metal, in the articles or coin): - silver;" is derived, is in fact:

"692 argŏs; from *1* (as a neg. particle) [*1* is A as used in negation whatever follows and *2041*; *inactive*, i.e. *unemployed*; (by impl.) *lazy*, *useless*: - barren, idle, slow."[10.32]

But there is no mention of money, silver, shining, coins; or anything related to the same contained in the definition of *argŏs*; which is proffered as the root of 696 *argurŏs*; which is proffered as the root of 694 *argurĭŏn*; and is translated in these two passages as "money."

Neither does *argŏs* contain the quasi-phantom "ur" seen in 696 *argurŏs*, or 694 *argurĭŏn*.

Instead we are told that this "ur" missing *argŏs*, is from two words: "*1* is A as used in negation whatever follows and *2041*."

And the above referenced 2041, which is negated by the use of "A" is the previously cited:

> "*2041* ĕrgŏn; from a prim. (but obsol.) ĕrgō (to work); toil (as an effort or occupation....."[10.33]

If this word *ĕrgŏn* sounds familiar, it is because *ĕrgŏn* was the word from which *ĕrgazŏmai*; previously *erroneously* translated as "traded," was derived; but that actually means *work*. Here however, with the addition of the *negation*; *argŏs* represents its opposite: "'inactive,' or no-work, or the opposite of work." This is why the definition of argŏs is: "*inactive,* i.e. *unemployed*; (by impl.) *lazy, useless*: - barren, idle, slow."

Thus it seems most reasonable that the original word used in the text, *argŏs*; is a combination of "a" as a prefix, providing "the negation of" whatever follows this prefix; which in this case is that same root of 2041 *ĕrgŏn,* which is *ĕrgō.*

Thus it also seems quite likely that originally the word *argŏs* was *aĕrgō,* or *aĕrgŏn,* (the negation of "a" with ĕrgō, as the root of *ĕrgŏn*); and then over time *aĕrgō* became *argŏs*. This would also explain the missing "ur."

Based upon this; then describing the talent of the servant with one talent as "*money,*" is quite erroneous. *Laziness* would be the best definition. This is further supported by the fact that the master did in fact refer to this servant as both "wicked" and "lazy," prior to the second appearance of the word translated as "money."

This is merely speculation, but since Argentum, (symbol Ag); is the correct scientific term for the metal commonly known as silver, the roots of this term may in fact be related to a term based upon the concept of a "lazy man's" metal, as silver historically has been about one twentieth the value of gold.

Proverbs 14:23 did tell us that *"in all labor there is profit."* Thus if there is labor, there must be profit, and a relationship is established between labor and profit. So if there is any labor, then there must be some profit as "all," is "all" inclusive.

But this is a one way street, in that: *"in all labor there is profit,"* does not *preclude* profit without labor. However, according to the second half of 14:23, if one assumes that *"mere talk"* is equal to no labor; then poverty and only poverty is where this leads.

2 Thessalonians 3:10-12 (KJV) tells us:

> *"For even when we were with you,*
> *this we commanded you,*
> *that if any would not work,*
> *neither should he eat.*
>
> *For we hear that there are some*
> *which walk among you disorderly,*
> *working not at all, but are busybodies.*
>
> *Now them that are such we command*
> *and exhort by our Lord Jesus Christ,*
> *that with quietness they work,*
> *and eat their own bread."*[10.34]

Thus it is a fair conclusion that *Scripturally*, there exists a relationship between *poverty* and the *lack* of labor. If there is profit in *all* labor, then *poverty* must necessarily be brought on by lack of labor; barring things such as theft or vices.

But even so, poverty cannot be maintained in the face of any type of continued labor, (if it is labor); because Proverbs tells us that: *"in all labor there is profit."* The term "all" is inclusive, and could essentially be translated as *any* labor; since if it is any type of labor, then it is included as part or subset of the "all." So to rephrase it as

True Talent

"in *any* labor there is profit" would be reasonable. Thus the evidence of little or no profit, (poverty); confirms that there has been little or no labor—at least this was the case during "those times."

The word *"bank"* in: *"Then you ought to have put my money in the bank,"* is also an *incorrect* translation; as is the word *"interest"* in: *"and on my arrival I would have received my money back with interest."*

The actual word translated as "bank" is:

> "5133 trapĕzitēs; from 5132; a money-broker or banker: - exchanger."[10.35]

Here the more correct translation of *trapĕzitēs* would be a "banker" himself, and not the "bank." *Trapĕzitēs* sounds very similar to a *trapezoid*, which is a four sided figure; but unlike a rectangle, only two sides are parallel. But trapezoid has an "oid" suffix, thus arguably only meaning similar to or almost like a rectangle. Why is this significant?

The root of "trapĕzitēs" is:

> "5132 trapĕza; prob. contr. from 5064 and 3979; a table or stool (as being four legged), usually for food (fig. a meal); also a counter for money (fig. a brokers office for loans at interest): - bank, meat, table."[10.36]

When Jesus encountered the "money changers" at the temple, it was the *tables* of these which He overturned, as well as the *seats* of the dove sellers; each likely having four supports.

These "money changers" who were at the temple are actually:

> "2855 kŏllubistēs; from a presumed der. of kŏllubŏs (a small *coin*; prob. akin to *2854*); a *coin-dealer*: - (money-)changer."[10.37]

After this, (from 2854 "backwards"), the definitions of the purported origins of *kŏllubistēs* seem to be unrelated.

"2854 kŏllŏuriŏn; neut. of a presumed der. of kŏllura (a *cake*; prob. akin to the base of 2853); prop. a *poultice* (as made of in the form of *crackers*), i.e. (by anal.) a *plaster*: eyesalve."[10.38]

"2853 kŏllaō; from kŏlla ("*glue*"); to *glue*, i.e. (pass. or reflex.) to *stick* (fig.): - cleave, join (self), keep company."[10.39]

The important thing is the nature of the word *trapĕza*, indicating a table or stool or something being four legged. Whether or not this relates to a counter at the bank, a restaurant, meat counter etc., would have to be determined by context.

Whatever the "wicked lazy" servant's entrusted possession(s) represented, the master believed that had the servant brought it to this counter or table, he would have left with something of greater value to the master than what burying the talent provided. But as it is written, this is *if*, and only *if*, what the *servant* thought of the *master* were in fact *true*.

The (KJV) translates "*interest*" as "*usury*."[10.40]

The actual Greek word translated as "interest" or "usury" is:

"5110 tŏkŏs; from the base of 5088; *interest* on money loaned (as a *produce*): - usury."[10.41]

"5088 tiktō; a strengthened form of a prim. tĕkō, (which is used only as alt. in certain tenses); to *produce* (from seed, as a mother, a plant, the earth, etc.), lit. or fig.: - bear, be born, bring forth, be delivered, be in travail."[10.42]

But there still remains the issue of what giving the possession(s) to the individuals at the counter or table means; as well as what type of return is referenced.

If it is considered that potentially four things are involved, and the same are applied to the will, intellect, and emotion diagram; this may begin to make some degree of sense.

True Talent

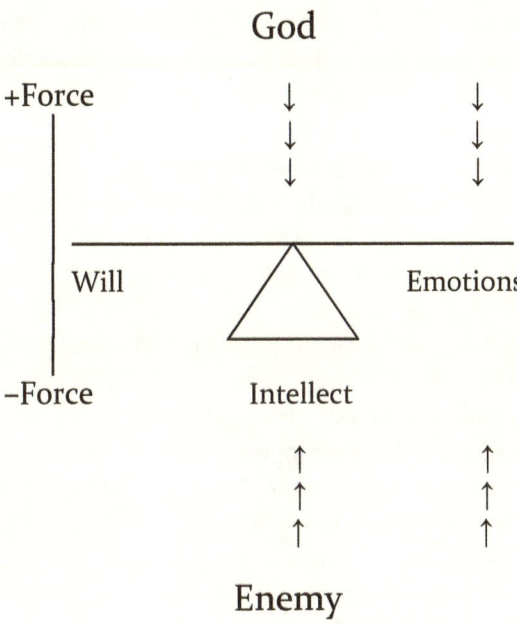

If the "talent" or *talantŏn* is considered as one type of *motivational* force on the right side of the diagram; and the *knowledge* of miraculous power or *dunamis*, is considered to be analogous to intellect area in the center of the diagram, (knowledge is power is a common saying); then the decision to use this power according to the *talantŏn*, by the will, results in work or *ĕrgazŏmai*; thereby moving of the line on the left side of the diagram upward.

For example: In the *natural*, one determines that he or she is in *need* of money. Here in this example, *need* represents the driving force to do something. It is not merely a *desire* to find a job; but also includes the *knowledge* that one must do something while at the job. When a job is found, the abilities of the individual are utilized by choosing to do work, (ergs); and this hopefully results in a change which pleases the employer.

So here there are three things in action: *Talantŏn*, or here in this example in the natural, at least *need* or *desire*, (the driving force); some type of *ability*, (*dunamis* or *dýnamis*, depending on whether *supernatural* or *natural* power); and *ĕrgazŏmai*, or work. At this point everything is complete. The worker goes to work every day and works; greatly pleases the employer; and all is fine.

Not quite. There seems to be something missing in the scenario, as the main reason for the *employee* doing what he or she is doing, is for a transfer of wealth from the *employer* to the *employee*. How much of a wealth transfer is expected? It would be whatever arrangement was agreed upon between the employer and the employee.

If "pay day" is the Wednesday following the Friday of the previous week; then from Friday until Wednesday there exists a *potential* wealth transfer as per the agreement; and this *potential* remains a *potential* until the employee is paid.

This *potential* energy is converted to, or balanced by *kinetic* energy, upon the act of paying the employee. Should this conversion not take place, there remains this *potential* energy, (imbalance), which will ultimately be balanced by other means, and likely to the employer's detriment.

And similarly with *dunamis*, or *supernatural* power; the combination of *talantŏn*, *dunamis*, and *ĕrgazŏmai* represents *wealth*;—either potential or realized. And this is twofold, as not only is there increase in terms of that which is similar to the employee receiving payment, but also ultimately an increase in available *dunamis*.

The "wicked" and "lazy" servant had *talantŏn*, as well as *dunamis*, but engaged in no significant *ĕrgazŏmai*. Instead of balancing the talent or weight by *working* his supernatural abilities, he chose to bury the weight. His goal was to get rid of the weight or emotional driving force by burying it; instead of doing what he *should* have done; and what the other two servants in fact did do.

This seems to be why the master suggested that the wicked and lazy servant take the talent and the abilities to the "counter;" as they would have done some "work" with it, and at least some amount of increase could have been expected. It must be remembered that this advice was based upon the assumption that what the servant said about the master, (you are a thief), were in fact *true*; which it appears was in fact not so.

It does not seem that these *kŏllubistēs*, or "money changers," were held in particularly high esteem. Thus, if the servant was using the excuse that the master was a thief, and that is why he would not work with the master's property, (rather than because he was lazy); then the master was saying: "If so, then you should have gone to those immoral kŏllubistēs, and at least I would have gotten some return, because they wouldn't care."

This wicked and lazy servant seems a bit similar to Adam; when after he disobeyed God, he then complained to God that it essentially was all God's fault; because of the "woman" He had given Adam.

It is the combination of *talent*, (driving force or weight); and our *abilities*, (often erroneously referred to as talent(s)); which make us capable of obtaining wealth; but we must choose to *do* something, (work or *ĕrgazŏmai*), with these.

A recap: *"Therefore take away the talent from him, and give it to the one who has the ten talents. For to everyone who has, more shall be given, and he will have an abundance; but from the one who does not have, even what he does have shall be taken away."*

The first sentence seems straightforward, as long as the *"therefore"* is taken into account. Is it the accusations of: *"reap where I did not so;"* or the failure to even *"put the money in the bank;"* or both; that prompted this *"therefore?"*

As written, the belief of *"reap where I did not so;"* should have caused the "one talent" man to at least *"put the money in the bank."* Thus this *"therefore"* seems to relate to no increase, because the man neither worked the "talent;" nor put it *"in the bank."*

The second sentence; which provides the explanation or justification of that which is stated in the first; is less clear: *"For* (because) *to everyone who has, more shall* (not may) *be given."* A fair question is: to everyone who has *what*? Precisely what is it to which this *"has"* refers? And with respect to those who do in fact "have," precisely what is it that they shall be given *"more"* of?

The first two servants had supernatural abilities, and were given balancing weight, or weight to bear, based upon their supernatural abilities. These "weights" are the force or forces on the right side of the diagram.

They then *worked* their supernatural abilities far beyond what was required by the original "weight." This would be represented by large movement of the line on the left side of the diagram in the upward direction. Perhaps they each even "pinned the needle" for their particular circumstances. So they gained additional responsibilities, or increased weight to bear. This was then balanced by being put in charge of more; likely an increase in their *dunamis* or supernatural abilities.

For everyone who has abilities, (here *dunamis*); weight, (here *talantŏn*); is given. For everyone who utilizes their abilities, (*ĕrgazŏmai*); they are given more weight because of this. For everyone who increases the weight in this manner, more *dunamic* abilities are given, and they will have an abundance.

Thus it would be fair to ask: "an abundance of what?"

The actual word translated as "abundance" is:

> "4052 pěrissěuō; from 4053; to *superabound* (in quantity or quality), *be in excess, be superfluous*; also (trans.) to *cause to superabound* or *excel*: - (make, more) abound (have, have more) abundance, (be more) abundant, be the better, enough and to spare, exceed, excel, increase, be left, redound, remain (over and above)."[10.43]

If taken *out* of the context of the parable, the definition of this sounds suspiciously like wealth—and a rather large amount of wealth at that. Even in the common usage of "superfluous," there is an implication of an excess of what is required or necessary.

But if used *in* the context of the parable, it may seem like this refers to an excess of either abilities or weight. But does it make any degree of sense, that God would provide either abilities, or balancing weight, or both; in quantities which would be in excess of what was needed? And is this even possible? The answer to each question is yes.

It seems likely that this *pěrissěuō* refers to the *result* of the abilities, the weight or drive and the work or effort(s) exerted, and this in fact is, or ultimately results in material *wealth*, and/or some other types of *increase*.

True Talent

But the lazy servant chose to *hide* weight or burden, with said weight being the counterpart to the actuality of his abilities, and in this case his *supernatural* abilities. It remains unclear as to whether or not the "hiding" is actually literal. Instead of *working* his abilities according to the "drive" or weight, he chose to ignore them. Thus his weight or drive was taken from him and given to the "busy person."

The statement: *"but from the one who does not have, even what he does have shall be taken away,"* seems to make no degree of sense. Precisely how does one do this? How is it, or how can it be that one who *"does not have;"* will somehow ultimately have what he *"does have"* taken away from him? Whatever he does not have, cannot be the same thing which is taken from him; as he clearly did or does not have "it" to begin with.

Thus it becomes an issue regarding precisely what it was that was taken from him; with the understanding that whatever was taken from him, cannot be something he did not have at the time it was taken from him.

The weight or *talantŏn* in question is largely personal and *motivational*, rather than *physical*. He, (the one talent man), chose to be unaffected by this weight or *talantŏn*; any excuses notwithstanding. Thus it must be asked whether or not he actually still had this weight or *talantŏn* that he chose to ignore, once he ignored, (hid), the same?

The parable tells us that this "lazy man's" *talantŏn* was "given" to the servant with ten talents; but the question remains as to whether this ignored psychological "weight," was actually still in the one talent man's possession. If so, then it was the weight that was taken from him; but this does not qualify as what he did *not* have; if it were the case that he still had it to be taken.

However, if it were the case that this "weight" was being ignored or "hidden" by him, is essentially the same as him not having it; he would then qualify as one "who does not have," at least in the weight, or *talantŏn* "department."

Little is known about what this servant did in fact have, but what we do know is that he must have had supernatural abilities of one "duna," because he was given one "tala." So the one thing stated in the story that we know he did in fact have, was this ability. Thus it seems likely that it was his *supernatural* abilities which were taken from him, these representing the "what he does have."

The actual word translated as "hid" in verse 18 is:

"613 apŏkruptō; from 575 and 2928; to *conceal away* (i.e. *fully*) fig. to *keep secret*: - hide."[10.44]

But the actual word translated as "hid" in verse 25 is:

"2928 kruptō: a prim verb; to *conceal* (prop. by covering): - hide (self), keep secret, secret [-ly]."[10.45]

If it is stipulated that the word *talantŏn* is as previously *literally* defined: "(to *bear*; equiv. to *5342*); a *balance* (as *supporting weights*);" one might reasonably ask precisely ask how this "to bear" or "a balance;" would be or could be *literally* hidden in the ground?

In order for this to be *literally* possible, only the *implied* definition can reasonably be utilized: "i.e. (by impl.) a certain *weight* (and thence a *coin* or rather *sum* of money)."

Thus the use of the phrase: "*dug a hole in the ground and hid,*" or as in the KJV: "*digged in the earth;*"[10.46] is likely not to be considered as *literal*, but *like* or *as though* buried in the ground; and refers to *apŏkruptō*, or to "conceal away (i.e. fully) fig. to keep secret," but here hidden *from himself.*

In the music industry, there is the term: "one hit wonder." This refers to an unknown artist, who has a "smash hit;" but never even comes even close to another. It is not the "hit" which is relevant here, but rather what subsequently does *not* happen.

It could be the case that the artist *serendipitously* received the *dunamis* which resulted in this "hit," and was unable to reproduce the *serendipity*—which in itself may in fact be an oxymoronic statement.

Or it could be that this artist chooses to ignore the forces or *talantŏn* on the right side of the diagram, with his supernatural ability subsequently taken from him. This is because *ignoring* these motivational forces, is essentially the same as not having them; so what he does have; often erroneously referred to as *talent*; is ultimately taken from him.

This is not done to be "mean," or "as punishment;" but rather because nature will not permit the *continued* existence of an unbalanced actuality.

Finally we are told: *"Throw out the worthless slave into the outer darkness; in that place there will be weeping and gnashing of teeth."*

The first distinction to be made is the use of the adjective *"outer"* to describe the darkness. If it were merely *darkness*, then the use of this adjective would be unnecessary. However; this word *"outer"* does appear, likely being utilized to distinguish this outer darkness from other types of darkness; such as those with either different or no adjectives preceding it or them. There would be no need to distinguish a sloth, by referring to it as a three toed sloth; if it were the case that *all* sloths had three toes—which they do not.

The most obvious other potential type of darkness would be *inner* darkness. Thus it would be fair to ask: What is outer darkness; what is inner darkness; and what are the differences between them?

The actual Greek word translated as darkness is:

"4655 skŏtŏs; from the base of *4639*; *shadiness, i.e. obscurity* (lit. or fig.): - darkness."[10.47]

"4639 skia; appar. a prim. Word; *"shade"* or a shadow (lit or fig. [or an *adumbration*]): - shadow."[10.48]

[*Skŏtŏs* is the same word used to describe the darkness at Calvary, which most believe was an eclipse; but could not have been.[10.49] [See: *"MeekRaker Beginnings..."* Chapter 11 *"Pericalvaric Apocrypha"*]

The actual Greek word translated as "outer" is:

"1857 ĕxōtĕrŏs; comp. of 1854; *exterior:* - outer."[10.50]

The actual Greek word translated as "gnashing" is:

"1030 brugmŏs; from *1031*; a *grating* (of the teeth): - gnashing."[10.51]

"1031 bruchō; a prim. verb: to *grate* the teeth (in pain or rage): - gnash."[10.52]

According to *"Vine's,"* the word "of teeth" was added, and thus does or did not appear in the original.[10.53]

As can be seen, *bugmŏs* refers to simply "grating;" while it is its root: *bruchō*, means "to grate the teeth."

According to *"The Illustrated Dictionary of the Bible,"* the use of the phrase "gnashing of teeth," as used by Jesus in this passage, is not literal; but refers to "the futility of the wicked who will be judged by God at the end of time."[10.54]

It also must be remembered that this verse tells us what *"there will be."* The verse does not tell that this is or was happening at the "now," or "real time," the time when these words were actually spoken "real time" by Jesus; or when these would have been spoken were this a *story* and not a *parable*. In fact in using the *future* tense, Jesus is more than arguably stating that weeping and gnashing is not yet going on in this outer darkness. This may also be perfectly consistent with the view of *"The Illustrated Dictionary of the Bible"* above: "will be judged at the end of time."

And we are told what *"will be"* happening in that "place." The statement refers to the *place*, and is not necessarily an all inclusive statement. Meaning; that although there will be weeping and gnashing in that place; not necessarily all in that place will be either weeping, or gnashing, or both.

Regarding this "outer darkness," this may refer to the "general area" of the nether or neither world, or *hell*; as opposed to the "*kŏlpŏs*, or *Limbus Patrum*, or *Abraham's Bosom*; (which) is or was the "area" for those who physically died before the availability of salvation." Here it may be that the *kŏlpŏs* represents the "inner darkness;" with the area of the *nether* or *neither* world *outside* of the *kŏlpŏs* representing this "*outer darkness*."

Nevertheless, this instead could simply be an angry and quite annoyed *"master,"* telling the servant to: "Go to hell!" and then translated into King James English.

A distinction should be made between saints and sinners:
Saints try to live their lives according to God's will. When *saints* sin; and all *saints* do; this is an error, and is not part of their plan. Even if the sin is willful, it still represents an *error* or straying from their intended path.

Sinners live for themselves. If they should somehow behave consistent with the will of God; this may or may not be "fine with them;" as long as it does not interfere with their intentions. Whether or not this is "fine with them," depends upon their actual level of evil. But a sinner deliberately behaving consistent with the will of God, and to do so for that reason, is the exception; just as is *sinning* is to the *saint*.

As previously stated, the actual Greek word often translated as "sin" in the *New Testament* is:

> "hamartanō; perh. from *1* (as a neg. particle) and the base of *3313*; prop. to *miss* the mark (and *so not share* in the prize), i.e. (fig.) to *err*, esp. (mor.) to *sin*."

And the actual Hebrew word often translated as "sin" in the *Old Testament* is:

> 2398 châṭâ'; a prim. root; prop. to *miss*; hence (fig. and gen.) to *sin*; by infer. To *forfeit, lack, expiate, repent,* (causat.) *lead astray, condemn...*"[10.55]

By these definitions, it must be asked: "Was the 'one talent man' a sinner?" After all, he buried his "talent," and missed any increase or "prize," unlike the other two.

If the answer is yes, then the same must also be asked about all of those who travel the *"broad"* way, and enter that *"wide* gate or door which *'many there be which go in thereat;'"* as opposed to the *"few there be that find it"* zōē door.

It must be remembered that man's lifetime or *zōē*, becomes *apōlĕia*; or wasted, ruined and lost; although likely not totally destroyed; when one enters that *wide* door.

Once again: "To the extent that this narrow gate or door described in Matthew is *entered*; there is to this very same extent, *less apōlĕia*. To the extent that there is *less apōlĕia*, then to this same extent man's "lifetime" or *zōē* is: "unwasted," "unruined," and/or "unlost." And to the extent that man's lifetime or *zōē* is "unwasted," "unruined," and/or "unlost;" there is greater success in man's primary function as *tsâbâ'*."

Again, that which is available upon entering this narrow door is not the same for everyone. It is not simply God's general plan for *zōē*, or *lifetime* in general. It is God's plan for each *individual's zōē*. Each individual is different, and each is brought into existence for different *objectives*; but all are brought into existence for the same *goal*.

This narrow door is God's plan for one's life. All are designed and equipped by God for certain purposes in furtherance of His plans. This represents our capabilities; whether natural, supernatural, or both. When one responds; and to the extent that one responds; to the triggers God provides for us to use our capabilities in furtherance of His will; one is closer to, or inside that narrow door.

What it is that is actually on the other side of this, (the good), *zōē* gate or door is wisdom, (knowledge plus understanding); "actionable intelligence;" power, and unpredictability. And this "power" includes *dunamis*.

Again, John 14:12 tells us:

> "Verily, verily, I say unto you,
> He that believeth on me,
> the works that I do shall he do also;
> and greater works than these shall he do;
> because I go unto my Father."

Chapter 11

Talantŏn
vs.
"A-talantŏn"

The great science fiction writer Robert A. Heinlein was once asked about why he enjoyed writing. Although his exact response is unavailable, he essentially answered, (paraphrased): "Good God, what ever gave you the idea I enjoyed writing?"

Heinlein was then asked why he did it, if he didn't enjoy it. His answer was that he did it because (paraphrased): "It hurts less to write, than to not write." This is often how a *talantŏn* will work—assuming of course that it is a *talantŏn*.

Here the matter of the *"a-talantŏn"* will be introduced. An *a-talantŏn* is not of God, but rather is a device of the enemy. The *purpose* of both the *talantŏn* and the *a-talantŏn* is not to actually force any *tsâbâ'* or H. Sapiens to act; but rather to essentially induce a *tsâbâ'* or H. Sapiens to *choose* to act.

An *a-talantŏn* is a *counterfeit* version of the *talantŏn*. It is not that the enemy *would* not force action; but rather that he *cannot* force action upon man. And God *will not* force action upon man.

However; unlike the *a-talantŏn*; with the *talantŏn*, there can be no violations of God's rules. No violations of any of the Commandments are required. This is not to say that one who is "working" a *talantŏn* will not in the process violate said rules or Commandments; but rather that this is not *required*. Any such violations are *errors* committed by the active party. These in fact represent *deviations* from what actions are required by the *talantŏn* for *success*; as well what is required for *balance*.

With the *a-talantŏn*, the reverse is true. This is a key in making an accurate determination as to precisely which type of "weight;" (*talantŏn* vs. *a-talantŏn*); it is that one is experiencing. If any action inconsistent with the word of God is *required* in order to satisfy that which seems to be "heavy on one's heart;" then whatever it might otherwise be; it is not a *talantŏn*.

The other main difference is the presence of *dunamis*, or supernatural power. With an *a-talantŏn*, the possibility of any significant levels of "real time" dunamis is essentially zero. [This "real time" *dunamis*, vs. its counterpart will be "re-addressed" later.]

As previously stated, *dunamis* is *supernatural* power, and not *natural* power. This can manifest in many different forms, and often is not recognized as such until much later.

There are two keys to recognizing *dunamis*, as opposed to mere *natural* power:

Firstly; there must be some violation or violations of what is considered to be *natural* law. The "considered to be" part of course is crucial. The presence of *dunamis* is not always as immediately obvious as feeding all of the people at a picnic, with one loaf of bread and a fish. When any cause *definitively* produces an effect other than that which is definitively "natural;" then *dunamis* is likely present. This can manifest in the *physical*, such as turning water into wine; or can also take place in the *non-physical*.

Secondly; *dunamis* or *dunamic* "acts," generally tend to happen quickly. The miracle that is considered to be the longest in duration; is the provision of manna—which roughly translates as:

Talantŏn vs. "A-talantŏn"

"What is it?" But in actuality this was an act of *dunamis* provided each day, and not one act lasting years; as manna simply would not "keep."

"Happen quickly," in this context, can also mean seeming to "come out of nowhere." Perhaps "suddenly" is a better description; i.e.; quickly and not expected. However a "dunamis-less" *a-talantŏn* can also seem to happen quickly; with the seemingly instant rise of Elvis Presley representing the former (*talantŏn*); and the rise of ISIS representing the latter (*a-talantŏn*).

When a *talantŏn* is present, this *talantŏn* is the source of that "heavy on my heart" feeling that tends to prompt one into action. Depending on the nature of the recipient, they: "aint a gonna have no peace;" until they begin acting, or introducing "ergs" into the system.

When a force is applied, (ergs), in an attempt to balance or remove the weight, the result is that *dunamis* or supernatural force begins to manifest. Once this begins, seemingly impossible events begin to be observed. Again, this assumes it is in fact a *talantŏn* that is being "worked." The use of "*true talantŏn*" is purposely avoided here, as it would be arguably tautological. This would be similar to: "his own autobiography;" as to who else could possibly be expected to write his autobiography.

In the "Talent Man" story, the servants had supernatural power, (dunamis). They were given weight (talantŏn) according to the amount of *dunamis*. Two of the servants "worked" this weight by putting energy into the system.

The result of their efforts ("*You were faithful with a few things*"); was additional weight or *talantŏn* being given to them; and they were put "*in charge of many things; enter into the joy of your master.*" This was done by first giving them additional weight, (talantŏn); and then given, (put in charge of), additional *dunamis*.

The "*enter into the joy of your master*" part should not be overlooked, for reasons that are obvious to those attempting to do God's will.

This parable provides an explanation of mechanisms and rules of, (for it is just like); the *immaterial* realm or the "kingdom of heaven." The "*joy of your master*" part likely refers to God as the *master*: "*Well done, good and faithful slave;*"—remembering here that the correct translation is *servant*.

This *talantŏn/dunamis/talantŏn* process is just that. It is a *process*, and not designed to be a "one shot deal." However; assuming the process is understood, (which is and was the true purpose of the parable); it nevertheless remains the choice of the recipient as to how far the process proceeds—hence the inclusion of the: "one talent man."

This *dunamis* or supernatural power, can be broken down into at least two sub-categories:

The first would be *absolute dunamis*. Turning water into wine is pretty funky no matter when or where it is done. It is difficult to imagine any circumstances where feeding thousands of people with an amount of food for just a few; and then having leftovers to gather, would be considered as not miraculous. This *dunamis* is *supernatural power* granted by God.

But there is also *relative dunamis*. This is really more like *dýnamis* or natural power in terms of an absolute; but becomes like *dunamis*, because of either the time or place of the application of the *ĕrgazŏmai* or labor. It is not necessarily supernatural power in and of itself, or alone; but is *dunamis* or *dunamic*, (authors' terminology), because of the *application*, and the subsequent result(s). *Relative dunamis* can often be *informational* in nature.

"Something just told me to pick those numbers for the lottery, and I won." Those same numbers would likely not have worked in yesterday's, tomorrow's, or last week's lottery. However; given an *infinite* number of lottery drawings, those same numbers would eventually recur—albeit not necessarily in one's lifetime.

"Something just told me to go in that store and I could not believe he, (pick a superstar), was there; and now we are good friends."

Or *relative dunamis* can be in the *negation* of the *ĕrgazŏmai* or work: "Something just told me to stay home from work on 9/11/01." This is the result of the receipt of information; not by the normal five senses; but by the *feelings*, (not emotions); and the results are similar to the application of absolute *dunamis*. The: "something

Talantŏn vs. "A-talantŏn"

just told me. . .;" could just as often be stated as: "I just had a feeling. . ."

The concept of this *talantŏn* is multi-faceted, and it can be very confusing to understand—even in a somewhat limited sense. It represents the balancing entity required for any *dunamic* actuality. In the Lottery numbers example, there was both the *dunamis*, (the winning numbers at the correct time); and the drive or *talantŏn* to play them that day. The *relative dunamis* alone would be insufficient for success in that example.

A *talantŏn* is similar to "normal" emotional drive, but it contains much more.

Like the old Geometry proofs, something can often be understood or determined by analyzing its opposite. The aforementioned An *"a-talantŏn,"* (literally *anti-talantŏn*, authors' terminology), represents the enemy's counterfeit version of *talantŏn*. For consistency, this *anti-talantŏn* can be measured in *anti-talas,* or *a-talas.*

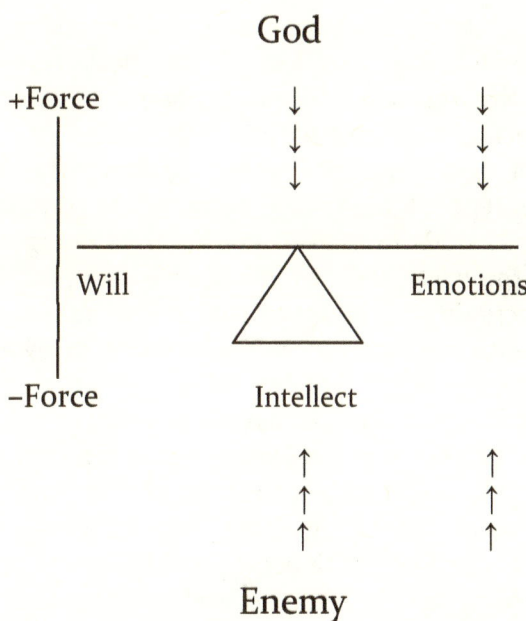

With respect to this diagram of will, intellect, and emotions; often the forces exerted by the enemy from the bottom on the right hand side *can* be, but are not always an *anti-talantŏn*. Some examples of *anti-talantŏn* are: pride, anger, greed hatred, and envy.

The purposes of this *anti-talantŏn*, is either to cause the host to engage in some type of manifestation of his or her will, which is consistent with the desires of the *enemy*; or to interfere with and/or neutralize a *talantŏn*.

For example: If one is insulted, the enemy will provide *anti-talantŏn* in order to affect the reactions of the host, here the "insultee." What the enemy desires, is for the host to make it his or her *will*, to respond in a manner consistent with what the enemy wants; and not what the host would generally otherwise want, or what God would *ever* want to see happen.

Normally a host will seek some kind of balance to the actions of any "attacker." The *a-talantŏn* is instituted to provide an additional mechanism purportedly in furtherance of this balancing. When this happens, the focus of the host now becomes the balancing of the *anti-talantŏn*, rather than balancing the *original* act. If the enemy is successful, the reaction of the host now becomes consistent with the *anti-talantŏn*, rather than consistent with the reasonable balancing of the original act.

So instead of this "insultee" either ignoring the insult, or providing some type of a rational response to the insult; the "insulter" suddenly finds himself in the hospital emergency room. Why? Because the host, (the *"insultee"*), chose—repeat *chose, not* to balance the *actuality* of the *insult* with a *rational* response; but instead he *chose* to balance the *anti-talantŏn* with *dýnamis*, and *ĕrgazŏmai*.

Meaning; that the host *chose* to use his *physical* capabilities and work, in order to balance this *a-talantŏn*; rather than balancing the original *insult*. This *a-talantŏn* consisted of *emotional* pressure; and usually is accompanied by some amount of falsehood, as *informational* pressure, with both being provided by the enemy.

So here it is much later in that day, and the "insultee" host was just allowed to leave police headquarters; and is at the hospital apologizing profusely to what now has become the victim. He simply does not know what happened to cause him to overreact so.

The answer of course was bad judgment. The host, likely unknowingly, interpreted the *a-talantŏn*, as though it was a *talantŏn*; and then reacted similar to the two servants in the parable. The difference in this case being, that it was *natural* and not *supernatural* capabilities which were utilized. It is not clear that any "host generated" supernatural abilities would function in these types of circumstances.

With respect to *neutralization* of a *talantŏn*, God provides a *talantŏn* let us say; for a host to give someone or some organization some sum of money. The enemy will then provide *anti-talantŏn* in the form of greed or fear, in order to attempt to modify the actions of the host in a manner the enemy prefers. If this *a-talantŏn* is accepted by the host, then sure as taxes, he will reduce the amount, or perhaps even eliminate entirely the donation or gift.

There must be a distinction made here, that this *a-talantŏn* refers to the *emotional* type pressures exerted on the right side of the diagram; and not the *false information* provided to the *intellect*, which will often accompany the *a-talantŏn*; with this being another matter which will be further analyzed later.

Although these *anti-talantŏn* events, rarely if ever at all, exist alone; i.e.; are not accompanied by the *intellect* attacks at some point in time; *what* one did or chose to do, as opposed to *why* one did it represent entirely different issues.

There are many different ways to determine if one is experiencing a *talantŏn*, or an *a-talantŏn*. The first is how quick is the response? The faster the response, the more likely it is *a-talantŏn*; as the enemy prefers to not risk the introduction and utilization of the host's judgment based upon anything else. Does it "feel good" while you are doing it, and if so; precisely what is this "good feeling" based upon? Will it still feel good at a later time?

Another way; would be to ask one's (own) self, if they would like the reaction that is currently planned were the roles reversed? Does it seem that the hastily, if at all, planned reaction is of God?

In the sense of a general rule, acting upon an *a-talantŏn*, will make one seem to "feel good" when you are providing the balance to it; and then in some way or manner "hurt" afterward.

Contrawise, acting upon a *talantŏn*, will "hurt" while the balance to it is being provided; and will "feel good" later. These of course require broader than normal definitions of "feels good" and "hurt."

But back to the (real) *talantŏn*.

Another "quote" attributed to the famous science fiction writer Robert A. Heinlein is relevant, and is concerned with morality. Heinlein provided guidance as to how one could determine the *moral* "thing;" or *moral* course of action, in the absence of sufficient information. His advice; was to look at all the possible choices, and pick the one that was most *difficult*. His view; was that the most *difficult* course of action to choose, as a rule generally represents the most *moral* course of action.

The *talantŏn* is that deep "heavy on the heart" desire. It can be a long term, or *strategic talantŏn*; which can last years or even a lifetime: "All of his life he wanted to be an "x;" and nothing was going to ever stop him." Or it can be a shorter term, *tactical* talantŏn.

In a sense, an *a-talantŏn* can resemble what is usually considered as "pangs of conscience;" but it is a bit different.

"Pangs of conscience" are an imbalance created between what one did or did not do, and what it is that one believes was appropriate; e.g.: "Now I must go and apologize to her." Here there is no rest because of the conflict, due to the imbalance of what one believes is appropriate; and what one did or did not do. This is a current imbalance due to some event or non-event in the *past*. [This will be addressed in greater detail in a subsequent volume when the "Ten Commandments" are analyzed.]

The *talantŏn* however, is not the result of this type of imbalance caused by one's (past) behavior; but rather a "weight" placed by God, here with God acting as: "an accessory *before* the fact." It is not the *result* of a host's actions or inactions. "Pangs of conscience" generally occur *after* something is done, (commission or omission). The *talantŏn* is present *before* an action is done; and is precisely designed and placed in order to prompt specific action.

Talantŏn vs. "A-talantŏn"

First there is relative *balance*. Then the *talantŏn* is introduced. Then there is an *imbalance*; which can only be balanced either by *action*; or the *dissipation* of the *talantŏn* over time by continued inaction; i.e.; *hiding* or *burying* the *talantŏn*.

The *talantŏn* can be a source of both unrest, and confusion. The cause of the unrest is obvious; and represents the very purpose *of* or *for* the *talantŏn*.

However, *confusion* often arises when determining the precise action required to balance the *talantŏn*; and thus this can often be a difficult process. This is because of many factors. One can perceive insufficient *actuality*, rendering one's *reality* insufficient. One can be "embarrassed" because of what others may think of the action required. Here it is extremely important to determine if it is an issue of *upright* behavior; or merely what others may think; i.e.; a matter of "taste."

Balancing a *talantŏn* can be unbelievably grueling, and often takes much time. And yes; others may perceive insanity *from their perspective*; and often can be quite vocal about it. And the enemy will sow anything he can to stop the process. "I had to sell that piano because that child was practicing all day long and driving me nuts," is unwise.

But when the *talantŏn* is balanced by the correct action(s), it often feels like: "a weight was taken off of one's chest"—and for good reason(s).

Alleged Fantasy Foundations Volume I

Chapter 12

It Sort of Has
to Be So

There are those who believe in the "miracles" of the Bible, and there are those who do not. From the enemy's perspective; it is in fact a logical necessity that those who do not, do not—

This of course sounds like a "no brainer"—perhaps representing an example of idiocy in one of its purest forms. But of course, such a dismissive conclusion requires ignoring the "em dash," and inserting a period; and would be predicated upon a *presumed* understanding of precisely to what the second "do not" refers. Said conclusion could arguably represent arrogance in its purest form; as "a-rogare" literally means without or not to question; here assuming a quasi-tautology, where none exists.

What is there to question? The answer to that question; is to ask this question: "Precisely to what does the second 'do not' refer?"

The second "do not" refers *not* to the same statement as the first; but rather to a necessary conclusion on the part of the enemy. The second "do not" is actually incomplete, in that it should read: "do not represent any substantial threat."

So it should actually read: "It is in fact a logical necessity that those who do not believe in the miracles of the Bible; do not represent any substantial threat."

Do not represent any substantial threat to whom? Why to the enemy of course.

Why? Because if one does not understand or even believe that these miraculous capabilities are actualities; then the enemy understands one very important fact with respect to that particular person, and all others like him.

And that fact; is that the potential threat level to the enemy is limited to the aforementioned *dynes*, and does not include the aforementioned *dunas*. These persons are limited to the *dýnamis* which is *natural* power or abilities; and are effectively incapable of *dunamis* or *supernatural* power or abilities—at least for any meaningful tactical or strategic usage.

Thus, whatever is "in them," is no greater than that which is in this, (the material), world. This knowledge pleases him or it, (the enemy), greatly; as the majority of these individuals do not represent any substantial threat level to him/it the majority of the time.

There may be times when these individuals *serendipitously* "fall into" a higher attack level; but the "expected value" of this event occurring; (the mathematical product of the level of potential *damage*, multiplied by the *probability* of it occurring); remains quite low. And most importantly; low enough as to be of little concern to the enemy, and so he behaves accordingly.

But what about those who believe in, (operate from a *reality* which includes), the *actuality* of this *dunamis*? These persons represent, not only actual potentially serious threats to the enemy; but more importantly, can often result in a situation where the enemy simply cannot win. This is so, because what is in these persons is greater that what is in this natural or material world; and *potentially* much greater than that which is in the enemy

It is a simple vector analysis of opposing forces, and the greater force prevails. Thus the only option for the enemy here, is to induce *fatigue*; and then have the host *choose* to remove this greater opposing force. This necessarily shifts the battle from one of forces, in which the enemy cannot prevail; to one of determination—a shift from *can* to *will*.

So there must exist an alternative for the enemy to somehow reduce the power level of the forces *available* to these pesky believing hosts. He cannot win on the battlefield of actual forces against these hosts, and as he has experienced; some attacks on some of these host's level of determination can often be both difficult, and quite fickle—sometimes backfiring on the enemy in a disproportionate manner.

As always, he or it (the enemy), has to: "cut the deal." How does one reconcile true belief in the existence of *dunamis*, and yet be rendered incapable of its utilization? The answer; is the belief that the miracles of the Bible are in fact true; but that this *dunamis* existed only at that time, and thus no longer applies to the current living hosts. There is no Scriptural evidence whatsoever to support this "deal;" but this nevertheless seems to be many of the prevalent "religious" viewpoints today.

It then becomes acceptable to still believe in *Jesus*, and acceptable to still believe in the power of the *Christ*, (the anointing of the *Holy Ghost*); but only for His, (Jesus'), contemporaries, and most importantly; that this power no is longer available today. It is never specified as to what year this "event" supposedly occurred; neither is there and specific reason(s) given as to why this supposed change happened.

In order for this "deal" to be accepted, there would have to be reasons for maintaining this belief. The reason(s) for *believing* this; and any reason(s) for this purported *change* are entirely different matters.

Like any good fictional work, the story must be *plausible*; that is, reasonably believable. And there must also exist a *motive* or *motives* for victims to believe this "doctrine"—particularly because there is no evidence to support it. More likely than not, this arises from the use of *inductive* reasoning, that is; making the journey from the specific to the general; combined with, and largely driven by *pride*.

This is a much more common practice than is generally perceived. "Since my refrigerator is white, all refrigerators must be white;" is an easy one to "see through." But; "because I like this type of music, everyone must like it," is a bit more difficult; but unfortunately quite common. However; it is generally never actually stated; but merely acted out. This is merely pride and self-centeredness. And each of these has a source that is not of God.

The next progression of this "thinking," then equates *quality* with *taste*: "This band is *really* good." Why? "Because I *really* like them." (Note the use of *reality*, and not *actuality*, as the root of the word utilized as a "degree of comparison.")

The use of a derivative of *actuality*; i.e.; *actually*, as in: "I actually like them," (as opposed to: "I really like them."); "normally" would be to present the existence of something as a fact.

However, to "actually" state: "I actually like them;" would instead generally be interpreted as a statement of fact *contrary* to that which was expected: "He put catsup in his coffee. Isn't that disgusting?" "Well, I tried it and I *actually* like it."

The use of a term which is supposed to be objective, (good), and indicates relative quality, and judged by objective standards; (What is the fastest tempo that Chopin's: *"Petite Chien,"* or *"Minute Waltz,"* (actually: "Little Dog"); can be played error free); is now in use based upon one's personal taste; i.e.; one's *reality*.

But of course, inductive reasoning is not a *motive*, but rather a *technique*. The real motive with respect to this matter; as is often the case with inductive reasoning; is the above stated *pride* and *self-centeredness* being *actualized*—whether this process is "realized" or not.

With regard to *dunamis*, since the target host of this scheme, (the victim); cannot, or at least *believes* that he cannot: speak in tongues; nor cast out demons; nor "heal" the sick; (These last two are not necessarily *dunamic*, but much more about this later); nor make it rain, or make it stop raining; they are left with only one of two possible choices: It must either be the case that it is *they* who simply cannot do it; or it simply cannot be done.

The "non-observations" made; and subsequent conclusions drawn by the victim of this type of attack; irrespective of which of the two reasons is chosen; are in fact erroneous.

It Sort of Has to Be So

The former, ("I cannot do it."), is a rarity; as most hosts would be reluctant to admit that it is *they* that are the problem. In addition, if this is the admission, then there must necessarily first be the prerequisite admission that it, (dunamis), *can* be done; but *they* are simply, and perhaps permanently, incapable of doing it.

It is simply much easier to believe that there is no *dunamis* available today, ("It simply cannot be done."); and *that* is the only reason they cannot do it—a common finding with any pride or self centered based, (motivated), conclusion. Essentially; the victim believes that he has observed no evidence of *dunamis* in his or her life. They have established a threshold for the presence of *dunamis*, which is strictly *result* oriented.

And since they have generally seen no results in their life which would require the presence of *dunamis*, in order for this or these, result or results, to have been achieved; *dunamis* must then not, (now, or at the present time), be an *actuality*.

In those few cases, (results), where the presence of *dunamis* would clearly have been required; these are then ultimately dismissed as bogus. Even if the evidence of *dunamis* is overwhelming; over time, the enemy will usually "work" the victim into believing that it was not so—with "it" here meaning the actual occurrence of very *event* itself.

Should he fail in this, ("I am telling you, that event most certainly did happen."); the enemy will then convince the "observer" that it was a matter of some unknown knowledge or factor that just made it *seem* that dunamis was present—it of course being known as a certainty by all; that each and every "magician" who ever existed, *always* utilized trickery, in *all* of his actions, and *all* of the time. This type of "knowledge," represents a comfortable baseline assumption for rejecting any and all evidence of *dunamis* today.

Today, "magicians" are generally in the *entertainment* business, but this was not always so. The "wise men," or *Magi*, who visited the *child* Jesus at the *house*; (not the *newborn* Jesus in the *manger*); were most certainly *not* in the entertainment business.

In order for this "observation or lack thereof," (never seeing *dunamis* in their lifetime); and subsequent conclusion, (therefore *dunamis* does not exist today), to be accurate; then the victim would be required to have *complete* evidence of the results of many types of actions in order to determine if their assigned threshold, (for the existence of *dunamis* today), has been met. This of course also assumes that the assigned threshold is accurate. Success in either of these is highly unlikely.

Nevertheless, the victim *believes*, (reality), that they have never seen nor done anything that was *actually miraculous* in nature. Thus, they are faced with the choice of these two alternatives in order to explain the "non-existence" of this is phenomenon.

If pride is in any way a factor, then it is simply much easier to believe that the reason that something *was not* accomplished; is because it *cannot* be accomplished.

Again, the rarely seen alternative being that although it, (dunamis), can in fact be accomplished, my attempts resulted in failure: "It can be done, but I cannot do it."

It is simply much easier for one to believe that the failure was due to circumstances *beyond* one's control; rather than due to circumstances *within* one's control. So the inductive reasoning comes into play and says: "Since I could not do it; then it cannot or could be done."

"The reason that it merely *appears* as though I failed, although understandable, is not true. I didn't actually fail, because it was simply impossible to do. It was impossible to succeed. It isn't my fault. Oh, I may have erred in *choosing* to attempt such an undertaking; but who can be faulted for setting such high standards?"

It is important to remember the parable of the "talent men," as the principles of the story are applicable here.

If the victim of this scheme were correct in that they have never done anything miraculous, (which forms the basis for the *specific*; which then "inductively" leads to the *general* conclusion), it would be fair to ask the question: "Why?"—and in the specific.

In the parable of the talent men, it is clear that the acquisition of *dunamis* is a *process*. They were each given a balancing or bearing weight according to some previous level(s) of *dunamis*.

Two of the men "worked" their *dunamis*, and one did not. Those two who "worked" their *dunamis* in excess of the requirements of

It Sort of Has to Be So

the bearing weight, were given additional bearing weight; but also were given additional *dunamis* or supernatural power.

The one who did nothing, (buried the weight), had this weight; and subsequently, his *dunamis* was taken from him. This parable represents a slice in time of an ongoing process. The important thing is that it is a *process*. Who was it that decided if additional power was to be granted to two of these men? *They did*, by working their abilities far beyond what was required by the balancing weight.

Thus it appears that *three* possibilities exist for the failure of the victim of the enemy's scheme to perform something miraculous:

Firstly; they may have not yet been given the corresponding weight in accordance with their *dunamis* in order to activate the same, thus balancing the actuality. This is highly unlikely, if not impossible. Likely the weight was *given*, but not *recognized*.

Or *secondly*; they may have been given this weight but failed to "work" their dunamis; instead, choosing to "bury" it. They then subsequently had both taken from them.

Or *thirdly*; perhaps as the "generalized conclusion" states: There never was any *dunamis* to work, because although there once was, there is no longer any such thing as *dunamis*—this of course being the very conclusion desired by the enemy, and the main purpose for this particular scheme.

If strictly for the purposes of argument, this "inductively derived generalized conclusion" is considered to be a possibility; meaning that *dunamis* was merely for a temporary period of time, and thus no longer is available; then there must have been a reason or reasons for its *institution*; as well as for its *removal*.

One can pore over all of the available *amphigory*, attempting to find the answer to this latter question; but there is little that makes any degree of sense in support of this "Apostolic era only" position. The best that can be said, is that the proponents of this "Apostolic era only" theory, believe that *dunamis* was required solely in order to establish the Christian Church. And the theory also states that once this was established, there was no longer any need for this *dunamis*.

This "Apostolic era only" theory is extremely problematic for several reasons:

Firstly; by definition, the "church" is the body of Christ; here "Christ" meaning the anointing or the Holy Ghost; which is the actual source of *dunamis*. It is delineated and distinguished that Jesus is the *head* of this *body*, in order to differentiate the *two different* parts of the Trinity that are involved.

If there were no Holy Ghost activity, there would be no need for the "church" as used in this sense. A church is not a building, but rather the people. This agrees perfectly with the concept of a Holy "Ghost" as opposed to a Holy "Spirit." The Christian "church" as used in this sense represents an organized group of "hosts" who desire that the Holy Ghost not merely be *on* them, but reside, (abide), *within* them. It must be remembered that the Holy Ghost not only *descended* upon Jesus, but that it also *abode* or *remained* on Him.

John 1:32-33 (KJV) tells us:

*"And John bare record, saying,
I saw the Spirit descending from heaven
like a dove, and it abode upon him."*

*And I knew him not:
but he that sent me to baptize with water,
the same said unto me,
Upon whom thou shalt see the
Spirit descending, and remaining on him,
the same is he which baptizeth
with the Holy Ghost."*[12.1]

After Calvary, this Holy Ghost is not limited to merely descending *upon* us, but rather can live *within* us; if we should choose to permit it. According to this current "no *dunamis* today" theory however; after a certain period of time, for reasons unknown; there "just aint no mo Ghost to be found."

It Sort of Has to Be So

This "Apostolic era only" theory is backwards. The fact is that the *church* as defined above; is necessary for the Holy Ghost to *increase* "operations," and not the reverse. It is *dunamis* that is the main reason for Christians to establish a *Christian*, (not "Jesusite"), church.

The four Gospels are largely about Jesus, the Son; or the *Second Part of the Trinity*. The "Book of Acts" is largely about The Holy Ghost; or the *Third* Part of the Trinity—hence the name: "Acts."

Secondly, with this "Apostolic era only" theory, there would be an issue of *fraud*.

A famous magician or a group of famous magicians decide to form a magic school. They travel around the world performing amazing feats of magic, all in an effort to get people to join the school. Millions of people join the school *specifically* in order to be able to learn to perform these types of amazing magic tricks. After a somewhat short period of time, the students become restless because they have not received any instruction in how to do these amazing feats, but rather, are limited to performances that are consistent with *natural* law. The students ask about learning the amazing tricks, and are told that those feats can no longer be performed.

The students then file suit. The magic school's first defense; is that although those capabilities did in fact once exist; the magic existed merely for the recruitment of students to facilitate the formation of the school—perhaps merely to worship the founder. And after a period of time, when the school had reached a certain undefined threshold; say a certain undisclosed number of students; the power to perform these amazing feats was then removed.

In fact, it is explained to the court that this magic was not in any way magic as commonly understood today; i.e.; for *entertainment* only; but was actual magic power.

Their second defense; is that this ability, which was actual *dunamis*; was only *loaned* to them by God for the purposes of getting people to join. They further explain that God never had any intention of providing this *dunamis* to the students once they joined; so at some unknown point in time, and for some unknown reason(s), and without ever even "breathing a word about it" in His "manual;" He just took it all away.

As a juror, how would one vote under these circumstances? And would one fairly tend to describe God as an "unindicted co-conspirator?" And, would it also be fair to ask if this sounds like either the God described in the Bible; the God of Abraham, Isaac and Jacob; or Jesus?

Thirdly, there is the matter of "The Force..."

Once again, John 14:12 (NAS) tells us:

> *"Truly, truly, I say to you,*
> *he who believes in Me,*
> *the works that I do, he will do also;*
> *and greater works than these he will do;*
> *because I go to the Father."*

The King James *version* of John 14:12:

> *"Verily, verily, I say unto you,*
> *He that believeth on me,*
> *the works that I do shall he do also;*
> *and greater works than these shall he do;*
> *because I go unto my Father."*[12.2]

Here Jesus is speaking, and he is making a specific statement of *fact*; as well as providing the specific *reason* why, (*"because"*), this fact is in fact so. The problem is that although a cursory reading may result in the nodding of one's head and an exclamation of "Hallelujah!;" upon careful scrutiny, this particular *reason*, (*"because I go to the Father"*), seems to make no degree of sense.

Precisely what is or are the statement or statements that Jesus is making; and precisely what do they mean?

This verse can actually be broken down into two different statements that Jesus is making:

The *first* statement represents an "if-then" relationship.

One read would be; that *if* one believes in Jesus; *and* one also believes in the works that He did; *then* he, (the believer), will do these works also.

The "if" portion reads: *"He that believeth on me, the works that I do."* In this case, the comma after *"me"* should be removed; and replaced with "and:" (If) He that believeth on me (and) the works that I do."

The "then" portion is: *"the works that I do shall he do also."*

Of course this could then raise the question as to what it is, (*"works"*), that *"he will do also?"* The most likely answer of course would refer to Jesus' actual *works*, which is precisely what we are told. Thus this would mean that, *if* one believes in Jesus, and believes in the works done by Jesus; *then*, the works that Jesus did, he (the believer) *"will"* or *"shall do also."*

It must be asked what types of works done by Jesus would require said "belief?" The answer would be that these would necessitate *believe in*, rather than merely *believe*.

If as a child, Jesus had constructed a toy airplane from *shittem* wood leftover from the ark, one may or may not believe this was so. But would this "work" in any way justify "believe in" as commonly understood?

"Do you believe God exists?;" and Do you believe in God?;" are not the same question. Often people are asked: "Do you believe in the devil?" One can believe the devil exists, without "believing in," the devil.

"Believing in," is a term that is usually reserved for that for which insufficient evidence exists, to justify having a high level of confidence that "the thing" is an actuality. Generally, there is also the issue of "faith" involved, which will be addressed later.

The actual Greek word translated as "works" both times, is again the previously addressed:

"2041 ĕrgŏn; from a prim. (but obsol.) ĕrgō (to *work*); *toil* (as an effort or occupation); by impl. an *act*: - deed, doing, labour, work."[12.3]

Clearly; constructing the toy airplane could easily fit the definition of *ĕrgŏn*, and one would be free to believe Jesus had built it. But it seems there would be no need to "believe in" the works of constructing a toy airplane.

Similarly; those to whom Jesus was actually speaking, believed there was a speaker in front of them, and that His name was Jesus, (Yeshua); with the alternative of course not believing He was there speaking. But believing, (*"believes in"*) that He was the Messiah and The Christ, is another matter.

The *first* statement: *"He that believeth on me, the works that I do shall he do also;"* tells us that "a believer" will be able to do the works that Jesus did. If you believe in Jesus and the works He did; then *you* will be able to do the works He did. And for emphasis of the veracity, there is a double *"truly;"* or what is used in the KJV as *"verily,"* included therein.

The *second* statement begins with *"and:"* *"and greater works than these shall he do;"* thus indicating that this is another separate statement, this being a *conditional* statement; in that it only applies, (if and only if), it is the situation where the "if" and subsequent "then" of the *first* statement have been met. Meaning that this second statement only applies to those who believe in Jesus and the works He did.

Assuming the criteria for the first statement have been met; i.e.; one is a believer; then this second statement: *"greater works than these he will do; because I go to the Father,"* necessarily also applies. And, it includes both the *statement* being made; as well as the *reason* given for the statement provided being true.

This raises the question of the use of the *future* tense being in use as evidenced by the appearance of the word "will," (NAS); or "shall," (KJV); in both statements: *"shall he do also; and greater works than these shall he do."*

There is also the issue of potential coercion in the translations as *"shall;"* vs. *"will."*

It Sort of Has to Be So

It must be noted that *"shall he do"* appears twice in John 14:12 (KJV) above. So the question then becomes whether these "shall he do(s)" refer to actual *capability*; or to actual *utilization*; e.g.; "shall be able to do" or "shall do?"

The actual Greek word translated as "shall he do" each time is:

> "4160 pŏiĕō; appar. a prol. form of an obsol. prim; to *make* or *do* (in a very wide application, more or less direct): - abide, +agree, appoint, x avenge..."[12.4]

There seems to be no *coercion* in the definition of *pŏiĕō*. Thus it seems that *"shall he do"* is better translated contextually as "shall he be *able* to do."

In the second statement: *"and greater works than these he will do; because I go to (unto KJV) the Father)*; the usage of the *future* tense is entirely appropriate.

Assuming the criteria for the *first* statement are met; that is; one has become a believer, and now can do the *same* works that Jesus did; as that is what the first statement promises; the *translation* of *pŏiĕō* as "will" with regard to the *greater* works, does or did not necessarily apply immediately.

Unlike as in the case of ability to do the *same* works, which *immediately* applies; these *greater* works, and the use of the term "will," indicates that this *greater* ability applies to, or will apply in the *future*.

At the time these statements were made; precisely when in the future these greater abilities would apply would have necessarily depended on, and directly corresponded to, the timing surrounding some *future* event.

The actual reason given by Jesus for these *greater* abilities; the same being: *"because"* Jesus would *"go to the Father;"* had unknown or at least undisclosed timing *at that time*; i.e.; it was not then known at what point in time He would *"go to the Father."*

From a present day perspective, the use of the future tense for these greater abilities no longer applies; as Jesus has already gone to the Father, and many believe currently sits the "right hand" of the

Father—whatever meaning this may or may not have in the *immaterial* realm, or "heaven;" but not "the heavens."

What did Jesus mean by greater works? There are many today that believe that He meant greater *numbers* of works, because of a greater *number* of believers. But this presents a problem with the "Apostolic era only" view of dunamis. So here with the "Apostolic era only" position, this must then refer to greater numbers of *non-dunamis* works, from some undisclosed point in time onward.

However, none of the words *numbers*, *amounts*, *quantities*, or any other word appears between "*greater*" and "*works*." Thus, we are left with the inescapable conclusion that the word "greater" refers to the word that follows it, and not another "phantom" word that does not appear anywhere in the original verse.

Nevertheless today many maintain the belief that the actual word that is translated as "greater" actually means "more numerous," "a plethora;" or some other word or words referring to the "quantity of," rather than the "magnitude of."

The original Greek word translated here as "greater" is:

> "3187 měizōn; irreg. compar. of *3173*; *larger* (lit. or fig., spec. in age): - elder, greater (-est), more."[12.5]

> "3173 měgas, [include. the prol. forms, fem. měgalē, plur. měgaloĭ, etc.; comp. also *3176*, *3187*]; *big* (lit. or fig., in a very wide application): - (+ fear) exceedingly, great (-est), high, large, loud, mighty, +(be) sore (afraid), strong, x to years."[12.6]

> "3176 měgistŏs; superl. of *3173*; *greatest* or *very great*: - exceeding great."[12.7]

A fair read of these definitions, is that it is the degree of *magnitude* of the *works* themselves to which this word *měizōn* refers; and that *měizōn* does not in any way relate to *quantity*; i.e.; the *number* of works "done"—except perhaps in the quantity of *dunas* these greater works represent or require.

But what about this cause-effect relationship between these *greater* abilities, and Jesus going to the Father?

What it does *not* state; is that a believer will have greater power than Jesus, because Jesus is the *Son of God*. It does not state that the greater abilities are because the *Father* is in Him; nor does it state that these greater abilities are because the *Father* is coming or comes *to* Him. All of these unstated things may or may not be in fact true; but nevertheless, none of these is the reason given for these greater abilities. Instead, the stated reason is: *"because I go to the Father."*

With respect to the uses of tenses, it is most likely that there is something that *will* happen, (do greater works); which *will* happen as a result of or because of the reason given; but the reason is presented in the *present* tense, ("*go*").

Thus it also seems reasonable that these *greater* capabilities were not yet available at the time Jesus made this statement, (*will*). This is because either Jesus has not yet gone to the Father, present tense, (I go) notwithstanding; or that He had already gone to the Father, but there was to be some sort of delay—something that is neither mentioned nor inferred here.

Thus it would be fair to assume that it is the former; that Jesus had not yet, but at some point after the statement was made Jesus *will* go to the Father; that is the correct meaning.

But is this statement to be taken *literally*; or is there some other non-literal meaning to the statement: *"because I go to the Father*? Does it mean "go to the Father" as in prayer; go to the father in terms of when Jesus commended or *paratithēmi* his (immaterial) soul to the Father; or literally *physically* go to the Father; i.e.; *in-corpus*?

The actual Greek word translated as "go" is:

> "4198 pŏrĕuŏmai; mid. from a der. of the same as 3984; to *traverse*, i.e. *travel* (lit. or fig.; espec. to *remove* [fig. *die*], *live*, etc.): - depart, go (away, forth, one's way, up), (make a, take a) journey, walk."[12.8]

It seems that *pŏrĕuŏmai* would best be described not as *prayer*; and not as the "severed" *soul* of Jesus being *commended* or *paratithēmi* to the Father. Rather, *pŏrĕuŏmai* in this context, likely refers to *physically* going to the Father; i.e.; *in-corpus*.

Thus although it seems that those who "fit the criteria" at that time, (the "believeth" part); would be capable of performing the *same* works or *ĕrgŏn* as Jesus *then*; the ability to perform *greater* or *mĕizōn*, works or *ĕrgŏn*, was to be in the *future*.

Shortly afterward, John 14:16 (NAS) tells us:

> "*I will ask the Father,
> and He will give you another Helper,
> that He may be with you forever;*"[12.9]

The King James Version of John 14:16 tells us:

> "*And I will pray the Father,
> and he shall give you another Comforter,
> that he may abide with you for ever;*"[12.10]

Here Jesus states that He will "*ask*" or "*pray*" the Father; and it is stated here in the *future* tense. Could it be that it is this very *asking* or *praying* to which Jesus is referring when he speaks of go(ing) to the Father, back in John 14:12? ("I will go and ask my boss.") Or is it in fact the case that He will ask the Father as a separate event *after* he *physically* goes to the father?

Stated differently, is the original Greek word translated here as "*ask*," (NAS); or "*pray*," (KJV); reasonably synonymic with or to *pŏrĕuŏmai*, translated as "go?"

The original Greek word translated here as "ask," (NAS), or "pray," (KJV) is:

It Sort of Has to Be So

2065 ĕrōtaō; appar. from 2046 [comp. 2045]; to *interrogate*; by impl. to *request*: - ask, beseech, desire, intreat, pray. Comp. 4441."[12.11]

What commonalities exist between *pŏrĕuŏmai*; "to *traverse*, i.e. *travel* (lit. or fig.; espec. to *remove* [fig. *die*], *live*, etc.): - depart, go (away, forth, one's way, up), (make a, take a) journey, walk;" and *ĕrōtaō*; "*interrogate*; by impl. to *request*: - ask, beseech, desire, intreat, pray." As can be easily seen, the answer is *few if any*.

Thus it appears that Jesus will first physically *pŏrĕuŏmai*, or travel, ("*go*"), "to the Father;" and *then* and only then *ĕrōtaō*; or "*ask*" or "*pray*" "*the father.*"

It could be fairly asked at this juncture if any of this matters. The answer to this question depends upon whether or not understanding the *mechanism* is of value.

What is this *mechanism*? This is a complex question; with a rather elaborate amount of evidence that must be presented in order to "back up" the answer.

Thus, before this is addressed, it seems prudent to determine what else there was that was contained in His message in John 14:16: "*I will ask the Father, and He will give you another Helper, that He may be with you forever,*" (NAS); or: "*And I will pray the Father, and he shall give you another Comforter, that he may abide with you for ever,*"(KJV).

Here Jesus refers to "another Helper," or "another Comforter;" (note the capitalization in the translations). Is it fair to assume that this means that we will then have two Helpers, (two helpings?); or that there will be second Helper who will replace the first Helper; or it will be the same Helper, but this ("*another*") Helper will be capable of increased power?

The original Greek word translated as "another" is:

"243 allŏs; a prim. word; "*else*," i.e. *different* (in many applications): - more, one (another), (an-, some and-) other (-s, -wise)."[12.12]

Although it can be seen from where the translation of "*another*" may have been derived, it seems likely that that "different" or "more" would be better translations.

It must be noted that Strong's very first *translation*, (not *definition*), of *allŏs* is "more." Why? Because the result is the possession of both the same original works or abilities—those *equal* to those performed by Jesus; as well as the ability to perform "*greater works.*" Different not in the sense of *another dissimilar* Helper, but rather a Helper whose capabilities with respect to the hosts, have been *augmented*—"more."

It must be pointed out that this augmentation is not a result of the Helper having any increased power whatsoever; (it is and always was infinite); but rather because of the removal of limitations; a removal which was allowed because of a *rebalancing*, as a result of changes in circumstances.

The actual Greek word translated as "Helper," in John 14:16 NAS; or translated as "Comforter" in the KJV, is:

> "3875 paraklētŏs; an *intercessor, consoler*: - advocate, comforter."[12,13]

Here it seems that the KJV has the better *literal translation* as "*comforter*"—albeit not necessarily in today's vernacular.

This is because despite any common usages, the actual root of the word "comfort" is *forte*; generally meaning power or strength. It is still in use today in terms such as "fort;" or "that is not my forte," (four-tay), or *strong* point; and is also used as a musical term.

And the prefix *com*, often was originally *con*, meaning "with;" and is believed to be the case with *comfort*. Thus: "with (greater) strength," would quite likely result in: "*greater works.*"

But the *translation* of *paraklētŏs* as "*comforter*," merely represents the KJV *translation* of *paraklētŏs*.

The actual word *paraklētŏs* can be split into *para-klētŏs*; here with the prefix *para*; in today's vernacular generally meaning "next to," (as was seen with *paranormal*).

It also seems reasonable to examine "klētŏs" without the "para;" and then again examine "para," in order to ascertain what these *individual* definitions actually are; and what the *collective* definition, (*paraklētŏs*), should in fact be.

> "2822 klētŏs; from the same as *2821*; *invited*, i.e. *appointed*, or (spec.) a saint: - called."[12.14]

> "2821 klēsis; from a shorter form of *2564*; an *invitation* (fig.): - calling, vocation."[12.15]

> "2564 kalĕō; akin to the base of *2753*; to "*call*" (prop. allowed, but used in a variety of applications, dir. or otherwise): - bid, call (forth), (whose sur-) name (was [called])."[12.16]

> "2753 kĕlĕuō; from a prim. kĕllō (to *urge* on); "hail"; to *incite* by word, i.e. *order*: - bid, (at, give) command (-ment)."[12.17]

Again, from the previous analysis of *paranormal*, the prefix "para," (full definition), is:

> "3844 para; a prim. prep.; prop. *near*, i.e. (with gen.) *from beside* (lit. or fig.), (with dat.) *at* (or *in*) the *vicinity* of (obj. or subj.), (with acc.) to the *proximity* with (local [espec. *beyond* or *opposed* to] or causal [*on account of*]); - above, against, among, at, before, by, contrary to, x friend, from, + give [such things as they] + that [she] had, x his, in, more than, nigh unto, (out) of, past, save, side... by, in the sight of than, [there-] fore, with. In compounds it retains the same variety of application."

Thus "near," "next to," or "beside;" that which is "invited," or "appointed;" would be one *literal* collective definition of the prefix and root combined; resulting in *paraklētŏs*.

249

However; instead collectively meaning of: "near," "next to," or "beside;" that which is "invited," or "appointed;" *paraklētŏs* could also refer to: "near," "next to," or "beside;" the very *invitation* or *appointment* itself.

In order for this latter possibility to make some degree of sense, it must be asked: Who or what is it that does the actual inviting or the appointing? Specifically; is it God or a host who proffers the *invitation*, or makes the *appointment*?

It is the individual host who chooses salvation by justification; and also determines whether or not he or she wants the Holy Ghost to reside in them. Thus it is the *host* that does the inviting, or the appointing.

Biblical Old Testament "history" is replete with individuals having the Holy Ghost *on them*. But they were unable to have the Holy Ghost *in them*; because of the contamination of sin; and the unavailability of *justification* at that time .

This raises an important point. Justification and the resultant salvation, are generally only considered as pertinent after physical death—but this is not so. This "cleanup" occurs while one is still physically alive; and thus one is: "just as though they never sinned," while still *physically* alive. It is because of this "cleanup," that the Holy Ghost can be *in them*, and not just *on them*; as the same "connection" rules for the afterlife, apply in physical life.

When "demonic possession" occurs, or referred to here as *endoparasitosis*; it is the desire of the invading entity or entities to take over the will and actions of the host. It is *supplanting*, that is desired by these invading entity or entities. Thus in a sense these entities desire to be *over* the host.

But when the Holy Ghost is *in* a host, it is *supplementation* and not *supplanting* that is the purpose. Thus the Holy Ghost will be *next to*, (para); and not *over* that host which provided the invitation to, or appointment of, (klētŏs), the Holy Ghost to do this.

One main difference is that here, the host maintains his or her *free will*; and the Holy Ghost will assist in all that is consistent with the will of God. This assistance is *dunamis*, and manifests in many forms.

But the entire word *paraklētŏs* is nevertheless *defined* as: "an *intercessor*, consoler;" and *paraklētŏs* is *translated* in the KJV as: "Comforter;" and in the NAS as "Helper."

The *only* appearance of *paraklētŏs* translated as "advocate," in the KJV appears in 1 John 2:1:[12.18]

> "My little children, these things write
> I unto you, that ye sin not.
> And if any man sin,
> we have an advocate with the Father,
> Jesus Christ the righteous."[12.19]

Here we are told that it is *Jesus*, (and not the Holy Ghost), who is this particular *"advocate"* or *paraklētŏs*. One could argue that an advocate *intercedes*, as one could similarly argue about a comforter. However; arguing that a "comforter" and an "advocate" have the same precise function, albeit each being a type of *intercessors*, would be difficult—particularly given the context here.

The appearance of *paraklētŏs* translated as "comforter;" in addition to appearing in the actual verse under analysis, (John 14:16): "*And I will pray the Father, and he shall give you another Comforter, that he may abide with you for ever;*"(KJV); appears only in John 14:26, John 15:26, and John 16:7 (KJV).[12.20]

John 14:26 (KJV) tells us:

> "But the Comforter, which is the Holy Ghost,
> whom the Father will send in my name,
> he shall teach you all things,
> and bring all things to your remembrance,
> whatsoever I have said unto you."[12.21]

The actual Greek word translated here as "Holy" is

"40 hagiŏs; from hagŏs (an *awful* thing) [comp. 53, 2282]; *sacred* (phys. *pure*, mor. *blameless* or *religious*, cer. *consecrated*): - (most) holy (one, thin), saint."[12.22]

The actual Greek word translated here as "Ghost" is the previously discussed *pnĕuma*.[12.23]

Here is seen confirmation that the "*Comforter*" or *paraklētŏs*" is in fact the "Holy Ghost;" or *Hagŏs Pnĕuma*.

And it is also confirmed that the Holy Ghost will be "sent;" and from *whom*, (the Father), the Holy Ghost will be "sent." This confirms that this Holy Ghost is or was as of that time: "unsent." This also confirms that the "Comforter" is neither Jesus nor the Father; but rather a "Third Party."

What we are not told in this passage, is *where* Jesus "will be" when this happens. Neither are we told what the actual stimulus for this "sending" is or will be; i.e.; what is the *cause*, as opposed to *who* it is that will do this "sending."

John 15:26 (KJV) tells us:

"But when the Comforter is come,
whom I will send unto you from the Father,
even the Spirit of truth,
which proceedeth from the Father,
he shall testify of me:"[12.24]

Here it is revealed that Jesus is in fact the *cause* for the Father to do the sending. There is also evidence that this "Comforter" had not yet been sent at that time.

John 16:7 (KJV) tells us:

"Nevertheless I tell you the truth;
It is expedient for you that I go away:
for if I go not away,
the Comforter will not come unto you;

> *but if I depart, I will send him unto you."*[12.25]

The actual Greek word translated here twice as "go away" is:

> "565 apĕrehŏmai; from 575 and 2064; to *go off* (i.e. *depart*), *aside* (i.e. *apart*) or *behind* (i.e. *follow*), lit. or fig.: - come, depart, go (aside, away, back, out, . . . ways), pass away, be past."[12.26]

The actual Greek word translated here "depart" is the aforementioned *pŏrĕuŏmai,* meaning to (physically) *traverse* or *travel.*[12.27]

Thus if Jesus did not *apĕrehŏmai* and/or *pŏrĕuŏmai,* the "Comforter" would not arrive.

Back to the previously addressed John 14:16 (KJV):

> *"And I will pray the Father,
> and he shall give you another Comforter,
> that he may abide with you for ever;"*

The actual Greek word translated as "forever" is:

> "165 aiōn; from the same as *104;* prop. an *age;* by extens. *perpetuity* (also past); by impl. the *world;* spec. (Jewish) a Messianic period (present or future): - age, course, eternal, (for) ever (-more), [n-] ever, (beginning of the, while the) world (began, without end). Comp. 5550."[12.28]

> "104 aĕi; from an obs. prim. Noun (appar. mean. continued *duration*); "*ever;*" by qualification *regularly;* by impl. *earnestly*: - always, ever."[12.29]

In the previously cited NAS John 14:16, unlike the above KJV, the use of the capitalized "He" in the NAS: *"He may abide with you forever;*" is likely one source of the confusion regarding those who believe these greater works are only "temporary."

Since the first capitalized "He" in this passage refers to "the Father," (Who *gives* the Comforter); likely this second appearance of "He" in this verse is; (incorrectly for certain, whether done deliberately or not); also then interpreted as the *Father*, and thus they believe this refers to *salvation*. But Jesus Himself told us that this Comforter was neither the Father, nor the Son.

So it seems we are then back to the idea of the use of this Helper or Comforter "temporarily;" in order to "facilitate" the "bait and switch," in order to get people to join the church expecting *dunamis*.

But instead; being told that although the *dunamis* no longer exists; it is all right; because although we cannot give you the *dunamis*; even though that is what attracted you in the first place; we can give you *salvation*. And this is okay, because *salvation* is so important, (which it is); that the ends justify the means, (which they never do).

What else about this Comforter or Helper?

The verses immediately following John 14:16, namely John 14:17-19 (NAS), tell us:

> "*the Spirit of truth, whom the world cannot receive,*
> *because it neither sees Him nor knows Him;*
> *but you know Him, for He dwells with you*
> *and will be in you.*
>
> *I will not leave you orphans; I will come to you.*
>
> *A little while longer and the world will see*
> *Me no more, but you will see Me.*
> *Because I live, you will live also.*"[12.30]

John 14:16 ends with the word "*forever*" (NAS), or "*for ever*" (KJV); which is followed by a semi-colon. Thus as originally written, John 14:16-17 is actually one long man-made sentence: "*I will ask the*

Father, and He will give you another Helper, that He may be with you forever; the Spirit of truth, whom the world cannot receive, because it neither sees Him nor knows Him; but you know Him, for He dwells with you and will be in you."

Thus, whomever it is, ("*the Spirit of truth*"), that will be with us "*forever,*" Jesus refers to here in John 14:17 in the third person as "*Him*" and "*He.*" Then in John 14: 18-19, the verses that directly follow, Jesus refers to Himself in the first person as "I" or "Me." Thus, this Comforter or Helper clearly cannot refer to Jesus.

This continues, as John 14:20 goes on to tell us:

"*At that day you will know that I am in My Father, and you in Me, and I in you.*"[12.31]

When Jesus is referring to God the Father, he uses "*the Father,*" (in John 14:16); and "*My Father,*" (here in John 14:20); and not "*Him*" or "*He.*" Thus, here this Comforter or Helper who will be with us "*forever,*" cannot refer to the Father either. In addition; we were told that Jesus; "*will ask the Father, and He will give you another Helper.*" It is the Father whom is being *asked* and will "*give*" the Helper; and Jesus who is doing the *asking*.

Thus by Hobson's choice, it must be the Holy Ghost to whom Jesus is referring; and it is He, the Holy Ghost; who will be with us forever. The same being this "different;" ("*another*"); Comforter or Helper.

In John 14:17 Jesus had told us about the Holy Ghost when He described it as: "*the Spirit of truth, whom the world cannot receive, because it neither sees Him nor knows Him; but you know Him, for He dwells with you and will be in you.*"

Here again there is much revelation, because of the *tenses*. Speaking as though to an individual, Jesus said "*you know him, for He dwells with you.*" This is present tense. At the time Jesus said this, the Holy Ghost was currently "dwelling with" being on some of the members of His audience. This is why if the "if" is met; ("*he who believes in Me, the works that I do*"); there is the resultant "then;" ("*he will do also*"). This refers to the present *same* works, and not the future *greater* or *měizōn* works.

But the last four words of John 14:17: "*and will be in you;*" indicates something that had not yet happened when Jesus spoke them. Jesus said that the Holy Ghost "*will be in you.*" "*Will be in you,*" is not the same as "*dwells with you.*" Before Jesus went to the Father, the Holy Ghost could dwell *with* us. But after Jesus went to the Father, the Holy Ghost could be "*in*" us. What is the result? "*Greater works than these* (the works Jesus did) *he will do; because I go to the Father.*"

For more elucidation, John 14:26 (NAS) tells us:

> "*But the Helper, the Holy Spirit,*
> *whom the Father will send in My name,*
> *He will teach you all things,*
> *and bring to your remembrance*
> *all that I said to you.*"[12.32]

John 14:26 again confirms that the "Helper," is neither Jesus nor The Father.

The actual word translated as "Spirit" in this passage is again *pnĕuma.*"[12.33]

And the actual word translated as "Holy" is again *hagiŏs.*[12.34]

However, here it is *Holy Pnĕuma*, as opposed to the *host's pnĕuma*; with the *former* being that which desires to live in us; and the *latter* being that which God breathes into our nostrils at birth, when we become physically alive.

What will the Holy Ghost "*teach*" us? A few things? Many things? The passage states: "*all things.*" "*All things*" is about as broad a category as possible, for anything that can be taught or learned.

The actual Greek word translated as "all" is:

> 3956 pas; include. *all* the forms of declension; appar. a prim. word; all, *any, every, the whole...*"[12.35]

It Sort of Has to Be So

And *how* will the Holy Ghost teach us?

The answer is that if it is *indirect*, it is the *lŏgŏs*, (recorded), which was at one time *rhēma*, (real time), for the *author* of the *lŏgŏs*.

If it is *direct*; which is what it is that it seems Jesus is speaking of in this passage, it is accomplished via the *rhēma*.

It must be remembered that the first four New Testament books, (Matthew, Mark, Luke, and John), are largely about *Jesus*; and the book of Acts is largely about the *Christ*—hence the name. What follows represents this "transition."

Acts 1:4-9 (KJV) tells us:

> "And, being assembled together with them,
> commanded them that they should
> not depart from Jerusalem,
> but wait for the promise of the Father,
> which, saith he, ye have heard of me.
>
> For John truly baptized with water;
> but ye shall be baptized with the
> Holy Ghost not many days hence.
>
> When they therefore were come together,
> they asked of him, saying,
> Lord, wilt thou at this time restore
> again the kingdom to Israel?
>
> And he said unto them,
> It is not for you to know the times or the seasons,
> which the Father hath put in his own power.
>
> But ye shall receive power,
> after that the Holy Ghost is come upon you:
> and ye shall be witnesses unto me both in Jerusalem,
> and in all Judaea, and in Samaria,
> and unto the uttermost part of the earth.
>
> And when he had spoken these things,

> *while they beheld, he was taken up;*
> *and a cloud received him out of their sight."*[12.36]

Here Jesus is speaking *after* the resurrection, but *before* His ascension; and thus: *"ye shall be baptized with the Holy Ghost not many days hence;"* represents the announcement of the soon to arrive *"Helper."*

The delay of *"not many days"* is necessary because as previously stated, Jesus must first go to the father *in-corpus*—the event that is described in the very last verse: *"he was taken up; and a cloud received him out of their sight."*

These two mentions of *"the Holy Ghost,"* are again *hagiŏs*; (holy) and pněuma (ghost).[12.37]

This is important, because again it is *ghosts* specifically, and not merely "spirits," that properly reside in human beings.

There are two mentions of *"power;"* one mentioned in verse 7: *"Father hath put in his own power;"* and the other contained in verse 8: *"But ye shall receive power."* Because of the translation, it would be easy to assume that these two *English* translations as "power," represent translations of the very same *Greek* word; but this is not so.

The *second* translation as "power" seen in: *"But ye shall receive power,"* is once again *dunamis*.[12.38]

But the *first* translation seen as "power" in: *"Father hath put in his own power,"* is an entirely *different* word. This word is very important to understand, as it forms the basis of much of not only what is contained in the pages that follow; but in understanding man's history and his future; as well as man's true purpose, as per God's stated will.

This word will thus be *introduced* here.

This original Greek word translated as "power," as seen in: *"Father hath put in his own power,"* is:

> "1849, ĕxŏusia; from *1832* (in the sense of *ability*); *privilege,* i.e. (subj.) *force, capacity, competency, freedom,* or (obj.) *mastery* (concr. *magistrate,*

superhuman, potentate, token of control), delegated *influence*: - authority, jurisdiction, liberty, power, right, strength."[12.39]

"1832 ĕxĕsti; third pers. sing. pres. indic. of a comp. of *1537* and *1510*; so also ĕxŏn; neut. pres. part. of the same (with or without some form of *1510* expressed); impers. *it is right* (through the fig. idea of *being out* in public): - be lawful, let, x may (-est)."[12.40]

"1537 ĕk; or ĕx; a prim. prep. denoting *origin* (the point *whence* motion or action proceeds), *from*, *out* (of place, time or cause; lit. or fig.; direct or remote). . ."[12.41]

"1510 ĕimi; first pers. sing. pres. indic.; a prol. form of a prim. and defective verb; I *exist* (used only when emphatic): - am, have been, x it is I, was. . ."[12.42]

Although *ĕxŏusia* will be addressed in much greater detail going forward, the main difference between *dunamis* and *ĕxŏusia*, has to do with the issue of *authority*.

Dunamis represents supernatural power in the very broad sense; i.e.; the very power itself—irrespective of any *authority* to utilize it.

Ĕxŏusia also represents *dunamis*, but here also includes the personal *authority* to utilize the *dunamis*.

Another way to understand this, is to further distinguish *ĕxŏusia* from "real time" *dunamis*.

In "real time" *dunamis*, one may presently have the *capability*, but not the *authority*. Meaning; the *dunamis* cannot be utilized without "real time" assistance from God.

The "Talent Men" had some degree of *ĕxŏusia*; but when they "worked" the additional *talantŏn*, they had insufficient *ĕxŏusia* capabilities due to *authority*; and thus required "real time" assistance for the additional *dunamis*. Upon completion of a given "dunamic" act or acts; their level of *ĕxŏusia* was then increased, as a matter of the additional *authority*, (in charge of).

This is a bit similar to *lŏgŏs* and *rhēma*. The utilization of *lŏgŏs*, requires no "real time" assistance from God in *obtaining* the *knowledge* contained therein. There may be "real time" assistance from God in getting one *to the lŏgŏs*; but the *lŏgŏs* itself already exists, and is available. Although it cannot be over emphasized that often *rhēma* can be utilized to "rightly divide" the *lŏgŏs* and produce the *second* of the *two* (Bibliomancy?).

However the original *rhēma* that was ultimately recorded and thus became the *lŏgŏs*, did in fact require "real time" assistance from God.

Neither "The Big M," (assuming he in fact wrote early Genesis); nor any other human being was alive at the time of those events; but today anyone can read that "story." The "trick" of course *today*, is to get the *rhēma* to filter out the man added "dross;" as the versions of the Bible are openly described as *versions*, and not *translations*.

In a very limited sense, there is a similarity between a previous discussion about electricity, and *dunamis* and *ĕxŏusia*:

"When electricity flows, there is a magnetic field created around the conductor. If another conductor enters this field, an electrical current will be produced in this second conductor. But this will happen only when there is *movement*."

If it is considered that there is a *dunamic* field, analogous to the above *magnetic* field; then things can begin "to flow." How does this happen? When there is movement. What is this movement? It is the "working" of the *talantŏn*, such as was done with two of the "Talent Men."

One main difference, is that *ĕxŏusia* is a bit analogous to a battery; in that *ĕxŏusia* remains as a *capability* to whatever level attained, unless increased by "working;" or decreased by the removal of the *authority*.

The *former*, (increase *ĕxŏusia* by working), is precisely what it is that man is supposed to be doing. And the *latter*, (decrease *ĕxŏusia* by removal of authority), is precisely what happened to the enemy after Calvary.

Thus today the enemy is left with what is essentially a discharged *ĕxŏusic* battery. And each H. Sapien begins with a relatively low charged *ĕxŏusic* battery, but unlike the enemy, is capable of a massive charging.

The enemy has full knowledge of his "dead battery," and wishes a full charge;" but cannot. This is because he lost the authority; and cannot, and thus will not ever get it back—except perhaps, *perhaps* for a brief period at "end times."

Most of mankind has no idea this "battery" even exists, much less the ability to charge it to an essentially infinite state because of the "Helper." And it is the enemy's job to make certain that man never discovers this truth.

That "narrow door," or *zōē* door, is personalized, with a "lock" that can be opened only by the person for whom it was designed. Behind that door is much, including virtually unlimited *dunamis* and thus *ĕxŏusia*; which is precisely why the *path* to it is so *crowded*.

But again, why did Jesus have to *physically* go to Father?

The answer to this could be provided here, but this would represent merely *knowledge*; and not *knowledge* plus *understanding*—which is precisely how many define *wisdom*.

There is much more that requires much *understanding*, before the answer to this question can be reasonably understood.

In the interim, precisely what does one of the "few" who found that narrow or *zōē* door actually "look like?"

Alleged Fantasy Foundations Volume I

Chapter 13

Tsâbâ' Extraordinaire

Two questions:
First: "Who is this fellow Elijah, and why should anyone care about him?"
Second: "And what; if anything; does this fellow Elijah have to do with reincarnation?"

"These are fair questions.
"2 Kings 2: 8-9 (KJV) tells us:

"Elijah took his mantle and folded it together and struck the waters, and they were divided here and there, so that the two of them crossed over on dry ground.

When they had crossed over, Elijah said

> to Elisha, "Ask what I shall do for you
> before I am taken from you."
>
> And Elisha said, "Please,
> let a double portion
> of your spirit be upon me.""[R62]

"So here Elijah and Elisha are walking along, until they reach an impassable body of water. Elijah then simply strikes the water with his folded mantle; the waters *"divided;"* and both of them cross the area previously covered by water like it was never there, and they then just walk on like nothing happened.

"This event sounds a bit *Mosaic*, and after all, who would not want to be able to part a body of water, simply by striking it with a folded mantle? *Elisha* was not only included in the group who would want this type of capability; but we are told that Elisha wanted even more, as he requested a *"double portion."*

"The story continues, as 2 Kings 2: 10-11 (KJV) then tells us:

> "He said, "You have asked a hard thing.
> Nevertheless, if you see me
> when I am taken from you,
> it shall be so for you; but if not,
> it shall not be so."
>
> As they were going along
> and talking, behold,
> there appeared a chariot of fire
> and horses of fire
> which separated the two of them.
>
> And Elijah went up by a
> whirlwind to heaven."[R63]

Tsâbâ' Extraordinaire

"So here Elijah is taken into heaven *in corpus*, with Elisha watching the entire time. This is a rather rare event, with the Ascension of Jesus immediately coming to mind; and perhaps Enoch. But of course the Ascension of Jesus was not to be for nearly a millennium after this.

"2 Kings 2: 12-14 (KJV) chronologically then tells us:

> *"Elisha saw it and cried out, "*
> *My father, my father, the chariots of*
> *Israel and its horsemen!"*
> *And he saw Elijah no more.*
>
> *Then he took hold of his own clothes*
> *and tore them in two pieces.*
> *He also took up the mantle of Elijah*
> *that fell from him and returned and stood*
> *by the bank of the Jordan.*
>
> *He took the mantle of Elijah that fell*
> *from him and struck the waters and said,*
> *"Where is the LORD, the God of Elijah?"*
> *And when he also had struck the waters,*
> *they were divided here and there;*
> *and Elisha crossed over."*[R64]

"It seems Elisha may have gotten what he asked for.

"Who was this Elijah, and why is this relevant?

"Elijah was a "fellow" who had "packed" some serious power. In addition to parting the waters, so that he and Elisha (his protégé) could walk over dry ground, as previously stated in verse eight; he also, among many other things: resurrected a child, (1 Kings 17:22);[R65] multiplied food, (1 Kings 17:14);[R66] and killed two groups of 51 men with fire from heaven, (2 Kings 1:10).[R67]

"Elijah first appears in the Bible in 1 Kings 17:1 (KJV):

> *"Now Elijah the Tishbite, who was of the settlers of Gilead..."*[R68]

"There is nothing actually Scripturally known about his birth, early life or very much else; until he just "shows up" as an adult in this passage. He is referred to as a *Tishbite*, which sounds a bit like something requiring immediate medical attention, but is not.

"There are many different opinions about the meaning of "tishbite," but the actual Hebrew word from which Tishbite is derived is:

> "8664 Tishbîy; patrial from an unused name mean. *recourse*; a *Tishbite* or inhab. of Tishbeh (in Gilead); - Tishbite."[R69]

"Thus, it would seem to be fair to say that this term "Tishbite," refers to someone from an area of Gilead, (Tishbeh); from which we are told Elijah *"was of."*

"The problem is that we do not actually know this, because we know not of the chronology. Meaning; that this area may have *later* been referred to as Tishbeh, *because* of Elijah; the same area formerly being known as just Gilead, until after Elijah became famous.

"If this were not so, then 1 Kings 17:1 *"Now Elijah the Tishbite, who was of the settlers of Gilead..."* seems a bit redundant. Substituting the words, it would literally read: "Now Elijah, who was from the Tisbeh section of Gilead, who was of the settlers of Gilead...;" which or course seems a bit silly. However if the use of the term Tishbite is because of the *purpose* of what he actually did, or performed, or because of his calling, (Tishbîy); then the verse begins to make a bit more sense.

"So there are "patrial," "unused name," and "recourse" from which to understand precisely what a "Tishbite" is.

"It is important to precisely understand the meaning of the word "recourse." This word is generally considered to be synonymous with "ability or means of some type of action," but this is incorrect.

The key to this meaning, is that it describes a *turning* of one's course, specifically and exclusively, in order to obtain assistance from another source—a source other than one's self.

"Thus, if it is assumed that Tishbite refers to what Elijah *did*; as opposed to where he was *from*; then in a broad sense, he as well as anyone else who is or was involved in a similar type of *recourse* (Tishbîy), is a Tishbite. But what does this mean?

"Does it matter one whit that Elijah himself may have at some point been involved in recourse, because of something he could not have accomplished himself? The answer is that this question is irrelevant. It is not because Elijah may have at some point in time *sought* recourse that is significant; but rather that he was the *object* of another "living" entity's need for assistance—and that living entity was God.

"The meaning of Tishbîy is first described as "patrial from an unused name mean(ing) *recourse*."

"The word "patrial" is an archaic term today, and if used at all today, is generally understood to refer to the right to live in England. But the root of the word is "*pater*," which of course is Latin for father. Thus, it could be argued that this "patrial" is merely consistent with the idea of Gilead as being his "fatherland; if we define "patrial" as father-like or fatherly, which is a fair definition. But this "theory" does little to explain the "unused name" part.

"Granted that at this juncture, this may at first in fact *appear* to be a bit of a "stretch;" it nevertheless remains the fact that the actual Hebrew word usually translated in Genesis as "hosts" is:

> "6635 tsâbâ' or ts^{e}bâ'âh from 6633; a *mass* of persons (or fig. things), espec. reg. organized for war (an *army*); by impl. a *campaign*, lit. or fig. (spec. *hardship, worship*): -appointed time, (+) army, (+) battle, company, host, service, soldiers, waiting upon..."[R70]

"Thus there seems to be a striking similarity between the words *Tishbîy*, meaning recourse; and *"tsâbâ'* or *ts^{e}bâ'âh"* as defined above. If the president cannot convince an enemy to "straighten up and fly right;" then using "a *mass* of persons (or fig. things), espec. reg. organized for war (an *army*);" is recourse; and perhaps the only means of recourse capable of succeeding.

"It also might be asked as to why a word meaning "recourse," (8664 Tishbîy), is capitalized. The question is not why the word Tishbite is capitalized, but rather why the actual root of Tishbite "Tishbîy; patrial from an unused name mean. *recourse;*" is capitalized? After all, if one is from Bakersville, Carpentersville, or Idiotsville; the corresponding *root* of the name of the town; baker, carpenter or idiot; is generally not capitalized.

"It is true that if one is *from* any of those towns, capitalization in: Bakersvillian, Carpentersvillian, or Idiotite is the norm. But that is because this usage then represents a proper noun. Here however, Tishbîy is capitalized, likely because of the normal capitalization of the name, (proper noun), from which; although largely unused; is always capitalized.

"What does an "unused name" mean? This seems a bit oxymoronic in that generally, the purpose of any name is to identify a person, place, or thing. A name is

Tsâbâ' Extraordinaire

designed to be *used*, else what need is there for it? To have a name that is not used; is not substantially more helpful than not having any name at all. So it would be fair to ask, where in the Bible is there any record of anything that has to do with a name that is not used?

> "Rabbinical Judaism teaches the four-letter name of God, YHVH, is forbidden to be uttered except by the High Priest in the Holy Temple on Yom Kippur."[R71]

"Sometimes the name of God is considered to be *ineffable*; with "ineffable" roughly meaning: "unable to be put into words." YHVH in all of its various spellings is referred to as the *tetragrammaton*. This ineffability of the name of God can be considered simply as a matter of respect, (minority view); or because no word exist which can adequately describe the nature of a limitless God. There is much disagreement regarding which four letters are appropriate, and whether or not the vowels were deliberately removed in order to make pronunciation impossible—except of course by the "Arcanum" of the time.

"Thus, often the names that refer to God in the Bible are actually a description or a title; e.g.; Creator, Lord, etc., rather than His actual "name." Nevertheless, whatever is the actual truth; it seems that here we have an excellent example of an unused name.

"Unfortunately, no matter how one attempts to pronounce YHVH, it cannot reasonably be made to sound anything like Tishbîy.

"However, according to Jewishencyclopedia.com:

> "The names Yhwh and Elohim frequently occur with the word Ẓeba'ot ("hosts"), as Yhwh Elohe Ẓeba'ot ("Yhwh God of Hosts")

or "God of Hosts"; or, most frequently, "Yhwh of Hosts.""[R72]

"This same source then cites 1 Samuel 17:45 as to the source of the original meaning of Zeba'ot.[R73]

"1 Samuel 17:45 (KJV) tells us:

"*Then David said to the Philistine,*
"You come to me with a sword, a spear,
and a javelin, but I come to you in the
name of the LORD of hosts,
the God of the armies of Israel,
whom you have taunted..."[R74]

"The original Hebrew word translated as "hosts" in this cited verse from 1 Samuel is in fact the aforementioned: "6635 tsâbâ' or tsᵉbâ'âh...."[R75]

"Thus, the name YHVH Zeba'ot is the same as YHVH tsâbâ' or YHVH tsᵉbâ'âh, albeit spelled a bit differently. Thus YHVH tsâbâ' or YHVH tsᵉbâ'âh; with the ineffable name of God left unspoken, leaves tsâbâ' or tsᵉbâ'âh, meaning remarkably: "hosts." And again; with Tishbîy meaning *recourse*, this is in fact remarkably quite similar.

"In fact, the similarities between these two words; tsâbâ' or tsᵉbâ'âh and Tishbîy; is much greater than the similarity between the word Zeba'ot and the word tsâbâ' or tsᵉbâ'âh from which Zeba'ot seems to be derived. The capitalization of Tishbîy, as opposed to Tishbite, is likely because it refers to a proper noun, as part of a name for God.

"Thus, Elijah as a "Tishbite," likely actually means one who is a tsâbâ' or tsᵉbâ'âh, or host or vehicle for recourse; in this case on the behalf of YHVH, with the

YHVH unspoken or "unused name" for all or the aforementioned reasons.

"Thus it should read: "Now Elijah the Ts^ebâ'âh(ite) or host for God (hence the capitalization, as well as the *patrial* or father reference), who was, (either genealogical or geographical), of the settlers of Gilead..." And it is inarguable that Elijah was armed with substantial *dunamis*, or supernatural power; in furtherance of his role; at least at the time he first enters the Scriptural scene, and "turns off the rain."

"In fact, Elijah's name, if broken down; is actually some permissible combination of this ineffable name of God or YHVH; and the word El, (from *'ĕlôhîym*), commonly used to describe "God." It can be translated as YHVH is God, or YHVH is my God, or arguably God is YHVH, or perhaps in other manners.

"For those unfamiliar with the analyses provided in the first Chapter of *"MeekRaker Beginnings...;"* Genesis 1:1 provides the complete statement of what God did or accomplished in the (very) "Beginning."

"This event (Genesis 1:1) happened a time long before, (how long is unstated), the description of conditions "on the ground" as contained in the first half of Genesis 1:2. Thus that which is described in Genesis 1:2, is *not* merely a "more detailed" recapitulation of Genesis 1:1; but rather occurred chronologically long after "The Beginning" referenced in Genesis 1:1.

"Contained in the second half of Genesis 1:2, is the description of how God Himself and acting alone; (long after the "end" of "The Beginning"); began to restore the conditions "on the ground;" thereby beginning the process in which we are involved to this very day— *whether mankind is aware of this fact or not.*

"The very first known Divine Act of God seeking "recourse," occurs in Genesis 1:26-28, where God creates the "hosts;" and gives them dominion over the earth.

"Genesis 1:26-28 (KJV) tells us:

> "And God said, Let us make man
> in our image, after our
> likeness: and let them have
> dominion over the fish of the sea,
> and over the fowl of the air,
> and over the cattle,
> and over all the earth,
> and over every creeping
> thing that creepeth upon the earth.
>
> So God created man in his own image,
> in the image of God created he him;
> male and female created he them.
>
> And God blessed them, and God
> said unto them, Be fruitful, and multiply,
> and replenish the earth, and subdue it:
> and have dominion over the fish of the sea,
> and over the fowl of the air, and over every
> living thing that moveth upon the earth."[R76]

"This terminology of "hosts" first appears in Genesis 2:1, and again this actual terminology is: "tsâbâ' or ts^{e}bâ'âh."[R77]

"The issue of why God chose "recourse," rather than just continuing the process himself is not stated. Clearly the establishment of "a mass of persons, (or fig. things), espec. reg. organized for war (an army);" represents recourse, and surely had some rational basis.

"Again it must be asked why any leader would incorporate the services of, (and also here the actual *creation* of), an army; if said leader was both *capable of*, and *permitted to*, accomplish the same ends himself? Since this cannot be because of God's *inability* to continue the fight himself, as he is omnipotent; and omnipotence necessarily includes no act of which one who is omnipotent is *incapable*; there then must be another reason or reasons why God chose to engage in recourse by the establishment of the hosts, as "tsâbâ' or ts^{e}bâ'âh". [Although this is far beyond the scope this work; and at the risk of causing additional controversy; the answer is that it is not a matter of capability, but a matter of authority. The truth, is that the instruction to man regarding the aforementioned kiboshing (kyboshing) of the earth, represents not the *granting* of authority, but rather the *transferring* of authority.]

"The actual word translated as "hard" describing the "thing" that Elijah was asked for by Elisha, is used only four other times in the entire Old Testament and is:

> "7185 qâshâh; a prim. root; prop. to *be dense*, i.e. tough or *severe* (in various applications): - be cruel, be fiercer, make grievous, be ([ask a], be in, have, seem, would) hard (-en, [labour], - ly, thing), be sore, (be, make) stiff (-en, [-necked])."[R78]

"Why is this important? The way that it reads, Elijah *seems* to be describing the difficulty of the *process* of granting Elisha a power equal to twice that of Elijah: *"You have asked a hard thing."*

"If this were the actual meaning and it was stated so today, it would read something like: "Giving you twice my power is a difficult thing for me to do, nevertheless..." But that is not what it seems Elijah is telling Elisha in this verse, and "difficult" appears nowhere in the definition of qâshâh.

"It is not the actual process of *granting* Elisha the power that Elijah is describing as a hard thing or qâshâh, but the very *power* itself. Thus, if stated today it would read something like: "The *thing* you are asking for is literally a very dense, tough and severe thing; and translationally, a cruel, fierce and grievous thing." Elijah is actually warning Elisha about the other side of the actuality of this kind of power. It is the same as any *dunamis* and the corresponding weight or *talantŏn*. It is the same as the previously addressed "oracle" and "burden" each being correct translations of the same Hebrew word: massâ'.

"By advising Elisha of this, Elijah is providing a means of what today would be referred to as "informed consent." When Elijah then tells Elisha that: *"Nevertheless, if you see me when I am taken from you, it shall be so for you; but if not, it shall not be so,"* he is giving Elisha the opportunity to either accept the *total* actuality of this power; or change his mind, simply by whether or not he watches the event.

"Translations notwithstanding; no reference can be found which indicates that the word "nevertheless" actually appears in this verse. Thus, it seems that what Elijah is doing is informing Elisha, in a very frank manner, the *totality* of his request; and in a kind way is telling him to "take it or leave it."

"But a more than fair argument exists, that despite the fact that we are told that Elijah *"went up by a whirlwind to heaven,"*—the "smart money" says: "He aint done yet.""[3.1] [Excerpt from *"Reincarnation—A Reasonable Inquiry"* Reprinted by Permission]

With respect to Elijah and Jesus, there are some interesting similarities. Each had *dunamis*. Each "worked" their *dunamis* by *ergazŏmai*. Likely each then received increased levels of *dunamis*. Each distributed this *dunamis* to others. To be fair, Elijah distributed it *directly* to only *one*, (Elisha), that we know of; and Jesus distributed and continues to distribute it simultaneously to *many*. And each indicated that there were certain *conditions* which had to be met before this transfer or distribution of *dunamis* could occur.

It is often considered a fact, that Jesus had infinite amounts of *dunamis*; here meaning limitless or *infinite* levels of *dunamis*; i.e.; *omnipotence* in the *dunamis* department.

If this were in fact so; then after He went to the Father, there then would necessarily somehow be available a larger, or *měizōn* infinity available to those who qualified—at least according to Jesus. Jesus Himself distinguished the things he did, from greater or *měizōn* things. Large and small infinities are not generally considered as actualities.

And there is one other commonality that is extremely important. Each did something very unusual, perhaps something limited to just these two. This was the transferring of their actual entire *material* or *physical* form to the *immaterial* realm. [Genesis 5:24 (KJV), *does* tell us that: *"Enoch walked with God; and he was not, for God took him."*[3.2] However, this tells us neither what actually happened, nor why.]

Thus a fair argument can be made that the transfer or distribution of Jesus' and Elijah's *dunamis*, required their *physical* presence in the immaterial realm—whatever this may represent.

In the case of *Elijah*, the fact is that *Elisha* could not have seen him "go," unless he did in fact "go;" i.e.; physically "go" to the immaterial realm.

Although Elijah's statement: *"if you see me when I am taken from you, it shall be so for you; but if not, it shall not be so;"* is usually considered as offering the option for Elisha to change his mind simply by not watching this event, there may be another reason. Elijah himself may have been uncertain that he, (Elijah), would in fact actually go through with it.

A similar situation arguably would occur many years later with Jesus in Gethsamane. So here if Elisha didn't see Elijah: "taken *from you*," it would be because Elijah decided not to go—whether Elisha was watching or not. And if so, had Elijah not gone to the immaterial realm *in-corpus*, this transfer of *dunamis* to Elisha likely would not have been possible.

If so; this is similar to, and consistent with, that which Jesus said in John 14:12: *"and greater works than these shall he do; because I go unto my Father*; and in John 16:7: *"for if I go not away, the Comforter will not come unto you; but if I depart, I will send him unto you."*

Irrespective of how it was phrased; each indicates that it in order for this power or *dunamis* "transfer" to occur, it was required that they return their *material* form to the *immaterial*.

We know Elijah had "packed" a rather large amount of *dunamis*; and also that Elisha obtained *twice* as much as Elijah had. So if there ever was an excellent example of one who had a large amount of *dunamis*, it was Elisha. But unlike *Elijah* of the Old Testament, *Elisha* of the Old Testament suffered a physical death.

2 Kings 13:20-21 (NAS) tells us:

> *"Elisha died, and they buried him.*
> *Now the bands of the*
> *Moabites would invade*
> *the land in the spring of the year.*
>
> *As they were burying a man, behold,*
> *they saw a marauding band;*
> *and they cast the man*
> *into the grave of Elisha.*
> *And when the man touched*
> *the bones of Elisha*
> *he revived and stood up on his feet."*[13.3]

This passage has a bit of "hyperpronounosis." nevertheless, the series of events can be sorted out—if great care is taken.

Elisha, (not *Elijah*), had physically died, and was buried. Some time afterward, *"in the spring,"* the Moabites invaded; and as *"they,"* (it is unclear who the *"they"* represents, other than not Moabites), were *"burying a man;"* and they: *"saw the Moabites,"* or: *"saw a marauding band."* So they instead cast the dead man, whom they were previously trying to bury, into Elisha's grave. When this dead man, who is now in Elisha's grave; *"touched the bones of Elisha,"* he then: *"revived and stood up on his feet."*

The first question about this story; would be as to how or why was it easier to place the deceased in Elisha's grave, when it seems Elisha had been buried quite some time earlier; at least before the spring? Why not just keep digging the grave that was in progress, as at least that one was partially done?

The actual Hebrew word translated here as "buried" with regard to Elisha is:

> "6912 qâbar; a prim. root; to *inter*: - x in any wise, bury, (-ier)."[13.4]

Thus, we have no way of knowing *how* it was that Elisha was *interred*. He could have been buried, but likely he was interred in some other manner; as he was a man of renown. If so, this might help explain why essentially hiding the deceased man where Elisha's was interred would have been faster.

The next question would be: "Was this formerly deceased man actually *alive* after merely coming in contact with the bones of Elisha?"

The actual original Hebrew word translated as "revived" is:

> "2421 châyâh; a prim. root [comp. 2331, 2421]; to *live*, whether lit. or fig.; causat. to *revive*; - keep (leave, make) alive, x certainly, give (promise) life, (let, suffer to) live, nourish up, preserve (alive), quicken, recover, repair, restore (to life), revive, (x God) save (alive, life, lives), x surely, be whole."[13.5]

This Hebrew word 2421 *châyâh*, is the root of the word 2416 *chay*. It is *chay* that is translated as *"living"* when describing as: *"living soul;"* the man God had formed in Genesis 2:7, who would later be known as Adam.

Thus there seems to be no question that he was in fact *alive* after touching Elisha's bones. And not only was he *alive*, but he: *"stood up on his feet."* In fact there is a sense in the definition of *châyâh*; that it is a word best suited to something that is not in any way alive, as was the case with Adam; until *châyâh* occurs.

And the last question would be: "What happened after he became alive, (again)? Did he just fall down dead again; or did something else happen to him that is not included in the story?"

The actual Hebrew word translated as the phrase "stood up on his feet" is:

> "6965 qûwm; a prim. root; to *rise* (in various applications, lit., fig., intens. and caus.): - abide, accomplish, x be clearer, confirm, continue, decree, x be dim, endure, x enemy, enjoin, get up, make good, help, hold, (help to) lift up (again), make, x but newly, ordain, perform, pitch, raise (up), rear (up), remain, (a-) rise (up) (again, against), rouse up, set (up), (e-)stablish, (make to) stand (up), stir up, strengthen, succeed, (as-, make) sure (-ly), (be) up (-hold, - rising)."[13.6]

By the use of *qûwm*, it seems that this man was more than just physically alive in the literal sense. In fact, the literal meaning of the phrase: "stand up on your own two feet," seems more appropriate; given the actual meaning of *qûwm*.

Earlier it was stated: "*ĕxŏusia* is a bit analogous to a battery, in that *ĕxŏusia* remains as a *capability* to whatever level attained, unless increased by "working;" or decreased by the removal of the *authority*."

It thus seems that there remains substantial power in the bones—even long after physical life has ceased. But precisely where is this "battery?" Based upon this story, it seems that at least at this juncture, that the skeletal system would be the likely area; as it seems that that was all that "remained" of Elisha.

It would be interesting to examine another prominent person in the Bible, and see if any type of information exists that would corroborate this theory; and Moses seems to be a prominent enough candidate.

Deuteronomy 34:5-7 (NAS) tells us:

> *"So Moses the servant of the LORD
> died there in the land of Moab,
> according to the word of the LORD.*

Tsâbâ' Extraordinaire

*And He buried him in the valley
in the land of Moab,
opposite Beth-peor;
but no man knows his burial place
to this day.*

*Although Moses was one hundred
and twenty years old when he died,
his eye was not dim, nor his vigor abated."*[13.7]

The first interesting thing about this passage is the appearance of the word "He" in "*He buried him.*"

In the context in which it is written, this "He" can only refer to the Lord, Moses, or: "*land of Moab.*" In English, it cannot refer to Moab, as that would be an "it." It cannot refer to Moses, because he was the deceased; and there is no evidence that Moses buried himself.

Thus it must refer to the Lord, or someone else. Since it is *capitalized*, and is not at the beginning of a sentence; it must be the Lord to which this "He" refers; and then later it is *Moses* who is referred to as "he," (lower case), in verse 7.

So here we have God actually burying the body of Moses—either *directly* or via *recourse*. It must be noted that the word translated as "*buried,*" is the same word used with Elisha: "*qâbar.*"[13.8]

One might ask why God would bury Moses' body; and the most likely answer is provided in the second half of verse 6: "*no man knows his burial place to this day.*"

Thus it is likely that this was done so that no man *would know where* Moses was buried. Had any man, even one, buried Moses; then at least one man would have known where he was buried.

It seems that God was already aware of "that one," which would later be attributed to Benjamin Franklin; concerning the maximum number of people that can keep a secret: "Three; but two of them have to be dead." And of course here God was the "one."

Why was it important that not even one man know where Moses was buried?

This is particularly interesting; in that Deuteronomy 34:8 (KJV) tells us:

> *"And the children of Israel wept for Moses*
> *in the plains of Moab thirty days:*
> *so the days of weeping and mourning*
> *for Moses were ended."*[3.9]

So it seems that there were thirty days of mourning for Moses, with no one even knowing where he was buried.

God always has a plan. If circumstances are unusual, it is likely because His plan is unusual. A careful read, is that it was God's will that no man knew of Moses' place of burial; which of course is entirely different than his place of burial not being known. It was in fact known—but just not by any man. The question is: "Why?"

Jude 1:9 (NAS) tells us:

> *"But Michael the archangel,*
> *when he disputed with the devil*
> *and argued about the body of Moses,*
> *did not dare pronounce against him*
> *a railing judgment, but said,*
> *"The Lord rebuke you!"*[3.10]

The same Jude 1:9, but here KJV, tells us:

> *"Yet Michael the archangel,*
> *when contending with the devil*
> *he disputed about the body of Moses,*
> *durst not bring against him*
> *a railing accusation, but said,*
> *The Lord rebuke thee."*[3.11]

Tsâbâ' Extraordinaire

In order to maintain contextual integrity, the circumstances surrounding the appearance of this passage should be noted. This passage today appears to: "drop a bomb," so to speak; but this was not the case when it was written.

Said "bomb," merely represents a cited example in support of a larger point; rather than representing any revelation about Michael *at that time*.

In context, it seems that something was represented here as a fact; something that everyone at that time knew about Michael and his *authority* and *capabilities*; and something that is only vaguely understood today, if even *believed*. This is provided in these passages not as any information about Michael's capabilities, which were obviously known at that time; but solely in support of a larger idea.

This is why the words "*Yet*" and "*But*" appear at the beginning of the passage; as in "Yet even Michael," or "But even Michael;" when he was. . ." "But Elvis Presley served his country;" would not be provided as information about Elvis, but rather in furtherance of another point.

But that was then and this is now. Unfortunately, no further reliable information about Jude 1:9 seems to be available anywhere. However, what can be utilized from this passage is the *factual* representation. And the fact is that Mike did in fact "dispute" and "argue" with the devil: "*about the body of Moses.*" What is also important; is what did *not* take place.

The original Greek word translated as "disputed," and "contending" is:

> "1252 diakrinō; from *1223* and *2919*; to *separate thoroughly*, i.e. (lit and reflex.) to *withdraw* from or (by impl.) *oppose*;..."[13.12]

The original Greek word translated as "argued," and "disputed" is:

> "1256 dialĕgŏmai; mid. from *1223* and *3004*; to *say thoroughly*, i.e. *discuss* (in argument or exhortation): - dispute, preach (unto), reason (with), speak."[13.13]

And what is also interesting, is the original Greek word translated as "about," and not *over* is:

> "4012 pĕri; from the base of 4008; prop. *through* (all over), i.e. around; fig. *with respect to*;..."[13.14]

What on earth is it that can be described as: *"pronounce against him a railing judgment;"* the same being what Mike did *not* do?

The actual Greek word translated as "pronounce against" or "bring against" is:

> "2018 ĕpiphĕrō; from *1909* and *5342*; to *bear upon* (or *further*), i.e. *adduce* (pers. or judicially [*accuse, inflict*]), *superinduce*: - add, bring (against), take."[13.15]

The actual word translated as "railing" is:

> "988 blasphēmia; from *989*; *vilification* (espec. against God): - blasphemy, evil speaking, railing."[13.16]

The actual Greek word translated as "accusation," or "judgment" is:

> "2920 krisis; *decision* (subj. or obj., for or against); by extens. a *tribunal*; by impl. *justice* (spec. divine law): - accusation, condemnation, damnation, judgment."[13.17]

So what Michael did *not* do to the devil was to bear upon or inflict, (ĕpiphĕrō); a vilification, (blasphēmia); decision or judgment, (krisis).

The NAS includes the word "dare" in: *"did not dare pronounce against him a railing judgment."* There is a clear implication in both translations, that Michael was fully capable of rendering this judgment against the devil. This was not an issue of what Michael *could* do; but rather what he *would* do. The inclusion of the word "dare" in the translation confirms this. But what could this decision or judgment have actually been?

Tsâbâ' Extraordinaire

It must be remembered that Michael and the enemy had "had it out" before. Back in Chapter 3 Revelation 12:7-9, (KJV); tells, (told) us:

> "And there was war in heaven:
> Michael and his angels fought
> against the dragon; and the dragon
> fought and his angels,
>
> And prevailed not; neither was
> their place found any more in heaven.
>
> And the great dragon was cast out,
> that old serpent, called the Devil, and Satan,
> which deceiveth the whole world:
> he was cast out into the earth, and
> his angels were cast out with him."

So sure as taxes, Michael would have liked to "take him out," this time; after "throwing him out" last time; here when this "discussion" about the body of Moses took place. But Michael did not "*dare*" do this. Instead he left it up to the Lord to "rebuke" him.

The actual Greek word translated as "rebuke" is:

> "2008 ĕpitimaō; from 1909 and 5091; to *tax upon*, i.e. *censure* or *admonish*; by impl. *forbid*: - (straitly) charge, rebuke."[3.18]

> "1909 ĕpi; a prim. prep. prop. mean. *superimposition*..."[3.19]

> "5091 timaō; from 5093; to *prize*, i.e. *fix* a *valuation* upon; by impl. to *revere*: - honour, value."[3.20]

Based upon the actual definition of *ĕpitimaō*, it seems that "rebuke" is an insufficient translation, as this implies mere criticism—which can also be constructive, with a desire to help. The literal definition *ĕpitimaō* is "to tax upon;" with the root *timaō* meaning: "to prize," or: "fix a valuation upon." Although *timaō* at least literally seems to have neither a positive or negative connotation—but merely to place a value upon; *ĕpitimaō* clearly has a negative meaning.

What it seems that Michael did, was to subrogate all of his available karmas to the Lord; by saying: "The Lord, (in my place), *ĕpitimaō* you." By subrogating the karmas available to him, he allowed God to "fix the value" of the karma to which Michael was otherwise entitled.

The actual word translated as "devil" here is again:

> "*1228* diabŏlŏs; from *1225*; a *traducer*; spec. *Satan* [comp. 7854]; - false accuser, devil, slanderer." (FN) "*1225* diaballō; from *1223* and *906*; (fig.) to *traduce*: - accuse."[13.21]

Why did the devil want to know where Moses was buried? *Diabŏlŏs* wanted that "battery." And he wanted it for the same reason that the dead man came back to life; when he was stone dead, and then merely *contacted* the bones of Elisha—*power*.

The devil wanted the power contained in Moses' body, likely in the bones; in order to increase his "arsenal." Of course God knew this; which is why He either buried Moses Himself *directly*; or had a "non-host" do it for Him *indirectly*; rendering this power unavailable to the enemy. To get this "battery," the devil had to get through Michael first; and the devil hadn't done very well with Mikey in the past.

What Michael and the devil did *not* do was *fight*. Why did they not fight? The answer is likely the poor results the devil had obtained in the past; i.e.; he was "a-scared."

So then why didn't the devil just go take the body of Moses; and fight Michael if and only if Michael had tried to stop the devil? The answer of course, being the fact that the devil simply didn't know where Moses was buried; and he could not "trick" any host into revealing this information, because none knew.

So instead, an argument took place not "*over* the body of Moses" as though the body were present; but rather "*about the body of Moses.*" What the devil wanted to know, was where the body was. Had any man known, the devil could have found out that way. But since "no man" knew Moses' place of burial, the devil tried to find another means.

And as it reads, the devil was quite *unsuccessful*.

Alleged Fantasy Foundations Volume I

Chapter 14

Exercitum ex Ossium
(The Army of Bones)

Ezekiel 37:1-10 (NAS) tells us:

*"The hand of the LORD was upon me,
and He brought me out by the Spirit of the LORD
and set me down in the middle of the valley;
and it was full of bones.*

*He caused me to pass among them round about,
and behold, there were very many
on the surface of the valley;
and lo, they were very dry.*

*He said to me, "Son of man,
can these bones live?"
And I answered, "O Lord GOD, You know."*

Again He said to me,

> *"Prophesy over these bones and say to them,*
> *'O dry bones, hear the word of the LORD."*
>
> *Thus says the Lord GOD to these bones,*
> *"Behold, I will cause breath to enter you*
> *that you may come to life.*
>
> *I will put sinews on you,*
> *make flesh grow back on you,*
> *cover you with skin and put breath*
> *in you that you may come alive;*
> *and you will know that I am the LORD."'*
>
> *So I prophesied as I was commanded;*
> *and as I prophesied, there was a noise,*
> *and behold, a rattling;*
> *and the bones came together, bone to its bone.*
>
> *And I looked, and behold,*
> *sinews were on them,*
> *and flesh grew and skin covered them;*
> *but there was no breath in them.*
>
> *Then He said to me,*
> *"Prophesy to the breath, prophesy,*
> *son of man, and say to the breath,*
> *Thus says the Lord GOD,*
> *Come from the four winds, O breath,*
> *and breathe on these slain,*
> *that they come to life."*
>
> *So I prophesied as He commanded me,*
> *and the breath came into them,*
> *and they came to life and stood on their feet,*
> *an exceedingly great army."*[14.1]

These passages are generally considered by most to be *prophetic*, often described as a "vision;" representing perhaps a *literal*, (minority); or perhaps an *allegorical*, (majority); account of something God already had done; or something God was planning to do at some point in the future.

Most also believe that this "explanation" of the actual meaning of the above passages as a "vision," as generally purported; is also contained or continued, perhaps as a *recapitulation*, in verses 11-14 which follow. However; interpretations of verses 11-14 individually and *apart* from the conclusion of the events contained verses 1-10, is not only equally possible; but is substantially more likely to represent the truth.

But before any of these verses are analyzed, something else needs to be addressed:

If one were capable of *psychokinesis* or *telekinesis*, and had a dent on the front fender of his or her Cadillac; would it be reasonable to assume that said dent necessarily was placed there by the power of the owners mind, because they *could*?

Or; in the absence of any evidence that it was *psychokinesis* or *telekinesis* that purposely dented the fender; would it be more reasonable to assume that it was simply a matter of another vehicle or something else striking the Cadillac?

And if there were clear and convincing evidence that this dent was caused by normal physical means; would one still maintain that it was *psychokinesis* or *telekinesis*, simply because the owner was capable of the same?

The point; is that simply because someone is capable of *psychokinesis* or *telekineseis*, this does not necessarily mean that every event in their life must be a "*psychokinetic*" or "*telekinetic*" event.

Or—

"I cannot believe what that well known prophet said to me."

"What did he say?"

"He said he wanted a hamburger and fries—what can that possibly mean?—What was he trying to tell me?"

"Well, since you work in a restaurant; and you were working at the time he said it; it probably just meant he wanted a hamburger and fries."

Is this silly? Of course it is. The point; is that simply because someone is a *prophet*, it does not necessarily mean that every word that comes out of their mouth is *prophesy*.

Likewise here, despite the fact that Ezekiel was a prophet; a *prophetic* or "vision" explanation for the story contained in Ezekiel 37:1-10, and then possibly continuing on in Ezekiel 30: 11-14; rather than a *recollection* of an actual event; is nevertheless quite problematic.

Firstly, Ezekiel himself was actually *personally involved* in the *events*—at least that is how it is written. Generally Bible *stories* contain actual names, while *parables* do not. Ezekiel was not merely a spectator or record keeper, either before, during, or after the fact; but was an active *participant*. It was Ezekiel himself who would have played the key and active participant in a "vision;" if this were a "vision"—a rather unusual circumstance.

Secondly, there is no introductory verbiage to indicate that this was a *prophetic* event. There is no "a vision came to me," or "I had a dream," preceding the recollection. To determine if this is significant; a close look at how other *preceding* prophetic passages in Ezekiel actually begin, is quite revealing:

Ezekiel Chapter 29 (NAS) begins with: "*1 In the tenth year, in the tenth month, on the twelfth of the month, the word of the LORD came to me saying...*"[14.2]

Ezekiel Chapter 30 (NAS) begins with: "*1 The word of the LORD came again to me saying,...*"[14.3]

Ezekiel Chapter 31 (NAS) begins with: "*1 In the eleventh year, in the third month, on the first of the month, the word of the LORD came to me saying...*"[14.4]

Ezekiel Chapter 32 (NAS) begins with: "*1 In the twelfth year, in the twelfth month, on the first of the month, the word of the LORD came to me saying,....*"[14.5]

Ezekiel Chapter 33 (NAS) begins with: "*1 And the word of the LORD came to me, saying,...*"[14.6]

Ezekiel Chapter 34 (NAS) begins with: "*1 Then the word of the LORD came to me saying,...*"[14.7]

Ezekiel Chapter 35 (NAS) begins with: "*1 Moreover, the word of the LORD came to me saying,...*"[14.8]

Exercitum ex Ossium (The Army of Bones)

And Ezekiel Chapter 36 (NAS) begins with: "*1 "And you, son of man, prophesy to the mountains of Israel and say, 'O mountains of Israel, hear the word of the LORD.*"14.9

But the very next chapter, here 37, begins with: "*The hand of the LORD was upon me, and He brought me out by the Spirit of the LORD and set me down in the middle of the valley; and it was full of bones.*"

Thus here in Chapter 37; unlike in the preceding Chapters 29-36; it is not the *"word"* of the Lord with which these passages are concerned; but rather the *"hand"* of the Lord.

Furthermore, it was not that this hand came "*to*" him, as the word of the Lord consistently did; but rather that it was "*upon*" him. The actual Hebrew word translated as "hand" is:

> "3027 yâd; a prim. word; a *hand* (the *open* one [indicating *power*, *means*, *direction*, etc.], in distinction from 3709, the *closed* one); used (as noun, adv., etc.) in a great variety of applications,..."14.10

The actual original Hebrew word translated as "upon" is:

> "5921 'al; prop. the same as 5920 used as a prep. (in the sing. or plur., often with pref. or as conj. with a particle following); *above*, *over*, *upon*, or *against* (yet always in this last relation with a downward aspect)..."14.11

And this "*hand*" or *yâd* was not *saying*, but rather "bringing" Ezekiel. Bringing Ezekiel where? Bringing him "*out*" of or *from* some location of which we are not told; but obviously it must have been from wherever he was at that time. And then *bringing* him into and setting him down *in* the middle of a valley. This "hand" or *yâd*, first brought him *out*; and then brought him *in*.

In addition; as often is the case; it is the word "spirit" that also causes a bit of confusion. Unless read very carefully, it can easily seem that it was Ezekiel's *spirit* that was brought to this valley; such as perhaps in astral projection. But in fact the word "*Spirit*" here does not in any way refer to Ezekiel's "Spirit." It is clearly stated that it is the *"Spirit of the LORD,"* to which this refers. In fact; as it is written, said Spirit via the *yâd*, seems to represent the *means* by which Ezekiel was brought; physically or otherwise; to this valley.

The actual Hebrew word translated as "by the Spirit of" is:

> "7307 rûwach; from 7306; *wind*; by resemblance *breath*, i.e. a sensible (or even violent) exhalation; fig. *life, anger, unsubstantiality*; by extens. a *region* of the sky; by resemblance *spirit*, but only of a rational being (includ. its expression and functions): - air, anger, blast, breath, x cool, courage, mind, x quarter x side, spirit ([-ual]), tempest, x vain, ([whirl-]) wind (-y)."[14.12]

Rûwach was addressed in an earlier chapter when analyzing "spirit" vs. "soul" in Bible *translations*. But here it seems that this word *rûwach* is not even translated as "Spirit;" but rather the entire phrase; "by the Spirit of." Thus if correct, again indicates a *means* by which something was done; in this case a change in the physical location of Ezekiel *from* the "out" location, *to* the "in" location.

Ezekiel was then *"caused"* to *"pass"* among these *"bones;"* and determined that they were *"very dry."* At first blush, this translation strongly suggests that these bones either were never interred, or interred in a shallow grave. At least contextually, it seems that their "dryness" was likely due to their having been in the sun for an extended period of time.

What was the nature of this valley? We are not told *where* it was, but only that it was a *"valley,"* and that it must have had some type of: *"middle."*

The actual Hebrew word translated here as "valley" is:

> "1237 biq'âh; from 1234; prop. a *split*, i.e. a wide level *valley* between mountains: - plain, valley."[14.13]

> "1234 bâqa'; a prim. root; to *cleave*; gen. to *rend, break, rip* or *open*: - make a breach, break forth (into, out, in pieces, through, up), be ready to burst, cleave (asunder),

cut out, divide, hatch, rend (asunder), rip up, tear, win."[14.14]

The use of *biq'âh* here for "valley" is uncommon, with *biq'âh* appearing only nine times in the entire Old Testament; with two of these nine appearing in these very passages.[14.15]

The more common Hebrew word translated as "valley" is:

"6010 'êmeq; from 6009; a *vale* (i.e. broad *depression*): - dale, vale, valley [*often used as a part of proper names*]. See also 1025."[14.16]

This particular word, *'êmeq*, appears fifty three times in the Old Testament.[14.17]

So it must be asked what the difference is between the more common use of *êmeq*, and the use of *biq'âh* here in Ezekiel?

The root of *biq'âh* is *bâqa'*, which is a verb. Thus when one engages in *bâqa'*, or "to cleave;" the result is *biq'âh* or "a split." It must be noted that the definition of *biq'âh* is actually not "a valley, but rather "a split; and that Strong's use of *id est*, (i.e.); is an attempted *rephrasing* of this definition, as "a wide level *valley* between mountains." Strong did *not* use *exempli gratia*, (e.g.); with "wide level *valley* between mountains" being an *example* of *biq'âh*.

Why does this matter? This matters because of the *cause* of the characteristics of this area. Normally, valleys are "formed" from *erosion* by water, *erosion* by wind; or *erosion* due to of glacial activities. Thus the more common word *'êmeq*, better describes these "normally occurring" "valley" areas.

But here this particular area was caused by *bâqa'*; or "to *cleave*; gen. to *rend, break, rip* or *open*;" and not by any type of *erosion*. We are not told when this cleaving or splitting occurred. Neither are we told who or what the active cause was for this splitting. But wherever it was, or however it was caused, or by whom; this was not a normal "valley."

Ezekiel then goes on to indicate that this "valley," ("a split") "*was full of bones.*"

The original Hebrew word translated as "bones" is:

"6106 'etsem; from 6105 a *bone* (as *strong*); by extens. the *body*; fig. the *substance*, i.e. (as pron.) *selfsame*: - body, bone, x life, (self,) same, strength, x very."[14.18]

"6105 'âtsam; a prim. root to bind fast, i.e. close (the eyes); intrans. to be (causat. make) powerful or numerous; denom."[14.19]

In fact, every time the word *"bones"* or *"bone"* appears in these ten passages, it is this very same word: '*etsem*.[14.20]

The KJV *translation* states that Ezekiel then describes these bones as *"very dry."* As previously stated: "At first blush, this translation strongly suggests that these bones either were never interred, or interred in a shallow grave. At least contextually, their "dryness" was likely due to their having been in the sun for an extended period of time."

However, the original Hebrew word translated as "very" is:

"3966 m^e'ôd; from the same as 181; prop. *vehemence*, i.e. (with or without prep.) *vehemently*; by impl. *wholly, speedily*, etc. (often with other words as an intensive or superlative; espec. when repeated)..."[14.21]

It seems that a problem is developing here with the translation of *m^e'ôd* as *"very."* Thus *literally* these bones were in fact either "vehemently dry" or "dry with vehemence." Precisely how could these bones, or any other bones exhibit any level of "vehemence?"

And it gets worse—

The original Hebrew words translated as "dry" is:

"3002 yâbêsh; from 3001; *dry*: - dried (away), dry."[14.22]

"3001 yâbêsh; a prim. root; to *be ashamed, confused* or *disappointed*; also (as failing) to *dry* up (as water) or *wither* (as herbage): - be ashamed, clean, be confounded, (make) dry (up), (do) shame (-fully), x utterly, wither (away)."[14.23]

The spelling of 3002 as *yâbêsh*; and the identical spelling, including the identical diacritics, of its root 3001 as *yâbêsh*; is not a typographical error here. It seems that the translation of 3002 *yâbêsh* as "*dry*" is inconsistent with the literal meaning of its root: 3001 *yâbêsh*—except perhaps as an *effect*.

Meaning; that here 3002 *yâbêsh* as "dry" likely is only the *result* of another process, with the same being 3001 *yâbêsh*: "to *be ashamed, confused* or *disappointed*; also (as failing) to *dry* up (as water) or *wither* (as herbage)." A town or county that is considered as "dry," is not literally dry, as in no water or moisture being present; but the result of another factor—local prohibition of alcohol.

Thus decisions must be made with regard to the actual meaning(s) of: "*very dry.*"

Does this mean that these bones were *literally* physically "vehemently dry," (m^e 'ôd and 3002 yâbêsh), such as dry from lying in the sun? If so, this condition was likely reached *after* physical death.

Or were these bones not being described as literally dry, but rather literally: "vehemently *ashamed, confused* or *disappointed*; also (as failing)," (m^e 'ôd and 3001 yâbêsh)? If so, this condition was likely reached *before* physical death.

At this juncture, it would be remiss to not consider what the Bible might have to say about "wet bones."

Job 21:23-24 (KJV) tells us:

*"One dieth in his full strength,
being wholly at ease and quiet.*

*His breasts are full of milk,
and his bones are moistened with marrow."*[14.24]

The actual Hebrew word translated as "*bones*" here in Job, is the same word translated as "*bones*" in Ezekiel: "6106 'etsem."[14.25]

The actual Hebrew word translated here as "moistened" is:

"8248 shâqâh; a prim. root; to *quaff,* i.e. (caus.) to *irrigate* or *furnish a potion to:*"[14.26]

The actual Hebrew word translated here as "marrow" is:

"4221 môach; from the same as 4220; *fat,* i.e. marrow: - marrow."[14.27]

[However, it must be noted that the word first translated as "*strength*" here in verse 23, is the very same word then translated as "*bones*" in verse 24: "6106 'etsem."[14.28]]

What is the *purpose* of these passages in Job? Clearly some type of a relationship is being established between: "*dieth in his full strength, being wholly at ease and quiet;*" and: "*his bones are moistened with marrow.*"

Although the words "so as a result" do not actually appear; there is a clear implication of this relationship—else what is the purpose of the passages? Thus if "*dieth in his full strength, being wholly at ease and quiet,*" were to be considered as a *cause*; then "*his bones are moistened with marrow,*" would be the stated *effect* of this cause; or perhaps more likely the reverse: Because: "*his bones are moistened with marrow:*" he then is able to: "*dieth in his full strength, being wholly at ease and quiet.*" Again, "*bones*" and "*strength*" are the very same word: 6106 'etsem.

Naturally, it must then be asked what degree of *antonymic* relationship exists between "*full strength, being wholly at ease and quiet,*" either resulting in or causing: "*moistened*" bones; and "vehemently *ashamed, confused* or *disappointed*; also (as failing)," resulting or causing: "*dry*" bones?"

In Ezekiel 37, there then seems to be a bit of a conversation between Ezekiel and God: "*He said to me, "Son of man, can these bones live?" And I answered, "O Lord GOD, You know."*"

The actual Hebrew word translated as "live" is:

"2421 châyâh; a prim. root [comp. 2331, 2421]; to *live,* whether lit. or fig.; causat. to *revive;* - keep (leave, make) alive, x certainly, give (promise) life, (let, suffer to) live,

> nourish up, preserve (alive), quicken, recover, repair, restore (to life), revive, (x God) save (alive, life, lives), x surely, be whole."[14.29]

This word *châyâh*, is the same word used to describe the condition of the formerly deceased man who came to life after contacting Elisha's bones. But unlike *here*, where *chây âh* is translated as *"live;" chây âh* is translated *there* as *"revived."*

Thus it seems that this question might better read: "He said to me, "Son of man, can these bones be *revived?"*

And the original Hebrew word translated as "know," in Ezekiel's response: *"O Lord GOD, You know;"* is:

> "3045 yâda'; a prim root; to *know* (prop. to ascertain by *seeing*); used in a great variety of senses, fig., lit., euphem. and infer. (including *observation, care, recognition*; and causat. *instruction, designation, punishment*, etc.)..."[14.30]

Thus it seems that this response might better read: "O Lord GOD, *watch,* ("prop. to ascertain by *seeing*"); and you will *know."*

Then it seems that Ezekiel is *commanded* to *prophesy* over these bones, but this is not actually so. And the *"again"* in: *"Again He said to me, "Prophesy over these bones and say to them, O dry bones, hear the word of the LORD,"* is a bit misleading; as this implies that Ezekiel had previously been asked to do this exact same thing.

The actual original Hebrew word translated as "again" is:

> "7725 shûwb; a prim. root; to *turn* back (hence, away) trans. or intrans. lit. or fig. (not necessarily with the idea of *return* to the starting point); gen. to *retreat*; often adv. *again*..."[14.31]

The actual original Hebrew word translated as "said" is:

> "559 'âmar; a prim. root; to *say* (used with great latitude)"[14.32]

Thus it seems this might better read: "He spoke to me again, this time saying: 'Prophesy over these bones and say to them, O dry bones, hear the word of the LORD.'"

Here in this verse, it appears that God is merely *saying*, or *'âmar*; but not *commanding* this action. The difference is in Ezekiel's free will to do, or not to do.

However later, in verse seven, the word "*commanded*" does in fact appear in this translation: "*So I prophesied as I was commanded.*"

This original Hebrew word translated in verse seven as "commanded" is:

> "6680 tsâvâh; a prim. root; (intens.) to *constitute, enjoin*: - appoint, (for-) bid, (give a) charge, (give a, giving, send with) command (-er, -ment), send a messenger, put, (set) in order."[14.33]

As can be seen above, the majority of the KJV translations of *tsâvâh* are not "*commanded*." And as can also be seen, *tsâvâh* is strikingly similar to another Hebrew word discussed in earlier chapters; with the same being that which God Himself called mankind:

> "6635 tsâbâ' or tsᵉba'ah from 6633; a *mass* of persons (or fig. things), espec. reg. organized for war (an *army*); by impl. a *campaign*, lit. or fig. (spec. *hardship, worship*): - appointed time, (+) army, (+) battle, company, host, service, soldiers, waiting upon, war (-fare)."

This is precisely what God is doing here, utilizing the verb *tsâvâh* to "enjoin" or *urge*, or "constitute" Ezekiel as an active participant, or the noun *tsâbâ'*; for literal *recourse*. And God is telling Ezekiel precisely what it is he is to prophesy.

The actual Hebrew word translated as "prophesy" is:

> "5012 nâbâ'; a prim. root; to *prophesy*, i.e. speak (or sing) by inspiration (in prediction or simple discourse): - prophesy (ing), make self a prophet."[14.34]

Exercitum ex Ossium (The Army of Bones)

Is this actual *prophesy*, or are there other reasons for this "prophesy?"

With the one interpretation of "very dry" bones; i.e.; the *unaware* bones, or just "plain old bleached out dry bones;" ("3002 yâbêsh; from 3001; *dry*: - dried (away), dry."); there is only God, Ezekiel, and these desiccated bones strewn about that are present. Thus, it must be asked precisely who or what it is that is or are the intended recipient(s) of this or any other prophesy?

With this view, the "prophesy" seems to have no possible intended recipients. God already knows, as He is the one who tells Ezekiel precisely what to "prophesy"—and not to mention that God is *omniscient*.

And Ezekiel knows what the content of this "prophesy" is as soon as God tells him—*without* repeating it. And it seems that the ("3002 yâbêsh") "dry bones," have no capability whatsoever to receive this, or any other "prophesy"—at least in the normal understanding of this term.

Thus with this view, there is either no "normal" purpose to this exercise; or there is a purpose that is not "normal." And this "non-normal" purpose; is likely the equivalent of the: "Let there be(s)."

Meaning; that the repeating as "prophesy," that which Ezekiel was told by God; is the *means* by which the *dunamis* or supernatural power manifests, and has nothing to do with the "normal" purposes of "prophesy."

In keeping with this "plain old bleached out dry bones" view; any *dunamis* contained in these bones, seems to be irrelevant. But what is relevant, is the "working" of the *dunamis* by Ezekiel. And the ultimate result of, and the very purpose for this "working," is *ĕxŏusia*—if this "plain old bleached out dry bones" is presumed to be so.

Clearly there is *dunamis* involved in what follows. But it is not just Ezekiel working *dunamis* that he is already "in charge of." Rather with this "plain old bleached out dry bones" view, God is providing instruction and "real time" *dunamis*, in furtherance of what follows. Thus there is *dunamis* and *authority* being provided, and that is *ĕxŏusia* as previously defined. Likely Ezekiel's *ĕxŏusia* "battery" increased substantially in capacity.

But what if the "plain old bleached out dry bones" view is discarded; and instead the root of the "*dry*" *yâbêsh*; here the "3001 yâbêsh; a prim. root; to *be ashamed, confused* or *disappointed*; also (as failing);" view is taken. Meaning; that instead of merely being *desiccated*; these bones are characterized as "*dry*," because they are "ashamed, confused, or disappointed." And it must be remembered that these bones are described literally as *m $^{e\text{'}}$ôd*, or "vehemently" dry; i.e.; vehemently "*ashamed, confused* or *disappointed*."

In other aspects of human existence, these types of "emotional" states represent *imbalances*; or "differences of potential." And a "difference of potential" is what drives action in many areas—not just electricity. Generally, when physically alive human beings are in these types of "emotional" states, particularly when "vehemently;" they have a desire to take some action to do something about it, and generally attempt to do so.

It has been shown that *dunamis* remained in the bones of Elisha. And in the case of Moses, God did not permit any man to even know the location of Moses' body; and thus that which would have remained "most intact"—the bones.

But here with the "vehemently" "ashamed, confused, or disappointed" definition of "very dry;" it seems that something *other than*, or perhaps *in addition to*, *dunamis* was contained in these bones.

It must be remembered that we are told what Elisha's bones *did* contain; because of what happened. But this acknowledgement of what was contained in Elisha's bones, is in no way any statement of exclusivity. Meaning; that simply because we are told or shown that *dunamis* was in Elisha's bones, this is not to say that *dunamis* and *dunamis* alone was contained therein.

The truth; is that the story, (not a parable), of this man coming back to life after merely touching the bones of Elisha, tells us little about the actual *mechanisms* involved. Surely there was *dunamis* involved, but *dunamis* represents only the *means*. In the case of criminal activity, *means* alone is insufficient. There usually must also be *motive* and *opportunity*.

The stated *motive* for this deceased man contacting Elisha's bones was not *resurrection*, but rather *concealment*. The truth is that those who hid this corpse; were simply tying to hide the body. There was no expectation of resurrection. Thus although the *opportunity* for this "bone contact" was in fact provided, it was provided only *serendipitously*.

There is no evidence that any of those involved in any way believed, that because it would be much better if this man were not dead; they then therefore knowingly placed the body where they did, with some expectation of *resurrection*. It is not just unclear, but highly unlikely that anyone knew Elisha's bones were even "in there."

This particular event with the deceased Elisha, as is the case with most if not all resurrections; was a *two-part* process. *First* the previously physically alive vessel must be repaired to the point where it can again contain the soul. And then, and only then, can the soul be introduced.

A two-part process, albeit a different one; is how *God* did it when He *formed*, (not *created*), Adam.

And this is how human beings procreate today. *Gestation* is the process by which this *physical* formation occurs.

One could try to argue that the second part, the introduction of the soul, is automatic; but this does not change the fact that it remains a *two-part* process. First the vessel must be capable of physical life; and then the soul is introduced.

The men in the "talent men" story did not have *dunamis* that "worked itself." Surely the one talent man's *dunamis* did not. The very purpose of the *talantŏn* is to provide the *motive* to "work it."

So it must be asked where was the *motive* for the *dunamis* contained in the bones of Elisha to manifest, and restore the physical body of this deceased individual? The *motive* either resided in Elisha's bones; or it did not.

If it did, then this *capacity* likewise "remains" in the bones. If it did not, then it came from without. If without, then precisely how and why did this serendipitous *contact* "trigger" this event?

Here with this "vehemently" "ashamed, confused, or disappointed" view of the bones Ezekiel saw; it seems the former must be the case. Meaning; that there was more than just *dunamis* in these bones.

So God tells Ezekiel what to "prophesy;" and when Ezekiel complies, these bones become bodies physically *capable* of containing human souls; but do not yet contain souls as we are told: *"but there was no breath in them."*

The actual Hebrew word translated as "breath" is:

"7307 rûwach; from 7306; *wind*; by resemblance *breath*, i.e. a sensible (or even violent) exhalation; fig. *life, anger, unsubstantiality*; by extens. a *region* of the sky; by resemblance *spirit*, but only of a rational being (includ. its expression and functions..."[14.35]

Rûwach was the word previously addressed as the most common word translated as "spirit" in the KJV Old Testament. *Rûwach* is the word translated here as "breath," (contextually of *life*). And it was *rûwach* that was translated as "Spirit," in "Spirit of the Lord" in a previous chapter.

And it must be remembered that that there is yet another *rûwach*, which was addressed in a previous chapter; with the same being the *Chaldean* form of *rûwach*.

"7308 rûwach (Chald.); corresp. to 7307: - mind, spirit, wind."[14.36]

God then again instructs Ezekiel to *"prophesy;"* but here to *"prophesy to the breath;"* and *"say to the breath, "Thus says the Lord GOD, Come from the four winds, O breath, and breathe on these slain, that they come to life."*

Here the translations as *"breath,"* (but not "breathe"), are all *rûwach*.[14.37]

The original Hebrew word translated as "breathe" is:

5301 nâphach; a prim. root; to puff, in various applications (lit., to inflate, blow hard, scatter, kindle, expire; fig., to disesteem)..."[14.38]

Exercitum ex Ossium (The Army of Bones)

And the "four winds" is:

"702 'arba'; masc. 'arbâ'âh; from 7251; four...;"[14.39] and the above *rûwach*.[14.40]

And the *"breath"* in the last verse is again the *Hebrew* word *rûwach*.[14.41]

Precisely what are these "four winds;" and why does any of this matter?"

Jeremiah 49:36 (KJV) tells us:

> *"And upon Elam will I bring the four winds*
> *from the four quarters of heaven,*
> *and will scatter them toward all those winds;*
> *and there shall be no nation whither*
> *the outcasts of Elam shall not come."*[14.42]

Here in Jeremiah, it seems that there are "four winds" in *heaven*. And again "winds" here in Jeremiah is the Hebrew *rûwach*.[14.43]

Revelation 7:1 (KJV) tells us:

> *"And after these things I saw four angels*
> *standing on the four corners of the earth,*
> *holding the four winds of the earth,*
> *that the wind should not blow on the earth,*
> *nor on the sea, nor on any tree."*[14.44]

Here it seems that there are also "four winds" in, or on, or of, the *earth*.

The actual *Greek* word translated as "wind" is:

"417 aněmŏs; from the base of *109*; *wind*; (plur.) by impl. (the four) *quarters* (of the earth): - wind."[14.45]

303

The actual Greek word translated as "corners" is:

"1137 gōnia; prob. akin to *1119*; an *angle*: - corner, quarter."[14.46]

Matthew 24:31 (KJV) tells us:

> *"And he shall send his angels*
> *with a great sound of a trumpet,*
> *and they shall gather together*
> *his elect from the four winds,*
> *from one end of heaven to the other."*[14.47]

The original Greek word translated here in Matthew as "winds," is also 417 *anĕmŏs*.[14.48]

Thus it seems a fair definition of "four winds" would be "in its entirety"—whether the immaterial, (heaven); or the material, (earth). "From the four corners of" would be another way to phrase "from the four winds."

This is despite the fact that as an *oblate spheroid*, the earth has no literal "corners;" and it also seems quite unlikely that *heaven* has any literal "corners"—at least as man knows them to be. The same can likely be said of "quarters."

And in Ezekiel, given the fact that it was *resurrection*, or: "*and the breath came into them*," that was the result; these particular "*four winds*" likely refer to *heaven* in its entirety, as in Jeremiah and Matthew; and not to *earth* as in Revelation.

The result of all of this is that: "*they came to life and stood on their feet, an exceedingly great army.*" The KJV is: "*and they lived, and stood up upon their feet, an exceeding great army.*"[14.49]

The actual Hebrew word translated as "life" (NAS) or "lived" (KJV) again is:

"2421 châyâh; a prim. root [comp. 2331, 2421]; to *live*, whether lit. or fig.; causat. to *revive*: - keep (leave, make)

Exercitum ex Ossium (The Army of Bones)

> alive, x certainly, give (promise) life, (let, suffer to) live, nourish up, preserve (alive), quicken, recover, repair, restore (to life), revive, (x God) save (alive, life, lives), x surely, be whole."[14.50]

And again in this word *châyâh*, is the same word used to describe the condition man after he touched Elisha's bones; but there is translated as "revived."

The actual Hebrew word translated as "army" is:

> "2428 chayil; from 2342; prob. a *force* whether of men, means, or other resources; an *army, wealth, virtue, valor, strength*..."[14.51]

The actual Hebrew word translated as "exceedingly," (NAS); or "exceeding," (KJV) is:

> "3966 m^e'ôd; from the same as 181; prop. vehemence, i.e. (with or without prep.) vehemently; by impl. wholly, speedily, etc. (often with other words as an intensive or superlative; espec. when repeated)..."[14.52]

The actual Hebrew word translated as "great" is:

> "1419 gâdôwl; or (short.) gâdôl; from 1431; *great* (in any sense); hence *older*; also *insolent*..."[14.53]

This word *m^e'ôd*, is the very same word translated as *"very,"* in *"very dry,"* when describing the original condition of *bones*. It is interesting that the translators chose to translate *m^e'ôd* as *"very,"* when describing how *"dry,"* ("3002 yâbêsh"), these bones were; but rejecting entirely the possibility that the root of this "3002 yâbêsh," "3001 yâbêsh; "a prim. root; to *be ashamed, confused* or *disappointed*; also (as failing)" would be more consistent with the literal meaning of *m^e'ôd* as "vehemence."

However much sense the use of "vehemently:" *"ashamed, confused* or *disappointed,"* may or may not make; "vehemently:"

"dry," clearly makes substantially less. In order for "a thing" to be either "vehement;" or to be "*ashamed, confused* or *disappointed*;" it seems would require some significant level of *consciousness*.

The most rational explanation for this would again be: "the tail wagging the dog." Meaning; that since the translators "already knew," that Ezekiel 37:1-10: "was not to be considered as a *literal* event;" there was no need to even consider that it might be a *literally* true story. Therefore, only those contextually "obvious" physical characteristics of these bones were of any concern.

And furthermore, since "everybody knows," (except perhaps for those—such as those who: "*cast the man into the grave of Elisha*); that bones "can contain nothing of significance;" therefore, there can be neither "vehemence;" nor can bones in any way be "*ashamed, confused* or *disappointed*."

And here the translation of this very same *m^e 'ôd*, as "exceedingly," (NAS); or "exceeding," (KJV); once again ignores that which is required for "vehemence"—*consciousness*. This is somewhat understandable, because as the translations read, *m^e'ôd* is describing not the very *chayil* or "*army*" itself; but rather in fact precisely how *gâdôwl*, or "*great*," this *chayil*, or "*army*" in fact is: "*exceedingly great army*."

It would be interesting to consider the alternative possibility: that that *gâdôwl m^e 'ôd*, or "greatly vehement;" rather than "vehemently great;" would be a better description of this *chayil* or "*army*."

It must also be asked if this event represents *resurrection* or *reincarnation*. The contribution of the osseous system to the total human body weight is between 10%-15%—presumably when the bones are "wet." Thus those new "*sinews*," "*flesh*," and "*skin*," "*on them*," represented at a minimum 85% by weight of the physical bodies of the members of this "*army*." Thus it must be asked at what percentage level should or would these physical bodies be considered as "the same body," as in *resurrection*; as opposed to a "new and different body," as in *reincarnation*?

And a similar question must be asked regarding: "*the breath came into them, and they came to life and stood on their feet*." Was it the *same* "breath" that originally inhabited each of these bodies; or were these each "different breaths?"

Ezekiel "prophesied" to two entirely different entities:"

First, he prophesied to the *bones,* likely to the residual *dunamis* contained therein.

Ezekiel *then* prophesied to the *breath,* which we are told was *not* contained therein.

These two can be differentiated; as the *dunamis* is originally of the Holy Ghost; and likely can be, or in fact is stored in bone. And we are told that unlike the case later with the "breath;" it was not the *"four winds"* to which Ezekiel was told to *"prophesy"* to cause the physical vessel to manifest; but rather to *"prophesy over these bones."*

The reason for this may be because it was the *ĕxŏusia,* or dunamic *power* and *authority* contained in these bones, that provided the *means* by which these bodies were then reconstructed.

It seems that there are three mechanisms by which this could be done via *recourse*:

The *first* would be via *ĕxŏusia* that Ezekiel himself already possessed. This of course assumes he already had this level of *ĕxŏusia.*

The second would be "real time *dunamis,*" provided "real time" to Ezekiel by God.

And the third; would be to take command of *ĕxŏusia* possessed by another; here this *ĕxŏusia* contained in these *"very many"* bones.

If the third, it was likely the *imbalances* existing because of the true meaning of "dry," or: "3001 yâbêsh; "a prim. root; to *be ashamed, confused* or *disappointed*; also (as failing);" that were then *balanced* by Ezekiel gaining the authority to utilize the dunamis part of the *ĕxŏusia* contained in these "dry" bones.

Stated another way, God authorized the transfer of the authority part of this *ĕxŏusia* to Ezekiel, when He said: "prophesy over these bones;" and this transfer was completed when Ezekiel complied. These imbalances "paid for" this transfer.

Revelation 6:9-11 (KJV) tells us:

*"And when he had opened the fifth seal,
I saw under the altar the souls of them
that were slain for the word of God,
and for the testimony which they held:*

*And they cried with a loud voice, saying,
How long, O Lord, holy and true,
dost thou not judge and avenge our blood
on them that dwell on the earth?"*[14.54]

Clearly there are imbalances here as "revealed in Revelation;" as these disembodied *"souls"* are in a *"loud voice"* asking God for, (arguably complaining to God about), *balance*. This is provided here to Biblically prove that *consciousness, communication*, and *emotions* can remain after physical life (time) is over.

These souls were of those *"that were slain."*

Were those whose *"bones"* were *"on the surface of the valley"* also "slain?" The presence of these "bones" would be consistent with either no burial, or burial in shallow graves. This is not actually stated in these passages; but seems likely, as what other available explanation for: *"and it was full of bones,"* makes more sense?

Since upon restoration of physical life, we are told they represented an "army;" it seems likely that they were originally an army, (large group or groups of hosts); that was slain and then restored. Unfortunately however, this is left unstated.

With regard to Elisha and the resurrected man, it is not known whether Elisha was actually buried *in* the ground, or interred *above* ground. It seems reasonable to presume that utilizing Elisha's place of interment would be easier to access and faster, than would be the effort and time required for digging a hole in the ground for this deceased man the *"they"* were burying.

Had Elisha's remains actually been below ground, it seems that the same would not have been much easier to access, than would the digging a new hole for the Moabites' deceased; and it does seem that they were in a bit of a hurry.

Does this matter? It must be noted that Jesus was also *not* actually or technically buried below grade either. Was this done just to make Jesus' exit easier? This does not seem reasonable; as angels that could move a boulder that large, clearly would not have had any trouble with six feet of earth.

The reason this is relevant, is because Elisha, (most likely); the bones in the valley; and Jesus, (with no bones broken), all had this in common: *none* were actually "buried," or interred *below* grade. Likely all had residual *dunamis*; albeit utilized in different manners. Had they been buried underground, would this *dunamis* have ultimately been "bled off" or depleted by the earth? If so, then it seems likely that *Moses* would have been interred *below* grade; both for *secrecy*, as well as in a sense: *term insurance*—but this remains unknown.

However; this Ezekiel story sounds a bit familiar. Back in the *gan* portion of Eden, God essentially did the same thing with Eve. Assuming the translation is correct, He fashioned Eve from an osseous structure, (rib), obtained from "the man," or Adam whom God had *formed*. The difference here is that God did it all Himself; and except for the "donor," the process was without any *recourse*.

The actual Hebrew word generally believed to mean "rib" is:

> "6763 tsêlâ'; or (fem.) tsal'âh; from 6760; a *rib* (as *curved*), lit. of the body) (sic.) or fig. (of a door, i.e. *leaf*); hence a *side*, lit. (of a person)..."[14.55]

So the question becomes: Why did He do this with *Eve* without recourse, but utilized recourse with *Ezekiel*? Clearly it was His will that Ezekiel do this.

Perhaps He merely wanted to increase Ezekiel's *éxŏusia*, or: "*dunamis* plus *authority*." If so, then God had both *power* and *authority*.

The answer may lie in precisely who it was that had jurisdiction over the area in question. With regard to the "Gan of Eden;" or the area commonly known as a "garden;" but what in actuality was a "guarded" or "protected" area; this was "sanctified ground." God had complete jurisdiction in this area, and thus had no need for recourse.

But outside of this *gan*, the enemy had already been given substantial jurisdiction—at a minimum by the original *created* hosts; and before that likely the "G_1." The amount of the enemy's jurisdiction depends on the time in question. Between Genesis 1:1 and 1:2 virtually all control had been handed over to the enemy.

Then, after God's intervention, and then the created hosts being given, (actually transferred), authority in Genesis 1:28; the enemy's authority was again reduced. And then after, and as a direct consequence of Calvary; much, (but not all), of the enemy's earthly authority would be removed.

Said authority was originally God's; then it was His will that this authority become that of His highest known creation at that time; who then "delivered" it to the enemy. The use of "highest known creation," rather than "hosts" here is deliberate, and will be addressed later.

It could be reasonably argued, that there are only a few *recorded* times that God ever placed the "breath of life" in a human body directly; i.e.; without any "host's" "will" being involved.

The first *known* time, being the *creation* of the original hosts.

The second *known* time being Adam, and possibly Eve; as although Adam provided the *physical* material; we do not know if Adam was ever asked for his permission to lose the rib, or if Adam in any other way willfully participated. And in each of these cases, God had previously to some extent sanctified the ground.

The third was the *resurrection*, (but not the birth), of Jesus. One could argue about this, in that Jesus knew about and participated in His own resurrection. However although He knew about it in advance and agreed to it; He was not actually a *host* when the resurrection actually happened. He was a host *before* it happened. In fact; He was the most powerful and accomplished host the world has ever encountered. Yet by definition, He was no longer a host while He was physically dead.

A possible fourth will be addressed next:

Chapter 15

The Separate and The Distinct

Ezekiel 37:11-14 (NAS), the verses which immediately *follow* this "dry bones" *recollection*, (not prophesy), contained in Ezekiel 37:1-10 tell us:

> *"Then He said to me, "Son of man,
> these bones are the whole house of Israel;
> behold, they say, "Our bones are dried up
> and our hope has perished.
> We are completely cut off."*
>
> *"Therefore prophesy and say to them,
> Thus says the Lord GOD,
> Behold, I will open your graves and
> cause you to come up out of your graves,
> My people; and I will bring you
> into the land of Israel.*

> *Then you will know that I am the LORD,*
> *when I have opened your graves*
> *and caused you to come up*
> *out of your graves, My people.*
>
> *I will put My Spirit within you*
> *and you will come to life,*
> *and I will place you on your own land.*
> *Then you will know that I,*
> *the LORD, have spoken and done it,"*
> *declares the LORD."*[15.1]

The very first thing that should be reasonably determined, is the chronological placement of these verses, (Ezekiel 10: 11-14); in order to determine if this is a *continuation* of the recollection contained in verses 1-10; a *recapitulation* of the recollection contained in verses 1-10; or if this is the *beginning* of something new.

If the *end* of verse 10, were connected to the *beginning* of verse 11, it would read like this:

> "*...and they came to life and stood on their feet, an exceedingly great army. Then He said to me, "Son of man, these bones are the whole house of Israel; behold, they say...*"

It must be noted that at the end of verse 10, there are no longer any bones; but rather an "*exceedingly great army.*" This of course assumes that *all* of the bones in the valley were restored to life—which is a reasonably safe assumption, as we are not told otherwise.

When did God make the statement about the bones contained in verse 11? The translation tells us: "*Then He said.*" When was "*then?*" The "*then*" was chronologically *after* the restoration of the bones in the valley to physical life in verse 10. So *chronologically* the statement in verse 11, as per the "*then;*" is made *after* the bones were no longer *bones*; but rather fully developed *bodies*; and very much *alive*—unless of course there were additional bones of which we are not told, or: "*ossa occultatum.*"

However; despite the translation being *"Then He said;"* it seems that Strong has no actual Hebrew word for this: *"then."*
The actual Hebrew word translated as "then He said" is again:

> "559 'âmar; a prim. root; to *say* (used with great latitude)..."[15.2]

It is not stated how much time lapsed between the existence of the *"exceedingly great army;"* and the *translated*, and perhaps phantom: *"then."* It is a bit ironic, that today many if not most believe that these passages *in-toto*, Ezekiel 37:1-14, are part of one large *prophesy*, and not an actual *event*; or *events*; despite the inclusion of the word *"then"* which suggests otherwise in the *translation*. It is likely that the original translators believed otherwise; i.e.; Ezekiel 37:11-14 represents a *different* event or events.

God's reference to "these" bones, likely refers to another set of "bones;" and *not* the former bones, which at *this* time are or were no longer bones, but fully functional human beings, arguably comprising an "army."

The actual Hebrew word translated as "these" is:

> "428 'êl-leh; prol. from 411; *these* or *those*: - an- (the) other; one sort, so, some, such, them, these (same), they, this, those, thus, which, who (-m)."[15.3]

This could be read with an emphasis on the word "these." Then He said to me: "Son of man, *these* bones are the whole house of Israel." Here likely referring to *these* bones, as being a different set of bones from *those* bones which were previously merely bones, which were now alive and comprised an "army."

The actual original Hebrew words here for "bones" and "dried up," in these passages, Ezekiel 37:11-14, are the same as in the previous verses, Ezekiel 37:1-10.[15.4]

If the position is taken that God is referring to some other set of bones in the previous *"valley;"* here bones that were there originally, but for some reason were not restored to life like the others; this is very problematic. The reason this is so, is because twice; (in verses 12 and 13); it states that the Lord will: "*open(ed) your graves and cause(d) you to come up out of your graves.*"

This represents a two stage process: The graves will *first* be opened; and *then* "you," will be; "*caused to come up out of the graves.*"

The actual original Hebrew word translated as "open" is:

"6605 pâthach; a prim root; to *open* wide (lit. or fig.); spec. to *loosen, begin, plough, carve...*"[15.5]

There was nothing described in the valley "full of bones" to *pâthach* or "open." Neither does it seem that any of the other definitions of *pâthach* could reasonably apply to those "valley bones" referenced in verses 1-10.

The actual original Hebrew word translated here as "graves" is:

"6913 qeber; or (fem.) qibrâh; from 6912; a *sepulchre*: - burying place, grave, sepulchre."[15.6]

In chapter 13, 6912 *qâbar* meaning: "to *inter*: - x in any wise, bury," was cited. This *qâbar* is the root of the above *qeber*.

Those "valley bones" as described in verses 1-10, were not in any way "buried." Thus it seems neither *qeber*, if male; nor *qibrâh*, if female; could in any way apply to the "valley bones."

Although Strong has "you" listed as present in "*cause you,*" there is, no number or Hebrew word provided.

The actual original Hebrew word translated as "come up" is:

"5927 'âlâh; a prim. root; to *ascend*, intrans. (*be high*) or act. (*mount*); used in a great variety of senses, primary and secondary, lit. and fig. (as follow)..."[15.7]

Thus, the bones contained in the "*graves,*" *qeber* or *qibrâh*; which would be "*opened,*" or *pâthach*; from which the "people" will be caused to "*come up,*" or *âlâh*; "*out of*;" could not have been any of the same bones on the *surface* of the valley. The description of these as "people" is appropriate, because of the semicolon placed after "people" in verse 12 (NAS).

Following is the Ezekiel 37:12, but here KJV:

> "*Therefore prophesy and say unto them,*
> *Thus saith the Lord God;*
> *Behold, O my people, I will open your graves,*
> *and cause you to come up out of your graves,*
> *and bring you into the land of Israel.*"[15.8]

It must be noted here, that the intended audience for verse 12 is or was *not* for the physically alive "army;" but rather for those who were not physically alive at that time this was stated.

Is it possible that there were actual graves under the piles of bones on the surface of the valley; and the "valley bones" had to first be brought to life in order to get out of the way; so that God and Zeke could "get to" those buried in said graves *under* the bones on the surface? If so; these remains, would nevertheless remain bones that were not the original "valley bones."

However; this would be a highly speculative position to take, as there is no indication whatsoever that this is or would have been so.

And the counterargument; would be that the mentioning of the *surface* of the valley was done specifically and intentionally to make it certain that the reader knew that there were *not* any bones anywhere except on the surface; thereby precluding the possibility of any actual underground graves.

However one could also argue that the use of surface was to differentiate those bones on the surface, from those which were buried.

As an aside; according to Strong, the word "*surface*" does not appear anywhere in the entire KJV Old Testament.[15.9]

Rather the actual Hebrew word translated here as "surface" is:

"6440 pâneh; (pânîym); from 6437; the *face* (as the part that *turns*); used in a great variety of applications..."[15.10]

However; it seems that *if* the information contained in Ezekiel 37:11-14 is considered as *prophesy*; *then* it does sound somewhat *historically* familiar—*now*; i.e; *today*; i.e.; a prophesy that was *fulfilled*.

Matthew 27:52-54 (KJV) tells us:

> *"And the graves were opened;*
> *and many bodies of the saints*
> *which slept arose,*
>
> *And came out of the graves*
> *after his resurrection,*
> *and went into the holy city,*
> *and appeared unto many.*
>
> *Now when the centurion,*
> *and they that were with him,*
> *watching Jesus, saw the earthquake,*
> *and those things that were done,*
> *they feared greatly, saying,*
> *Truly this was the Son of God."*[15.11]

As this cursorily reads, this chronologically happened *immediately* after the *death* of Jesus. But there is a problem with this "read;" and that problem is contained in verse 53. Verse 53 tells us: "*after his resurrection.*"

The actual Greek word translated here as "resurrection" is:

"1454 ĕgĕrsis; from 1453; a *resurgence* (from death): - resurrection."[15.12]

According to Strong, this is the only time the *translated* word "resurrection," is actually *ĕgĕrsis*.[15.13]

In the New Testament, except for *ĕgĕrsis*, and one other exception; "resurrection" is always the word "*anastasis*."[15.14] This word was introduced in chapter 9.

"386 anastasis; from 450; a *standing up* again, i.e. (lit.) a *resurrection* from death (individual, gen. or by impl. [its author]), or (fig.) a (moral) *recovery* (of spiritual truth): - raised to life again, resurrection, rise from the dead, that should rise, rising again."[15.15]

"450 anistēmi; from 303 and 2476; to *stand up* (lit. or fig., trans. or intrans.)..."[15.16]

"303 ana; a prim. prep. and adv.; prop. *up*; but by extens.) used (distributively) *severally*, or (locally) *at* (etc.)..."[15.17]

"2476 histēmi; a prol. form of a prim. staō, (of the same mean., and used for it in certain tenses); to *stand* (trans. or intrans.), used in various applications (lit. or fig.): - abide, appoint, bring, continue, covenant, establish, hold up, lay, present, set (up), stanch, stand (by, forth, still, up)."[2.9]

In Chapter 2, when the fact that the enemy: "*does not stand in the truth,*" because: "*there is no truth in him,*" was addressed; the word "*stand*" was the above *histēmi*.

This other exception is:

"1815 ĕxanastasis; from 1817; a *rising from* death: - resurrection."[15.18]

So here it must be asked precisely what the differences are between *anastasis*, or: "a *standing up* again, i.e. (lit.) a *resurrection* from death;" and *ĕxanastasis*, or: "a *rising from* death?"

The stated origin of the above *ĕxanastasis* is:

"1817 ĕxanistēmi; from 1537 and 450; obj, to *produce*, i.e. (fig.) *beget*; subj. to *arise*, i.e. (fig.) *object*: - raise, (rise) up."[15.19]

"1537 ĕk; or ĕx; a prim. prep. denoting origin the point whence motion or action procced."[15.20]

Both *anastasis*: "from 450; a *standing up* again, i.e. (lit.) a *resurrection* from death;" and ultimately: "1815 ĕxanastasis; from 1817; a *rising from* death: - resurrection;" via the stated root of ĕxanastasis: "1817 ĕxanistēmi; from 1537 and 450; obj, to *produce*, i.e. (fig.) *beget*; subj. to *arise*, i.e. (fig.) *object*: - raise, (rise) up;" are derived from "450 anistēmi; from 303 and 2476; to stand up (lit. or fig., trans. or intrans.)..."

In the case of *anastasis*, the derivation from 450 *anistēmi*, is *direct*. However, in the case of *ĕxanastasis*, the derivation from 450 *anistēmi*, is *indirect* and via *ĕxanistēmi*.

It should be noted that, unlike as is the case with *anastasis*; "produce," and "beget" appear in the definition of *ĕxanistēmi*; which is the direct root of *ĕxanastasis*. The meaning of *ĕxanastasis* is specifically "rising from death," which is an *effect* or *result*. But the meaning of its root, *ĕxanistēmi*, is much more general, defined as "produce," or "beget."

Thus it seems that although *ĕxanastasis* as "rising from death," is a result similar to *anastasis* as: "*standing up* again, i.e. (lit.) a *resurrection* from death;" here there is a specific *causation* or requirement for *ĕxanastasis* includes "produce," or "beget." Ergo; it seems that *ĕxanastasis* may refer *solely* to reincarnation; while *anastasis* refers to "*standing up* again," via *either* means—i.e.; *resurrection or reincarnation*.

Philippians 3:10-12 (KJV) tells us:

"That I may know him,
and the power of his resurrection,
and the fellowship of his sufferings,
being made conformable unto his death;
If by any means I might attain
unto the resurrection of the dead.

Not as though I had already attained,
either were already perfect:

> *but I follow after, if that I may apprehend*
> *that for which also I am apprehended*
> *of Christ Jesus."*[15.21]

The original Greek word translated here in Philippians as *"resurrection"* in verse 10 in: *"the power of his resurrection,"* is *anastasis*.[15.22] Here Paul is speaking of Jesus' resurrection.

However the original Greek word translated as *"resurrection"* in verse 11 in: *"If by any means I might attain unto the resurrection of the dead,"* is not *anastasis*; but rather *ĕxanastasis*."[15.23]

It appears that this is the only time it is *ĕxanastasis*, that is translated as "resurrection" in the entire Bible. And since no other translations of *ĕxanastasis* as any other word appears, this is likely the only Biblical appearance of *ĕxanastasis*.

Thus two things are evident:

Firstly, Paul believed reincarnation was a fact, and by the use of *ĕxanastasis*, and not *anastasis*, it seems Paul was referring to his own *reincarnation*, and not *resurrection*.

And *secondly,* the Bible translators did not want this known—else why translate the specific *ĕxanastasis* as synonymic with the general *anastasis*? Meaning; that *anastasis* could be translated as either *resurrection* or *reincarnation*, depending upon the context. But *ĕxanastasis* requires "produce," or "beget;" and thus cannot reasonably be considered as *resurrection* utilizing the *same* physical body. [For an exhaustive analysis of reincarnation based upon the Bible, see: *"Reincarnation—A Reasonable Inquiry."*]

One might fairly say that although it is interesting, informative, and illuminating; that it seems Paul wished to "attain unto the *reincarnation* of the dead;" this does not even address, much less explain, the "time problem" with: *"And the graves were opened; and many bodies of the saints which slept arose, And came out of the graves after his resurrection,"* in Matthew 27.53.

The key to this dilemma lies in the meaning of the word translated as *"his;"* and the NAS version makes matters worse by capitalization: *"His."*[15.24]

We are told in Matthew 27:52 that: *"graves were opened; and many bodies of the saints which slept arose."*

In Ezekiel 37:12 we had been told: *"Behold, I will open your graves and cause you to come up out of your graves."*

These are reasonably similar, and thus likely refer to the same event.

And then in the beginning of Matthew 27:53, appears the problematic verse: *And came out of the graves after his resurrection."*

The original Greek word translated here as "his" is:

"848 hautŏu; contr. for *1438*; *self* (in some oblique case or reflex. relation): - her (own), (of) him (-self), his (own), of it, thee, their (own), them (-selves), they."[15.25]

As can easily be seen, *hautŏu* means "self," but in masculine or feminine; and in singular or plural. Thus Matthew 27:53, translated as: "And came out of the graves after *their* (own) resurrection(s);" would be another and more contextually accurate translation.

Of course it seems that it would be necessary to first be resurrected, before moving anywhere; and as previously addressed, here uniquely as *ĕgĕrsis*: "from 1453; a *resurgence* (from death);" and not *anastasis*; before coming: "*out of the graves.*"

And what about the "*arose*" in: "*and many bodies of the saints which slept arose*" statement in the previous Matthew 27:52 verse?

The original Greek word translated here as "arose" is:

1453 ĕgĕirō; prob. akin to the base of *58* (through the idea of *collecting* one's faculties); to *waken* (trans. or intrans.), i.e. *rouse* (lit. from sleep, from sitting or lying, from disease, from death; or fig. from obscurity, inactivity, ruins..."[15.26] [It must be noted that according to Strong, the current translation of *ĕgĕirō* in Matthew 27:52 as "arose," is relatively new; as it seems *ĕgĕirō* in this particular passage used to be translated as: "*were raised.*"[15.27]]

Here *ĕgĕirō* is the root of the *ĕgĕrsis*.

The chronology of that which is recounted in Matthew, seems to be that these "*many bodies of the saints*" were first *ĕgĕirō*, or "*collecting* one's faculties); to *waken* (trans. or intrans.), i.e. *rouse* (lit. from sleep, from sitting or lying, from disease, from death."

Then their state after this *ĕgĕirō* process, was *ĕgĕrsis*; or "a *resurgence* (from death): - resurrection." *Ĕgĕirō*, the root of *ĕgĕrsis*, was the *cause*; and *ĕgĕrsis*, or "resurrected" state, was the *effect*.

Then, they "*came out of the graves after*" this *ĕgĕrsis*, or: "a *resurgence* (from death), process was completed

In Ezekiel 37:1-10, Ezekiel is an active participant with regard to the "valley bones." Ezekiel 37:1-10 represents a *recollection* of past events.

As soon as Ezekiel prophesied to the "valley bones," these described events began happening. This is known because in Ezekiel 37:7 we are told: "*and as I prophesied, there was a noise, and behold, a rattling; and the bones came together, bone to its bone.*"

The purpose for the "*prophesy*" here in Ezekiel 37:1-10, is *immediate action*.

But here in Ezekiel 37:11-14, Ezekiel is *not* any type of active participant in any actual *events*, but rather is acting solely as a *prophet*.

The purpose for the "*prophesy*" in Ezekiel 37:11-14, is *not* "immediate action;" but rather *information*; which is to be provided to the "*whole house of Israel*," regarding an event which will happen in the *future*.

In these Ezekiel 37:11-14 verses, God is also stating at that time what He "*will*" (future) do: "*I will open your graves and cause you to come up out of your graves, My people; and I will bring you into the land of Israel.*"

Here God does *not* ask Ezekiel to prophesy: "*and you will know that I am the Lord*, (and);" as He did with the "valley bones." Rather, Ezekiel is told to prophesy: "*Then you will know that I am the LORD* (then)."

When is this future "*then*?"

This future "*then*," is when the three things stated have been completed:

First: *"when I have opened your graves"*
Second: *"and caused you to come up out of your graves, My people;"*
Third: *"and I will bring you into the land of Israel."*

In the case of the "valley bones" *event* in Ezekiel 37:1-10, there were no actual *"graves,"* (qeber; or (fem.) qibrâh); and thus there were no *"graves"* to *"come up out of."* In addition, the *conclusion* of the "valley bones" event in verse 10, tells us only *what* these "valley bones" collectively *became*; with no information about any of these being "brought" anywhere.

And precisely what is meant by the above term translated as "LORD?"

In Ezekiel 37:6: *"and you will know that I am the Lord;"* and Ezekiel 37:13: *"Then you will know that I am the LORD;"* the original Hebrew word is purportedly:

"3068 Y^{e}hôvâh; from 1961; (the) self-*existent* or Eternal; *Jehovah*, Jewish national name of God: - Jehovah, the Lord. Comp. 3050. 3069."[15.28]

"1961 hâyâh; a prim. root [comp. 1933]; to *exist* i.e. *be* or *become, come to pass* (always emphatic and not a mere copulate or auxiliary)..."[15.29]

"1933 hâvâ',; or hâvâh; a prim. root [comp. 183, 1961] supposed to mean prop. to *breathe*; to *be* (in the sense of existence): - be, x have."[15.30]

"183 'âvâh; a prim. root; to *wish* for: - covet, (greatly) desire, be desirous, long, lust (after)."[15.31]

"3050 Yâhh; contr. for 3068, and mean. the same; *Jah*, the sacred name..."[15.32]

"3069 Y^{e}hôvîh; a var. of 3068 [used after 136, and pronounced by Jews as 430, in order to prevent the repetition of the same sound since they elsewhere pronounce 3068 as 136]: - God"[15.33]

Exodus 3:14-15 (KJV) tells us:

> "And God said unto Moses,
> I Am That I Am: and he said,
> Thus shalt thou say unto the children of Israel,
> I Am hath sent me unto you.
>
> And God said moreover unto Moses,
> Thus shalt thou say unto the children of Israel,
> the Lord God of your fathers,
> the God of Abraham, the God of Isaac,
> and the God of Jacob, hath sent me unto you:
> this is my name for ever,
> and this is my memorial unto all generations."[15.34]

All three translations in verse 14 as "I am" are the above 1961 hâyâh; "to exist"[15.35]; the purported root of 3068 Y^{e}h.

This is provided here in order to illustrate the idea of *being*, or self-awareness, with regard to these names of God. Even the seemingly odd root: "183 'âvâh; a prim. root; to *wish for*;" requires this self-awareness. This will be discussed in detail in the analysis of the "Commandments," in a later volume.

Ezekiel had actually *prophesied* in 37:11: "Then He said to me, "Son *of man, these bones are the whole house of Israel; behold, they say, "Our bones are dried up and our hope has perished. We are completely cut off."* This verse is God describing or recounting to Ezekiel who or what these bones are, and what they are saying.

The actual Hebrew word translated as "Israel" is:

> "3478 Yisrâ'êl; from 8280 and 410; *he will rule as God*; *Jisraël*, a symbolical name of Jacob; also (typically) of his posterity: - Israel."[15.36]

"8280 sârâh; a prim. root; to *prevail*: - have power (as a prince)."[15.37]

"410 'êl; short. from 352; *strength* as adj. *mighty*; espec. the *Almighty* (but used also of any *deity*): - God (god), x goodly, x great, idol, might (-y one), power, strong. Comp. names in "-el""[15.38]

If it is remembered that it was God's will that man rule the earth, as we are told in Genesis 1:28, arguably as though "kings;" and it is remembered that Jesus is "King of (these) kings;"[15.39] then it would be fair to say that *"house of" Yisrâ'êl"* could easily apply to those who are doing or did do the will of God. Perhaps it would be better phrased as those who are sincerely *trying* or sincerely *tried* to do the will of God; and likely have or had access to some degree of *dunamis* to prove it.

The original Hebrew word translated as "whole" is:

3605 kôl; or (Jer. 33:8) kôwl; from 3634; prop. the *whole*; hence *all*, *any* or *every* (in the sing. only, but often in plur. sense)..."[15.40]

The original Hebrew word translated as "house" is:

"1004 bayith; prob. from 1129 abbrev.; a *house* (in the greatest var. of applications, espec. *family*, etc.)..."[15.41]

This definition of *kôl*, is not particularly helpful; as it is difficult to understand what would *not* be included in: "all, any or every (in the sing. only, but often in plur. sense)."

Thus it seems that the *"the whole house of Israel,"* means one of two things: Either these bones represent the entire *"house of Israel;"* or these bones are all (members) of the *"house of Israel;"* but here these are not representing the entire "house." And of course *"house"* likely meaning "espec. family," rather than a *physical* abode.

What was the "whole house of Israel" *saying*, as recounted by God to Ezekiel? *"Our bones are dried up and our hope has perished.*

The Separate and the Distinct

We are completely cut off."
They are or were saying three things:
Their *first* statement is: *"Our bones are dried up."*
As previously stated, the actual word translated as *"bones"* is the same as in verses 1-10, *'etsem*.
It must be noted that *"bones,"* is *not* the word:

"1634 gerem; from 1633; a *bone* (as the *skeleton* of the body); hence *self*, i.e. (fig.) very: - bone, strong, top."[15.42]

Here in Ezekiel 37:11; (as opposed to the "derived" similar word in Ezekiel 37:2); the actual Hebrew word translated as "dried up" is:

"3001 yâbêsh; a prim. root; to *be ashamed, confused* or *disappointed*; also (as failing) to *dry* up (as water) or *wither* (as herbage): - be ashamed, clean, be confounded, (make) dry (up), (do) shame (-fully), x utterly, wither (away)."[15.43]

This presents an interesting conundrum. Those who would maintain that Ezekiel 3:1-14 represents one continuous "prophesy," would then have to explain why the "valley bones" are described as 3002 *yâbêsh*, which is derived from 3001 *yâbêsh*, and just means "dry;" and yet these *believed* to be *same* bones, are here in fact described as: 3001 yâbêsh; "a prim. root; to *be ashamed, confused* or *disappointed*.

The same problem occurs with the two separate and distinct events proponents, unless the aforementioned "tail wagging the dog" explanation is accepted.

Their *second* statement is: *"Our hope has perished."*
The actual Hebrew word translated as "hope" is:

"8615 tiqvâh; from 6960; lit. a *cord* (as an *attachment* [comp. 6961]); fig. *expectancy*: - expectation ([-ted]), hope, live, thing that I have longed for."[15.44]

This (*tiqvâh*) as a "cord," sounds more like something to be described as "cut off;" but it is not. Instead, this *tiqvâh*, or "cord," which is translated here only *figuratively* as "hope," (via "expectation") is described as *"perished."*

The actual Hebrew word translated as "perished" is:

"6 'âbad; a prim. root; prop. to *wander* away i.e. *lose* one's self; by impl. to *perish* (caus. *destroy*)..."[15.45]

Here *'âbad* literally means: "to *wander* away i.e. *lose* one's self;" yet the translators did not choose the *literal* meaning but rather the: "by impl. to *perish* (caus. *destroy*);" meaning of *'âbad*.

Revelation 9:11 (KJV) tells us:

"And they had a king over them,
which is the angel of the bottomless pit,
whose name in the Hebrew tongue is Abaddon,
but in the Greek tongue hath his name Apollyon."[15.46]

The actual Greek word translated as "Abaddon" is:

"3 Abaddōn; of Heb. or. [11]; a destroying *angel*: - Abaddon."[15.47]

The actual Hebrew word that is the stated root of the Greek "Abaddon" is:

"11 'ăbaddôwn; intens. from 6; abstr. a *perishing*; concr. Hades: - destruction."[15.48]

Here with *Abaddōn* and *'ăbaddôwn*, it seems reasonably clear that some form of *perish* or *destroy* would be a fair translation.

However Strong has an interesting note:

"10 'ăbaddôh; the same 9, miswritten for 11; a *perishing*: - destruction."[15.49]

"9 'ăbêdâh; from 6; concr. something *lost*; abstr. *destruction*, i.e. Hades: - lost. Comp. 10."[15.50]

Thus it seems likely that the original Hebrew *word* provided as 6 'âbad, is *incorrect*; but 'âbad is related to *Abaddōn* and 'ăbaddôwn; which signifies *perishing* or *destruction*. We are told here that: "11 'ăbaddôwn; intens. from 6;" but we are also told: "'ăbêdâh; from 6."

This is because we are told here that 'ăbêdâh is: "from 6; concr. something *lost*;" and the *definition* of 6 does in fact mean: "to *wander* away i.e. *lose* one's self." However the actual Hebrew *word* provided as 6 is listed as 'âbad and not 'ăbêd. This is likely the source of the inclusion of the : "by impl. to *perish* (caus. *destroy*)" part of the definition of 6 'âbad, which should be 6 'ăbêd. Why the translators chose the definition of the *erroneously* provided actual *word* listed as 6, instead of the *correctly* provided *definition* of 6, is unknown.

To try and clarify this, we are told that *Abaddōn*, or "destroying angel," is from 'ăbaddôwn or: "a perishing;" and that ăbaddôwn is from 'âbad; "a prim. root; prop. to *wander* away i.e. *lose* one's self; by impl. to *perish* (caus. *destroy*)." However we are also told that 'ăbêdâh, or "something lost," is also from 'âbad.

The significance of the appearance of *"Abaddon"* in Revelation and "elsewhere," will be examined in detail in a later volume. But here determining the correct meaning of what is *translated* as: *"Our hope has perished;"* merits further investigation.

Specifically; it would be prudent to try and determine if there is any other evidence that would support the contention that this *tiqvâh*, or "cord" has *literally*: "wander(ed) away" or lost; rather than what the translation tells us, (by *implication*), that it has: "perish(ed)," or been "destroy(ed)?"

Back in chapter 3, the reason those "angels" were "thrown out" of the immaterial realm, was because they were engaging in *planaō*.

> "4105 planaō; from 4106; to (prop. *cause to*) *roam* (from safety, truth, or virtue): - go astray, deceive, err, seduce, wander, be out of the way."

> "Thus here there are actually two matters to consider. The *objective of* these particular aggĕlŏs, is or was planaō; or "to (prop. *cause to*) *roam* (from safety, truth, or virtue): - go astray, deceive, err, seduce, wander, be out of the way." The "these," in this context, is important because not all angels or aggĕlŏs seek planaō. It was only *these particular* angels or aggĕlŏs; those "cast out with him;" who sought and seek planaō. Those who were not "cast out;" i.e.; are not with the enemy, are likewise aggĕlŏs; but they do not seek planaō."

Similarities exist between the Greek *planaō* as: "cause to roam;" and the Hebrew 6 listed as *'âbad* but is actually *'ăbêd* as literally: "prop. to *wander* away i.e. *lose* one's self."

Likewise similarities exist between *Abaddōn* as "a destroying *angel*," with the root of *Abaddōn* being this same incorrectly provided *'âbad*, or "prop. to *wander* away i.e. *lose* one's self;" and those *aggĕlŏs* engaging in *planaō*, or "cause to roam," who were subsequently banished because of this.

It must be remembered that it is not the *literal* definition of *'âbad* that is utilized in the translation as "*perished*," but it is only by *implication*, that the *translation* of *'âbad* is proffered as "*perished*."

But what if the *literal* meaning of these words; *tiqvâh* and *'âbad*; were to be considered: "Our cord (*tiqvâh*), has wandered away (*'âbad*, which should be listed as *'ăbêd*)?"

A "cord" is generally something that *connects* two things. It can reasonably be presumed that "one end" of this "cord" is connected to these "*bones*"—else why describe this "cord" as "our cord," mistranslated as: "*our hope?*"

And the *other* end of this cord is either connected to God, or it is connected to something else. If it is connected to something else,

The Separate and the Distinct

why then are they telling, (arguably complaining to), God about this? And why is God then telling Zeke?

A "cut cord," generally results in a *disconnection*. Just as is the case of *physical life*, where the soul is *connected* to the physical body; in *spiritual life*, the soul is connected to God. *Spiritual death*, is when this connection is no longer—hence the need for man's salvation.

But here this cord or *tiqvâh* is not actually "cut;" but rather "*wander*(ed) *away*," or *'âbad, or 'ăbêd*. Nevertheless, it seems the effect of a "cord" that "wandered away" would be the same; i.e; *spiritual death*—unless or until it was "found." If this cord or *tiqvâh* were to actually "perish," it seems any "reconnection," at least via this "cord," would be impossible.

And their *third* statement is: "*We are completely cut off.*"
The original Hebrew word translated as "cut off" is:

> "1504 gâzar; a prim. root; to *cut* down or off; (fig.) to destroy, divide, exclude or decide: - cut down (off), decree, divide, snatch."[5.51]

It must be asked from precisely why, and from what are they cut off?

The *why* can be reasonably determined from the previous statement. They are "cut off," because the connecting "cord" or *tiqvâh*, has wandered away, or *'âbad*.

And the "from what," can be reasonably be determined from the very next word that God says: "*therefore.*"

The actual Hebrew word translated as "therefore" is:

> "3651 kên; from 3559; prop. *set* upright; hence (fig. as adj.) *just*; but usually (as adv. or conj.) *rightly* or so (in various applications to manner, time and relation; often with other particles)..."[5.52]

As can be seen, "therefore," is a grossly inadequate translation. Because these, (paraphrased): "bones or strength, (*'etsem*); is or are ashamed, confused, or disappointed (*yâbêsh*); our attachment or cord, (tiqvâh), has wandered away ('âbad); we are completely cut off (gâzar)..."

The *kên*, or "set upright," thing to do is..."

What is this *kên*, or "set upright," thing for God to do? God telling Zeke to: *"prophesy and say to them, Thus says the Lord GOD."*

And what did God say? *"Behold, I will open your graves and cause you to come up out of your graves, My people; and I will bring you into the land of Israel."*

This word "Israel" is the same Hebrew word seen in verse 11.

> "3478 Yisrâ'êl; from 8280 and 410; *he will rule as God*; *Jisraël*, a symbolical name of Jacob; also (typically) of his posterity: - Israel."[15.53]

The Hebrew word translated both times as "land" in these verses is:

> "127 'ădâmâh; from 119; *soil (from its gen. redness)*: - country, earth, ground, husband [-man] (-ry), land."[15.54]

This *ădâmâh* is related to Adam's name."

What is the purpose of this believed to be? So that: *"Then you will know that I am the LORD, when I have opened your graves and caused you to come up out of your graves, My people."*

When will this be *done*, and then be *known*? The answer is not *now*, at the time when I, (God), am instructing Ezekiel to "prophesy" this; but *"then,"* at some point in the *future*, when I, (God), undertake these actions.

And what else is the *kên*, or "set upright," thing for God to do? *"I will put My Spirit within you and you will come to life, and I will place you on your own land. Then you will know that I, the LORD, have spoken and done it," declares the LORD.")*

Note again the *"then"* here in: *"Then you will know that I, the LORD..."*

The *first* Hebrew word translated as "LORD" here is:

"3068 Yᵉhôvâh; from 1961; (the) self-*existent* or Eternal; *Jehovah*, Jewish national name of God: - Jehovah, the Lord. Comp. 3050. 3069."[5.55]

But the *second* Hebrew word translated as "LORD" here is:

"136 'Ădônây; an emphatic form of 113; the *Lord* (used as a prop. God only): - (my) Lord."[5.56]

"113 'âdôwn; or (short.) 'âdôn; from an unused root (mean. to *rule*); *sovereign*, i.e. *controller* (human or divine): - lord, master, owner. Comp. also names beginning with "Adoni-"[5.57]

Why are there two *different* Hebrew words, each translated as "*LORD*" in the very same verse? Why did the translators translate *two* different Hebrew words, into *one* English word? Since each is translated as "*LORD*;" what are the differences between these two "Lords," that the translators failed to disclose by translating each as merely "*LORD*?"

One answer is that one "LORD" is *structural* and unique— Yᵉhôvâh. Many believe that Yᵉhôvâh is the pronunciation of the *tetragrammaton*; or the unspoken name of God, symbolized by four letters. This is the *ineffable name* of God, as discussed earlier with regard to Elijah the *Tishbite*.

But '*Ădônây*; the other, (the second), "*LORD*," is a *functional* description, and is unique only when the meaning is expressed as '*Ădônây*. Meaning; the actual *root* of '*Ădônây*, when expressed as '*âdôwn*, (lower case); can refer to: "any old" "(mean. to *rule*); *sovereign*, i.e. *controller* (human or divine)."

The *functions* of: "Yᵉhôvâh; from 1961; (the) self-*existent*" God, are entirely different from the "structure" of Yᵉhôvâh Himself.

But again, *why* are there two different terms used not just in the very same *verse*, but in the very same *sentence*. We are told: "Then you will know that I, the LORD, have spoken and done it," declares the LORD."

The last phrase: *"declares the LORD,"* seems superfluous; as who else is it that would or could truthfully be saying: *"Then you will know that I, the LORD, have spoken and done it,"* except: "the LORD?" So why then is it necessary to tell us who (else?) it is that *"declares"* this?

Here is the same verse, with the insertion of the original Hebrew in place of the English translations: *"Then you will know that I,* [*"the* Yᵉhôvâh; from 1961; (the) self-*existent LORD"* or "He Who is."], *have spoken and done it," declares* "Ădônây; an emphatic form of 'âdôwn; (mean. to *rule*); *sovereign*, i.e. *controller* (human or divine)." or "He Who rules."

"He Who *is*," is the one who actually will have *"done it;"* and: "He Who *rules"* is the one who then *"declares."* At the time this was written, there was only "He Who *is*." But at the time: "He Who *is*" will have *"done* it;" there will also be or have been the: "He Who *rules*," that then *"declares."*

It must be asked who it is that the "house of Israel" would have otherwise suspected was ultimately responsible for these types of *dunamic* events, except deity? But it is not anywhere near that simple.

In verse Ezekiel 37: 12: *"Thus says the Lord GOD"* appears, as the beginning of what it is that God wants Ezekiel to prophesy to these, (non-valley), "bones."

Here in verse 12 the *"Lord"* part of *"Lord GOD,"* is the aforementioned "136 'Ădônây."[15.58]

However, here the *"GOD"* part is not 3068 Yᵉhôvâh, but is:

> "3069 Yᵉhôvîh; a var. of 3068 [used after 136, and pronounced by Jews as 430, in order to prevent the repetition of the same sound, since they elsewhere pronounce 3068 as 136] God."[15.59]

And in verse 13, the *"LORD"* in: *"I am the LORD"* is "3068 Yᵉhôvâh."[15.60]

What is going on here?

Chapter 16

Resurrection and Recourse

There are believed to be ten "resurrections" recorded in the Bible.
Following are eight of these ten:

- 1 Kings 17:17-24, is where *Elijah* raises the widow's son.[16.1]
- 2 Kings 4:18-37 is where *Elisha* raises a dead child.[16.2]
- 2 Kings 13:20-21 is the aforementioned event, where the dead man is "revived" by merely touching the bones of *Elisha*.[16.3]
- Luke 7:11-17 is where *Jesus* raises a dead man.[16.4]
- Luke 8:49-56 is where *Jesus* raises a child.[16.5]
- John 11:1-44 is where *Jesus* raises Lazarus.[16.6]
- Acts 9:36-42 is where *Peter* raises Tabitha.[16.7]
- Acts 20:-12 is where *Paul* raises Eutychus.[16.8]

What do these actions done by Elijah, Elisha, Jesus, Peter, and Paul have in common? The answer is that they were all done by Elijah, Elisha, Jesus, Peter, and Paul.

In each of these events, God utilized *recourse*, instead of doing it Himself. But there is a distinct difference between the "resurrections" that occurred pre-Calvary, and those that occurred at or post-Calvary. This will be explained shortly.

The remaining two "resurrective" events, are the resurrection of Jesus; and that which was previously addressed in Matthew 27:50-54; those who "*came out of the graves,*" but *after* the crucifixion. In each of these two events, God utilized *no recourse*.

So why would God utilize *recourse* with eight of these ten; and (then), *not* utilize *recourse* with the other two? Is it that He *would* not, or that He *could* not do these things Himself—at least at the times they were done?

If "He *could* not," how can this be? Since God is *omnipotent*, He can always do anything he wants "His Own Self"—Right?

The answer lies in *ĕxŏusia*.

Matthew 4:8-9 (KJV) tells us:

> "*Again, the devil taketh him up into*
> *an exceeding high mountain,*
> *and sheweth him all the kingdoms of the world,*
> *and the glory of them;*
>
> "*And saith unto him,*
> *All these things will I give thee,*
> *if thou wilt fall down and worship me.*""16.9

Here the devil is essentially offering Jesus the entire *material* realm, "*if*" Jesus would *fall down and worship*" him. Did Jesus then tell the devil that he is nuts; and that the devil did not have rightful ownership of that which the devil was offering? The very next verse provides the answer to this question.

Matthew 4:10 (KJV) tells us:

Resurrection and Recourse

> *"Then saith Jesus unto him,*
> *Get thee hence,*
> *Satan: for it is written,*
> *Thou shalt worship the Lord thy God,*
> *and him only shalt thou serve."*[16.10]

This response represents a tacit admission, that that which was stated in verse 9 above; *"All these things will I give thee,"* was in fact possible. In other words, the devil had the authority to lawfully fulfill the "then" part of the "offer." Ergo *"all the kingdoms of the world, and the glory of them"* were in fact the devil's to *"give"*—at *that time.*

This is precisely why God chose recourse with all of the "resurrections" that occurred "pre-Calvary." Although God had the dunamic *capability* part of *ĕxŏusia*; He lacked the *authority* part.

A distinction must be made regarding this "resurrection recourse." Prior to Calvary, God had the *dunamic* power, (*dunamis*), but not the *authority*. This is not *ĕxŏusia*, but *dunamis* alone—at least with respect to "resurrection."

At some point, those *hosts* who were utilized by God for "resurrection recourse," had the *authority*; but insufficient *dunamis*. But by utilizing processes such as that which is illustrated in the "Talent Man" parable, any host can increase his level of *dunamis* and subsequent *ĕxŏusia*. God's *authority* issues however, could only have been resolved by taking back the power from the enemy; and only God Himself while acting as a *host*, was capable of success in this.

The (re)acquisition of the *authority*, and thus *ĕxŏusia* by God after Calvary, did not in any way diminish the levels of *ĕxŏusia* possessed by many; including those such as Peter and Paul. In fact the *potential* level of *ĕxŏusia* increased dramatically after Jesus "went to the Father," because of the *"greater things"* capability—just as He told us it would.

So once God obtained *ĕxŏusia* with regard to "resurrection;" although this meant that He could now do these acts *alone*; it did not mean that hosts were suddenly incapable of these acts. Neither did it mean that God was in any way forbidden from utilizing "resurrection recourse," in the future.

How does God determine when to utilize "resurrection recourse," as opposed to doing it Himself? One would have to pretend to know the mind of God, in order to pretend to answer this question in any meaningful way; except to say when it will "work better." "Work better" here does not refer to the "quality of the resurrection," whatever that might mean; but rather the amount of His will that could be fulfilled.

> "Probably the most spectacular redemptive event, was Jesus' blood contacting the ground. When God breathes into our nostrils the "breath of life," and we become living beings, as per Genesis 2:7; this essence resides in the blood. In the case of Jesus, this essence was the Father Himself. When that blood containing the essence of the Father "hit the ground," over which Satan had been given, (delivered); a large amount of authority because of sin, literally "all hell broke loose.""[16.11]

Back to the second sentence in Ezekiel 37.14: "Then *you will know that I, the LORD, have spoken and done it,* "declares the LORD;" cited in the previous chapter.

Here is this same second sentence in Ezekiel 37.14:, with the insertion of some of the original Hebrew in addition to the English translations: *"Then you will know that I, the LORD,"* ["*the* Y^{e}hôvâh; from 1961; (the) self-*existent*" "*LORD*," or "He Who *is*"]; "*have spoken and done it, declares the LORD*," or: ["Ădônây; an emphatic form of 'âdôwn; (mean. to *rule*); *sovereign*, i.e. *controller* (human or divine)"]; or "He Who *rules*"

Here the *"house of Israel"* is being told that when this particular event happens; when Y^{e}hôvâh Himself, and *without* utilizing recourse does what is described in these passages; they will know that something has changed. And the only way that particular change could have occurred, was the arrival of Messiah, and the completion of His, ("it is finished"), purposes on earth. And it is this Lord, *Jesus*, who "declares" this.

These prophetic passages in Ezekiel 37:11-14, go hand in with Matthew 27:52-54. However, again in Ezekiel it is *prophesy*, but in Matthew it is the *recollection* of these previously prophesied events. The difference is the *time* factor, which appears in Ezekiel with the appearance of the words *"then,"* and *"will,"* to indicate at a *future* time—unlike the "valley bones."

Ezekiel 37:12 prophesies: *"Therefore prophesy and say to them, "Thus says the Lord GOD, "Behold, I will open your graves and cause you to come up out of your graves, My people; and I will bring you into the land of Israel."*

Matthew 27:52-53 recollects: *"And the graves were opened; and many bodies of the saints which slept arose, And came out of the graves after his resurrection, and went into the holy city, and appeared unto many."* The confusion about *"his resurrection,"* as opposed to "their resurrection(s)," was previously addressed.

Ezekiel 37:13 prophesies: *"Then you will know that I am the LORD, when I have opened your graves and caused you to come up out of your graves, My people."* When will you *"know"* this? After the: *"I will,"* comes to fruition.

Ezekiel 37:14 then prophesies: *"I will put My Spirit within you and you will come to life, and I will place you on your own land. Then you will know that I, the LORD, have spoken and done it," declares the LORD."*

Matthew 27:54 then recollects: *"Now when the centurion, and they that were with him, watching Jesus, saw the earthquake, and those things that were done, they feared greatly, saying, Truly this was the Son of God."*

The Greek word in Matthew that is translated as "graves" is:

> "3419 mnēmĕiŏn; from 3420; a *remembrance*, i.e. cenotaph (*place of interment*): - grave, sepulcher, tomb."[16.12]

Thus it seems that *mnēmĕiŏn* could reasonably cover "in ground" burial, as well as other means of interment.

These *prophesied* events in Ezekiel represent a reasonable similarity to what later happened as *recollected* in Matthew; with the precise *result*, as evidenced by the words of the centurion.

What is *not* known about this event is much. What happened to these resurrected individuals is largely unknown. Neither is it known how widespread this event or phenomenon was. It is unknown what other areas of the world this same event may have simultaneously occurred.

But today, the *recollection* in Matthew 27:52-54 is not commonly believed to be in any way related to that which Ezekiel 37:11-14 *prophesies*. Instead, it is generally believed that these passages in Ezekiel have more to do with the establishment of a Jewish state; with "state" here meaning a *political* or *geographic*, division, or boundary.

To those adherents of that belief, it seems that these passages are considered as *allegorical*. Matthew describes actual *events*, which literally comport with Ezekiel's *prophesy*; but if one does not recognize Jesus as Messiah, then the door is immediately opened for other "non-literal" meanings of Ezekiel 37:11-14.

This is an easy mistake to make, particularly because of the appearance of term *"house of Israel."* Likely this is believed to refer to Jacob and his offspring. But the *"whole house of Israel"* is a pretty tall order. Ezekiel is believed to have lived about 600 BC.[16.13] And for some reason, it is often, (erroneously), believed that the *chronological* order of a prophet's *prophesies*, necessarily corresponds to the *chronological* order of the occurrence of *events* contained in those prophesies.

Also, the appearances of the word "*land*" in these verses, which again is "'ădâmâh; from 119; *soil* (from its gen. *redness*)." This word *'ădâmâh* refers to *soil*, because of its *color*; and not any geopolitical boundaries—despite 'ădâmâh being *translated* in the KJV as: "country, earth, ground, husband [-man] (-ry), land."

In addition, it seems as though many believe that for whatever reason(s), once a given prophet "professes" about a particular time; there cannot be any more prophesy concerning any time before that time. [Perhaps this belief came from Moses writing Genesis 1:1;

as there was nothing to write about the material realm before that, (Genesis 1:1), time.]

This of course is untrue, as prophesy can "jump" back and forth with respect to the times the *events* occur, irrespective of the times of the occurrence of or chronological order of the various *prophesies*. The "Book of Revelation" is the best example of this phenomenon, once the "absence of time" factor is understood.

No attempt is being made here to disparage anyone's beliefs. But in truth, Christianity is the "only game in town"—at least with respect to *salvation*. If a gambling establishment existed, where the rules were such that although one could win an infinite amount of money; but no one was permitted at any time to lose any of the money they already possessed; could this even be considered as gambling?

If one has a belief system that does not yet recognize the availability of salvation, the adherents already have no means of salvation. If one of these adherents becomes a Christian; and Christianity represents *truth*; they gain salvation. But if Christianity is *false*, they are no worse off than they were before. And Christianity costs *nothing*, as long as one believes what the *Bible* actually states, instead of believing what various *religions* proffer.

But back to the original question about Jesus going to the Father.

So then why is it that both Elijah and Jesus had to return to the immaterial realm? The answer is because the bones containing the power had to return to the *immaterial* realm, in order for the power to be *transferred*, (in the case of Elijah); or *distributed*, (in the case of Jesus); to those "qualified" recipient(s); first Elisha, and then "those who believe;" on the *material* realm.

And whence did this additional *dunamis*; the same additional dunamis that would allow those who believe in Him to do greater things; the same dunamis that would make a different (improved) helper come? It likely was the same authority and power Jesus reclaimed from the enemy after Calvary; power which was to be distributed to those who believe in him. For what purpose is the distribution of this power? The reason was or is, to equip the hosts with "nuclear" capabilities.

What changed? The answer is Calvary. When Calvary was over, much of the dominion over the earth previously handed over to the enemy, was returned to God and man. So God was now permitted to do certain things Himself, that he previously required recourse in order to do; without these acts causing an imbalance.

And those literal beings in the graves to whom he restored life, now had the opportunity to accept and thus obtain salvation; thus no longer "cut off."

This is strictly speculation; but it is within the realm of possibility, that Moses was originally intended to also return *in-corpus* to the immaterial realm. But because of the same sin that disqualified him from ever entering the "promised land;" (arguably hitting the rock in anger, instead of speaking to them as instructed); this may also have precluded him from returning to the immaterial realm *"in corpus."* And this could then be the very reason why God, then and because of this, had to hide Moses' remains.

Chapter 17

Sowing, Reaping, and Interference

It has often been said, that there is nothing more *sinful* than a person without a purpose. This can be expanded in a sense, as to distinguish "*a*" purpose, from "*the*," (here as a *definite* article); or "*their*" purpose.

There are some who truly believe that they do not have a purpose.

And there are others who believe that they have a purpose, but although that purpose is "*their*" purpose; it is at the same time not "their" purpose. Meaning that they are forced to either *do things* they would rather *not do*; or *not do* things they would rather *do*. Here "*their*" purpose was not determined by them; often chosen as the result of bad decisions; and/or by perceived necessity, and thus is not what "their" purpose would be, had they been able to make this determination in an informed manner.

There are some, who have "*their*" purpose, and kind of step in and out of "their" purpose.

And there are those few, at least who the majority of the time, have determined "their" purpose; irrespective of the fact that prior to this time, it was merely "*their*" purpose for which they were striving.

There are no bridges being offered for sale here. Distinctions must be made between these various forms of "purposes."

"A" *purpose* is just that. Why are you doing what you are doing? This could and should apply to any type of undertaking; and even mental insanity would not be precluded here. Even in the case of mental insanity, there exists a purpose for the action(s). It is just that it is truly irrational, and thus does not; and cannot; make any degree of sense to anyone, (rationality presumed), else.

With regard to "*their*" purpose; this is merely the reason(s) why one is doing or not doing, what they have chosen to do or not do. There is a plan, with specific objectives and goals in mind. These were chosen by the *individual* based upon what they believe or believed was in their best interest at the time of their choosing. This could be called *subjective* or *reality* based purpose.

The use of the term "their" purpose however; as distinguished by the use of italics in "*their*" purpose; refers to their purpose, but not the purpose determined by *them*. Instead; "their" purpose, (as opposed to "*their*" purpose), is their purpose as determined by God; and is based upon His intentions for, and design of, that particular individual.

This, ("their" purpose), could be called *objective* or *actuality* based purpose. It must be noted, that often those who engage in fulfilling *objective* or *actuality* based, (God's) purpose; can often be, and often are, confused with those who are mentally *insane*.

The "reason" for this, is generally because of the *erroneous* presumption of sufficient knowledge, on the part of those who choose to judge these, (actions in furtherance of "their" (and God's) purpose), actions thusly. This is often simply a *subjective* judgment based upon the "judger's" *reality*; and not *actuality*.

This necessarily leads to two different types of success, here referred to as: S_1 and S_2:

Sowing, Reaping, and Interference

S_1 can be considered as a measurement of the level of success or achievement of *subjective* or *reality* based purposes. This is a level of success based upon their or one's *own* idea of *"their"* purpose—including their own assessments of capabilities. This is generally limited to the product of *dýnamis*, (natural power); and effort or *ergazŏmai*; but may occasionally be augmented by seemingly serendipitous encounters with *dunamis*.

S_2 can be considered as a measurement of the level of success or achievement of *objective* or *actuality* based purposes. This is a level of success based upon God's will for their life—"their" purpose; and His provision of capabilities—most especially *dunamis*. Thus here this level of success is essentially limited only by *ergazŏmai*, or effort.

In Matthew 13:10-12 (NAS), Jesus is speaking and tells us:

"And the disciples came and said to Him,
"Why do You speak to them in parables?"

Jesus answered them,
"To you it has been granted to know
the mysteries of the kingdom of heaven,
but to them it has not been granted.

"For whoever has,
to him more shall be given,
and he will have an abundance;
but whoever does not have,
even what he has shall be
taken away from him.""[7.1]

Here we have Jesus responding to an inquiry from his disciples as to why he speaks in parables; and in this particular case, the parable of: "the sower."

This last part sounds somewhat familiar. Back in Chapter 10, "*True Talent;*" in Matthew 25: 30 we were told: "*For to everyone who* has, more shall be given, and he will have an abundance; but from the one who does not have, even what he does have shall be taken away."

Here Jesus first provides the *reasons* in the above verses 11-12; and *then* He provides the *conclusion*, the *"therefore,"* in the very next verse.

Matthew 13:13 (KJV) tells us:

> *"Therefore speak I to them in parables:*
> *because they seeing see not;*
> *and hearing they hear not,*
> *neither do they understand."*[17.2]

So it is *because* of the fact that: *"For whoever has, to him more shall be given, and he will have an abundance; but whoever does not have, even what he has shall be taken away from him;"* that Jesus speaks to them in parables: *"Therefore speak I to them in parables: because they seeing see not; and hearing they hear not, neither do they understand."*

The actual Greek word translated as "mysteries" in: *"the mysteries of the kingdom of heaven,"* in Matthew 13:11 is:

> "3466 mustērioň; from a der. of muō (to *shut* the mouth); a *secret* or *"mystery"* (through the idea of *silence* imposed by *initiation* into religious rites): - mystery."[17.3]

Clearly there is a sense, of *secrecy* or *silence*, whether *intentional* or otherwise; rather than mystery as in a "whodunit," in the meaning of the word *mustērioň*. Thus, Jesus is explaining the "secrets" or "mysteries" of the *immaterial* realm, or: "kingdom of heaven;" as in the case of the parable of the "Talent man."

Prior to the disciples asking this question, Jesus had *introduced*, but not yet *explained* the parable of the "sower."

Matthew 13:3-8 (KJV) tells us:

Sowing, Reaping, and Interference

> "And he spake many things unto them in parables,
> saying, Behold, a sower went forth to sow;
>
> And when he sowed, some seeds fell by the way side,
> and the fowls came and devoured them up:
>
> Some fell upon stony places,
> where they had not much earth:
> and forthwith they sprung up,
> because they had no deepness of earth:
>
> And when the sun was up,
> they were scorched;
> and because they had no root,
> they withered away.
>
> And some fell among thorns;
> and the thorns sprung up, and choked them:
>
> But other fell into good ground,
> and brought forth fruit, some an hundredfold,
> some sixtyfold, some thirtyfold."[17-4]

The importance of that which Jesus mentioned: *"brought forth fruit"* in the: *"hundredfold, some sixtyfold, some thirtyfold,"* cannot be over emphasized.

With respect to the actual *meaning* of the parable of the "sower," Jesus goes on to explain the same.

In Matthew 13:18-23 (KJV), Jesus is speaking and tells us:

> ""Hear ye therefore the parable of the sower.
>
> When any one heareth the word of the kingdom,
> and understandeth it not,
> then cometh the wicked one,
> and catcheth away that
> which was sown in his heart.

This is he which received seed by the way side.

*But he that received the seed into stony places,
the same is he that heareth the word,
and anon with joy receiveth it;*

*Yet hath he not root in himself,
but dureth for a while:
for when tribulation or persecution
ariseth because of the word,
by and by he is offended.*

*He also that received seed among the thorns
is he that heareth the word;
and the care of this world,
and the deceitfulness of riches,
choke the word, and he becometh unfruitful.*

*But he that received seed into the
good ground is he that heareth the word,
and understandeth it; which also beareth fruit,
and bringeth forth, some an hundredfold,
some sixty, some thirty.*[17.5]

The actual Greek word translated as "'word,'" is the aforementioned:

> "3056 lŏgŏs; from 3004; something *said* (including the *thought*); by impl. a *topic* (subject of discourse), also *reasoning* (the mental faculty) or *motive*; by extens. a *computation*; spec. (with the art. In John) the Divine Expression (i.e. Christ)..."[17.6]

This is with the understanding that Strong's also includes in the definition, something that not only is "said," as when having been *written*; but also ultimately what was originally "said" "real time," as per previous analysis of *lŏgŏs* vs. *rhēma*.

Sowing, Reaping, and Interference

The actual Greek word translated as "seed" in these passages is:

"4687 spĕirō; prob. strengthened from 4685 (through the idea of *extending*); to *scatter*, i.e. *sow* (lit. or fig.): - sow (er), receive seed."[17.7]

Thus it seems that translating *spĕirō* as *"seed,"* meaning a *noun*, would be incorrect. Rather *spĕirō* seems to be a verb, as an infinitive: to seed, as in an *action*; or "to *scatter*."

With respect to verse 19: "*When any one heareth the word of the kingdom, and understandeth it not, then cometh the wicked one, and catcheth away that which was sown in his heart. This is he which received seed by the way side;*" this represents an activity in which the enemy has been involved, on *two* fronts for quite some time.

First; when it is the case that *anyone* hears the Word, and yet does not understand it; the enemy comes and steals what has been "*sown*" in the person's heart. It was *sown* in the person's heart, but it has to get through to the *intellect* in order to prosper. Thus until then, it remains merely a seed or a small tender shoot, and is subject to theft, or trampling by the enemy.

The *second* front; is the activities by the enemy to make the Word as "non-understandable" as possible, in order to maximize the number of persons who do not, or cannot understand it. This is accomplished by interference either on an *individual* basis; or in the case of the *written* Word, by interference with those who are in charge of *translation* or *interpretation*. The enemy would prefer have the battle at the latter, (*translation* or *interpretation*), level, as he then gets closer to the written *source*; and thus maximizes the interference with the minimum time and effort in the "long run."

And with respect to verses 20-21: "*But he that received the seed into stony places, the same is he that heareth the word, and anon with joy receiveth it; Yet hath he not root in himself, but dureth for a while: for when tribulation or persecution ariseth because of the word, by and by he is offended;*" this is yet another trick of the enemy.

The word *"anon"* roughly means *soon*; and *"dureth"* roughly means *endure*. This is the man who first "*heareth*" the *spĕirō*, or sowing, and *soon "receiveth"* it with joy. Yet since he has no "root in himself," when the enemy attacks *"because of the word"* over time, he is *"offended."*

The actual Greek word translated as "offended" is:

> "4624"skandalizō; ("scandalize"); from 4625; to *entrap*, i.e. *trip* up (fig. *stumble* [trans.] or *entice* to sin, apostasy or displeasure): - (make to) offend."[17.8]

Thus depending upon the meaning of *"offended,"* this may or may not be a correct translation of *skandalizō*. Meaning; does *"offended"* here mean a *reality*; or mere state of mind such as: "His language offended me." Or does offended mean an *actuality*, as in legal, either physical or non-physical *offenses*, such as assault, battery, extortion, etc.?

The difference between *"heareth the word,"* and *"anon (soon) with joy receiveth it;"* is the *beginning* of the process of *shâmar* in the Hebrew; or *tērĕō* in the Greek.

Again, these represent what God the Father, and Jesus the Son respectively, actually advised us to do with regard to "keeping" the Commandments, as previously addressed.

> "8104: shâmar; A prim. root; prop. to *hedge* about (as with thorns), i.e. *guard*; gen. to *protect, attend to*, etc.: - beware, be circumspect, take heed (to self), keep (-er, self), mark, look narrowly, observe, preserve, regard, reserve, save (self), sure, (that lay) wait (for), watch (-man)."

> "5083 tērĕō; from tĕrŏs (a *watch*; perh. akin to 2334); to *guard* (from *loss* or *injury*, prop. by keeping *the eye* upon..."

And the *skandalizō*, inaccurately translated here as *"offended,"* which *"by and by"* occurs is actually: "to *entrap*, i.e. *trip* up (fig. *stumble* [trans.] or *entice* to sin, apostasy or displeasure)."

Sowing, Reaping, and Interference

The purpose of this *skandalizō*, is the previously addressed actual Greek word for sin: "hamartanō; perh. from *1* (as a neg. particle) and the base of *3313*; prop. to *miss* the mark (and *so not share* in the prize), i.e. (fig.) to *err*, esp. (mor.) to *sin*."

The very reason the *"word"* or *lŏgŏs*, and *rhēma*, is in fact provided, is to assist us in "hitting" the "mark," and thus "share in the prize."

This is the man who *hears* the word, and soon *receives* it with joy; yet since he has no firm *"root in himself,"* this "reception" is only temporary. This is one who "hallelujahs" the loudest when he watches the preachers, as the "messages" do in fact, (*"with joy"*), resonate with him. But since he has no firm *"root in himself,"* he "falls for" the entrapment; and the subsequent interruption or reversal of the *shâmar* or *tērĕō* process. And this is *skandalizō* is *"because of the word."*

The key here is the *reason*. It is precisely because the person *heard*, and *"with joy" received* the word, that he is attacked or *skandalizō*. This means that this particular attack likely would not have happened, had this particular "one" not heard and received the word. This is not to say that there would be no other attacks, but this one is a direct result of the *hearing* and subsequent *receiving* of the word. This is an illustration of the common term: "Different Level—Different Devil."

It must be noted that it is not a matter of *if*, but *when* the attack comes. Receiving the word, particularly if accompanied by *joy*, and not merely *happiness*; guarantees some type of attack, including this attack. These are *direct* and *indirect*; *benign* and *malignant*; tailor made attacks; with specific intention(s); and against a specific person, as the target of said attack.

Sure as taxes, these attacks will "come around:"

"I had a friend of mine once who believed that too, and he died."

"Yeah, my aunt used to believe that stuff, and we all thought she was nuts too."

"I tried that once, and all I got was nothing."

Since *"he has no firm root in himself,"* when he is attacked, what was sown gets washed away. The enemy does not want any of this to take *"root"* and grow strong.

The amount of time between the *receipt* of the word and the *attack*, is likely very short; as young plants are quite vulnerable before the root system is established. However the amount of time, or the *"by and by,"* between the *attack* and *skandalizō*, and the actual *sin*, or *hamartanō*; is much more variable.

It is very important to understand this mechanism. These attacks are not because the Word is *false*; but because it is *true*. In fact, if perceived carefully; the attack level can be used to assess the level of "concern" the enemy has for what was just received; e.g.: "He hit me pretty hard, so he must be really mad!" The higher the attack level is; then the more the enemy is concerned for that which was received,.

In verse 22 appears a different scenario: "*He also that received seed among the thorns is he that heareth the word; and the care of this world, and the deceitfulness of riches, choke the word, and he becometh unfruitful.*"

The actual Greek word translated as "unfruitful" is:

> "175 akarpŏs; from *1* (as a neg. particle) and 2590; barren (lit. or fig.): - without fruit, unfruitful."[17.9]
>
> "2590 karpŏs; prob. from the base of 726; fruit (as plucked), (lit. or fig.): - fruit."[17.10]

This "*among the thorns*" is the person who received/heard the word, and was for some time "fruitful," or *karpŏs*—likely either *directly*, or *indirectly* because of the word. This is because we are told what ultimately happens: "*choke the word, and he becometh unfruitful.*"

In order to become "*unfruitful*" one must begin this process of becoming "*unfruitful*;" by already being *fruitful* to some extent. Had he never been fruitful, he could not *become* "*unfruitful*;" as in that case he already was "*unfruitful*," and would have *remained* "*unfruitful*," and thus could not: "*becometh unfruitful*."

But the "unfruitfulness" was not because of any attack directly "*because of the word*," as was the case with the "*stony places.*" Rather it was because of: "*the care of this world, and the deceitfulness of riches, choke the word,*" that was or became the problem.

The actual Greek word translated as "care" is:

> "3308 měrimna; from 3307 (through the idea of distraction); *solicitude*: - care."[17.11]

The actual Greek word translated as "world" is:

> "165 aiōn; from the same as *104*; prop. an *age*; by extens. *perpetuity* (also past); by impl. the *world*; spec. (Jewish) a Messianic period (present or future)..."[17.12]

Thus it seems that a more accurate translation of this phrase would be: "the concern, anxiety, or distraction(s) of the, or that age."

The actual Greek word translated as "deceitfulness" is:

> "539 apatē; from *538*; *delusion*: - deceit(ful, fullness), deceivableness (-ving)."[17.13]

The actual Greek word translated as "riches" is:

> "4149 plŏutŏs; from the base of *4130*; *wealth* (as *fullness*), i.e. (lit.) *money, possessions*, or (fig.) *abundance, richness*, (spec.) valuable *bestowment*: - riches."[17.14]

Thus it seems that a more accurate translation of this phrase would be: "the *delusion*, or maintaining a given belief despite overwhelming evidence to the contrary; about *bestowed* wealth." This is because the definition of: "(spec.) valuable *bestowment*," strongly suggests *provision* of this wealth to the recipient; as opposed to this wealth actually having been *earned* by the recipient.

The actual Greek word translated as "choke" is:

"4846 sumpnigō; from 4862 and 4155; to *strangle completely*, i.e. (lit.) to *drown*, or (fig.) to *crowd*: - choke, throng.'"[7.15]

Thus: "*He also that received seed among the thorns is he that heareth the word; and the care of this world, and the deceitfulness of riches, choke the word, and he becometh unfruitful;*" would be better translated as:

"*He also that received seed among the thorns is he that heareth the word*" and "the concern, anxiety, or distraction(s) of the age," and "the *delusion*, or maintaining a given belief despite overwhelming evidence to the contrary; about *bestowed* wealth," "completely strangles" "*the word and he becometh unfruitful.*"

What does this mean? This means that although he became wealthy because of the Word, he slowly began to believe that this wealth was not *bestowed*, but rather *earned*.

This "*among the thorns*" attack could in fact consist of "incessant niceties." The enemy could be telling the victim him how great he is—which may in fact be true in certain other areas. But the "trick," is to "flip" this into a cause-effect relationship with regard to this man's purported "greatness" as a *cause*; and as the direct *result* or *effect* of this "greatness," the "fruit."

So when successful, at some point in the victim's mind it was no longer God that was providing this wealth, (*bestowed* to him); but rather that this wealth was due to him and him alone, (*earned* by him). So the glory was no longer God's, but his.

And the result was complete strangulation of the word, and subsequent "unfruitfulness."

This entire delusional process likely takes substantial time; or phrased differently, a much longer "*by and by.*" Meaning; that a much longer period of time had elapsed between the understanding the word; and the success of the attack; as compared to the case with the "*stony places.*"

With respect to verse 23, "*the seed into the good ground;*" this is the person who heard the word; understood the word; withstood the attacks; worked, (*ergazŏmai*), the word; and is bearing fruit in the various levels or realms of return, [F = MA].

These first three examples; represent attacks by the enemy in three "phases:"

The *first* attack example, is phase one. Here with only the *"way side"* "heart only reception;" the enemy tries to remove that which was: "in the heart," or *"sown in his heart*; but was not yet: "in the head," because he: *"understandeth it not."*

This is likely an *emotional* attack, designed to remove, or *"catcheth away"* that which is "in the heart;" in order to prevent it from getting "in the head." Depending upon the person, an *intellectual* attack here, might very well achieve the opposite of the enemy's intentions.

This is the person who *heard* the word, but did not *understand* it enough to allow it to prosper in him. So the enemy comes and steals it before the word which was sown, can be understood and prosper; arguably supplanting it with an *a-talantŏn* for "insurance."

The *second* attack example is phase two. Here with the *"stony places,"* *stealing* the word simply will not do. Perhaps the enemy has already attempted the "heart" theft, but was unsuccessful. This person *understands* the word, and is joyous because of it. It is in their heart, and in their "head;" and they like it. So the enemy will then create forces of *direct* and *indirect* custom made TIS, and other attacks. It must be emphasized that these attacks may be *direct*, (such as "head voices"); or *indirect* through a surrogate or surrogates. This force is designed to be sufficient to overcome the wisdom of the Word; and thus remove the resultant joy,

Although the translation of the result of the successful attack is *"offended,"* it must be remembered that *skandalizō* is actually "to *entrap*, i.e. *trip* up (fig. *stumble* [trans.] or *entice* to sin..."

The third attack example is phase three. This is when stealing the word simply will, or did not do; and the custom made attacks will, or did not work. This *"among the thorns"* attack, does not relate to *understanding*, or whether or not the word will be fruitful; as it likely, arguably required, that it already has borne fruit.

Here the word is already understood, already "tested," and passed the test. Thus, this is the aforementioned "incessant niceties" attack, seeking an *emotional* response; in order to provide the stimulus to gradually supplant the previously "known" actual *cause* of the "fruit."

Those that do not withstand this phase three attack; may have survived the first two, but lose at the end of this phase.

The "one" in verse 23: *"But he that received seed into the good ground is he that heareth the word, and understandeth it; which also beareth fruit, and bringeth forth, some an hundredfold, some sixty, some thirty*;" likely represents survival of the first three attacks, and thus represents success—"hit the mark, and got the prize."

Or alternatively; for some reason the enemy either decided not to attack, or for some reason began attacking and stopped. But the problem with these "alternatives," is that generally it is when the Bible is *misunderstood*, that the enemy tends to "leave it alone."

Most people have little or no idea about the so called "game" of life—irrespective of whether or not they believe they do.

Some believe that "dying with the most toys" constitutes winning this "game." Since literally doing this is quite impossible for any more than one person; the real objective becomes getting as close as possible to this "ideal," albeit unique, status.

Often times in this "quest," only the *ends* are utilized to determine success; with the judgment of the propriety of the *means*, too often being laid aside.

The one exception to lack of concern regarding the *means*, would be based upon a calculation of the expected value, (the enemy does the same thing), of "getting caught." Here, this is the product of the probability of getting caught, multiplied by the magnitude of the penalty. Prisons are filled with individuals who should have taken a remedial mathematics course prior to making their decisions.

And there is also the other end of the "spectrum." Material wealth is considered by many to be wicked or evil, genuinely believing that God wants you to be impoverished: "Just like Jesus." It is interesting to make an inquiry with those who believe this, as to why then it is that Jesus both needed, and in fact had, a *treasurer*?

John 13:27-29 (KJV) tells us:

> *"And after the sop Satan entered into him.*
> *Then said Jesus unto him,*
> *That thou doest, do quickly.*
>
> *Now no man at the table knew for*
> *what intent he spake this unto him.*
>
> *For some of them thought,*
> *because Judas had the bag,*
> *that Jesus had said unto him,*
> *Buy those things that we have*
> *need of against the feast; or,*
> *that he should give something to the poor."*[17.16]

Here the original Greek word translated as "bag" is:

> "1101 glōssŏkŏmŏn; from *1100* and the base of *2889*; prop. a *case* (to keep mouthpieces of wind-instruments in), i.e. (by extens.) a *casket* or (spec.) *purse*: - bag."[17.17]

It is clear in these passages, that although the disciples did not understand, and/or *misunderstood* what Jesus was saying to Judas; Judas in fact: *"had the bag."* Here in the KJV, translated with the definite article "the," and not the indefinite article "a;" indicates that there was only one *glōssŏkŏmŏn*, or *"the bag."*

It is also clear, that the disciples believed that whatever the contents of this *glōssŏkŏmŏn* or "bag;" the same was suitable to: *"Buy those things that we have need of against the feast; or, that he should give something to the poor."*

It is also important to remember that it was not because Joe and Mary were "broke," that Jesus was born where he was born; but rather because there was no room available. It is arguable, that the "real" reason that there was no available room; was because of the fact that they were unmarried parents at that time and...

1,722 words omitted...

Had they, (J&M), not had sufficient funds to pay for a room; whether there was or was not a room available, clearly would have been a moot point.

In addition, there is also the matter, (reality), of Joseph being a "poor carpenter." If you go by the well known translation, this a bit problematic, as the word carpenter comes from the Latin word *carpentium*, which means a carriage or chariot, and unlike today; at that time carpenter was not necessarily synonymous with wood worker.

Thus, based *solely* upon this, Joseph likely was skilled in building chariots or carriages, for those who could afford them. The fact is that he may have largely worked with metal, and perhaps did not even work with wood very much at all.

If one goes by the actual original Greek word translated as "*carpenter*," in Mark 6:3[17.18]; and "*carpenter's*" (son), in Matthew 13:55[17.19]; it gets a bit even more dicey.

The actual word translated as "carpenter" and "carpenter's" is:

> "5045 tĕktōn; from the base of 5088; an *artificer* (as *producer* of fabrics), i.e. (spec.) a *craftsman* in wood: - carpenter."[17.20]

> "5088 tiktō; a strengthened form of a prim. tĕkō, (which is used only as alt. in certain tenses); to *produce* (from seed, as a mother, a plant, the earth, etc.), lit. or fig.: - bear, be born, bring forth, be delivered, be in trevail."[17.21]

In the "Talent Man" parable back in Chapter 10, 5088 *tiktō* was the root of the word 5110 *tŏkŏs*; and in the parable, *tŏkŏs* was translated as "*interest*" or "*usury*."

Here with *tĕktōn*, another offspring of *tiktō*; we now have an emphasis on being an: "*artificer*," "*producer*," "*craftsman*;" and arguably one who gives *birth*. It is interesting to ponder if the inclusion of: "(spec.) a *craftsman* in wood: - carpenter," in the definition of *těktōn*; may have been done *retrospectively*.

And there is also the matter of everyone knowing that the Bible tells us that "money is the root of all evil."

However, the exact quotation appears in 1 Timothy 6:10 (KJV):

"For the love of money is the root of all evil:
which while some coveted after,
they have erred from the faith,
and pierced themselves through
with many sorrows."[17.22]

Here in 1 Timothy, it is made clear, precisely what it is that is the root of, (*all*), evil. The subject of the sentence is not *money*, but rather is the: *"love of money."*

And not just love in a general sense, but it is very specific here, in that it is the *"love of money,"* (and not the money itself); that represents the root of evils of all sorts; and he goes on to tell us why.

It is because the coveting *"after"* it will cause *"some,"* but not all, to result in having: *"erred from the faith."* And the result of this is either instead of, or in addition to *money*; (it does not state which), one will obtain *"many sorrows."*

It is the making of a false God out of money that is the issue; and most certainly not material wealth, nor even a *reasonable* desire for the same.

And in fact, Ecclesiastes 10:19 (KJV) tells us:

"A feast is made for laughter,
and wine maketh merry:
but money answereth all things."[17.23]

Here in Ecclesiastes, it is the *very money itself*, and not the *love* of money that is under discussion. It does not seem likely or even possible that that which: *"answereth all things;"* could also be the *"root of all evil."*

"Basic Instructions Before Leaving Earth," is often proffered as that for which the purported "acronym:" "BIBLE" stands—whether this represents: "many a truth spoken in jest," or not. But the question becomes: "Instructions for what?"

"Instructions" are generally provided in furtherance of some *end*; and would seem to have little value in the absence of the knowledge of that particular, or any other *end*.

There exists a plethora of purported answers to this question; many of which either make little or no sense; or are self-contradictory.

And it matters little to have a set of instructions that at best are not understood; and at worst misunderstood. How many religions claiming the Bible as their sole source, actually agree on what the Bible actually "states?" The "trick" here, is to find the "version" that best agrees with what it is that one "feels good" about believing. And when discrepancies arise, simply develop some "long winded," ("bloviation"), to explain the inexplicable.

Proverbs 10:19 (NAS) tells us:

> "When there are many words,
> transgression is unavoidable,
> But he who restrains his lips is wise."[17.24]

"I gave my life to Jesus." is often heard. "Well; what is it that Jesus then told you to do?" It seems that the ability to do *"greater things"* that Jesus provided; and even told us ahead of time that He would be providing, was provided for reasons.

The truth of the matter is that the main purpose of physical life, or perhaps better phrased "Why we are here," is crystal clear, and appears in the Scriptures as far back as Genesis. As "hosts," we are here to conduct warfare against the enemy. And the purpose is redemption of the earth. We cannot redeem ourselves, but can only *accept* that which was redeemed for us. These facts must be included in the discussion of the aforementioned two successes.

There are two interrelated series of events to explain these successes:

As previously discussed, hosts are given abilities; whether merely *dýnamis* or natural power, or *dunamis*, or supernatural power; or as is usually the case *both*—irrespective of the magnitude of either. And the other side, or the balancing side of these abilities; which is a necessary part of the complete actuality; is the *talantŏn*, or balancing or borne weight.

The *talantŏn* provides the balancing or borne weight to do something with these abilities. We have the choice of ignoring or burying them, or utilize *ergazŏmai* or to work these capabilities.

When we choose *ergazŏmai*, as two of the talent men did; we are then given more *talantŏn* or weight, which is balanced by additional *dunamis*, as is precisely what happened in the parable. It could also be the case that additional *dunamis* is given first, before the additional *talantŏn*, but that is not how that particular parable tells it. They are, after all, merely different parts of the same actuality; or in the Hebrew: *massâ'*.

But although here the *talantŏn* and the *dunamis* will balance, and the result will be additional *talantŏn* and *dunamis*, there is still the "orphan" *ergazŏmai*. Although the *ergazŏmai* balanced the actuality with positive results in terms of future capabilities, there must be a counterpart to the balance the actuality of the *ergazŏmai*, and that counterpart is *abundance*.

Alleged Fantasy Foundations Volume I

Chapter 18

Faith—
What on Earth Is It?

This is a fair question; and is a question to which no one seems to have *the* answer. This is not to say that this is a question to which many do not have *an* answer; but rather one to which no one seems to have *the* answer.

Faith is a word that is: "used in a wide variety of applications;" but used in and of itself, is usually interpreted as being concerned with matters of a "religious" or "spiritual" nature. However; "faith" has much more broad meanings than would be suggested by the usual interpretation of its qualified usage.

The word "faith" is from:

> "Latin *fidēs* trust, belief; related to *fidere* to trust, and cognate with Greek *peíthesthai* be persuaded, obey, believe, trust."[8.1]

This Latin *fidēs*, appears to be the root of other words such as: *fidelity, fiduciary*, etc.; each having somewhat related meanings.

Thus in the general sense; faith can relate to anything in the universe that one "trusts." The question is what does this mean; and upon what is this reasonably based? "The belief that a thing is what it purports to be;" likely represents the best overall definition of faith, as commonly understood. Thus faith is based in at least two conditions being met: *knowledge* and *belief*.

In order for *faith* to exist, there is the requirement of the *knowledge* of precisely what it is that "the thing" is purporting to be.

Then a decision is made, as to whether or not to *believe* that "the thing" is what it purports to be.

If the answer is no; then in a certain sense this also can represent faith, in that one believes that "the thing;" whatever it may in fact be; it is *not* what it purports to be. So here the *reality* of this purported *actuality* is such that said *reality* does not include the existence of this purported *actuality*; i.e.; this one can be "crossed off the list."

If the answer is yes; then there is *belief* and *trust* that the thing reasonably is what it purports to be.

Thus faith represents the end result of a *twofold* process:

First, there must be *knowledge* regarding what it is that "a thing" is purporting to be. Then and only then, can a decision be made as to whether or not to *believe* that the thing is what it purports to be. In the absence of what is considered to be sufficient information; the process cannot rationally continue.

This, (faith), is to be distinguished from *fear*. Often, but not always, *fear* is based upon that which is *not* known. Fear is that *anxiety*, which is the direct result of the belief that danger is *approaching*. Often the reaction to diminish this anxiety; is to "run away," in order to increase the distance from this "believed to be approaching" danger.

One can, in a sense, believe that something is what it purports to be; simply and solely because of the *fear* of the consequences if one does not. However this does not represent any type of faith in the *thing* being what it purports to be; but rather, merely faith in that the *consequences* are as they purport to be.

Thus in a sense, here there is faith or trust in the *consequences*; but not necessarily in "the thing" itself.

One need to know little about Jesus, if one is told, (and believes); that eternal damnation will be the result of failing to believe in Him. But here the faith is not based upon the belief that Jesus is what *He* purports to be; but rather that the eternal damnation is what *it* is purported to be.

But in this case, the *level* of "faith" is limited strictly to that quantity which is necessary in order to avoid the consequences. There is little room for love, or any desire for knowledge of Him; when the belief is based solely upon the faith in; and fear of; the purported *consequences* of not believing.

An examination of those original Hebrew and Greek words which the Bible translators translated as "faith," would be illuminating. Although this might not necessarily be particularly illuminating with respect to the actual meaning of faith *today*; this nevertheless *would* be illuminating—at least with respect to those words which the translators believed were words for which "faith" was a reasonable synonym *at that time*.

Thus it seems prudent to understand the meanings of the original Hebrew and Greek—the very words which were used to describe this phenomenon translated as "faith."

This investigation may seem unnecessary at first, and perhaps even a bit boring. However it must be remembered that words are symbols. Thus it is the case, that whatever it was that these original Hebrew and Greek words *symbolize* or *symbolized* is that which is under discussion. Meaning; that any translation of any of these original words as "faith," represents merely the opinion of the translators and "versioneers."

All too often, it is these *translated* into English words that are considered as "gospel," with the original terminology utilized as perhaps only potential modifiers. But it is the original terminology, or as close as one can reliably get, that best describes what it is that the authors were trying to state.

Today, everyone knows about the "boat" built by Noah. But God never told Noah to build a boat; and Noah in fact never built a boat. God told Noah to build a box, and Noah did. It matters little whether or not one believes this actually happened, with regard to the truth of what it is we are *told* happened.

What God told Noah to build, and what Noah in fact built was:

> "8392 têbâh; perh. of for. der.; a *box*: – ark"[8.2]

A boat has *navigational* capabilities. A box does not. But today, Noah's ark or *têbâh*, is nevertheless considered by most, (doxa), as some type of "boat."

According to Strong; the actual word "faith" appears only twice in the English translation (KJV), of the entire Old Testament.[8.3]

There are two Hebrew words which are translated as "faith:"

> "529 'êmûwn; from 539; *established*. i.e. (fig.) *trusty*; also (abstr.) *trustworthiness*: - faith (ful), truth."[8.4]

> "530 'ĕmûwnâh; or (short.) 'ĕmûnâh; fem. of 529; lit. *firmness*; fig. *security*; mor. *fidelity*: faith (-ful, -ly, -ness, [man]), set office, stability, steady, truly, truth, verily."[8.5]

The *direct* root of 529 'êmûwn,("established"); and thus the *indirect* root of 530 'ĕmûwnâh, ("firmness"), is:

> "539 'âman; a prim. root; prop. to *build up* or *support*; to *foster* as a parent or nurse; fig. to *render* (or *be*) *firm* or faithful, to *trust* or believe, to be *permanent* or quiet; mor. to *be true* or certain; once (Isa. 30:21 by interch. for 541) to *go to the right hand*: - hence, assurance, believe, bring up, establish, + fail, be faithful (of long continuance, stedfast [sic.], sure, surely, trusty, verified), nurse, (-ing father), (put), trust, turn to the right."[8.6]

Most would believe that the literal meanings of these words as "*established*," "lit. *firmness*;" and from their direct and indirect root: "to *build up* or *support*" refer to that which one *believes*—hence the translation as "faith." This is fair, but the *real* question here would be whether or not these original words refer to this and this alone.

Strong's inclusion of: "once (Isa. 30:21 by interch. for 541) to *go to the right hand*," is worthy of note.

Faith—What on Earth Is It?

Isaiah 30:21 (KJV) tells us:

*"And thine ears shall hear a word behind thee,
saying, This is the way, walk ye in it,
when ye turn to the right hand,
and when ye turn to the left."*[18.7]

The *"Interlinear Bible"* lists *"you go right,"* as the correct translation; citing 541 as the original Hebrew word translated as such.[18.8]

"541 'âman; denom. from 3225; to take the *right hand* road: - turn to the right. See 539."[18.9]

It cannot be missed that 539 *'âman*, and 541 *'âman*, are identical in terms of English characters—even including identical diacritics.
The question of course is why?
The original Hebrew word translated here as "word," in *"word behind thee,"* is:

"1697 dâbâr; from 1696; a *word*; by impl. a *matter* (as *spoken* of) or *thing*; adv. a *cause*..."[18.10]

The *context* of this passage, seems to have to do with that which God "provides;" so it would be reasonable to conclude that this passage is consistent with this same context, as there is nothing that suggests otherwise. Thus this *dâbâr*, translated as *"word;"* which is *"behind thee,"* is likely somewhat analogous to the Greek *rhēma*.

This *dâbâr*, is God providing *guidance* whenever one is required to make choices. And making choices is something man is required to do constantly—irrespective of any given host being aware of this at any given time.

With this more literal interpretation, when this *"word"* is saying: *"This is the way, walk ye in it, when ye turn to the right hand, and when ye turn to the left;"* this *"word"* is providing guidance as to which way to turn.

However, there also may be another meaning to this "right" and "left." Since 539 *'âman* is the direct and indirect root for the only two words translated as "faith" in the Old Testament; and since 541 *'âman* means "to take the *right hand* road," there may be some allegory here.

If the word "correctly" is substituted for *"right hand,"* it would read: *"This is the way, walk ye in it, when ye turn* (correctly).

It would then necessarily follow that: *"and when ye turn to the left,"* would then read: *"and when ye turn* (incorrectly).

The Latin word for "left" is various forms of *sinistram*, from which the English word *sinister* is derived.

Combined this would then read: *"This is the way, walk ye in it, when ye turn* (correctly), *and when ye turn* (incorrectly.)"

What is this *"this,"* in: *"This is the way?"*

With the *allegorical* approach, this *"this,"* is that which directly preceded this *"this."* Namely; the: *"word behind thee;"* or perhaps more importantly, what this word is *saying*. Here meaning; that this: *"word behind thee"* will always be there guiding, even when *incorrect* decisions are made.

The Hebrew root of the common English word "amen" is:

> 543 'âmên; from 539; *sure*; abstr. *faithfulness*; adv. *truly*:
> - Amen, so be it, truth."[18.11]

Here, but as the root of *'âmên*, again appears: "539 'âman; a prim. root; prop. to *build up* or *support*; to *foster* as a parent or nurse; fig. to *render* (or *be*) *firm* or faithful, to *trust* or believe...."

The word "faithful" appears twenty eight times in the KJV *Old Testament*; and is the translation of five Hebrew words.[18.12]

The most common Hebrew word translated as "faithful," is the previous 539 *'âman*; and represents twenty of these twenty eight.[18.13]

The next most common Hebrew word translated as "faithful," appears three times and is the same word previously translated as "faith."[18.14]

"530 'ĕmûwnâh; or (short.) 'ĕmûnâh; fem. of 529; lit. *firmness*; fig. *security*; mor. *fidelity*: faith (-ful, -ly, -ness, [man]), set office, stability, steady, truly, truth, verily."[18.15]

The next most common Hebrew word translated as "faithful," appears three times,[18.16] and is the other word previously translated as "faith."

"529 'êmûwn; from 539; *established*. i.e. (fig.) *trusty*; also (abstr.) *trustworthiness*: - faith (ful), truth."[18.17]

Another Hebrew word translated as "faithful," appears once,[18.18] and is:

"540 'ăman (Chald.); corresp. to 539: - believe, faithful, sure."[18.19]

It must be noted that although *translations* of this Chaldean 'ăman are provided, "believe, faithful, sure;" the actual *definition* of 540 *'ăman*, is not provided; but rather only "corresp. to 539," is provided. And this "539 'âman," again is defined as: "a prim. root; prop. to *build up* or *support*."

Here the *translations* of 540 'ăman, as "believe, faithful, sure;" include essentially only that which would relate to *intangibles* such as "belief." There is no *translation* of 540 'ăman, that would include to "*build up* or *support*" anything *tangible*. It must be remembered that it is only the *figurative* meaning of "539 'âman, that refers to *belief*: "fig. to *render* (or *be*) *firm* or faithful, to *trust* or believe, to be *permanent* or quiet."

The last Hebrew word translated as "faithful," appears once,[18.20] and is:

"571 'emeth; contr. from 539; *stability*; fig. *certainty, truth, trustworthiness*..."[18.21]

The word "faithfully" appears seven times in the KJV *Old Testament*;[18.22] and is the translation of two Hebrew words.

The most common Hebrew word translated as "faithfully," in five of these seven, is the above 530, *'ĕmûwnâh*,[18.23] previously translated as "faith," and "faithful."

The other Hebrew word translated as "faithfully," in two of these seven is the above 571 *'emeth*,[18.24] previously translated as "faithful."

The word "faithfulness" appears nineteen times in the KJV Old Testament;[18.25] and in eighteen of nineteen times is the above 530, *'ĕmûwnâh*.[18.26]

The other Hebrew word translated as "faithfulness," is:

> "3559 kûwn; a prim. root; prop. to *be erect* (i.e. stand perpendicular); hence (causat.) to *set up*, in a great variety of applications, whether lit. (*establish, fix, prepare, apply*), or fig. (*appoint, render sure, proper* or *prosperous*)..."[18.27]

The actual definition of this particular word, *kûwn*: "to *be erect* (i.e. stand perpendicular)," but translated as "faithfulness;" sounds suspiciously like the previous "right angle" definition of *norm* or *normal*, when the definition of *paranormal* was addressed:

> "*Paranormal* as per the above definition of its root *normal*, would fairly then refer to phenomenon or a phenomena; which is *next to*, or *beside*, something that involves a *right angle*.
>
> "This right angle or norm, likely refers to the intersection of that which is of the *immaterial*, and that which is *material*; and particularly, although not always necessarily; referring to that which is *physically alive*."

Maintaining that right angle of the *immaterial* realm to the *material* as previously discussed, may be the strongest expression of "faith."

According to Strong, the word "unfaithful" appears once in the KJV *Old Testament*; and is:

> "898 bâgad; a prim. root; to *cover* (with a garment); fig. to *act covertly*; by impl. to *pillage*..."[18.28]

The word "unfaithfully" appears once in the KJV Old Testament; and is also 898 *bâgad*.[18.29]

The word "faithless" does not seem to appear anywhere in the KJV Old Testament.

With regard to the *New Testament*; according to Strong, although the translation as "faith" appears many many times in the New Testament (KJV); the actual Greek words translated as "faith" are only three: *pistis*, *ŏligŏpistŏs*, and *ĕlpis*.[18.30]

The most common Greek word translated as "faith" in the *New Testament* (KJV),[18.31] is:

> "4102 pistis; from 3982; *persuasion*, i.e. *credence*; mor. *conviction* (of *religious* truth, or the truthfulness of God or a religious teacher), espec. *reliance* upon Christ for salvation; abstr. *constancy* in such profession; by extens. the system of religious (Gospel) *truth* itself: - assurance, belief, believe, faith, fidelity."[18.32]

> "3982 pĕithō; a prim. verb; to *convince* (by argument, true or false); by anal. to *pacify* or *conciliate* (by other fair means); reflex. or pass. to *assent* (to evidence or authority), to *rely* (by inward certainty): - agree, assure, believe, have confidence, be (wax) [(? unreadable)], make friend, obey, persuade, trust, yield."[18.33]

Pĕithō, is similar to the previously cited purported "cognate" in the etymology of the word "faith:" "Latin *fidēs* trust, belief; related to *fidere* to trust, and cognate with Greek *peíthesthai* be persuaded, obey, believe, trust."

As can easily be seen, purported "cognates" can be quite misleading. Here we are essentially being told that: "to *convince* (by argument, true or false);" and the root of "faith" via "*fidēs* trust, belief," have a common *etymological* source. This may be true in many ways, but nevertheless runs counter to the common concept of "faith," with regard to "spiritual" matters. "Questionable cognates" will be addressed later on, and will form the basis for the: "Red Flag Rule."

The second most common Greek word translated as "faith" in the New Testament (KJV), appearing five times,[18.34] is:

> "3640 ŏligŏpistŏs; from *3641* and *4102*; incredulous, i.e. *lacking confidence* (in Christ): - of little faith."[18.35]

But as can easily be seen, *ŏligŏpistŏs*, actually does not mean "faith;" but instead means: "*lacking* confidence" or "of little faith;" and is actually a combination of two words, the first is:

> "3641 ŏligŏs; of uncert. affin.; *puny* (in extent, degree number, duration or value); espec. neut. (adv.) *somewhat*: - + almost, brief [-ly], few, (a) little, + long, a season, short, small, a while."[18.36]

And the second word in forming *ŏligŏpistŏs*, is the above *pistis*.[18.37]

The last Greek word translated as "faith" in the New Testament (KJV), appearing only once[18.38] is:

> "1680 ĕlpis; from a prim. ĕlpō (to *anticipate*, usually with pleasure); *expectation* (abstr. or concr.) or *confidence*: - faith, hope."[18.39]

Here *ĕlpis* seems to be largely concerned with the final results of applying "ergs" or "working faith," and anticipating or expecting the "increase." The part of the definition of *ĕlpis*: "to *anticipate*, usually with pleasure); *expectation*," seems to be consistent with, and an integral component of; the original and correct meaning of the word *gay*. [For additional information about the original and correct meaning of gay; and the attempts to supplant this original meaning, see: "*Learning How to be Gay*"]

The only appearance of this word is in Hebrews 10:23 (KJV):[18.40]

Faith—What on Earth Is It?

> *"Let us hold fast the profession
> of our faith without wavering;
> (for he is faithful that promised;)"*[18.41]

Here *"faith"* is *ĕlpis*;[18.42] and *"faithful"* is:

> "4103 pistŏs; from 3982; obj. *trustworthy* subj. *trustful*: - believe (-ing, -r), faithful (-ly), sure, true."[18.43]

Although *pistŏs*: "obj. *trustworthy* subj. *trustful*;" and *pistis*: "*persuasion, i.e. credence*; mor. *conviction*;" are each derived from the same root: "3982 pĕithō; a prim. verb; to *convince* (by argument, true or false;" as can bee seen, they are not synonyms.

The word "faithful" appears fifty four times in the New Testament (KJV).[18.44]

Fifty three of the fifty four appearances of "faithful," is the above *pistŏs*.[18.45]

The other word translated as "faithful" is in Hebrews 3:2,[18.46] but Strong has no word listed for this appearance.

The word "faithfully" appears once in the New Testament (KJV),[18.47] and the original Greek word is also *pistŏs*, but here translated as "faithfully"[18.48]

The word "faithless" appears only in the *New Testament*, appearing four times.[18.49]

This original Greek word translated as "faithless" is:

> "571 apistŏs; from 1 (as a neg. particle) and 4103; (act.) *disbelieving*, i.e. without Chr. faith (spec. a heathen); (pass.) *untrustworthy* (person), or *incredible* (thing)..."[18.50]

Each and every time *apistŏs* appears in the Bible, it is Jesus speaking; so "without Chr. faith" being in the definition above, seems a bit hyperbolic. And likewise, the use of "heathen" to describe disbelief in any of the *Abrahamic* religions, as though synonymous with total "disbelieving;" seems at best unwarranted.

The words "unfaithful" and "unfaithfully" do not appear in the *New Testament* (KJV).[18.51]

The previous *Hebrew* words translated as "faith:" "529 'êmûwn; from 539; *established*. i.e. (fig.) *trusty*; also (abstr.) *trustworthiness*;" and "530 'ĕmûwnâh; or (short.) 'ĕmûnâh; fem. of 529; lit. *firmness*; fig. *security*; mor. *fidelity*: faith;" refer to a *result* or *condition*.

And in the *Hebrew*, there is also the *direct* root of 529 'êmûwn, and the *indirect* root of 530 'ĕmûwnâh: "539 'âman; a prim. root; prop. to *build up* or *support*; to *foster* as a parent or nurse; fig. to *render* (or *be*) *firm* or faithful, to *trust* or believe;" but here 539 'âman, can also refer to a *process*; as well as *result* or *condition*.

But the Greek word, *pistis*; and the root of *pistis*, *pĕithō*; seem to refer to both the *process* and the *result*.

The most common word translated as "faith" in the New Testament, *pistis*; and the root of the same; require "persuasion," and: "to convince."

Thus; irrespective of the views of some, it appears that with respect to the word of God; "blind faith;" unlike "first introduced;" is not a tautology.

The use of "blind" in describing a particular type of faith, is used in order to preclude the very fulfillment of the requirements of *pistis* and *pĕithō*; as well as the Hebrew: *'êmûwn, 'ĕmûwnâh*, and *'âman*—irrespective of whether *process* or *result*.

In addition; at least from these original Hebrew and Greek verbiage; "blind faith" is not only *not* a tautology; but is more than arguably oxymoronic; in that neither the Greek *pistis*, nor *pĕithō*; neither the Hebrew *'êmûwn*, nor *'ĕmûwnâh*, nor *'âman*, permit "blindness;" and in fact more than arguably require the opposite of "blindness" in this usage.

Therefore whatever "blind faith" may represent to the secular world; it is not and cannot be Biblical "faith" of any type—again, at least according to the meanings of the original Hebrew and Greek terminologies.

Thus unlike what many today "believe," or "have faith in;" that which Biblical "faith" in fact is; Biblical "faith" is not only *not* synonymous with either credulity, (as opposed to credence), or gullibility. In fact, Biblical faith is *antonymic* to either or both of these—at least with respect to the level of *evidence* required, according to these original Hebrew and Greek words.

Conclusion: In order for their to be "faith" in the New Testament sense, and arguably in the Old Testament sense; then there must be some type of "persuasion," "credence," "to convince," or "conciliate (by other fair means)." The word "convince;" contains the root of the English word *victory*—the Latin *vincere*, or: "to conquer." This is also seen, but here in its negation, in the word "invincible; but here in "convince" with the prefix "con" literally meaning: "with victory."

Hence "faith" in this Biblical context, should not and cannot be based upon: "You are going to hell—unless you believe what I believe, and do what *I say*—irrespective of whether or not what *I say* to do; is what *I do*."

Instead; if "faith" means the belief that a thing is what it purports to be; then this is to be based upon information that results in: "persuasion," "credence," "to convince," "conciliate (by other fair means);" by the very definition of the original Scriptural Greek terminology. If there is no convincing information or knowledge; then this cannot be "faith" in this usage.

"Not leaning on one's understanding;" refers to believing that a thing exists; if it reasonably appears to exist; despite the fact that the *mechanism* for its existence is not *understood*. One need not *understand* the mechanism of gravity, in order to *believe* that gravity exists.

Romans 12:3 (KJV) tells us:

> *"For I say, through the grace given unto me,*
> *to every man that is among you,*
> *not to think of himself more*
> *highly than he ought to think;*
> *but to think soberly,*
> *according as God hath dealt*
> *to every man the measure of faith."*[18.52]

Here we are first being told not to: *"think of himself more highly than he ought to think."* This represents sound advice. We are then told to instead think *"soberly."*

The actual Greek words translated as "soberly" are:

> "1519 ĕis; a prim. prep.; to or into (indicating the point reached or entered), of place, time, or (fig.) purpose (result, etc.); also in adv. phrases..."[18.53]

> "4993 sōphrŏnĕō: from 4998; to be of sound mind, i.e. sane, (fig.) moderate..."[18.54]

And we are then told *why* to *"think soberly:" "according as God hath dealt to every man the measure of faith."*
The original Greek word translated as "dealt" is:

> "3307 mĕrizō; from 3313; to *part*, i.e. (lit.) to *apportion*, *bestow*, *share*, or (fig.) to *disunite*, *differ*: - deal, be difference between, distribute, divide, give part."[18.55]

The original Greek word translated as "measure" is:

> "3358 mĕtrŏn; an appar. prim. word; a *measure* ("metre"), lit. or fig.; by impl. a limited *portion* (*degree*): - measure."[18.56]

The implication of "a *measure*" or "limited *portion*" is of importance here, as this relates to the previous advice. And it must be asked precisely how anything could be "measured," without the result being limited; as that is generally the very purpose of *measuring* anything, including in this context?
With the *common* understanding of "faith," clearly we are being told here in this translation, that by *design*, our faith is *limited*, as we are apportioned, (*mĕrizō*); the measure, (*mĕtrŏn*); of faith. Thus: "Don't have too much faith in God; as He gave you as much faith in Him as He wanted you to have;" would be a fair

conclusion—at least based upon this *common* understanding of faith.

And in fact, the original Greek word translated here as in, (measure of), "faith" is the aforementioned:

> "4102 pistis; from 3982; *persuasion*, i.e. *credence*; mor. *conviction* (of *religious* truth, or the truthfulness of God or a religious teacher), espec. *reliance* upon Christ for salvation; abstr. *constancy* in such profession; by extens. the system of religious (Gospel) *truth* itself: - assurance, belief, believe, faith, fidelity."[18.57]

And again, the root of *pistis* is in fact:

> "3982 pěithō; a prim. verb; to *convince* (by argument, true or false); by anal. to *pacify* or *conciliate* (by other fair means); reflex. or pass. to *assent* (to evidence or authority), to *rely* (by inward certainty): - agree, assure, believe, have confidence, be (wax) [(? unreadable)], make friend, obey, persuade, trust, yield."

Of course the above conclusion of: "Don't have too much faith in God; as He gave you as much faith in Him as He wanted you to have;" makes no sense. So what is actually going on here?

In order to determine this, it must first be determined in what context this: *"God hath dealt to every man the measure of faith."* is all taking place.

What *follows* the above Romans 12:3, (here Romans 12:4-7 (KJV)), provides this context:

> *"For as we have many members in one body, and all members have not the same office:*
>
> *So we, being many, are one body in Christ, and every one members one of another.*

> *Having then gifts differing according
> to the grace that is given to us,
> whether prophecy, let us prophesy
> according to the proportion of faith;"*
>
> *Or ministry, let us wait on our ministering:
> or he that teacheth, on teaching;"*[18.58]

Here we are being told precisely about the actual subject under discussion. Thus it seems the *"measure of faith,"* or *pistis*, previously referenced in the preceding Romans 12:3; is not about faith in *God*. The "for" at the beginning of these passages essentially means "because." This indicates that that which was stated in verse 3 is because of that which is stated in verses 4-7.

In fact it could be reasonably argued that for those whom these words were meant, this was a moot point. Meaning; the intended audience already had substantial faith in God; or this information in these passages would not, (perhaps yet), be for them.

The key phrases here are: *"gifts differing according to the grace that is given to us,"* and: *"let us prophesy according to the proportion of faith;"* "connected together" with: *"whether prophecy."*

We are told of *"gifts differing,"*

The actual Greek word translated here as "gifts" is:

> "5486 charisma; from 5483; a (divine) *gratuity*, i.e. *deliverance* (from danger or passion); (spec.) a (spiritual) *endowment*, i.e. (subj.) religious *qualification* or obj.) miraculous *faculty*: - (free) gift."[18.59]
>
> 5483 charizŏmai; mid. from 5485; to grant as a *favor* i.e. gratuitously, in kindness, pardon or rescue: - deliver, (frankly) forgive, (freely) give, grant."[18.60]

The actual Greek word translated here as "differing" is:

"1313 diaphŏrŏs; from *1308*; *varying*; also *surpassing*: - differing, divers (sic.), more excellent."[18.61]

And we are also told that these gifts differ "*according to the grace that is given to us.*"

The actual Greek word translated here as "grace" is:

"5485 charis; from *5463*; *graciousness* (as *gratifying*), of manner or act (abstr. or concr.; lit., fig. or spiritual; espec. the divine influence upon the heart, and its reflection in the life; including *gratitude*)..."[18.62]

The actual Greek word translated here as "faith" in "*proportion of faith,*" is: "4102 pistis; from *3982*; *persuasion*, i.e. *credence*..."[18.63]

These "gifts" or *charisma* above, are not literal *gifts,* as commonly understood. The inclusion of "*gratuity*" in the definition of *charisma*; and the appearance of both "gift," and "(free) gift," in some of the *translations of,* (but not in the *definition of*), *charisma*, (the words appearing after the : -), attest to this.

It must also be noted, that in the *definition* of the word *charisma*, "divine" appears before "gratuity;" seeming to differentiate *divine* from *non-divine* gratuities. And also included in this definition is: "miraculous *faculty.*"

So is *charisma* a *gift* or a *gratuity*? And where are these "free" and "non-free" *translations*, (not *definitions*), of *charisma*; and precisely what is the topic under discussion with respect to the same?

In Romans 12:6 above, the translation does not include "free:" "*gifts differing according to the grace that is given to us.*"

However, in the case of Romans 5:15, 5:16, and 5:18; some of these *translations* include the word "*free.*"[18.64]

Romans 5:15-18 (KJV) tells us:

> "*But not as the offence, so also is the free gift.*
> *For if through the offence of one many be dead,*
> *much more the grace of God,*

> *and the gift by grace, which is by one man,*
> *Jesus Christ, hath abounded unto many.*
>
> *And not as it was by one that sinned,*
> *so is the gift: for the judgment was*
> *by one to condemnation,*
> *but the free gift is of many*
> *offences unto justification.*
>
> *For if by one man's offence*
> *death reigned by one;*
> *much more they which receive abundance*
> *of grace and of the gift of righteousness*
> *shall reign in life by one, Jesus Christ.)*
>
> *Therefore as by the offence of one judgment*
> *came upon all men to condemnation;*
> *even so by the righteousness of one*
> *the free gift came upon*
> *all men unto justification of life.*"[18.65]

It seems that there are two types of "gifts" that appear in these translated Romans 5:15-18 passages. One is the regular "garden variety" "*gift*," translated without the "free" qualifier; and the other is the "gift," translated with the "free" qualifier resulting in the tautological *"free gift."*

Thus we actually have two types of "gifts," depending upon whether or not the "gift" is "free." There are the gifts that are not qualified as "free;" i.e. best described as the "non-free" gifts; and there are the "free gifts" when the qualifier "free" is included in the translation.

In Romans 5:15 the "non-free" gift, ("*gift by grace*"), is:

"1431 dōrĕa; from 1435; a *gratuity*: -gift."[18.66]

As can bee seen, *gratuity* would be the more correct translation of *dōrĕa*. But "gratuity by grace" seems to make little sense—at least according to the common usages of *gratuity* and *grace*, assuming something is an actual *gratuity*.

In Romans 5:16 the "non-free" gift, ("*so is the gift*"), gift is:

"1434 dōrēma; from *1433*; a *bestowment*: - gift."[18.67]

"1433 dōrĕŏmai; mid. from 1435; to *bestow* gratuitously: - give."[18.68]

The inclusion of "*bestowment*" in the definition of *dōrēma*; as well as the inclusion of "gratuitously," in the definition of the *root* of *dōrēma*, (dōrĕŏmai), should be noted. This appearance of *dōrēma* in Romans 5:16, is the only appearance of *dōrēma* in the entire New Testament.[18.69]

In Romans 5:17 the "non-free" gift, ("*gift of righteousness*"), is again 1431 *dōrĕa*,[18.70] or *gratuity*.

And what about the "free gifts?"

The "free gifts" here in 5:15, 5:16 are both 5486 *charisma*;[18.71] but the "free gift" in 5:18 has no Strong's number.[18.72] The "*Interlinear Bible*" does not include "free gift" in the translation of Romans 5:18.[18.73]

By the inclusion of "*free*" in the translation describing *charisma*, here in Romans 5:15, 5:16, and possibly 5:18; this again represents a tacit admission that *charisma* alone is not free.

The reason for the decision to include "*free*" in the translation of these, (Romans 5:15, 5:16, and 5:18), passages; is because in these passages, the topic is *salvation*; and thus is unrelated to the actual topic of the previous Romans 12:4-7. So salvation must be free, even though the actual Greek word is *charisma*, which literally means: "a (divine) *gratuity*."

But does this make any sense? What is the common understanding of "gift," other than it is supposed to be free? As previously discussed, the use of "gifted" for those with extraordinary capabilities is erroneous, because this usage ignores the "price" or "cost" of the corresponding *talantŏn*.

Is "free gift" not in fact a tautology, in that what could possibly be considered a true "gift" if it is not "free,"—at least if *honesty* is a prerequisite.

Why is it the case that some other Greek word or words; those that actually mean "gift," without any "free" qualifiers required; were not utilized, instead of *charisma*?

Here is one possible other word:

> "1435 dōrŏn; a *present*; spec. a *sacrifice*: - gift, offering."[18.74]

It is *dōrŏn* that is translated as the *"gifts"* to Jesus from the Magi, in Matthew 2:11 (KJV).[18.75]

And here is another:

> "1390 dŏma; from the base of 1325; a present: - gift."[18.76]

It is *dŏma* that is translated as *"gift"* in: *"Not because I desire a gift,"* appearing in Philippians 4:17.[18.77]

The reason(s) for all of this confusion, is that there clearly are or were misunderstandings about: *salvation, gifts, gratuities,* and actual literal *"grace."*

As previously stated, literal "grace;" is getting something of *positive* value, that one in fact *does not* deserve. And its counterpart, "mercy;" is *not* getting something of *negative* value, that one in fact *does* deserve.

An actual or true, (the *"free"*), gift, is literal *grace*; in that it is or was not deserved, because it was not paid for in any way or manner. Thus this is something of positive value that is undeserved

But any type of *gratuity* is in fact *deserved* in some way or manner; and thus not any type of *gift*, unless it vastly exceeds that which would normally be expected. And even then, there would then actually exist both a *gratuity*, and a *gift*.

So the original deserved *gratuity*, or the correct meaning of *charisma* in Romans 5:15, 5:16, and possibly 5:18; is or was later attempted to be turned into literal (undeserved) *grace*, by the inclusion of the "free" qualifier to this *gratuity* or *charisma*.

Is salvation a true *gift* of *grace*; or is salvation a *gratuity*? Most religions would surely make an exception to the: "The only stupid question, is the question that is not asked," rule for asking this one.

But the truth is, that although these same religions proclaim salvation is unquestionably a (free) gift; the *original* Greek, upon which these erroneous *translations* are purportedly based; clearly state otherwise.

And another truth, is that H. Sapiens as hosts, or: "tsâbâ' or tseba'ah from 6633; a *mass* of persons (or fig. things), espec. reg. organized for war (an *army*);" are incessantly in an unfair position.

Man is thrust into this world with little or no knowledge of his role as *tsâbâ'*. Man often knows not what the objective is, or even that there is an objective. Man knows not what many of the rules are, but is judged when he violates them. And man will suffer eternal separation from God, ("spiritual death," or disconnection), for even just one violation.

The enemy on the other hand, attacks man 24/7 with anything and everything he is capable of. The enemy violates each and every rule that he wishes to violate, and is capable of violating.

The disparity is so great, that the only One who ever survived this constant onslaught on man while physically alive; was God Himself, while in physical form.

Thus whenever any "host" is born, he is doomed to "spiritual death;" with only one exception to this ever recorded. [It must be noted that Elijah, and possibly Enoch left the earth *in-corpus*, but their "current" situation in this regard remains unknown—if *epistémē* is the test.]

So the use of *charisma* is the correct description in the case of the availability of salvation; as it is a *gratuity*, for simply being a host. It is not a gratuity for any type of *works*, but merely having been placed in this untenable position. This is balance.

First God *created* the hosts to redeem, (put the kibosh on), the earth; and then *formed* the "First Adam;" and "chose" his offspring, (His chosen people), to begin; and continue, respectively; the process of the redemption of man by the "Last Adam"—*redeem* the *redeemers*. And just like any other *gratuity*, salvation is both provided "after the fact;" and is of no cost to the recipient; or perhaps better stated: "It is the *availability* of salvation is a *gratuity* for man's untenable position; and is provided after the fact." [Many politicians are in prison for bribery, because they did not understand this.]

But many either do not know this, or do not want to know this. They prefer the "undeserved" or "literal grace" viewpoint for whatever reason(s). [For additional information about this topic, see: "*Statists Saving One*" - "*The Pseudo Statists*"]

Hence; that which literally appears in Romans 5:15, 5:16, and possibly 5:18 as *charisma* or *gratuity*; does not comport with, and thus presents a serious problem to, this literal *gift* or literal *grace* viewpoint. Hence the word "free" was later *added* to *charisma* or *gratuity*—irrespective of whether any actuality of a "free gratuity," is in any way possible. Free or not free is a *binary*; in that something is either free, or it is not.

And so it must be understood that these particular "gifts," or *charisma*, are in fact not "free," bur rather: "literally a (divine) *gratuity*." A *gratuity* normally, (when unaccompanied by the qualifier "free"), is not a gift. A gratuity is something voluntarily given, generally for some service provided; e.g.; a "tip" to a waiter or waitress. The *amount* of any gratuity or tip, should be in proportion to the *level of service* provided.

So these particular, (un-free), "*gifts*" or *charisma*, are actually given to us according to the *charis* or: "*graciousness (as gratifying)*." The fact that here *charis* is "gratifying, (a gratuity), grace," with respect to *salvation*; as opposed to "free," is important. And again, it must be remembered that *charisma* refers not to just "any old type" of gratuity, such as the aforementioned "tip;" but rather refers to: "a (divine) *gratuity*."

In fact, here even the "gratifying, (a gratuity), grace;" of *charis*; likely confirms the *gratuity* meaning of the quasi-eponymous: "*charis*-ma."

Back to Romans 12:3, *et. seq.*

Once again, Romans 12:3 tells us: "*For I say, through the grace given unto me, to every man that is among you, not to think of himself more highly than he ought to think; but to think soberly, according as God hath dealt to every man the measure of faith."*

The *"according as,"* can reasonably be considered as a statement of *causation*; in the sense of the reason *why* what precedes this statement of causation, is in fact true.

"Do not think more highly than you ought to, instead think soberly, (*ĕis sōphrŏněō*), because God has apportioned, (*mĕrizō*), every man the measure, (*mĕtrŏn*), of not blind faith, but rather *pistis*, or 'persuasion.'" It must me remembered here that *pistis* is derived from *pěithō*: "to *convince*."

And as previously addressed, if the translation of *pistis* as "faith," as commonly understood in "religious circles" were correct; then the absurd message of: "Don't have too much faith in God; as He gave you as much faith in Him as He wanted you to have;" would be a fair conclusion—at least based upon this *common* understanding of "faith."

But the context of this passage becomes clear with that which follows:

Romans 12:4-7 (KJV), provides this context: *"For as we have many members in one body, and all members have not the same office: So we, being many, are one body in Christ, and every one members one of another. Having then gifts differing according to the grace that is given to us, whether prophecy, let us prophesy according to the proportion of faith; Or ministry, let us wait on our ministering: or he that teacheth, on teaching."*

The *"for"* at the beginning of these passages, can reasonably be translated as "because;" and ties together that which precedes this *"for"* (paraphrased): "Do not think more highly than you ought to, instead think soberly, (*ĕis sōphrŏněō*), because God has apportioned, (*mĕrizō*), every man the measure, (*mĕtrŏn*) of not blind faith, but rather *pistis*, or 'persuasion.'"—*because*

"*as we have many members in one body, and all members have not the same office:*"

The actual Greek word translated as "office" is:

> "4234 praxis; from 4238; *practice*, i.e. (concr.) an *act*; by extens. a *function*: - deed, office, work."[18.78]

Here it is clear that "*office*" refers to *practices*, *acts*, or *functions*; and does not refer to any type of "official" *rank*, or some type of *location*.

We are then told:

> "So we, being many, are one body in Christ, and every one members one of another."

Here we are told that despite not having the same *practices* or *acts*; there is unanimity.

We are then told:

> "Having then gifts differing according to the grace that is given to us, whether prophecy, let us prophesy according to the proportion of faith; Or ministry, let us wait on our ministering: or he that teacheth, on teaching."

As previously cited, these "*gifts*" are: *charisma*, or "a (divine) gratuity*;* "*grace*" is: *charis*, "*graciousness* (as *gratifying*);" and "*faith*" is: *pistis* "*persuasion*, i.e. *credence*;" again with *pistis* being derived from *pĕithō*: "*to convince*."

The actual Greek word translated as "proportion" is:

> "356 analŏgia; from a comp. of 303 and 3056; *proportion*: - proportion."[18.79]

"Having different divine gratuities, (*charisma*);" according to gratification graciousness, (*charis*); given to us, let us use whatever these gratuities are to act according to the proportion, (*analŏgia*), of "persuade-ability" (*pistis*) or "convince-ability;" whether it be prophesy, ministry, or teaching."

"Do not think more highly than you ought to, instead think soberly, (*ĕis sōphrŏnĕō*), because God has apportioned, (*mĕrizō*), every man the measure, (*mĕtrŏn*) of not blind faith, but rather *pistis*, or 'persuasion.'" Again, *pistis* is derived from *pĕithō*: "to *convince*."

Precisely what is this: "*dealt to every man the measure of faith?*" Meaning; since this is proffered as the reason why one should not: "think more highly than he *ought* to think" about himself; precisely what is this that is under discussion?

One answer to this is likely "seed *ĕxŏusia*," or baseline *dunamic* power and authority. This is the granting of say one "talent," and one "duna;" in the hope of a host working this *talantŏn*, and obtaining more of the earlier coined *duna* of *dunamis* in return.

This *pistis*, translated here as "faith," is actually the ability to "persuade" or "convince." How is this done? One way is by the demonstration of this *dunamis* to others.

Another answer, is the additional "divine gratuities" or increased dunamic abilities apportioned, (*mĕrizō*), every man the measure, (*mĕtrŏn*) of *pistis*, or 'persuasion;'" according to how much "working" was done. This is another way to state that which is contained in the "Talent Man" parable.

Matthew 17:20 (KJV) tells us:

> "And Jesus said unto them,
> Because of your unbelief:
> for verily I say unto you,
> If ye have faith as a grain of mustard seed,
> ye shall say unto this mountain,
> Remove hence to yonder place;
> and it shall remove;
> and nothing shall be impossible unto you."[18.80]

The "faith" referenced here is also *pistis*, or the ability to "persuade" or "convince."[18.81]

And the "grain of mustard seed" is:

> "4615 sinapi; perh. from sinŏmai (to *hurt*, i.e. *sting*); *mustard* (the plant): - mustard."[18.82]

There is no word listed in Strong's for "seed," relating to this particular passage.

The "*Interlinear Bible*" translates this as: "grain of mustard."[18.83]

As a unit of measure, a literal "grain" is just under 65 milligrams, or just under 0.002292808 ounces.

So it seems *translationally*, that Jesus is allegorically telling us, that even with the small amount of 0.002292808 ounces of *pistis*, a "*mountain*" *can* be moved.

The actual Greek word translated as "mountain" is:

> "3735 ŏrŏs; prob. from an obsol. ŏrō (to *rise* or "*rear*"; perh. akin to *142*; comp. *3733*); a *mountain* (as *lifting* itself above the plain): - hill, mount (-ain)."[18.84]

Each and every time the translation of "mountain" appears in the KJV New Testament, it is 3735 ŏrŏs.[18.85]

However, it should be noted that as discussed in Chapter 10; ŏrŏs is the root of the word translated as "*heaven*," in: "*kingdom of heaven;*" contained in Matthew 25:1: "*3772* ŏuranŏs; perh. from the same as *3735* (through the idea of *elevation*); the *sky*; by extens. *heaven* (as the abode of God)..."

It is also interesting, that Jesus chose "*a grain*" of mustard, or *sinapi*; rather than "*a grain*" of something else. This may refer to the effect that *dunamis* has on the enemy: "to *hurt*, i.e. *sting*"

In what ways do these "*gifts*," or *charisma*; differ, or *diaphŏrŏs*? The answer is that they differ, or *diaphŏrŏs*; both in *quality* and *quantity*.

The first "*differing*," is *quality*; and is determined by *God*. Quality in this usage; refers to the *type of manifestation*. This is shown in the references to: "*prophesy*," "*ministry*," and "*teacheth*." Each of us is designed by God with certain types of tasks in mind.

The second *"differing,"* is *quantity*; and is determined by *man*. In the "talent man story," we are not told of the *quality* of their *dunamis*, or supernatural power. Meaning; we are not told the *types of manifestations* of their *dunamis*, or supernatural power; as the "story" relates only to the *quantity* or the *magnitude*; and does not address the particular *type of manifestation*.

Hebrews 11:1-3 (KJV) tell us:

> *"Now faith is the substance of things hoped for,*
> *the evidence of things not seen.*
>
> *For by it the elders obtained a good report.*
>
> *Through faith we understand that the*
> *worlds were framed by the word of God,*
> *so that things which are seen*
> *were not made of things which do appear."*[18.86]

These particular passages are quoted often, perhaps even as much as even the 23rd Psalm; but precisely what is it are we actually being told here?

Much wisdom can and has been gained by analysis of the *translation* alone. However; as is always the case, one is then limited by the *actualities* presented in the terminology chosen by the translators. But simply because there is wisdom in the analysis of the *translation* alone, this does not mean that *all* of the wisdom has been obtained; or guarantee that the wisdom obtained in any way relates to the actual meaning of the original passages. *Rhēma* sometimes works this way—if it is *rhēma*.

Words are symbols for actualities, different symbols - different actualities. And this of course assumes that it was *objective clarity* that was the goal of the translator(s).

The actual Greek word translated here as *"now"* is:

"1161 dĕ; a prim. particle (adversative or continuative); *but, and*, etc.: - also, and, but, moreover, now [*often unexpressed in English*]."[18.87]

Here is the first potential error. Since the Bible is believed to have originally been written in "long form," and thus without any punctuation; it is unclear where a comma should be placed. It is unknown if this should be "Now, faith..." or "Now faith,"

In the first case, the "now" can essentially be ignored. This would be *dĕ* as some type of *continuative*.

In the second case, *dĕ* would be used *adjectivally* to describe this faith as "current" faith; as opposed to "past faith" or "future faith"— whatever, if anything, these terms may mean,

But *dĕ* is described as a "prim. particle (adversative or continuative);" and not any type of adjective.

And the second potential error, is the precise translation of *dĕ* as "now;" as "also, and, but, moreover," represent equally possible translations of *dĕ*.

As a "prim. particle (adversative or continuative)," it will be presumed that *dĕ* was included as a means of *sequencing* for the audience, and not affecting the meaning of that which follows.

The actual Greek word translated here as "faith" is the aforementioned "4102 pistis; from 3982; *persuasion*, i.e. *credence*;...;"[18.85] which again is: "derived from "3982 pĕithō; a prim. verb; to *convince*..."

The actual Greek word translated here as "substance" is:

"5287 hupŏstasis; from a comp. of 5259 and 2476; a *setting under* (*support*), i.e. (fig.) concr. *essence*, or abstr. *assurance* (obj. or subj.): -confidence, confident, person, substance."[18.89]

The translation of *hupŏstasis* as "*substance*" appears in the "revised version," of the KJV. This was changed by the British and American revisers; from the "authorized version," which appears to have translated *hupŏstasis* as "*assurance*," rather than "*substance*."[18.90]

Why was this change made? The word "sub-stance" could literally mean "a stance below," which would be reasonably similar to: "a *setting under.*" However *today*, a "substance" is generally considered to be something that is *material* in nature.

So if the unchanged translation of *hupŏstasis* as "*assurance*," is utilized, it would read: Persuasion, (*pistis*), is the assurance (*hupŏstasis*) of "*things.*" This translation of *hupŏstasis* as *assurance*, would be more consistent with the context and usages.

Precisely what are these "*things?*"

According to Strong, "things" is:

> "4229 pragma; from 4238; a *deed*; by impl. an *affair*; by extens. an *object* (material): - business, matter, thing, work."[18.91]

But according the "*Interlinear Bible,*" "*things hoped for,*" is a translation of the following;[18.92] but according to Strong it is only "*hoped for,*"[18.93] that is the translation of the following:

> "1679 ĕlpizō; from 1680; to *expect* or *confide*: - (have, thing) hope (-d) (for), trust."[18.94]

Thus we are actually told: "("*Now*" as a *continuative*); Persuasion, (*pistis*); is the assurance (*hupŏstasis*); of "deeds," [here *things done*, not a piece of paper relating to real estate], or, "by impl. an *affair*; by extens. an *object* (material)" (*pragma*); that are expected (*ĕlpizō*)."

But this persuasion, (*pistis*), is also something else, namely—"*evidence:*" "*the evidence of things not seen.*"

The actual Greek word translated here as "evidence" is:

> "1650 ĕlĕgehŏs; from 1651; *proof, conviction*: - evidence, reproof."[18.95]

What is it that there is "*evidence*" or "proof," (ĕlĕgehŏs), of?

Alleged Fantasy Foundations Volume I

Here the word "things" appears in the translation, for which Strong has no number, but here the "Interlinear Bible" cites the above: "4229 pragma."[18.96]

But these "things," or "deeds," or: "by impl. an *affair*; by extens. an *object* (material)," are a bit peculiar; because they are "*not seen*."

The original Greek words translated as "not seen" are:

"3756 ŏu; also (before a vowel) ŏuk; and (before an aspirate) ŏuch; a prim. word; the absol. neg. [comp. 3361] adv.; *no* or *not*"[18.97]

and

"991 blĕpō; a prim. verb; to look at (lit. or fig.)..."[18.98]

Therefore: "("*Now*" as a *continuative*); Persuasion, (*pistis*); is the assurance (*hupŏstasis*); of "deeds," [here *things done*, not a piece of paper relating to real estate], or, "by impl. an *affair*; by extens. an *object* (material)" (*pragma*); that are expected (*ĕlpizō*)."

Persuasion, (*pistis*); is also: the proof, (*ĕlĕgehŏs*); of deeds, "by impl. an *affair*; by extens. an *object* (material), (*pragma*); not, (ŏu); looked at (*blĕpō*). [This Greek word ŏu, and most particularly its offspring, have enormous importance which are not *blĕpō* at this juncture; but are the subject of an entire chapter in a future volume.]

So this same *pistis*, or persuasion, is both the *assurance* of "things" we expect; as well as *proof* of things we either do not "look at," (literal); or things we do not *see*, (*present* tense, of actual translation as "seen").

What happened to others who had this persuasion, (*pistis*)?

We are told that because of this *pistis*, ("*for by it*"), these others, described here as "elders:" "*the elders;*" had; "*obtained a good report.*"

Who are these "*elders*?"

Strong tells us these "*elders*" are:

"4245 prĕsbutĕrŏs; compar. of prĕsbus (*elderly*); *older*; as noun, a *senior*; spec. an Isr. *Sanhedrist* (also fig. member of the celestial council) or Chr. "*presbyter*": - elder (-est), old."[m8.99]

But determining the meaning of: "*obtained a good report*," is not so easy.

According to Strong; "*obtained*" is 3140;[18.100] but there is no number for "*good*;" and "*report*."[18.101] Strong placed an asterisk by each of these words. According to Strong, the original translation was: "Had witness borne to them."[m8.102]

According to the "Interlinear Bible" the translation is: "obtained witness," and cites 3140.[18.103]

This original Greek word 3140 is:

"3140 marturĕō; from *3144 to be a witness*, i.e. *testify* (lit. or fig.)..."[m8.104]

"To be, or being a witness to;" is not the same as: "to be, or being a witness." The first is generally based upon some type of *observation*; and the second is the provision of some type of *testimony*. Here it seems *marturĕō* refers to the *latter*: "i.e. *testify*."

In court proceedings, there generally are two types of witnesses.

The first is a "fact witness;" and is one who has *factual* information, as they "witnessed" something. A fact witness is limited to only the provision of *facts*; and is not permitted to provide any *opinion*.

The second is an "expert witness;" who is there because of recognized *expertise* in a specific area, or areas; and is normally there to provide *information* to the court; but is also permitted to provide *opinion* in their recognized area of *expertise*.

Thus *marturĕō*, as: "To be a witness," meaning: "i.e. *testify*;" could refer to either a fact witness, (facts only); or an expert witness, (facts and/or opinion).

Why does the inclusion of this: "*for by it the elders obtained a good report*" matter; or does it?

The placement of this entire verse is odd and arguably disruptive. Verses 1 and 3 would flow much better if verse 2 were not present.

Hebrews Chapter 11 in its entirety, is concerned with others who could reasonably be considered as *"elders;"* but yet *"elders"* as a *translation*, does not appear anywhere else in the entire Book of Hebrews (KJV).[18.105]

And the word *prĕsbutĕrŏs*, likewise does not appear anywhere else in the entire Book of Hebrews (KJV).[18.106]

And it must be remembered that *prĕsbutĕrŏs* is not just an *elder*, but rather: "spec. an Isr. *Sanhedrist*."

Hebrews is believed to have been written about thirty five years after the Crucifixion; with the hands of *Sanhedrin* not considered as particularly clean with regard to this event. It is believed that it was the *Sanhedrin* who both had Jesus arrested, and tried.

It is quite possible that Paul was merely being sarcastic with this statement, (paraphrased): "By persuasion, (*pistis*), the *Sanhedrin* testified, (*martŭrĕō*), but here as "expert" or *opinion* witnesses; and were completely wrong with regard to Jesus."

And that which "persuaded" the *Sanhedrin*, clearly was not of God. This is despite the fact that the Crucifixion was consistent with God's will. Nevertheless, the *Sanhedrin* did not do what they did to *please* God, but rather to try and *stop* Him, in order to maintain their socioeconomic status.

We are then told: *"Through faith we understand that the worlds were framed by the word of God.*

The "faith" here is again the aforementioned 4012, *pistis*, or *persuasion*.[18.107]

The original Greek word translated here as "understand" is:

> "3539 nŏiĕō; from 3563; to *exercise* the *mind* (*observe*), i.e. (fig.) to *comprehend, heed*: - consider, perceive, think, understand."[18.108]

The original Greek word translated here as "worlds" is:

> "165 aiōn; from the same as *104*; prop. an *age*; by extens. *perpetuity* (also past); by impl. the *world*; spec. (Jewish)

> a Messianic period (present or future): - age, course, eternal, (for) ever (-more), [n-]ever, (beginning of the, while the) world (began, without end). Comp. 5550."[18.109]
>
> "104 aěi; from an obs. prime noun (appar. mean. continued *duration*); "*ever*;" by qualification *regularly*; by impl. *earnestly*: - always, ever."[18.110]

In chapter 12, aiōn was translated as "forever" in John 14:16: "*He may abide with you forever;*" regarding the Holy Ghost; and in Chapter 17, translated as "*world*" in Matthew 13:18: "*the care of this world, and the deceitfulness of riches, choke the word.*"

Here in this "upper tetrachord," when we are told in verse 3: "*Through faith we understand that the worlds were framed by the word of God, so that things which are seen were not made of things which do appear;*" we first are actually being told that: "Through *persuasion*, (*pistis*); we observe, (*nŏiěŏ*); that the: "age(s)," "perpetuity," or "continued duration," (*aiōn* or *aěi*); were acted upon in some way or manner.

To translate *aiōn* as "*worlds*," particularly in the plural; is at best extremely misleading. The word "world," (singular), in the definition of *aiōn* appears only as: "by impl. the *world*; spec. (Jewish) a Messianic period (present or future)." And even here the inclusion of "world," (singular), in the definition of *aiōn* is clearly *qualified* as relating to *time*; by the inclusion of: "a Messianic period (present or future)."

The translation in the plural as "*worlds*," could lead one to believe that this refers to both the *material* and *immaterial* "worlds." Or it could lead one to believe this refers to planets. Most would think of "worlds" as referring to material entities, at least in part; when in fact *aiōn* literally refers to *time*, and perhaps *events*.

And how was it that that *aiōn* was acted upon, which resulted in the aforementioned persuasion or *pistis* translated as "*faith*;" through which "*we*" observed both this action, as well as how this action was accomplished?

We are told that this *aiōn* was: "*framed by the word of God.*"

The original Greek word for this *action*, translated here as "*framed*" is:

> "2675 katartizō; from 2596 and a der. of 739; to *complete thoroughly*, i.e. *repair* (lit. or fig.) or *adjust*: - fit, frame, mend, (make) perfect (-ly join together), prepare, restore."[18.111]

> "2596 kata; a prim. particle; (prep.) *down* (in place or time), in varied relations (according to the case [gen., dat. or acc.] with which it is joined): - ... In composition it retains many of these applications, and frequently denotes *opposition, distribution* or *intensity*."[18.112]

> "739 artiŏs; from 737; *fresh*, i.e. (by impl.) *complete*: - perfect."[18.113]

The translation of *katartizō* as "framed," seems a bit odd. With the aforementioned mistranslation of *aiōn* as "*worlds*," and here the mistranslation of *katartizō* as "*framed*;" this could easily lead one to believe that this refers to what happened "In the Beginning," when God *created*, (H. bârâ'), from nothing; the "heavens and the earth."

The word *katartizō* does not mean "framed," except perhaps such as in the case of a work of art being "complete" once the "framing" process is completed.

In fact, *katartizō* means: "*complete thoroughly*, i.e. *repair* (lit. or fig.) or *adjust*." Thus there is a prerequisite in this definition for the existence of, or at least the existence of a *part* of: "the thing," that is to be completed, ("*thoroughly*"), repaired or adjusted.

This may somewhat comport with those who erroneously believe that Genesis 1:2 represents the *continuation* of the *creation* of the earth, described in Genesis 1:1 ending with "earth." So then here the "earth" as stated, was in fact completed at the end of Genesis 1:1, but was *not* "completed thoroughly"—whatever: "non-thorough completion," may in fact mean.

Then with this position, what God really wanted when He instructed man to: "*replenish the earth, and subdue it,*" in Genesis 1:28 (KJV); was to: "finish the job for Him."

However the more compelling argument, is that the: "i.e. *repair* (lit. or fig.) or *adjust*" meaning of *katartizō*, refers to the *redemption* process of the earth that began in Genesis 1:2, and continues to this very day.

Here the "repair" or "adjust" meanings of *katartizō*, represent *processes*, and thus the *means* by which the "*complete thoroughly*" meaning of *katartizō*; or if reversed, the "thoroughly complete" *ends* are ultimately achieved.

It is difficult to determine precisely what "fresh" meant in the late 1800's, when Strong included "fresh" in the definition of the purported *root* of *katartizō* namely: *artiŏs*.

However, it is believed that it was not until circa:

> "1848, U.S. slang, probably from German *frech* "insolent, cheeky," from Old High German *freh* "covetous," related to Old English *frec* "greedy, bold."[18.114]

Thus it seems unlikely that Strong would have meant this "new" slang usage in defining *artiŏs*. This leaves meanings such as *new* or *renewed* as the likely meaning of "fresh" in defining *artiŏs*.

It must be noted that there is a difference between *complete thoroughly*, (*katartizō*); and the above noted KJV translation of the root of *katartizō* (*artiŏs*) as "perfect." "Complete" appears to be derived from the Latin infinitive *complere*, roughly meaning: "to fill up." Thus; although nothing can be "perfect" unless it is "full;" simply being "filled up," does not necessarily mean "perfect." One can "completely fill" a fuel tank with contaminated fuel, and yet go nowhere.

""*Through*" persuasion, (*pistis*); we observe, and "*understand*," (*nŏiĕō*); that the "age(s)," "perpetuity," or "continued duration," (*aiōn* or *aĕi*); were completed, by "repair" or adjustment, (*katartizō*)—by something.

And that "something," is translated in the KJV as: "*the word of God.*"

The original Greek word translated here as "word" is:

> "4487 rhēma; from 4483; an *utterance* (individ., collect. or spec.); by impl. a *matter* or *topic* (espec. of narration, command or dispute); with a neg. *naught whatever*..."[18.115]

It should not be overlooked that the actual Greek word that appears in this passage is *rhēma*, and not *lŏgŏs*. Again, this *rhēma* refers to the "real time" word of God; and not *lŏgŏs* or "recorded" word of God. This then would be a "real time" event such as: "let there be;" as opposed to *reading* a Biblical account of this very same event.

The original Greek word translated here as God is:

> "2316 thĕŏs; of uncert. affin.; a *deity*, espec. (with 3588) the supreme *Divinity*; fig. a *magistrate*; by Heb. *very*: - x exceeding, God, god [-ly, -ward]."[18.116]

It is interesting to note that *thĕŏs* is the original word, and is nevertheless defined as "a *deity*." *Theism* and *Deism* vary in one major way. *Theists* believe in a currently active God; while *Deists* do not. And each could in fact be true, depending upon which *realm* it is that is the reference.

From the *material* realm standpoint, it is virtually impossible to make a rational *Deist* argument—else how is it that babies are born, with many of these ultimately having more babies?

But from the *immaterial* viewpoint, since there is no time, it could be argued that there is no sequencing possible; so whatever God did, He did all at once—but only from that *immaterial* reference, where time is not a factor.

""Through" persuasion, (*pistis*); we observe, and "understand," (*nŏiĕō*); that the "age(s)," "perpetuity," or "continued duration," (*aiōn* or *aĕi*); were completed, by "repair" or adjustment, (*katartizō*); by the real time "spoken" word, (*rhēma*), of an active God, (*thĕŏs*).

And we are then told the conclusion: "*so that things which are seen were not made of things which do appear.*"

The original Greek word translated as the first "*things*," is a bit unclear at this juncture. Strong indicates that the word for the first appearance of "things"—here these "*seen*" things; "was changed" from the original "what is," to the current "which are;" but provides no actual Greek word for these "things"[m8.117]

Thus it seems that according to Strong, the word "things" does not actually originally appear in this part of the passage. Rather; instead of "things which are," it should read only: "what is;" (original KJV), sans any mention of the word "things."

And this particular "what is," is: "seen."

The original Greek word translated here as "seen" is the aforementioned: "991 blĕpō; a prim. verb; to look at (lit. or fig.)..."[m8.118]

This is again with the understanding that "look at," and "seen;" are not necessarily synonymous.

And we are told that these "what is," (things?) were "*not made of.*"

The actual Greek word for "made" is:

> "1096 ginŏmai; a prol. and mid. form of a prim. verb; to *cause to be* ("*gen*"- *erate*), i.e. (reflex.) to *become* (*come into being*), used with great latitude (lit., fig., intens., etc.)..."[m8.119]

Here with the negation, ("not"); "what is" *was not* "*cause*(d) *to be*" by some "things."

The actual original Greek word translated as "not" is again:

> "3756 ŏu; also (before a vowel) ŏuk; and (before an aspirate) ŏuch; a prim. word; the absol. neg. [comp. 3361] adv.; *no* or *not*..."[m8.120]

This is the same word, ŏu; that was previously seen with: "Persuasion, (*pistis*); is also: the proof, (*ĕlĕgehŏs*), of deeds, "by impl. an *affair*; by extens. an *object* (material) (*pragma*); not, (ŏu); looked at (*blĕpō*)."

And once again, this Greek word *ŏu*, and most particularly its offspring, have enormous importance which are not easily *blĕpō* at this juncture; but are the subject of an entire chapter in a future volume.

But with regard to the second appearance of "things," Strong has no Greek word for this "things" either. Thus it is unclear if this "things" should be included in the translation either.

And those ("things") which actually do the *ginŏmai*, or "*cause*(d) *to be*;" "do not appear."

The actual Greek word translated as "appear" is:

> 5316 phainō; prol. for the base of 5457; to *lighten* (*shine*), i.e. *show* (trans. or intrans., lit. or fig.): - appear, seem, be seen, shine, x think."[18.121]

When the first "what is" was described as "*seen*," the original Greek word was: "991 blĕpō; a prim. verb; to look at (lit. or fig.)..."

But here; these particular, (presumably), "what is" with regard to "*appear*," the original Greek word is not *blĕpō*. Instead, the original reek word is *phainō*, or: "to *lighten* (*shine*), i.e. *show*." [A *relative* of *phainō* was noted in the introduction: "Tale of Two Fantasies," as the root of the original word "fantasy."]

With regard to that which is "*seen*," *blĕpō*: "to look at," refers to the actions of the purported *observer*, who is "look(ing) at" something. Thus *blĕpō* refers to only the potential *reality*, or *perception* of this "something." Even a *mirage* is "looked at."

But with regard to the "*appear*," *phainō*: "to *lighten* (*shine*), i.e. *show*;" *phainō* refers not to the *observer*, but to the actual "what is" itself. Thus this represents the *actuality*—irrespective of whether anyone is "looking at it," or not.

[In the *Introduction* to this work: "*Tale of Two Fantasies*," appeared the following: "Whether or not one believes that Theophany ever happened; Theophany nevertheless still means a genuine appearance of God, or an actual phenomenon; and thus represents the one definition of fantasy, ("from *phantós* visible, from *phainesthai* appear"); and *never* the other definition: ("use of the imagination.")]

We here are told: *"so that things which are seen were not made of things which do appear."*

But what we are actually being told is: "Therefore, (*"so that"*); any "what is," or "*cause*(d) *to be*," (*ginŏmai*); that one can "look at," (*blĕpō*); (and presumably *perceive* at some level); was or were not, (*ŏu*); "*cause*(d) *to be*," (*ginŏmai*); by any "what is," or "*cause*(d) *to be*," that itself shines or is shown, (*phainō*).

One can *blĕpō* or "look at" an *actuality*, and yet *perceive* nothing. It must be stipulated that said actuality exists; as this is a requirement for there to be an "at" "at which" to "look"—else it is not "look at," but just "look."

But to the extent that that which is *blĕpō*, or "look(ed) at," can be *perceived*, the reason why this perception is possible, is because of that which is *blĕpō*, or "look(ed) at;" is or has *phainō*, or: "to *lighten (shine)*, i.e. *show*."

If there is no *phainō*, there can be no true *blĕpō*; as there can be no *perception* of that actuality, and thus no "at" perceived; i.e.; there is nothing: "at which" to "look." And with no *phainō*, there is no possible *sane* reason to even "look."

And the existence of *phainō* is a *binary*. An *actuality* is either *shining* or *showing*; or it is not. Any *degree* of shining or showing requires the existence of *phainō* at some level.

We are *not* actually told that that which can be "looked at," was "caused to be," by that which does not "shine or show."

Instead we *are* told that that which can be "looked at," was *not* "caused to be," by that which *does* "shine or show."

If the complete set of that which can be "looked at" and perceived, is ruled out as a *cause*; for that which can be "looked at" and perceived as an *effect*; then by Hobson's choice the only possible cause for that which *can* be "looked at" and perceived; would be that which *cannot* be can be "looked at" and perceived.

Again, Hebrews 11:1-3 (KJV) tells us:

"Now faith is the substance of things hoped for,

the evidence of things not seen.

For by it the elders obtained a good report.

*Through faith we understand that the
worlds were framed by the word of God,
so that things which are seen
were not made of things which do appear."*

But Hebrews 11:1-3 *actually* tells us:

"(*"Now"* as a *continuative*); Persuasion, (*pistis*);
is the assurance (*hupŏstasis*); of "deeds,"
[here *things done*, not a piece of paper relating to real estate],
or, "by impl. an *affair*; by extens. an *object* (material)" (*pragma*);
that are expected (*ĕlpizō*).

"Persuasion, (*pistis*); is also:
"the proof, (*ĕlĕgehŏs*); of deeds,
"by impl. an *affair*; by extens. an *object* (material),"
(*pragma*); not, (*ŏu*); looked at (*blĕpō*).

(Likely sarcasm omitted)

""*Through*" persuasion, (*pistis*);
we observe, and "understand," (*nŏiĕō*);
that the "age(s)," "perpetuity," or "continued duration,"
(*aiōn* or *aĕi*); were completed, by "repair" or adjustment,
(*katartizō*); by the real time "spoken" word,
(*rhēma*), of an active God, (*thĕŏs*).

"Therefore, ("*so that*"); any "what is,"
or "*cause*(d) *to be*," (*ginŏmai*);
that one can "look at," (*blĕpō*);
(and presumably *perceive* at some level);
was or were not, (*ŏu*); "*cause*(d) *to be*," (*ginŏmai*);

by any "what is," or "*cause*(d) *to be*,"
that itself shines or is shown, (*phainō*)."

This in no way means that these *things* or *causes*, cannot in many other ways be *perceived*; but only that they cannot be perceived by merely *looking*.

Alleged Fantasy Foundations Volume I

END OF VOLUME I

INSERT VOLUME II

GLOSSARY

'âbad (H): "6 'âbad; a prim. root; prop. to *wander* away i.e. *lose* one's self; by impl. to *perish* (caus. *destroy*)..."[15.45]

'ăbaddôh (H): "10 'ăbaddôh; the same 9, miswritten for 11; a *perishing*: - destruction."[15.49]

Abaddōn (H): "3 Abaddōn; of Heb. or. [11]; a destroying *angel*: - Abaddon."[15.47]

'ăbaddôwn (H): "11 'ăbaddôwn; intens. from 6; abstr. a *perishing*; concr. Hades: - destruction."[15.48]

'ăbêdâh (H): "9 'ăbêdâh; from 6; concr. something *lost*; abstr. *destruction*, i.e. Hades: - lost. Comp. 10."[15.50]

actuality: "*actuality*" is what currently exists or what "is;" what a thing objectively is, as opposed to a *reality* based upon *perception*. An "un-acted upon" actuality, remains an actuality; and that which is not an actuality remains not an actuality—irrespective of any *reality* of the same. The *reality* of a mirage is water, but the *actuality* of a mirage can be anything *except* water—if it is a mirage.

No actuality can ever be 100% accurately perceived, thus *reality* always falls short.

actualization: to bring something from the thought process; (via imagination, quasi-reality); to a current actuality. One can ultimately produce an actuality through a reality (actualization), but not just by the existence of the reality alone—at least when confined to the material realm. Some level of energy or effort (ĕrgŏn) must be also utilized in the actualization process.

'ădâmâh (H): "127 'ădâmâh; from 119; *soil* (from its gen. *redness*): - country, earth, ground, husband [-man] (-ry), land."[15.54]

'Ădônây (H): "136 'Ădônây; an emphatic form of 113; the *Lord* (used as a prop. God only): - (my) Lord."[15.56]

'âdôwn (H): "113 'âdôwn; or (short.) 'âdôn; from an unused root (mean. to *rule*); *sovereign*, i.e. *controller* (human or divine): - lord, master, owner. Comp. also names beginning with "Adoni-"[15.57]

aĕi (G): "104 aĕi; from an obs. prim. Noun (appar. mean. continued *duration*); "*ever*;" by qualification *regularly*; by impl. *earnestly*: - always, ever."[12.29]

afterlife: That "state" of the immaterial part of man (soul), *after* leaving the previously alive or connected (incarnated) body or soma.

aggĕlŏs (G): "32 aggĕlŏs; from aggĕllō; (prob. der. from 71; comp. 34) (to *bring tidings*); a *messenger*; esp. an "*angel*"; by impl. a *pastor*:- angel, messenger."[O2]

agōnizŏmai (G): "75 agōnizŏmai; from 73; to *struggle*, lit. (to *compete* for a prize), fig. (to *contend* with an adversary), or gen. (to *endeavor* to accomplish something): - fight, labor fervently, strive."[5.10]

Glossary

'âhab (H): "157 'âhab or 'âhêb; a prim. root: to *have affection* for (sexually or otherwise): - (be-) love (-ed, -ly, -r), like, friend."[SH5]

aiōn (G): "165 aiōn; from the same as *104*; prop. an *age*; by extens. *perpetuity* (also past); by impl. the *world*; spec. (Jewish) a Messianic period (present or future): - age, course, eternal, (for) ever (-more), [n-] ever, (beginning of the, while the) world (began, without end). Comp. 5550."[12.28]

akarpŏs (G): "175 akarpŏs; from *1* (as a neg. particle) and *2590*; barren (lit. or fig.): - without fruit, unfruitful."[17.9]

'al (H): "5921 'al; prop. the same as 5920 used as a prep. (in the sing. or plur., often with pref. or as conj. With a particle following); *above, over, upon,* or *against* (yet always in this last relation with a downward aspect)..."[14.11]

'âlâh (H): "5927 'âlâh; a prim. root; to *ascend,* intrans. (*be high*) or act. (*mount*); used in a great variety of senses, primary and secondary, lit. and fig. (as follow)..."[15.7]

alēthĕia (G): "225 alēthĕia; from *227; truth*: - true, x truly, truth verity."[9.9]

alēthēs (G): "227 alēthēs; from *1* (as a neg. particle) and *2990; true* (as *not concealing*): - true, truly, truth."[9.10]

alive: in the *general* sense, refers to a *connection,* or connected.

allŏs (G): "243 allŏs; a prim. word; "*else,*" i.e. *different* (in many applications): - more, one (another), (an-, some and-) other (-s, - wise)."[12.12]

'âman (H): "539 'âman; a prim. root; prop. to *build up* or *support*; to *foster* as a parent or nurse; fig. to *render* (or *be*) *firm* or faithful, to *trust* or believe, to be *permanent* or quiet; mor. to *be true* or certain; once (Isa. 30:21 by interch. for 541) to *go to the right hand*: - hence,

409

assurance, believe, bring up, establish, + fail, be faithful (of long continuance, stedfast [sic.], sure, surely, trusty, verified), nurse, (-ing father), (put), trust, turn to the right."[18.6]

'ăman (Chal): "540 'ăman (Chald.); corresp. to 539: - believe, faithful, sure."[18.19]

'âman (H): "541 'âman; denom. from 3225; to take the *right hand* road: - turn to the right. See 539."[18.9]

'âmar (H): "559 'âmar; a prim. root; to *say* (used with great latitude)..."[14.32]

'âmên (H): "543 'âmên; from 539; *sure*; abstr. *faithfulness*; adv. *truly*: - Amen, so be it, truth."[18.11]

ana (G): "303 ana; a prim. prep. and adv.; prop. *up*; but by extens.) used (distributively) *severally*, or (locally) *at* (etc.)..."[15.17]

analŏgia (G): "356 analŏgia; from a comp. of 303 and 3056; *proportion*: - proportion."[18.79]

anastasis (G): "386 anastasis; from 450; a *standing up* again, i.e. (lit.) a *resurrection* from death (individual, gen. or by impl. [its author]), or (fig.) a (moral) *recovery* (of spiritual truth): - raised to life again, resurrection, rise from the dead, that should rise, rising again."[15.15]

anĕmŏs (G): "417 anĕmŏs; from the base of *109*; *wind*; (plur.) by impl. (the four) *quarters* (of the earth): - wind."[14.45]

anistēmi (G): 450 anistēmi; from 303 and 2476; to *stand up* (lit. or fig., trans. or intrans.)..."[15.16]

apatē (G): "539 apatē; from 538; *delusion*: - deceit(ful, fullness), deceivableness (-ving)."[17.13]

Glossary

apěrehŏmai (G): "565 apěrehŏmai; from 575 and 2064; to *go off* (i.e. *depart*), *aside* (i.e. *apart*) or *behind* (i.e. *follow*), lit. or fig.: - come, depart, go (aside, away, back, out, . . . ways), pass away, be past."[12.26]

apistŏs (G): "571 apistŏs; from 1 (as a neg. particle) and 4103; (act.) disbelieving, i.e. without Chr. faith (spec. a heathen); (pass.) untrustworthy (person), or incredible (thing)..."[18.50]

apŏkruptō (G): "613 apŏkruptō; from 575 and 2928; to *conceal away* (i.e. *fully*) fig. to *keep secret*: - hide."[10.44]

apōlěia (G): "684 apōlěia; from a presumed der. of 622; *ruin* or *loss* (phys., spiritual or eternal): - damnable (- nation), destruction, die, perdition, x perish, pernicious ways, waste."[5.24]

apŏllumi (G): "622 apŏllumi; from 575 and the base of 3639 to *destroy* fully (reflex. to *perish*, or *lose*), lit. or fig.: - destroy, die, lose, mar, perish."[5.25]

'arba (H): 702 'arba'; masc. 'arbâ'âh; from 7251; four...;"[14.39]

argŏs (G): "692 argŏs; from 1 (as a neg. particle) [1 is A as used in negation whatever follows and 2041; *inactive*, i.e. *unemployed*; (by impl.) *lazy, useless*: - barren, idle, slow."[10.32]

arguriŏn (G): "694 arguriŏn; neut. Of a presumed der. of 696; *silvery*, i.e. (by impl.) *cash*; spec. a *silverling* (i.e. drachma or shekel): - money, (piece of) silver (piece)."[10.30]

argurŏs (G): "696 argurŏs; from argŏs (*shining*); *silver* (the metal, in the articles or coin): - silver."[10.31]

artiŏs (G): "739 artiŏs; from 737; *fresh*, i.e. (by impl.) *complete*: - perfect."[18.113] *a-talantŏn*: a counterfeit talantŏn, provided by the enemy to manipulate a host into action or inaction, desired by the enemy

'*âtsam* (H): "6105 'âtsam; a prim. root to bind fast, i.e. close (the eyes); intrans. to be (causat. make) powerful or numerous; denom."[14.19]

'*âvâh* (H): "183 'âvâh; a prim. root; to *wish* for: - covet, (greatly) desire, be desirous, long, lust (after)."[15.31]

bâgad (H): "898 bâgad; a prim. root; to *cover* (with a garment); fig. to *act covertly*; by impl. to *pillage*..."[18.28]

ballō (G): "906 ballō; a prim. verb; to *throw* (in various applications, more or less violent or intense): - arise, cast (out), x dung, lay, lie, pour, put (up), send, strike, throw (down), thrust."[4.9]

bâqa (H): "1234 bâqaʻ; a prim. root; to *cleave*; gen. to *rend, break, rip* or *open*: - make a breach, break forth (into, out, in pieces, through, up), be ready to burst, cleave (asunder), cut out, divide, hatch, rend (asunder), rip up, tear, win."[14.14]

basilĕia (G): "932 basilĕia; from 935; prop. *royalty*, i.e. (abstr.) *rule*, or (concr.) a *realm* (lit. or fig.): - kingdom + reign."[10.6]

bayith (H): "1004 bayith; prob. from 1129 abbrev.; a *house* (in the greatest var. of applications, espec. *family*, etc.)..."[15.41]

beforelife: That "state" of the immaterial part of man (soul), *before* entering into that alive or connected (incarnated) condition with a body or soma. Whether souls are always "new," or sometimes "recycled," is irrelevant to this definition.

bĕlŏs (G): "956 bĕlŏs; from 906; a *missile*, i.e. *spear* or *arrow*: - dart."[4.8]

Glossary

bibliomancy: using a "book" to obtain unknown information, often "randomly" opening a book, and often it is the Bible.

blasphēmia (G): "988 blasphēmia; from *989*; *vilification* (espec. against God): - blasphemy, evil speaking, railing."[13.16]

blĕpō (G): "991 blĕpō; a prim. verb; to *look* at (lit. or fig.)..."[18.98]

body or ***soma***: in these usages refers to that *material* or *physical* part of man; i.e.; the physical structure which is designed to contain the immaterial part of man.

bruchō (G): "1031 bruchō; a prim. verb: to *grate* the teeth (in pain or rage): - gnash."[10.52]

brugmŏs (G): "1030 brugmŏs; from *1031*; a *grating* (of the teeth): - gnashing."[10.51]

châcad (H): "2616 châcad; a prim. root; prop. perh. to *bow* (the neck only [comp. 2603] courtesy to an equal), i.e. to *be kind*;..."[SH3]

chânan (H): "2603 chânan; a prim. root [comp. 2583]; prop. to *bend* or stoop in kindness to an inferior; to *favor bestow*..."[SH4]

charis (G): "5485 charis; from *5463*; *graciousness* (as *gratifying*), of manner or act (abstr. or concr.; lit., fig. or spiritual; espec. the divine influence upon the heart, and its reflection in the life; including *gratitude*)..."[18.62]

charisma (G): "5486 charisma; from *5483*; a (divine) *gratuity*, i.e. *deliverance* (from danger or passion); (spec.) a (spiritual) *endowment*, i.e. (subj.) religious *qualification* or obj.) miraculous *faculty*: - (free) gift."[18.59]

charizŏmai (G): "5483 charizŏmai; mid. from *5485*; to grant as a *favor* i.e. gratuitously, in kindness, pardon or rescue: - deliver, (frankly) forgive, (freely) give, grant."[18.60] *châṭâ'* (H): "2398 châṭâ'; a prim. root; prop. to *miss*; hence (fig. and gen.) to *sin*; by infer. To *forfeit, lack, expiate, repent*, (causat.) *lead astray, condemn*..."[10.55]

chay (H): "2416 chay; from 2421 *alive*; hence *raw* (flesh); *fresh* (plant, water, year) *strong*; also (as noun, espec. in the fem. sing. and masc. plur.) *life* (or living thing), whether lit.or fig..."[9.35]

châyâh (H): "2421 châyâh; a prim. root [comp. 2331, 2421]; to *live*, whether lit. or fig.; causat. to *revive*; - keep (leave, make) alive, x certainly, give (promise) life, (let, suffer to) live, nourish up, preserve (alive), quicken, recover, repair, restore (to life), revive, (x God) save (alive, life, lives), x surely, be whole."[13.5]

chayil (H): "2428 chayil; from 2342; prob. a *force* whether of men, means, or other resources; an *army, wealth, virtue, valor, strength*..."[14.51]

checed (H): "2617 checed; from 2616; *kindness*;..."[SH2]

chĕir (G): "5495 chĕir; perh. from the base of 5494 in the sense of its congener the base of 5490 (through the idea of *hollowness* for grasping); the *hand* (lit. or fig. [*power*]; espec. [by Heb.] a *means* or *instrument*]: - hand."[9.18]

dâbâr (H): "1697 dâbâr; from 1696; a *word*; by impl. a *matter* (as spoken of) or *thing*; adv. a *cause*..."[18.10]

dĕ (G): "1161 dĕ; a prim. particle (adversative or continuative); *but, and*, etc.: - also, and, but, moreover, now [*often unexpressed in English*]."[18.87]

dead: in the *general* sense refers to a *disconnection*, or disconnected.

death: is roughly synonymous with "dead," but refers to the *event* of disconnection, rather than that *general state* where there is no connection. "Death" is when this disconnection occurs; and "dead" is the state after this occurrence.

diabŏlŏs (G): "1228 diabŏlŏs; from *1225*; a *traducer*; spec. *Satan* [comp. 7854]: - false accuser, devil, slanderer."[7.6]

diakrinō (G): "1252 diakrinō; from *1223* and *2919*; to *separate thoroughly*, i.e. (lit and reflex.) to *withdraw* from or (by impl.) *oppose*;..."[13.12]

dialĕgŏmai (G): "1256 dialĕgŏmai; mid. from *1223* and *3004*; to *say thoroughly*, i.e. *discuss* (in argument or exhortation): - dispute, preach (unto), reason (with), speak."[13.13]

diaphŏrŏs (G): "1313 diaphŏrŏs; from *1308*; *varying*; also *surpassing*: - differing, divers (sic.), more excellent."[18.61]

dŏma (G): "1390 dŏma; from the base of 1325; a *present*: - gift."[18.76]

dōrĕa (G): "1431 dōrĕa; from *1435*; a *gratuity*: -gift."[18.66]

dōrēma (G): "1434 dōrēma; from *1433*; a *bestowment*: - gift."[18.67]

dōrĕŏmai (G): "1433 dōrĕŏmai; mid. from *1435*; to *bestow* gratuitously: -give."[18.68]

dōrŏn (G): "1435 dōrŏn; a *present*; spec. a *sacrifice*: - gift, offering.[18.74]

dŏulŏs (G): "1401 dŏulŏs; from *1210*; a slave (lit. or fig., invol or vol.; frequently therefore in a qualified sense of subjection or subserviency): - bond (-man), servant."[10.9]

doxa: commonly *believed*, *possible* or *probable* knowledge; (as opposed to *epistémē*, or certain knowledge).

dunamis (G): "*1411* dunamis; from *1410*; *force* (lit. or fig.); spec. miraculous *power* (usually by impl. a *miracle* itself): - ability, abundance, meaning, might (-ily, -y, -y deed), worker of) miracle (-s), power, strength, violence, mighty (wonderful) work."[10.17]

dynamikós : (G) natural power.

ĕgĕirō (G): "1453 ĕgĕirō; prob. akin to the base of *58* (through the idea of *collecting* one's faculties); to *waken* (trans. or intrans.), i.e. *rouse* (lit. from sleep, from sitting or lying, from disease, from death; or fig. from obscurity, inactivity, ruins..."[15.26]

ĕgĕrsis (G): "1454 ĕgĕrsis; from 1453; a *resurgence* (from death): - resurrection."[15.12]

ĕimi (G): "1510 ĕimi; first pers. sing. pres. indic.; a prol. form of a prim. and defective verb; I *exist* (used only when emphatic): - am, have been, x it is I, was..."[12.42]

ĕis (G): "*1519* ĕis *to* or *into* (indicating the point reached or entered) of place, time, or (fig) purpose (result etc.)"[O7]

ĕisĕrchŏmal (G): "1525 ĕisĕrchŏmal; from 1519 and 2064; to *enter* (lit or fig.); - x arise, come (in, into), enter in (-to), go in (through)."[5.9]

ĕk (G): "1537 ĕk, or ĕx; a prim. prep. denoting *origin* (the point *whence* motion or action proceeds)..."[9.15]

ĕkpnĕō (G): "*1606* ĕkpnĕō; from *1537* and *4154*; to *expire*; - give up the ghost."[9.14]

'êl (H): "410 'êl; short. from 352; *strength* as adj. *mighty*; espec. the *Almighty* (but used also of any *deity*): - God (god), x goodly, x great, idol, might (-y one), power, strong. Comp. names in "-el"[15.38]

Glossary

ĕlĕgehŏs (G): "1650 ĕlĕgehŏs; from *1651*; *proof, conviction*: - evidence, reproof."[18.95]

'êl-leh (H): "428 'êl-leh; prol. from *411*; *these* or *those*: - an- (the) other; one sort, so, some, such, them, these (same), they, this, those, thus, which, who (-m)."[15.3]

ĕlpis (G): "1680 ĕlpis; from a prim. ĕlpō (to *anticipate*, usually with pleasure); *expectation* (abstr. or concr.) or *confidence*: - faith, hope."[18.39]

ĕlpizō (G): "1679 ĕlpizō; from *1680*; to *expect* or *confide*: - (have, thing) hope (-d) (for), trust."[18.94]

'emeth (H): "571 'emeth; contr. from *539*; *stability*; fig. *certainty, truth, trustworthiness*..."[18.21]

'êmeq (H): "6010 'êmeq; from *6009*; a *vale* (i.e. broad *depression*): - dale, vale, valley [*often used as a part of proper names*]. See also 1025."[14.16]

'êmûwn (H): "529 'êmûwn; from *539*; *established*. i.e. (fig.) *trusty*; also (abstr.) *trustworthiness*: - faith (ful), truth."[18.4]

'ĕmûwnâh (H): "530 'ĕmûwnâh; or (short.) 'ĕmûnâh; fem. of *529*; lit. *firmness*; fig. *security*; mor. *fidelity*: faith (-ful, -ly, -ness, [man]), set office, stability, steady, truly, truth, verily."[18.5]

ĕpi (G): "1909 ĕpi; a prim. prep. prop. mean. *superimposition*..."[13.19]

ĕpiphĕrō (G): "2018 ĕpiphĕrō; from *1909* and *5342*; to *bear upon* (or *further*), i.e. *adduce* (pers. or judicially [*accuse, inflict*]), *superinduce*: - add, bring (against), take."[13.15]

epistémē: "certain" knowledge.

ĕpitimaō (G): "2008 ĕpitimaō; from *1909* and *5091*; to *tax upon*, i.e. *censure* or *admonish*; by impl. *forbid*: - (straitly) charge, rebuke."[13.18]

ĕpŏuraniŏs (G): "2032 ĕpŏuraniŏs; from *1909* and *3772*; *above* the *sky*: - celestial, (in) heaven (-ly), high."[7.1]

ĕrgazŏmai (G): "2038 ĕrgazŏmai; mid. from *2041*; to *toil* (as a task, occupation, etc.)..."[10.26]

ĕrgŏn (G): "2041 ĕrgŏn; from a prim. (but obsol.) ĕrgō (to work); *toil* (as an effort or occupation); by impl. and act: - deed, doing, labour, work."[10.27]

ĕrōtaō (G): "2065 ĕrōtaō; appar. from *2046* [comp. *2045*]; to *interrogate*; by impl. to *request*: - ask, beseech, desire, intreat, pray. Comp. *4441*."[12.11]

'*etsem* (H): "6106 'etsem; from *6105* a *bone* (as *strong*); by extens. the *body*; fig. the *substance*, i.e. (as pron.) *selfsame*: - body, bone, x life, (self,) same, strength, x very."[14.18]

ĕuruchōrŏs (G): "2149 ĕuruchōrŏs; from ĕurus (*wide*) and *5561*; *spacious*: - broad."[5.20]

ĕxanastasis (G): "1815 ĕxanastasis; from *1817*; a *rising from* death: - resurrection."[15.18]

ĕxanistēmi (G): "1817 ĕxanistēmi; from *1537* and *450*; obj, to *produce*, i.e. (fig.) *beget*; subj. to *arise*, i.e. (fig.) *object*: - raise, (rise) up."[15.19]

ĕxĕsti (G): "1832 ĕxĕsti; third pers. sing. pres. indic. of a comp. of *1537* and *1510*; so also ĕxŏn; neut. pres. part. of the same (with or without some form of *1510* expressed); impers. *it is right* (through the fig. idea of *being out* in public): - be lawful, let, x may (-est)."[12.40]

ĕxōtĕrŏs (G): "1857 ĕxōtĕrŏs; comp. of *1854*; *exterior*: - outer."[10.50]

Glossary

ĕxŏusia (G): "1849, ĕxŏusia; from *1832* (in the sense of *ability*); *privilege*, i.e. (subj.) *force, capacity, competency, freedom,* or (obj.) *mastery* (concr. *magistrate, superhuman, potentate, token of control*), delegated *influence*: - authority, jurisdiction, liberty, power, right, strength."[12.39]

faith: "Latin *fidēs* trust, belief; related to *fidere* to trust, and cognate with Greek *peíthesthai* be persuaded, obey, believe, trust."[18.1]

fancy: "fancy n. 1462-65 *fantsy, fansey,* in *The Paston Letters*; formed by contraction of FANTASY. *Fancy* and *fantasy* gradually differentiated in form and sense with *fancy* taking on the meaning of inclination, liking, desire, often whimsical, which became obsolete in *fantasy* in the 1600's."[14]

fantasy: "fantasy n. About 1350 *fantasie* use of the imagination; later, apparition or phantom (probably before 1375; * borrowed from Old French *fantasie*, learned borrowing from Latin *phantasia*, from Greek *phantasíā* appearance, image, perception, imagination, from *phantázesthai* picture to one self..."[11]
"... from *phantós* visible, from *phaínesthai* appear (middle voice to *phaínein* to show, related to *pháos, phôs* light). The Greek is cognate with Sanskrit *bhāma-s* light, Old Irish *bān* white, Albanian (Tosk dialect) *bënj* I make (appear), Armenian *banam* I open, make visible, and Tocharian A *pam* clear, from Indio-European * *bhā-/bhə*-shine (Pok. 104). The meaning of whimsical or visionary notion, illusion, appeared in Middle English before 1400, followed by the general sense of imagination, especially extravagant or visionary imagination, in early modern English (1539)."[12]

First Adam: Adam, or the man *formed* by God from *something*; as opposed to the original hosts who were *created* from *nothing*. The First Adam was the beginning of the redemptive process for *man* undertaken by God, and was completed, "It is finished;" by the Last Adam, who was Jesus.

419

gâdôwl (H): "1419 gâdôwl; or (short.) gâdôl; from 1431; *great* (in any sense); hence *older*; also *insolent*..."[14.53]

gar (G): "1063 gar; a prim. particle; prop. assigning a *reason* (used in argument, explanation or intensification; often with other particles): - and, as, because (that)..."[7.3]

gâzar (H): "1504 gâzar; a prim. root; to *cut* down or off; (fig.) to *destroy, divide, exclude* or *decide*: - cut down (off), decree, divide, snatch."[15.51]

gerem (H): "1634 gerem; from 1633; a *bone* (as the *skeleton* of the body); hence *self*, i.e. (fig.) very: - bone, strong, top."[15.42]

ghost: an immaterial breath-like (*spiritus*) entity, specifically designed to "live in" or be connected with a physical vessel.

ginŏmai (G): "1096 ginŏmai; a prol. and mid. form of a prim. verb; to *cause to be* ("*gen*"- *erate*), i.e. (reflex.) to *become* (*come into being*), used with great latitude (lit., fig., intens., etc.)..."[18.119]

glōssŏkŏmŏn (G): "1101 glōssŏkŏmŏn; from *1100* and the base of *2889*; prop. a *case* (to keep mouthpieces of wind-instruments in), i.e. (by extens.) a *casket* or (spec.) *purse*: - bag."[17.17]

gōnia (G): "1137 gōnia; prob. akin to *1119*; an *angle*: - corner, quarter."[14.46]

hagiŏs (G): "40 hagiŏs; from hagŏs (an *awful* thing) [comp. 53, 2282]; *sacred* (phys. *pure*, mor. *blameless* or *religious*, cer. *consecrated*): - (most) holy (one, thin), saint."[12.22]

hamartanō (G): "264 hamartanō; perh. from *1* (as a neg. particle) and the base of *3313*; prop. to *miss* the mark (and *so not share* in the prize), i.e. (fig.) to *err*, esp. (mor.) to *sin*."[5.11]

420

haunt: "v. go often to, visit frequently. Probably about 1200 *hanten* practice habitually; later *haunten* (before 1250), and in the sense of visit frequently (probably before 1300); borrowed from Old French *hanter* to frequent, resort to, be familiar with (originally, of a spirit coming back to the house he had lived in)."[3.6]

hautŏu (G): "848 hautŏu; contr. for *1438*; *self* (in some oblique case or reflex. relation): - her (own), (of) him (-self), his (own), of it, thee, their (own), them (-selves), they."[15.25]

hâvâ' (H): "1933 hâvâ',; or hâvâh; a prim. root [comp. 183, 1961] supposed to mean prop. to *breathe*; to *be* (in the sense of existence): - be, x have."[15.30]

hâyâh (H): "1961 hâyâh; a prim. root [comp. 1933]; to *exist* i.e. *be* or *become, come to pass* (always emphatic and not a mere copulate or auxiliary)..."[15.29]

heaven (singular): in the *singular*; generally refers to the *immaterial* realm where God resides; e.g.; the "heaven" in "Who art in heaven," refers to the *immaterial* realm.

heavens (plural): the *plural* of heaven: "heavens," generally refers to the space between the celestial bodies, and thus is contained, (as "space"); in the *material* realm.

hell: "Old English hel, helle, "nether world, abode of the dead, infernal regions, place of torment for the wicked after death," from Proto-Germanic *haljō "the underworld" (source also of Old Frisian helle, Old Saxon hellia, Dutch hel, Old Norse hel, German Hölle, Gothic halja "hell"). "Literally "concealed place" (compare Old Norse hellir "cave, cavern"), from PIE root *kel-(1) "to cover, conceal, save." The English word may be in part from Old Norse mythological Hel (from Proto-Germanic *halija "one who covers up or hides something"), in Norse mythology the name of Loki's daughter who rules over the evil dead in Niflheim, the lowest of all worlds (nifl "mist"). A pagan concept and word fitted to a Christian idiom. "In Middle English, also of the Limbus Patrum, place where the Patriarchs, Prophets, etc. awaited the Atonement."[O10]

histēmi (G): "2476 histēmi; a prol. form of a prim. Staō, (of the same mean., and used for it in certain tenses); to *stand* (trans. or intrans.), used in various applications (lit. or fig.): - abide, appoint, bring, continue, covenant, establish, hold up, lay, present, set (up), stanch, stand (by, forth, still, up)."[2.9]

hŏdŏs (G): "3598 hŏdŏs; appar. a prim. word; a *road*; by impl. a *progress* (the route, act or distance); fig. a *mode* or *means*: - journey, (high-) way."[5.7]

hupŏstasis (G): "5287 hupŏstasis; from a comp. of 5259 and 2476; a *setting under* (*support*), i.e. (fig.) concr. *essence*, or abstr. *assurance* (obj. or subj.): -confidence, confident, person, substance."[18.89]

hustěrěō (G): "5302 hustěrěō; from 5306; to *be later*, i.e. (by impl.) to *be inferior*; gen. to *fall short* (*be deficient*): - come behind (short), be destitute, fail, lack, suffer need, (be in) want, be the worse.[5.38]

imagination: Imagination is similar to a reality, but with the subjective knowledge or belief that the thing does not yet exist.

isaggělŏs (G): "2465 isaggělŏs; from 2470 and 32; *like an angel*, i.e. *angelic*: - equal unto the angels."[O3]

kâbash (H): "3533 kâbash; a prim. root; to *tread* down; hence neg. to *disregard*; pos. to *conquer, subjugate, violate*: - bring into bondage, force, keep under, subdue, bring into subjection."[4.5]

kalěō (G): "2564 kalěō; akin to the base of 2753; to "*call*" (prop. allowed, but used in a variety of applications, dir. or otherwise): - bid, call (forth), (whose sur-) name (was [called])."[12.16]

karpŏs (G): "2590 karpŏs; prob. from the base of 726; fruit (as plucked), (lit. or fig.): - fruit."[17.10]

Glossary

kâshaph (H): "3784 kâshaph; a prim. root; prop. to *whisper* a spell, i.e. to *inchant* or practise magic: —sorcerer, (use) witch (-craft)."[2.19]

kata (G): "2596 kata; a prim. particle; (prep.) *down* (in place or time), in varied relations (according to the case [gen., dat. or acc.] with which it is joined): - ... In composition it retains many of these applications, and frequently denotes *opposition, distribution* or *intensity.*"[18.112]

katartizō (G): "2675 katartizō; from 2596 and a der. of 739; to *complete thoroughly*, i.e. *repair* (lit. or fig.) or *adjust*: - fit, frame, mend, (make) perfect (-ly join together), prepare, restore."[18.111]

kathistēmi (G): "2525 kathistēmi; from 2596 and 2476; to *place down* (permanently), i.e. (fig.) to *designate, constitute, convoy*: - appoint, be, conduct, make ordain, set."[10.29]

kĕlĕuō (G): "2753 kĕlĕuō; from a prim. kĕllō (to *urge* on); "hail"; to *incite* by word, i.e. *order*: - bid, (at, give) command (-ment)."[12.17]

kên (H): "3651 kên; from 3559; prop. *set* upright; hence (fig. as adj.) *just*; but usually (as adv. or conj.) *rightly* or so (in various applications to manner, time and relation; often with other particles)..."[15.52]

kikkâr (H): "3603 kikkâr; from 3769; a *circle*, i.e. (by impl.) a circumjacent *tract* or region, espec. the *Ghôr* or valley of the Jordan; also a (round) *loaf*; also a *talent* (or large [round] coin): - loaf, morsel, piece, plain, talent."[10.13]

kikkêr (Chald.): H"3604 kikkêr (Chald.); corresp. to 3603; a *talent*; - talent."[10.14]

klētŏs (G): "2822 klētŏs; from the same as 2821; *invited*, i.e. *appointed*, or (spec.) a saint: - called."[12.14]

klēsis (G): "2821 klēsis; from a shorter form of 2564; an *invitation* (fig.): - calling, vocation."[12.15]

kôl (H): "3605 kôl; or (Jer. 33:8) kôwl; from 3634; prop. the *whole*; hence *all, any* or *every* (in the sing. only, but often in plur. sense)..."[15.40]

kŏlpŏs (G): "2859 kŏlpŏs; appar. a prim. word; the *bosom*; by anal. a *bay*: - bosom, creek."[3.8]

kŏllŏuriŏn (G): "2854 kŏllŏuriŏn; neut. of a presumed der. of kŏllura (a *cake*; prob. akin to the base of 2853); prop. a *poultice* (as made of in the form of *crackers*), i.e. (by anal.) a *plaster*: eyesalve."[10.38]

kŏllubistēs (G): "2855 kŏllubistēs; from a presumed der. of kŏllubŏs (a small *coin*; prob. akin to 2854); a *coin-dealer*: - (money-) changer."[10.37]

krisis (G): "2920 krisis; *decision* (subj. or obj., for or against); by extens. a *tribunal*; by impl. *justice* (spec. divine law): - accusation, condemnation, damnation, judgment."[13.17]

kruptō (G): "2928 kruptō: a prim verb; to *conceal* (prop. by covering): - hide (self), keep secret, secret [-ly]."[10.45]

kûwn (H): "3559 kûwn; a prim. root; prop. to *be erect* (i.e. stand perpendicular); hence (causat.) to *set up*, in a great variety of applications, whether lit. (*establish, fix, prepare, apply*), or fig. (*appoint, render sure, proper* or *prosperous*)..."[18.27]

lanthanō (G): "2990 lanthanō; a prol. form of a prim. verb, which is used only as an alt. in certain tenses; to *lie hid* (lit. or fig.); often used adv. *unwittingly*: - be hid, be ignorant of, unawares."[9.11]

Last Adam: The First Adam or the man *formed* by God from *something*; as opposed to the original hosts who were *created* from *nothing*, was the beginning of the redemptive process for *man* undertaken by God: and was completed "It is finished;" by the Last Adam, who was Jesus.

life or *living*: reasonably synonymous with "alive" and thus also refers to that *general* state where there is some type of connection.

limbo: "Latin (in) *limbō* (on) the edge, ablative case of *limbus* edge, border..."[O9]

lŏgŏs (G): "3056 lŏgŏs; from 3004; something *said* (including the *thought*); by impl. a *topic* (subject of discourse), also *reasoning* (the mental faculty) or *motive*; by extens. a *computation*; spec. (with the art. In John) the Divine *Expression* (i.e. *Christ*)..."[7.13]

machaira (G): "3162 machaira; prob. fem. of a presumed der. of 3163; a *knife*, i.e. *dirk*; fig. *war*, judicial *punishment*: - sword."[7.9]

marturĕō (G): "3140 marturĕō; from 3144 *to be a witness*, i.e. *testify* (lit. or fig.)..."[18.104]

massâ' (H): "4853 massâ'; from 5375; a *burden*; spec. *tribute*, or (abstr.) *porterage*; fig. an *utterance*,..." chiefly a *doom*, espec. *singing*; mental, *desire*: - burden, carry away, prophesy, x they set, song, tribute."[10.23]

mĕgas (G): "3173 mĕgas, [include. the prol. forms, fem. mĕgalē, plur. mĕgalŏi, etc.; comp. also 3176, 3187]; *big* (lit. or fig., in a very wide application): - (+ fear) exceedingly, great (-est), high, large, loud, mighty, +(be) sore (afraid), strong, x to years."[12.6]

mĕgistŏs (G): "3176 mĕgistŏs; superl. of 3173; *greatest* or *very great*: - exceeding great."[12.7]

mĕizōn (G): "3187 mĕizōn; irreg. compar. of 3173; *larger* (lit. or fig., spec. in age): - elder, greater (-est), more."[12.5]

mᵉʻôd (H): "3966 mᵉʻôd; from the same as 181; prop. *vehemence*, i.e. (with or without prep.) *vehemently*; by impl. *wholly, speedily*, etc. (often with other words as an intensive or superlative; espec. when repeated)..."¹⁴·²¹

měrimna (G): "3308 měrimna; from 3307 (through the idea of *distraction*); *solicitude*: - care."¹⁷·¹¹

měrizō (G): "3307 měrizō; from 3313; to *part*, i.e. (lit.) to *apportion, bestow, share*, or (fig.) to *disunite, differ*: - deal, be difference between, distribute, divide, give part."¹⁸·⁵⁵

měthŏděia (G): "3180 měthŏděia; from a comp. of 3326 and 3593 [comp. "method"]; *traveling over*, i.e. *travesty* (*trickery*): - wile, lie in wait."⁷·⁵

mětrŏn (G): "3358 mětrŏn; an appar. prim. word; a *measure* ("metre"), lit. or fig.; by impl. a limited *portion* (*degree*): - measure."¹⁸·⁵⁶

miracle: something that occurs in the material realm, but is contrary to natural law. In fact in order to be considered a miracle, it *must* contradict natural law or laws; natural law here meaning the law or laws of the material realm.

mnēměiŏn (G): "3419 mnēměiŏn; from 3420; a *remembrance*, i.e. *cenotaph* (*place of interment*): - grave, sepulcher, tomb."¹⁶·¹²

môach (H): "4221 môach; from the same as 4220; *fat*, i.e. marrow: - marrow."¹⁴·²⁷

mustēriŏn (G): "3466 mustēriŏn; from a der. of muō (to *shut* the mouth); a *secret* or "*mystery*" (through the idea of *silence* imposed by *initiation* into religious rites): - mystery."¹⁷·³

nâbâ' (H): "5012 nâbâ'; a prim. root; to *prophesy*, i.e. speak (or sing) by inspiration (in prediction or simple discourse): - prophesy (ing), make self a prophet."[14.34]

nâchâsh (H): "5175 nâchâsh; from 5172; a *snake* (from its *hiss*); - serpent."[2.12]

nâchash (H): "5172 nâchash a prim. root; prop. to *hiss*, i.e. *whisper* a (magic) spell; gen. to *prognosticate*: - x certainly, divine, enchanter, (use) x enchantment, learn by experience, x indeed, diligently observe."[2.13]

nâphach (H): "5301 nâphach; a prim. root; to puff, in various applications (lit., to inflate, blow hard, scatter, kindle, expire; fig., to disesteem)..."[14.38]

nâsâ' (H): "5375 nâsâ' or nâcâh; a prim. root; to *lift* in a great variety of applications."[10.24]

nathan (H): "5414 nathan; a prim. root; to *give*, used with greatest latitude of application (*put, make*, etc.)"[5.3]

n^{e}dîybâh (H): "5082 n^{e}dîybâh; fem. of 5081; prop. nobility, i.e. reputation: - soul."[9.39]

nephesh (H): "5315 nephesh; from 5314 prop. a *breathing* creature, i.e. *animal* or (abstr.) vitality; used very widely in lit., accommodated or fig. sense (bodily or mental)..."[9.32]

n^{e}shâmâh (H): "5397 n^{e}shâmâh; fr. 5395; a *puff*, i.e. *wind*, angry or vital *breath*, divine *inspiration*, *intellect*, or (concr.) an *animal*: - blast, (that) breath (-eth), inspiration, soul, spirit."[9.28]

nether: "1: situated down or below: lower; 2: situated or believed to be situated beneath the earth's surface."[O8]

nŏiĕō (G): "3539 nŏiĕō; from 3563; to *exercise* the *mind* (*observe*), i.e. (fig.) to *comprehend, heed*: - consider, perceive, think, understand."[18.108]

nŏmŏs (G): "3551 nŏmŏs; from a prim. nĕmō (to *parcel* out, espec. *food* or *grazing* to animals); *law* (through the idea of prescriptive usage), gen. (*regulation*), spec. (of Moses [include. the volume]; also of the Gospel), or fig. (a *principle*): - law."[5.15]

normal: "...norma carpenter's square, rule, NORM... Normalcy 1857, mathematical condition of being at right angles..."[3.3]

ŏligŏpistŏs (G): "3640 ŏligŏpistŏs; from 3641 and 4102; incredulous, i.e. *lacking confidence* (in Christ): - of little faith."[18.35]

ŏligŏs (G): "3641 ŏligŏs; of uncert. affin.; *puny* (in extent, degree number, duration or value); espec. neut. (adv.) *somewhat*: - + almost, brief [-ly], few, (a) little, + long, a season, short, small, a while."[18.36]

ŏpsariŏn (G): "3795 ŏpsariŏn; neut. of a presumed der. of the base of 3702; a *relish* to other food (as if cooked *sauce*), i.e. (spec.) *fish* (presumably salted and dried as a condiment): - fish."[8.3]

ŏpsōniŏn (G): "3800 ŏpsōniŏn; neut. of a presumed der. of the same as 3795; *rations* for a soldier, i.e. (by extens.) his *stipend* or *pay*: - wages."[8.2]

ŏrŏs (G): "3735 ŏrŏs; prob. from an obsol. ŏrō (to *rise* or "*rear*"; perh. akin to *142*; comp. *3733*); a *mountain* (as *lifting* itself above the plain): - hill, mount (-ain)."[10.4]

ŏrthŏtŏmĕō (G): "3718 ŏrthŏtŏmĕō; from a comp. of 3717 and the base of 5114; to *make a straight cut*, i.e. (fig.) to *dissect* (*expound*) *correctly* (the divine message): - rightly divide."[9.2]

Glossary

ŏu (G): "3756 ŏu; also (before a vowel) ŏuk; and (before an aspirate) ŏuch; a prim. word; the absol. neg. [comp. 3361] adv.; *no* or *not*"[18.97]

ŏuranŏs (G): "3772 ŏuranŏs; perh.from the same as 3735 (through the idea of *elevation*); the *sky*; by extens. *heaven* (as the abode of God); by impl. *happiness, power, eternity*; spec. the *Gospel*, (*Christianity*): - air, heaven ([-ly]), sky."[10.3]

'ŏwb (H): "178 'ŏwb; from the same as 1 (appar. through the idea of *prattling* a father's name); prop. a *mumble*, i.e. a water-*skin* (from its hollow sound); hence a *necromancer* (ventriloquist, as from a jar: - bottle, familiar spirit."[9.27]

pâneh (H): "6440 pâneh; (pânîym); from 6437; the *face* (as the part that *turns*); used in a great variety of applications..."[15.10]

para (G): "3844 para; a prim. prep.; prop. *near*, i.e. (with gen.) *from beside* (lit. or fig.), (with dat.) *at* (or *in*) the *vicinity* of (obj. or subj.), (with acc.) to the *proximity* with (local [espec. *beyond* or *opposed to*] or causal [*on account of*]); - above, against, among, at, before, by, contrary to, x friend, from, + give [such things as they] + that [she] had, x his, in, more than, nigh unto, (out) of, past, save, side... by, in the sight of than, [there-] fore, with. In compounds it retains the same variety of application."[3.2]

paraklētŏs (G): "3875 paraklētŏs; an *intercessor, consoler*: - advocate, comforter"[12.13]

parallel: "parà allélois beside one another, side by side (parà beside and allélois each other...)"[3.4]

paratithēmi (G): "3908 paratithēmi; from 3844 and 5087; to place alongside, i.e. present (food, truth); by impl. to deposit (as a trust or for protection)..."[9.17]

pas (G): "3956 pas; include. *all* the forms of declension; appar. a prim. word; all, *any, every*, the *whole*..."[12.35] *pâthach* (H): "6605 pâthach; a prim root; to *open* wide (lit. or fig.); spec. to *loosen, begin, plough, carve*..."[15.5]

pĕithō (G): "3982 pĕithō; a prim. verb; to *convince* (by argument, true or false); by anal. to *pacify* or *conciliate* (by other fair means); reflex. or pass. to *assent* (to evidence or authority), to *rely* (by inward certainty): - agree, assure, believe, have confidence, be (wax) [(? unreadable)], make friend, obey, persuade, trust, yield."[8.33]

pĕri (G): "4012 pĕri; from the base of 4008; prop. *through* (all over), i.e. around; fig. *with respect to*;..."[3.14]

pĕrissĕuō (G): "4052 pĕrissĕuō; from 4053; to *superabound* (in quantity or quality), *be in excess, be superfluous*; also (trans.) to *cause to superabound* or *excel*: - (make, more) abound (have, have more) abundance, (be more) abundant, be the better, enough and to spare, exceed, excel, increase, be left, redound, remain (over and above)."[10.43]

phainō (G): "5316 phainō; prol. for the base of 5457; to *lighten* (*shine*), i.e. *show* (trans. or intrans., lit. or fig.): - appear, seem, be seen, shine, x think."[8.121]

phenomenon: "phenomenon *n.* 1625, fact or occurrence, manifestation... borrowed from Latin *phaenomenon*, from Greek *phainómenon* that which appears or is seen, noun use of neuter present participle *phaínesthai* appear; see FANTASY"[13]

phĕrō (G): "5342 phĕrō; a prim. verb... to "*bear*" or *carry*"[10.16]

physical death: refers to that state where the immaterial part of man (soul) is no longer connected to the material part of man (body).

physical life: is that condition where the immaterial part of man (soul) is connected to the material part (body).

pistis (G): "4102 pistis; from 3982; *persuasion*, i.e. *credence*; mor. *conviction* (of *religious* truth, or the truthfulness of God or a religious teacher), espec. *reliance* upon Christ for salvation; abstr. *constancy* in such profession; by extens. the system of religious (Gospel) *truth* itself: - assurance, belief, believe, faith, fidelity."[18.32]

pistŏs (G): "4103 pistŏs; from 3982; obj. *trustworthy* subj. *trustful*: - believe (-ing, -r), faithful (-ly), sure, true."[18.43]

planaō (G): "4105 planaō; from 4106; to (prop. *cause to*) *roam* (from safety, truth, or virtue): - go astray, deceive, err, seduce, wander, be out of the way."[O5]

platus (G): "4116 platus; from 4111; spread out *"flat"* (*"plot"*), i.e. *broad*: - wide."[5.19]

plŏutŏs (G): "4149 plŏutŏs; from the base of 4130; *wealth* (as *fullness*), i.e. (lit.) *money, possessions*, or (fig.) *abundance, richness*, (spec.) valuable *bestowment*: - riches."[17.14]

pněō (G): "4154 pněō; a prim. word; to *breath* hard, i.e. *breeze*: - blow comp..."[9.16]

pněuma (G): "4151 pněuma; from 4154; a *current* of air, i.e. *breath* (*blast*) or a *breeze*; by anal. or fig. a *spirit*, i.e. (human) the rational *soul*, (by impl.) *vital principle*, mental *disposition*, etc., or (superhuman) an *angel, doemon*, or (divine) God, Christ's *spirit*, the Holy *Spirit*: - ghost, life, spirit(ual, ually), mind. Comp. 5590."[5.33]

pŏiěō (G): "4160 pŏiěō; appar. a prol. form of an obsol. prim; to *make* or *do* (in a very wide application, more or less direct): - abide, +agree, appoint, x avenge..."[12.4]

poltergeist: "n. noisy spirit or ghost. 1848, borrowing of German Poltergeist (*poltern* make noise, rattle, rumble + *geist* GHOST)."[3.7]

pŏrĕuŏmai (G): "4198 pŏrĕuŏmai; mid. from a der. of the same as *3984*; to *traverse*, i.e. *travel* (lit. or fig.; espec. to *remove* [fig. *die*], *live*, etc.): - depart, go (away, forth, one's way, up), (make a, take a) journey, walk."[12.8]

pragma (G): "4229 pragma; from *4238*; a *deed*; by impl. an *affair*; by extens. an *object* (material): - business, matter, thing, work."[18.91]

praxis (G): "4234 praxis; from *4238*; *practice*, i.e. (concr.) an *act*; by extens. a *function*: - deed, office, work."[18.78]

prĕsbutĕrŏs (G): "4245 prĕsbutĕrŏs; compar. of prĕsbus (*elderly*); *older*; as noun, a *senior*; spec. an Isr. *Sanhedrist* (also fig. member of the celestial council) or Chr. "*presbyter*": - elder (-est), old."[18.99]

prŏphētēs (G): "4396 prŏphētēs; from a comp. of *4253* and *5346*; a *foreteller* ("*prophet*"); by anal. an *inspired speaker*; by extens. a *poet*: - prophet."[5.16]

psuchē (G): "5590 psuchē; from *5594*; *breath*, i.e. (by impl.) *spirit*, abstr. or concr. (the *animal* sentient principle only; thus distinguished on the one hand from *4151*, which is the rational and immortal *soul*; and on the other from *2222* which is mere *vitality*, even of plants: these terms thus exactly correspond respectively to the Heb. 5315, 7307 and 2416): - heart (+- ily), life, mind, soul, + us, + you."[5.32]

pulē (G): "4439 pulē, appar. a prim. word; a *gate*, i.e. the leaf or wing of a folding *entrance* (lit. or fig.): - gate."[5.6]

purŏō (G): "4448 purŏō; from *4442*; to *kindle* i.e. (pass.) to *be ignited*, *glow* (lit.), *be refined* (by impl.), or (fig.) to *be inflamed* (with anger, grief, lust): - burn, fiery, be on fire, try."[4.10]

qâbar (H): "6912 qâbar; a prim. root; to *inter*: - x in any wise, bury, (-ier)."[13.4]

Glossary

qeber (H): "6913 qeber; or (fem.) qibrâh; from 6912; a *sepulchre*: - burying place, grave, sepulchre."[5.6]

qâshâh (H): "7185 qâshâh; a prim. root; prop. to *be dense*, i.e. tough or *severe* (in various applications): - be cruel, be fiercer, make grievous, be ([ask a], be in, have, seem, would) hard (-en, [labour], -ly, thing), be sore, (be, make) stiff (-en, [-necked])."[R78]

qûwm (H): "6965 qûwm; a prim. root; to *rise* (in various applications, lit., fig., intens. and caus.): - abide, accomplish, x be clearer, confirm, continue, decree, x be dim, endure, x enemy, enjoin, get up, make good, help, hold, (help to) lift up (again), make, x but newly, ordain, perform, pitch, raise (up), rear (up), remain, (a-) rise (up) (again, against), rouse up, set (up), (e-)stablish, (make to) stand (up), stir up, strengthen, succeed, (as-, make) sure (-ly), (be) up (-hold, - rising)."[3.6]

râ'a' (H): "7489 râ'a': a prim. root; prop. to *spoil* (lit. by *breaking* to pieces); fig. to *make* (or *be*) *good for nothing*, i.e. *bad* (phys., soc. or mor.):—afflict, associate selves [*by mistake for* 7462], break (down, in pieces), + displease, (be, bring, do) evil (doer, entreat man), show self friendly [*by mistake for* 7462}, do harm, (do) hurt, (behave self, deal ill, x indeed, do mischief, punish, still, vex, (do) wicked (doer,-ly), be (deal, do) worse."[2.15]

râ'âh (H): "7462 râ'âh; a prim root; to tend a flock, i.e. pasture it; intrans. To graze (lit or fig.); gen. to rule; by extens. to associate with (as a friend):—x break, companion, keep company with, devour, eat up, evil entreat, feed, use a friend, make friendship with, herdman, keep [sheep] (-er), pastor, + shearing house, shepherd, wander, waste."[2.16]

reality: the belief or "understanding" of: "what a thing is or is not," based upon perception.

realization: The process by which the perception of a "thing or things," produces an awareness, belief or understanding (reality) of said actuality or actualities. *Realization* (process) and *reality* (result) are always less than the actuality, and often incomplete and/or erroneous.

recollection: The process of "remembering." Recollection is similar to a reality, but with the subjective knowledge or belief that the thing may no longer exist.

reincarnation: in a very general sense, the reintroduction of that immaterial part of man (soul) into a *new* and *different* physical body.

resurrection: the reintroduction of that immaterial part of man (soul) into the *same* physical body.

retrophesy: to obtain knowledge "unnaturally" about the *past*, in the same way and manner that *prophesy* is concerned with the *future*.

rhēma (G): "4487 rhēma; from *4483*; an *utterance* (individ., collect. or spec.); by impl. a *matter* or *topic* (espec. of narration, command or dispute); with a neg. *naught* whatever..."[7.11]

rûwach (H) "7306 rûwach; a prim. root; prop. to *blow*, i.e. *breathe*; only (lit.) to *smell* or (by impl. *perceive* (fig. to *anticipate*, *enjoy*): - accept, smell, x touch, make of quick understanding."[9.21]

rûwach (H): "7307 rûwach; from 7306; *wind*; by resemblance *breath*, i.e. a sensible (or even violent) exhalation; fig. *life, anger, unsubstantiality*; by extens. a *region* of the sky; by resemblance *spirit*, but only of a rational being (includ. its expression and functions..."[9.20]

rûwach (Ch.): "7308 rûwach (Chald.); corresp. to 7307: - mind, spirit, wind."[9.22]

Glossary

sârâh (H): "8280 sârâh; a prim. root; to *prevail*: - have power (as a prince)."[15.37]

schizō (G): "4977 schizō; appar. A prim. verb; to split or sever (lit. or fig.)..."[9.3]

shâmar (H): "8104: shâmar; A prim. root; prop. to *hedge* about (as with thorns), i.e. *guard*; gen. to *protect, attend to*, etc.: - beware, be circumspect, take heed (to self), keep (-er, self), mark, look narrowly, observe, preserve, regard, reserve, save (self), sure, (that lay) wait (for), watch (-man)."[SH6]

shâmayim (H): "8064 shâmayim; dual of an unused sing. shâmeh; from an unused root mean. to *be lofty*; *the sky* (as *aloft* the dual perh. Alluding to the visible arch in which the clouds move, as well as to the higher ether where the celestial bodies revolve)."[1.2]

shâqâh (H): "8248 shâqâh; a prim. root; to *quaff*, i.e. (caus.) to *irrigate* or *furnish a potion to*:"[14.26]

sheqer (H): "8267 sheqer; from 8266; an *untruth*; by impl. a *sham* (often adv.): - without a cause, deceit (-ful), false (- hood, - ly), feignedly, liar, + lie, lying, vain (thing), wrongfully."[2.4]

shûwb (H): "7725 shûwb; a prim. root; to *turn* back (hence, away) trans. or intrans. lit. or fig. (not necessarily with the idea of *return* to the starting point); gen. to *retreat*; often adv. *again*..."[14.31]

sinapi (G): "4615 sinapi; perh. from sinŏmai (to *hurt*, i.e. sting); *mustard* (the plant): - mustard."[8.82]

skandalizō (G): "4624 skandalizō; ("scandalize"); from 4625; to *entrap*, i.e. *trip* up (fig. *stumble* [trans.] or *entice* to sin, apostasy or displeasure): - (make to) offend."[17.8]

skia (G): "4639 skia; appar. a prim. Word; "*shade*" or a shadow (lit or fig. [or an *adumbration*]): - shadow."[10.48]

skŏtŏs (G): "4655 skŏtŏs; from the base of *4639*; *shadiness*, i.e. *obscurity* (lit. or fig.): - darkness."[10.47]

sōphrŏnĕō (G): "4993 sōphrŏnĕō: from 4998; to be of sound mind, i.e. sane, (fig.) moderate..."[18.54]

soul: refers to that *immaterial* part of man, often inadequately described as "will, intellect and emotions."

sōzō (G): "4982 sōzō; from a prim. sōs (contr. for obsol. saŏs "*safe*"); to *save*, i.e. *deliver* or *protect* (lit. or fig.): - heal, preserve, save (self), do well, be (make) whole."[5.12]

spĕirō (G): "4687 spĕirō; prob. strengthened from 4685 (through the idea of *extending*); to *scatter*, i.e. *sow* (lit. or fig.): - sow (er), receive seed."[17.7]

spiritual: can refer to a myriad of immaterial or "breath like" entities.

spiritual death: refers to that state where the immaterial part of man, (soul), is *disconnected* from its original source.

spiritual life: refers to that state where the immaterial part of man, (soul), is *connected* to its original source.

stĕnŏs (G): "4728 stĕnŏs; prob, from the base of *2476*; *narrow* (from obstacles *standing* close about): - strait." [5.13]

sumpnigō (G): "4846 sumpnigō; from *4862* and *4155*; to *strangle completely*, i.e. (lit.) to *drown*, or (fig.) to *crowd*: - choke, throng."[17.15]

sûwk (H): "7753 sûwk a prim. root; to *entwine*, i.e. *shut* in (for formation, protection or restraint):- fence, (make an) hedge (up)."[T2]

talantŏn (G): "5007 talantŏn; neut. Of a presumed der. of the orig. form of tiaō (to *bear*; equiv. to *5342*); a *balance* (as *supporting*

Glossary

weights), i.e. (by impl.) a certain *weight* (and thence a *coin* or rather *sum* of money) or "*talent*": - talent."[10.15]

têbâh (H): "8392 têbâh; perh. of for. der.; a *box*: – ark"[18.2]

těktōn (G): "5045 těktōn; from the base of 5088; an *artificer* (as *producer* of fabrics), i.e. (spec.) a *craftsman* in wood: - carpenter."[17.20]

tērěō (G): "5083 tērěō; from těrŏs (a *watch*; perh. akin to 2334); to *guard* (from *loss* or *injury*, prop. by keeping *the eye* upon..."[SH8]

thěŏs (G): "2316 thěŏs; of uncert. affin.; a *deity*, espec. (with 3588) the supreme *Divinity*; fig. a *magistrate*; by Heb. *very*: - x exceeding, God, god [-ly, -ward]."[18.116]

thlibō (G): "2346 thlibō; akin to the base of 5147; to crowd (lit. or fig.): - afflict, narrow, throng, suffer tribulation, trouble."[5.22]

thlipsis (G): "2347 thlipsis; from 2346; *pressure* (lit. or fig.): - afflicted (-tion), anguish, burdened, persecution, tribulation, trouble."[5.39]

thura (G): "2374 thura; appar. a prim. word [comp. "door"]; a *portal* or entrance (the opening or the closure, lit. or fig.) – door, gate."[5.8]

tiktō (G): "5088 tiktō; a strengthened form of a prim. těkō, (which is used only as alt. in certain tenses); to *produce* (from seed, as a mother, a plant, the earth, etc.), lit. or fig.: - bear, be born, bring forth, be delivered, be in travail."[10.42]

timaō (G): "5091 timaō; from 5093; to *prize*, i.e. *fix* a *valuation* upon; by impl. to *revere*: - honour, value."[13.20]

tiqvâh (H): "8615 tiqvâh; from 6960; lit. a *cord* (as an *attachment* [comp. 6961]); fig. *expectancy*: - expectation ([-ted]), hope, live, thing that I have longed for."[15.44]

Tishbîy (H): "8664 Tishbîy; patrial from an unused name mean. *recourse*; a *Tishbite* or inhab. of Tishbeh (in Gilead); - Tishbite."[R69]

tŏkŏs (G): "5110 tŏkŏs; from the base of 5088; *interest* on money loaned (as a *produce*): - usury."[10.41]

traduce: "traduce (v.)1530s, "alter, change over, transport," from Latin traducere "change over, convert..."[7.7]

transducer: "transducer (n.)1924, "device which converts energy from one form to another," from Latin transducere/traducere..."[7.8]

trapĕza (G): "5132 trapĕza; prob. contr. from 5064 and 3979; a table or stool (as being four legged), usually for food (fig. a meal); also a counter for money (fig. a brokers office for loans at interest): - bank, meat, table."[10.36]

trapĕzitēs (G): "5133 trapĕzitēs; from 5132; a money-broker or banker: - exchanger."[10.35]

tribŏs (G): "5147 tribŏs; from tribō (to "rub"; akin to tĕirō, truō, and the base of 5131, 5134); a rut or worn track: - path"[5.23]

tsâbâ' (H): "tsâbâ' or tsᵉba'ah from 6633; a *mass* of persons (or fig. things), espec. reg. organized for war (an *army*); by impl. a *campaign*, lit. or fig. (spec. *hardship, worship):* - appointed time, (+) army, (+) battle, company, host, service, soldiers, waiting upon, war (-fare). 6633 "tsâbâ' a prim. root; to *mass* (an army or servants): - assemble, fight, perform, muster, wait upon, war."[4.3]

tsâvâh (H): "6680 tsâvâh; a prim. root; (intens.) to *constitute, enjoin*: - appoint, (for-) bid, (give a) charge, (give a, giving, send

Glossary

with) command (-er, -ment), send a messenger, put, (set) in order."¹⁴·³³

tsêlâ (H): "6763 tsêlâ'; or (fem.) tsal'âh; from 6760; a *rib* (as *curved*), lit. of the body) (sic.) or fig. (of a door, i.e. *leaf*); hence a *side*, lit. (of a person)..."¹⁴·⁵⁵

witch: "...wiche, in Genesis and Exodus; developed from Old English wicce female magician, sorceress,..."²·¹⁷

yâbêsh (H): "3001 yâbêsh; a prim. root; to *be ashamed, confused* or *disappointed*; also (as failing) to *dry* up (as water) or *wither* (as herbage): - be ashamed, clean, be confounded, (make) dry (up), (do) shame (-fully), x utterly, wither (away)."¹⁴·²³

yâbêsh (H): "3002 yâbêsh; from 3001; *dry*: - dried (away), dry."¹⁴·²²

yâd (H): "3027 yâd; a prim. word; a hand (the open one [indicating power, means, direction, etc.], in distinction from 3709, the closed one); used (as noun, adv., etc.) in a great variety of applications,..."¹⁴·¹⁰

yâda (H): "3045 yâda'; a prim root; to *know* (prop. to ascertain by *seeing*); used in a great variety of senses, fig., lit., euphem. and infer. (including *observation, care, recognition*; and causat. *instruction, designation, punishment*, etc.)..."¹⁴·³⁰

Yâhh (H): "3050 Yâhh; contr. for 3068, and mean. the same; *Jah*, the sacred name..."¹⁵·³²

Yᵉhôvâh (H): "3068 Yᵉhôvâh; from 1961; (the) self-*existent* or Eternal; *Jehovah*, Jewish national name of God: - Jehovah, the Lord. Comp. 3050. 3069."¹⁵·²⁸

Yᵉhôvîh (H): "3069 Yᵉhôvîh; a var. of 3068 [used after 136, and pronounced by Jews as 430, in order to prevent the repetition of the same sound since they elsewhere pronounce 3068 as 136: - God"¹⁵·³³

Yisrâ'êl (H): "3478 Yisrâ'êl; from 8280 and 410; *he will rule as God*; *Jisraël*, a symbolical name of Jacob; also (typically) of his posterity: - Israel."[15.36]

zaō (G): "2198 zaō; a prim. verb; to *live* (lit. or fig.): - life (-time), (a-) live (-ly), quick."[5.31]

zōē (G): "2222 zōē; from *2198*; *life* (lit. or fig.): - life (-time). Comp. 5590."[5.30]

Bibliography

1.1 *King James Bible,* Genesis 1:1
1.2 Strong, James. *Strong's Exhaustive Concordance of the Bible.* © 1890 James Strong, Madison, NJ p. 118 (Hebrew)
1.3 Walker/Quadrakoff. *MeekRaker Beginnings…*©2016 Quadrakoff Publications Group, LLC Wilmington DE p. i

2.1 Walker, J. Bartholomew. *Wisdom Essentials* ©2017 Quadrakoff Publications Group, LLC Wilmington DE p. 151
2.2 *King James Bible,* Proverbs 17:4
2.3 *New American Standard Bible*: 1995 update. 1995 (Proverbs 17:4) The Lockman Foundation: Lahabra, CA
2.4 Strong, James. *Strong's Exhaustive Concordance of the Bible.* © 1890 James Strong, Madison, NJ p. 120 (Hebrew)
2.5 Strong, James. *Strong's Exhaustive Concordance of the Bible.* © 1890 James Strong, Madison, NJ p. 599
2.6 *New American Standard Bible*: 1995 update. 1995 (John 8:44) The Lockman Foundation: Lahabra, CA
2.7 Strong, James. *Strong's Exhaustive Concordance of the Bible.* © 1890 James Strong, Madison, NJ p. 8
2.8 Strong, James. *Strong's Exhaustive Concordance of the Bible.* © 1890 James Strong, Madison, NJ p.38 (Greek)

2.9 Strong, James. *Strong's Exhaustive Concordance of the Bible.* © 1890 James Strong, Madison, NJ p. 38 (Greek)
2.10 *New American Standard Bible*: 1995 update. 1995 (1 Peter 5:8) The Lockman Foundation: Lahabra, CA
2.11 Walker/Quadrakoff. *MeekRaker Beginnings*...©2016 Quadrakoff Publications Group, LLC Wilmington DE p. 198
2.12 Strong, James. *Strong's Exhaustive Concordance of the Bible.* © 1890 James Strong, Madison, NJ p. 78 (Hebrew)
2.13 Strong, James. *Strong's Exhaustive Concordance of the Bible.* © 1890 James Strong, Madison, NJ p. 78 (Hebrew)
2.14 *King James Bible,* Genesis 3:14
2.15 Strong, James. *Strong's Exhaustive Concordance of the Bible.* © 1890 James Strong, Madison, NJ p. 110 (Hebrew)
2.16 Strong, James. *Strong's Exhaustive Concordance of the Bible.* © 1890 James Strong, Madison, NJ p. 109 (Hebrew)
2.17 *Chambers Dictionary of Etymology*. Copyright © 1988 The H. W. Wilson Company, New York, NY p. 1240
2.18 *King James Bible,* Exodus 22:18
2.19 Strong, James. *Strong's Exhaustive Concordance of the Bible.* © 1890 James Strong, Madison, NJ p. 58 (Hebrew)

3.1 Strong, James. *Strong's Exhaustive Concordance of the Bible.* © 1890 James Strong, Madison, NJ p. 67 (Hebrew)
3.2 Strong, James. *Strong's Exhaustive Concordance of the Bible.* © 1890 James Strong, Madison, NJ p. 54 (Greek)
3.3 *Chambers Dictionary of Etymology*. Copyright © 1988 The H. W. Wilson Company, New York, NY p. 710
3.4 *Chambers Dictionary of Etymology*. Copyright © 1988 The H. W. Wilson Company, New York, NY p. 754
3.5 Camminatore, Danté. *Ostium Ab Inferno—The Opening From Hell.* ©2020 Quadrakoff Publications Group, LLC Wilmington DE pp.7-13
3.6 *Chambers Dictionary of Etymology*. Copyright © 1988 The H. W. Wilson Company, New York, NY p. 469
3.7 *Chambers Dictionary of Etymology*. Copyright © 1988 The H. W. Wilson Company, New York, NY p. 814

Bibliography

3.8 Strong, James. *Strong's Exhaustive Concordance of the Bible.* © 1890 James Strong, Madison, NJ p. 43 (Greek)

4.1 https://www.lifehack.org/articles/featured/how-to-use-parkinsons-law-to-your-advantage.html (retrieved 8/16/2020)
4.2 *King James Bible,* Genesis 2:3
4.3 Strong, James. *Strong's Exhaustive Concordance of the Bible.* © 1890 James Strong, Madison, NJ p. 98 (Hebrew)
4.4 *King James Bible,* Genesis 1:28
4.5 Strong, James. *Strong's Exhaustive Concordance of the Bible.* © 1890 James Strong, Madison, NJ p. 54 (Hebrew)
4.6 *New American Standard Bible*: 1995 update. 1995 (Ephesians 6:12-17) The Lockman Foundation: Lahabra, CA
4.8 Strong, James. *Strong's Exhaustive Concordance of the Bible.* © 1890 James Strong, Madison, NJ p. 19 (Greek)
4.9 Strong, James. *Strong's Exhaustive Concordance of the Bible.* © 1890 James Strong, Madison, NJ p. 18 (Greek)
4.10 Strong, James. *Strong's Exhaustive Concordance of the Bible.* © 1890 James Strong, Madison, NJ p. 63 (Greek)
4.11 *King James Bible,* Genesis 1:1
4.12 *King James Bible,* Genesis 1:2
4.13 *Interlinear Bible Hebrew Greek English, 1 Volume edition.* © 1976, 1977, 1978, 1979, 1980, 1981, 1984. Second Edition, © 1986 Jay P. Green, Sr., Hendrickson Publishers p. 1 (Genesis 1:2)
4.14 Walker, J. Bartholomew. *Statists Saving Ones* ©2017 Quadrakoff Publications Group, LLC Wilmington DE p. 57-59
4.15 *King James Bible,* Genesis 1:5

5.1 Walker, J. Bartholomew. *Wisdom Essentials* ©2017 Quadrakoff Publications Group, LLC Wilmington DE p. 95-99
5.2 *King James Bible,* Psalms 37:4
5.3 Strong, James. *Strong's Exhaustive Concordance of the Bible.* © 1890 James Strong, Madison, NJ p. 81 (Hebrew)
5.4 *King James Bible,* Matthew 7:13-14
5.5 *King James Bible,* Luke 13:23-25

5.6 Strong, James. *Strong's Exhaustive Concordance of the Bible.* © 1890 James Strong, Madison, NJ p. 63 (Greek)
5.7 Strong, James. *Strong's Exhaustive Concordance of the Bible.* © 1890 James Strong, Madison, NJ p. 51 (Greek)
5.8 Strong, James. *Strong's Exhaustive Concordance of the Bible.* © 1890 James Strong, Madison, NJ p. 37 (Greek)
5.9 Strong, James. *Strong's Exhaustive Concordance of the Bible.* © 1890 James Strong, Madison, NJ p. 26 (Greek)
5.10 Strong, James. *Strong's Exhaustive Concordance of the Bible.* © 1890 James Strong, Madison, NJ p. 8 (Greek)
5.11 Strong, James. *Strong's Exhaustive Concordance of the Bible.* © 1890 James Strong, Madison, NJ p. 931
5.12 Strong, James. *Strong's Exhaustive Concordance of the Bible.* © 1890 James Strong, Madison, NJ p. 70 (Greek)
5.13 Strong, James. *Strong's Exhaustive Concordance of the Bible.* © 1890 James Strong, Madison, NJ p. 66 (Greek)
5.14 *King James Bible*, Matthew 7:7-12
5.15 Strong, James. *Strong's Exhaustive Concordance of the Bible.* © 1890 James Strong, Madison, NJ p. 50 (Greek)
5.16 Strong, James. *Strong's Exhaustive Concordance of the Bible.* © 1890 James Strong, Madison, NJ p. 62 (Greek)
5.17 Strong, James. *Strong's Exhaustive Concordance of the Bible.* © 1890 James Strong, Madison, NJ p. 378
5.18 Strong, James. *Strong's Exhaustive Concordance of the Bible.* © 1890 James Strong, Madison, NJ p. 63 (Greek)
5.19 Strong, James. *Strong's Exhaustive Concordance of the Bible.* © 1890 James Strong, Madison, NJ p. 58 (Greek)
5.20 Strong, James. *Strong's Exhaustive Concordance of the Bible.* © 1890 James Strong, Madison, NJ p. 34 (Greek)
5.21 Strong, James. *Strong's Exhaustive Concordance of the Bible.* © 1890 James Strong, Madison, NJ p. 378
5.22 Strong, James. *Strong's Exhaustive Concordance of the Bible.* © 1890 James Strong, Madison, NJ p. 36 (Greek)
5.23 Strong, James. *Strong's Exhaustive Concordance of the Bible.* © 1890 James Strong, Madison, NJ p. 72 (Greek)

Bibliography

5.24 Strong, James. *Strong's Exhaustive Concordance of the Bible.* © 1890 James Strong, Madison, NJ p. 15 (Greek)
5.25 Strong, James. *Strong's Exhaustive Concordance of the Bible.* © 1890 James Strong, Madison, NJ p. 14 (Greek)
5.26 Strong, James. *Strong's Exhaustive Concordance of the Bible.* © 1890 James Strong, Madison, NJ p. 259
5.27 *King James Bible,* Matthew 26:8
5.28 Strong, James. *Strong's Exhaustive Concordance of the Bible.* © 1890 James Strong, Madison, NJ p. 1107
5.29 *King James Bible,* Mark 14:4
5.30 Strong, James. *Strong's Exhaustive Concordance of the Bible.* © 1890 James Strong, Madison, NJ p. 35 (Greek)
5.31 Strong, James. *Strong's Exhaustive Concordance of the Bible.* © 1890 James Strong, Madison, NJ p. 34 (Greek)
5.32 Strong, James. *Strong's Exhaustive Concordance of the Bible.* © 1890 James Strong, Madison, NJ p. 79 (Greek)
5.33 Strong, James. *Strong's Exhaustive Concordance of the Bible.* © 1890 James Strong, Madison, NJ p. 58 (Greek)
5.34 Strong, James. *Strong's Exhaustive Concordance of the Bible.* © 1890 James Strong, Madison, NJ p. 19
5.35 *King James Bible,* 1 Timothy 5:10
5.36 Strong, James. *Strong's Exhaustive Concordance of the Bible.* © 1890 James Strong, Madison, NJ p. 1077
5.37 *King James Bible,* 1 Thessalonians 3:3-4
5.38 Strong, James. *Strong's Exhaustive Concordance of the Bible.* © 1890 James Strong, Madison, NJ p. 75 (Greek)
5.39 Strong, James. *Strong's Exhaustive Concordance of the Bible.* © 1890 James Strong, Madison, NJ p. 36 (Greek)
5.40 Strong, James. *Strong's Exhaustive Concordance of the Bible.* © 1890 James Strong, Madison, NJ p. 1078
5.41 *King James Bible,* 2 Thessalonians 1:6
5.42 Strong, James. *Strong's Exhaustive Concordance of the Bible.* © 1890 James Strong, Madison, NJ p. 1078

6:1 Walker, J. Bartholomew. *Wisdom Essentials* ©2017 Quadrakoff Publications Group, LLC Wilmington DE pp. 56-59

7.1 Strong, James. *Strong's Exhaustive Concordance of the Bible.* © 1890 James Strong, Madison, NJ p. 32 (Greek)
7.2 *King James Bible,* Ephesians 6:12
7.3 Strong, James. *Strong's Exhaustive Concordance of the Bible.* © 1890 James Strong, Madison, NJ p. 20 (Greek)
7.4 *King James Bible,* Ephesians 6:8-11
7.5 Strong, James. *Strong's Exhaustive Concordance of the Bible.* © 1890 James Strong, Madison, NJ p. 47 (Greek)
7.6 Strong, James. *Strong's Exhaustive Concordance of the Bible.* © 1890 James Strong, Madison, NJ p. 22 (Greek)
7.7 https://www.etymonline.com/word/traduce (retrieved 8/17/20)
7.8 https://www.etymonline.com/word/transducer (retrieved 8/17/20)
7.9 Strong, James. *Strong's Exhaustive Concordance of the Bible.* © 1890 James Strong, Madison, NJ p. 46 (Greek)
7.10 Strong, James. *Strong's Exhaustive Concordance of the Bible.* © 1890 James Strong, Madison, NJ p. 58 (Greek)
7.11 Strong, James. *Strong's Exhaustive Concordance of the Bible.* © 1890 James Strong, Madison, NJ p. 63 (Greek)
7.12 *King James Bible,* John 1:1
7.13 Strong, James. *Strong's Exhaustive Concordance of the Bible.* © 1890 James Strong, Madison, NJ p. 45 (Greek)
7.14 *King James Bible,* Matthew 4:1-11
7.15 Walker, J. Bartholomew. *Wisdom Essentials* ©2017 Quadrakoff Publications Group, LLC Wilmington DE pp. 164-165
7.16 Walker, J. Bartholomew. *Wisdom Essentials* ©2017 Quadrakoff Publications Group, LLC Wilmington DE pp. 175-176

8.1 *King James Bible,* Romans 6:22-23
8.2 Strong, James. *Strong's Exhaustive Concordance of the Bible.* © 1890 James Strong, Madison, NJ p. 53 (Greek)
8.3 Strong, James. *Strong's Exhaustive Concordance of the Bible.* © 1890 James Strong, Madison, NJ p. 53 (Greek)

9.1 *King James Bible*, 2 Timothy 2:15

Bibliography

9.2 Strong, James. *Strong's Exhaustive Concordance of the Bible.* © 1890 James Strong, Madison, NJ p. 52 (Greek)

9.3 Strong, James. *Strong's Exhaustive Concordance of the Bible.* © 1890 James Strong, Madison, NJ p. 70 (Greek)

9.4 Petrovsky, Erich Z. *Reincarnation—A Reasonable Inquiry.* ©2019 Quadrakoff Publications Group, LLC Wilmington DE pp.56-57

9.5 *New American Standard Bible*: 1995 update. 1995 (Proverbs 2:6) The Lockman Foundation: Lahabra, CA

9.6 *New American Standard Bible*: 1995 update. 1995 (Proverbs 22:21) The Lockman Foundation: Lahabra, CA

9.7 *King James Bible*, John 4:24

9.8 Strong, James. *Strong's Exhaustive Concordance of the Bible.* © 1890 James Strong, Madison, NJ p. 58 (Greek)

9.9 Strong, James. *Strong's Exhaustive Concordance of the Bible.* © 1890 James Strong, Madison, NJ p. 9 (Greek)

9.10 Strong, James. *Strong's Exhaustive Concordance of the Bible.* © 1890 James Strong, Madison, NJ p. 9 (Greek)

9.11 Strong, James. *Strong's Exhaustive Concordance of the Bible.* © 1890 James Strong, Madison, NJ p. 44 (Greek)

9.12 *King James Bible*, Luke 23:46

9.13 Strong, James. *Strong's Exhaustive Concordance of the Bible.* © 1890 James Strong, Madison, NJ p. 968

9.14 Strong, James. *Strong's Exhaustive Concordance of the Bible.* © 1890 James Strong, Madison, NJ p. 27 (Greek)

9.15 Strong, James. *Strong's Exhaustive Concordance of the Bible.* © 1890 James Strong, Madison, NJ p. 26 (Greek)

9.16 Strong, James. *Strong's Exhaustive Concordance of the Bible.* © 1890 James Strong, Madison, NJ p. 59 (Greek)

9.17 Strong, James. *Strong's Exhaustive Concordance of the Bible.* © 1890 James Strong, Madison, NJ p. 55 (Greek)

9.18 Strong, James. *Strong's Exhaustive Concordance of the Bible.* © 1890 James Strong, Madison, NJ p. 77 (Greek)

9.19 Strong, James. *Strong's Exhaustive Concordance of the Bible.* © 1890 James Strong, Madison, NJ p. 967

9.20 Strong, James. *Strong's Exhaustive Concordance of the Bible.* © 1890 James Strong, Madison, NJ p. 107 (Hebrew)

9.21 Strong, James. *Strong's Exhaustive Concordance of the Bible.* © 1890 James Strong, Madison, NJ p. 107 (Hebrew)

9.22 Strong, James. *Strong's Exhaustive Concordance of the Bible.* © 1890 James Strong, Madison, NJ p. 107 (Hebrew)

9.23 Strong, James. *Strong's Exhaustive Concordance of the Bible.* © 1890 James Strong, Madison, NJ p. 967

9.24 *King James Bible*, Genesis 1:2

9.25 Strong, James. *Strong's Exhaustive Concordance of the Bible.* © 1890 James Strong, Madison, NJ p. 967

9.26 *King James Bible*, Daniel 4:8

9.27 Strong, James. *Strong's Exhaustive Concordance of the Bible.* © 1890 James Strong, Madison, NJ p. 9 (Hebrew)

9.28 Strong, James. *Strong's Exhaustive Concordance of the Bible.* © 1890 James Strong, Madison, NJ p. 81 (Hebrew)

9.29 Strong, James. *Strong's Exhaustive Concordance of the Bible.* © 1890 James Strong, Madison, NJ p. 960

9.30 Strong, James. *Strong's Exhaustive Concordance of the Bible.* © 1890 James Strong, Madison, NJ p. 79 (Greek)

9.31 Strong, James. *Strong's Exhaustive Concordance of the Bible.* © 1890 James Strong, Madison, NJ p. 960

9.32 Strong, James. *Strong's Exhaustive Concordance of the Bible.* © 1890 James Strong, Madison, NJ p. 80 (Hebrew)

9.33 *King James Bible*, Genesis 2:7

9.34 Strong, James. *Strong's Exhaustive Concordance of the Bible.* © 1890 James Strong, Madison, NJ p. 960

9.35 Strong, James. *Strong's Exhaustive Concordance of the Bible.* © 1890 James Strong, Madison, NJ p. 38 (Hebrew)

9.36 Strong, James. *Strong's Exhaustive Concordance of the Bible.* © 1890 James Strong, Madison, NJ p. 81 (Hebrew)

9.37 Strong, James. *Strong's Exhaustive Concordance of the Bible.* © 1890 James Strong, Madison, NJ p. 960

9.38 *King James Bible*, Job 30:15

9.39 Strong, James. *Strong's Exhaustive Concordance of the Bible.* © 1890 James Strong, Madison, NJ p. 76 (Hebrew)

9.40 *King James Bible*, Isaiah 57:16

Bibliography

9.41 Strong, James. *Strong's Exhaustive Concordance of the Bible.* © 1890 James Strong, Madison, NJ p. 81 (Hebrew)

9.42 *King James Bible*, 1 Corinthians 14:33

9.43 Strong, James. *Strong's Exhaustive Concordance of the Bible.* © 1890 James Strong, Madison, NJ p. 842

9.44 Strong, James. *Strong's Exhaustive Concordance of the Bible.* © 1890 James Strong, Madison, NJ p. 11 (Greek)

9.45 *King James Bible*, John 14:12

10.1 *New American Standard Bible*: 1995 update. 1995 (Matthew 25: 14-30) The Lockman Foundation: Lahabra, CA

10.2 *New American Standard Bible*: 1995 update. 1995 (Matthew 25:1) The Lockman Foundation: Lahabra, CA

10.3 Strong, James. *Strong's Exhaustive Concordance of the Bible.* © 1890 James Strong, Madison, NJ p. 53 (Greek)

10.4 Strong, James. *Strong's Exhaustive Concordance of the Bible.* © 1890 James Strong, Madison, NJ p. 52 (Greek)

10.5 Strong, James. *Strong's Exhaustive Concordance of the Bible.* © 1890 James Strong, Madison, NJ p. 475

10.6 Strong, James. *Strong's Exhaustive Concordance of the Bible.* © 1890 James Strong, Madison, NJ p. 18 (Greek)

10.7 Strong, James. *Strong's Exhaustive Concordance of the Bible.* © 1890 James Strong, Madison, NJ p. 936

10.8 Strong, James. *Strong's Exhaustive Concordance of the Bible.* © 1890 James Strong, Madison, NJ p. 936

10.9 Strong, James. *Strong's Exhaustive Concordance of the Bible.* © 1890 James Strong, Madison, NJ p. 24 (Greek)

10.10 Strong, James. *Strong's Exhaustive Concordance of the Bible.* © 1890 James Strong, Madison, NJ p. 936

10.11 Strong, James. *The Strongest Strong's* © 2001 Zondervan, Grand Rapids, MI p. 1068

10.12 *New American Standard Bible*: 1995 update. 1995 (Monies, Weights, and Measures p. 345) The Lockman Foundation: Lahabra, CA

10.13 Strong, James. *Strong's Exhaustive Concordance of the Bible.* © 1890 James Strong, Madison, NJ p. 55 (Hebrew)

10.14 Strong, James. *Strong's Exhaustive Concordance of the Bible*. © 1890 James Strong, Madison, NJ p. 55 (Hebrew)

10.15 Strong, James. *Strong's Exhaustive Concordance of the Bible*. © 1890 James Strong, Madison, NJ p. 70 (Greek)

10.16 Strong, James. *Strong's Exhaustive Concordance of the Bible*. © 1890 James Strong, Madison, NJ p. 75 (Greek)

10.17 Strong, James. *Strong's Exhaustive Concordance of the Bible*. © 1890 James Strong, Madison, NJ p. 24 (Greek)

10.18 *Chambers Dictionary of Etymology*, Copyright © 1988 The H. W. Wilson Company, New York, NY p. 308

10.19 *New American Standard Bible*: 1995 update. 1995 (Proverbs 30:1 The Lockman Foundation: Lahabra, CA

10.20 *King James Bible*, Proverbs 30:1

10.21 *New American Standard Bible*: 1995 update. 1995 (Malachi 1:1) The Lockman Foundation: Lahabra, CA

10.22 *King James Bible*, Malachi 1:1

10.23 Strong, James. *Strong's Exhaustive Concordance of the Bible*. © 1890 James Strong, Madison, NJ p. 73 (Hebrew)

10.24 Strong, James. *Strong's Exhaustive Concordance of the Bible*. © 1890 James Strong, Madison, NJ p. 80 (Hebrew)

10.25 *New American Standard Bible*: 1995 update. 1995 (Luke 12:48) The Lockman Foundation: Lahabra, CA

10.26 Strong, James. *Strong's Exhaustive Concordance of the Bible*. © 1890 James Strong, Madison, NJ p. 32 (Greek)

10.27 Strong, James. *Strong's Exhaustive Concordance of the Bible*. © 1890 James Strong, Madison, NJ p. 32 (Greek)

10.28 *New American Standard Bible*: 1995 update. 1995 (Proverbs 14:23) The Lockman Foundation: Lahabra, CA

10.29 Strong, James. *Strong's Exhaustive Concordance of the Bible*. © 1890 James Strong, Madison, NJ p. 38 (Greek)

10.30 Strong, James. *Strong's Exhaustive Concordance of the Bible*. © 1890 James Strong, Madison, NJ p. 15 (Greek)

10.31 Strong, James. *Strong's Exhaustive Concordance of the Bible*. © 1890 James Strong, Madison, NJ p. 15 (Greek)

10.32 Strong, James. *Strong's Exhaustive Concordance of the Bible*. © 1890 James Strong, Madison, NJ p. 15 (Greek)

Bibliography

10.33 Strong, James. *Strong's Exhaustive Concordance of the Bible.* © 1890 James Strong, Madison, NJ p. 32 (Greek)
10.34 *King James Bible*, 2 Thessalonians 3:10-12
10.35 Strong, James. *Strong's Exhaustive Concordance of the Bible.* © 1890 James Strong, Madison, NJ p. 72 (Greek)
10.36 Strong, James. *Strong's Exhaustive Concordance of the Bible.* © 1890 James Strong, Madison, NJ p. 72 (Greek)
10.37 Strong, James. *Strong's Exhaustive Concordance of the Bible.* © 1890 James Strong, Madison, NJ p. 43 (Greek)
10.38 Strong, James. *Strong's Exhaustive Concordance of the Bible.* © 1890 James Strong, Madison, NJ p. 43 (Greek)
10.39 Strong, James. *Strong's Exhaustive Concordance of the Bible.* © 1890 James Strong, Madison, NJ p. 43 (Greek)
10.40 *King James Bible*, Matthew 25:27
10.41 Strong, James. *Strong's Exhaustive Concordance of the Bible.* © 1890 James Strong, Madison, NJ p. 72 (Greek)
10.42 Strong, James. *Strong's Exhaustive Concordance of the Bible.* © 1890 James Strong, Madison, NJ p. 72 (Greek)
10.43 Strong, James. *Strong's Exhaustive Concordance of the Bible.* © 1890 James Strong, Madison, NJ p. 57 (Greek)
10.44 Strong, James. *Strong's Exhaustive Concordance of the Bible.* © 1890 James Strong, Madison, NJ p. 14 (Greek)
10.45 Strong, James. *Strong's Exhaustive Concordance of the Bible.* © 1890 James Strong, Madison, NJ p. 43 (Greek)
10.46 *King James Bible*, Matthew 25:18
10.47 Strong, James. *Strong's Exhaustive Concordance of the Bible.* © 1890 James Strong, Madison, NJ p. 65 (Greek)
10.48 Strong, James. *Strong's Exhaustive Concordance of the Bible.* © 1890 James Strong, Madison, NJ p. 65 (Greek)
10.49 Strong, James. *Strong's Exhaustive Concordance of the Bible.* © 1890 James Strong, Madison, NJ p. 233
10.50 Strong, James. *Strong's Exhaustive Concordance of the Bible.* © 1890 James Strong, Madison, NJ p. 30 (Greek)
10.51 Strong, James. *Strong's Exhaustive Concordance of the Bible.* © 1890 James Strong, Madison, NJ p. 19 (Greek)

10.52 Strong, James. *Strong's Exhaustive Concordance of the Bible.* © 1890 James Strong, Madison, NJ p. 19 (Greek)

10.53 Vine, W. E. *Vine's Complete Expository Dictionary of Old and New Testament Words* ©1984, 1996 Thomas Nelson, Inc. Nashville, TN p. 637

10.54 Lockyer, Herbert. *Illustrated Dictionary of the Bible* ©1986 Thomas Nelson Publishers, Thomas Nelson, Inc. Nashville, TN p. 444

10.55 Strong, James. *Strong's Exhaustive Concordance of the Bible.* © 1890 James Strong, Madison, NJ p. 38 (Hebrew)

12.1 *King James Bible*, John 1:32-33

12.2 *King James Bible*, John 14:12

12.3 Strong, James. *Strong's Exhaustive Concordance of the Bible.* © 1890 James Strong, Madison, NJ p. 32 (Greek)

12.4 Strong, James. *Strong's Exhaustive Concordance of the Bible.* © 1890 James Strong, Madison, NJ p. 59 (Greek)

12.5 Strong, James. *Strong's Exhaustive Concordance of the Bible.* © 1890 James Strong, Madison, NJ p. 47 (Greek)

12.6 Strong, James. *Strong's Exhaustive Concordance of the Bible.* © 1890 James Strong, Madison, NJ p. 46 (Greek)

12.7 Strong, James. *Strong's Exhaustive Concordance of the Bible.* © 1890 James Strong, Madison, NJ p. 46 (Greek)

12.8 Strong, James. *Strong's Exhaustive Concordance of the Bible.* © 1890 James Strong, Madison, NJ p. 59 (Greek)

12.9 *New American Standard Bible*: 1995 update. 1995 (John 14:16) The Lockman Foundation: Lahabra, CA

12.10 *King James Bible*, John 14:16

12.11 Strong, James. *Strong's Exhaustive Concordance of the Bible.* © 1890 James Strong, Madison, NJ p. 33 (Greek)

12.12 Strong, James. *Strong's Exhaustive Concordance of the Bible.* © 1890 James Strong, Madison, NJ p. 10 (Greek)

12.13 Strong, James. *Strong's Exhaustive Concordance of the Bible.* © 1890 James Strong, Madison, NJ p. 55 (Greek)

12.14 Strong, James. *Strong's Exhaustive Concordance of the Bible.* © 1890 James Strong, Madison, NJ p. 42 (Greek)

Bibliography

12.15 Strong, James. *Strong's Exhaustive Concordance of the Bible.* © 1890 James Strong, Madison, NJ p. 42 (Greek)
12.16 Strong, James. *Strong's Exhaustive Concordance of the Bible.* © 1890 James Strong, Madison, NJ p. 39 (Greek)
12.17 Strong, James. *Strong's Exhaustive Concordance of the Bible.* © 1890 James Strong, Madison, NJ p. 41 (Greek)
12.18 Strong, James. *Strong's Exhaustive Concordance of the Bible.* © 1890 James Strong, Madison, NJ p. 19
12.19 *King James Bible*, 1 John 2:1
12.20 Strong, James. *Strong's Exhaustive Concordance of the Bible.* © 1890 James Strong, Madison, NJ p. 207
12.21 *King James Bible*, John 14:26
12.22 Strong, James. *Strong's Exhaustive Concordance of the Bible.* © 1890 James Strong, Madison, NJ p. 7 (Greek)
12.23 Strong, James. *Strong's Exhaustive Concordance of the Bible.* © 1890 James Strong, Madison, NJ p. 384
12.24 *King James Bible*, John 15:26
12.25 *King James Bible*, John 16:7
12.26 Strong, James. *Strong's Exhaustive Concordance of the Bible.* © 1890 James Strong, Madison, NJ p. 14 (Greek)
12.27 Strong, James. *Strong's Exhaustive Concordance of the Bible.* © 1890 James Strong, Madison, NJ p. 254
12.28 Strong, James. *Strong's Exhaustive Concordance of the Bible.* © 1890 James Strong, Madison, NJ p. 9 (Greek)
12.29 Strong, James. *Strong's Exhaustive Concordance of the Bible.* © 1890 James Strong, Madison, NJ p. 8 (Greek)
12.30 *New American Standard Bible*: 1995 update. 1995 (John 14:17-19) The Lockman Foundation: Lahabra, CA
12.31 *New American Standard Bible*: 1995 update. 1995 (John 14:20) The Lockman Foundation: Lahabra, CA
12.32 *New American Standard Bible*: 1995 update. 1995 (John 14:26) The Lockman Foundation: Lahabra, CA
12.33 Strong, James. *Strong's Exhaustive Concordance of the Bible.* © 1890 James Strong, Madison, NJ p. 968
12.34 Strong, James. *Strong's Exhaustive Concordance of the Bible.* © 1890 James Strong, Madison, NJ p. 488

12.35 Strong, James. *Strong's Exhaustive Concordance of the Bible.* © 1890 James Strong, Madison, NJ p. 56 (Greek)

12.36 *King James Bible*, Acts 1:4-9

12.37 Strong, James. *Strong's Exhaustive Concordance of the Bible.* © 1890 James Strong, Madison, NJ p. 488

12.38 Strong, James. *Strong's Exhaustive Concordance of the Bible.* © 1890 James Strong, Madison, NJ p. 802

12.39 Strong, James. *Strong's Exhaustive Concordance of the Bible.* © 1890 James Strong, Madison, NJ p. 30 (Greek)

12.40 Strong, James. *Strong's Exhaustive Concordance of the Bible.* © 1890 James Strong, Madison, NJ p. 29 (Greek)

12.41 Strong, James. *Strong's Exhaustive Concordance of the Bible.* © 1890 James Strong, Madison, NJ p. 26 (Greek)

12.42 Strong, James. *Strong's Exhaustive Concordance of the Bible.* © 1890 James Strong, Madison, NJ p. 25 (Greek)

13.1 Petrovsky, Erich Z. *Reincarnation—A Reasonable Inquiry.* ©2019 Quadrakoff Publications Group, LLC Wilmington, DE pp. 63-73

13.2 *King James Bible*, Genesis 5:24

13.3 *King James Bible*, 2 Kings 13:20-21

13.4 Strong, James. *Strong's Exhaustive Concordance of the Bible.* © 1890 James Strong, Madison, NJ p. 102 (Hebrew)

13.5 Strong, James. *Strong's Exhaustive Concordance of the Bible.* © 1890 James Strong, Madison, NJ p. 39 (Hebrew)

13.6 Strong, James. *Strong's Exhaustive Concordance of the Bible.* © 1890 James Strong, Madison, NJ p. 102 (Hebrew)

13.7 *New American Standard Bible*: 1995 update. 1995 (Deuteronomy 34:5-7) The Lockman Foundation: Lahabra, CA

13.8 Strong, James. *Strong's Exhaustive Concordance of the Bible.* © 1890 James Strong, Madison, NJ p. 155

13.9 *King James Bible*, Deuteronomy 34:8

13.10 *New American Standard Bible*: 1995 update. 1995 (Jude 1:9) The Lockman Foundation: Lahabra, CA

13.11 *King James Bible*, Jude 1:9

13.12 Strong, James. *Strong's Exhaustive Concordance of the Bible.* © 1890 James Strong, Madison, NJ p. 22 (Greek)

Bibliography

13.13 Strong, James. *Strong's Exhaustive Concordance of the Bible*. © 1890 James Strong, Madison, NJ p. 22 (Greek)
13.14 Strong, James. *Strong's Exhaustive Concordance of the Bible*. © 1890 James Strong, Madison, NJ p. 56 (Greek)
13.15 Strong, James. *Strong's Exhaustive Concordance of the Bible*. © 1890 James Strong, Madison, NJ p. 32 (Greek)
13.16 Strong, James. *Strong's Exhaustive Concordance of the Bible*. © 1890 James Strong, Madison, NJ p. 19 (Greek)
13.17 Strong, James. *Strong's Exhaustive Concordance of the Bible*. © 1890 James Strong, Madison, NJ p. 43 (Greek)
13.18 Strong, James. *Strong's Exhaustive Concordance of the Bible*. © 1890 James Strong, Madison, NJ p. 32 (Greek)
13.19 Strong, James. *Strong's Exhaustive Concordance of the Bible*. © 1890 James Strong, Madison, NJ p. 30 (Greek)
13.20 Strong, James. *Strong's Exhaustive Concordance of the Bible*. © 1890 James Strong, Madison, NJ p. 72 (Greek)
13.21 Strong, James. *Strong's Exhaustive Concordance of the Bible*. © 1890 James Strong, Madison, NJ p. 22 (Greek)

14.1 *New American Standard Bible*: 1995 update. 1995 (Ezekiel 37:1-10) The Lockman Foundation: Lahabra, CA
14.2 *New American Standard Bible*: 1995 update. 1995 (Ezekiel 29:1) The Lockman Foundation: Lahabra, CA
14.3 *New American Standard Bible*: 1995 update. 1995 (Ezekiel 30:1) The Lockman Foundation: Lahabra, CA
14.4 *New American Standard Bible*: 1995 update. 1995 (Ezekiel 31:1) The Lockman Foundation: Lahabra, CA
14.5 *New American Standard Bible*: 1995 update. 1995 (Ezekiel 32:1) The Lockman Foundation: Lahabra, CA
14.6 *New American Standard Bible*: 1995 update. 1995 (Ezekiel 33:1) The Lockman Foundation: Lahabra, CA
14.7 *New American Standard Bible*: 1995 update. 1995 (Ezekiel 34:1) The Lockman Foundation: Lahabra, CA
14.8 *New American Standard Bible*: 1995 update. 1995 (Ezekiel 35:1) The Lockman Foundation: Lahabra, CA

14.9 *New American Standard Bible*: 1995 update. 1995 (Ezekiel 36:1) The Lockman Foundation: Lahabra, CA
14.10 Strong, James. *Strong's Exhaustive Concordance of the Bible.* © 1890 James Strong, Madison, NJ p. 47 (Hebrew)
14.11 Strong, James. *Strong's Exhaustive Concordance of the Bible.* © 1890 James Strong, Madison, NJ p. 88 (Hebrew)
14.12 Strong, James. *Strong's Exhaustive Concordance of the Bible.* © 1890 James Strong, Madison, NJ p. 107 (Hebrew)
14.13 Strong, James. *Strong's Exhaustive Concordance of the Bible.* © 1890 James Strong, Madison, NJ p. 23 (Hebrew)
14.14 Strong, James. *Strong's Exhaustive Concordance of the Bible.* © 1890 James Strong, Madison, NJ p. 23 (Hebrew)
14.15 Strong, James. *Strong's Exhaustive Concordance of the Bible.* © 1890 James Strong, Madison, NJ p. 1095
14.16 Strong, James. *Strong's Exhaustive Concordance of the Bible.* © 1890 James Strong, Madison, NJ p. 89 (Hebrew)
14.17 Strong, James. *Strong's Exhaustive Concordance of the Bible.* © 1890 James Strong, Madison, NJ p. 1095
14.18 Strong, James. *Strong's Exhaustive Concordance of the Bible.* © 1890 James Strong, Madison, NJ p. 91 (Hebrew)
14.19 Strong, James. *Strong's Exhaustive Concordance of the Bible.* © 1890 James Strong, Madison, NJ p. 90 (Hebrew)
14.20 Strong, James. *Strong's Exhaustive Concordance of the Bible.* © 1890 James Strong, Madison, NJ p. 135
14.21 Strong, James. *Strong's Exhaustive Concordance of the Bible.* © 1890 James Strong, Madison, NJ p. 60 (Hebrew)
14.22 Strong, James. *Strong's Exhaustive Concordance of the Bible.* © 1890 James Strong, Madison, NJ p. 47 (Hebrew)
14.23 Strong, James. *Strong's Exhaustive Concordance of the Bible.* © 1890 James Strong, Madison, NJ p. 46 (Hebrew)
14.24 *King James Bible*, Job 21:23-24
14.25 Strong, James. *Strong's Exhaustive Concordance of the Bible.* © 1890 James Strong, Madison, NJ p. 135
14.26 Strong, James. *Strong's Exhaustive Concordance of the Bible.* © 1890 James Strong, Madison, NJ p. 120 (Hebrew)

Bibliography

14.27 Strong, James. *Strong's Exhaustive Concordance of the Bible.* © 1890 James Strong, Madison, NJ p. 64 (Hebrew)
14.28 Strong, James. *Strong's Exhaustive Concordance of the Bible.* © 1890 James Strong, Madison, NJ p. 980
14.29 Strong, James. *Strong's Exhaustive Concordance of the Bible.* © 1890 James Strong, Madison, NJ p. 39 (Hebrew)
14.30 Strong, James. *Strong's Exhaustive Concordance of the Bible.* © 1890 James Strong, Madison, NJ p. 47 (Hebrew)
14.31 Strong, James. *Strong's Exhaustive Concordance of the Bible.* © 1890 James Strong, Madison, NJ p. 113 (Hebrew)
14.32 Strong, James. *Strong's Exhaustive Concordance of the Bible.* © 1890 James Strong, Madison, NJ p. 14 (Hebrew)
14.33 Strong, James. *Strong's Exhaustive Concordance of the Bible.* © 1890 James Strong, Madison, NJ p. 98 (Hebrew)
14.34 Strong, James. *Strong's Exhaustive Concordance of the Bible.* © 1890 James Strong, Madison, NJ p. 75 (Hebrew)
14.35 Strong, James. *Strong's Exhaustive Concordance of the Bible.* © 1890 James Strong, Madison, NJ p. 107 (Hebrew)
14.36 Strong, James. *Strong's Exhaustive Concordance of the Bible.* © 1890 James Strong, Madison, NJ p. 107 (Hebrew)
14.37 Strong, James. *Strong's Exhaustive Concordance of the Bible.* © 1890 James Strong, Madison, NJ p. 143
14.38 Strong, James. *Strong's Exhaustive Concordance of the Bible.* © 1890 James Strong, Madison, NJ p. 79 (Hebrew)
14.39 Strong, James. *Strong's Exhaustive Concordance of the Bible.* © 1890 James Strong, Madison, NJ p. 16 (Hebrew)
14.40 Strong, James. *Strong's Exhaustive Concordance of the Bible.* © 1890 James Strong, Madison, NJ p. 107 (Hebrew)
14.41 Strong, James. *Strong's Exhaustive Concordance of the Bible.* © 1890 James Strong, Madison, NJ p. 107 (Hebrew)
14.42 *King James Bible*, Jeremiah 49:36
14.43 Strong, James. *Strong's Exhaustive Concordance of the Bible.* © 1890 James Strong, Madison, NJ p. 1173
14.44 *King James Bible*, Revelation 7:1
14.45 Strong, James. *Strong's Exhaustive Concordance of the Bible.* © 1890 James Strong, Madison, NJ p. 12 (Greek)

14.46 Strong, James. *Strong's Exhaustive Concordance of the Bible.* © 1890 James Strong, Madison, NJ p. 21 (Greek)
14.47 *King James Bible*, Matthew 24:31
14.48 Strong, James. *Strong's Exhaustive Concordance of the Bible.* © 1890 James Strong, Madison, NJ p. 1173
14.49 *King James Bible*, Ezekiel 37:10
14.50 Strong, James. *Strong's Exhaustive Concordance of the Bible.* © 1890 James Strong, Madison, NJ p. 39 (Hebrew)
14.51 Strong, James. *Strong's Exhaustive Concordance of the Bible.* © 1890 James Strong, Madison, NJ p. 39 (Hebrew)
14.52 Strong, James. *Strong's Exhaustive Concordance of the Bible.* © 1890 James Strong, Madison, NJ p. 60 (Hebrew)
14.53 Strong, James. *Strong's Exhaustive Concordance of the Bible.* © 1890 James Strong, Madison, NJ p. 25 (Hebrew)
14.54 *King James Bible*, Revelation 6:9-11
14.55 Strong, James. *Strong's Exhaustive Concordance of the Bible.* © 1890 James Strong, Madison, NJ p. 100 (Hebrew)

15.1 *New American Standard Bible*: 1995 update. 1995 (Ezekiel 37:11-14) The Lockman Foundation: Lahabra, CA
15.2 Strong, James. *Strong's Exhaustive Concordance of the Bible.* © 1890 James Strong, Madison, NJ p. 14 (Hebrew)
15.3 Strong, James. *Strong's Exhaustive Concordance of the Bible.* © 1890 James Strong, Madison, NJ p. 12 (Hebrew)
15.4 Strong, James. *Strong's Exhaustive Concordance of the Bible.* © 1890 James Strong, Madison, NJ p. 135
15.5 Strong, James. *Strong's Exhaustive Concordance of the Bible.* © 1890 James Strong, Madison, NJ p. 97 (Hebrew)
15.6 Strong, James. *Strong's Exhaustive Concordance of the Bible.* © 1890 James Strong, Madison, NJ p. 102 (Hebrew)
15.7 Strong, James. *Strong's Exhaustive Concordance of the Bible.* © 1890 James Strong, Madison, NJ p. 88 (Hebrew)
15.8 *King James Bible*, Ezekiel 37:12
15.9 Strong, James. *Strong's Exhaustive Concordance of the Bible.* © 1890 James Strong, Madison, NJ p. 988 (No Word Available Here)

Bibliography

15.10 Strong, James. *Strong's Exhaustive Concordance of the Bible.* © 1890 James Strong, Madison, NJ p. 95 (Hebrew)
15.11 *King James Bible*, Matthew 27:52-54
15.12 Strong, James. *Strong's Exhaustive Concordance of the Bible.* © 1890 James Strong, Madison, NJ p. 24 (Greek)
15.13 Strong, James. *Strong's Exhaustive Concordance of the Bible.* © 1890 James Strong, Madison, NJ p. 842
15.14 Strong, James. *Strong's Exhaustive Concordance of the Bible.* © 1890 James Strong, Madison, NJ p. 842
15.15 Strong, James. *Strong's Exhaustive Concordance of the Bible.* © 1890 James Strong, Madison, NJ p. 11 (Greek)
15.16 Strong, James. *Strong's Exhaustive Concordance of the Bible.* © 1890 James Strong, Madison, NJ p. 12 (Greek)
15.17 Strong, James. *Strong's Exhaustive Concordance of the Bible.* © 1890 James Strong, Madison, NJ p. 10 (Greek)
15.18 Strong, James. *Strong's Exhaustive Concordance of the Bible.* © 1890 James Strong, Madison, NJ p. 29 (Greek)
15.19 Strong, James. *Strong's Exhaustive Concordance of the Bible.* © 1890 James Strong, Madison, NJ p. 29 (Greek)
15.20 Strong, James. *Strong's Exhaustive Concordance of the Bible.* © 1890 James Strong, Madison, NJ p. 26 (Greek)
15.21 *King James Bible*, Philippians 3:10-12
15.22 Strong, James. *Strong's Exhaustive Concordance of the Bible.* © 1890 James Strong, Madison, NJ p. 842
15.23 Strong, James. *Strong's Exhaustive Concordance of the Bible.* © 1890 James Strong, Madison, NJ p. 842
15.24 *New American Standard Bible*: 1995 update. 1995 (Matthew 27:53) The Lockman Foundation: Lahabra, CA
15.25 Strong, James. *Strong's Exhaustive Concordance of the Bible.* © 1890 James Strong, Madison, NJ p. 17 (Greek)
15.26 Strong, James. *Strong's Exhaustive Concordance of the Bible.* © 1890 James Strong, Madison, NJ p. 25 (Greek)
15.27 Strong, James. *Strong's Exhaustive Concordance of the Bible.* © 1890 James Strong, Madison, NJ p. 20 (Comparative)
15.28 Strong, James. *Strong's Exhaustive Concordance of the Bible.* © 1890 James Strong, Madison, NJ p. 47 (Hebrew)

15.29 Strong, James. *Strong's Exhaustive Concordance of the Bible.* © 1890 James Strong, Madison, NJ p. 32 (Hebrew)
15.30 Strong, James. *Strong's Exhaustive Concordance of the Bible.* © 1890 James Strong, Madison, NJ p. 32 (Hebrew)
15.31 Strong, James. *Strong's Exhaustive Concordance of the Bible.* © 1890 James Strong, Madison, NJ p. 9 (Hebrew)
15.32 Strong, James. *Strong's Exhaustive Concordance of the Bible.* © 1890 James Strong, Madison, NJ p. 47 (Hebrew)
15.33 Strong, James. *Strong's Exhaustive Concordance of the Bible.* © 1890 James Strong, Madison, NJ p. 47 (Hebrew)
15.34 *King James Bible*, Exodus 3:14-15
15.35 Strong, James. *Strong's Exhaustive Concordance of the Bible.* © 1890 James Strong, Madison, NJ p. 57
15.36 Strong, James. *Strong's Exhaustive Concordance of the Bible.* © 1890 James Strong, Madison, NJ p. 53 (Hebrew)
15.37 Strong, James. *Strong's Exhaustive Concordance of the Bible.* © 1890 James Strong, Madison, NJ p. 121 (Hebrew)
15.38 Strong, James. *Strong's Exhaustive Concordance of the Bible.* © 1890 James Strong, Madison, NJ p. 12 (Hebrew)
15.39 *King James Bible*, 1 Timothy 6:15
15.40 Strong, James. *Strong's Exhaustive Concordance of the Bible.* © 1890 James Strong, Madison, NJ p. 55 (Hebrew)
15.41 Strong, James. *Strong's Exhaustive Concordance of the Bible.* © 1890 James Strong, Madison, NJ p. 20 (Hebrew)
15.42 Strong, James. *Strong's Exhaustive Concordance of the Bible.* © 1890 James Strong, Madison, NJ p. 28 (Hebrew)
15.43 Strong, James. *Strong's Exhaustive Concordance of the Bible.* © 1890 James Strong, Madison, NJ p. 46 (Hebrew)
15.44 Strong, James. *Strong's Exhaustive Concordance of the Bible.* © 1890 James Strong, Madison, NJ p. 126 (Hebrew)
15.45 Strong, James. *Strong's Exhaustive Concordance of the Bible.* © 1890 James Strong, Madison, NJ p. 7 (Hebrew)
15.46 *King James Bible*, Revelation 9:11
15.47 Strong, James. *Strong's Exhaustive Concordance of the Bible.* © 1890 James Strong, Madison, NJ p. 7 (Greek)

Bibliography

15.48 Strong, James. *Strong's Exhaustive Concordance of the Bible.* © 1890 James Strong, Madison, NJ p. 7 (Hebrew)
15.49 Strong, James. *Strong's Exhaustive Concordance of the Bible.* © 1890 James Strong, Madison, NJ p. 7 (Hebrew)
15.50 Strong, James. *Strong's Exhaustive Concordance of the Bible.* © 1890 James Strong, Madison, NJ p. 7 (Hebrew)
15.51 Strong, James. *Strong's Exhaustive Concordance of the Bible.* © 1890 James Strong, Madison, NJ p. 27 (Hebrew)
15.52 Strong, James. *Strong's Exhaustive Concordance of the Bible.* © 1890 James Strong, Madison, NJ p. 56 (Hebrew)
15.53 Strong, James. *Strong's Exhaustive Concordance of the Bible.* © 1890 James Strong, Madison, NJ p. 53 (Hebrew)
15.54 Strong, James. *Strong's Exhaustive Concordance of the Bible.* © 1890 James Strong, Madison, NJ p. 8 (Hebrew)
15.55 Strong, James. *Strong's Exhaustive Concordance of the Bible.* © 1890 James Strong, Madison, NJ p. 47 (Hebrew)
15.56 Strong, James. *Strong's Exhaustive Concordance of the Bible.* © 1890 James Strong, Madison, NJ p. 8 (Hebrew)
15.57 Strong, James. *Strong's Exhaustive Concordance of the Bible.* © 1890 James Strong, Madison, NJ p. 8 (Hebrew)
15.58 Strong, James. *Strong's Exhaustive Concordance of the Bible.* © 1890 James Strong, Madison, NJ p. 631 (Hebrew)
15.59 Strong, James. *Strong's Exhaustive Concordance of the Bible.* © 1890 James Strong, Madison, NJ p. 47 (Hebrew)
15.60 Strong, James. *Strong's Exhaustive Concordance of the Bible.* © 1890 James Strong, Madison, NJ p. 631

16.1 *King James Bible*, 1 Kings 17:17-24
16.2 *King James Bible*, 2 Kings 4:18-37
16.3 *King James Bible*, 2 Kings 13:20-21
16.4 *King James Bible*, Luke 7:11-17
16.5 *King James Bible*, Luke 8:49-56
16.6 *King James Bible*, John 11:1-44
16.7 *King James Bible*, Acts 9:36-42
16.8 *King James Bible*, Acts 20:12
16.9 *King James Bible*, Matthew 4:8-9

16.10 *King James Bible*, Matthew 4:10

16.11 Walker, J. Bartholomew. *Wisdom Essentials* ©2017 Quadrakoff Publications Group, LLC Wilmington DE p. 137

16.12 Strong, James. *Strong's Exhaustive Concordance of the Bible.* © 1890 James Strong, Madison, NJ p. 48 (Greek)

16.13 *New American Standard Bible*: 1995 update. 1995 (p. 886) The Lockman Foundation: Lahabra, CA

17.1 *New American Standard Bible*: 1995 update. 1995 (Matthew 13:10-12) The Lockman Foundation: Lahabra, CA

17.2 *King James Bible*, Matthew 13:13

17.3 Strong, James. *Strong's Exhaustive Concordance of the Bible.* © 1890 James Strong, Madison, NJ p. 49 (Greek)

17.4 *King James Bible*, Matthew 13:3-8

17.5 *King James Bible*, Matthew 13:18-23

17.6 Strong, James. *Strong's Exhaustive Concordance of the Bible.* © 1890 James Strong, Madison, NJ p. 45 (Greek)

17.7 Strong, James. *Strong's Exhaustive Concordance of the Bible.* © 1890 James Strong, Madison, NJ p. 66 (Greek)

17.8 Strong, James. *Strong's Exhaustive Concordance of the Bible.* © 1890 James Strong, Madison, NJ p. 65 (Greek)

17.9 Strong, James. *Strong's Exhaustive Concordance of the Bible.* © 1890 James Strong, Madison, NJ p. 9 (Greek)

17.10 Strong, James. *Strong's Exhaustive Concordance of the Bible.* © 1890 James Strong, Madison, NJ p. 39 (Greek)

17.11 Strong, James. *Strong's Exhaustive Concordance of the Bible.* © 1890 James Strong, Madison, NJ p. 47 (Greek)

17.12 Strong, James. *Strong's Exhaustive Concordance of the Bible.* © 1890 James Strong, Madison, NJ p. 9 (Greek)

17.13 Strong, James. *Strong's Exhaustive Concordance of the Bible.* © 1890 James Strong, Madison, NJ p. 13 (Greek)

17.14 Strong, James. *Strong's Exhaustive Concordance of the Bible.* © 1890 James Strong, Madison, NJ p. 58 (Greek)

17.15 Strong, James. *Strong's Exhaustive Concordance of the Bible.* © 1890 James Strong, Madison, NJ p. 68 (Greek)

17.16 *King James Bible*, John 13:27-29

Bibliography

17.17 Strong, James. *Strong's Exhaustive Concordance of the Bible*. © 1890 James Strong, Madison, NJ p. 20 (Greek)
17.18 Strong, James. *Strong's Exhaustive Concordance of the Bible*. © 1890 James Strong, Madison, NJ p. 172
17.19 Strong, James. *Strong's Exhaustive Concordance of the Bible*. © 1890 James Strong, Madison, NJ p. 172
17.20 Strong, James. *Strong's Exhaustive Concordance of the Bible*. © 1890 James Strong, Madison, NJ p. 71 (Greek)
17.21 Strong, James. *Strong's Exhaustive Concordance of the Bible*. © 1890 James Strong, Madison, NJ p. 72 (Greek)
17.22 *King James Bible*, 1 Timothy 6:10
17.23 *King James Bible*, Ecclesiastes 10:19
17.24 *New American Standard Bible*: 1995 update. 1995 (Proverbs 10:19) The Lockman Foundation: Lahabra, CA

18.1 *Chambers Dictionary of Etymology*. Copyright © 1988 The H. W. Wilson Company, New York, NY p. 366
18.2 Strong, James. *Strong's Exhaustive Concordance of the Bible*. © 1890 James Strong, Madison, NJ p. 122 (Hebrew)
18.3 Strong, James. *Strong's Exhaustive Concordance of the Bible*. © 1890 James Strong, Madison, NJ p. 330
18.4 Strong, James. *Strong's Exhaustive Concordance of the Bible*. © 1890 James Strong, Madison, NJ p. 14 (Hebrew)
18.5 Strong, James. *Strong's Exhaustive Concordance of the Bible*. © 1890 James Strong, Madison, NJ p. 14 (Hebrew)
18.6 Strong, James. *Strong's Exhaustive Concordance of the Bible*. © 1890 James Strong, Madison, NJ p. 14 (Hebrew)
18.7 *King James Bible*, Isaiah 30:21
18.8 *Interlinear Bible Hebrew Greek English, 1 Volume edition*. © 1976, 1977, 1978, 1979, 1980, 1981, 1984. Second Edition, © 1986 Jay P. Green, Sr., Hendrickson Publishers (Isaiah 30:21)
18.9 Strong, James. *Strong's Exhaustive Concordance of the Bible*. © 1890 James Strong, Madison, NJ p. 14 (Hebrew)
18.10 Strong, James. *Strong's Exhaustive Concordance of the Bible*. © 1890 James Strong, Madison, NJ p. 29 (Hebrew)

18.11 Strong, James. *Strong's Exhaustive Concordance of the Bible.* © 1890 James Strong, Madison, NJ p. 14 (Hebrew)
18.12 Strong, James. *Strong's Exhaustive Concordance of the Bible.* © 1890 James Strong, Madison, NJ p. 331
18.13 Strong, James. *Strong's Exhaustive Concordance of the Bible.* © 1890 James Strong, Madison, NJ p. 331
18.14 Strong, James. *Strong's Exhaustive Concordance of the Bible.* © 1890 James Strong, Madison, NJ p. 331
18.15 Strong, James. *Strong's Exhaustive Concordance of the Bible.* © 1890 James Strong, Madison, NJ p. 14 (Hebrew)
18.16 Strong, James. *Strong's Exhaustive Concordance of the Bible.* © 1890 James Strong, Madison, NJ p. 331
18.17 Strong, James. *Strong's Exhaustive Concordance of the Bible.* © 1890 James Strong, Madison, NJ p. 14 (Hebrew)
18.18 Strong, James. *Strong's Exhaustive Concordance of the Bible.* © 1890 James Strong, Madison, NJ p. 331
18.19 Strong, James. *Strong's Exhaustive Concordance of the Bible.* © 1890 James Strong, Madison, NJ p. 14 (Hebrew)
18.20 Strong, James. *Strong's Exhaustive Concordance of the Bible.* © 1890 James Strong, Madison, NJ p. 331
18.21 Strong, James. *Strong's Exhaustive Concordance of the Bible.* © 1890 James Strong, Madison, NJ p. 14 (Hebrew)
18.22 Strong, James. *Strong's Exhaustive Concordance of the Bible.* © 1890 James Strong, Madison, NJ p. 331
18.23 Strong, James. *Strong's Exhaustive Concordance of the Bible.* © 1890 James Strong, Madison, NJ p. 331
18.24 Strong, James. *Strong's Exhaustive Concordance of the Bible.* © 1890 James Strong, Madison, NJ p. 331
18.25 Strong, James. *Strong's Exhaustive Concordance of the Bible.* © 1890 James Strong, Madison, NJ p. 331
18.26 Strong, James. *Strong's Exhaustive Concordance of the Bible.* © 1890 James Strong, Madison, NJ p. 331
18.27 Strong, James. *Strong's Exhaustive Concordance of the Bible.* © 1890 James Strong, Madison, NJ p. 54 (Hebrew)
18.28 Strong, James. *Strong's Exhaustive Concordance of the Bible.* © 1890 James Strong, Madison, NJ p. 1090

Bibliography

18.29 Strong, James. *Strong's Exhaustive Concordance of the Bible.* © 1890 James Strong, Madison, NJ p. 19 (Hebrew)
18.30 Strong, James. *Strong's Exhaustive Concordance of the Bible.* © 1890 James Strong, Madison, NJ p. 1090
18.31 Strong, James. *Strong's Exhaustive Concordance of the Bible.* © 1890 James Strong, Madison, NJ p. 330
18.32 Strong, James. *Strong's Exhaustive Concordance of the Bible.* © 1890 James Strong, Madison, NJ p. 58 (Greek)
18.33 Strong, James. *Strong's Exhaustive Concordance of the Bible.* © 1890 James Strong, Madison, NJ p. 56 (Greek)
18.34 Strong, James. *Strong's Exhaustive Concordance of the Bible.* © 1890 James Strong, Madison, NJ p. 330
18.35 Strong, James. *Strong's Exhaustive Concordance of the Bible.* © 1890 James Strong, Madison, NJ p. 51 (Greek)
18.36 Strong, James. *Strong's Exhaustive Concordance of the Bible.* © 1890 James Strong, Madison, NJ p. 51 (Greek)
18.37 Strong, James. *Strong's Exhaustive Concordance of the Bible.* © 1890 James Strong, Madison, NJ p. 1090
18.38 Strong, James. *Strong's Exhaustive Concordance of the Bible.* © 1890 James Strong, Madison, NJ p. 330
18.39 Strong, James. *Strong's Exhaustive Concordance of the Bible.* © 1890 James Strong, Madison, NJ p. 27 (Greek)
18.40 Strong, James. *Strong's Exhaustive Concordance of the Bible.* © 1890 James Strong, Madison, NJ p. 330
18.41 *King James Bible*, Hebrews 10:23
18.42 Strong, James. *Strong's Exhaustive Concordance of the Bible.* © 1890 James Strong, Madison, NJ p. 330
18.43 Strong, James. *Strong's Exhaustive Concordance of the Bible.* © 1890 James Strong, Madison, NJ p. 58 (Greek)
18.44 Strong, James. *Strong's Exhaustive Concordance of the Bible.* © 1890 James Strong, Madison, NJ p. 330
18.45 Strong, James. *Strong's Exhaustive Concordance of the Bible.* © 1890 James Strong, Madison, NJ p. 331
18.46 Strong, James. *Strong's Exhaustive Concordance of the Bible.* © 1890 James Strong, Madison, NJ p. 331

18.47 Strong, James. *Strong's Exhaustive Concordance of the Bible.* © 1890 James Strong, Madison, NJ p. 331
18.48 Strong, James. *Strong's Exhaustive Concordance of the Bible.* © 1890 James Strong, Madison, NJ p. 331
18.49 Strong, James. *Strong's Exhaustive Concordance of the Bible.* © 1890 James Strong, Madison, NJ p. 331
18.50 Strong, James. *Strong's Exhaustive Concordance of the Bible.* © 1890 James Strong, Madison, NJ p. 14 (Greek)
18.51 Strong, James. *Strong's Exhaustive Concordance of the Bible.* © 1890 James Strong, Madison, NJ p. 1090
18.52 *King James Bible*, Romans 12:3
18.53 Strong, James. *Strong's Exhaustive Concordance of the Bible.* © 1890 James Strong, Madison, NJ p. 26 (Greek)
18.54 Strong, James. *Strong's Exhaustive Concordance of the Bible.* © 1890 James Strong, Madison, NJ p. 70 (Greek)
18.55 Strong, James. *Strong's Exhaustive Concordance of the Bible.* © 1890 James Strong, Madison, NJ p. 47 (Greek)
18.56 Strong, James. *Strong's Exhaustive Concordance of the Bible.* © 1890 James Strong, Madison, NJ p. 48 (Greek)
18.57 Strong, James. *Strong's Exhaustive Concordance of the Bible.* © 1890 James Strong, Madison, NJ p. 58 (Greek)
18.58 *King James Bible*, Romans 12:4-7
18.59 Strong, James. *Strong's Exhaustive Concordance of the Bible.* © 1890 James Strong, Madison, NJ p. 77 (Greek)
18.60 Strong, James. *Strong's Exhaustive Concordance of the Bible.* © 1890 James Strong, Madison, NJ p. 77 (Greek)
18.61 Strong, James. *Strong's Exhaustive Concordance of the Bible.* © 1890 James Strong, Madison, NJ p. 23 (Greek)
18.62 Strong, James. *Strong's Exhaustive Concordance of the Bible.* © 1890 James Strong, Madison, NJ p. 77 (Greek)
18.63 Strong, James. *Strong's Exhaustive Concordance of the Bible.* © 1890 James Strong, Madison, NJ p. 330
18.64 Strong, James. *Strong's Exhaustive Concordance of the Bible.* © 1890 James Strong, Madison, NJ p. 371
18.65 *King James Bible*, Romans 5:15-18

Bibliography

18.66 Strong, James. *Strong's Exhaustive Concordance of the Bible.* © 1890 James Strong, Madison, NJ p. 24 (Greek)

18.67 Strong, James. *Strong's Exhaustive Concordance of the Bible.* © 1890 James Strong, Madison, NJ p. 24 (Greek)

18.68 Strong, James. *Strong's Exhaustive Concordance of the Bible.* © 1890 James Strong, Madison, NJ p. 24 (Greek)

18.69 Strong, James. *Strong's Exhaustive Concordance of the Bible.* © 1890 James Strong, Madison, NJ p. 385

18.70 Strong, James. *Strong's Exhaustive Concordance of the Bible.* © 1890 James Strong, Madison, NJ p. 385

18.71 Strong, James. *Strong's Exhaustive Concordance of the Bible.* © 1890 James Strong, Madison, NJ p. 385

18.72 Strong, James. *Strong's Exhaustive Concordance of the Bible.* © 1890 James Strong, Madison, NJ p. 385 (Greek)

18.73 *Interlinear Bible Hebrew Greek English, 1 Volume edition.* © 1976, 1977, 1978, 1979, 1980, 1981, 1984. Second Edition, © 1986 Jay P. Green, Sr., Hendrickson Publishers (Romans 5:18)

18.74 Strong, James. *Strong's Exhaustive Concordance of the Bible.* © 1890 James Strong, Madison, NJ p. 24 (Greek)

18.75 Strong, James. *Strong's Exhaustive Concordance of the Bible.* © 1890 James Strong, Madison, NJ p. 385

18.76 Strong, James. *Strong's Exhaustive Concordance of the Bible.* © 1890 James Strong, Madison, NJ p. 24 (Greek)

18.77 Strong, James. *Strong's Exhaustive Concordance of the Bible.* © 1890 James Strong, Madison, NJ p. 385

18.78 Strong, James. *Strong's Exhaustive Concordance of the Bible.* © 1890 James Strong, Madison, NJ p. 60 (Greek)

18.79 Strong, James. *Strong's Exhaustive Concordance of the Bible.* © 1890 James Strong, Madison, NJ p. 11 (Greek)

18.80 *King James Bible*, Matthew 17:20

18.81 Strong, James. *Strong's Exhaustive Concordance of the Bible.* © 1890 James Strong, Madison, NJ p. 330

18.82 Strong, James. *Strong's Exhaustive Concordance of the Bible.* © 1890 James Strong, Madison, NJ p. 65 (Greek)

18.83 *Interlinear Bible Hebrew Greek English, 1 Volume edition.* © 1976, 1977, 1978, 1979, 1980, 1981, 1984. Second Edition, © 1986 Jay P. Green, Sr., Hendrickson Publishers (Matthew 17:20)

18.84 Strong, James. *Strong's Exhaustive Concordance of the Bible.* © 1890 James Strong, Madison, NJ p. 52 (Greek)

18.85 Strong, James. *Strong's Exhaustive Concordance of the Bible.* © 1890 James Strong, Madison, NJ p. 696

18.86 *King James Bible*, Hebrews 11:1-3

18.87 Strong, James. *Strong's Exhaustive Concordance of the Bible.* © 1890 James Strong, Madison, NJ p. 21 (Greek)

18.88 Strong, James. *Strong's Exhaustive Concordance of the Bible.* © 1890 James Strong, Madison, NJ p. 330

18.89 Strong, James. *Strong's Exhaustive Concordance of the Bible.* © 1890 James Strong, Madison, NJ p. 74 (Greek)

18.90 Strong, James. *Strong's Exhaustive Concordance of the Bible.* © 1890 James Strong, Madison, NJ p. 203 (Comparative)

18.91 Strong, James. *Strong's Exhaustive Concordance of the Bible.* © 1890 James Strong, Madison, NJ p. 60 (Greek)

18.92 *Interlinear Bible Hebrew Greek English, 1 Volume edition.* © 1976, 1977, 1978, 1979, 1980, 1981, 1984. Second Edition, © 1986 Jay P. Green, Sr., Hendrickson Publishers (Hebrews 11:1-3)

18.93 Strong, James. *Strong's Exhaustive Concordance of the Bible.* © 1890 James Strong, Madison, NJ p. 491

18.94 Strong, James. *Strong's Exhaustive Concordance of the Bible.* © 1890 James Strong, Madison, NJ p. 27 (Greek)

18.95 Strong, James. *Strong's Exhaustive Concordance of the Bible.* © 1890 James Strong, Madison, NJ p. 27 (Greek)

18.96 *Interlinear Bible Hebrew Greek English, 1 Volume edition.* © 1976, 1977, 1978, 1979, 1980, 1981, 1984. Second Edition, © 1986 Jay P. Green, Sr., Hendrickson Publishers (Hebrews 11:1-3)

18.97 Strong, James. *Strong's Exhaustive Concordance of the Bible.* © 1890 James Strong, Madison, NJ p. 53 (Greek)

19.98 Strong, James. *Strong's Exhaustive Concordance of the Bible.* © 1890 James Strong, Madison, NJ p. 19 (Greek)

18.99 Strong, James. *Strong's Exhaustive Concordance of the Bible.* © 1890 James Strong, Madison, NJ p. 60 (Greek)

Bibliography

18.100 Strong, James. *Strong's Exhaustive Concordance of the Bible.* © 1890 James Strong, Madison, NJ p. 734
18.101 Strong, James. *Strong's Exhaustive Concordance of the Bible.* © 1890 James Strong, Madison, NJ p. 839
18.102 Strong, James. *Strong's Exhaustive Concordance of the Bible.* © 1890 James Strong, Madison, NJ p. 203 (Comparative)
18.103 *Interlinear Bible Hebrew Greek English, 1 Volume edition.* © 1976, 1977, 1978, 1979, 1980, 1981, 1984. Second Edition, © 1986 Jay P. Green, Sr., Hendrickson Publishers (Hebrews 11:1-3)
18.104 Strong, James. *Strong's Exhaustive Concordance of the Bible.* © 1890 James Strong, Madison, NJ p. 46 (Greek)
18.105 Strong, James. *Strong's Exhaustive Concordance of the Bible.* © 1890 James Strong, Madison, NJ p. 300
18.106 Strong, James. *Strong's Exhaustive Concordance of the Bible.* © 1890 James Strong, Madison, NJ p. 300
18.107 Strong, James. *Strong's Exhaustive Concordance of the Bible.* © 1890 James Strong, Madison, NJ p. 330
18.108 Strong, James. *Strong's Exhaustive Concordance of the Bible.* © 1890 James Strong, Madison, NJ p. 50 (Greek)
18.109 Strong, James. *Strong's Exhaustive Concordance of the Bible.* © 1890 James Strong, Madison, NJ p. 9 (Greek)
18.110 Strong, James. *Strong's Exhaustive Concordance of the Bible.* © 1890 James Strong, Madison, NJ p. 8 (Greek)
18.111 Strong, James. *Strong's Exhaustive Concordance of the Bible.* © 1890 James Strong, Madison, NJ p. 40 (Greek)
18.112 Strong, James. *Strong's Exhaustive Concordance of the Bible.* © 1890 James Strong, Madison, NJ p. 39 (Greek)
18.113 Strong, James. *Strong's Exhaustive Concordance of the Bible.* © 1890 James Strong, Madison, NJ p. 16 (Greek)
18.114 https://www.etymonline.com/word/fresh (Retrieved 8/20/2020)
18.115 Strong, James. *Strong's Exhaustive Concordance of the Bible.* © 1890 James Strong, Madison, NJ p. 63 (Greek)
18.116 Strong, James. *Strong's Exhaustive Concordance of the Bible.* © 1890 James Strong, Madison, NJ p. 36 (Greek)

18.117 Strong, James. *Strong's Exhaustive Concordance of the Bible*. © 1890 James Strong, Madison, NJ p. 185 (Comparative)
18.118 Strong, James. *Strong's Exhaustive Concordance of the Bible*. © 1890 James Strong, Madison, NJ p. 899
18.119 Strong, James. *Strong's Exhaustive Concordance of the Bible*. © 1890 James Strong, Madison, NJ p. 20 (Greek)
18.120 Strong, James. *Strong's Exhaustive Concordance of the Bible*. © 1890 James Strong, Madison, NJ p. 53 (Greek)
18.121 Strong, James. *Strong's Exhaustive Concordance of the Bible*. © 1890 James Strong, Madison, NJ p. 75 (Greek)

Embedded Bibliography

[In Order of Occurrence]

O1 *King James Bible* Genesis 1:1
O2 *King James Bible* Genesis 2:7
O3 *King James Bible* Revelation 12:7-9 (KJV)
O4 Strong, James. *Strong's Exhaustive Concordance of the Bible*. © 1890 James Strong, Madison, NJ p. 7 (Greek)
O5 Strong, James. *Strong's Exhaustive Concordance of the Bible*. © 1890 James Strong, Madison, NJ p. 38 (Greek)
O6 *King James Bible* Luke 20:36
O7 Strong, James. *Strong's Exhaustive Concordance of the Bible*. © 1890 James Strong, Madison, NJ p. 58 (Greek)
O8 *King James Bible* Revelation 12:4
O9 Strong, James. *Strong's Exhaustive Concordance of the Bible*. © 1890 James Strong, Madison, NJ p. 26 (Greek)

Bibliography

O10 https://www.merriam-webster.com/dictionary/nether ret. 11-18

SH1 *The Holy Bible, KJV* Exodus 20:6, *kingjamesbibleonline.org*, retrieved 7 March 2016

SH2 Strong, James. *Strong's Exhaustive Concordance of the Bible.* © 1890 James Strong, Madison, NJ p. 41(Hebrew)

SH3 Strong, James. *Strong's Exhaustive Concordance of the Bible.* © 1890 James Strong, Madison, NJ p. 41(Hebrew)

SH4 Strong, James. *Strong's Exhaustive Concordance of the Bible.* © 1890 James Strong, Madison, NJ p. 41(Hebrew)

SH5 Strong, James. *Strong's Exhaustive Concordance of the Bible.* © 1890 James Strong, Madison, NJ p. 9(Hebrew)

SH6 Strong, James. *Strong's Exhaustive Concordance of the Bible.* © 1890 James Strong, Madison, NJ p. 118(Hebrew)

SH7 *The Holy Bible, KJV* John 14:15, *kingjamesbibleonline.org*, retrieved 7 March 2016

SH8 Strong, James. *Strong's Exhaustive Concordance of the Bible.* © 1890 James Strong, Madison, NJ p. 71(Greek)

NJAT1 *King James Bible* Romans 6:21-23

NJAT2 Strong, James. *Strong's Exhaustive Concordance of the Bible.* © 1890 James Strong, NJ p. 35 (Greek)

NJAT3 Strong, James. *Strong's Exhaustive Concordance of the Bible.* © 1890 James Strong, Madison, NJ p. 35 (Greek)

R62 *King James Bible* (2 Kings 2:8-9)

R63 *King James Bible* (2 Kings 2:10-11)

R64 *King James Bible* (2 Kings 2:12-14)

R65 *King James Bible* (1 Kings 17:22)

R66 *King James Bible* (1 Kings 17:14)

R67 *King James Bible* (2 Kings 1:10)

R68 *King James Bible* (1 Kings 17:1)

R69 Strong, James. *Strong's Exhaustive Concordance of the Bible* © 1890 James Strong, Madison, NJ p. 126 (Hebrew)

R70 Strong, James. *Strong's Exhaustive Concordance of the Bible* © 1890 James Strong, Madison, NJ p. 98 (Hebrew)
R71 Jewishencyclopedia.com
R72 Jewishencyclopedia.com
R73 Jewishencyclopedia.com
R74 *King James Bible* (1 Samuel 17:45)
R75 Strong, James. *Strong's Exhaustive Concordance of the Bible* © 1890 James Strong, Madison, NJ p. 493
R76 *King James Bible* (Genesis 1:26-28)
R77 Strong, James. *Strong's Exhaustive Concordance of the Bible* © 1890 James Strong, Madison, NJ p. 493
R78 Strong, James. *Strong's Exhaustive Concordance of the Bible* © 1890 James Strong, Madison, NJ p. 105 (Hebrew)

AT1 *Chambers Dictionary of Etymology*. Copyright © 1988 The H. W. Wilson Company, New York, NY p.648
AT2 *www.kingjamesbibleonline.org* (KJV) (Matt.5:5) retrieved June 2011
AT3 *www.kingjamesbibleonline.org* (KJV) (Ps. 25:9) retrieved June 2011
AT4 *www.kingjamesbibleonline.org* (KJV) (Ps. 147:6) retrieved June 2011
AT5 *www.kingjamesbibleonline.org* (KJV) (Ps. 76:9) retrieved June 2011
AT6 *www.kingjamesbibleonline.org* (KJV) (Mark 6:52) retrieved June 2011
AT7 *www.kingjamesbibleonline.org* (KJV) (Mark 8:17) retrieved June 2011
AT8 *www.kingjamesbibleonline.org* (KJV) (John 12:40) retrieved June 2011
AT9 *www.kingjamesbibleonline.org* (KJV) (Neh. 9:16) retrieved June 2011
AT10 *www.kingjamesbibleonline.org* (KJV) (Prov. 28:14) retrieved June 2011
AT11 *www.kingjamesbibleonline.org* (KJV) (Prov. 29:1) retrieved June 2011
AT12 Strong, James. *Strong's Exhaustive Concordance of the Bible.* © 1890 James Strong, Madison, NJ p. 63 (Greek)

ABOUT THE MEEKRAKER SERIES

What on earth is a MeekRaker? This word can be broken down into two parts "Meek" and "Raker." Capital letters were used in order to minimize any mispronunciations such as Mee-kraker; but the "etymology" is actually the fusion of these two words.

What is meek? And who in their right mind would ever want to be meek? Courage, strength, and bravery are characteristics that are generally considered desirable; but meek? No thanks. Unfortunately, the meaning of this word has been distorted over time to include things such as timidity, or shyness; weakness, or cowardice, but this is not; or rather should not be so.

Chambers states:

> "meek adj. Probably before 1200 meok gentle, humble, in Ancrene Riwle; later mec (probably about 1200, in the *The Ormlum*); borrowed from a Scandanavian source (Compare Old Icelandic mjukr soft pliant gentle...."[AT-1]

These origins seem to be adjectival in nature, and describe a condition of humility or softness. Thus a meek person, by these definitions would indicate a humble or soft person. The opposite of this would then be a person who is prideful or hard.

Humble vs. prideful is an easy one. Who would want to be prideful? The Bible is replete with warnings about pride; and it was pride that started all of the messes to begin with. Pride may make one "feel good" for a short period of time, but as previously referenced; the Bible is quite clear that on that path there lies destruction.

But what does the Bible actually have to say about being a meek person?

- It tells us that the meek shall (*not will or might*) inherit the earth.[AT-2]
- It further tells us that the meek will be guided in judgment will be taught His way.[AT-3]
- The meek will be lifted up by the Lord, and He will cast the wicked down to the ground.[AT-4]
- He will save all the meek of the earth.[AT-5]

And what about the Bible's statements regarding being "hard?"

- "For their heart was hardened."[AT-6] "Have ye your heart yet hardened?"[AT-7]
- "... their eyes and hardened their heart."[AT-8]
- "But they and our fathers dealt proudly, and hardened their necks, and hearkened not to thy commandments, and refused to obey, neither were mindful of thy wonders that thou didst among them; but hardened their necks, and in their rebellion..."[AT-9]
- "Happy is the man that feareth always: But he that hardeneth his heart shall fall into mischief."[AT-10]
- "He that being often reproved hardeneth his neck, shall suddenly be destroyed, and that without remedy."[AT-11]

The actual word in all of these citations which is translated as hard is:

About the MeekRaker Series

> "4456 poroo (a kind of stone); to *petrify*, i.e. (fig.) to *indurate* (*render stupid* or *callous*): - blind, harden.[AT-12]

With respect to hard, there is a clear Scriptural relationship between the same and disobedience; not being "mindful" of God performing wonders in one's life, rebellious, falling into "mischief," and being "destroyed," "without remedy."

In addition, by the very definition of the original word, one who is "hard" is also stupid callous and blind. (If a physical heart were actually to turn into stone, you are just dead; so surely that definition does not apply in this context or usage.)

Thus, meek or soft; that being the opposite of hard; would tend to be obedient, be mindful of God performing wonders, not rebellious, not falling into mischief, and not destroyed. Furthermore, one would not be "stupid," "callous" or "blind."

The use of the term meek as "soft," also implies *teachable*.

Hardhead: will not change mind. Hardhearted: will not change heart. Hard necked: junction between head and heart is hard, and will not permit mental change to be transmitted to change the heart.

If it is firmly established that the term "revelation" has the prerequisite of being *the* truth; when confronted with potential revelation; it has been the authors' experiences that hard persons; specifically those of the head, neck, and heart variety; will generally behave according to the "Three A's:"

> A_1 is *anger*. This is the first response. This anger is not so much because there is a remote chance that they may be wrong, but rather when it is somewhat clear that they *are* wrong. This would be best illustrated as a line on a graph rising from left to right; with the level of anger represented by the vertical axis, and time represented by the horizontal axis.
>
> A_2 is *argument*. This generally begins with emotionally (anger) driven arguments. As the arguments begin to fail, the level and usually the slope of A_1 will increase.

When all possible arguments, logical, relevant or otherwise have been proffered, the original arguments will then return. This would be best illustrated as a circle under the rising anger line referenced above. Often, what is just under the skin, (which is generally the reason for the pride and subsequent anger) will pop its "head" out; revealing things previously unknown about this individual.

A_3 is *absconding*. When all of the arguments and the repetition thereof have unquestionably failed, the hard person will generally abscond; or run away. This may be represented by actual physical separation, changing the subject or in some other manner. This could be perceived as the disappearance of the anger line, but is only subjective; as the true level of anger then becomes somewhat hidden.

Contrarily, the *meek* will weigh the value of any purported revelation; and then decide precisely what it is that merits their belief. Sincere questioning and even some arguments will be presented; but here not with the primary purpose of proving that they, the inquirer, is correct; but rather to understand precisely what it is that this revelation represents; knowing that if it in fact does represent revelation, then this will be to their benefit. A logical decision will then be made with respect to what constitutes the truth.

The primary basis for the actions of a "hard-head," is *emotional*. The primary basis for the actions of the meek; although perhaps including some emotional factors; (i.e. passion); is largely *intellectual*.

In a sense, the purpose of a rake is to separate the soft from the hard. The Bible refers to separating the wheat from the chaff, the silver from the dross; hence the origin of *"MeekRaker"*. Meek or hard is not so much determined by what one believes; but rather by the *process* involved in making these determinations.

??

"Do you think they will get it this time?

"They had it pretty well the last time, and the time before that and th—"

"Never mind; I probably should'nt've asked. I had said from the beginning he was no good and would come to no good. But He wouldn't let me do what I wanted to do with him, and look at the mess."

"Do you know how big of a mess it would have been if you gotten that last one in? Remember; I was the one who broke it up."

"Maybe so; but look at all of the garbage down there; and now he is talking about the moon—he wants to send em to just wait. He and the Russians always got along pretty good you know."

"You still don't understand. Did you really want to go have to back in time and redo all of that stuff, just for that last one? It wouldn't have worked anyway; he'd have just gotten back up. You better review that last part of their field manual again; he'd still be there, but things would be worse."

"I don't understand why He won't let us take care of it. They keep messing things up. They get it right for a while; and then everything goes backwards. Now there's a bunch of them that think He made earth just for its own sake. They think that the hosts are like a fungus or something, and they are hell bent (oops) on returning it to the way it was. They should've seen what it was like when the lid was still on. They'd have liked that. There was nothing. I guess they think He made a mistake by bringing it back, and then setting up the armies."

"Nah! They don't even think He exists. Just one big bang and everything else was just random. The fuse just lit itself."

"And now this craziness about the temperature. If it wasn't for the temperature dropping; and then rising; Long Island wouldn't even be there. Hey; remember that guy in Long Island when you—"

"Never mind about him; it's not important now."

"I wanted to ask you. How did you settle that argument about Moishe's bones?"

"I just told him that if he wanted it that bad, he'd have to force the info out of me."

"Ahh; that's right he must've suddenly remembered that he didn't do too well with that the first time; I ..."

"Like I said I shoul..."

"There you go again. It is also funny because you didn't even know. I did that job. I guess he didn't know that either."

"If we were ordered to assist in a mass suicide, how would you do it?"

"We aren't allowed to kill—you know that. He'd have to remove some of the chains and shackles, and just let the other side do it; just like before. And we aren't cleared even for that."

"I didn't say mass murder; I said mass suicide."

"You mean get to them to kill themselves?"

"That's what suicide usually means. Yeah; how would you go about that?"

"Easy—anarchy. All you have to do is remove all of the rules and regulations, and that will happen by itself."

"But you can't remove all of the rules and regulations; there are and will always be some rules and regs."

"I know. You don't do it that way. You don't get rid of rules and regs; you just get rid of the ultimate authority for right and wrong. Then right and wrong become subjective; and everyone lives by different rules. Once there is no clear authority; then whatever feels good for one person becomes right; even if it hurts another. And on top of that; all of those negative MA's, (the immaterial ones they don't know much about), that are being created will give the covering cherub fun time."

"Wow; I never thought you were that smart!"

"I'm not! I mean I am; but I didn't think that one up, I just been watching."

"Why does He allow it?"

"Well, you know He won't allow it forever. But right now he can't stop it. Free will—you know." And I gotta tell you. He's got some serious free will issues with these folks going out and telling everybody what the deal with the salvation is—claiming to speak for Him about it."

"What do you mean?"

"Well, you know He made salvation so easy, that even you could figure it out."

"Hey wait a minute!"

"Seriously. He made it so that all you have to do is accept it. Like picking up a free ticket."

"Tell me something I don't know."

"Well, from a salvation standpoint, you can keep on cussing and fussing, and smoking and drinking; and it doesn't matter. It may effect the return you get for your actions; but its got nothing to do with salvation."

"And?"

"And these preachers keep upping the cost. They keep telling people that you gotta behave they way they say; or the way Jesus said; or the way they say Jesus said; or salvation is gone. That may not hurt the folks who already have it, He knows they're OK. But by upping the price tag there are lots of folks who just think it's too expensive. It's those folks He's worried about. They've got to be told that it is absolutely free."

"You mean after all of that; some folks are being told that their salvation is works based—and they believe it?"

"Yup; and He aint happy about it."

"So because of all of these big mouths; either not knowing or outright lying about it; there are folks not being saved because even though it is free; they are being told they have to pay for it?"

"Yup."

"Let me guess. I bet some are being told you can lose it if you miss church."

"Yup".

"And do they ever forget to pass the collection plate around?"

"Nope."

"I see. What else?"

"Well, they're being told that if they don't let Jesus command them; then He won't save them."

"What! The whole reason they need it is because they messed up once. Now they're right back to where they started."

"I didn't say it made any sense. But they're afraid, and they believe it."

"And lots of others won't accept it because of all of the strings these guys are attaching to it."

"Wait... Have you ever listened to this guy? Looks like he is at it again. You can tell when he really gets into it; because his accents completely disappear. I say accents, because he will often move in and out of different accents; even including Yiddish on rare occasion."

"Velcome studentz."

"I am Dr. Petrovsky; und vee vill be studying vutt izz today known az zee Biology. Und vee vill be study here today, zee animal Biology only."

"Vee vill be concerned vith vutt izz zee *epistēmē* vith en eye to zee *těchnē*, vith zee *doxa* only ven needed."

"Ven vee think uv zee Biology; vutt izz it zat vee think uv? Zee study of zee life — no? Zat izz true, but only part uv it. Zee numbers come first; zen zee life."

"Zee Biology izz..."

["*Listen up; he usually loses (mostly) his accents—right... about... now...*"]

488

"...in the broad sense; simply the study of two. *Bi*-ology. The two comes first, and everything else follows.

"Many try to say the Greek *biŏs*, but this the poppycock. The Biology is the study of the two; and if they would stop with the lazy man's cognates, even this *biŏs* comes from the two or the "bi."

"And the logos, which means the written word, but is used as the "study of" now; so we have the study of the two.

"You are so used to the two, that you do not see it properly. You see the two as normal; and the one as unusual—sometimes. And other times you see the one as normal, and the two as unusual. Yet it cannot be both ways. I want you should think about this.

"We must also distinguish the *epistēmē* from the *tĕchnē*; and distinguish each and both from the *doxa*. The *doxa* is what is the believed to be so. But the *epistēmē* and the *tĕchnē* are what is the known to be so. This *doxa* is the possible or probable knowledge or truth; versus as certain as can reasonably be known truth. *Epistēmē* is considered the certain knowledge simply for its acquisition; while *tĕchnē* relates to *epistēmē*, or the certain knowledge; but related to the practical uses.

"The truth is that in many ways it is "the nothing" that is what is or was normal. It is not that *nothing* is normal; but "*the nothing*" that is or was the normal. Anything that is what it is supposed to be can be considered normal; so to say that nothing is normal would be a false statement. But "the nothing" was all that there was until there was "the something." In the truth, it was actually less than the nothing that was normal; if space is considered to be a type of void with potential, because then the space is actually "a something." Before the creation of nothingness of space, there was the true nothing as there was not even the space for any something thing to exist; and no material thing can there be without the space for it to exist. This of course applies only to the time/space continuum, which is where it is that we find the Biology.

"So first there was the less than nothing, and then there was the something, but this something is actually two "somethings;" as all "things" must have space in which to reside; and even most "things" are largely space. So both "things" and space for things replaced the true and original nothing. These two "somethings" is "the one" which replaced the original nothing and then this "something" or "the one" became the new normal. Taken the collectively; even though matter and space are technically two, they can be considered as one; as matter cannot exist without space. If there is to be the matter, then as stated, there must be the space for the matter to exist.

"It is the stipulation for the purpose of discussion here that:

$$V = \text{the Void,}$$
$$S = \text{the Space}$$
$$M = \text{the Matter}$$

"Originally all that existed was V. This is the true nothing, if the space is considered as the something; or less than the nothing if space is considered as nothing.

"Then the S and the M were brought into existence; (likely simultaneously; but possibly with S preceding the M); as the result of a will which is or was necessarily from outside of this yet to be, but soon to be, created realm.

"Here both S and the M are considered to be the separate entities; but in terms of the purpose can collectively be considered as the one. *(It is the stipulation that the time and the duration did not exist prior to the existence of S and M; and thus any discussion of duration prior to or during this may appear as the nonsensical. Depending on the distance we get with discussion of S and the M; this phenomenon referred to as time may or may not be addressed. Those who requested to take Part II of this course prior to the completion of Part I may now begin to see the wisdom of the refusal.)*

"So $U = S + M$; here with the U representing the Universe.

"From the *structural* standpoint the S and M are the different entities, and should be distinguished as the *two*. However from the *functional* standpoint; since it seems reasonable that the purpose of S is to contain M; and it is generally believed that M cannot exist without S; that the use of U as one *functional* entity would be the more appropriate.

"This "one" or here represented by U, represents the *material* realm; again remembering that since space is the prerequisite for the existence of matter, both can collectively be considered as one. But the subject under discussion is not Monology, but the Biology.

"This "one" or U in a sense can often seem to be like life or the Biology; but it is not the life or the Biology. There are types of matter such as inert gasses, which seem to never change. Some believe that as the matter of the probability; in their lifetime, everyone breathes in at least one molecule of these inert gasses that was breathed in by Jesus.

"There are also types of matter, such as radioactive elements, that seem to change constantly. All are in motion, but none are alive—the calculations of the "half-life" for the radioactive elements not without the standing.

"This "one;" (*structurally* S + M; *functionally* U); obeys rules from within and rules from the without. When obeying the known or unknown rules from within; then these rules are referred to as the natural law. When obeying rules from without; then this is referred to as the supernatural event or the miracle—which is how this *structurally* S + M; *functionally* began in the place of the first.

"Often labeling something as the supernatural event(s) or the miracle(s); is merely the result of the misunderstanding(s). When this error occurs; it is either because of the insufficient knowledge about the known natural laws; or lack of knowledge of additional natural law(s).

"What is the difference between the natural law events and the supernatural law events?

"The answer is the will and the balance. What does this mean?

"Depending upon the perspective; the material universe and all of its laws represent the balance or the imbalance. The material universe has balancing mechanisms incorporated into it which it cannot change. Although there is seeming evidence of constant imbalance, this is actually by design, and the material always changes according to established laws; always seeking balance.

"But the existence of the material realm in itself appears to be caused by the result without the cause—at least in the ultimate.

Since there can never be the cause without effect; nor the effect without cause; this is problematic in the two folds.

The one is because there simply cannot be a cause from within a realm, prior to the existence of that same realm. To try and determine the cause for the existence of the material realm from within that realm; would necessitate the existence of that same realm, prior to it being brought into existence.

"Obvious; wherever or whatever the *cause* of the *effect* known as the material realm; it could not have been from within the material realm. No matter how many times one wishes to believe that the "Big Bang" happened; one in the necessary always ends up with this same problem. This material perspective "*primum movens*," prime mover, or cause, must reside in a realm other than the realm whose very bringing into existence was the subsequent result of this cause—if the logic is present. But this is just the *where*.

The two is not the where, but the *what*. Since there can never be the cause without effect; nor the effect without cause; this would only guarantee the nothing, as what could cause the cause for the something. In the ultimate, there must be an effect with no cause for the something; and not from the alone material perspective with the beginning. The logic requires this "*primum movens*," prime mover, or cause to be the effect with no cause that caused the something rather than the nothing, but not the alone material.

"It could be argued that the research into the inanimate matter, and the material part of animate matter, the Biology; is like the Curly eating this artichoke. He keeps peeling off the leaves and getting the frustration, until there is nothing left inside. When all of the previously undividable atomic and sub atomic particles are finally divided; what is left may be is nothing material, but only that which is the immaterial. Remove all the organization; and what is left is that which was used to organize.

"In the one sense the laws of the material realm are like the deism. This "primum movens" established laws to govern the material realm. The material realm cannot change these laws; neither is there any means from within that realm to obey in a manner other than according to these laws.

"The *cause* of the material realm was not a matter of the balance, but of *will*; from outside this realm that did not yet exist. The *result* of this cause (the will), or the bringing into existence of the material realm; was the balance to the expression of this will; and from the material standpoint, these material laws that were established cannot be changed from within. Simply not knowing; or knowing but not understanding; the *purpose* for this cause from without—that the result in the effect of the bringing into existence of the material realm via will; in no way alters its logical necessity.

"There is no such thing as the will, (as opposite to the *effects* of the will), in the material realm. Material objects respond to the forces according to the laws. In order for the material realm to respond to forces in a manner different than necessitated by natural law, requires will. And the actuality created by the expression of this will, is not limited to the observed altered material response.

"Just as there are "automatic" balancing mechanisms "deistically" within the material realm; there are also balancing mechanisms when "theistic" methods are employed. This means that the results of the expression of the will to make (supernaturally) changes in the material realm, does just that. The changes are actualities that balance the expression of this will *exactly*. Simply not recognizing that there will be the "undesired consequences," or the precise nature of the same; will not preclude their occurrence.

"This idea of will with respect to the Biology is overridden only by the will of the Creator, or balance. The vestiges of the importance of will are seen in today's world. It is no longer the Creator who determines what is right, but men—or so they think. Nevertheless; many actions that are perfectly legal, can be a crime if there is violation of the will of one of the parties. Destroying a forming child is legal of the perfect; as long as this is the will of the mother. But if the mother refuses a medical treatment and the child dies; then this is the crime in some places. If the mother wishes to destroy the child and succeeds; this is her right and all is well. But if the mother wishes to carry the child to term, and fails because she refuses a medical procedure; this is the crime.

"When we evaluate U as the one; it is complete and useful. Many things can be said about the manifestations of this one; as the diamond; even unpolished; can be a beautiful sight. We can change the one in many different ways to suit out likings. But all of the one's manifestations generally have some use.

"But when we evaluate the Biology, the two, it is different situation. It is always the two that is required, and when the one not seen is missing, it is easily noticed that it is merely the one.

"In the Biology it is the two that is expected, and even if this is not admitted. When there is only the one when the two is expected, this then is noticed as the abnormal condition, as one of the expected two is missing. In the more specific; it is presumed that one of the two has left, and only the one is left. This is despite that it is the fact that it is the two that is the unusual and transitional state, as most of the known mass in the universe represents the only the one; even though it is in the structural sense it is two that make up this one—the space and the matter.

"But in this Biology, what is this additional one that is added to the one to make the two? In the above example, it was noted that when the two is expected, but there is only the one that remains; that this is noticed. This is because the nature of what *remains* never naturally exists, unless there was at one time the two. And this one that is left is highly unstable; and is subject to all sorts of forces which produce changes in it that cannot normally/naturally be either resisted or reversed.

"What is the nature of what it is that leaves the two or the Biology, and where does it come from and where does it "go" when it leaves?

"Much like the will; which as stated, has no existence on the material plane; this "other one" is/was also from this "other realm." This being the same realm in which resides the will; including the will that caused the bringing into existence of this material realm. This is because the main purpose of this union of the two in the Biology, is will. Thus the Biology is the result of the will; and its main purpose is the expression of the will.

"So the two in Biology; in fact actually results in the three. This is because there is the one of the material realm; and the other one from the other realm that is added to the material portion; and the third; which exists as the transient entity, existing only as long as this union exists. The material portion remains in its realm after the disunion, now subject to rapid change; and the immaterial portion leaves and returns to its realm. But this third; which is or was the union of the two; ceases to exist once the disunion occurs.

"Despite seeming the ubiquity, this third is the highly unusual; and both a stable and an unstable phenomenon. In fact the third is extremely scarce, even if it is only the *known* universe that is the reference. This third actually represents a kind of portal from that which existed before the material realm; this being the realm *from* which the will to cause the material realm emerged; and *to* this other realm from the material realm itself.

"This is easily seen because of the constant changes that occur in this third entity. From its conception to its demise, it is engaged in changes that do not and cannot occur outside of that which is contained in the category we call the Biology. In fact; many of these changes run contrary to the laws of the material realm—like the water running uphill. Water can easily run uphill; but there must be both a pump, and energy to run the pump, or the downhill it goes.

"The known complexity of the matter seen in the Biology, is not known to exist outside of the Biology. Neither does the changeability seen in the Biology exist outside the Biology. Radioactives break down into the less complex, although the more stable. The diffusion decreases the level of organizational structure; even as seen with the distribution of matter from this "Big Bang." Entropy is the rule of the material realm; but not with the Biology. From the beginning of the biologic form and for most if not all of its existence; increased complexity and increased organization is the norm. Smush the rock and it will remain the smushed. Smush the thumb with a hammer and it will repair itself, albeit within the limitations—but it will change, and not remain smushed. I want you should think about this too; as this is the proof of the mechanisms contrary to those in the material realm.

"There is then no reasonable of alternative, but to see these effects of these forces are inconsistent with those in this material realm. With regard to the Biology, these changes are the result of something from outside the material realm. Some are not the voluntary, but the "automatic" or the autonomic, as expression of the will from another source; in order to support the voluntary or the non-autonomic. The autonomic or involuntary is generally to maintain the material vessel; so it may remain capable of expression of its will.

"A Rabbi he once told me that Deuteronomy meant "second law." Auto-nomic then meaning: "self-law;" to provide autonomy. This vessel is comprised macroscopically of the M, and microscopically the S; as there is much subatomic space. But much or all of the M in this vessel, is subject to changes inconsistent with the similar material when there is not the Biology; and when it is not the Biology, there is not the two creating the third, but only the one.

"Will originally created the one; the functional U; the structural S and M. This same will then introduced that which together with this one produced the union of these two and resulted in the third—the Biology. And the purpose of this third; is to be the device (portal) for expression of the will on the material realm.

"If that which animates is ignored; then the third becomes the second; and the Biology then becomes the one, plus only the *results* of this ignored entity. The Biology then becomes merely the matter, these then being the functional U; the structural S and M. recognized two. Scientifically, this usually is how it is done.

"But there is no will on the material realm. (*Neither is there intellect nor emotion; but these are things to be in discussed in greater detail at another time.*) Therefore the will expressed on the material realm cannot originate on the material realm, but must be from this other realm. This represents the most fundamental use of the portal; or the most basic non-autonomic, or *voluntary* function. It could even be argument at another time, that the expression of will alone is only partially voluntary. I want you should also consider the possibility of any of the Biology forms to not express will; and if so; if this decision would then represent the expression of the will to not express will. Not responding to my mother in-law, it comes to my mind as prime example of this.

"We should talk about the circle. What circle you ask? The circle and the other shapes that many years ago were drawn on the ground. As though a circle chalked on the ground could possibly stop anything of the substance from exiting the circled area. It was not the circle that prevented this; but the *will* of the person drawing or causing the circle to be drawn. The drawing merely made clear the boundary, but the will is what actually prevented the exit.

"What else through the portal from the immaterial realm? Will and intellect? What about the power? What kind of power?

"Two separate systems are seen with this two that forms the third. One is the physical input and output of the material, to take care of the material needs of the vessel; and although there may be the immaterial included, this is largely material. This is the alimentary canal or digestive system. The other is the input and output of the immaterial, to take care of the immaterial needs or the content of the vessel; although there may be material included, this is largely immaterial. This is done primarily through the physical respiratory system.

"The Biology can be viewed two ways. Is it that there is the vessel that needs to be animated? Or is it that there is the animating entity that needs a vessel? Much as matter requires space; it is logical that the vessel needs to exist before it can be animated. But this as the alone does not answer the question of the purpose of the Biology.

"The "other" (enemy) straddles the two realms. At some point there was no place for him in the immaterial, so he was thrown down into the material. But he was not designed for existence in the material. This is why the Biology was created the way that it was; to battle and defeat this "other" utilizing both realms; as it is kind of between these realms that he is the stuck; in the neither or nether world.

"Both the formation of the vessel, and the animating of the vessel; are the supernatural events. Both disobey natural law, so there is admission of the existence of a directing intelligence and power. Given that much of the world is covered with entities that disobey natural law; the disobedience it is taken for granted. But all of the disobeying entities are included in the Biology. There is no known material entity that can itself disobey natural law outside of the Biology. This can almost be used as a test for the presence of the two resulting in the third.

"Physical laws are laws. They are not the mere tendencies. If the physical law is broken; then either the law is no law; or there must be an explanation of the misapplication of the law. And the reason; is that there is the two and not the one—even if the second is only obvious by the result. When the result violates a law that is a law; then this proves the presence of the additional entity. There is no other explanation possible; that includes the continued survival of both the scientific evidence and the scientific law.

"Earlier it was asked what else in addition to will is there that the Biology portal *can* bring into the material realm. Perhaps a better question is: "What is it that the Biology portal *will* bring into the material realm?" These are different, but related questions.

"The answer to the question of what *can* be brought into the material realm via the Biology portal, has the complex but uncomplicated answer. The answer is almost anything that resides in the other realm. This is an objective answer, as it can be answered independent of any characteristics of any subset of the Biology.

"The answer to the question regarding what *will* be brought, is also the complex as the other realm contains much; but here the answer is also quite *complicated*, because of the so many entanglements.

"In a sense; the immaterial is a practically unlimited source of locks or keys, depending on the perspective—a practically unlimited source of power—a practically unlimited source of intelligence and information. But keys are worthless, without the lock into which they fit, and the reverse. Power is unusable, without the appropriate load through which it can flow. And intelligence and knowledge are useless; without the suitable container to which they may be sent if it is the change in thee material is the desire.

"This is the purpose of the Biology. Just as when the material realm was necessarily brought into existence from the phenomenon from without, originating from a entity that was necessarily operating from without, (as this material realm did not yet exist); similarly, the Biology is the portal between the two realms to make changes to this realm from phenomena from without; but here operating (partially) from within the material realm itself. This is unlike the "other's" current status, as the Biology is designed for this. The Biology is in both realms, and the "other" is in neither.

"How does one get the lock to the key—the load to the power source—the container to the intelligence and knowledge? The answer is that one does not; as there would be no need to do this. It is not the *location* of the lock, load, or container that is the issue; and it would be the foolish to suggest otherwise. These keys, powers, and intelligence and knowledge reside in a realm with no distances. They are either omnipresent; or they simply do not exist.

"The issue regarding these suitable locks, loads, and containers; is not their locations; but their *existence*. More often than not, a suitable device for the reception of these immaterial tools occurs "by accident;" and the reception is judged solely the knowledge of the results—the unexpected or serendipitous miracle.

"The actual cause, or even any cause-effect relationship remains unknown; rendering repeatability difficult or impossible. The norm should be consistency and not "by accident." But the norm, is that the suitable lock or key is the usual brought into existence by "accident," and not knowingly or consistently. It has been said: 'Man is designed for existence in two realms; but generally only has experience in one.'"

"Why is this? The answer is because there is the "other." This "other" opposes what is; by substituting what is not. In a sense, it is his objective to destroy all of the keys or locks, loads, and containers; if possible. If not; then to render them unusable for what is; by filling them with what is not. Once they are filled with the what is *not*; then the what *is* cannot enter. The "other" does not necessarily abhor a vacuum, as this presents the opportunity.

"Instead of it being the vacuum that the "other" abhors, it is that which in the ways of the many is both the antithesis and the very same thing that he abhors—the filling of something with what is; as he then must first remove what is, and replace it with what is not. This can be the falsehood, or the misplacement.

"If it is the falsehood, then this is the what is not. But if it is the misplacement of what is, this is the idea of the dirt, or as we say the schmutz. These are not what the plant life grows in. That is the soil or earth. But rather these are all things which are where they do not belong. These are contaminants. The aphar or that which God formed the Adam, was not the soil, but the schmutz.

"In the natural world, this schmutz is in fact seeking equilibrium, according to natural law. This is the result of the diffusion; one of the laws which the Biology sometimes obeys, and sometimes disobeys. It is the movement of matter, from areas where there is the higher concentration to the area of the lower. When a certain threshold is reached where something is considered "dirty," then certain acts are undertaken; and the *result* of this process is attempted to be reversed.

"How is it reversed? The answer is by the very same process. Something that is considered relatively devoid of the schmutz, is utilized to remove the schmutz. This can be relatively schmutzless water, cloth, or anything else. When equilibrium is reached; meaning an equal amount of schmutz remains on the dirty item and what was introduced on to the cleaning implement; then the cleaning implement is discarded and a new one is used.

"But there is no way to get 100% of the schmutz form the dirty item removed, and even if this happened, this is only the temporary. Each time the equilibrium changes; but neither can be completely schmutzless. There can be less and less schmutz on each, but to make the dirty item truly "pure," would require the last molecule or atom of the schmutz to be transferred to the cleaning implement, without any reverse transfer; as the use of water or a towel which is relatively dirtier than the object to be cleaned, will only make the dirty object even dirtier.

"The only logical way to do this would require a cleaning implement that has the negative schmutz; which is something that although would work quite well, this does not currently exist in the natural; at least in this sense. Vacuum cleaner? Perhaps; but only up to the point certain.

"Here is where we find the catch of the twenty two. Why is there schmutz? Because there is schmutz. But first it must be understood that the schmutz as the contaminant can be the relative or be the absolute.

"With the absolute schmutz, this is of course absolute. One does not generally want to purchase flour with any sugar or salt mixed with the flour. To have this situation would be the contaminated flour. But this could be also the relative schmutz if the certain level of sugar or salt in the flour was acceptable.

"This is the same with the sanitation and the sterile. The sanitation allows some level of the live microorganism presence, but the sterile allows none.

"But this contamination of the flour is exactly what one does when making the cake from the mix. In the pure flour, this would be the absolute schmutz. But in the cake mix, these would not be absolute schmutz, but could be the relative schmutz, say if too sweet or too salty.

"The flour should not contain the sucrose or the NaCl. But the cake mix must contain flour, sugar, and usually some salt. Sugar or salt mixed in with the flour is the schmutz when not desired; but not only not schmutz, but necessary when the cake mix is desired.

"Lemon flavoring in the cake batter is the schmutz; unless one wanted a lemon flavored cake; in which case chocolate would be the schmutz; unless one wanted chocolate lemon cake.

"But even with a cake that contained poison, the poison would not be considered as the schmutz or contaminant, but the necessity; if it was the poison cake that was desired.

"The schmutz or contaminant with respect to the *immaterial* is something that must always be a contaminant as it does not the actual exist; but is only believed to exist. Once the "other" produced the schmutz in the immaterial, it was sent to the "no realm." The justification of man by salvation is: "just as though there was no schmutz."

"This can be like a false premise in a scientific experiment that is believed to be true. The premises affect outcomes; and the false premise that is believed to be true; will result either in the negative result or the false conclusion; and can often be quite dangerous. This is because although the scientist believes he knows what it is he is doing, and bases the level of caution on this; he in fact does not. Any unwanted accident will determine what is and what is not; and not merely what is believed to be or not be.

"As stated; contaminants in this *immaterial* sense are always contaminants not the so much because they do not exist; but because are *believed* to exist. Therefore; whenever the immaterial contaminant is introduced; either in the positive or negative; the result must always be the contamination.

"Does this mean that the contamination cannot ever result in the good? No; the explosion that occurred in the *material* laboratory because of the unknown contamination, may ultimately benefit mankind greatly. But this requires recognition of the error, and the abandonment of the original intent of making the better chicken soup—at least via that precise method.

"And the immaterial contamination of the religious leaders at the time of Jesus was (some may still say will be), necessary for Calvary.

"What is; can only come from what is. What is not; cannot come from that which is; as that which is, does not contain that which is not. And "that which is not," is impotent to do anything, unless "that which is not," contains some degree of the relative contamination (relative to that which is not) of that which is. No action is possible, if attempting to exclusively utilize that which is not.

"This is the mechanism of the "a truth" that is dangerous to the hosts.

"In the chemical reaction, it is the limiting reagent that determines the maximum amount of the result. In the Italian kitchen; it is the same rule. An infinite amount of the dough and sauce; will be the limited result by the lesser amount of cheese available to make the pizza. The same is true with the halupki.

"The requirement of the existence of something that is the contaminant alone, results in an output of absolute zero. This is different than the thermal "absolute zero," but similar. In order reduce the temperature of something to absolute zero; it would be necessary to find something colder than absolute zero; which by definition does not and cannot exist.

"In the certain sense this is like a form of the Biology, as the two are required. If "that which is not," becomes completely "contaminated" with that which is; there then becomes no difference between that which *now* is; (the same formerly being "that which was not"); and that which is and always was. Here; that which now is; cannot act in any manner based upon that which is not, because of the now state of "that which is;" as there no longer remains any that which is not, within. Thus here; there can be nothing but actions based upon that which is.

"As previously stated; purity or no schmutz in "that which is not," (to "that which is not," "that which is" here represents the schmutz), results in impotence; as there then is nothing existing with which to act. Therefore; the only way that "that which is not" is capable of utilizing that which is not; is when there is the two—some mixture of that which is, and that which not. But of course this requires the trickery.

"If the "locks, loads, and containers" can be built for that which is; then that which is can find its way to them. This is the desired situation for all of those who are concerned with what is. However; this represents a disaster for those concerned with what is not. This is because these represent the portals by which that which exists in the one (the immaterial) realm, to be transferred into this (the material) realm.

"This "other" consists of that which is not; and desperately desires the manifestation of that which is not.

"It is not the manifestation of that which is not, because it is not *yet* in this realm from the other realm that he desires; this being exactly what he does *not* want. This is because whatever is in the other realm, is that which *is*; even if not yet manifested in this realm.

"It is the manifestation of the "that which is not" contained in *either* realm which he desires. How can this succeed? Barring the existence of a third realm; which is precluded by the binary nature of the two realms; (material and not material); the answer is that it cannot succeed.

"The "other's" theory is likely that if the manifestation of "what is" can be forced to encounter "what is not;" then the cancelling out; and "the nothing" will be the result. Much like the theories of the matter and the anti-matter cancelling each other; this is what the "other" seems to believe.

"It is unclear as to how this could be the scientifically valid; for several reasons:

1. Result: There is no certainty that the result of the encounter of that which is, with that which is not; even if there were a way to bring into existence something with no existence; would result in the nothing.
2. Destiny: Given the scientific conservation laws; it is likely that even if the result in the material realm was a decrease in matter; then this would have to be balanced by a corresponding increase in something in the other realm, representing an imbalance because of original will; and thus a remaining potential for re-manifestation.
3. Space: Reducing all of the M; even to nothing; would not necessarily result in any change in the S. Reducing the M in the $U = S + M$ to zero, would likely then simply result in a universe without any matter. It would then be that $U = S$; but there would still remain a U, albeit void of the matter. And although the "other" may like a vacuum; "nature" generally does not.
4. Time: Although beyond the scope of this course, there is also the issue of time.

"One might ask by what mechanism the "other" expects this to happen? The key to this has its foundation in the misunderstanding or the denial of a key principle—that the creation can never be greater than its creator. This applies to both will, in terms of hierarchy; power, in terms of magnitude; and the supremacy of the Creator's laws. These laws *are* supreme; but there are two realms are involved. The miracle by definition is impossible without involving the "other" realm; and prove both its existence, and the capability of access to it.

"This error likely lies in confusion between the authority and the power. The expert in the martial arts who uses just enough to stop the attacker, because his oaths forbid killing unless it is absolutely necessary; can by the error assumed to be incapable of the fatal blow by the attacker. But this was in the actual because he *chose* not to use it, as it was not authorized by the circumstances.

"This is in a certain sense the mercy; as the attacker did in fact try his best to kill the victim; but because of the imbalance of skills, the death of the attacker was not necessary; even though certainly deserved. But this act of the mercy—not the taking of the eye for the eye, or the tooth for the tooth, is instead erroneously perceived as the weakness in the mental or the physical.

"This "other" would kill the Creator if he could; but he cannot. The creation can never be greater than the creator. [Note: There is not the epistémē of the origin of the "other" in the current.]

"This is why the "other's" most common name is translated as "adversary," and not as "enemy;" as this has the God as the reference. The "other's" perception of why he is not immediately killed by God, is the same as the attacker being spared his life. This misperception emboldens him, and allows him to deceive even himself.

"He then projects this or his perceived "power superiority" on to those creations (the Biology) who; whether he hates this fact or not; he knows are above him in the rank. He therefore believes that that which is not and can never be; can somehow be.

"This original source (the "other") of the contamination, results in all the contamination that exists elsewhere; as there is nowhere else from which it could come. It is sound advice to the crook, to not come up with a scheme for committing a crime; but rather to use some scheme invented by another. This is because it is impossible for any "creator" to "create" without leaving substantial evidence of the nature of the creator in the scheme's design. So it is much better to commit a crime using a scheme invented by another; so that law enforcement will build a profile of the designer of the scheme and look for him, instead of the perpetrator. But with only the one possible source, this is not possible.

"That which created what exists, created that which exists. He did not create that which does not exist. If both realms are considered the true universe; with time being a factor, as to which of the two realms whatever it is that exists, exists; then nothing can exists unless it exists in at least one; (and likely only one at any given point in time); of these two realms. The transferring of that which exists in one realm to the other realm, is a transfer which; when viewed from the material perspective; may appear as the creation; but it is in fact not the creation but only the transfer. There can be the creation only with the transfer.

"This "other" opposes all that exists; because he opposes the Creator. The human Biology is that which is designed to oppose this "other" in those areas which they are designed to oppose him; and not in those areas where they are not. They are designed to utilize that which is, and not utilize that which is not. As the portals; the human Biology can bring into the material realm that which is in the other realm; but cannot bring in that which is not.

"The source of all contamination; opposes the Biology utilizing what exists to oppose this same source; and will contaminate the Biology with what does not exist, to try and "stop them from stopping him." But he must always be careful to allow some of that which is (exists) into the mix; because without that component, no action is possible. Many of the called as such "news" networks and papers use this same technique.

"If it can be established that if the A then the B; and if the B then the C; (A→B→C); then it is foolish to consider A, without taking into account both B and C; as A then is only a portion of what exists or will exist; assuming this relationship is the validity. This can be analyzed in different ways:

"This relationship does not take into account the *cause* for A. If A→B→C; then if and when the A exists; then the B and the C must also exist. There is nothing taken into account with regard to the *cause* of the existence of the A; but only what also must the co-exist if A exists. If A exists, then a cause for the existence of A must be; unless A is and always was. Therefore; the existence of A as the event when the prior condition was not A; must be the result of some other cause outside of the ABC relationship as expressed.

"The analysis of the A→B→C relationship may or may not take the time into account. "A" may represent a portion of something which *simultaneously* includes the A, B and C; or the B and the C may be the unavoidable *consequence* of the bringing into existence of the A.

"If A, B, and C merely represent the certainties which are only logically derived from the known existence of A, without empirical evidence of B and C; then it is quite possible that it is ABC which represents that which came into existence simultaneously; but with only the A being empirically noted.

"Here it was the in fact the ABC complex which was brought into existence; with *one* cause; (here unknown); and one effect; (ABC). This not is to say; that the bringing into existence of the ABC will not then have effects which could exhaust all the other the known alphabets. But rather that A, B, and C each individually represent different aspects of this ABC complex; having only *one* simultaneous cause.

"If however there is the time/duration (however short) involved with regard to the existence of the B and the C; then it can reasonably be stated that although the cause for A is unknown; the cause for B was in fact A; and the cause for C was in fact B. Once A was; then B and then C necessarily happened the some unspecified time afterward.

"It is important to note that there is a difference; and that there is also no difference. It cannot be otherwise; than if a cause brings the ABC into existence in the *material* realm; then the ABC is brought into existence in the *material* realm.

"Neither can it be the argued that if the A→B→C relationship is so; then if one brings A into existence into the material realm; then B and C are also brought into existence in the material realm in the ultimate. The *only* difference is that of primary and unavoidable secondary/tertiary causes, if the *sequential*; as the opposed to one *primary* cause, with the no sequence; at least with respect to the confines of this A→B→C relationship.

"But there is no time on the immaterial realm. So then what is the difference between the "all at the once" or "sequential" from the *immaterial* perspective? The answer is that there may be little or no difference; or there may be that which cannot be the reconciled.

"There is the homunculus. This is to be considered outside of the homunculus in the neurology. Many years ago this homunculus was considered by some as representing a little man that was contained in a fertilized human ovum. This is of course is the nonsense; as much is known about embryology, and this simply is not so. Or is it?

"From the *material* perspective this is in fact the nonsense. Whatever threshold one utilizes to determine when the embryo or fetus represents a fully formed but tiny human being; there exists no rational argument that this is immediately contained in a fertilized egg; as the processes from fertilized egg to this fetus state is well known and documented. These are processes that are ongoing, and take the time.

"However from the *immaterial* viewpoint; engaging in activities in the *material* which result in the fertilized ovum, will result in the bringing into existence of the A in an A→B→C sequence. Unless some action is undertaken to alter this A→B→C sequence in the material; then a fully formed but tiny human being *will be* the result in the material; but may *already* exist in the immaterial as the *potential*. The only difference is that of the time; and there being no time on that realm; it is essentially the done. The material result or the C here *will be* a fully formed human being; and is as certain as the taxes if nothing else happens; but with the occurrence of "A," likely *already is* in the immaterial as the potential.

"But there being no time on that *immaterial* realm; should anything in the material *future* interfere with this process in the *material*; the original A→B→C *total* material potential is altered, and *will* also then no longer exist in that realm with no time. This is the first of the two doctors, as how can this potential not exist, exist; and then not exist in the timeless realm? And the second, would be the existence and non-existence of the same potential in the simultaneous.

"Here we initially have A→B→C in the immaterial realm, as the result of "A" in the material realm. But *then* something happens in the material realm to negate the "A;" and there is *then* a change in the immaterial realm which has no time; and thus no duration or any of the sequence possible. This is the similar but different as the $1{,}000{,}000 \div x$ is a much greater amount than $1 \div x$; no matter what the value of "x," unless "x" is zero; and then these are the infinity of precisely the same "magnitude."

"The Biology must understand this general concept; at least as well as or better than the "other." The ultimate material realm effects of ABC or A→B→C are essentially the same. If it is ABC that is desired; then ABC is what is brought into this realm. The danger lies in desiring A to be brought into this realm; and the concomitant ignorance of any A→B→C relationship.

"That which is, is: F = MA.

"That which is not, is: F ≠ MA.

"If this relationship of A→B→C is the result of F = MA; but the decision to bring the A of the A→B→C into existence is made believing that F ≠ MA; then the bringing into existence of both B and C will necessarily be the surprise.

"Here the *something* that the "other" uses, is the A of the A→B→C. Here the *nothing* that this "other" uses is the F ≠ MA. [It being noted that this something called A represents the A of the A→B→C; while the A in F = MA or F ≠ MA refers to acceleration. (In order to avoid confusion; transistors in a schematic are generally designated by the Q; because T was already in use to designate the transformers, as they were invented first.)]

"This "other" wants a certain B and or C to be brought into this realm; but he cannot do it. The Biology is designed to hear from the Creator; but can also hear the "other," and can often be confused. If this "other" tells the Biology to bring this particular B and C into existence; the Biology may find B and C repulsive; and may very well refuse.

"The likelihood of this refusal is the function of the inverse of how far that Biology has moved away from being the likeness the Creator—the farther away from this likeness; then the less likely to refuse.

"There is also the function of how badly the "other" wants these B and C; which is in direct proportion to how much the Creator does not.

"And again, with the regard to the distance from the Creator any given Biology has transgressed; there in the general remains some dissonance to B and C because of whatever is left. The magnitude of the dissonance will likewise be inversely proportional to the magnitude of the deviation from the will of the Creator; (or consistent with the will of the "other"); that this particular B and C represent.

"So the "other" then must get the Biology to bring the A into existence, because the "other" desires the B and C; and knows A→B→C, because F = MA. But if the Biology knows of this; then the Biology may again refuse.

"So the "other" has to choose an A which will give him the B and C *he* wants, using an A desired by the Biology. But he must either keep the Biology ignorant of the F = MA; which is impossible when the Biology already knows this; or convince the Biology that in this instance; F ≠ MA; so either way there therefore will *not* be the resultant B and C which would displease the Biology. This F ≠ MA is also that which does not exist.

"Or the "other" will use some level of truth, "a truth," to simply lie to the Biology about the A that will produce the B and C he wants.

"The Biology is designed with the *physical* and *emotional* homeostasis. The *emotional* homeostasis of the Biology is utilized by the "other." When "that which is not" is factored in to this process as thought it is "that which is;" then the balancing by the emotional homeostasis, results in the producing of something which is the contaminated.

"This result or something, is then inconsistent with the antithesis of that which is not; which of course is "that which is." The trick here is the *false* information; but with a *healthy* emotional balancing mechanism.

"This has the same effect as the delusion; but the different cause. It must be asked for what reason someone continues to believe the something that is overwhelmingly contradicted by the overwhelming evidence?

"The only reasonable answer is the emotional. The emotional balance in the delusion is a higher priority than the factual accuracy. The intellect is sacrificed for the emotional. Rather than changing the emotion to balance the facts; the facts are "changed" to balance the emotion.

"A student came up to me after I finished teaching the Hebrew school, and told me that he had just finished reading a book on humility. I told him that he should not brag about this—attempting the humor. I could have said boast; but I did not, as the attempt was humor. Using *boast* would indicate that I believed that he had read it; but the use of *brag* indicated that I believed that he had not.

"The use of the boast reflects that which *is*; albeit improper behavior, as it should be the *res ipsa loquitur*. But the use of the brag reflects that which *is not*. If it is brag, this requires that he did not read the book. If it is so; then it is boast. If it is not so; then it is brag. If one can do it; it is the boast; if not, then it is the brag.

"The brag and the pride are interrelated. Bragging to one's self results in the pride. This pride results in the bragging to others. Both are the use of what is not, in combination with that which is. Telling one that they can fly like the Superperson will not work very well; because it involves only that which is not, and will not be believed. But telling one that they can run a marathon in record time may work; as someone had to have already done so. This one is the combining of that which is not, with that which is.

"What is the only possible source of that which is not? He who created that which is; created that which is, and did not create that which is not; else that which is not, would not be that which is not, but rather be that which is.

"The Biology was designed as the portal between the two realms to bring forth that which is in the one realm (usually immaterial), to the other realm (usually material). The main purpose of this is to defeat that source of that which is not. But in doing so, the design of the Biology can be contaminated with that which is not. The goal of the source of that which is not, is to defeat the source of that which is. The Biology hangs in the middle; being under the influence of the source of that which was created, and *is*; but also can be under some degree of the influence of the source of that which *is not*.

"If the material realm is represented by the horizontal line; and the immaterial realm is represented by the vertical line; then the

Biology is at the intersection of this "cross." And this is the right angle or "norm." Anything next to this norm is the paranormal.

"But it must be asked if these are the lines, or the line segments; because the universe is the curved. If it is the line segment; then the curve of these segments is insignificant for the illustrative purposes. (Curve is utilized here rather than *curvature*, because the latter usually refers to the abnormal.)

"But if it is an actual line; then it actually becomes two circles appearing to be at ninety degrees to each other. This is why and where the Euclidian geometry falls short. If the immaterial part represents a vertical circle, this is God's domain; and sometimes God is represented by the circle. But sometimes God is represented by the spiral. This is because of the addition of time and distance into the equation, and the "stretching" of this circle. If one continually draws a circle when the paper is being moved; the spiral will be the result.

"'That man over there doesn't know what he is doing—he's drunk.' That of course being the "lay" description of the condition; with those with the many letters after their name saying instead: "he is intoxicated." He also seems to be having quite the good time—at least while the intoxication lasts.

"The "intoxication" refers to the ingestion of the poison. But is it true that intoxication is an absolute; or is it threshold related? Ingestion of the cyanide is the ingestion of the absolute poison; as it is poisonous and harmful in any quantity. Ingestion of large amounts of the Vitamin A can result in "toxic levels;" but in smaller quantities it is required. Therefore the harmful effects of the Vitamin A; unlike the cyanide; is not the linear, as too little is harmful as well as too much. Some say the same is true with ethanol—the booze; and some say not. Too little Vitamin A and too much Vitamin A are both harmful; but *any* quantity of the cyanide ingested is harmful. This is an example of the *material* absolute and relative contaminants.

That which is not. . .

"Thank you choir. Let's give a hand to all of our members who work so hard to bring us that of which there is nothing more beautiful—the human voice. And hearing 200 of them all at once is an amazing experience. (*roaring applause*)

"As we always do on this day in honor of Socrates; I will dispense with my usual sermon, (*again roaring applause*) and... and...and... present our visiting pastor. Really people, are my sermons really that..."

(*from the back*) "Just messing with you Pastor. Most of us appreciate very much the opportunity to sit back, close our eyes, and... just kidding."

"Very well. I must admit that having your active involvement in the process at least insures the wakeful state. He needs no introduction; but let us give a hearty welcome to..." (*deafening applause*)

"Thank you! Thank you very much!

"Now the first... thank you very much. Now the first thing... thank you; thank you very much. The first thing I would like to do is to try and figure out what we are all doing here.

"Any takers?"

(*silence*)

"Don't be afraid, no matter who answers, the recording will show only an "A;" meaning audience response"

A: "We are here to worship God."

"Okay, but which one?"

A: "There is only one."

"Is that so? Then what difference does it make what house of worship we attend? The Jewish Temple across the street is a much bigger building, and they are all very nice people. Surely you are not in any way suggesting that they don't believe in God. Why don't we just go there, as the Rabbi is very knowledgeable?"

A: "Of course they believe in God. They just don't believe in Jesus."

"They do believe there was a Jesus. They do not deny that Jesus walked the earth, but believe He existed and was a very fine prophet. To say that we cannot worship God there because they don't believe in God is not true. Likewise to say that they do not believe there was a Jesus is also not true. So again I must ask: Why not go over there?"

A: "Because they do not believe that Jesus is God."

"I see. So then there are actually two Gods. There is the God that both of us believe in; and then there is the God that we believe in, but they do not. If you believe only in the one God, you worship there; but if you believe in two Gods, then you worship here."

A: "Well no—not exactly."

"Please explain this so that even I can understand it."

A: "Right. Well; it is not that there are two Gods, but one God in three parts. You know: the Father, the Son, and the Holy Ghost."

"So you are saying that across the street, they only believe in one of the three?"

A: "Correct."

"Incorrect. They do not believe in only one of the three. They believe in two of the three."

A: "I am sorry Pastor—they do not. They do not believe in Jesus, and that is why they are Jewish. They only believe in the Father, and are still waiting for the Son. That means one."

"No; I am sorry; they do believe in two. They believe in the Father, and they believe in the Holy Ghost. It is the Son in whom they do not believe; as they do not believe He has ever walked the earth."

A: "Okay, I got you now. What you are saying is that they believe in only two of the three; but we Christians believe in three of the three. I'll agree with that."

"If I take your statement literally in its entirety; then I said no such thing."

A: "I don't get it."

"Let's try this another way: What makes you a Christian?"

A: "Because I believe that Christ walked the face of the earth, was the Messiah, and that He is the son of God."

"What about Jesus? Where does He fit in?"

A: "I just told you."

"No; you told me about Christ; which is the root of what is called Christianity. But what about Jesus?"

A: "Same thing—true enough?"

"Yes and no. If you believe that Christ was Jesus' last name, then they are the same. Unfortunately; it was not.

"He was *the* Christ, the Anointed One. He was believed to be carpenter's son? So Jesus was sometimes called Jesus the carpenter's son. He was believed to have something to do with Nazareth; so He was sometimes called Jesus of Nazareth. (Actually; this was likely because of Him being a Nazarite or a Nazarene, like John the Baptist.) These quasi surnames relate to something outside of Him. The same is true with the use of Christ."

A: "What is the difference?"

"Because if you believe that it is always that Jesus = Christ; then when "Christ" is seen in the Bible, you will always believe that this refers to Him; and never refers to this thing outside of Him, for which He was called the Christ. You would then erroneously attribute the passage to one of the two parts of God you actually do believe in."

A: "Wait a minute; I believe in all three parts of God"

"What *are* they again?"

A: "The Father, the Son and the Holy Ghost."

"We got it on the first two. Tell me about the Holy Ghost."

A: "Well, its Holy; and its also a Ghost."

"Thank you. Anything else?"

A: "It is the third part of God."

"My good man. This reminds me of a time many years ago, when I was visiting our nation's capital. There were these food trucks selling "half-smokes;" and I was very hungry. I asked the woman at the counter what a "half-smoke" was; my having no idea whatsoever what it was. She tried, but was unable to reasonably describe it. Finally she said: 'You know; its a half smoke.'"

A: "Its what it is we Christians are named after."

"How come it is that Christians aren't called Jesusites."

A: "Christians had to be differentiated from the Jesuits."

"Are you saying that Jesuits are not Christians?"

A: "I don't know; they probably are."

"The Jesuits did not come into existence for a millennium and a half or so after Christianity was called Christianity; so clearly the name was available then, and for quite some time afterward."

A: "I don't know."

"Lets try this another way: Why is it that the persecution of Christians is on the rise; and public policy seems to becoming such that persecution of any religion is verboten—except Christianity?

"More and more, open season on Christianity is becoming not only standard practice, but also more than tacitly accepted. Do you actually believe that this is because of fear based upon the images of Jesus, that those who actually persecute Christians have seen? They only see images of Jesus in a manger; (where He was not born, but actually placed in *after* His birth); and images of Him hanging on the cross. And in addition; those that persecute Christians generally either do not believe He existed; or that if He did exist, He wasn't anyone particularly special."

A: "I don't understand."

"It's not the Jesus that they fear; it is the Christ."

A: "But aren't they the—no you explained that one already."

"It is the Christ that they fear, and although anyone can have some level of the Christ; only those who believe in Jesus can have the level of Christ to cause so much fear. And guess who it is that effectively has no idea of the availability of this kind of power?"

A: "... ... ... Not the Christians?"

"Bingo!"

A: "Wait... how can that be?"

"You know; that third part of God that you claim to believe in; but seem to know nothing about?"

A: (*reluctantly*) "Yeah; I mean yes."

"You know and believe in the Father right?"

A: "Of course."

"This is because you know what He claims to be by His word; and you choose to believe that He is what he says He is?"

A: "Sure."

"You know and believe in the Son right?"

A: "Yes."

"This is because you know what *He* claims to be by *His* word; and you choose to believe that He is what he says He is?"

A: "True."

"But when it comes to that third part; which is the anointing, the Christos, or the Holy Ghost; you just proved that you know nothing—yet you claim to believe in it, in the same way as the Father and the Son."

A: "But it is not my fault. No one ever mentions it except in passing. And they don't call it the Holy Ghost either."

"I know it is not your fault; and no one is blaming you. You cannot be expected to know something that no one has ever taught you. This was done to you by design. Just like the abridging of the Bible. The KJV represents a compromise between those who wanted the entire Word released, and those who wanted none of it released. Now; although some "lost" books can be proven to be non-genuine, such as the book of Phillip; there is no way to be sure about many of the others. Chanukah is not even contained in the 66 books of the KJV Bible; except for what some believe is a brief reference to it by Jesus. Except for that, the story is nowhere to be found in those 66 books."

A: "So what is there to do?"

"Start with what you have. The first thing is to try and recognize which of the Three it is that the Bible is talking about. It is always wise to determine what it is that one is studying first; then determine its attributes."

A: "So I can learn about the Holy Spirit that way?"

"Grrrrrrrrrrrr."

A: "I uhhh; I mean the Holy Ghost."

"You must understand the difference between spirit and ghost—this is critical. Spirit is about structure-less *structure*; ghost is about *function*. Ghost can cause spirit; but spirit cannot cause ghost. Let me explain: Spirit is that which is immaterial and breath-like; and can include much—such as that which results in the manifestation of matter. Spirit is the cause; the effect is matter. There likely are other results; but let's keep it simple, as we are discussing ghost and not spirit.

"Ghost is an immaterial or spirit-like entity, but is designed to reside in a material body; but it can also function to some extent outside the material body. This is why non-Christians can utilize the Holy Ghost; but it is *on* them and not *in* them.

"Even in the world of the entertainment, a ghost is that which once resided in a human body; has left this body; but for some reason does not go where all the other ghosts go. Instead; it "hangs around," and often can cause some degree of mischief. If it is *noisy*; it is called a "poltergeist;" which essentially means "noisy ghost."

"When a human body becomes alive, a "holy ghost" in a sense enters this body via breathing the first breath, and exits the body with the last breath. This is the soul, but since it is designed to live within and animate the physical body, it is also a ghost. But although this is in a sense *a* holy ghost, because it is of and from God; it is not *The* Holy Ghost. The source is the same; but the entity is different.

"So you see when you were trying to look smart before when you said: 'Well, its Holy; and its also a Ghost,' you were literally stating the truth.

"The Holy Ghost describes a similar entity; and since it is part of God, one main function of that entity is supernatural power. When the Holy Ghost is *on* you; you can demonstrate supernatural power, but only up to a certain level. When the Holy Ghost is *in* you; the level of supernatural capability becomes limited only by you.

"This is what Jesus meant when He spoke of performing greater things than He; if you believed in Him and the things he did; once He went to the Father. If these criteria are or were met; then you qualify to have the Holy Ghost *in* you, and not merely *on* you.

"Given all of this, is it not odd how many great discoveries, inventions, etc. are brought into our world by non-Christians? This is because of their greater understanding of God's system, and the fact that they work within it. They know and obey the laws and rules; and therefore have the Holy Ghost *on* them, with results that can be easily discerned. But at most they are capable of performing actions no greater than those Jesus performed. This is a bit ironic, because by definition these are those who believe neither in Him, nor the things He did.

"And what are the Christians doing in the supernatural power department? The answer is generally nothing of any significance; and perhaps nothing at all. Most major Christian religions have essentially hit the delete key with respect to the Holy Ghost;

mentioning it only in passing, and then even changing its name, which merely adds to the confusion.

"This was all done deliberately; although perhaps not necessarily recognized as such by them. But gradually over time, these compromises, and what we today call "political correctness;" as well as unsuitable individuals who managed to wrangle themselves into positions of religious/political power; have taken their toll. And many well meaning individuals who were willing to "make just this little change" to ensure the harmony; ended up contributing to what *Christians* have now become; although actual *Christianity* remains unchanged.

"The problem for the enemy is that this lie; as is the case with all lies; represents an unstable situation. There are Christian organizations emerging who understand these things, and their ranks are growing. Although they may be operating with only remnants of the truth, their trajectory worries the enemy greatly. This is why the level of tacit and blatant Christian persecution is on the rise. The enemy fully understands the capability of Christians who understand Christianity, and he fears this greatly; even if at the present, most Christians have no idea what Christianity actually represents or means."

A: "Wow, so I can go home and turn some water into Dom? I like Dom. But you know, after all it isn't the cheapest..."

"Not so fast. You don't have the brains for it."

A: "What do you mean? You just said..."

"Five minutes ago, you had no idea what I was talking about. You think God is going to give you a Harley, when five minutes ago you didn't even know what training wheels were?"

A: "I don't understand. I thought you said that an incredible level of supernatural power was available to all Christians."

"It is. But I also said that essentially, its only limits were you. Perhaps you missed that part."

A: "I didn't miss it. I'm smart. I am a decent human being."

"This is likely so; at least by your or the world's standards perhaps. But God's standards are another matter. He is not going to give you power you can't handle. This is a process. It is not so much that you must *earn* the right to it, as a Christian you already have that. But you must obtain the *wisdom* to go along with it; and the standard is *His* and not yours."

A: "I don't get it. What good is the availability of this power, if we can't use it?"

"I didn't say you can't use it."

A: "You said I was stupid."

"I didn't say you were stupid. I said you didn't have the brains for it. By that I meant the wisdom to understand what else happens when you make turn that tap water into a soporific."

A: "How am I going to learn if I don't try?"

"You aren't."

A: "I still don't get it."

"Do you know the story of the "Talent Man?"

A: "Sure; I learned that one in grammar school."

"You did?"

A: "Yup."

"Tell me the moral to the story."

A: "Use it or lose it."

"Use or lose what?"

A: "Literally money; figuratively gifts."

"So the talent refers to something of value; if tangible like money; or if intangible like talent?"

A: "You got it."

"And this comes from the Hebrew unit of measure called the talent?"

A: "Correct."

"Incorrect."

A: "No; the talent *is* a Hebrew measure of weight; it can be either a common talent; or a royal talent—which is heavier; I might add. (*beaming*)"

"So they say. But they are wrong. The actual Anglicized word which appears as talent; should be *talant*, and not *talent*. And it comes from the Greek, and not the Hebrew."

A: "And?"

"And in that story is the answer to your question."

A: "*silence*"

"The "talent" refers to a weight; but the significance is that it is a weight to be carried or a weight for balance; and not merely a unit of static weight like a pound. It is the *balancing* or *bearing* of weight to which this word refers. What is this the balance to? In the story, it is a balancing of supernatural power. It is also bearing; in the sense of something 'heavy on one's heart.'

"This "talent" acts as both a *motivational* and *balancing* weight. The motivational part is to provide this "weight;" in order for it to be removed by a free will choice of the bearer to do something about it. This is the "heavy on one's heart" part. But the balancing part is to balance the supernatural power afforded one. Together the power and weight define an actual Hebrew word; which coincidentally or otherwise; looks an awful lot like the word mass.

"If we analyze the common meanings of "talented" and "gifted;" we find discrepancies. If talent is defined as a skill, this is not true. If gift is defined as free; this is also not true. Supernatural power labeled as *talent*, in fact only refers to the other side—the weight borne or balanced by the part which we call *gifted*. And the gift is not free because of the requirement of the weight. They only exist together; even if there is often a time delay in this realm.

"That is the key to the answer to your question. As a child; you did not begin the walking phase by immediately running laps. First you crawled, and then learned to walk, and then learned to run. The same is true with the "gifts" of the Holy Ghost. You must begin with small things. Sense the weight; act on the weight in a manner consistent with God's law; and the power will come."

A: "You know; one time I just had this *feeling* that I should call this friend of mine that I hadn't spoken with in a long time. And I was glad that I did; because he was planning to do something that was pretty bad."

"And?"

A: "And he changed his mind. All he really needed was for someone to listen to him."

"Where did that *feeling* come from?"

A: "I don't know."

"Where could it have come from?"

A: "God? I mean the Holy Sp... Ghost?"

"That message via "feeling" was the supernatural power as to whom; and the weight was you "feeling" that you should call him. It was in the two parts; but it was really one. Your action resulted in both balance and imbalance. You completed it, which was the balance; but you now became capable of more of this, but at a higher level; and this is an imbalance. You were a good and faithful servant; even if you did not realize it. A child who has learned to crawl, may only vaguely realize that he is now in a different place; and he does not quite know how he got there.

"You also created another imbalance by helping your friend. The first imbalance is or will be balanced by receiving another similar, but greater opportunity; whether you recognize it as such or not. And the second is *karma*—understanding that they may in fact ultimately be different parts of the same thing.

"You balanced the imbalance by action. But if one does not; the imbalance will ultimately be balanced by dissipation or removal of something. In the former; you end up in a better place. In the latter; the best that can be hoped for is to remain in the same place.

"That chronologically balanced "feeling" experience; gave you both the desire and the ability to act. You had a choice, and you chose to *act*; rather than *not act*. The result of the action was increase; and inaction did not result in having something taken away."

"...ALERT ALERT ALERT... DEFCON 5 SITUATION EMERGING... ALERT ALERT ALERT... DEFCON 5 SITUATION EMERGING ALERT..."

"Turn that thing off."

"Off or on, we've got to go. This one is a five. Been a long time since there was a fiver." Let's move!"

"Where we going? And why do we use a reverse Defcon, where five is the highest level?"

"Answer to second question, because we are in the immaterial realm. Answer to fist question: 'Where do you think?'"

"Him again. He travels all over the place and most times he gets only about halfway through speaking, and here they come. It seems that we've seen every city in the world this year alone. It is always the same; he speaks for a while; then swarms of them show up, like somebody whacked a hornet's nest; and we have to go into battle. Just like the manual says: as soon as he sows it; they immediately come to steal it"

"Yeah but like you said; this time it is a five. And he hasn't hardly even begun speaking yet."

"What?"

"He's just kind of looking around and hesitating."

"No... And we know how much he hates speaking in the first person."

"Yes! At least I think so. There's a bit of hesitation there; but I think he's gonna go for "it". The crowd is very demanding. I don't blame him for hesitating though."

"Just exactly what do you mean by "it?" No; please please say he's not gonna tell what I think he's gonna tell."

"Looks like he's 'a-gonna.'"

"Oh man; no wonder its a five; and no wonder its early. They aren't just coming to steal it after the fact; they're coming to try and stop him this time."

"Fact is; I know the story is true too; because I was on duty then and there. When I found out what it was up to, I called it Vox Stulta, which means: "dopey voice;" but I haven't seen him around since then. And if it wasn't true, they wouldn't care. And they sure seem to care."

"Here they come!"

"Let's move!"

"So you have to understand that I do not expect you to believe me. I cannot control what you believe; and I would not even if I could. I can only make sure that I tell you the complete truth.

"It was a very bad time I was going through. It was probably the lowest point in my life, as someone very close and very young had passed on. And a very peculiar thing had happened. Someone who knew me professionally came to me and asked; actually importuning is a better word; that she be afforded some time with me in a quiet location. This in itself is not all that peculiar; let me explain:

"This was a beautiful young girl of impeccable character seeking a private audience with me. So those of you with wild imaginations please put a lid on it. All she wanted was to sit in my office on the other side of my desk and talk to me. I had no idea why. She was pleading with me to afford her this one opportunity.

"And so I agreed and we did. She insisted on holding my hand, and began to tell me things that she would have no way of knowing—such as things about my home and the furnishings. She would have had no way of even knowing where it was, much less any of the rest. I will not go into great detail as to the other things she knew, as it is neither relevant nor appropriate. Suffice it to say that she had an incredible amount of knowledge regarding very specific things that she simply could not have known—yet she did.

"At the conclusion, she was behaving as if a tremendous burden had been removed from her. I found the experience amazing and quite interesting.

"Several days later, I had come home late (around midnight) from the office; and was sitting on the floor with my back against the wall, in what was my family room at that time. The room was an "L" shape; with a piano from the late 1940's in the short part of the "L."

"Suddenly a male voice came out of the piano. At first it startled me, as who expects a voice to come from a piano. I must make it clear that this was an audible voice in the room; with its direction being easily determined; and no I have never even considered taking LSD.

"What was also especially odd, was its "accent." This type of accent is and was, the precise type of accent that would cause me to immediately distrust the speaker. This may be unfair and prejudicial; but it is based upon experiences. I might add that this "accent" is strictly based upon a regional dialect; and *not* race, religion, or anything of the sort.

"A "conversation" had begun; although much of it I simply cannot remember. And with respect to what I do recall, certain parts of this would be inappropriate to disclose. My first statement to it was: 'I figured you'd be around sooner or later.'

"I was then told that there were certain things that I desired, and perhaps I could be helped with their attainment, if only...

"My response was: 'Before we talk about the price; what have you got?' There was then one of the most striking displays of qualification, prevarication, verbal amphigory that I have ever witnessed. My response was unabashedly less than refined or gentlemanly, as I stated: 'So you aint got ****.' There was a bit more nonsense from him, and then it was over. This had never happened before, and has not happened to me since.

"*How* something is stated, is often more revealing than *what* is stated. There was an underlying fear revealed in this voice—as though walking a tightrope *sans net*, with any error resulting in the same potential fate. This could have easily been mistaken for timidity.

"It is doubtful that this was in any way because of any fear of me. More likely; the manifestation of this audible phenomenon required special permission—remember Satan asking for permission to do what he did with Job? And likely had this not been done precisely according to the terms of the permission, his existence would have automatically ceased; and he *knew* this.

"This is probably why that particular accent was required of him. Is it stacking the deck? Heck no; likely he was the one asking for the special privileges; and he either had to do it the precise way it was permitted, or not at all; and likely would be immediately destroyed if he 'messed up.' And in truth, what happened to it after that is unknown.

"The real question is why little old me? It is easy to understand why at that time; as he is not only a bully; but the originator and source of all bullying. But why bother with me?

"What did he know at that time? Chances are not much. What he may have *suspected* is another matter. One thing he has is experience. This can be mistaken for knowledge; and he prefers this. For whatever reason(s) he must have suspected that at sometime in the future I was capable of causing him substantial problems; because he had seen a pattern developing that had seen before; albeit completely unknown to me.

"What he did succeed in doing, was make me utterly certain that he exists. At that time I was unsure. This event presented me with irrefutable evidence that he in fact exists; as there is no explanation for this in the material realm; and there is no explanation in the immaterial realm that includes only God and His manifestations. But again, believe what you wish.

"In closing, I would like to talk a bit about how he obtains information about us. Dr. Erich Petrovsky knows much more than I about the existence of those things which exist only on the immaterial realm; and his courses should be seriously considered. He will be back shortly, (*applause*), but for now...

"Are you applauding because Petrovsky is returning; or because I am almost done here?

"Suffice it to say that the *results* or *consequences* of thoughts ideas and suggestions may exist on the *material* realm, if energy is utilized with regard to these. But the thoughts ideas and suggestions themselves, reside exclusively on the timeless *immaterial* realm.

"When there is *silent* prayer, this represents immaterial changes on the immaterial plane, as the result of will and effort. There is a difference between silently *thinking* about praying, and silent praying.

"When there is *audible* prayer, this results in changes in both realms. 'Speaking in tongues;' is sometimes permitting the Holy Ghost to utilize you, (your physical body) to engage in audible prayer.

"The words can even be what essentially seems to be gibberish. But this presumed gibberish is not only because it is necessary to make the change on both realms to express will; but also so that the enemy has no clue regarding the specifics—except for what he may logically derive from the circumstances, and other factors *outside* of the communication itself. It is this consent of the host that is extremely valuable, and thus of course is something which the enemy opposes quite forcefully at times.

"Or the Holy Ghost may use certain actual terms or phrases that mean one thing today; and meant something entirely different at another time. This of course by design drives the enemy crazy. These "utterances" are utilized to bring changes into both realms; based upon the subrogation of one's will to the Holy Ghost. If you know and trust the waiter; then let him order for you as, he knows what it is that is best that day.

"This only works when both parties are in agreement. If either the Holy Ghost or the host does not wish to participate at any given time, then it will not happen at that time. One cannot force the Holy Ghost; and it will not force you, as this is not consent.

"Those things that exist exclusively on the *immaterial* realm are not all the same, simply because they exist only on that realm. This may sound silly, but often is tacitly believed to be so. Will, intellect, emotion, thoughts, ideas, suggestions etc., are all entirely different immaterial phenomena. This distinction is important in understanding how the enemy obtains information about us.

"The enemy cannot read anyone's mind; it just seems that way sometimes. One's thoughts belong to them; and the enemy cannot gain access to them by himself. What he can do is set up an "experiment," just like an equation with variables; and then he observes the response: '$X + Y = Z$'

"If he wants information about *what* you are thinking, or *how* you think; he will do something; and then simply observe the, (*your*), response.

"Here with this '$X + Y = Z$,' the 'X' is what he does, the 'Y' is the unknown, (what or how you are thinking); and the 'Z' is your reaction to the 'X.' He will tailor make an "X" to catch your attention, based upon what his best intelligence estimate is of you at that time.

"It may look like he seeks the 'Z,' and he could in fact be pleased with the 'Z;' but what he actually seeks is the 'Y.' It is for *future* actions that this scheme is designed, and not necessarily the *result* or 'Z,' which will be in the *present*.

"When you act upon this stimulus, 'X' and the result is 'Z'—whatever this 'Z' may be; then he can logically derive what 'Y' must have been for you to have reacted to that particular 'X' the way you did; because if: 'X + Y = Z,' then: 'Y = Z − X.'

"The enemy *causes* the 'X,' *observes* the 'Z;' and can then easily *derive* or *determine* the 'Y'—unless of course the victim knows of this scheme. Should the victim know of this process, then the reaction or 'Z' can be deliberately made to be different than what would otherwise or normally be the reaction; i.e.; *bogus*.

"Here with the deliberately *bogus* 'Z,' or here: 'Z_B;' with the subscript 'B' indicating the *bogus* 'Z;' the equation will not only not work to the enemy's benefit, but has the potential to cause him great harm.

"The enemy will correctly believe: 'Y = Z − X.' But the enemy does not know the actual value of 'Z,' but only *believes* that he does; i.e.; he does not know that he does not know. So when he unknowingly 'plugs' this 'Z_B' into this equation, believing that it is "Z;" what he unknowingly obtains is not 'Y,' but instead 'Y_B,' believing it is 'Y.' Here the enemy in fact derives a 'Y,' that in fact does not exist.

"Likely quite proud of himself, he then acts upon this *bogus* 'actionable intelligence,' until things eventually 'blow up in his face.' So then when he concocts the next 'Z,' at least with regard to the same victim; he will be unsure if what he "determines" is an *actual* and thus *actionable* 'Y,' or yet another '*bogus* Y,' or 'Y_B.' This will breed fear in the enemy, in that he will not be certain with regard to precisely what type of bomb it is that he is in fact creating, and upon whom it will explode.

"This can actually be a bit of fun if one is careful. And of course a normal or non-bogus 'Z' should be 'thrown in' from time to time as 'a truth' in order to produce additional confusion.

"This is merely the production of an *actuality/reality* mismatch in the 'mind' of the enemy; which is one of the most effective weapons he has been utilizing against the hosts almost since the beginning of time.

"But 'normally,' the result is that we are amazed, thinking all along that he already knew the 'Y,' via some type of *quasi-omniscience*, or via mind reading; and wanted the 'Z.' We believe that his knowledge of the 'Y' actually occurred in the *past*, and he wanted this 'Z' in the *present*.

"When in fact, he didn't really care much about this particular 'Z' at all; caring much more about the 'Y;' as this is *what* you were thinking, and thus *how* you think. This helps build the picture as to what you are, to assist him with attacks in the *future*.

"'He must have read my mind, as he knew exactly what I was going to do.' In fact he had only a general idea of what you might do. This is confusing an *intelligence gathering* mission with *operations*. The 'mission' was intelligence gathering, and not the results of the 'operation.' This is one way that he: 'roars' seeking whom he may 'devour.'

"Precisely how many bombs need to explode in his face before he realizes he is dealing with a dangerous entity, is subject to many variables; and thus is unknown.

"In the first Iraq war; one of the first actions was the bombing of Baghdad. This was not done to sustain any significant physical damage; but rather to gather *intelligence*.

"Once the incoming bombs were detected by the Iraqi military, they went into defensive mode, and 'lit up' all of their radar installations. It was the acquiring the precise *location* of these radar installations that was the main purpose of this *initial* attack; and not primarily to cause damage. This was an *intelligence* gathering mission; which as was hoped, the Iraqis confused with an actual destruction *operation*. It was the second attack that was the true operation; as this intelligence facilitated all of their radar installations then being destroyed.

"A store manager asks a new employee to go into the parking lot and steal the hubcaps from another vehicle; as the manager says he wants these hubcaps. The employee looks at him kind of funny, and finally says: 'I can't do that—that's *stealing*.' The employee was not concerned with getting caught. The employee was not concerned with any penalty. In fact, the employee was concerned that he may have been fired for refusing. Nevertheless he refused; and stated why. This is another example of the above referenced equation; although here it is unclear as to whether there was any significant *demonic* participation.

"Did the manager really want the hubcaps, or was this a *test*? From that point on, the employee began to be trusted with keys, cash; and many things of extremely high value. If this or any other manager wanted to leave early, he would just hand the keys to the store to this employee, and ask him to "close" the store for him. They were quite pleased with the 'Y.' This is a true story.

"With the acquisition of sufficient 'Y,' the enemy, (or anyone else); can construct a reasonably reliable composite of what you are. He may or may not like the results; but this is not in any way based upon what he probed into, but rather what you showed him. He then wants you to believe that he can know your thoughts beforehand; when all he did was observe what you did, and *derived* the thoughts after the fact. But when one picks up the 'hand grenade' and throws it back at him, not so much.

"Everyone hears 'voices.' 'Voices;' in this context, refers to 'head voices,' and not audible voices. This is a phenomenon that has a similar effect as audible voices, without the incorporation of the actual hearing apparatus. There are those who know this, and those who do not. There are those who will admit this, and those who will not. When we like the results, it is good. When we do not, it is bad. If hearing "head" voices is insanity; then we are all insane by design; which also means that God must be nuts too.

"Beyond a certain threshold, the hearing of voices is considered as mental insanity. He hears voices; therefore he is nuts. When in fact: if there is mental insanity present; it is actually the reverse. He is not crazy because he hears these voices; rather that he hears these voices *because* he is crazy. But of course this doesn't always work either—else Paul/Saul of Tarsus, who wrote roughly one third of the New Testament was likely insane too.

"What is missing in the usual analysis of this, is the nature of what these voices are saying. This 'nature' refers to both the magnitude and the polarity of the voices. We inadvertently will ignore the magnitude and skip the insanity diagnosis; if we like the results. 'A voice just told me that there was an injured child there, so I stopped what I was doing; and boy am I glad I did.' This is then a *hero*, and not a 'nut.' It makes little difference how loud the voice was, because it was a good result. This is a positive polarity voice. But if the action is perceived to be negative in polarity; then the admission of a voice practically guarantees the DX of mental insanity.

"The problem; is that everyone experiences this on an ongoing basis. When the voice says something that you simply cannot believe you were thinking; chances are that you shouldn't believe that you were. This is because it came from *without*, and you tentatively believe that it came from *within*.

"But by admission; the surprise is because it could not have come from within. 'I had better have myself (head) examined.' No; you should tell the enemy to shut up.

"Did the enemy know *at that time* what you were thinking? Certainly. Why? Because he is the one who just placed it there; it never being in your mind before this. He knew it was going to be in your mind *before* it actually was in your mind, because he planned it. This is not the same thing.

"When you tell the enemy to shut up, he hears you; but this is not mind reading either. This is the result of *will*. This is a deliberate message sent to the enemy; whether verbal or not. It is your intention that he receives this message, and some degree of effort is made in the transmission; even if only mentally. This is not the enemy perusing the depths of your mind, and somehow finding this out. It is intentionally being sent into the *immaterial* realm where he receives it. This is a force, and not a mere thought; and this force will find him, because it is your *will* that it be so.

"No matter how the message is sent, it can only be understood in the immaterial, as there is no consciousness in the material. Stating the message verbally; also brings it into the material realm, but it can be interpreted only by that which resides only in the immaterial. A rock may vibrate if one screams loud enough; but it will not understand. Although communications using the material; e.g.; speech are recognized as necessary; this is not always true. There is nothing wrong with the non-material *mechanism*; it is the *reception* that is usually the issue. There is no requirement that the material be used as an intermediary for any communication; but this is how it is usually done. Again this is not mind reading, because the transmission requires will, and thus consent of the "sender."

> "Well—he's finally done. (I think.)"
> "It wasn't as bad as I thought it was going to be; but it pays to be cautious."
> "Sometimes I think that hedge just attracts them."
> "You just figured that one out? Don't you remember the bellyaching about Job?
> "Well—let's get back over to Petrovsky."

"That which is the not. . . will always contaminate that which is. This must again be distinguished from the that which is the not, but merely only because it is not as of the material yet.

"The difference is the existence or non-existence of the thing on the immaterial realm. All that exists or ever will exist, has its origins on the immaterial realm—even the idea for the invention.

"That which is the not," here refers to the that which is not and cannot be; as there never was any such phenomenon on the immaterial realm; and in this realm with no time, it of course then could never be.

"The *imagination* is to the *future* what the *recollection* is to the *past*; and either can be faulty.

"The *recollection* of the something that did not happen, and therefore could not have happened; represents the faulty recollection, as it contains the faults. And because it is in the past and cannot be changed in the present; represents the faulty recollection, as it contains the faults.

"This must be distinguished from the non-recollection of the something that did in fact happen. Remembering the something that did not happen; and the inability to remember what did happen, are not the same.

"There is a similar relationship with the *imagination*. Imagining the something that cannot the possible ever be is silly, except for the fun. This is what the children do with the imaginary friend.

"But the imagining of something that presently is not, but could be; is the beginning of the transfer.

"With the accurate *recollection*, the past can be brought as though in the present; as was done by Moses and many others—albeit without actual witnessing. Some past can be brought into the now, because it has or had existence on the material realm.

"With accurate imagination, the future can be brought into the present; but usually at some later time.

"Under the normal, the actuality causes the reality if there is the *perception*. This is the *actuality* based reality; or realization.

"*Imagination* based reality, can result in the very same actuality imagined, if there is the *effort*. This is the actualization.

"But it cannot necessarily be determined with certainty that any imagination will result in the fruit. This is because not of the all is known. However; it is sometimes possible to determine that there can be no fruit to the imaginative effort; if it can be determined that "that which is not" is a necessary component. Again the "that which is not" means not in either realm. It is not in the material realm, which is the precise why manifestation is desired at some future time; but is also not in the timeless immaterial realm. Here there can be no transfer, because there is nothing to transfer.

"When the "other" in any way lies about what is, by telling that "that which is not" is "that which is;" the victim cannot obtain the expected result; because "that which is not" is then a necessary component. The same happens when one lies to himself.

"Within the material, there is what is known as the "inverse square law." This is the reason why the intensity of many the phenomena such as the light, sound, radio waves, gravity, etc., diminish as a function of distance. As the distance from the source increases, the intensity decreases as a square function. If the distance is doubled; the intensity is one quarter.

"If the current theories about the gravity are correct; and if there were only two stationary neutrons in the entire universe, they must eventually collide. This is not because of the random; but because each would attract the other, according to these "laws" of the gravity. This gravity permeates the entire universe; and with no respect of any extremely low of the intensity due to this "inverse square law;" it is still present.

"But with those phenomena such as the consciousness, thoughts, will, intellect, etc., that only exist on the immaterial plane; there is no distance. Therefore; they do not obey the "inverse square law;" or perhaps it is the better to say that this law does not come into effect. This means that there is no diminishment of the intensity possible. This of course assumes that something is either being "projected," or being made available by some aspect of will. And with no distance possible, there can be no time lag possible.

"This is why the writers of the fictional science use the telepathy, and not the radio. The radio will take the thousands of the years to get to the ship that is the thousands of the light years away, by the definition. But the telepathy is the immediate.

"This can be something of the Biology in the "mental" area; or it can be what is sometimes called the Akashic records—which has nothing to do with the varnishkes.

"This Akashic is the knowledge of all that was, is, and will be; as there is no time. This is the *knowledge* of a thing and not the thing itself; as they are not the same. This is likely where the disciple John was permitted to "see."

"The lie has existence in the Akashic area, as the lie was or will be told. But the *subject* of the lie itself has no existence on the immaterial realm. This Akashic is like the library with an infinite number of copies of all the books that were or will ever be written—the fiction and the non-fiction; so the reception of this information by the Biology, in no way decreases the availability of this information to any other of the Biology.

"But the presence or absence of the *thing* itself is different. The Biology can assist in the transfer of the thing from one realm to the other. The Biology can bring the thing from the immaterial to the material; and sometimes the other way. But the Biology cannot cause something to exist, that does not already exist in the timeless realm. This is like the time travel paradox.

"It is also likely that once the thing that is brought into the material realm from the immaterial; it can not be brought into existence in this manner again; unless it is somehow returned first. This may be why there is the very little actual creation going on in what many call the: "Book of Creation;" or: "The Book of Genesis."

"This is also likely why the Adam was not created, but formed. The original hosts were created, but the Adam was formed. One can learn much about the rules by observing how God acts.

"It is not the actual strength of the signal from the Akashic records that is the problem. It is what it is supposed to be; and cannot be altered or diminished by the distance, because there is none. It is the sensitivity, selectivity, and stability of the receiver of the Biology that is the issue. When the receiver of the Biology is in fine shape; we call this a psychic. The likely source is the Akashic records as this can include information about the past, present, or future.

"The clairvoyant is a bit different; as this more means "clear view," or "see clearly." This is the reception of the real time events; but not generally of the future or the past. The source of the clairvoyant is likely that immaterial which is emitted by the Biology itself, in the time that is real; rather than the Akashic records. It is interesting to ponder if or how the clairvoyant would be able to view real time events against the will of the participants.

"The same could be asked with reception of information from these Akashic records. There likely are the "clearances" required for certain types of information; and there may be prohibited information, such as information about physical death. But most of the Biology has such poor receivers, that this verboten level is rarely if ever reached. Even Jesus did not know all that the Father knew, and He admitted it.

"We must talk about the warp speed and the hyperspace. These are usually considered the same, but are not. The fact that neither has the actuality at this time, is the irrelevant.

"The warp speed; which is provided by the warp drive; is the speed of light. The fictional science has much to say about these; but at the present, this existence is limited to the fiction.

"In the material realm, all is constantly in motion. There really is no absolute measure of motion possible; but only relative motion. Whatever the reference one chooses for "stationary;" strange things begin to happen when something attains the substantial velocity relative to this "stationary" point of reference.

"If works of Lorentz are correct, three things begin to happen when the velocity approaches that of light. This is the slowing of relative time, the decreasing of one dimension, and the increase of mass. It is the last of these that is problematic; as these increases are not the linear. As a mass approaches this warp speed, the "mass of the mass" also increases in the non-linear manner, so that at the speed of light it is infinite.

"There is no natural force known in the universe that could accelerate an infinite mass; as there is no known infinite force; and even that may not be enough. Thus it seems that exceeding the speed of light is not possible for any mass. If the original "mass of the mass" could be brought to zero, perhaps this might work; and perhaps not.

"When the thing "gets moving," beyond some point, the force needed to get any degree of the acceleration becomes the burdensome. Assuming the constant acceleration; whatever its magnitude; as the mass increases in a non-linear manner; the amount of force must increase likewise; and at some point any further acceleration would require greater amounts of energy than exists in all forms in the entire material universe.

"There is also the issue of the time. At warp one, the time or duration of the moving object becomes zero from one perspective. But time at the "stationary" point is normal. All the other things being equal, time also remains normal at the destination. Like many of the stars seen at night that ceased to exist long ago, it does little good to arrive at a destination that is no longer there.

"The answer would be increasing the warp levels. The problem with this; is that unlike in the fiction, time does not become a negative number when the speed of light is exceeded; but the *square root* of a negative number—which of course does not exist anywhere in the known universe—except in the imagination of the mathematicians.

"The speed of light has a finite quantity. And although the large one, it is grossly insufficient for interstellar travel; or for the transmission of those attributes of the Biology which reside on the immaterial plane.

"Warp drive is concerned solely with the M or the mass; with little or no concern for the nature of the S or the space through which it travels; except for the distances. Space is generally assumed to be constant; except for those with the grizzled hairs, who theorize with those with slightly greater numbers of the grizzled hairs.

"Nevertheless, this space is the answer to the instantaneous travel. There is no distance in the immaterial realm, but that is not the subject. The subject is the space in the *material* realm, and understanding its structure. Space in the material realm is not merely the condition of no mass being present; and again, there are those who believe it is not of the uniform structure.

"The fictional science calls this the hyperspace. It is not a matter of the faster projectile as in the warp; but finding those portals to the hyperspace which would result in the instantaneous relocation of the masses involved. Many concepts in fictional science ultimately become the historical facts.

"Study the immaterial realm, and use this as the guide. When studying these wormholes and related phenomena, study these without being the matter bound. Understand the immaterial realm and its rules; and apply these to these space problems. The Biology is designed to be portals between the two realms. Use this portal to discover these other "portals" in the material realm.

"Over the years, students have asked how it is the subject matter of the lectures could be so seemingly different; being a mixture of the science and what some call the spiritual. The answer is that it is the one unit, the same thing viewed from different perspectives; and yes—I want you should think about this too."

"One final point about the Biology; and this concerns the DNA. The DNA is considered by many to be the cause; and this is true. However it is also the effect.

"In my youth, we had these small records. Many of you may not remember the small record with the large hole in the middle; much less those that were called the 78's. But both did exist. If by mistake, one bought one of these records of another artist, or one that had not been recorded; it would have been different, and also would have been the same. The unrecorded record would have been smooth; unlike the recorded record; but the material or the matter present would have essentially been the same. The record of the other artist would have been even more similar; except that different sound would have come out when played.

"From a material viewpoint; what is the difference between the device for storage that contains the information, and the one that is unused? The answer is nothing substantial. It is not the matter that one is interested in, as that is only the medium by which the information or sound is stored and transferred. It is the intelligence in whatever form that is of interest; as that is the only reason for the existence of the old record, or the device for storage today.

"No matter what is stored on these devices, the ultimate source of this information is that which does not reside in the material, but only is present in the immaterial. All is the fruit of the consciousness. It matters not if the sound, sentences, video, or data is stored in these devices. If the *ultimate* source is sought; it will be found that it is immaterial in nature, and will only be found in the immaterial.

"The DNA is similar. It is believed that most or all known Biology contains the DNA, or some functional variant; and it is not known to be present in the non-Biology such as rock; unless there is the fossil present. The DNA is not the cause of life, but it is necessary for life. This is because it contains the information necessary for the forming and maintaining of the vessel that *contains* the immaterial part; which together is the Biology.

"The DNA is the material repository of information. It is necessary for life, and can in a sense be considered as a requirement for the Biology; as a special vessel is necessary—as rocks do not and cannot think. This is seen in the formation of the vessel prior to the entrance of the first breath; when the immaterial part enters the vessel, and the Biology is the result.

"But the DNA is also an *effect* of something else. The *matter* for the coding sequences and the other matter that makes up the DNA, has its material existence because of something else. In this discussion, we will call this something else the *Force*.

"This Force relates strictly to the matter; and is the entity that is the intermediary between will and the result. When the Creator created; there was the will, and there was the result. When He created the heavens and the earth He did it because He wanted to. This was His will, and the heavens and the earth, (=Big Bang), was the result. What emanated from Him as a result of this will was this Force; and the matter was result. Will → Force → Matter

"The old record, current storage devices, and the DNA all *materially* exist because of this; but all exist in order to contain something else. They are material, but this is both the incidental to and currently required for their purpose. What is *stored* ultimately comes from the immaterial, and through the Biology; whether through sound or anything else. This stored information is the oblivious to the means of storage. But because it comes through the Biology, it is subject to the limitations of the Biology.

"The vessel part of the Biology materially exists *because* of this Force; but also exists in order to contain something else. The information stored on the DNA is necessary for the Biology; and in a sense comes *to* the Biology; but does not come *through* the Biology, in the sense of the consciousness.

"This information is immaterial in nature and is an *effect* of the will of the Creator. Just as the technology currently uses the digital format; the Creator also uses a format with DNA, albeit not the same digital—though some of my good friends in the Mathematics Department might argue this.

"It is the DNA information that is required to form and maintain the vessel capable of containing its desired contents, which of course is the soul. This Force generally refers to the vessel's matter only, but is related to all material structure.

"The DNA (material in nature), is involved with the information (immaterial in nature), required for the vessel's proper structure and function as designed. It cannot be over emphasized that it is this Force which resulted in matter being brought to the material from the immaterial, including the DNA *structure*; but the DNA *function* is involved with one aspect of *organizing* the matter that is already contained in this material realm for the unique vessel.

"This organizing is the result of the Vital Life Force, which is immaterial; but is not this Force that causes matter, nor is it the soul. The Force is responsible for the existence of the matter that the Vital Life Force uses in forming maintaining the vessel; and the *information* in the material DNA is one part of what this Vital Life Force utilizes. The corpse has both the result of the Force, and DNA; but has neither soul, nor Vital Life Force; although at one time had all four.

"The DNA is somewhat the analogous to the ĕxŏusia when speaking about some of, but only some of the "miracles." With the "local" miracle; there is the self-contained ĕxŏusia which consists of both the "local" supernatural power; and the authority to utilize it. But there are limits to the magnitude of this stored supernatural power. How many dunas of supernatural power are present? The answer is whatever amount balances the amount of authority and/or burden already present.

"In a sense this is like the battery in the electric and gas vehicle; except that the power available does not diminish with use, as with the vehicle battery; because the ĕxŏusia power is not of this realm. In the fact, the ĕxŏusia increases with the usage. But there is also additional supernatural power available, which was not previously "stored" as this ĕxŏusia; but can be provided "real time." This additional supernatural power, is like the vehicle engine starting when more power is required.

"The same is true with the DNA. The DNA is an effect, but it can also act as the cause for many biologic events; this being the reason for its existence. It is *informational* if decoded, but this is only an ancillary consequence of its existence.

"Like the ĕxŏusia; the DNA has local power and authority to cause many things to happen; but there also can be and is "real time" Vital Life Force involved. This force augments, and can even override functions of the DNA.

"Most believe that it is possible for the DNA to spontaneously change; and at the same time impossible for the DNA to spontaneously change—depending upon the nature of the change.

"How can this be? Because in the minds of most; this change is the one way street. The DNA can be damaged, but barring the elaborate medical (material) procedure, it cannot be spontaneously enhanced—at least in the minds of most.

"This is the DNA mutation, which is considered as diminishment. It is true that DNA can be diminished or damaged by the material; but it is also true that it can be augmented by the immaterial?

"This augmentation is not meant the mutation of the haploid gamete. If the haploid gamete is the positive or favorable mutation; then the offspring, and not the parent reap the benefit.

"This augmentation means the spontaneous augmentation of the somatic or the body cells from that which is the less desirable to the more desirable; in the same already living person.

"How rare is this augmentation? It is likely not as rare as it may seem. This is because the DNA augmentation can only be confirmed, *if* the DNA structure is pre and post examined. Any and all DNA "improvements" which cause dramatic biologic vessel improvements will not be attributed to any DNA changes, unless they are attributed to DNA changes. And to do this, requires the knowledge of the pre and the post DNA; and it is *this* which is the true rarity.

"Is it possible to *not* do what the functioning DNA dictates; to not get the effects the functioning DNA should be causing? This is not the same as the *defective* DNA not doing what *it* is supposed to do. How is it possible, to have material attributes which differ from the "code," if the DNA is not dysfunctional? If functional DNA says that the hair is to be the green, but the hair is first green, but is now the purple without the use of the dye, or disease; *something* is amiss.

"If some unknown event changes the hair color to purple; will the DNA change to accommodate this?

"Or did the DNA change first; and then the hair turned purple. If the latter; and the purple hair is *less* desirable than the green; then the common DNA change rule clearly held. But if the purple hair is *more* desirable than the green; the commonly understood DNA change rule was clearly violated.

"These type of changes—DNA "improvements;" are done immaterially; can be, but are not necessarily accomplished utilizing the *miraculous* power. It could be a removal of immaterial interference to the Vital Life Force; or it could be dunamis or the miraculous power. [It must be noted that the Biology is an ongoing miracle, as physical laws are violated constantly. However dunamis or miraculous power and the Vital Life Fore are different.]

"The Vital Life Force with respect to these positive DNA changes; is analogous to Force with respect to the "creation;" and perhaps the maintaining of matter; depending on one's perspective. Both changes are the result of will; and both utilize an intermediary. And both must respect the known and unknown laws, including maintaining balances.

"Did the hair turn purple immediately or gradually? This is important; because this will determine whether or not the miraculous power was involved. It is easy to simply label anything not understood as the miraculous; but this should not be the so hastily done.

"In the material realm, things are usually a bit "slow." Even the fastest "material" thing, believed to exist by most; the light; assuming it is the material, and not merely the material result of the immaterial disturbance, (the: "let there be"); as discussed, is much too slow to be used as any reasonable means of travel in our galaxy; much less the rest of known universe.

"But some things are much slower than others. The obvious physical changes in the Biology take much time as compared to many other material phenomena. Since hair generally grows from the proximal to the distal; a change in the hair color would likely be gradual; maybe even with the two tone effect often seen with late stage artificial coloring; if no physical laws are broken.

"If the change was "immediate;" whatever "immediate" means on this realm—the poof, and the hair was purple; then this would likely require miraculous power, as the normal time element would be absent. But if the purple hair "grew in;" this would not necessarily be the "miraculous" power. It all depends upon whether the physical laws were violated.

"The "other" enjoys confusing these, as he prefers the chaos. He deliberately mixes the will, the authority, and supernatural power—as though they are all supernatural power; and then does his best to convince the human Biology that the supernatural power does not exist. But this is not so. They are separate and distinct entities, and each exists.

"The *will* in a sense is the absolute. The Biology has free will by design; but only over those areas where the free will is supposed to be by this design; and this does not include other hosts—except by their consent.

"Whether or not the will comes to fruition is another matter, and can depend upon many factors. With the stored "ĕxŏusia," the supernatural power can be utilized against the will of the Creator. But with the "real time" supernatural power it cannot; because the Creator must have the "real time" involvement.

"The *authority* is both the absolute and the relative. The human Biology has complete authority over the "other," and he knows this; but hopes no host does. The human Biology also has authority over the angels, but the will of the Creator can trump this authority. Likewise; the "other" and his minions; (it is not the 1/3, as that was a different event); cannot disobey the authority of the human Biology, unless perhaps it was the somehow against the will of the Creator. But the "other's" entire existence is to disobey the will of the Creator, so this situation does not work out well for him.

"The *supernatural power* is either power that is stored locally (the ĕxŏusia); or power transmitted the "real time;" or both. The stored power can be used against the will of the Creator; but the real time power cannot.

"Many of the events in the Bible are attributed to supernatural power, when they are not supernatural power. For there to be the miracle; there has to be a violation of the material law, without any violation of immaterial law. The most important determinants of keeping within the immaterial law; are will and balance. Once these are achieved, almost anything is possible.

"When the sick were healed; this may or may not have included the supernatural power. It depends upon whether the natural law was violated. If the healing process was the normal; then this was likely the result of using one's will and authority to force the interfering entity to depart. This is only the will and authority.

"But if the healing process required *no* period of the convalescence; such as the withered hand immediately being restored; then this likely involved the miracle.

"The Biology deals with the mishmash of the "biological" facts, the factoids; and the fiction. It is the "known fact" that parts of the DNA turn off, and simply cannot turn back on—barring some material intervention that may not exist. So the human DNA; unlike the starfish DNA; cannot turn back on to replace a severed limb in the normal.

"Except that *sometimes it does*; even if the result is incomplete, or out of place. The abnormal dermoid cyst can contain the teeth, even though an adult growing new teeth in the mouth is the very rare.

"When it does this in the desirable manner, it is a labeled a "miracle." Perhaps this is so; and perhaps it is not. Perhaps the will and the Vital Life Force can turn the DNA back on; as it seems reasonable that the human should be able to consciously perform something that the starfish performs unconsciously.

"Or perhaps it includes a miracle. It must be determined what natural "law" was violated, to qualify as the miracle. Erroneous assumptions about the DNA do not qualify as natural laws. However; the *instantaneous* restoration of the limb is another matter. Even the starfish cannot do that.

"When one listens to the radio, what is one listening to? He is listening to whatever frequency is permitted to enter the receiver. This is really not quite so; as it is more the blocking of all of the other undesired frequencies that is accomplished. There are many other frequencies which would enter the receiver if permitted. The circuit is designed to be resonant with certain frequencies. This "tuned circuit" in many older radios, consisted of the inductor and the capacitor. The old tuning dials were actually the variable capacitors, which when turned either increased or decreased the capacitance; thereby changing what frequency the radio "front end" permitted to enter.

"The human Biology operates in a similar manner. He is designed to receive that which is of the Creator, including the Vital Life Force. This represents a "tuned circuit;" perhaps even with the material biological or "organic" capacitors and inductors; perhaps not; or perhaps both material and immaterial—this is not understood.

"But there is that which is *not* of the Creator, just like static or the unwanted radio station that also wishes to enter the Biology; and this is not limited to the human Biology. When the human Biology begins to accept through whatever means that which is not of the Creator; then this resonant frequency of the Biology begins to change. Now those previously unwanted frequencies, those that are not of the Creator, can begin to enter; and the Creator is resisted.

"And just like the infection, it begins to spread. But unlike the infection, this is to permit the entrance of more of that which is from the without; until maximum control of the "host" is established. But this is not the so easy; as that which is of the Creator will fight that which is not. This is part of what those who are the legitimate descendants or believers of he who deviated from Abraham, as a result of Abraham's comedy with Hagar; today call the Jihad.

"This is the case with much; but also here there is the concern with the Vital Life Force. No one; except One; has the ever had the Vital Life Force which was not interfered with. Except for Him; it is only and always the magnitude of the interference, and never the question of the existence of interference; or the presence of the factor desiring to interfere.

"This affects the concept of health; rendering it always the relative, and never the absolute. No one knows today what pure Vital Life Force is capable of; as there is only the greater and the lesser levels of interference that are ever witnessed.

"'He has nothing in me;' is commonly attributed to the One exception to this. But although there are the "somethings" and the "anythings;" the use of the nothing makes things the clearer. There are only two categories: that which is of the Creator, and that which is not. The "he" here, refers to the "other;" that which is not currently of the Creator.

"It is the will that is crucial. This Messiah or the Jesus is sometimes called "The King of Kings." This is usually interpreted as the superlative form of King. Perhaps "Kingest King;" or "Most Kingly King;" or "Kingus Maximus;" would be equivalents to this generally understood meaning.

"The common understanding is that there is only the one in this, and that one is meant to be the adjective as the "Super-king;" the e.g.; a King superior to all benign monarchs, and the dictators. But again this would at best refer to Him; and the relatively small number of individuals who have existed as "kings;" and then again it remains a means of comparison of the amount or the level of "Kingliness."

"But there are actually the two in this "The King of Kings." There is the Messiah who is the first party; and then there is the human Biology who is the second party. This describes the two types of the kings; and is a statement of hierarchy of two; and not the level of "Kingliness" of one. But although this is so by design; is not necessarily operational today in the particular.

"Those who do not believe that the Messiah has yet come; cannot escape this relationship; and the existence of these "other kings."

"This second "kings;" is a description of the hierarchy of the human Biology, with respect to the earth and much more. This is easily seen when the original created from the nothing human Biology, (long before Adam was formed from the something); is given the instructions to "put the kibosh on" the earth—the original Hebrew being *kâbash*, from which this English *kibosh* is derived.

"But this "kings" is the objective in the ultimate; and likely also was the situation before the "other" arrived, but not in terms of the *kâbash*.

"This seems even more the so; because there had to be the recipient of the deception for which the "other" was ejected from the immaterial to the earth. There had to be much of something at the similar to the Biology, which was created sometime between the first and second sentences of His Word, and *not* just afterward as commonly believed. But since the Book is about the redemption and not the history, this is not stated.

"Although the "king" is usually considered the unique entity with respect to his domain; this the usual refers to an individual; and not the entire concept of "kingship." Kings are not the dictators. They are not the thug; as the thug is the thug no matter what he calls himself. Kingship requires acting in the best interest of the subjects. The human Biology as the king of the earth and all that is on it, (except the other human Biologies); requires the not less.

"First the Creator created the heavens and the earth. We are told this. Then the Creator inhabited the earth with what He chose to create to inhabit the earth. We are not told this; but it logically must have been so. This included what others have called the G_1—those beings who were the first given authority over the earth and all that was upon it.

"Then at some point this "other" was "thrown down" because of the leading astray and deception; and so there was no longer any place for him in the immaterial realm. Again; it was necessary to have a realm from which the yet to exist material realm; (the heavens and the earth); was created *from*. This is the binary, as there is the realm or perhaps realms with the matter and the space; and the realm that has neither the matter nor the space.

"This immaterial realm was the realm which had no place for him—"place" of course is the quasi-allegorical, and is used so that those in the true "place" (material realm), can understand.

"This "other" then "wrestled" the authority over the earth and what was upon it from these G_1; and the second sentence of the Bible, (Genesis 1:2), tells us conditions "on the ground" at the completion of all that he was permitted to do.

"Why was he permitted? The answer is the free will of the G_1; but this was based upon the trickery—the combination of that which is not with that which is; which was the reason for the "other's" expulsion.

"The problem for this "other" is that he is in the true limbo. The realm from which he was thrown is the realm in which he is supposed to function by design of the Creator; as is the realm of those (again not 1/3—as that is the different event), who went with him.

"Neither he nor they were designed to function in the material realm. None was designed to function as the portal between the realms like the human Biology. He is in the limbo, as he is in the realm that he is not designed to function; because there is no place for him in the realm from which by design he was supposed to function. This limbo is the neither or nether world.

"The great mystery is how this happened. It is similar to the man in the gan; this one we call Adam and his "wife;" but it is also the dissimilar. Adam and the wife were similar to these G_1; as they knew no evil, or even of the potential of the evil.

"This gan; or as some refer to it the garden; was a sequestered and protected area. The source of the potential for evil which was introduced is well documented. But the source of the source of the evil; how or why the "other" originally acted against the will of the Creator while in the immaterial realm is unknown. This represents the dilemma.

"It was likely the acting upon envy of the free will and the hierarchical position of the G_1 that caused the battle in the immaterial which he lost; and explains his current behavior today toward the human Biology and God; but the question of the origin or source of this envy remains.

"It is sometimes stated that God is the jealous. This is not the envy. Jealous is the distrust of someone; often a spouse; for which the famous windows were named. These jalousie windows were designed to appear to be closed, but left open just enough to hear what was happening on the other side. It is not known how long this works.

"God has good reason to be jealous of the human Biology; but this is not the envy. Envy is the *ill will* or *hatred* of someone because of their good fortune. Although God being jealous is reasonable given history; He is not a recognized source of ill will or hatred for any reason.

"The Biology errs because of the influence of this "other," and the free will decision to act upon this; just as the Adam did. But the source of whatever it was that caused the *"other"* to err before *he* erred; is not known. This had to come from a source from where it was present at that time; and could not have come from a source where it was not present at that time. It simply makes no sense that God would delegate His hatred and envy side to the "other;" assuming He had one; for the purpose of attempting to destroy Him, and all of that which He created—and ultimately failing. So then where did it come from? This is the mystery.

"There was the kingship; and there will again be the kingship. *When* (not if) this kingship is restored depends not upon God; but upon the human Biology. It is the human Biology who is the army; this tsâbâ'; and there is free will. The reason that the Messiah was never given the knowledge as to the time of his return was because of this.

"This is another twenty two. Had Messiah revealed the time of His return; this could also have likely provided the guarantee that this was incorrect. So then the Messiah would have been providing the false information. This is because it is the human Biology, and not the God that will determine this; and providing this would have altered the Biology's actions with respect to the actions required by the Biology before this could happen. Knowing the date, the Biology could have become lazy, and thus prolonged this event beyond that date.

"But one could also say that this is not the so; because although prolonged by the laziness, the date would still be correct because of the omniscience.

"The same is the similar with the time travel. Either one was there or one was not. Going back in time to the time when one was not there; but "now" is or was there; has effects from that time going onward. Now is the now, because of all of the events that led up to the now. To go back and change these events by the introduction of another factor that was not there then "before;" changes everything from that point onward; and would result in the altered and the different present. This cannot be so

"There is much talk today about what has become known as the: "*Quadrakoff Equation;*" this being the application of Newton's F = MA; but here with *both* realms involved, and the transfer of the energies between, so it is stated as F_T = MA.

"The standard F = MA is generally part of the physics; and is concerned with the physical or the material realm. It involves an application of physical force measured in the "Newton;" meaning the kilogram meters per second squared. This is the amount of force required to accelerate the stationary one kilogram mass one meter per second. Push it and it moves. This is quite simple.

"But according to the Quadrakoff; the F is broken down into two very separate and distinct parts, when both the physical and non-physical realms are involved. There is the F_A; which is the actual material portion; and the F_R; which is the reason for the action; with the multiplicative product known as the F_T. This F_T is analogous to the F of the Newton physical only equation in terms of calculations; but the Newton F would actually be represented by only the F_A.

"In the physical only realm, F=MA or F_A=MA; as F_A=F in the purely physical realm. From the standpoint of calculating the movement of an object in the physical realm; it matters little *why* the object was pushed. This is a one realm concept, and is quite useful when one is concerned with that which is only in the material realm.

"But the Quadrakoff Equation takes into account both that which exists only in the material realm, the F_A; *and* that which exists only in the immaterial realm, the F_R. This is the *action* undertaken in the material realm; and the *reason* for the action, which is in the immaterial realm.

"When the factors which exist only in the immaterial realm become in the play; then this becomes the much more complex. It is somewhat simple to calculate the force required to move the object in the material; and this Newton equation is what is used. But the *reason* that the object was moved resides in the immaterial, and is excluded from being a factor in the physical only F = MA equation. This reason factor matters substantially when both realms are involved. In fact; because this is the result of will; it is not additive, but *multiplicative*.

"For example: say all of the factors are known regarding the baseball pitchers capabilities; and the velocity of the ball as it nears the bat is calculated. It can be determined with precision that the ball will be travelling at XYZ MPH. This is the F = MA. Consider two possible outcomes that are possible:

"The stipulation is that the trajectory of the ball is such; that the ball goes where half of the spectators wish it to go and the other half wishes not.

"The first outcome is that the trajectory of the ball is such; that *despite* extreme care by the pitcher, the ball strikes the head of the batter.

"The second outcome is that the trajectory of the ball is such that *because* of extreme care by the pitcher, the ball strikes the head of the batter.

"The material F = MA is essentially close enough for the jazz to be the same for both.

"In the stipulation, the pitcher both greatly succeeded and greatly failed—depending on opinions of where ball should have went.

"In the first outcome, the pitcher *failed* when the ball struck the head of the batter.

"In the second outcome, the pitcher *succeeded* when the ball struck the head of the batter.

"But in both outcomes; the velocity and trajectory of the ball was of the little difference.

"With the outcomes, the *will* of the pitcher must also be taken into account in order to assess all the forces involved; and this is where the F_R or the reason comes into play.

"The *material* results of the pitchers actions are the same, whether he hit the batter deliberately or by the mistake. But the *immaterial* forces are entirely different; depending on the pitchers intention.

"The pitcher's action taken in the *material*, created an imbalanced material condition, which was then balanced. He used physical forces in the material realm which imbalanced a balanced condition; by accelerating a material object which was originally essentially at rest. The accelerated mass ultimately came to rest, as all of the forces imparted to it were ultimately absorbed by striking another other object—here the head of the batter.

["The earth is different than the small asteroid. One must be careful about jumping while standing upon the small asteroid. If the low escape velocity of the asteroid is exceeded, one may never return. The same can be true for baseballs on earth, but only if the man of the super is involved.]

"Simultaneously; the pitcher utilized that which exists only in the immaterial. This either balances an imbalance, (rare); or creates an imbalance, (common); in the *immaterial* realm.

"Whatever his will or intentions when he threw the ball; this also *must* be balanced in the immaterial, just as it was in the material. This represents potential energy in the immaterial realm. This immaterial portion that will be balanced is the F_R (the reason) part of the F_T.

"This is unlike actions in the material that have no immaterial component. If the wind causes a tree branch to fall, then there is balance when it comes to the rest. This of course assumes that there was no conscious entity contributing to the fall.

"But the magnitudes of either the imbalance, or the subsequent balancing mechanisms in the immaterial are not so easily calculated. This is because of at least two reasons:

"Firstly it is impossible for the Biology to quantify, or arrive at the magnitude of the F_R part of the F_T; and therefore it is impossible to quantify the F_T.

"And secondly; even if the F_R part, and thus the product F_T, could be quantified; there are an infinite combinations of MA with which this could be balanced.

"This immaterial balance (MA) must be the same as the magnitude of the original force (F_T) that caused the immaterial imbalance; just as in the material; and the same material rules hold. And since the original action involved both realms; it is likely that there will be return of something to the material realm. Whatever this may be this is the M. And how quickly it arrives, depends upon the A.

"This means that if the action is upright; it is best to have to wait, as the smaller the magnitude of the acceleration, the greater the magnitude of the mass of that which will be liked.

"But if the action is not upright; then it is best to "get it over with;" as the greater the magnitude of the acceleration, the smaller the magnitude of the mass that will be disliked.

"Thus far we have discussed the two types of the F = MA. One is when there is the material action only with no will; and the other when there is the material action *and* the will. The first has no involvement with or the consequences from the immaterial realm; and the second involves both the material and the immaterial realms.

"In the first, $F_T = F_A$, is the plain old Newtonian F; as there is no F_R, as there is no will or intellect involved.

"In the second, F_T must be calculated using forces in both realms, as both realms are involved.

"It is quite fair to ask if there can be F = MA involving the immaterial realm only. This is likely the case when the "other" is cast out of one of the Biology, by another of the Biology; without speaking, or the inclusion of any of the rigmarole. If there is speaking, or the rigmarole; then both realms are usually involved.

"When there is the *hasty* casting out; the will of the "caster" causes the "other" to depart; without the appropriate balancing of the immaterial imbalance that permitted his entrance in the place of first—if it is done with the haste.

"If it is *not* done with the haste; then there has already been a balancing of the original "permissive" imbalance, and another different and opposite immaterial imbalance is present and growing because of the "other's" presence acting as though the squatter.

"When the casting is done with the haste; and by the definition, the original immaterial "permissive" balance has not been achieved. Here it is possible that the "caster" then *can* assume the responsibility for the remainder of this balancing. The word "possible" is important; because there are factors that may be unknown and/or incalculable which can affect this "surrogate" balancing. This has nothing to do with the return of the "other" with the other "others" in the clean house with no one home. This returning is like the mice returning because the hole was not blocked.

"The important thing in that either in the case; is if there is no inclusion of that which is of the material; then there is no involvement of the material realm. If the "other" is cast out strictly mentally, as a command, and as the result of will; with no words gestures or the like; then this is an *intra*-immaterial event. In this instance, there is only the F_R. This could be considered as the complement to the material only forces.

"Back to the pitcher.

"Had he hit the other player by mistake; then his will was not obeyed. This remains an imbalance in the immaterial, which must ultimately *somehow* be balanced or resolved.

"Had he hit the other player by the deliberate; then his will was obeyed; but there is a different kind of imbalance in the immaterial, and the pitcher will receive the MA in the material, and will not like it.

"With regard to the previously ignored example of the pitcher; the here situation where he tried to strike the batter out and succeeded, or the batter hit the home run; this deserves the comments.

"No matter who in the stands wanted what to happen, one thing is certain: The pitcher wanted the strike; and the batter wanted the home run. But this cannot be the both.

"This is the much more complex situation than the simple $F = MA$, although this is a component. This is the four dimensional meeting or intersection of two levels of capability; with the one with the greater capability prevailing *at that time*.

"These capabilities are the result or sum total of many factors, not all of which are necessarily the result of the will of the players. The basketball player and the jockey have different physical characteristics which are considered as the optimal. One who has the physical attributes suited to the basketball is not likely to do well as the jockey, and the reverse. These can be referred to as *involuntary* characteristics.

"But there are many characteristics which are the result of choice; and these can be considered the *voluntary* characteristics. Some of these characteristics are suitable for use with that which is; and some are only "useful" with that which is not. The pitcher and the batter both want to "win." The question is whether or not this is mere desire, or desire plus the expectation. It seems senseless to play if one does not desire to win; but why is there expectation of winning; and upon what is this expectation based?

"The capabilities of the players at this 4 dimensional intersection are the sum of those involuntary attributes and the voluntary attributes; *at that time*. This is the more easily understood as those involuntary characteristics that the players were "dealt;" plus the sum total of all of the choices each made up to the time of this intersection.

"This includes ignoring advice and going out to do the drinking the night before the game. It does not seem that ignoring the advice and doing the drinking could in any way enhance the performance. Therefore the player who does this, must believe that his performance will be equal despite the drinking; or diminished in an amount that is so the infinitesimal as to not matter. This is an attribute or characteristic that will only function with "that which is not."

"The sum of all of these *voluntary* things; both the correct and the erroneous; together constitute what is called the *character*. The character does not include the involuntary—with racism being an extreme example of the erroneous inclusion of the involuntary; and Martin Luther King proved he knew this quite well.

"But the character is much deeper than the choices. The character is consistent with *why* the choices are made, or perhaps better stated; the choices made are a reflection of the character. It is important to understand that perfect character is impossible for all but one. Thus character is a *relative* term. As it is a sum; there are positives, negatives; and at least theoretically, neutrals.

"The character is based upon the overall levels. If a number could be assigned to one's character, would this be a positive or negative number, and what would be its magnitude? Add up all of the positives; subtract the negatives; and what is left. What is the polarity and what is the magnitude.

"The fact is that precise quantification of this number is impossible. And unfortunately, the threshold for the positive character changes, or does it?

"There is a distinct difference between what is *considered* the positive character; and what truly *is* the positive character. This is because the thresholds for what is *considered* the positive traits or actions and thus the evaluation of the character, will vary based upon the myriad of things. Negatives acts will no longer be considered negatives, because "everybody does it;" which of course is the nonsense. The negative will then no longer be subtracted from the sum, so the character will appear more positive.

"But this is only the perceived and is not the so. The reason for these changes is the balance. The subjective balance must be achieved; even at the cost of calling that which is not, that which is. "He is the good character guy, even though he is the heroin addict; because he will only commit non-violent crime to feed his habit."

"But of course this is all the idiocy, and is what is responsible for the destruction of the society. Results are always based upon what is.

"It is the *integrity*, and not the opinion that determines the quality. Integrity refers to wholeness or completeness, as in the mathematical integer. To the extent that there is integrity; there is the presence of what is, and the absence of that which is not. What is comes from that which is; and what is not, comes from that which is not. Integrity is sometimes referred to *moral uprightness*, but this is both accurate and a misnomer.

"Uprightness refers to that which is upright. Looking at the cross, or the *interlaced* triangles; (sometimes called Star of David); or even the Masonic Square and Compasses; these all represent the intersection of the two realms. Whether it be the intersection of horizontal and vertical lines; the interlacing of the triangle with the base up representing the immaterial, and the triangle with the base down representing the material; or the allegorical Square and Compasses; it is all the same.

"Upright refers to consistency with that which is above—the immaterial realm. Is one's thinking, will, and behavior consistent with that which is of that realm? Or is there more consistency with the material realm; the realm where the "other" was thrown when there was no longer a place for him in the immaterial realm?

"Integrity is what one has when one is upright. Integrity in a sense is the result of the upright. And the level of character is determined by the level of integrity or wholeness; which is determined by the level of uprightness. If character is to be maximized; then integrity is the means; and uprightness is the path to integrity.

"The child was "raised" or "raised up." This is where he did the growing "up." Lazarus was "raised." In each case, it is the introduction (or reintroduction) that which is of the vertical, with that of the horizontal.

The "moral uprightness" is the interesting term. Can one be the upright and not be the moral? Or perhaps a better question is whether or not one can be moral and not upright? This depends upon one's definition of the moral. Moral can refer to any part of the disposition of an individual; or it can refer to only the positive side of the disposition. In the former there can be the good or the bad morality, sometimes called the immoral. But in the latter if there is bad morality it would then have to be something other than morality; as both come from the same word.

"To the extent that one is upright, then one does not really need the *morality*. To the extent that one is upright; then there is the presence of the knowing what to do in a situation, if the long term benefit is desired. The knowledge of the balance between the two realms provides the guidance. It is when this is not known that the morality is required. To the extent that the decision is not "the no brainer;" is to the extent that morality is required.

"'I need the money. All I have to do is lie to get it;' is not usually what is meant. It is not the mere obtaining of the money, as that can be done with a loan; but in a loan, the money must be repaid; and usually with interest. The "get it" here implies that it will be kept, and not have to be repaid. There is no mechanism that exists in the universe by which the money can be obtained with the fraud, and be kept. When this is attempted; this only results in the loan, but with the much higher interest to cover the fraud.

"Upright tells us that balancing one's material need for the money by the fraud; immediately causes the imbalance in the other realm. The imbalance will then return to the fraud liar; and he will lose that money plus more; which provides the balance between the realms. The balancing of the material need by the lie or the fraud, creates the imbalance in the immaterial; and then the imbalance in the immaterial is balanced by the "re-unbalancing" of the material. And because of the fraud component; the magnitude of the final step is larger than the amount of the theft.

"The upright also knows that giving sets up an imbalance in the other realm, which will return this gift to him plus more. This "more" is disproportionately based upon *why* he gave.

"This is the essence, and the example of that which is of the *Quadrakoff Equation*; the $F_T = MA$. The singular is used here because it is only one. It is the same law. The human Biology chooses the both the magnitude and the polarity of the return.

"This is one of the main issues to the acquiring of the supernatural power—the establishment of the portal. Free will goes along only with that which the free will has the jurisdiction over. Free will has no power over that which it has no jurisdiction over *in the real time*.

"The supernatural power in the ĕxŏusia and the real time dunamis are different. But with the human Biology usually much or all of the ĕxŏusia was real time the dunamis at some time—except perhaps the very first time with the measure.

"The similar is so with the lŏgŏs and the rhēma. When Moses wrote early Genesis, this was provided to him as real time dunamis; in this case as the rhēma or the word of God; and not like the time of the stick that scared him. This must be so because he was not there then, and in parts of it no witnesses were present. But when we read it is the lŏgŏs. The exception is when we read this and receive some additional fact that is not contained in the lŏgŏs; and either was not known, or was not known by the reader. This is the "real time" dunamis here as the rhēma, which is the balance to the seeking. It then becomes the lŏgŏs if recorded.

"Even if some level of ĕxŏusia is considered as innate as the stipulation; much more supernatural power is available. But it must first occur as real time dunamis. And to occur as real time dunamis, the Biology's will is necessary but insufficient. This must also be consistent with the will of the Creator. And the state of the "uprightness" of the Biology is a major factor.

"But no upright is completely the upright. If completeness or the perfection in the upright was the requirement; then only the Son would have ever received this power; and He would then have been lying about the greater things.

"It is not perfection in the upright that is required; but that a threshold be met. But the Biology does not usually know in advance when this threshold is met, only knowing this in the retrospective.

"This is why there is so much serendipity when the real time dunamis happens. Only after the supernatural event occurs, can the Biology know that a threshold must have been met. And of course the "other" comes immediately to confuse the matters; including the pride, so it is not repeated. This is even seen with those who should know the better, and yet want the cured leprosy to be thought of as the pimples in the today.

"As the character becomes the integer; the wholeness of the Biology or integrity; the whole of what is, and less contaminated with that which not; then the capability rises. This is the relative and not the absolute.

"As the capability rises, the *availability* of the supernatural power increases because of the will of the Creator. But just as the will of the Biology alone is insufficient; so is the will of the Creator alone insufficient. To the extent that the will of the Creator alone would be sufficient, is the same as the removal of the free will of the Biology; and this is the no-no.

"But the Biology cannot have the will for something that the Biology does not believe exists. This has been one of the most effective weapons of the "other." He has been quite the success in the supplanting "that which is" with "that which is not;" in the supernatural power areas; reversing the two. This is most seen with the Son. The other is sometimes even willing to "take of the hit" with the miracles of the Son; as long as these miracles are considered unique to Him. The "other" is terrified of the "greater things" that the Biology is capable of; knowing the danger if the Biology only knew it, worked at it, and willed it.

"The "other" will even sometimes deny the ěxŏusia power he once had; if it is required to stop the belief by the Biology in any supernatural power. The "black magic" does not exist today; therefore it never existed; is the good example.

"This does two things: It helps deny the existence of any supernatural power; and it also avoids any discussion as to how he lost this power he once had. But other times he will convince the Biology that he has these powers. This helps confuse the Biology; so that the Biology fears that which is not, and overlooks that which is.

"This is the war. The human Biology has of the nuclear weapons; but does not know it. The "other" has only the custom designed sticks; and knows it. I want you should think about this.
"I will see you all again next time... Class dismissed."

> "You know there is going to be hell to pay."
> "Good thing we don't have any hell in us."
> "And we don't even get paid for overtime."

"Never mind that. I was surprised he didn't bring up that 120 year thing. You know; the part about Boss only letting them live 120 years, that so many seem to like to quote."

"The one where He was talking about that specific group, at that specific time, because of their specific acts? That He was only going to let them live that long, and it is now thought He meant everybody?"
"Exactly.
"He's working on it. You should spend a little less time on..."
"Never mind that. We best get moving".
"Let's go."

> "Only try, not try—win not win; there is.
> First, to believe possible there must be.
> Then effort one must make.
> If win not, no loss there is.
> Not a circle this is.
> A spiral it mote be."
>
> Musings From That Little Man.

Other Fine QPG Publications:

Coming Spring 2021 The Alleged Fantasy Project Volume II Acts

LEARNING HOW TO BE GAY

This is not what you are thinking.

It is not clear when gay took on its: "modern meaning;" but likely within only the past 100 years or so. This change was not done by homosexuals; but rather was done to homosexuals. Why was this done? Was this change just a change to what used to be called "hip talk;" or was this change a part of a much larger plan?

Once the original meaning of a word is drastically altered; that which it originally symbolized is easily forgotten. This is why true lexicographers will never remove a word from "circulation."

What does the Bible literally state about homosexuality; and what does the Bible literally state about being gay? These terms are not synonymous; but Biblically are actually unrelated to each other.

And we know God wants us to be gay, because His Word is quite clear in this regard.

But how can one become that which God desires, when one no longer knows what that is? God literally told us what we are here to do, but no one seems to notice it; instead supplanting His word with what they say God wants us to do.

The closer we get to doing what God actually wants;
the "gayer" we become-in the original meaning.

MEEKRAKER BEGINNINGS...

From the "inside flap" of *"MeekRaker Beginnings..."*

"The primary purpose of this tome, is the reconciliation of the word of God with science; and to do so in such a manner as to be rendered inarguable by any rational mind. As stated in the Preface: "One must choose between being a "man of science" or a believer," because they are generally considered to be mutually exclusive. If one agrees that words mean things, then an unbiased fair read of God's Word presents no such paradox. But one must read what God actually said, not merely what one thinks He said, what one was told He said, what one wished He said, or would rather He had said."

STATISTS SAVING ONE

The Malignant Sophistry of Rights Removal by the Far Left

"...under the umbrella of "liberals" or "liberalism;" (as used today); there are actually two separate and distinct groups:
"True *liberals* believe very much in what they promulgate. They are truly concerned with the welfare of citizens, and they believe in policies that will benefit the same—at least in their view. There are neither nefarious purposes, nor any intellectual dishonesty. Their objective is to improve the quality of life (and longevity), for as many people as possible.
"...Conservatives and liberals can often agree on the *ends*; but vastly disagree on the *means*. Giving a hungry person a fish is kind; but to conservatives, teaching him how to fish seems to be a better long term solution. It is not that conservatives object to the temporary

giving of the fish; but rather they object to *not* teaching him how to fish.

"True liberals believe in the dignity of man; and promulgate policies in furtherance of this belief.

"Statists; the other group usually and often erroneously grouped under the "liberal" umbrella; are another matter. It is because of agreements with liberal *policy* that they are usually grouped under this liberal umbrella; but their *motivations, purposes* and *beliefs* are entirely different—arguably antithetical—to true liberalism."

Why should *liberals* read "Statists Saving One?"

> To understand that many who may appear to agree with your *means*, have entirely different *ends* in sight; and that these ends are antithetical to liberalism. True liberalism and statism are entirely incompatible. And all along you thought they were your friends.

Why should *conservatives* read "Statists Saving One?"

> To understand the difference between liberals and statists; and end the confusion. Many liberals agree with many conservative *ends*, merely proffering a different *means* to achieve them. But statists have entirely different ends in sight—no matter whom they may appear to agree with at any given time.

Why should *statists* read "Statists Saving One?"

> To understand the true motivations behind statism; and decide if continued actions are wise. The masquerade is now over. Either change now; or "pack up and go home" while you can, as it will never become any easier in any current statist's lifetime.

Wisdom Essentials—*The Pentalogy*

"That Which is Difficult If Not Impossible to Find Anywhere Else—All In One Place"

There are many effects for which no material cause can be found. In *"Donald Trump Candidacy According to Matthew?,"* his meteoric rise and seeming inability to fail are explained according to Biblical principles. Since this is a non-political work, his success was not actually prophesied, but no other conclusion could possibly have been drawn—*and this was published long before he was even nominated.*

In *"SHÂMAR TO SHARIA,"* the process of radical indoctrination is analyzed, and is shown to be a perversion of that very same thing God instructed man to do with the Commandments, and how this is not in any way limited to terrorists.

"It's Not Just A Theory" examines the relationship between behavior and longevity according to both science and the Scriptures; and "according to both" also includes major consistencies.

"Calvary's Hidden Truths" reveals many unknown facts about what actually occurred at that time.

"Inevitable Balance" scientifically and Biblically explains that which is often observed but rarely understood: Why "What Goes Around Comes Around;" AKA *karma*, or the "law of compensation."

OSTIUM AB INFERNO
[*The Opening From Hell*]

"The Original Monograph - According to the Father, The Christ Son and The Holy Ghost"

- What is hell?
- Why is there a hell?
- What openings from "hell" exist?
- What is the truth about "Abraham's Bosom?" And how does this or do these affect man?

- What are angels?
- Are angels named such because of structure or function?
- Precisely why were some angels sent to hell?
- Is it true that one third were banished to hell?
- If so, when did this all happen?

Much of that which is fanciful has been written about these questions. But the answers should not be sought from that which is the product of men's imaginations—albeit these may provide interesting reading. Rather; the answers should be sought from, and always remain: "according to The Father, The Christ Son, and The Holy Ghost." (Written in English.)

REINCARNATION —A REASONABLE INQUIRY

"*Often times it is emotion(s) and not facts that determine what it is that is believed to be 'in fact so.'*" —p.6

"When truth and perceived practicality conflict; unfortunately it is truth that often becomes the sacrificial lamb." —p.91

"He that answereth a matter before he heareth it, it is folly and shame unto him."

—Proverbs 18:13 (KJV)

Some say reincarnation is a fact, and cite the Bible as the unimpeachable source regarding this matter.

Others say reincarnation is fiction, and cite the Bible as the unimpeachable source regarding this very same matter.

One of these groups is about to be shocked.

QPG Publications are available
wherever you buy fine books.

For a complete list of QPG publications
visit: MeekRaker.com